To Stella Suhrin Sisk, whose genotype spans two continents, and whose
peace will, I hope, encompass all of them.

Brief Contents

Contents

Preface

I t is often with a sense of quiet celebration that an author begins work on succeeding editions of a previously published book. After all, the very fact that a third, or thirty-third, edition is warranted speaks to the success of the project itself. In this case, although the book *Approaches to Peace* has been successful, as measured by the enthusiasm of instructors and students, or the number of course adoptions, it simply cannot be concluded that we have been especially successful in approaching peace. There is regrettably little in the fourteen years that intervene between the first and third editions that warrant patting ourselves on our collective backs for a job well done.

Indeed, it is difficult in the year 2013 to maintain the same cautious optimism that many of us felt in 1999, when memories of democratic successes were fresh and the prospect beckoned of building a worldwide consensus in favor of negative peace (the prevention of war) as well as positive peace, in its diverse and alluring manifestations. Since then, the possibility of a "peace dividend" following the end of the Cold War has been squandered, the specter of terrorism has been horribly enhanced, the United States has engaged directly in two wars that have not only cost tens of thousands of lives but has also diminished its status as well as the ability of cooperative international institutions to solve our shared, planetary problems. Among these are economic inequity, continued denial of human rights, the ever-increasing pressure of population, and the largely unaddressed emergence of world-wide environmental threats including (but not limited to) drastic and potentially irreversible climate change. If this weren't bad enough, the threat of nuclear proliferation has if anything accelerated, such that it may well now constitute a greater danger to planetary survival than in the immediate aftermath of the US-Soviet arms race.

But this is no time for despair, and not only because "hope springs eternal." More than ever before, the world has become a "global village," with nearly instantaneous, real-time information-sharing that makes it increasingly difficult for wrong-doing to go unnoticed. Even though human rights are still not universally enjoyed, they are universally aspired to (although they may be defined differently by different people), and even the most egregious governments have been unable to keep their citizens isolated in their aspirations. If our problems are great – and they are – the human potential for solving problems has never been greater. Major new actors have entered the scene . . . actually, old actors, notably India, China, and a revitalized Russia which brings both new threats and new opportunities in an increasingly multipolar world. The field of Peace Studies has itself expanded, and not simply because the need for it has grown; so too has awareness of human potential, deriving at least in part from enthusiasm over past successes as well as frustration over how close we have come to getting things right.

For those endeavoring to approach peace, there is no shortage of challenges, practical as well as intellectual. Fortunately, there is also no shortage of inspiration and of insight. I hope this revised Reader will help its readers to appreciate those challenges, while profiting from the inspiration and insight of others, even as they develop their own.

As we proceed into the second decade of the twenty-first century, and despite our remarkable technological advances, some things remain depressingly the same: notably humanity's frequent recourse to war and other violent means of "solving" disputes, as well as many other problems confronting our planet and ourselves. Nonetheless, there are glimmers of hope, not least being the election of an African American (twice!) to the presidency of the United States, pro-democracy movements worldwide (including within the US itself), increasing tolerance of alternative lifestyles, and maybe even more.

NEW TO THIS EDITION

One of my goals in *Approaches to Peace* has been to bring together material that has a relatively long "shelf life," that transcends the latest crisis or fad. Nonetheless, some adjustments seem appropriate, as times change. Just as it has been difficult to choose among the many excellent contenders for inclusion in the third, it was extremely painful to delete selections that had graced the second. But considerations of space and expense left no alternative. For students and faculty wanting to increase their perspective, here is a list of selections that appeared in the second edition, but which, to my regret, are not included in the 3rd (all are worthwhile; some, even more than that):

Chapter 1 – Johan Galtung's "A Structural Theory of Imperialism," Michael Klare's "Redefining Security – the new global schisms," and a number of poems reflecting "glamorized nationalism"; Chapter 2 – Lloyd J. Dumas's "Finding the Future: the Role of Economic Conversion in Shaping the Twenty-First Century"; Chapter 3 – Richard D. Falk's "Defining a Just War" and Charles P. Webel's "Terror – the Neglected but Inescapable Core of Terrorism"; Chapter 6 – "Religious Inspiration" – has been deleted altogether, not because I don't consider this material important, but because a number of professors have informed me that they didn't find it a "good fit" for their classes. The following had been included in that chapter: selections from *The Bhagavad Gita*, from Thich Nhat Hanh's *Being Peace*, the *Tao De Ching*, the Old Testament, the New Testament, from A. J. Muste's "Holy Disobedience," and Thomas Merton's "A Devout Meditation on Behalf of Adolf Eichmann." Also deleted, from Chapter 7 – Elise Boulding's "Building Utopias in History," and Chalmers Johnson's "Empire v. Democracy: Why Nemesis Is at Our Door," as well as several poetic visions concerning peace.

Despite these painful cuts, the third edition of *Approaches to Peace* is somewhat longer than the 2nd, because the following new selections have been added:

Chapter 1 – Michael Klare: "Resource Competition in the 21st Century," Peter Singer: "Battlefields of the Future" and "Do Drones Undermine Democracy?" and Andrew Bacevich: "The Revisionist Imperative: Rethinking Twentieth Century Wars";

Chapter 2 – Volha Charnish: "Nuclear Proliferation," Lloyd J. Dumas: "Transforming the War Economy into the Peacekeeping Economy: Using Economic Relationships to Build A More Peaceful, Prosperous and Secure World," A semi-official Catholic statement on "Just War doctrine," David P. Barash: "World Government," Steven Pinker: "Violence Vanquished," and Douglas P. Fry: "Life Without War"; Chapter 3 – Noam Chomsky: "The Evil Scourge of Terrorism" and Haviland Smith: "The U.S. Response to Terrorism"; Chapter 5 – Gene Sharp: "Seeking a Solution to the Problem of War" and Joseph S. Nye, Jr.: "Soft Power"; and Chapter 6 – Rebecca Solnit: "Vision: Revolution is as Unpredictable and Beautiful as Spring." Several of these were written just for this book.

As you encounter and evaluate the material in *Approaches to Peace*, third edition, I very much hope that you will deepen and broaden your own personal approach to peace, while doing whatever you can to help all people approach this goal. The bad news is that peace itself may never be achieved, in the definitive sense of, say, landing on the moon, or eliminating smallpox, but it can certainly be approached, as with the mathematical concept of an asymptote. As the Hebrew Rabbinic saying goes, "It is not incumbent upon you to complete the work, but neither are you at liberty to desist from it."

ACKNOWLEDGMENTS

I thank my students at the University of Washington, particularly those from my class, Psychology 207, "Psychology of Peace," for serving as guinea pigs as I tried out various inclusions and exclusions and—even more so—for making useful suggestions. In this regard, special thanks are owed to Aditya Ganapathiraju, a remarkable young man, as dedicated as he is brilliant. Also, deep gratitude to Jennifer Carpenter for encouraging me to undertake the revised third edition of this project and to Maegan Sherlock, who worked hard and wonderfully well to make it a reality. Finally, I thank, Richard W. Coughlin, Florida Gulf Coast University; Stephen Crowley, Oberlin College; Katalin Fabian, Lafayette College; Warren R. Haffar, Arcadia University; Reina Neufeldt, American University; Richard T. Peterson, Michigan State University; Harry Targ, Purdue University; Robert R. Tomes, St. John's University; Craig Warkentin, State University of New York, Oswego for their suggestions.

David P. Barash
Redmond, Washington

Approaches to *Approaches to Peace*

"There is no way to peace," wrote theologian and antiwar activist A. J. Muste. "Peace is the way." Maybe so, but there are, at least, ways of *approaching* peace, and this book investigates some of them.

Rephrasing Muste, we might say that peace is never fully achieved; it can only be approached. Mathematicians call something "asymptotic" if it can be infinitely (or rather, infinitesimally) approached but never quite reached. Peace, then, may be an asymptote. Unfortunately, we do not yet have the luxury of bemoaning a "near miss," regretting that although we approach peace very closely, it continues to elude us, remaining just beyond our grasp. The hard reality is that peace can barely be glimpsed, never mind grasped; what is frustrating, therefore, is not that peace is so close but that it remains so far away.

Yet there is cause for hope. The Cold War is over. From Berlin to Johannesburg, seemingly intractable systems of oppression have collapsed, with remarkably little overt violence, and, in at least some cases, with the beginning of genuine reconciliation. More people—especially in Latin America—live under democracy than ever before. Environmental consciousness is widespread and increasingly acknowledged, along with the importance of human rights. Nonetheless, human beings are faced with many problems: a polluted and otherwise threatened planet composed of resources that are finite and whose limits may soon be reached (or may in many cases have already been exceeded); gross maldistribution of wealth, as a result of which the great majority of human beings are unable to realize their potential and vast numbers die prematurely; and persistent patterns of social and political injustice, in which racism, sexism, and other forms of unfairness abound and in which representative government is relatively rare and torture and other forms of oppression distressingly common. And this is only a partial list.

Despite all of these difficulties, daunting enough even if the world were to cooperate actively in their solution, the remarkable fact is that enormous sums of money and vast reserves of material, time, and energy are expended, not in solving what we might call the "problems of peace," but rather in threatening and actually making war on one another. If it wasn't so tragic, the situation would be so absurd as to be high comedy.

It seems unlikely that human beings will ever achieve anything approaching heaven on earth; however, it also seems reasonable to hope—and perhaps even to demand—that we will someday behave far more responsibly and establish a society based on the needs of the entire planet and the beings that inhabit it, a society that is just and sustainable and is not characterized by major outbreaks of self-defeating violence.

In this book, we'll explore some of the prospects of, and the obstacles to, achieving such a world. We shall do so by sampling an array of classic, near-classic, and potentially "future classic" readings. My hope is that *Approaches to Peace* will serve as a kind of core curriculum around which courses in peace studies can cohere. This book, then, will have been successful if it proves to be a convenient source of certain essential and provocative writings, a useful touchstone from which students and instructors can voyage out into the important and exciting field of peace studies, defining it for themselves as they go.

A quick explanation and apology is therefore called for: assembling a collection of such readings is unavoidably arbitrary. Different editors would doubtless come up with different selections, particularly as the field of peace studies is itself a "work in progress." There is no shortage of suitable readings, however, and it has been painful to omit so many excellent candidates. Similarly, it has been difficult—and a bit arrogant—to abridge many of them. But to some extent, *Approaches to Peace* may be useful insofar as it doesn't go too far in indulging anyone's preference, even its editor's! So if this book whets the appetite but doesn't entirely satisfy, if it leaves the reader wanting more, then so much the better.

Students of peace are, ironically, a feisty and even occasionally combative lot . . . perhaps because their enterprise is especially likely to attract its share of dissidents. Different instructors may therefore want to branch out from this book and devote special attention to those topics of special concern to them: feminism and women's rights, for example, or specific regions of current violence and war; the history of recent conflicts; detailed proposals for a peaceful future; ideas of environmental and economic amelioration; exposés of egregious human rights abuses; additional sources of religious and/or ethical inspiration; case studies of particular crusaders for peace, human rights, and nonviolence; and so forth.

Approaches to Peace reflects the assumption—characteristic of peace studies—that peace can and must include not only the absence of war ("negative peace") but also the establishment of life-affirming and life-enhancing values and structures ("positive peace"). Thus, an important concept in peace studies is that, as logicians might put it, negative peace is a necessary but not sufficient condition for positive peace. This book also assumes that there are no simple solutions to the problems of either peace or war; the war–peace dilemma is complex, interconnected, and often poorly understood. On the other hand, there is much to be gained by exploring the various dimensions of war and peace, including the prospects of achieving a just, sustainable world: in short, a way of living that will nurture life itself and of which its citizens can be proud. A degree of optimism seems warranted, not simply as an article of faith, but based on the realistic premise that once human beings understand the situation and their own best interests, they can behave rationally, creatively, and with compassion. As we shall see, there are positive steps to be taken that will diminish humanity's reliance on organized violence to settle conflicts and that will begin the construction of a better, more truly peaceful world.

To some scholars, peace studies may appear redundant because most of its subject matter can legitimately be covered in various other academic disciplines, nearly all of which are better established: history, psychology, anthropology, sociology, literature, political science, economics, and so forth. But the reality is that students are unable to take courses in all of these fields, and if they wanted to cover the peace-related material, they would have to pick and choose, like a gourmet eating just a couple of shrimp from one casserole, picking out a few candied raisins from the dessert, and so on. Peace studies offers, instead, a unique focus on peace, just as women's studies selects material from traditional disciplines that relate specifically to women, or environmental studies focuses on the environment.

There is another way in which peace studies is special. Unlike the usual social science approach, which prides itself on being "value free," peace studies unblushingly acknowledges biases and preferences. It is scholarly but not disinterested. It does not simply encourage the study of peace but is in *favor* of peace: peace, we proclaim, is better than war, just as social justice is better than injustice, environmental integrity is better than destruction, and so forth. Peace studies is thus similar to medical science, which freely admits to a preference for health over disease. (Think of it as offering a kind of "planetary medicine.")

Despite the enormous ills of our planet, there is reason to believe that our most pressing problem is not hunger, disease, poverty, social inequity, overpopulation, or environmental degradation but rather the violence that human beings commit and threaten to commit against others. This is especially true in modern times, with the invention of nuclear weapons, but is valid, too, in a world of "merely" conventional arms. Consider the deep irony of a planet beset with desperate crises whose inhabitants nonetheless spend their time and energies fighting with each other, thereby making things even worse: imagine a small, overcrowded lifeboat facing severe shortages of food and water, springing leaks, tossed about in stormy seas, and facing a long trip to safe harbor. Imagine further that within this lifeboat there are sufficient resources to patch the leaks,[1] keep everyone nourished, and build adequate oars and makeshift sails so as to complete the voyage safely (maybe even enjoyably) . . . but squabbling breaks out among the occupants. Precious supplies, including the compass, get thrown overboard, and the boat itself is in danger of capsizing.

Perhaps try a different image. Imagine that a space probe headed for Mars has run into serious technical difficulties: the air supply is endangered, the energy source has begun to fail, and the craft has entered an unexpected meteor shower . . . whereupon the astronauts, instead of dealing with their problems, begin a fistfight among themselves!

It is indeed paradoxical that in a time of unique danger and difficulty, the inhabitants of planet Earth waste their time, resources, and energy—as well as their lives— fighting among themselves and/or preparing to do so. Sadly, there is nothing new in

---

[1] Or, for an even more disquieting scenario, imagine that resources are *not* sufficient.

the human experience about recourse to war. What is new, however, is its profound inappropriateness: with the wolf at the door, we leap to our feet, grab a gun . . . and begin shooting each other!

It is also noteworthy that after decades on the brink of nuclear annihilation, the world situation has changed dramatically, notably with the dissolution of the former Soviet Union and the widespread disavowal of communism. This has deprived many of the most war-prone individuals of a feared (or favorite) enemy. And yet, such extraordinary reworking of the global map has not resulted in a comparable reworking of military expenditures, at least on the part of the United States. This may be because there has not been a comparable restructuring of the intellectual and emotional map or of social relationships based on power, violence, or the threat of violence.

Any attempt to approach peace, if it is to be meaningful, must also approach this problem of redrawing the "conceptual cartography" through which most people structure their view of the world and their place in it. *Approaches to Peace* is perhaps best approached this way: as an offering to help its readers make some progress in approaching peace in as many ways as possible and regardless of whether—or even, where—they eventually arrive.

Understanding War

It may seem perverse to begin our survey of "approaches to peace" by looking at the causes of war. But it can't be helped. War is humanity's most inhumane and destructive endeavor. Destroying not only lives, property, the environment, hopes, and dreams, it also wreaks havoc with any prospects for "positive peace," the goal for which most workers in peace studies strive. Accordingly, we must understand some of the causes of war. And this, alas, is easier said than done.

Mark Twain is reputed to have said that it was easy to stop smoking; he had done it hundreds of times! Similarly, it is easy to identify the causes of war: it seems there are hundreds of them.

"War" does not exist as a generality. There are, instead, individual wars, just as there are individual human beings. And just as every person is unique (not only genetically but also in the private trajectory of his or her experience), it can be argued that the causes of *each* war require detailed study. The danger thus exists that in attempting to unravel the causes of war, or even of a particular war, we will fall into the error portrayed by poet John Saxe, when he depicted the blind men and the elephant:

> It was six men from Industan, to learning much inclined,
> Who went to see the elephant (though all of them were blind),
> that each by observation might satisfy his mind . . .

Each felt a different part of the elephant, and so the one touching the legs thought it was a tree, the one touching the tail thought it was a snake, and so forth. As it turned out, the blind men

> disputed loud and long, each in his opinion stiff and strong,
> though each was partly in the right, and all of them were wrong.

In trying to comprehend the cause(s) of war, each of the efforts presented in this chapter is similarly "wrong." But if we put them all together—and add a number of others, which considerations of space have prevented inclusion of in this book—it

5

is possible to get a comprehensive view of the peculiar, complex elephant that is war. Despite the fact that every person is unique, it is also true that useful generalizations can be made about *Homo sapiens*. Similar generalizations can be made about that "species" of human behavior known as war.

It goes almost without saying that—at least from the Western perspective—every effect must have a preexisting cause, and war should be no exception, even though there has been vigorous debate as to how best to categorize these causative factors. Not surprisingly, and not inappropriately, the search for war's causes has often become an effort to finger a limited number of identifiable culprits, or villains:

> In the eighteenth century, many philosophers thought that the ambitions of absolute monarchs were the main cause of war; pull down the mighty, and wars would become rare. Another theory contended that many wars came from the Anglo-French rivalry for colonies and commerce: restrain that quest, and peace would be more easily preserved. The wars following the French Revolution fostered an idea that popular revolutions were becoming the main cause of international war. In the nineteenth century, monarchs who sought to unite their troubled country by a glorious foreign war were widely seen as culprits. At the end of that century the capitalists' chase for markets or investment outlets became a popular villain. The First World War convinced many writers that armaments races and arms salesmen had become the villains, and both world wars fostered the idea that militarist regimes were the main disturbers of the peace.[1]

Circumstances thus do not only influence not only events but also the interpretation of events. During the U.S.–Soviet Cold War for example (not a direct shooting war but a period of heightened tensions, characterized by a vigorous nuclear arms race in addition to many "proxy wars," as in Korea, Vietnam, and Afghanistan), peace researchers tended to emphasize the clash of ideologies, and the role of misunderstandings and misperceptions, as well as the potential danger of false alarms, while attributing roughly equal blame to expansionist tendencies on the part of the United States and the Soviet Union. Much attention was also given to the dynamics of arms races and the dangers of crisis decision making. With the Cold War gone—but with war and warlike situations continuing—emphasis has shifted to nationalist passions as well as to religious and ethnic conflicts.

Some researchers, attempting a more detached perspective, have looked to possible causes that are less situation-linked, in the process coming up with theories connecting the onset of wars to factors as diverse as grand cycles of history and sunspots; population pressure; sexual competition and frustration; early childhood experiences; protein shortage; and even the existence of pure, unmitigated evil.

Preferred explanations are also influenced by political orientation. Thus, capitalism is often blamed by leftists, communism by conservatives, religion by atheists and atheism by the religious! Progressive and left-leaning thinkers are generally more likely to attribute war to misunderstandings and other psychological factors, whereas those of the political right are generally more comfortable identifying what they see as innate human

---

[1] Geoffrey Blainey, *The Causes of War* (New York: Free Press, 1973).

depravity. Nor is professional orientation irrelevant: biologists, for example, are prone to suggest that insight into the causes of war can be derived from consulting the human gene pool as well as by from examining aggressive behavior in animals. Psychologists are likely to emphasize the importance of individual experience, whether early in life or as a result of learning and social conditioning, perceptions, and misperceptions. For many anthropologists, nontechnological war among "primitive" people can provide models for the more elaborate war of modern nation-states. Sociologists are inclined toward explanations that involve complex group processes, such as stability, national image, and the dynamics of industrialization, religious teachings or militarization. For political scientists, war-proneness cannot be meaningfully separated from the governmental systems involved or from reigning political ideologies. Economists, not surprisingly, are struck not only by the economic consequences of war and preparation for war but also by the role of markets, competition, and economic systems in predisposing a country toward war. Mathematically inclined analysts examine quantitative models, including the so-called Prisoner's Dilemma, whereas theologians, psychiatrists, lawyers, and military specialists all have their own favored interpretations of why and under what conditions people are likely to resort to war.

This diversity should be seen as a source of hope, not discouragement. After all, it would be absurd to think that anything as complex as war could be "explained" in a single, simple way. (If it could, then the problem of war would probably have been solved long ago, and this book would be concerned only with "positive peace!") When it comes to understanding the causes of war, diversity is not only a source of strength, it is also more likely to yield answers.

In attempting to assess the causes of any war, or of war in general, it is important to distinguish between the announced reason(s) for its outbreak, which are often excuses concocted as public justification, and the actual, underlying causes, which may not even be accessible to the participants. One must also identify not only immediate precipitating factors (often military, political, or economic) but also preexisting historical antecedents as well as any other causes that may lie deeper yet, within the specific individuals involved, and also, perhaps, within human beings generally.

Take an undeclared war, the so-called Gulf War of 1991, in which the United States mobilized and led a multinational, United Nations coalition that drove Iraqi forces out of Kuwait. What was its cause? Here are just a few possibilities.

1. The role of leaders: The Iraqi leader, Saddam Hussein, was a violent, aggressive dictator, who took an opportunity to invade his defenseless neighbor, hoping to enhance his political prestige; and/or, the United StatesU.S. president George Bush was largely responsible because he felt personally challenged and perceived a need to banish his "wimp" image before the next presidential election.
2. Economic factors: Iraq sought to gain the economic benefits that would come from capturing Kuwaiti oil fields; and/or U.S. economic dependence on Middle Eastern oil made it willing to "trade blood for oil."
3. Psychological decision-making factors: Saddam Hussein misunderstood the position of the United States when the U.S. ambassador indicated that Iraq's border dispute with Kuwait was

an Iraqi–Kuwaiti matter and not one that the United States considered vital to its "national interest"; and/or the American public's fears and hatreds were aroused by reports of Iraqi brutality toward Kuwaitis; and/or the Iraqi public was envious of the ostentatious wealth of the neighboring Kuwaitis; and/or Arab people, frustrated by their inability to defeat Israel, were eager to vent their rage against other enemies.

4. Historical factors: British colonialism actually caused the war, for when the British withdrew from the area, they created an artificial border between Iraq and Kuwait because the British wanted to establish a pliant sheikdom that would permit Western oil companies to dominate the extraction of petroleum from the region; and/or the U.S. military and political leadership wanted to prove that it had outgrown the "Vietnam syndrome," a supposed hesitancy in the aftermath of the U.S. military debacle in Vietnam.

5. The military-industrial complex: The U.S. military wanted to test an array of newly developed weapons and also to demonstrate its importance because, with the ending of the Cold War, people had begun to question the value of maintaining a huge military establishment; and/or the U.S. "military-industrial complex" was eager for a war so it could profit from greater demand for new weapons systems.

6. International politics and law: Iraq's invasion of Kuwait was a clear invasion violation of international law, such that the maintenance of long-term peace and stability required a clear and vigorous response; and/or with the end of the Cold War, the United States no longer felt constrained by the prospect that the Soviet Union (previously Iraq's ally) would support Iraq

For better or worse, a different list—similar in its complexity, unique in its specifics—can be constructed for every war. It would be a useful exercise, in fact, to select a few wars and do just that. The fact that the causes of war are often complex, diffuse, and multidimensional does not mean that searching for them is a waste of time. Out of that search can come a deeper understanding of the dilemma that is war; moreover, our insights into the causes of war will have great influence on methods of preventing specific ones as well as on the prospects for eliminating war altogether.

Sigmund Freud

WHY WAR?

Psychiatric theories of war emphasize the role of individuals, both as leaders and as personal participants. Carl G. Jung, for example, attached special importance to the existence of a "dark side" within human nature. For Jungian analysts, this dark side, unacceptable to one's consciousness, is "projected" onto an Other, who becomes the Enemy, imbued with an array of hateful traits . . . which actually originate within one's self. Jung was impressed with what he considered the human "collective unconscious," including powerful images such as those of heroes and enemies. Alfred Adler attributed great importance to interpersonal struggles for social dominance and to the "inferiority complex."

The American psychiatrist Harry Stack Sullivan felt that human fears and anxieties derived from inhibited communication, which in turn gave rise to terror-ridden distortions, which in their turn produce a tendency to strike out at those one does not understand and who are different. For Erik Erikson, personal wholeness and healthy integration can be threatened by confusing social ambiguity, both at home and in the society; as a result, according to Erikson, the confused individual may seek refuge in "totalism," which leads to unquestioning identification of the Self with the State, along with equally total rejection of the selfhood of others. Another important psychiatric theorist of war was Erich Fromm, who examined the formation of various "malignant," pathological personalities, especially among despotic, violence-prone leaders such as Hitler and Stalin.

The towering figure among psychiatrists looking for the causes of war, however, was Sigmund Freud, founder of psychoanalysis. For Freud, there is a direct link between aggression—a behavior of individuals—and the social phenomenon that is war, in that both are manifestations of the same underlying drive system. He believed that much "inhumane" behavior was in fact all too human, deriving from the operation of "Thanatos," or the death instinct, which he saw as opposed to "Eros," the life instinct. Although many of Freud's notions appear quaint today, and some of them could be seen as downright crackpot, his identification of the unconscious remains central to nearly all efforts to explain war (and most other behavior) at the level of the individual.

In 1932 Albert Einstein was invited by the League of Nations to initiate an exchange of views with another renowned person on a subject of Einstein's choosing. Einstein selected the question, "Is there any way of delivering mankind from the menace of war?" and his chosen correspondent was Sigmund Freud. A selection from Freud's famous response is reprinted here.

Conflicts of interest between man and man are resolved, in principle, by the recourse to violence. It is the same in the animal kingdom, from which man cannot claim exclusion; nevertheless, men are also prone to conflicts of opinion touching, on occasion, the loftiest peaks of abstract thought, which seem to call for settlement by quite another method. This refinement is, however, a late development. To start with, brute force was the factor which, in small communities, decided points of ownership and the question which man's will was to prevail. Very soon physical force was implemented, then replaced, by the use of various adjuncts; he proved the victor whose weapon was the better or handled the more skillfully. Now, for the first time, with the coming of weapons, superior brains began to oust brute force, but the object of the conflict remained the same: one party was to be constrained, by the injury done him or impairment of his strength, to retract a claim or a refusal. This end is most effectively gained when the opponent is definitively put out of action—in other words, is killed. This procedure has two advantages; the enemy cannot renew hostilities, and, second, his fate deters others from following his example. Moreover, the slaughter of a foe gratifies an instinctive craving—a point to which we shall revert hereafter. However, another consideration may be set off against this will to kill: the possibility of using an enemy for servile tasks if his spirit be broken and his life spared. Here violence finds an outlet not in slaughter but in subjugation. Hence springs the practice of giving quarter; but the victor, having from now on to reckon with the craving for revenge that rankles in his victim, forfeits to some extent his personal security.

Thus, under primitive conditions, it is superior force—brute violence or violence backed by arms—that lords it everywhere. We know that in the course of evolution this state of things was modified, a path was traced that led away from violence to law. But what was this path? Surely it issued from a single verity: that the superiority of one strong man can be overborne by an alliance of many weaklings, that *l'union fait la force*. Brute force is overcome by union, the allied might of scattered units makes good its right against the isolated giant. Thus we may define "right" (i.e., law) as the might of a community. Yet it, too, is nothing else than violence, quick to attack whatever individual stands in its path, and it employs the selfsame methods, follows like ends, with but one difference; it is the communal, not individual, violence that has its way. But, for the transition from crude violence to the reign of law, a certain psychological condition must first obtain. The union of the majority must be stable and enduring. If its sole *raison d'être* be the discomfiture of some overweening individual and, after his downfall, it be dissolved, it leads to nothing. Some other man, trusting to his superior power, will seek to reinstate the rule of violence, and the cycle will repeat itself unendingly. Thus the union of the people must be permanent and well organized; it must enact rules to meet the risk of possible revolts, must set up machinery ensuring that its rules—the laws—are observed and that such acts of violence as the laws demand are duly carried out. This recognition of a community of interests engenders among the members of the group a sentiment of unity and fraternal solidarity which constitutes its real strength.

So far I have set out what seems to me the kernel of the matter: the suppression of brute force by the transfer of power to a larger combination, founded on the community of sentiments linking up its members. All the rest is mere tautology and glosses. Now, the position is simple enough so long as the community consists of a number of equipollent individuals. The laws of such a group can determine to what extent the individual must forfeit his personal freedom, the right of using personal force as an instrument of violence, to ensure the safety of the group. But such a combination is only theoretically possible; in practice the situation is always complicated by the fact that, from the outset, the group includes elements of unequal power, men and women, elders and children, and, very soon, as a result of war and conquest, victors and the vanquished—that is, masters and slaves—as well. From this time on the common law takes notice of these inequalities of power, laws are made by and for the rulers, giving the servile classes fewer rights. . . .

Thus we see that, even within the group itself, the exercise of violence cannot be avoided when conflicting interests are at stake. But the common needs and habits of men who live in fellowship under the same sky favor a speedy issue of such conflicts and, this being so, the possibilities of peaceful solutions make steady progress. Yet the most casual glance at world history will show an unending series of conflicts between one community and another or a group of others, between large and smaller units, between cities, countries, races, tribes, and kingdoms, almost all of which were settled by the ordeal of war. Such wars end either in pillage or in conquest and its fruits, the downfall of the loser. No single all-embracing judgment can be passed on these wars of aggrandizement. Some, like the war between the Mongols and the Turks, have led to unmitigated misery; others, however, have furthered the transition from violence to law, since they brought larger units into being, within whose limits a recourse to violence was banned and a new regime determined all disputes. Thus the Roman conquests brought that boon, the *Pax Romana*, to the Mediterranean lands. The French kings' lust for aggrandizement created a new France, flourishing in peace and unity. Paradoxical as it sounds, we must admit that warfare well might serve to pave the way to that unbroken peace we so desire, for it is war that brings vast empires into being, within whose frontiers all warfare is proscribed by a strong central power. In practice, however, this end is not attained, for as a rule the fruits of victory are but short-lived, the new-created unit falls asunder once again, generally because there can be no true cohesion between the parts that violence has welded. Hitherto, moreover, such conquests have only led to aggregations which, for all their magnitude, had limits, and disputes between these units could be resolved only by recourse to arms. For humanity at large the sole result of all these military enterprises was that, instead of frequent not to say incessant little wars, they had now to face great wars which, for all they came less often, were so much the more destructive. . . .

I now can comment on another of your statements. You are amazed that it is so easy to infect men with the war fever, and you surmise that man has in him an active instinct for hatred and destruction, amenable to such stimulations. I entirely agree with you. I believe in the existence of this instinct and have been recently at pains to study its manifestations. In this connection may I set out a fragment of that knowledge of the instincts, which we psychoanalysts, after so many tentative essays and gropings in the dark, have compassed? We assume that human instincts are of two kinds: those that conserve and unify, which we call "erotic" (in the meaning Plato gives to *eros* in his *Symposium*) or else "sexual" (explicitly extending the popular connotation of "sex"); and, second, the instincts to destroy and kill, which we assimilate as the aggressive or destructive instincts. These are, as you perceive, the well-known opposites, love and hate, transformed into theoretical entities; they are, perhaps, another aspect of those eternal polarities, attraction and repulsion, which fall within your province. But we must be chary of passing overhastily to the notions of good and evil. Each of these instincts is every whit as indispensable as its opposite, and all the phenomena of life derive from their activity, whether they work in concert or in opposition. It seems that an instinct of either category can operate but rarely in isolation; it is always blended ("alloyed," as we say) with a certain dosage of its opposite, which modifies its aim or even, in certain circumstances, is a prime condition of its attainment. Thus the instinct of self-preservation is certainly of an erotic nature, but to gain its ends this very instinct necessitates aggressive action. In the same way the love instinct, when directed to a specific object, calls for an admixture of the acquisitive instinct if it is to enter into effective possession of that object. It is the difficulty of isolating the two kinds of instinct in their manifestations that has so long prevented us from recognizing them.

If you travel with me a little further on this road, you will find that human affairs are complicated in yet another way. Only exceptionally does an action follow on the stimulus of a single instinct, which is per se a blend of *eros* and destructiveness. . . . Thus, when a nation is summoned to engage in war, a whole gamut of human motives may respond to this appeal; high and low motives, some openly avowed, others slurred over. The lust for aggression and destruction is certainly included; the innumerable cruelties of history and man's daily life confirm its prevalence and strength. The stimulation of these destructive impulses by appeals to idealism and the erotic instinct naturally facilitates their release. Musing on the atrocities recorded on history's page, we feel that the ideal motive has often served as a camouflage for the lust of destruction; sometimes, as with the cruelties of the Inquisition, it seems that, while the ideal motives occupied the foreground of consciousness, they drew their strength from the destructive instincts submerged in the unconscious. Both interpretations are feasible.

You are interested, I know, in the prevention of war, not in our theories, and I keep this fact in mind. Yet I would like to dwell a little longer on this destructive instinct which is seldom given the attention that its importance warrants. With the least of speculative efforts we are led to conclude that this instinct functions in every living being, striving to work its ruin and reduce life to its primal state of inert matter. Indeed it might well be called the "death instinct," whereas the erotic instincts vouch for the struggle to live on. The death instinct becomes an impulse to destruction when, with the aid of certain organs, it directs its action outward, against external objects. The living being, that is to say, defends its own existence by destroying foreign bodies. But, in one of its activities, the death instinct is operative *within* the living being, and we have sought to trace back a number of normal and pathological phenomena to this *introversion* of the destructive instinct. We have even committed the heresy of explaining the origin of human conscience by some such "turning inward" of the aggressive impulse. Obviously when this internal tendency operates on too large a scale, it is no trivial matter, rather a positively morbid state of things; whereas the diversion of the destructive impulse toward the external world must have beneficial effects. Here is then the biological justification for all those vile, pernicious propensities which we now are combating. We can but own that they are really more akin to nature than this our stand against them, which, in fact, remains to be accounted for. . . .

The upshot of these observations, as bearing on the subject in hand, is that there is no likelihood of our being able to suppress humanity's aggressive tendencies. In some happy corners of the earth, they say, where nature brings forth abundantly whatever man desires, there flourish races whose lives go gently by, unknowing of aggression or constraint. This I can hardly credit; I would like further details about these happy folk. The Bolshevists, too, aspire to do away with human aggressiveness by ensuring the satisfaction of material needs and enforcing equality between man and man. To me this hope seems vain. Meanwhile they busily perfect their armaments, and their hatred of outsiders is not the least of the factors of cohesion amongst themselves. In any case, as you too have observed, complete suppression of man's aggressive tendencies is not in issue; what we may try is to divert it into a channel other than that of warfare.

From our "mythology" of the instincts, we may easily deduce a formula for an indirect method of eliminating war. If the propensity for war be due to the destructive instinct, we have always its counteragent, *eros*, to our hand. All that produces ties of sentiment between man and man must serve us as war's antidote. These ties are of two kinds. First, such relations as those toward a beloved object, void though they be of sexual intent. The psychoanalyst need feel no compunction in mentioning "love" in this connection; religion uses the same language: "Love thy neighbor as thyself." A pious injunction easy to announce, but hard to carry out! The other bond of sentiment is by way of identification. All that brings out the significant resemblances between men calls into play this feeling of community, identification, whereon is founded, in large measure, the whole edifice of human society.

. . . The ideal conditions would obviously be found in a community where every man subordinated his instinctive life to the dictates of reason. Nothing less than this could bring about so thorough and so durable a union between men, even if this involved the severance of mutual ties of sentiment. But surely such a hope is utterly Utopian, as things are. The other indirect methods of preventing war are certainly more feasible, but entail no quick results. They conjure up an ugly picture of mills which grind so slowly that, before the flour is ready, men are dead of hunger.

As you see, little good comes of consulting a theoretician, aloof from worldly contacts, on practical and urgent problems! Better it were to tackle each successive crisis with means that we have ready to our hands. However, I would like to deal with a question which, though it is not mooted in your letter, interests me greatly. Why do we, you and I and many another, protest so vehemently against war, instead of just accepting it as another of life's odious importunities? For it seems a natural thing enough, biologically sound and practically unavoidable. I trust you will not be shocked by my raising such a question. For the better conduct of an inquiry it may be well to don a mask of feigned aloofness. The answer to my query may run as follows: because every man has a right over his own life, and war destroys lives that were full of promise; it forces the individual into situations that shame his manhood, obliging him to murder fellow men, against his will; it ravages material amenities, the fruits of human toil, and much besides. Moreover, wars, as now conducted, afford no scope for acts of heroism according to the old ideals, and, given the high perfection of modern arms, war today would mean the sheer extermination of one of the combatants, if not of both. This is so true, so obvious, that we can but wonder why the conduct of war is not banned by general consent. Doubtless either of the points I have just made is open to debate. It may be asked if the community, in its turn, cannot claim a right over the individual lives of its members. Moreover, all forms of war cannot be indiscriminately condemned; so long as there are nations and empires, each prepared callously to exterminate its rival, all alike must be equipped for war. But we will not dwell on any of these problems; they lie outside the debate to which you have invited me. I pass on to another point, the basis, as it strikes me, of our common hatred of war. It is this: we cannot do otherwise than hate it. Pacifists we are, since our organic nature wills us thus to be. Hence it comes easy to us to find arguments that justify our standpoint.

This point, however, calls for elucidation. Here is the way in which I see it. The cultural development of mankind (some, I know, prefer to call it civilization) has been in progress since immemorial antiquity. . . . It well may lead to the extinction of mankind, for it impairs the sexual function in more than one respect, and even today the uncivilized races and the backward classes of all nations are multiplying more rapidly than the cultured elements. This process may, perhaps, be likened to the effect of domestication on certain animals—it clearly involves physical changes of structure—but the view that cultural development is an organic process of this order has not yet become generally familiar. The psychic changes which accompany this process of cultural change are striking and not to be gainsaid. They consist in the progressive rejection of instinctive ends and a scaling down of instinctive reactions. Sensations which delighted our forefathers have become neutral or unbearable to us; and, if our ethical and aesthetic ideals have undergone a change, the causes of this are ultimately organic. On the psychological side two of the most important phenomena of culture are, first, a strengthening of the intellect, which tends to master our instinctive life, and, second, an introversion of the aggressive impulse, with all its consequent benefits and perils. Now war runs most emphatically counter to the psychic disposition imposed on us by the growth of culture; we are therefore bound to resent war, to find it utterly intolerable. With pacifists like us it is not merely an intellectual and affective repulsion, but a constitutional intolerance, an idiosyncrasy in its most drastic form. And it would seem that the aesthetic ignominies of warfare play almost as large a part in this repugnance as war's atrocities.

How long have we to wait before the rest of men turn pacifist? Impossible to say, and yet perhaps our hope that these two factors—man's cultural disposition and a well-founded dread of the form future wars will take—may serve to put an end to war in the future.

Konrad Z. Lorenz

ON AGGRESSION

Maybe human beings are "instinctively" aggressive. Not surprisingly, this approach to understanding aggression has been especially prominent among biologists, themselves strongly influenced by a Darwinian approach to human nature. Of these, perhaps the most influential has been the Austrian ethologist Konrad Z. Lorenz, who shared a Nobel Prize in 1973 for his research on animal behavior. According to his thinking, there are a variety of positive, adaptive advantages to animal—and human—aggression. This is not to say that Lorenz extolled human aggressiveness; rather, he sought to understand its origin, pointing out that with the advent of modern technology, the human penchant for violence has become *Homo sapiens'* greatest danger, especially in conjunction with "militant enthusiasm" and, ironically, a *lack* of human instincts when it comes to restraints on violence.

In recent years, a more sophisticated version of instinctivism has gained currency. Known as "sociobiology," this approach is even more avowedly evolutionary, emphasizing that the capacity for aggressiveness is within the biological repertoire of human beings, just as it is for many other living things. But so are cooperation and altruism. The key, then, is to identify circumstances in which people are predisposed to one behavior pattern or the other. Although biologists no longer accept "good of the species" arguments, I have chosen the following selection because the writings of Konrad Lorenz have been so influential.

What is the value of all this fighting? In nature, fighting is such an ever-present process, its behavior mechanisms and weapons are so highly developed and have so obviously arisen under the selection pressure of a species-preserving function, that it is our duty to ask this Darwinian question.

The layman, misguided by sensationalism in press and film, imagines the relationship between the various "wild beasts of the jungle" to be a bloodthirsty struggle, all against all. In a widely shown film, a Bengal tiger was seen fighting with a python, and immediately afterward the python with a crocodile.

With a clear conscience I can assert that such things never occur under natural conditions. What advantage would one of these animals gain from exterminating the other? Neither of them interferes with the other's vital interests.

Darwin's expression, "the struggle for existence," is sometimes erroneously interpreted as the struggle between different species. In reality, the struggle Darwin was thinking of and which drives evolution forward is the competition between near relations. What causes a species to disappear or become transformed into a different species is the profitable "invention" that falls by chance to one or a few of its members in the everlasting gamble of hereditary change. The descendants of these lucky ones gradually outstrip all others until the particular species consists only of individuals who possess the new "invention."

There are, however, fightlike contests between members of different species: at night an owl kills and eats even well-armed birds of prey, in spite of their vigorous defense, and when these birds meet the owl by day they attack it ferociously. Almost every animal capable of self-defense, from the smallest rodent upward, fights furiously when it is cornered and has no means of escape. Besides these three particular types of inter-specific fighting, there are other, less typical cases; for instance, two cave-nesting birds of different species may fight for a nesting cavity. Something must be said here about these three types of inter-specific fighting in order to explain their peculiarity and to distinguish them from the *intra*-specific aggression which is really the subject of this book.

The survival value of inter-specific fights is much more evident than that of intra-specific contests. The way in which a predatory animal and its prey influence each other's evolution is a classical example of how the selection pressure of a certain function causes corresponding adaptations. The swiftness of the hunted ungulate forces its feline pursuers to evolve enormous leaping power and sharply armed toes. Paleontological discoveries have shown impressive examples of such evolutionary competition between weapons of attack and those of defense. The teeth of grazing animals have achieved better and better grinding power, while, in their parallel evolution, nutritional plants have devised means of protecting themselves against being eaten, as by the storage of silicates and the development of hard, wooden thorns. This kind of "fight" between the eater and the eaten never goes so far that the predator causes extinction of the prey: a state of equilibrium is always established between them, endurable by both species. The last lions would have died of hunger long before they had killed the last pair of antelopes or zebras; . . .

The opposite process, the "counteroffensive" of the prey against the predator, is more nearly related to genuine aggression. Social animals in particular take every possible chance to attack the "eating enemy" that threatens their safety. This process is called "mobbing." Crows or other birds "mob" a cat or any other nocturnal predator, if they catch sight of it by day. . . .

All the cases described above, in which animals of different species fight against each other, have one thing in common: every one of the fighters gains an obvious advantage by its behavior or, at least, in the interests of preserving the species it "ought to" gain one. But intra-specific aggression, aggression in the proper and narrower sense of the word, also fulfills a species-preserving function. Here, too, the Darwinian question "What for?" may and must be asked. Many people will not see the obvious justification for this question, and those accustomed to the classical psychoanalytical way of thinking will probably regard it as a frivolous attempt to vindicate the life-destroying principle or, purely and simply, evil. The average normal civilized human being witnesses aggression only when two of his fellow citizens or two of his domestic animals fight, and therefore sees only its evil effects. In addition there is the alarming progression of aggressive actions ranging from cocks fighting in the barnyard to dogs biting each other, boys thrashing each other, young men throwing beer mugs at each other's heads, and so on to barroom brawls about politics, and finally to wars and atom bombs.

With humanity in its present cultural and technological situation, we have good reason to consider intra-specific aggression the greatest of all dangers. We shall not improve our chances of counteracting it if we accept it as something metaphysical and inevitable, but on the other hand, we shall perhaps succeed in finding remedies if we investigate the chain of its natural causation. Wherever man has achieved the power of voluntarily guiding a natural phenomenon in a certain direction, he has owed it to his understanding of the chain of causes which formed it. Physiology, the science concerned with the normal life processes and how they fulfill their species-preserving function, forms the essential foundation for pathology, the science investigating their disturbances. Let us forget for a moment that the aggression drive has become derailed under conditions of civilization, and let us inquire impartially into its natural causes. For the reasons already given, as good Darwinians we must inquire into the species-preserving function which, under natural—or rather precultural—conditions, is fulfilled by fights within the species, and which by the process of selection has caused the advanced development of intra-specific fighting behavior in so many higher animals. It is not only fishes that fight their own species: the majority of vertebrates do so too, man included.

Darwin had already raised the question of the survival value of fighting, and he has given us an enlightening answer: It is always favorable to the future of a species if the stronger of two rivals takes possession either of the territory or of the desired female. . . .

Unless the special interests of a social organization demand close aggregation of its members, it is obviously most expedient to spread the individuals of an animal species as evenly as possible over the available habitat. To use a human analogy: if, in a certain area, a larger number of doctors, builders, and mechanics want to exist, the representatives of these professions will do well to settle as far away from each other as possible.

The danger of too dense a population of an animal species settling in one part of the available biotope and exhausting all its sources of nutrition and so starving can be obviated by a mutual repulsion acting on the animals of the same species, effecting their regular spacing out, in much the same manner as electrical charges are regularly distributed all over the surface of a spherical conductor. This, in plain terms, is the most important survival value of intra-specific aggression. . . .

I think it has been adequately shown that the aggression of so many animals toward members of their own species is in no way detrimental to the species but, on the contrary, is essential for its preservation. However, this must not raise false hopes about the present situation of mankind. Innate behavior mechanisms can be thrown completely out of balance by small, apparently insignificant changes of environmental conditions. Inability to adapt quickly to such changes may bring about the destruction of a species, and the changes which man has wrought in his environment are by no means insignificant.

An unprejudiced observer from another planet, looking upon man as he is today, in his hand the atom bomb, the product of his intelligence, in his heart the aggression drive inherited from his anthropoid ancestors, which this same intelligence cannot control, would not prophesy long life for the species. Looking at the situation as a human being whom it personally concerns, it seems like a bad dream, and it is hard to believe that aggression is anything but the pathological product of our disjointed cultural and social life.

And one could only wish it were no more than that! Knowledge of the fact that the aggression drive is a true, primarily species-preserving instinct enables us to recognize its full danger: it is the spontaneity of the instinct that makes it so dangerous. If it were merely a reaction to certain external factors, as many sociologists and psychologists maintain, the state of mankind would not be as perilous as it really is, for, in that case, the reaction-eliciting factors could be eliminated with some hope of success. It was Freud who first pointed out the essential spontaneity of instincts, though he recognized that of aggression only rather late. He also showed that lack of social contact, and above all deprivation of it (*Liebesverlust*), were among the factors strongly predisposing to facilitate aggression. However, the conclusions which many American psychologists drew from this correct surmise were erroneous. It was supposed that children would grow up less neurotic, better adapted to their social environment, and less aggressive if they were spared all disappointments and indulged in every way. An American method of education, based on these surmises, only showed that the aggressive drive, like many other instincts, springs "spontaneously" from the inner human being, and the results of this method of upbringing were countless unbearably rude children who were anything but nonaggressive. . . .

It is a curious paradox that the greatest gifts of man, the unique faculties of conceptual thought and verbal speech which have raised him to a level high above all other creatures and given him mastery over the globe, are not altogether blessings, or at least are blessings that have to be paid for very dearly indeed. All the great dangers threatening humanity with extinction are direct consequences of conceptual thought and verbal speech. They drove man out of the paradise in which he could follow his instincts with impunity and do or not do whatever he pleased. There is much truth in the parable of the tree of knowledge and its fruit, though I want to make an addition to it to make it fit into my own picture of Adam: that apple was thoroughly unripe! Knowledge springing from conceptual thought robbed man of the security provided by his well-adapted instincts long, long before it was sufficient to provide him with an equally safe adaptation. Man is, as Arnold Gehlen has so truly said, by nature a jeopardized creature. . . .

I have spoken of the inhibitions controlling aggression in various social animals, preventing it from injuring or killing fellow members of the species. As I explained, these inhibitions are most important and consequently most highly differentiated in those animals which are capable of killing living creatures of about their own size. A raven can peck out the eye of another with one thrust of its beak, a wolf can rip the jugular vein of another with a single bite. There would be no more ravens and no more wolves if reliable inhibitions did not prevent such actions. Neither a dove nor a hare nor even a chimpanzee is able to kill its own kind with a single peck or bite; in addition, animals with relatively poor defense weapons have a correspondingly great ability to escape quickly, even from specially armed predators which are more efficient in chasing, catching, and killing than even the strongest of their own species. Since there rarely is, in nature, the possibility of such an animal's seriously injuring one of its own kind, there is no selection pressure at work here to breed in killing inhibitions. The absence of such inhibitions is apparent to the animal keeper, to his own and to his animals' disadvantage, if he does not take seriously the intra-specific fights of completely "harmless" animals. Under the unnatural conditions of captivity, where a defeated animal cannot escape from its victor, it may be killed slowly and cruelly. In my book *King Solomon's Ring*, I have described in the chapter "Morals and Weapons" how the symbol of peace, the dove, can torture one of its own kind to death, without the arousal of any inhibition.

Anthropologists concerned with the habits of Australopithecus have repeatedly stressed that these hunting progenitors of man have left humanity with the dangerous heritage of what they term "carnivorous mentality." This statement confuses the concepts of the carnivore and the cannibal, which are to a large extent, mutually exclusive. One can only deplore the fact that man has definitely not got a carnivorous mentality! All his trouble arises from his being a basically harmless, omnivorous creature, lacking in natural weapons with which to kill big prey, and, therefore, also devoid of the built-in safety devices which prevent "professional" carnivores from abusing their killing power to destroy fellow members of their own species. A lion or a wolf may, on extremely rare occasions, kill another by one angry stroke, but, all heavily armed carnivores possess sufficiently reliable inhibitions which prevent the self-destruction of the species.

In human evolution, no inhibitory mechanisms preventing sudden manslaughter were necessary, because quick killing was impossible anyhow; the potential victim had plenty of opportunity to elicit the pity of the aggressor by submissive gestures and appeasing attitudes. No selection pressure arose in the prehistory of mankind to breed inhibitory mechanisms preventing the killing of conspecifics until, all of a sudden, the invention of artificial weapons upset the equilibrium of killing potential and social inhibitions. When it did, man's position was very nearly that of a dove which, by some unnatural trick of nature, has suddenly acquired the beak of a raven. One shudders at the thought of a creature as irascible as all prehuman primates are, swinging a well-sharpened handax. Humanity would indeed have destroyed itself by its first inventions, were it not for the very wonderful fact that inventions and responsibility are both the achievements of the same specifically human faculty of asking questions.

Not that our prehuman ancestor, even at a stage as yet devoid of moral responsibility, was a fiend incarnate; he was by no means poorer in social instincts and inhibitions than a chimpanzee, which, after all, is—his irascibility not withstanding—a social and friendly creature. But whatever his innate norms of social behavior may have been, they were bound to be thrown out of gear by the invention of weapons. If humanity survived, as, after all, it did, it never achieved security from the danger of self-destruction. If moral responsibility and unwillingness to kill have indubitably increased, the ease and emotional impunity of killing have increased at the same rate. The distance at which all shooting weapons take effect screens the killer against the stimulus situation which would otherwise activate his killing inhibitions. The deep, emotional layers of our personality simply do not register the fact that the crooking of the forefinger to release a shot tears the entrails of another man. No sane man would even go rabbit hunting for pleasure if the necessity of killing his prey with his natural weapons brought home to him the full, emotional realization of what he is actually doing.

The same principle applies, to an even greater degree, to the use of modern remote-control weapons. The man who presses the releasing button is so completely screened against seeing, hearing, or otherwise emotionally realizing the consequences of his action, that he can commit it with impunity—even if he is burdened with the power of imagination. Only thus can it be explained that perfectly good-natured men, who would not even smack a naughty child, proved to be perfectly able to release rockets or to lay carpets of incendiary bombs on sleeping cities, thereby committing hundreds and thousands of children to a horrible death in the flames. The fact that it is good, normal men who did this, is as eerie as any fiendish atrocity of war! . . .

Militant enthusiasm is particularly suited for the paradigmatic illustration of the manner in which a phylogenetically evolved pattern of behavior interacts with culturally ritualized social norms and rites, and in which, though absolutely indispensable to the function of the compound system, it is prone to miscarry most tragically if not strictly controlled by rational responsibility based on causal insight. The Greek word *enthousiasmos* implies that a person is possessed by a god; the German *Begeisterung* means that he is controlled by a spirit, a *Geist*, more or less holy.

In reality, militant enthusiasm is a specialized form of communal aggression, clearly distinct from and yet functionally related to the more primitive forms of petty individual aggression. Every man of normally strong emotions knows, from his own experience, the subjective phenomena that go hand in hand with the response of militant enthusiasm. A shiver runs down the back and, as more exact observation shows, along the outside of both arms. One soars elated, above all the ties of everyday life, one is ready to abandon all for the call of what, in the moment of this specific emotion, seems to be a sacred duty. All obstacles in its path become unimportant; the instinctive inhibitions against hurting or killing one's fellows lose, unfortunately, much of their power. Rational considerations, criticisms, and all reasonable arguments against the behavior dictated by militant enthusiasm are silenced by an amazing reversal of all values, making them appear not only untenable but base and dishonorable. Men may enjoy the feeling of absolute righteousness even while they commit atrocities. Conceptual thought and moral responsibility are at their lowest ebb. As a Ukrainian proverb says: "When the banner is unfurled, all reason is in the trumpet." . . .

Anybody who has ever seen the corresponding behavior of the male chimpanzee defending his band or family with self-sacrificing courage will doubt the purely spiritual character of human enthusiasm. The chimp, too, sticks out his chin, stiffens his body, and raises his elbows; his hair stands on end, producing a terrifying magnification of his body contours as seen from the front. The inward rotation of his arms obviously has the purpose of turning the longest-haired side outward to enhance the effect. The whole combination of body attitude and hair-raising constitutes a bluff. This is also seen when a cat humps its back, and is calculated to make the animal appear bigger and more dangerous than it really is. Our shiver, which in German poetry is called a *"heiliger Schauer,"* a "holy" shiver, turns out to be the vestige of a prehuman vegetative response of making a fur bristle which we no longer have.

To the humble seeker of biological truth there cannot be the slightest doubt that human militant enthusiasm evolved out of a communal defense response of our prehuman ancestors. The unthinking single-mindedness of the response must have been of high survival value even in a tribe of fully evolved human beings. It was necessary for the individual male to forget all his other allegiances in order to be able to dedicate himself, body and soul, to the cause of the communal battle . . .

The object which militant enthusiasm tends to defend has changed with cultural development. Originally it was certainly the community of concrete, individually known members of a group, held together by the bond of personal love and friendship. With the growth of the social unit, the social norms and rites held in common by all its members became the main factor holding it together as an entity, and therewith they became automatically the symbol of the unit. . . .

Like the triumph ceremony of the greylag goose, militant enthusiasm in man is a true autonomous instinct: it has its own appetitive behavior, its own releasing mechanisms, and, like the sexual urge or any other strong instinct, it engenders a specific feeling of intense satisfaction. The strength of its seductive lure explains why intelligent men may behave as irrationally and immorally in their political as in their sexual lives. Like the triumph ceremony, it has an essential influence on the social structure of the species. Humanity is not enthusiastically combative because it is split into political parties, but it is divided into opposing camps because this is the adequate stimulus situation to arouse militant enthusiasm in a satisfying manner. . . .

The first prerequisite for rational control of an instinctive behavior pattern is the knowledge of the stimulus situation which releases it. Militant enthusiasm can be elicited with the predictability of a reflex when the following environmental situations arise. First of all, a social unit with which the subject identifies himself must appear to be threatened by some danger from outside. That which is threatened may be a concrete group of people, the family or a little community of close friends, or else it may be a larger social unit held together and symbolized by its own specific social norms and rites. . . .

A second key stimulus which contributes enormously to the releasing of intense militant enthusiasm is the presence of a hated enemy from whom the threat to the above "values" emanates. This enemy, too, can be of a concrete or of an abstract nature. It can be "the" Jews, Huns, Boches, tyrants, etc., or abstract concepts like world capitalism, Bolshevism, fascism, and any other kind of ism; it can be heresy, dogmatism, scientific fallacy, or whatnot. Just as in the case of the object to be defended, the enemy against whom to defend it is extremely variable, and demagogues are well versed in the dangerous art of producing supranormal dummies to release a very dangerous form of militant enthusiasm.

A third factor contributing to the environmental situation eliciting the response is an inspiring leader figure. Even the most emphatically antifascistic ideologies apparently cannot do without it, as the giant pictures of leaders displayed by all kinds of political parties prove clearly enough. . . .

A fourth, and perhaps the most important, prerequisite for the full eliciting of militant enthusiasm is the presence of many other individuals, all agitated by the same emotion. Their absolute number has a certain influence on the quality of the response. Smaller numbers at issue with a large majority tend to obstinate defense with the emotional value of "making a last stand," while very large numbers inspired by the same enthusiasm feel the urge to conquer the whole world in the name of their sacred cause. Here . . . the excitation grows in proportion, perhaps even in geometrical progression, with the increasing number of individuals. This is exactly what makes militant mass enthusiasm so dangerous.

Margaret Mead

WARFARE IS ONLY AN INVENTION—NOT A
BIOLOGICAL NECESSITY

Instinctivist theories of human aggressiveness have been criticized, especially because such views seem to promote the notion that warfare is "in our genes" and, hence, cannot be prevented. There is, indeed, some evidence that people who are politically conservative and typically promilitary disproportionately tend to believe that human beings are "naturally" aggressive, untrustworthy, and incapable of changing. In any event, the prevailing view among social scientists is that there is no "war instinct," even though aggressiveness may sometimes be readily evoked.

Anthropologists concern themselves largely with the activities of non-Western, typically nontechnological societies. There is legitimate debate about whether such study casts valuable light on modern, technological war-making. Some emphasize that the two situations are quite different, whereas others argue that examination of "primitive" war might help illuminate the conditions under which group violence has evolved. Some anthropologists, for example, claim that the capacity for warfare developed along with adaptations for hunting large game; others have emphasized competition for mates, for social prestige, or between rival bands.

A cross-cultural perspective on war reveals, among other things, a widespread tendency to dehumanize members of other tribes, often through the using use of literally animalizing terms to describe strangers and enemies. War-making is also typically associated with an array of rituals, with the enhancement of group cohesion, as well asand with ritual purification connected with the taking of human life. A schism of sorts also exists among anthropologists, with some convinced that "primitive war" is functional (although not necessarily good) in meeting various ecological and social needs, whereas and others claiming that it is essentially dysfunctional, a social pathology.

In general, however, anthropologists have contributed less heavily to the study of war than might be expected. An exception is Margaret Mead, whose brief essay, reprinted here, has become a classic statement of the anti-instinctivist school.

⎯⎯⎯⎯⎯⎯⎯⎯⎯⎯ ✥ ⎯⎯⎯⎯⎯⎯⎯⎯⎯⎯

Is war a biological necessity, a sociological inevitability, or just a bad invention? Those who argue for the first view endow man with such pugnacious instincts that some outlet in aggressive behavior is necessary if man is to reach full human stature. . . . A basic, competitive, aggressive, warring human nature is assumed, and those who wish to outlaw war or outlaw competitiveness merely try to find

From "Warfare Is Only an Invention—Not a Biological Necessity" by Margaret Mead. 1940. *Asia*, XL:402–5.

new and less socially destructive ways in which these biologically given aspects of man's nature can find expression. Then there are those who take the second view: warfare is the inevitable concomitant of the development of the state, the struggle for land and natural resources of class societies springing not from the nature of man, but from the nature of history. War is nevertheless inevitable unless we change our social system and outlaw classes, the struggle for power, and possessions; and in the event of our success warfare would disappear, as a symptom vanishes when the disease is cured.

One may hold a sort of compromise position between these two extremes; one may claim that all aggression springs from the frustration of man's biologically determined drives and that, since all forms of culture are frustrating, it is certain each new generation will be aggressive and the aggression will find its natural and inevitable expression in race war, class war, nationalistic war, and so on. All three of these positions are very popular today among those who think seriously about the problems of war and its possible prevention, but I wish to urge another point of view, less defeatist, perhaps, than the first and third and more accurate than the second: that is, that warfare, by which I mean recognized conflict between two groups *as groups,* in which each group puts an army (even if the army is only fifteen pygmies) into the field to fight and kill, if possible, some of the members of the army of the other group—that warfare of this sort is an invention like any other of the inventions in terms of which we order our lives, such as writing, marriage, cooking our food instead of eating it raw, trial by jury, or burial of the dead, and so on. Some of this list anyone will grant are inventions: trial by jury is confined to very limited portions of the globe; we know that there are tribes that do not bury their dead but instead expose or cremate them; and we know that only part of the human race has had the knowledge of writing as its cultural inheritance. But, whenever a way of doing things is found universally, such as the use of fire or the practice of some form of marriage, we tend to think at once that it is not an invention at all but an attribute of humanity itself. And yet even such universals as marriage and the use of fire are inventions like the rest, very basic ones, inventions which were,

perhaps, necessary if human history was to take the turn that it has taken, but nevertheless inventions. At some point in his social development man was undoubtedly without the institution of marriage or the knowledge of the use of fire.

The case for warfare is much clearer because there are peoples even today who have no warfare. Of these the Eskimos are perhaps the most conspicuous examples, but the Lepchas of Sikkim described by Geoffrey Gorer in *Himalayan Village* are as good.[2] Neither of these peoples understands war, not even defensive warfare. The idea of warfare is lacking, and this idea is as essential to really carrying on war as an alphabet or a syllabary is to writing. But, whereas the Lepchas are a gentle, unquarrelsome people, and the advocates of other points of view might argue that they are not full human beings or that they had never been frustrated and so had no aggression to expand in warfare, the Eskimo case gives no such possibility of interpretation. The Eskimos are not a mild and meek people; many of them are turbulent and troublesome. Fights, theft of wives, murder, cannibalism, occur among them—all outbursts of passionate men goaded by desire or intolerable circumstance. Here are men faced with hunger, men faced with loss of their wives, men faced with the threat of extermination by other men, and here are orphan children, growing up miserably with no one to care for them, mocked and neglected by those about them. The personality necessary for war, the circumstances necessary to goad men to desperation are present, but there is no war. When a traveling Eskimo entered a settlement, he might have to fight the strongest man in the settlement to establish his position among them, but this was a test of strength and bravery, not war. The idea of warfare, of one *group* organizing against another *group* to maim and wound and kill them was absent. And, without that idea, passions might rage but there was no war.

But, it may be argued, is not this because the Eskimos have such a low and undeveloped form of social organization? They own no land, they move from place to place, camping, it is true, season after season on the same site, but this is not something to fight for as the modern nations of the world fight

---

[2] G. Gorer, *Himalayan Village* (London: M. Joseph, 1938).

for land and raw materials. They have no permanent possessions that can be looted, no towns that can be burned. They have no social classes to produce stress and strains within the society which might force it to go to war outside. Does not the absence of war among the Eskimos, while disproving the biological necessity of war, just go to confirm the point that it is the state of development of the society which accounts for war and nothing else?

We find the answer among the pygmy peoples of the Andaman Islands in the Bay of Bengal. The Andamans also represent an exceedingly low level of society; they are a hunting and food-gathering people; they live in tiny hordes without any class stratification; their houses are simpler than the snow houses of the Eskimo. But they knew about warfare. The army might contain only fifteen determined pygmies marching in a straight line, but it was the real thing nonetheless. Tiny army met tiny army in open battle, blows were exchanged, casualties suffered, and the state of warfare could only be concluded by a peacemaking ceremony.

Similarly, among the Australian aborigines, who built no permanent dwellings but wandered from water hole to water hole over their almost desert country, warfare—and rules of "international law"—were highly developed. The student of social evolution will seek in vain for his obvious causes of war, struggle for lands, struggle for power of one group over another, expansion of population, need to divert the minds of a populace restive under tyranny, or even the ambition of a successful leader to enhance his own prestige. All are absent, but warfare as a practice remained, and men engaged in it and killed one another in the course of a war because killing is what is done in wars.

From instances like these it becomes apparent that an inquiry into the causes of war misses the fundamental point as completely as does an insistence upon the biological necessity of war. If a people have an idea of going to war and the idea that war is the way in which certain situations, defined within their society, are to be handled, they will sometimes go to war. If they are a mild and unaggressive people, like the Pueblo Indians, they may limit themselves to defensive warfare, but they will be forced to think in terms of war because there are peoples near them who have warfare as a pattern, and offensive, raiding, pillaging warfare at that. When the pattern of warfare is known, people like the Pueblo Indians will defend themselves, taking advantage of their natural defenses, the mesa village site, and people like the Lepchas, having no natural defenses and no idea of warfare, will merely submit to the invader. But the essential point remains the same. There is a way of behaving which is known to a given people and labeled as an appropriate form of behavior; a bold and warlike people like the Sioux or the Maori may label warfare as desirable as well as possible, a mild people like the Pueblo Indians may label warfare as undesirable, but to the minds of both peoples the possibility of warfare is present. Their thoughts, their hopes, their plans are oriented about this idea—that warfare may be selected as the way to meet some situation.

So simple peoples and civilized peoples, mild peoples and violent, assertive peoples, will all go to war if they have the invention, just as those peoples who have the custom of dueling will have duels and peoples who have the pattern of vendetta will indulge in vendetta. And, conversely, peoples who do not know of dueling will not fight duels, even though their wives are seduced and their daughters ravished; they may on occasion commit murder but they will not fight duels. Cultures which lack the idea of the vendetta will not meet every quarrel in this way. A people can use only the forms it has. So the Balinese have their special way of dealing with a quarrel between two individuals: if the two feel that the causes of quarrel are heavy, they may go and register their quarrel in the temple before the gods, and, making offerings, they may swear never to have anything to do with each other again. . . . But in other societies, although individuals might feel as full of animosity and as unwilling to have any further contact as do the Balinese, they cannot register their quarrel with the gods and go on quietly about their business because registering quarrels with the gods is not an invention of which they know. . . .

In many parts of the world, war is a game in which the individual can win counters—counters which bring him prestige in the eyes of his own sex or of the opposite sex; he plays for these counters as he might, in our society, strive for a tennis championship. Warfare is a frame for such prestige-seeking merely because it calls for the display of certain skills and certain virtues; all of these skills—riding straight, shooting straight, dodging the missiles of the enemy and sending one's own straight to the mark—can be equally well exercised in some other framework and, equally, the virtues—endurance, bravery, loyalty, steadfastness—can be displayed in other contexts. The tie-up between proving oneself a man and proving this by a success in organized killing is due to a definition which many societies have made of manliness. And often, even in those societies which counted success in warfare a proof of human worth, strange turns were given to the idea, as when the plains Indians gave their highest awards to the man who touched a live enemy rather than to the man who brought in a scalp—from a dead enemy—because the latter was less risky. Warfare is just an invention known to the majority of human societies by which they permit their young men either to accumulate prestige or avenge their honor or acquire loot or wives or slaves or sago lands or cattle or appease the bloodlust of their gods or the restless souls of the recently dead. It is just an invention, older and more widespread than the jury system, but nonetheless an invention.

. . . Grant that war is an invention, that it is not a biological necessity nor the outcome of certain special types of social forms, still, once the invention is made, what are we to do about it? . . . Warfare is here, as part of our thought; the deeds of warriors are immortalized in the words of our poets, the toys of our children are modeled upon the weapons of the soldier, the frame of reference within which our statesmen and our diplomats work always contains war. If we know that it is not inevitable, that it is due to historical accident that warfare is one of the ways in which we think of behaving, are we given any hope by that? What hope is there of persuading nations to abandon war, nations so thoroughly imbued with the idea that resort to war is, if not actually desirable and noble, at least inevitable whenever certain defined circumstances arise?

In answer to this question I think we might turn to the history of other social inventions, and inventions which must once have seemed as firmly entrenched as warfare. Take the methods of trial which preceded the jury system: ordeal and trial by combat. Unfair, capricious, alien as they are to our feeling today, they were once the only methods open to individuals accused of some offense. The invention of trial by jury gradually replaced these methods until only witches, and finally not even witches, had to resort to the ordeal. . . . In each case the old method was replaced by a new social invention. The ordeal did not go out because people thought it unjust or wrong; it went out because a method more congruent with the institutions and feelings of the period was invented. And, if we despair over the way in which war seems such an ingrained habit of most of the human race, we can take comfort from the fact that a poor invention will usually give place to a better invention.

For this, two conditions, at least, are necessary. The people must recognize the defects of the old invention, and someone must make a new one. Propaganda against warfare, documentation of its terrible cost in human suffering and social waste, these prepare the ground by teaching people to feel that warfare is a defective social institution. There is further needed a belief that social invention is possible and the invention of new methods which will render warfare as out of date as the tractor is making the plow, or the motor car the horse and buggy. A form of behavior becomes out of date only when something else takes its place, and, in order to invent forms of behavior which will make war obsolete, it is a first requirement to believe that an invention is possible.

Chris Hedges

WAR IS A FORCE THAT GIVES US MEANING

There is an irony in the public's attention to war. On the one hand, most people detest it, considering war among the greatest misfortunes to befall human beings. But on the other hand, people eagerly listen to war stories, songs, and marches; avidly read accounts of battles; flock to parades and movies that celebrate armed conflict; and revere war heroes. Because war is almost universally reviled—as opposed to soldiers, who are typically admired—only rarely are the *attractions* of war faced honestly and openly; yet those attractions are undeniable, as indicated not only by the public's almost insatiable appetite for war-related material but—even more troublesome—by the persistence of war itself. Even those peace activists who agree with Margaret Mead's claim that "warfare is only an invention—not a biological necessity," believe that there is a need to confront its appeal.

There are many reasons for war's perverse attractiveness, ranging from sheer thrill seeking, with its physical and sexual opportunities, to its potential for expressing genuine altruism and, indeed, heroism. High on the list is a connection to other combatants, including even, on occasion, the opponents. A U.S. combat veteran of World War II wrote that

> we are liberated from our individual impotence and are drunk with the power that union with our fellows brings. In moments like these many have a vague awareness of how isolated and separate their lives have hitherto been. . . . With the boundaries of the self expanded, they sense a kinship never known before. Their "I" passes insensibly into a "we." . . . At its height, this sense of comradeship is an ecstasy.[3]

Reflections of this sort may be discomfiting to those of us seeking to eliminate war, or, at least, to reduce its frequency and intensity. But an honest approach to peace requires nothing less than an honest recognition of war's appeal, including the extent to which it offers many a sense of "meaning." In this regard, former war correspondent Chris Hedges offers an honest and troubling account.

—————————— ⌘ ——————————

War and conflict have marked most of my adult life. I have been in ambushes on desolate stretches of Central American roads, locked in unnerving firefights in the marshes in southern Iraq, imprisoned in the Sudan, beaten by Saudi military police, deported from Libya and Iran, captured and held for a week by Iraqi Republican Guards, strafed by Russian MiG-21s in central Bosnia, shot at by Serb snipers, and shelled with deafening rounds of artillery in Sarajevo that threw out thousands of

[3] J. Glen Gray, *The Warriors: Reflections on Men in Battle* (New York: Harper & Row, 1967).

deadly bits of iron fragments. I have seen too much of violent death. I have tasted too much of my own fear. I have painful memories that lie buried most of the time. It is never easy when they surface.

And yet there is a part of me that remains nostalgic for war's simplicity and high. The enduring attraction of war is this: even with its destruction and carnage, it gives us what we all long for in life. It gives us purpose, meaning, a reason for living. Only when we are in the midst of conflict does the shallowness and vapidness of our lives become apparent. Trivia dominates our conversations and increasingly our news. And war is an enticing elixir. It gives us resolve, a cause. It allows us to be noble. And those that have the least meaning in their lives—the impoverished refugees in Gaza, the disenfranchised North African immigrants in France, even the lost legions of youth that live in the splendid indolence and safety of the industrialized world—are all susceptible to war's appeal.

WAR AS CULTURE

I learned early on that war forms its own culture. The rush of battle is a potent and often lethal addiction, for war is a drug, one I ingested for many years. It is peddled by mythmakers—historians, war correspondents, filmmakers, novelists, and the state— all of whom endow it with qualities it often does possess: excitement, exoticism, power, chances to rise above our small stations in life, and a bizarre and fantastic universe that has a grotesque and dark beauty. It dominates culture, distorts memory, corrupts language, and infects everything around it, even humor, which becomes preoccupied with the grim perversities of smut and death. Fundamental questions about the meaning, or meaninglessness, of our place on the planet are laid bare when we watch those around us sink to the lowest depths. War exposes the capacity for evil that lurks just below the surface within all of us.

And so it takes little in wartime to turn ordinary men into killers. Most give themselves willingly to the seduction of unlimited power to destroy, and all feel the peer pressure. Few, once in bottle, can find the strength to resist.

The historian Christopher Browning noted the willingness to kill in *Ordinary Men*, his study of Reserve Police Battalion 101 in Poland during World War ll. On the morning of July 12, 1942, the battalion was ordered to shoot 1,800 Jews in the village of Jozefow in a daylong action. The men in the unit had to round up the Jews, march them into the forest, and one by one order them to lie down in a row. The victims, including women, infants, children, and the elderly, were shot dead at close range.

Battalion members were offered the option to refuse, an option only about a dozen men took, although more asked to be relieved once the killing began. Those who did not want to continue, Browning says, were disgusted rather than plagued by conscience. When the men returned to the barracks, they "were depressed, angered, embittered, and shaken." They drank heavily. They were told not to talk about the event, "but they needed no encouragement in that direction."

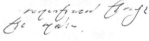

WAR AS MYTH

The most recent U.S. conflicts have insulated the public and U.S. troops from both the disgust and pangs of conscience. The Gulf War—waged from bombers high above the fray and reported by carefully controlled journalists—made war fashionable again. It was a cause the nation willingly embraced. It exorcised the ghosts of Vietnam. It gave us heroes and the heady belief in our own military superiority and technology. It almost made war fun. And the chief culprit was, as in many conflicts, not the military but the press. Television reporters happily disseminated the spoon-fed images that served the propaganda effort of the military and the state.

These images did little to convey the reality of war. Pool reporters, those guided around in groups by the military, wrote once again about "our boys" eating packaged army food, practicing for chemical weapons attacks, and bathing out of buckets in the desert. It was war as spectacle—war, if we are honest, as entertainment. The images and stories were designed to make us feel good about our nation, about ourselves. The families and soldiers being blown to bits by iron fragmentation bombs just over the border in Iraq were faceless and nameless phantoms.

The moment I stepped off an Army C-130 military transport in Dhahran, Saudi Arabia, to cover the Persian Gulf War, I was escorted to a room with several dozen other reporters and photographers. I was told to sign a paper that said I would abide by the severe restrictions placed on the press. The restrictions authorized "pool reporters" to be escorted by the military on field trips. Most of the press sat in hotel rooms and rewrote the bland copy filed by the pool or used the pool video and photos. I violated this agreement the next morning when I went into the field without authorization. The rest of the war, most of which I spent dodging military police and trying to talk my way into units, was a forlorn and lonely struggle against the heavy press control.

The notion that the press was used in the war is incorrect. The press wanted to be used. It saw itself as part of the war effort. Most reporters sent to cover a war don't really want to go near the fighting. They do not tell this to their editors and indeed will moan and complain about restrictions. The handful who actually head out into the field have a bitter enmity with the hotel room warriors. But even those who do go out are guilty of distortion—maybe more so. For they not only believe the myth, feed off the drug, but also embrace the cause. They may do it with more skepticism. They certainly expose more lies and misconceptions. But they believe. We all believe. When you stop believing, you stop going to war.

I knew a Muslim soldier, a father, who fought on the front lines around Sarajevo. His unit, in one of the rare attempts to take back a few streets controlled by the Serbs, pushed across Serb lines. They did not get very far. The fighting was heavy. As he moved down the street, he heard a door swing open and fired a burst from his AK-47 assault rifle. A twelve-year-old girl dropped dead. He saw in the body of the unknown girl lying prostrate in front of him the image of his own twelve-year-old daughter. He broke down. He had to be helped back to the city. He was lost for the rest of the war, shuttered inside his apartment, nervous, morose, and broken. This experience is far more typical of warfare than the Rambo heroics we are fed by the state and the

entertainment industry. The cost of killing is all the more bitter because of the deep disillusionment that war usually brings.

WAR AS CRUSADE

The disillusionment comes later. Each generation again responds to war as innocents. Each generation discovers its own disillusionment—often at a terrible price.

"We believed we were there for a high moral purpose," wrote Philip Caputo in his book on Vietnam, *Rumor of War*. "But somehow our idealism was lost, our morals corrupted, and the purpose forgotten."

Once again the United States stands poised on the threshold of war. "We go forward," President George W. Bush assures us, "to defend freedom and all that is good and just in the world." He is not shy about warning other states that they either stand with us in the war on terrorism or will be counted as aligned with those that defy us. This too is a crusade.

But the war on terrorism is different in that we Americans find ourselves in the dangerous position of going to war not against a state but a phantom. The crusade we have embarked upon in the war on terrorism is targeting an elusive and protean enemy. The battle we have begun is never-ending. But it may be too late to wind back the heady rhetoric. We have embarked on a campaign as quixotic as the one mounted to destroy us. As it continues, as terrorist attacks intrude on our lives, as we feel less and less secure, the acceptance of all methods to lash out at real and perceived enemies will distort and deform our democracy.

And yet, the campaign's attraction seems irresistible. War makes the world understandable, a black-and-white tableau of them and us. It suspends thought, especially self-critical thought. All bow before the supreme effort. We are one. Most of us willingly accept war as long as we can fold it into a belief system that paints the ensuing suffering as necessary for a higher good; for human beings seek not only happiness but also meaning. And tragically, war is sometimes the most powerful way in human society to achieve meaning.

William Graham Sumner

WAR AND OTHER ESSAYS

Sociological perspectives on war tend to fall into two camps. A German school, under the influence of the philosopher Georg Hegel, and, later, sociologists such as von Bernhardi, Gumplowicz, and Ranzenhofer, developed a "sociology of conflict," which saw warfare as necessary and desirable for the evolution of society. "War," wrote Hegel, in *Philosophy of Right*, "has the higher meaning that through it . . . the ethical health of nations is maintained; . . . war prevents a corruption of nations which a perpetual peace would produce."

By contrast, an Anglo-French-American tradition, represented initially by John Stuart Mill, Auguste Comte, and Émile Durkheim, focused on the differentiation and integration of social groups, the role of group consensus, and what they saw as the problem of "in-group amity, out-group enmity." They were interested in the role of war in the development of the nation-state, and they treated national competition less as a desired outcome than as an objective fact of life to be analyzed and understood.

Others have sought to clarify the relationship between industrialization and war as well as the powerful and complex phenomenon of nationalism. The following selection is by William Graham Sumner, one of the founders of American sociology.

We have heard our political leaders say from time to time that, "War is necessary," "War is a good thing." They were trying to establish a major premise which would suggest the conclusion, "Therefore let us have a little war now," or "It is wise, on general principles, to have a war once in a while." That argument may be taken as the text of the present essay. It has seemed to me worthwhile to show from the history of civilization just what war has done and has not done for the welfare of mankind.

In the eighteenth century it was assumed that the primitive state of mankind was one of Arcadian peace, joy, and contentment. In the nineteenth century the assumption went over to the other extreme—that the primitive state was one of universal warfare. This, like the former notion, is a great exaggeration. Man in the most primitive and uncivilized state known to us does not practice war all the time; he dreads it. He might rather be described as a peaceful animal. Real warfare comes with the collisions of more developed societies. . . .

War arises from the competition of life, not from the struggle for existence. In the struggle for existence a man is wrestling with nature to extort from her the means of subsistence. It is when two men are striving side by side in the struggle for existence to extort from nature the supplies they need that they come into rivalry, and a collision of interest with each other takes place. This collision may be light and unimportant, if the supplies are large and the number of men small, or it may be harsh and violent, if there are many men striving for a small supply. This collision we call the competition of life. Of course, men are in the competition of life

From *War and Other Essays* by William Graham Sumner (New Haven: Yale University Press, 1911).

with beasts, reptiles, insects, and plants—in short, with all organic forms; we will, however, confine our attention to men. The greater or less intensity of the competition of life is a fundamental condition of human existence. . . . The members of the unit group work together. The Australian or Bushman hunter goes abroad to seek meat food, while the woman stays by the fire at a trysting place with the children and collects plant food. They cooperate in the struggle for existence, and the size of the group is fixed by the number who can work together to the greatest advantage under their mode of life. Such a group, therefore, has a common interest. It must have control of a certain area of land; hence it comes into collision of interest with every other group. The competition of life, therefore, arises between groups not between individuals, and we see that the members of the ingroup are allies and joint partners in one interest while they are brought into antagonism of interest with all outsiders. . . .

Each group must regard every other as a possible enemy on account of the antagonism of interests, and so it views every other group with suspicion and distrust, although actual hostilities occur only on specific occasion. Every member of another group is a stranger; he may be admitted as a guest, in which case rights and security are granted him, but, if not so admitted, he is an enemy. We can now see why the sentiments of peace and cooperation inside are complementary to sentiments of hostility outside. It is because any group, in order to be strong against an outside enemy, must be well disciplined, harmonious, and peaceful inside; in other words, because discord inside would cause defeat in battle with another group. Therefore the same conditions which made men warlike against outsiders made them yield to the control of chiefs, submit to discipline, obey law, cultivate peace, and create institutions inside. The notion of rights grows up in the ingroup from the usages established there securing peace. There was a double education, at the same time, out of the same facts and relations. It is no paradox at all to say that peace makes war and that war makes peace. There are two codes of morals and two sets of mores, one for comrades inside and the other for strangers outside, and they arise from the same interests. Against outsiders it was meritorious to kill, plunder, practice blood revenge, and to steal women and slaves, but inside none of these things could be allowed because they would produce discord and weakness. Hence, in the ingroup, law (under the forms of custom and taboo) and institutions had to take the place of force. Every group was a peace group inside, and the peace was sanctioned by the ghosts of the ancestors who had handed down the customs and taboos. Against outsiders religion sanctioned and encouraged war, for the ghosts of the ancestors, or the gods, would rejoice to see their posterity and worshipers once more defeat, slay, plunder, and enslave the ancient enemy.

. . . A peaceful society must be industrial because it must produce instead of plundering; it is for this reason that the industrial type of society is the opposite of the militant type. In any state on the continent of Europe today these two types of societal organization may be seen interwoven with each other and fighting each other. Industrialism builds up; militancy wastes. If a railroad is built, trade and intercourse indicate a line on which it ought to run; military strategy, however, overrules this and requires that it run otherwise. Then all the interests of trade and intercourse must be subjected to constant delay and expense because the line does not conform to them. Not a discovery or invention is made but the war and navy bureaus of all the great nations seize it to see what use can be made of it in war. It is evident that men love war; when two hundred thousand men in the United States volunteer in a month for a war with Spain which appeals to no sense of wrong against their country and to no other strong sentiment of human nature, when their lives are by no means monotonous or destitute of interest, and where life offers chances of wealth and prosperity, the pure love of adventure and war must be strong in our population. Europeans who have to do military service have no such enthusiasm for war as war. The presence of such a sentiment in the midst of the most purely industrial state in the world is a wonderful phenomenon. At the same time the social philosophy of the modern civilized world is saturated with humanitarianism and flabby sentimentalism. The humanitarianism is in the literature; by it the reading public is led to suppose that the world is advancing along some line which they call "progress" toward peace and brotherly love. Nothing could be more mistaken. We read of fist law and constant war in the Middle Ages and think that life must have been full of conflicts and bloodshed then, but modern warfare bears down on the whole population with a frightful weight through all the years of peace. Never, from the day of barbarism down to our own time, has every man in a society been a soldier until now, and the armaments of today are immensely more costly than ever before. There is only one limit possible to the war preparations of a modern European state; that is, the last man and the last dollar it can control. What will come of the mixture of sentimental social philosophy and warlike policy? There is only one thing rationally to be expected, and that is a frightful effusion of blood in revolution and war during the century now opening.

It is said that there are important offsets to all the burden and harm of this exaggerated militancy. That is true. Institutions and customs in human society are never either all good or all bad. We cannot adopt either peacefulness or warlikeness as a sole true philosophy. Military discipline educates; military interest awakens all the powers of men, so that they are eager to win and their ingenuity is quickened to invent new and better weapons. In history the military inventions have led the way and have been afterward applied to industry. Chemical inventions were made in the attempt to produce combinations which would be destructive in war; we owe some of our most useful substances to discoveries which were made in this effort. The skill of artisans has been developed in making weapons, and then that skill has been available for industry. The only big machines which the ancients ever made were battering rams, catapults, and other engines of war. The construction of these things familiarized men with mechanical devices which were capable of universal application. Gunpowder was discovered in the attempt to rediscover Greek fire; it was a grand invention in military art, but we should never have had our canals, railroads, and other great works without such explosives. Again, we are indebted to the chemical experiments in search of military agents for our friction matches. . . . We find, then, that in the past, war has played a great part in the irrational nature

process by which things have come to pass. But the nature processes are frightful; they contain no allowance for the feelings and interests of individuals—for it is only individuals who have feelings and interests. The nature elements never suffer, and they never pity. If we are terrified at the nature processes, there is only one way to escape them; it is the way by which men have always evaded them to some extent; it is by knowledge, by rational methods, and by the arts. The facts which have been presented about the functions of war in the past are not flattering to the human reason or conscience. They seem to show that we are as much indebted for our welfare to base passion as to noble and intelligent endeavor. At the present moment things do not look much better. We talk of civilizing lower races, but we never have done it yet; we have exterminated them. Our devices for civilizing them have been as disastrous to them as our firearms. At the beginning of the twentieth century the great civilized nations are making haste, in the utmost jealousy of each other, to seize upon all the outlying parts of the globe; they are vying with each other in the construction of navies by which each may defend its share against the others. What will happen? As they are preparing for war, they certainly will have war, and their methods of colonization and exploitation will destroy the aborigines. In this way the human race will be civilized—but by the extermination of the uncivilized—unless the men of the twentieth century can devise plans for dealing with aborigines which are better than any which have yet been devised. No one has yet found any way in which two races, far apart in blood and culture, can be amalgamated into one society with satisfaction to both. Plainly, in this matter which lies in the immediate future, the only alternatives to force and bloodshed are more knowledge and more reason. . . .

Can peace be universal? There is no reason to believe it. It is a fallacy to suppose that, by widening the peace group more and more, it can at last embrace all mankind. What happens is that, as it grows bigger, differences, discords, antagonisms, and war begin inside of it on account of the divergence of interests. Since evil passions are a part of human nature and are in all societies all the time, a part of the energy of the society is constantly spent in repressing them. If all nations should resolve to have no armed ships anymore, pirates would reappear upon the ocean; the police of the seas must be maintained. We could not dispense with our militia; we have too frequent need of it now. But police defense is not war in the sense in which I have been discussing it. War in the future will be the clash of policies of national vanity and selfishness when they cross each other's path.

If you want war, nourish a doctrine. Doctrines are the most frightful tyrants to which men ever are subject, because doctrines get inside of a man's own reason and betray him against himself. Civilized men have done their fiercest fighting for doctrines. The reconquest of the Holy Sepulcher, "the balance of power," "no universal dominion," "trade follows the flag," "he who holds the land will hold the sea," "the throne and the altar," the revolution, the faith—these are the things for which men have given their lives. What are they all? Nothing but rhetoric and phantasms. Doctrines are always vague; it would ruin a doctrine to define it, because then it could be analyzed, tested, criticized, and verified; but nothing ought to be tolerated which cannot be so tested. Somebody asks you with astonishment and horror whether you do not believe in the Monroe Doctrine. You do not know whether you do or not because you do not know what it is, but you do not dare to say that you do not because you understand that it is one of the things which every good American is bound to believe in. Now when any doctrine arrives at that degree of authority, the name of it is a club which any demagogue may swing over you at any time and apropos of anything. In order to describe a doctrine, we must have recourse to theological language. A doctrine is an article of faith. It is something which you

are bound to believe not because you have some rational grounds for believing it true, but because you belong to such and such a church or denomination. The nearest parallel to it in politics is the "reason of state." The most frightful injustice and cruelty which has ever been perpetrated on earth has been due to the reason of state. . . .

What has just been said suggests a consideration of the popular saying, "In time of peace prepare for war." If you prepare a big army and navy and are all ready for war, it will be easy to go to war; the military and naval men will have a lot of new machines, and they will be eager to see what they can do with them. There is no such thing nowadays as a state of readiness for war. It is a chimera, and the nations which pursue it are falling into an abyss of wasted energy and wealth. When the army is supplied with the latest and best rifles, someone invents a new field gun; then the artillery must be provided with that before we are ready. By the time we get the new gun, somebody has invented a new rifle, and our rival nation is getting that; therefore we must have it—or one a little better. It takes two or three years and several millions to do that. In the meantime somebody proposes a more effective organization which must be introduced; signals, balloons, dogs, bicycles, and every other device and invention must be added, and men must be trained to use them all. There is no state of readiness for war; the notion calls for never-ending sacrifices. It is a fallacy. It is evident that to pursue such a notion with any idea of realizing it would absorb all the resources and activity of the state; this the great European states are now proving by experiment. A wiser rule would be to make up your mind soberly what you want, peace or war, and then to get ready for what you want; for what we prepare for is what we shall get.

Irving Janis

VICTIMS OF GROUPTHINK

The preamble to the UNESCO[4] constitution states that "since wars begin in the minds of men, it is in the minds of men that the defenses of peace must be constructed." This is generally interpreted to mean that all individuals (of both sexes!) are crucial to preventing war. However, some students of peace and war would amend this sentence to begin, "Since wars begin in the minds of the crucial, decision-making elite of each country. . . . " It is widely acknowledged that the psychology of decision- making plays a key role in influencing the immediate outcome (although this is not to deny the importance of other factors—historical, economic, sociological, etc.—in setting the stage).

Psychologically minded researchers have identified a number of factors involved in going to war, decisions that have often proved ill-advised not only on moral grounds but also based on their immediate, practical outcomes. Here is but a sample: Robert Jervis has inquired into the various patterns of misperception, by which decision-makers labor under inaccurate views of reality. Ole Holsti has investigated the costly consequences of stress during decision making under crisis conditions. Morton Deutsch has analyzed the process of hostile interactions by which the mutually reinforcing impressions of adversaries can spiral out of control. Ralph White has pointed out the role of fear and of such "motivated misperceptions" as the "diabolical enemy image" combined with a self-righteous "moral self-image."

Irving Janis, a social psychologist, has provided a great service by identifying an especially important syndrome, which that he calls "groupthink," whereby small groups tend to be vulnerable to a dangerous psychological process. In the following selection, from his book, *Victims of Groupthink*, Janis examines the ill-conceived and ill-fated Bay of Pigs invasion in 1961. More than 40 forty years after his path-breaking research, Janis's concept of groupthink was revisited to help explain the lack of dissent and debate within the Bush Administration prior to the U.S. invasion of Iraq in 2003.

NOBODY IS PERFECT

Year after year newscasts and newspapers inform us of collective miscalculations—companies that have unexpectedly gone bankrupt because of misjudging their market, federal agencies that have mistakenly authorized the use of chemical insecticides that poison our environment, and White House executive committees that have made ill-conceived foreign

---

[4] United Nations Educational, Scientific, and Cultural Organization.

---

policy decisions that inadvertently bring the major powers to the brink of war. Most people, when they hear about such fiascoes, simply remind themselves that, after all, "organizations are run by human beings," "to err is human," and "nobody is perfect." But platitudinous thoughts about human nature do not help us to understand how and why avoidable miscalculations are made.

Fiasco watchers who are unwilling to set the problem aside in this easy fashion will find that contemporary psychology has something to say (unfortunately not very much) about distortions of thinking and other sources of human error. The deficiencies about which we know the most pertain to disturbances in the behavior of each individual in a decision-making group—temporary states of elation, fear, or anger that reduce a person's mental efficiency; chronic blind spots arising from a person's social prejudices; shortcomings in information processing that prevent a person from comprehending the complex consequences of a seemingly simple policy decision. One psychologist has suggested that because the information processing capabilities of every individual are limited, no responsible leader of a large organization ought to make a policy decision without using a computer that is programmed to spell out all the probable benefits and costs of each alternative under consideration. The usual way of trying to counteract the limitations of individuals' mental functioning, however, is to relegate important decisions to groups.

IMPERFECTIONS OF GROUP DECISIONS

Groups, like individuals, have shortcomings. Groups can bring out the worst as well as the best in man. Nietzsche went so far as to say that madness is the exception in individuals but the rule in groups. A considerable amount of social science literature shows that in circumstances of extreme crisis, group contagion occasionally gives rise to collective panic, violent acts of scapegoating, and other forms of what could be called group madness. Much more frequent, however, are instances of mindless conformity and collective misjudgment of serious risks, which are collectively laughed off in a clubby atmosphere of relaxed conviviality. . . .

Lack of vigilance and excessive risk taking are forms of temporary group derangement to which decision-making groups made up of responsible executives are not at all immune. Sometimes the main trouble is that the chief executive manipulates his advisers to rubber-stamp his own ill-conceived proposals. . . . I shall be dealing mainly with a different source of defective decision making, which often involves a much more subtle form of faulty leadership: During the group's deliberations, the leader does not deliberately try to get the group to tell him what he wants to hear but is quite sincere in asking for honest opinions. The group members are not transformed into sycophants. They are not afraid to speak their minds. Nevertheless, subtle constraints, which the leader may reinforce inadvertently, prevent a member from fully exercising his critical powers and from openly expressing doubts when most others in the group appear to have reached a consensus. . . .

I use the term "groupthink" as a quick and easy way to refer to a mode of thinking that people engage in when they are deeply involved in a cohesive in-group, when the members' strivings for unanimity override their motivation to realistically appraise alternative courses of action. "Groupthink" is a term of the same order as the words in the newspeak vocabulary George Orwell presents in his dismaying *1984*—a vocabulary with terms such as "doublethink" and "crimethink." By putting groupthink with those Orwellian words, I realize that groupthink takes on an invidious connotation. The invidiousness is intentional: groupthink refers to a deterioration of mental efficiency, reality testing, and moral judgment that results from in-group pressures. . . .

At least six major defects in decision making contribute to failures to solve problems adequately. First, the group's discussions are limited to a few alternative courses of action (often only two) without a survey of the full range of alternatives. Second, the group fails to reexamine the course of action initially preferred by the majority of members from the standpoint of non-obvious risks and drawbacks that had not been considered when it was originally evaluated. Third, the members neglect courses of action initially evaluated as unsatisfactory by the majority of the group: They spend little or no time discussing whether they have overlooked non-obvious gains or whether there are ways of reducing the seemingly prohibitive costs that had made the alternatives seem undesirable. Fourth, members make little or no attempt to obtain information from experts who can supply sound estimates of losses and gains to be expected from alternative courses of action. Fifth, selective bias is shown in the way the group reacts to factual information and relevant judgments from experts, the mass media, and outside critics. The members show interest in facts and opinions that support their initially preferred policy and take up time in their meetings to discuss them, but they tend to ignore facts and opinions that do not support their initially preferred policy. Sixth, the members spend little time deliberating about how the chosen policy might be hindered by bureaucratic inertia, sabotaged by political opponents, or temporarily derailed by the common accidents that happen to the best of well-laid plans. Consequently, they fail to work out contingency plans to cope with foreseeable setbacks that could endanger the overall success of the chosen course of action.

I assume that these six defects and some related features of inadequate decision-making result from groupthink. But, of course, each of the six can arise from other common causes of human stupidity as well—erroneous intelligence, information overload, fatigue, blinding prejudice, and ignorance. Whether produced by groupthink or by other causes, a decision suffering from most of these defects has relatively little chance of success. . . .

At first I was surprised by the extent to which the groups in the fiascoes I have examined adhered to group norms and pressures toward uniformity. Just as in groups of ordinary citizens, a dominant characteristic appears to be remaining loyal to the group by sticking with the decisions to which the group has committed itself, even when the policy is working badly and has unintended consequences that disturb the conscience of the members. In a sense, members consider loyalty to the group the highest form of morality. That loyalty requires each member to avoid raising controversial issues, questioning weak arguments, or calling a halt to softheaded thinking.

Paradoxically, softheaded groups are likely to be extremely hard-hearted toward out-groups and enemies. In dealing with a rival nation, policy makers comprising an amiable group find it relatively easy to authorize dehumanizing solutions such as large-scale bombings. An affable group of government officials is unlikely to pursue the difficult and controversial issues that arise when alternatives to a harsh military solution come up for discussion. Nor are the members inclined to raise ethical issues that imply that this "fine group of ours, with its humanitarianism and its high-minded principles, might be capable of adopting a course of action that is inhumane and immoral."

Many other sources of human error can prevent government leaders from arriving at well worked out decisions, resulting in failures to achieve their practical objectives and violations of their own standards of ethical conduct. But, unlike groupthink, these other sources of error do not typically entail increases in hard-heartedness along with softheadedness. Some errors involve blind spots that stem from the personality of the decision-makers. Special circumstances produce unusual fatigue and emotional stresses that interfere with efficient decision making. Numerous institutional features of the social structure in which the group is located may also cause inefficiency and prevent adequate communication with experts. In addition, well-known interferences with sound thinking arise when the decision-makers comprise a noncohesive group. For example, when the members have no sense of loyalty to the group and regard themselves merely as representatives of different departments, with clashing interests, the meetings may become bitter power struggles, at the expense of effective decision making.

The concept of groupthink pinpoints an entirely different source of trouble, residing neither in the individual nor in the organizational setting. Over and beyond all the familiar sources of human error is a powerful source of defective judgment that arises in cohesive groups—the concurrence-seeking tendency, which fosters overoptimism, lack of vigilance, and sloganistic thinking about the weakness and immorality of out-groups. This tendency can take its toll even when the decision-makers are conscientious statesmen trying to make the best possible decisions for their country and for all mankind.

I do not mean to imply that all cohesive groups suffer from groupthink, though all may display its symptoms from time to time. Nor should we infer from the term "groupthink" that group decisions are typically inefficient or harmful. On the contrary, a group whose members have properly defined roles, with traditions and standard operating procedures that facilitate critical inquiry, is probably capable of making better decisions than any individual in the group who works on the problem alone. And yet the advantages of having decisions made by groups are often lost because of psychological pressures that arise when the members work closely together, share the same values, and above all face a crisis situation in which everyone is subjected to stresses that generate a strong need for affiliation. In these circumstances, as conformity pressures begin to dominate, groupthink and the attendant deterioration of decision-making set in.

The central theme of my analysis can be summarized in this generalization, which I offer in the spirit of Parkinson's laws: *The more amiability and esprit de corps among the members of a policymaking in-group, the greater is the danger that independent critical thinking will be replaced by groupthink, which is likely to result in irrational and dehumanizing actions directed against out-groups. . . .*

The Kennedy administration's Bay of Pigs decision ranks among the worst fiascoes ever perpetrated by a responsible government. Planned by an overambitious, eager group of American intelligence officers who had little background or experience in military matters, the attempt to place a small brigade of Cuban exiles secretly on a beachhead in Cuba with the ultimate aim of overthrowing the government of Fidel Castro proved to be a "perfect failure." The group that made the basic decision to approve the invasion plan included some of the most intelligent men ever to participate in the councils of government. Yet all the major assumptions supporting the plan were so completely wrong that the venture began to founder at the outset and failed in its earliest stages.

THE "ILL-STARRED ADVENTURE"

Ironically, the idea for the invasion was first suggested by John F. Kennedy's main political opponent,

Richard M. Nixon. As vice president during the Eisenhower administration, Nixon had proposed that the United States government secretly send a trained group of Cuban exiles to Cuba to fight against Castro. In March 1960, acting on Nixon's suggestion, President Dwight D. Eisenhower directed the Central Intelligence Agency to organize Cuban exiles in the United States into a unified political movement against the Castro regime and to give military training to those who were willing to return to their homeland to engage in guerrilla warfare. The CIA put a large number of its agents to work on this clandestine operation, and they soon evolved an elaborate plan for a military invasion. Apparently without informing President Eisenhower, the CIA began to assume in late 1960 that they could land a brigade of Cuban exiles not as a band of guerrilla infiltrators but as an armed force to carry out a full-scale invasion.

Two days after the inauguration in January 1961, President John F. Kennedy and several leading members of his new administration were given a detailed briefing about the proposed invasion by Allen Dulles, head of the CIA, and General Lyman Lemnitzer, chairman of the Joint Chiefs of Staff. During the next eighty days, a core group of presidential advisers repeatedly discussed this inherited plan informally and in the meetings of an advisory committee that included three Joint Chiefs of Staff. In early April 1961, at one of the meetings with the president, all the key advisers gave their approval to the CIA's invasion plan. Their deliberations led to a few modifications of details, such as the choice of the invasion site.

On April 17, 1961, the brigade of about fourteen hundred Cuban exiles, aided by the United States Navy, Air Force, and the CIA, invaded the swampy coast of Cuba at the Bay of Pigs. Nothing went as planned. On the first day, not one of the four ships containing reserve ammunition and supplies arrived; the first two were sunk by a few planes in Castro's air force, and the other two promptly fled. By the second day, the brigade was completely surrounded by twenty thousand troops of Castro's well-equipped army. By the third day, about twelve hundred members of the brigade, comprising almost all who had not been killed, were captured and ignominiously led off to prison camps. . . .

An important symptom of groupthink is the illusion of being invulnerable to the main dangers that might arise from a risky action in which the group is strongly tempted to engage. Essentially, the notion is that "If our leader and everyone else in our group decides that it is okay, the plan is bound to succeed. Even if it is quite risky, luck will be on our side." A sense of "unlimited confidence" was widespread among the "New Frontiersmen" as soon as they took over their high government posts, according to a Justice Department confidant, with whom Robert Kennedy discussed the secret CIA plan on the day it was launched:

> It seemed that, with John Kennedy leading us and with all the talent he had assembled, *nothing could stop us.* We believed that if we faced up to the nation's problems and applied bold, new ideas with common sense and hard work, we would overcome whatever challenged us. . . .

Once this euphoric phase takes hold, decision making for everyday activities, as well as long-range planning, is likely to be seriously impaired. The members of a cohesive group become very reluctant to carry out the unpleasant task of critically assessing the limits of their power and the real losses that could arise if their luck does not hold. They tend to examine each risk in black-and-white terms. If it does not seem overwhelmingly dangerous, they are inclined simply to forget about it, instead of developing contingency plans in case it materializes. The group members know that no one among them is a superman, but they feel that somehow the group is a supergroup, capable of surmounting all risks that stand in the way of carrying out any desired course of action: "Nothing can stop us!" Athletic teams and military combat units may often benefit from members' enthusiastic confidence in the power and luck of their group. But policymaking committees usually do not.

We would not expect sober government officials to experience such exuberant esprit de corps, but a subdued form of the same tendency may have been operating—inclining the president's advisers to become reluctant about examining the drawbacks of the invasion plan. In group meetings, this groupthink tendency can operate like a low-level noise that prevents warning signals from being heeded.

Everyone becomes somewhat biased in the direction of selectively attending to the messages that feed into the members' shared feelings of confidence and optimism, disregarding those that do not. . . .

In a concurrence-seeking group, there is relatively little healthy skepticism of the glib ideological formulas on which rational policymakers, like many other people who share their nationalistic goals, generally rely in order to maintain self-confidence and cognitive mastery over the complexities of international politics. One of the symptoms of groupthink is the members' persistence in conveying to each other the cliché and oversimplified images of political enemies embodied in long-standing ideological stereotypes. Throughout their deliberations they use the same old stereotypes, instead of developing differentiated concepts derived from an openminded inquiry enabling them to discern which of their original ideological assumptions, if any, apply to the foreign policy issue at hand. Except in unusual circumstances of crisis, the members of a concurrence-seeking group tend to view any antagonistic out-group against whom they are plotting not only as immoral but also as weak and stupid. These wishful beliefs continue to dominate their thinking until an unequivocal defeat proves otherwise, whereupon—like Kennedy and his advisers—they are shocked at the discrepancy between their stereotyped conceptions and actuality. . . .

The sense of group unity concerning the advisability of going ahead with the CIA's invasion plan appears to have been based on superficial appearances of complete concurrence, achieved at the cost of self-censorship of misgivings by several of the members. From post-mortem discussions with participants, Sorensen concluded that among the men in the State Department, as well as those on the White House staff, "doubts were entertained but never pressed, partly out of a fear of being labelled 'soft' or undaring in the eyes of their colleagues." Schlesinger was not at all hesitant about presenting his strong objections in a memorandum he gave to the president and the secretary of state. But he became keenly aware of his tendency to suppress objections when he attended the White House meetings of the Kennedy team, with their atmosphere of assumed consensus:

In the months after the Bay of Pigs I bitterly reproached myself for having kept so silent during those crucial discussions in the Cabinet Room, though my feelings of guilt were tempered by the knowledge that a course of objection would have accomplished little save to *gain me a name as a nuisance*. . . .

Schlesinger says that when the Cuban invasion plan was being presented to the group, "virile poses" were conveyed in the rhetoric used by the representatives of the CIA and the Joint Chiefs of Staff. He thought the State Department representatives and others responded by becoming anxious to show that they were not softheaded idealists but really were just as tough as the military men. Schlesinger's references to the "virile" stance of the militant advocates of the invasion plan suggest that the members of Kennedy's in-group may have been concerned about protecting the leader from being embarrassed by their voicing "unvirile" concerns about the high risks of the venture. . . .

At a large birthday party for his wife, Robert Kennedy, who had been constantly informed about the Cuban invasion plan, took Schlesinger aside and asked him why he was opposed. The president's brother listened coldly and then said, "You may be right or you may be wrong, but the president has made his mind up. Don't push it any further. Now is the time for everyone to help him all they can." Here is another symptom of groupthink, displayed by a highly intelligent man whose ethical code committed him to freedom of dissent. What he was saying, in effect, was, "You may well be right about the dangerous risks, but I don't give a damn about that; all of us should help our leader right now by not sounding any discordant notes that would interfere with the harmonious support he should have."

When Robert Kennedy told Schlesinger to lay off, he was functioning in a self-appointed role that I call being a "mindguard." Just as a bodyguard protects the president and other high officials from injurious physical assaults, a mindguard protects them from thoughts that might damage their confidence in the soundness of the policies to which they are committed or to which they are about to commit themselves. . . .

The group pressures that help to maintain a group's illusions are sometimes fostered by various leadership practices, some of which involve subtle ways of making it difficult for those who question the initial consensus to suggest alternatives and to raise critical issues. The group's agenda can readily be manipulated by a suave leader, often with the tacit approval of the members, so that there is simply no opportunity to discuss the drawbacks of a seemingly satisfactory plan of action. This is one of the conditions that fosters groupthink.

President Kennedy, as leader at the meetings in the White House, was probably more active than anyone else in raising skeptical questions; yet he seems to have encouraged the group's docility and uncritical acceptance of the defective arguments in favor of the CIA's plan. At each meeting, instead of opening up the agenda to permit a full airing of the opposing considerations, he allowed the CIA representatives to dominate the entire discussion. The president permitted them to refute immediately each tentative doubt that one of the others might express, instead of asking whether anyone else had the same doubt or wanted to pursue the implications of the new worrisome issue that had been raised. . . .

Although the available evidence consists of fragmentary and somewhat biased accounts of the deliberations of the White House group, it nevertheless reveals gross miscalculations and converges on the symptoms of groupthink. My tentative conclusion is that President Kennedy and the policy advisers who decided to accept the CIA's plan were victims of groupthink. If the facts I have culled from the accounts given by Schlesinger, Sorensen, and other observers are essentially accurate, the groupthink hypothesis makes more understandable the deficiencies in the government's decision making that led to the enormous gap between conception and actuality.

The failure of Kennedy's inner circle to detect any of the false assumptions behind the Bay of Pigs invasion plan can be at least partially accounted for by the group's tendency to seek concurrence at the expense of seeking information, critical appraisal, and debate. The concurrence-seeking tendency was manifested by shared illusions and other symptoms, which helped the members to maintain a sense of group solidarity. Most crucial were the symptoms that contributed to complacent overconfidence in the face of vague uncertainties and explicit warnings that should have alerted the members to the risks of the clandestine military operation—an operation so ill-conceived that among literate people all over the world the name of the invasion site has become the very symbol of perfect failure.

Michael Howard

THE CAUSES OF WAR

The defining quality of war is violence: organized, armed violence on the part of large groups of people. Yet, war does not always involve strong, out-of-control emotion. For soldiers, boredom (either repetitive drill or prolonged periods of inaction) is typically more prominent than "action," such that actual combat is sometimes seen as a relief. It has also been argued that for political and military elites as well, war-making is more likely to involve a reasoned decision than a spasm of aggressiveness.

Deterrence—whether nuclear or nonnuclear—is supposed to rely on such a careful, rational calculus, in which a would-be aggressor is expected to be "deterred" by recognizing that the cost of launching a war will be greater than any potential benefits that might accrue. The thinking is similar to the so-called "rational actor" model used by economists, in which consumers are expected to get the maximum value for their money, and businesses are predicted to behave in a way that (rationally) maximizes their profits. It is, of course, debatable whether human beings limit their motivations to such dry and reasoned decisions, especially when issues of pride, prestige, fear, hope, revenge, anger, and so on—not to mention life and death!—are involved. There is also the fact that whatever their "best judgment," people are prone to making mistakes. After all, because most wars do not end in a tie, roughly half the participants were incorrect if, when the war began, they assumed they would win. Furthermore, wars may begin in the reasoned hope of generating greater political support and internal cohesiveness within a country, although as they drag on, they often become destabilizing instead.

In any event, historians and political scientists in particular have been partial to emphasizing the role of coolly reasoned, hardheaded "realpolitik," or "power politics," in the causation of war. In his book *On War*, Carl von Clausewitz, Prussian spokesperson for the military aspects of realpolitik, made the renowned observation that war is "the continuation of politics by other means." For Clausewitz, war, although often brutal, should not be senseless but rather "an act of violence to compel the enemy to fulfill our will."

In this view, war is merely one of many tools employed by politicians and strategists. This is essentially the perspective of most conservative students of war, including British military historian Michael Howard. Whether or not one agrees with this perspective, it is clearly important and deserves attention.

It is true, and it is important to bear in mind . . . that before 1914 war was almost universally considered an acceptable, perhaps an inevitable and for many people a desirable, way of settling international differences, and that the war generally foreseen was expected to be, if not exactly brisk and cheerful, then certainly brief; no longer, certainly, than the war of 1870 between France and Prussia that was consciously or unconsciously taken by that generation as a model. Had it not been so generally felt that war was an acceptable and tolerable way of solving international disputes, statesmen and soldiers would no doubt have approached the crisis of 1914 in a very different fashion.

But there was nothing new about this attitude to war. Statesmen had always been able to assume that war would be acceptable at least to those sections of their populations whose opinion mattered to them, and in this respect the decision to go to war in 1914—for continental statesmen at least—in no way differed from those taken by their predecessors of earlier generations. The causes of the Great War are thus in essence no more complex or profound than those of any previous European war, or indeed than those described by Thucydides as underlying the Peloponnesian War: "What made war inevitable was the growth of Athenian power and the fear this caused in Sparta." In Central Europe, there was the German fear that the disintegration of the Habsburg Empire would result in an enormous enhancement of Russian power—power already becoming formidable as French-financed industries and railways put Russian manpower at the service of her military machine. In Western Europe, there was the traditional British fear that Germany might establish a hegemony over Europe which, even more than that of Napoleon, would place at risk the security of Britain and her own possessions, a fear fueled by the knowledge that there was within Germany a widespread determination to achieve a world status comparable with her latent power. Considerations of

this kind had caused wars in Europe often enough before. Was there really anything different about 1914?

Ever since the eighteenth century, war had been blamed by intellectuals upon the stupidity or the self-interest of governing elites (as it is now blamed upon "military-industrial complexes"), with the implicit or explicit assumption that if the control of state affairs were in the hands of sensible men—businessmen, as Richard Cobden thought, the workers, as Jean Jaurès thought—then wars would be no more.

By the twentieth century, the growth of the social and biological sciences was producing alternative explanations. As Quincy Wright expressed it in his massive *A Study of War* (1942), "Scientific investigators . . . tended to attribute war to immaturities in social knowledge and control, as one might attribute epidemics to insufficient medical knowledge or to inadequate public health services." The Social Darwinian acceptance of the inevitability of struggle, indeed of its desirability if mankind was to progress, the view, expressed by the elder Moltke but very widely shared at the turn of the century, that perpetual peace was a dream and not even a beautiful dream, did not survive the Great War in those countries where the bourgeois-liberal culture was dominant, Britain and the United States. The failure of these nations to appreciate that such bellicist views, or variants of them, were still widespread in other areas of the world, those dominated by Fascism and by Marxism-Leninism, was to cause embarrassing misunderstandings, and possibly still does.

For liberal intellectuals, war was self-evidently a pathological aberration from the norm, at best a ghastly mistake, at worst a crime. Those who initiated wars must in their view have been criminal, or sick, or the victims of forces beyond their power to control. Those who were so accused disclaimed responsibility for the events of 1914, throwing it on others or saying the whole thing was a terrible mistake for which no one was to blame. None of them, with their societies in ruins around them and tens of millions dead, were prepared to say courageously: "We only acted as statesmen always have in the past. In the circumstances then prevailing, war seemed to us to be the best way of protecting or forwarding the national interests for which we were responsible. There was an element of risk, certainly, but the risk might have been greater had we postponed the issue. Our real guilt does not lie in the fact that we started the war. It lies in our mistaken belief that we could win it."

⌒

The trouble is that if we are to regard war as pathological and abnormal, then all conflict must be similarly regarded; for war is only a particular kind of conflict between a particular category of social groups: sovereign states. It is, as Clausewitz put it, "a clash between major interests that is resolved by bloodshed—that is the only way in which it differs from other conflicts." If one had no sovereign states, one would have no wars, as Rousseau rightly pointed out—but, as Hobbes equally rightly pointed out, we would probably have no peace either. As states acquire a monopoly of violence, war becomes the only remaining form of conflict that may legitimately be settled by physical force. The mechanism of legitimization of authority and of social control that makes it possible for a state to moderate or eliminate conflicts within its borders or at very least to ensure that these are not conducted by competitive violence—the mechanism to the study of which historians have quite properly devoted so much attention—makes possible the conduct of armed conflict with other states, and on occasion—if the state is to survive—makes it necessary.

These conflicts arise from conflicting claims, or interests, or ideologies, or perceptions; and these perceptions may indeed be fueled by social or psychological drives that we do not fully understand and that one day we may learn rather better how to control. But the problem is the control of social

conflict *as such*, not simply of war. However inchoate or disreputable the motives for war may be, its initiation is almost by definition a deliberate and carefully considered act and its conduct, at least at the more advanced levels of social development, a matter of very precise central control. If history shows any record of "accidental" wars, I have yet to find them. Certainly statesmen have sometimes been surprised by the nature of the war they have unleashed, and it is reasonable to assume that in at least 50 percent of the cases they got a result they did not expect. But that is not the same as a war begun by mistake and continued with no political purpose.

⌒

Statesmen in fact go to war to achieve very specific ends, and the reasons for which states have fought one another have been categorized and recategorized innumerable times. Vattel, the Swiss lawyer, divided them into the necessary, the customary, the rational, and the capricious. Jomini, the Swiss strategist, identified ideological, economic, and popular wars, wars to defend the balance of power, wars to assist allies, wars to assert or to defend rights. Quincy Wright, the American political scientist, divided them into the idealistic, the psychological, the political, and the juridical. Bernard Brodie in our own times has refused to discriminate: "Any theory of the causes of war in general or any war in particular that is not inherently eclectic and comprehensive," he stated, ". . . is bound for that very reason to be wrong." Another contemporary analyst, Geoffrey Blainey, is on the contrary unashamedly reductionist. All war aims, he wrote, "are simply varieties of power. The vanity of nationalism, the will to spread an ideology, the protection of kinsmen in an adjacent land, the desire for more territory . . . all these represent power in different wrappings. The conflicting aims of rival nations are always conflicts of power."

In principle, I am sure that Bernard Brodie was right: no single explanation for conflict between states, any more than for conflict between any other social groups, is likely to stand up to critical examination. But Blainey is right as well. Quincy Wright provided us with a useful indicator when he suggested that "while animal war is a function of instinct and primitive war of the mores, civilized war is primarily a function of state politics."

Medievalists will perhaps bridle at the application of the term "primitive" to the sophisticated and subtle societies of the Middle Ages, for whom war was also a "function of the mores," a way of life that often demanded only the most banal of justifications. As a way of life, it persisted in Europe well into the seventeenth century, if no later. For Louis XIV and his court war was, in the early years at least, little more than a seasonal variation on hunting. But by the eighteenth century, the mood had changed. For Frederick the Great, war was to be preeminently a function of *Staatspolitik*, and so it has remained ever since. And although statesmen can be as emotional or as prejudiced in their judgments as any other group of human beings, it is very seldom that their attitudes, their perceptions, and their decisions are not related, however remotely, to the fundamental issues of *power*, that capacity to control their environment on which the independent existence of their states and often the cultural values of their societies depend.

⤙

And here perhaps we do find a factor that sets interstate conflict somewhat apart from other forms of social rivalry. States may fight—indeed as often as not they do fight—not over any specific issue such as might otherwise have been resolved by peaceful means, but in order to acquire, to enhance, or to preserve their capacity to function as independent actors in the international system at all. "The stakes of war," as Raymond Aron has reminded us, "are the existence, the creation, or the elimination of States." It is a somber analysis, but one which the historical record very amply bears out.

It is here that those analysts who come to the study of war from the disciplines of the natural sciences, particularly the biological sciences, tend, it seems to me, to go astray. The conflicts between states which have usually led to war have normally arisen, not from any irrational and emotive drives, but from almost a superabundance of analytic rationality. Sophisticated communities (one hesitates to apply to them Quincy Wright's word, "civilized") do not react simply to immediate threats. Their intelligence (and I use the term in its double sense) enables them to assess the implications that any event taking place anywhere in the world, however remote, may have for their own capacity, immediately to exert influence, ultimately perhaps to survive. In the later Middle Ages and the early Modern period, every child born to every prince anywhere in Europe was registered on the delicate seismographs that monitored the shifts in dynastic power. Every marriage was a diplomatic triumph or disaster. Every stillbirth, as Henry VIII knew, could presage political catastrophe.

Today, the key events may be different. The pattern remains the same. A malfunction in the political mechanism of some remote African community, a coup d'état in a minuscule Caribbean republic, an insurrection deep in the hinterland of Southeast Asia, an assassination in some emirate in the Middle East—all these will be subjected to the kind of anxious examination and calculation that was devoted a hundred years ago to the news of comparable events in the Balkans: an insurrection in Philippopoli, a coup d'état in Constantinople, an assassination in Belgrade. To whose advantage will this ultimately redound, asked the worried diplomats, ours or *theirs*? Little enough in itself, perhaps, but will it not precipitate or strengthen a trend, set in motion a tide whose melancholy withdrawing roar will strip us of our friends and influence and leave us isolated in a world dominated by adversaries deeply hostile to us and all that we stand for?

There have certainly been occasions when states have gone to war in a mood of ideological fervor like the French republican armies in 1792; or of swaggering aggression like the Americans against Spain in 1898 or the British against the Boers a year later; or to make more money, as did the British in the War of Jenkins' Ear in 1739; or in a generous desire to help peoples of similar creed or race, as perhaps the Russians did in helping the Bulgarians fight the Turks in 1877 and the British dominions certainly did in 1914 and 1939. But, in general, men have fought during the past two hundred years neither because they are aggressive nor because they are acquisitive animals, but because they are reasoning ones: because they discern, or believe that they can discern, dangers before they become immediate, the possibility of threats before they are made.

⌒

But be this as it may, in 1914 many of the German people, and in 1939 nearly all of the British, felt justified in going to war, not over any specific issue that could have been settled by negotiation, but *to maintain their power*; and to do so while it was still possible, before they found themselves so isolated, so impotent, that they had no power left to maintain and had to accept a subordinate position within an international system dominated by their adversaries. "What made war inevitable was the growth of Athenian power and the fear this caused in Sparta." Or, to quote another grimly apt passage from Thucydides:

> The Athenians made their Empire more and more strong . . . [until] finally the point was reached when Athenian strength attained a peak plain for all to see and the Athenians began to encroach upon Sparta's allies. It was at this point that Sparta felt the position to be no longer tolerable and decided by starting the present war to employ all her energies in attacking and if possible destroying the power of Athens.

You can vary the names of the actors, but the model remains a valid one for the purposes of our analysis. I am rather afraid that it still does.

Something that has changed since the time of Thucydides, however, is the nature of the power that appears so threatening. From the time of Thucydides until that of Louis XIV, there was basically only one source of political and military power—control of territory, with all the resources in wealth and manpower that this provided. This control might come through conquest, or through alliance, or through marriage, or through purchase, but the power of princes could be very exactly computed in terms of the extent of their territories and the number of men they could put under arms.

In seventeenth-century Europe, this began to change. Extent of territory remained important, but no less important was the effectiveness with which

the resources of that territory could be exploited. Initially there were the bureaucratic and fiscal mechanisms that transformed loose bonds of territorial authority into highly structured centralized states whose armed forces, though not necessarily large, were permanent, disciplined, and paid.

⌒

Then came the political transformations of the revolutionary era that made available to these state systems the entire manpower of their country, or at least as much of it as the administrators were able to handle. And finally came the revolution in transport, the railways of the nineteenth century that turned the revolutionary ideal of the "Nation in Arms" into a reality. By the early twentieth century, military power—on the continent of Europe, at least—was seen as a simple combination of military manpower and railways. The quality of armaments was of secondary importance, and political intentions were virtually excluded from account. The growth of power was measured in terms of the growth of populations and of communications; of the number of men who could be put under arms and transported to the battlefield to make their weight felt in the initial and presumably decisive battles. It was the mutual perception of threat in those terms that turned Europe before 1914 into an armed camp, and it was their calculations within this framework that reduced German staff officers increasingly to despair and launched their leaders on their catastrophic gamble in 1914, which started the First World War.

But already the development of weapons technology had introduced yet another element into the international power calculus, one that has in our own age become dominant. It was only in the course of the nineteenth century that technology began to produce weapons systems—initially in the form of naval vessels—that could be seen as likely in themselves to prove decisive, through their qualitative and quantitative superiority, in the event of conflict. But as war became increasingly a matter of competing technologies rather than competing armies, so there developed that escalatory process known as the "arms race." As a title, the phrase, like so many coined by journalists to catch the eye, is misleading.

⤳

"Arms races" are in fact continuing and open-ended attempts to match power for power. They are as much means of achieving stable or, if possible, favorable power balances as were the dynastic marriage policies of Valois and Habsburg. To suggest that they in themselves are causes of war implies a naive if not totally mistaken view of the relationship between the two phenomena. The causes of war remain rooted, as much as they were in the preindustrial age, in perceptions by statesmen of the growth of hostile power and the fears for the restriction, if not the extinction, of their own. The threat, or rather the fear, has not changed, whether it comes from aggregations of territory or from dreadnoughts, from the numbers of men under arms or from missile systems. The means that states employ to sustain or to extend their power may have been transformed, but their objectives and preoccupations remain the same.

"Arms races" can no more be isolated than wars themselves from the political circumstances that give rise to them, and like wars they will take as many different forms as political circumstances dictate. They may be no more than a process of competitive modernization, of maintaining a status quo that commands general support but in which no participant wishes, whether from reasons of pride or of prudence, to fall behind in keeping his armory up to date. If there are no political causes for fear or rivalry, this process need not in itself be a destabilizing factor in international relations. But arms races may, on the other hand, be the result of a quite deliberate assertion of an intention to *change* the status quo, as was, for example, the German naval challenge to Britain at the beginning of this century.

This challenge was an explicit attempt by Admiral Alfred von Tirpitz and his associates to destroy the hegemonic position at sea which Britain saw as essential to her security, and, not inconceivably, to replace it with one of their own. As British and indeed German diplomats repeatedly explained to the German government, it was not the German naval program in itself that gave rise to so much alarm in Britain. It was the intention that lay behind it. If the status quo was to be maintained, the German challenge had to be met.

⤳

The naval race could quite easily have been ended on one of two conditions. Either the Germans could have abandoned their challenge, as had the French in the previous century, and acquiesced in British naval supremacy; or the British could have yielded as gracefully as they did, a decade or so later, to the United States and abandoned a status they no longer had the capacity, or the will, to maintain. As it was, they saw the German challenge as one to which they could and should respond, and their power position as one which they were prepared, if necessary, to use force to preserve. The British naval program was thus, like that of the Germans, a signal of political intent; and that intent, that refusal to acquiesce in a fundamental transformation of the power balance, was indeed a major element among the causes of the war. The naval competition provided a very accurate indication and measurement of political rivalries and tensions, but it did not cause them; nor could it have been abated unless the rivalries themselves had been abandoned.

It was the general perception of the growth of German power that was awakened by the naval challenge, and the fear that a German hegemony on the Continent would be the first step to a challenge to her own hegemony on the oceans, that led Britain to involve herself in the continental conflict in 1914 on the side of France and Russia. "What made war inevitable was the growth of *Spartan* power," to reword Thucydides, "and the fear which this caused in *Athens.*" In the Great War that followed, Germany was defeated, but survived with none of her latent power destroyed. A "false hegemony" of Britain and France was established in Europe that could last only so long as Germany did not again mobilize her resources to challenge it. German rearmament in the 1930s did not of itself mean that Hitler wanted war (though one has to ignore his entire philosophy if one is to believe that he did not); but it did mean that he was determined, with a great deal of popular support, to obtain a free hand on the international scene.

With that free hand, he intended to establish German power on an irreversible basis; this was the message conveyed by his armament program. The armament program that the British reluctantly adopted in reply was intended to show that, rather than submit to the hegemonic aspirations they feared from such a revival of German power, they would fight to preserve their own freedom of action. Once again to recast Thucydides:

> Finally the point was reached when German strength attained a peak plain for all to see, and the Germans began to encroach upon Britain's allies. It was at this point that Britain felt the position to be no longer tolerable and decided by starting this present war to employ all her energies in attacking and if possible destroying the power of Germany.

What the Second World War established was not a new British hegemony, but a Soviet hegemony over the Euro-Asian landmass from the Elbe to Vladivostok; and that was seen, at least from Moscow, as an American hegemony over the rest of the world; one freely accepted in Western Europe as a preferable alternative to being absorbed by the rival hegemony. Rival armaments were developed to define and preserve the new territorial boundaries, and . . . arms competition began. . . .

⌣⟍

The trouble is that what is seen by one party as the breaking of an alien hegemony and the establishment of equal status will be seen by the incumbent powers as a striving for the establishment of an alternate hegemony, and they are not necessarily wrong. In international politics, the appetite often comes with eating; and there really may be no way to check an aspiring rival except by the mobilization of stronger military power. An arms race then becomes almost a necessary surrogate for war, a test of national will and strength; and arms control becomes possible only when the underlying power balance has been mutually agreed.

We would be blind, therefore, if we did not recognize that the causes which have produced war in the past are operating in our own day as powerfully as at any time in history. . . .

But times *have* changed since Thucydides. They have changed even since 1914. These were, as we have seen, bellicist societies in which war was a normal, acceptable, even a desirable way of settling differences. The question that arises today is, how widely and evenly spread is that intense revulsion against war that at present characterizes our own society? For if war is indeed now *universally* seen as being unacceptable as an instrument of policy, then all analogies drawn from the past are misleading, and although power struggles may continue, they will be diverted into other channels. But if that revulsion is not evenly spread, societies which continue to see armed force as an acceptable means for attaining their political ends are likely to establish a dominance over those which do not. Indeed, they will not necessarily have to fight for it.

My second and concluding point is this: whatever may be the underlying causes of international conflict, even if we accept the role of atavistic militarism or of military-industrial complexes or of sociobiological drives or of domestic tensions in fueling it, wars begin with conscious and reasoned decisions based on the calculation, made by *both* parties, that they can achieve more by going to war than by remaining at peace.

Kenneth Boulding

NATIONAL IMAGES AND INTERNATIONAL SYSTEMS

Nationalism is one of the most powerful forces of modern times. It can be beautiful, reflecting the yearning of people to associate themselves with others, as well as evoking compassion, love, respect for one's past, one's culture, and even the natural environment. In offering perhaps its most famous definition, French philosopher and historian J. Ernest Renan suggested that nationalism is

> a grand solidarity constituted by the sentiment of sacrifices which one has made and those that time is disposed to make again. . . . The existence of a nation is an everyday plebiscite.[5]

At the same time, nationalism can become malevolent, fostering chauvinism, group intolerance, and violent divisions between people, which that threaten to destroy the values it claims to venerate. "By nationalism," wrote George Orwell,

> I mean first of all the habit of assuming that human beings can be classified like insects and that whole blocks of millions or tens of millions of people can be confidently labeled "good" or "bad." But secondly—and this is much more important—I mean the habit of identifying oneself with a single nation or other unit, placing it beyond good or evil and recognizing no other duty than that of advancing its own interests.[6]

Here Kenneth Boulding—one of the founders of peace studies—discusses the phenomenon of national "images."

We must recognize that the people whose decisions determine the policies and actions of nations do not respond to the "objective" facts of the situation, whatever that may mean, but to their "image" of the situation. It is what we think the world is like, not what it is really like, that determines our behavior. If our image of the world is in some sense "wrong," of course, we may be disappointed in our expectations, and we may therefore revise our image; if this revision is in the direction of the "truth" there is presumably a long-run tendency for the "image" and the "truth" to coincide. Whether this is so or not, it is always the image, not the truth, that immediately determines behavior. We act according to the way the world appears to us, not necessarily according to the way it "is." Thus . . . it is one nation's image of the hostility of another, not the "real" hostility, which determines its reaction. The "image," then,

---

[5] J. Ernest Renan, *What Is a Nation?* (Paris: Calmann-Levy, 1882).
[6] George Orwell, *Such, Such Were the Joys* (New York: Harcourt, Brace, 1953).

---

must be thought of as the total cognitive, affective, and evaluative structure of the behavior unit, or its internal view of itself and its universe.

Generally speaking, the behavior of complex organizations can be regarded as determined by *decisions*, and a decision involves the selection of the most preferred position in a contemplated field of choice. Both the field of choice and the ordering of this field by which the preferred position is identified lie in the image of the decision-maker. Therefore, in a system in which decision-makers are an essential element, the study of the ways in which the image grows and changes, both of the field of choice and of the valuational ordering of this field, is of prime importance. The image is always in some sense a product of messages received in the past. It is not, however, a simple inventory or "pile" of such messages but a highly structured piece of information capital, developed partly by its inputs and outputs of information and partly by internal messages and its own laws of growth and stability.

The images which are important in international systems are those which a nation has of itself and of those other bodies in the system which constitute its international environment. At once a major complication suggests itself. A nation is some complex of the images of the persons who contemplate it, and as there are many different persons, so there are many different images. The complexity is increased by the necessity for inclusion, in the image of each person or at least of many persons, his image of the image of others. This complexity, however, is a property of the real world, not to be evaded or glossed over. It can be reduced to simpler terms if we distinguish between two types of persons in a nation—the powerful, on the one hand, and the ordinary, on the other. This is not, of course, a sharp distinction. The power of a decision-maker may be measured roughly by the number of people which his decisions potentially affect, weighted by some measure of the effect itself. Thus the head of a state is powerful, meaning that his decisions affect the lives of millions of people; the ordinary person is not powerful, for his decisions affect only himself and the lives of a few people around him. There is usually a continuum of power among the persons of a society: thus in international relations there are usually a few very powerful individuals in a state—the chief executive,

the prime minister, the secretary of state or minister of foreign affairs, the chiefs of staff of the armed forces. There will be some who are less powerful but still influential—members of the legislature, of the civil service, even journalists, newspaper owners, prominent businessmen, grading by imperceptible degrees down to the common soldier, who has no power of decision even over his own life. For purposes of the model, however, let us compress this continuum into two boxes, labeled the "powerful" and the "ordinary," and leave the refinements of power and influence for later studies.

We deal, therefore, with two representative images, (1) the image of the small group of powerful people who make the actual decisions which lead to war or peace, the making or breaking of treaties, the invasions or withdrawals, alliances, and enmities which make up the major events of international relations, and (2) the image of the mass of ordinary people who are deeply affected by these decisions but who take little or no direct part in making them. The tacit support of the mass, however, is of vital importance to the powerful. The powerful are always under some obligation to represent the mass, even under dictatorial regimes. In democratic societies the aggregate influence of the images of ordinary people is very great; the image of the powerful cannot diverge too greatly from the image of the mass without the powerful losing power. On the other hand, the powerful also have some ability to manipulate the images of the mass toward those of the powerful. This is an important object of instruments as diverse as the public education system, the public relations departments of the armed services, the Russian "agitprop," and the Nazi propaganda ministry.

In the formation of the national images, however, it must be emphasized that impressions of nationality are formed mostly in childhood and usually in the family group. It would be quite fallacious to think of the images as being cleverly imposed on the mass by the powerful. If anything, the reverse is the case: the image is essentially a mass image, or what might be called a "folk image," transmitted through the family and the intimate face-to-face group, both in the case of the powerful and in the case of ordinary persons. Especially in the case of the old, long-established nations, the powerful share the mass image rather than impose it; it is passed on from the value systems of the parents to those of the children, and agencies of public instruction and propaganda merely reinforce the images which derived essentially from the family culture. This is much less true in new nations which are striving to achieve nationality, where the family culture frequently does not include strong elements of national allegiance but rather stresses allegiance to religious ideals or to the family as such. Here the powerful are frequently inspired by a national image derived not from family tradition but from a desire to imitate other nations, and here they frequently try to impose their images on the mass of people. Imposed images, however, are fragile by comparison with those which are deeply internalized and transmitted through family and other intimate sources.

Whether transmitted orally and informally through the family or more formally through schooling and the written word, the national image is essentially a *historical* image—that is, an image which extends through time, backward into a supposedly recorded or perhaps mythological past and forward into an imagined future. The more conscious a people is of its history, the stronger the national image is likely to be. To be an Englishman is to be conscious of "1066 and All That" rather than of "Constantine and All That," or "1776 and All That." A nation is the creation of its historians, formal and informal. The written word and public education contribute enormously to the stability and persistence of the national images. The Jews, for instance, are a creation of the Bible and the Talmud, but every nation has its bible, whether formed into a canon or not—noble words like the Declaration of Independence and the Gettysburg Address—which crystallize the national image in a form that can be transmitted almost unchanged from generation to generation. It is no exaggeration to say that the function of the historian is to pervert the truth in directions favorable to the images of his readers or hearers. Both history and geography as taught in national schools are devised to give "perspective" rather than truth: that is to say, they present the world as seen from the vantage point of the nation. The national geography is learned in great detail, and the rest of the world is a fuzzy outline; the national history is emphasized and exalted; the

history of the rest of the world is neglected or even falsified to the glory of the national image.

It is this fact that the national image is basically a lie, or at least a perspective distortion of the truth, which perhaps accounts for the ease with which it can be perverted to justify monstrous cruelties and wickednesses. There is much that is noble in the national image. It has lifted man out of the narrow cage of self-centeredness, or even family-centeredness, and has forced him to accept responsibility, in some sense, for people and events far beyond his face-to-face cognizance and immediate experience. It is a window of some sort on both space and time and extends a man's concern far beyond his own little lifetime and petty interests. Nevertheless, it achieves these virtues usually only at the cost of untruth, and this fatal flaw constantly betrays it. Love of country is perverted into hatred of the foreigner, and peace, order, and justice at home are paid for by war, cruelty, and injustice abroad.

In the formation of the national image the consciousness of great *shared* events and experiences is of the utmost importance. A nation is a body of people who are conscious of having "gone through something" together. Without the shared experience, the national image itself would not be shared, and it is of vital importance that the national image be highly similar. The sharing may be quite vicarious; it may be an experience shared long ago but constantly renewed by the ritual observances and historical memory of the people, like the Passover and the Captivity in the case of the Jews. Without the sharing, however, there is no nation. It is for this reason that war has been such a tragically important element in the creation and sustenance of the national image. There is hardly a nation that has not been cradled in violence and nourished by further violence. This is not, I think, a necessary property of war itself. It is rather that, especially in more primitive societies, war is the one experience which is dramatic, obviously important, and shared by everybody. . . .

We now come to the central problem, which is that of the impact of national images on the relations among states, that is, on the course of events in international relations. The relations among states can be described in terms of a number of different dimensions. There is, first of all, the dimension of simple geographical space. It is perhaps the most striking single characteristic of the national state as an organization, by contrast with organizations such as firms or churches, that it thinks of itself as occupying, in a "dense" and exclusive fashion, a certain area of the globe. The schoolroom maps which divide the world into colored shapes which are identified as nations have a profound effect on the national image. Apart from the very occasional condominium, it is impossible for a given plot of land on the globe to be associated with two nations at the same time. The territories of nations are divided sharply by frontiers carefully surveyed and frequently delineated by a chain of customs houses, immigration stations, and military installations. We are so accustomed to this arrangement that we think of it as "natural" and take it completely for granted. It is by no means the only conceivable arrangement, however. In primitive societies the geographical image is not sharp enough to define clear frontiers; there may be a notion of the rough territory of a tribe, but, especially among nomadic peoples, there is no clear concept of a frontier and no notion of a nation as something that has a shape on a map. In our own society the shape on the map that symbolizes the nation is constantly drilled into the minds of both young and old, both through formal teaching in schools and through constant repetition in newspapers, advertisements, cartoons, and so on. A society is not inconceivable, however, and might even be desirable, in which nations governed people but not territories and claimed jurisdiction over a defined set of citizens, no matter where on the earth's surface they happened to live.

The territorial aspect of the national state is important in the dynamics of international relations because of the *exclusiveness* of territorial occupation. This means that one nation can generally expand only at the expense of another; an increase in the territory of one is achieved only at the expense of a decrease in the territory of another. This makes for a potential conflict situation. This characteristic of the nation does not make conflict inevitable, but it does make it likely and is at least one of the reasons why the history of international relations is a history of perpetual conflict.

The territorial aspect of international relations is complicated by the fact that in many cases the territories of nations are not homogeneous but are composed of "empires," in which the populations do not identify themselves with the national image of the dominant group. Thus when one nation conquers another and absorbs the conquered territory into an empire, it does not thereby automatically change the culture and allegiances of the conquered nation. The Poles remained Polish for a hundred and twenty-five years of partition between Germany, Austria, and Russia. The Finns retained their nationality through eight hundred years of foreign rule and the Jews, through nearly two thousand years of dispersion. If a nation loses territory occupied by disaffected people, this is much less damaging than the loss of territory inhabited by a well-disposed and loyal population. Thus Turkey, which was the "sick man of Europe" as long as it retained its heterogeneous empire, enjoyed a substantial renewal of national health when stripped of its empire and pushed back to the relatively homogeneous heartland of Anatolia. In this case the loss of a disaffected empire actually strengthened the national unit.

The image of the map shape of the nations may be an important factor affecting the general frame of mind of the nation. There is a tendency for nations to be uneasy with strong irregularities, enclaves, detached portions, and protuberances or hollows. The ideal shape is at least a convex set, and there is some tendency for nations to be more satisfied if they have regularly round or rectangular outlines. Thus the detachment of East Prussia from the body of Germany by the Treaty of Versailles was an important factor in creating the fanatical discontent of the Nazis.

A second important dimension of the national image is that of hostility or friendliness. At any one time a particular national image includes a rough scale of the friendliness or hostility of, or toward, other nations. The relationship is not necessarily either consistent or reciprocal—in nation A the prevailing image may be that B is friendly, whereas in nation B itself the prevailing image may be one of hostility toward A; or again in both nations there may be an image of friendliness of A toward B but of hostility of B toward A. On the whole, however, there is a tendency toward both consistency and reciprocation—if a nation A pictures itself as hostile toward B, it usually also pictures B as hostile toward it, and the image is likely to be repeated in B. One exception to this rule seems to be observable: most nations seem to feel that their enemies are more hostile toward them than they are toward their enemies. This is a typical paranoid reaction; the nation visualizes itself as surrounded by hostile nations toward which it has only the nicest and friendliest of intentions.

An important subdimension of the hostility-friendliness image is that of the stability or security of the relationship. A friendly relationship is frequently formalized as an alliance. Alliances, however, are shifting; some friendly relations are fairly permanent, others change as the world kaleidoscope changes, as new enemies arise, or as governments change. Thus. . . . most people in the United States visualized Germany and Japan, even before the outbreak of the war, as enemies, and after Hitler's invasion of Russia, Russia was for a while regarded as a valuable friend and ally. . . . We can roughly classify the reciprocal relations of nations along some scale of friendliness-hostility. At one extreme we have stable friendliness, such as between Britain and Portugal or between Britain and the Commonwealth countries. At the other extreme we have stable hostility—the "traditional enemies" such as France and Germany. Between these extremes we have a great many pairs characterized by shifting alliances. On the whole, stable friendly relations seem to exist mainly between strong nations and weaker nations which they have an interest in preserving and stable hostile relations between adjacent nations, each of which has played a large part in the formation of the other.

Samuel P. Huntington

THE CLASH OF CIVILIZATIONS

For some students of international affairs, the fundamental war/peace issue facing modern societies is a conflict between "civilizations." This perspective was most forcefully developed by political scientist Samuel Huntington, initially in an influential article in the journal *Foreign Affairs* (excerpted here) and then later expanded into a book by the same title. Although Huntington's initial thesis was broader than simply warning about a clash between Islam and the West, that component has been the most dramatic part of his argument, one that has subsequently been taken up by many observers, especially those of a more conservative bent.

Critics of Huntington's perspective have pointed out that with the end of the U.S.-Soviet rivalry, "cold warriors" may well have felt threatened by the *absence* of a designated enemy, which led, in turn, to identifying a forthcoming "clash of civilizations," less because of its likely reality than as a form of post–Cold War job insurance. In addition, the danger exists that identifying such "clashes" may well serve as a self-fulfilling prophecy, whereby preparing for some eventualities has the effect of generating responses by the other side that cause the original prediction to become true. Moreover, others point out that "civilizations" are hardly unitary or homogeneous and that by identifying "Islam," for example, as a single entity, the "clash of civilizations" approach errs greatly by failing to recognize the complex heterogeneity of, for example, Sunni and Shiite, Arab and non-Arab, moderate and fundamentalist, and so forth.

On the other hand, it can be argued that this perspective has proven remarkably prescient: note that it initially appeared in 1993. Only time will tell whether a "clash of civilizations" explains past history, underlies current events, or—more to the point—anticipates the future. In any event, by understanding the argument, those seeking to pursue peace will be in a better position to reject or learn from it.

THE NEXT PATTERN OF CONFLICT

World politics is entering a new phase, and intellectuals have not hesitated to proliferate visions of what it will be—the end of history, the return of traditional rivalries between nation-states, and the decline of the nation-state from the conflicting pulls of tribalism and globalism, among others. Each of these visions catches aspects of the emerging reality. Yet they all miss a crucial, indeed a central, aspect of what global politics is likely to be in the coming years.

It is my hypothesis that the fundamental source of conflict in this new world will not be primarily ideological or primarily economic. The great divisions among humankind and the dominating source of conflict will be cultural. Nation-states will remain the most powerful actors in world affairs, but the principal conflicts of global politics will occur between nations and groups of different civilizations. The clash of civilizations will dominate global politics. The fault lines between civilizations will be the battle lines of the future.

Conflict between civilizations will be the latest phase in the evolution of conflict in the modern world. For a century and a half after the emergence of the modern international system with the Peace of Westphalia, the conflicts of the Western world were largely among princes—emperors, absolute monarchs, and constitutional monarchs attempting to expand their bureaucracies, their armies, their mercantilist economic strength and, most important, the territory they ruled. In the process they created nation-states, and beginning with the French Revolution the principal lines of conflict were between nations rather than princes. In 1793, as R. R. Palmer put it, "The wars of kings were over; the wars of peoples had begun." This nineteenth-century pattern lasted until the end of World War I. Then, as a result of the Russian Revolution and the reaction against it, the conflict of nations yielded to the conflict of ideologies, first among communism, fascism-Nazism, and liberal democracy, and then between communism and liberal democracy. During the Cold War, this latter conflict became embodied in the struggle between the two superpowers, neither of which was a nation-state in the classical European sense and each of which defined its identity in terms of its ideology.

These conflicts between princes, nation-states, and ideologies were primarily conflicts within Western civilization, "Western civil wars," as William Lind has labeled them. This was as true of the Cold War as it was of the world wars and the earlier wars of the seventeenth, eighteenth, and nineteenth centuries. With the end of the Cold War, international politics moves out of its Western phase, and its centerpiece becomes the interaction between the West and non-Western civilizations and among non-Western civilizations. In the politics of civilizations, the peoples and governments of non-Western civilizations no longer remain the objects of history as targets of Western colonialism but join the West as movers and shapers of history. . . .

Westerners tend to think of nation-states as the principal actors in global affairs. They have been that, however, for only a few centuries. The broader reaches of human history have been the history of civilizations. In *A Study of History*, Arnold Toynbee identified twenty-one major civilizations; only six of them exist in the contemporary world.

WHY CIVILIZATIONS WILL CLASH

Civilization identity will be increasingly important in the future, and the world will be shaped in large measure by the interactions among seven or eight major civilizations. These include Western, Confucian, Japanese, Islamic, Hindu, Slavic-Orthodox, Latin American, and possibly African civilization. The most important conflicts of the future will occur along the cultural fault lines separating these civilizations from one another.

Why will this be the case?

First, differences among civilizations are not only real; they are basic. Civilizations are differentiated from each other by history, language, culture, tradition, and, most important, religion. The people of different civilizations have different views on the relations between God and man, the individual and the group, the citizen and the state, parents and children, husband and wife, as well as differing views of the relative importance of rights and responsibilities, liberty and authority, equality and hierarchy. These differences are the product of centuries. They will not soon disappear. They are far more fundamental than differences among political ideologies and political regimes. Differences do not necessarily mean conflict, and conflict does not necessarily mean violence. Over the centuries, however, differences among civilizations have generated the most prolonged and the most violent conflicts.

Second, the world is becoming a smaller place. The interactions between peoples of different civilizations are increasing; these increasing interactions intensify civilization-consciousness and awareness of differences between civilizations and commonalities within civilizations. North African immigration to France generated hostility among Frenchmen and at the same time increased receptivity to immigration by "good" European Catholic Poles. Americans react far more negatively to Japanese investment than to larger investments from Canada and European countries. Similarly, as Donald Horowitz has pointed out, "An Ibo may be . . . an Owerri Ibo or an Onitsha Ibo in what was the Eastern region of Nigeria. In Lagos, he is simply an Ibo. In London, he is a Nigerian. In New York, he is an African." The interactions among peoples of different civilizations

enhance the civilization-consciousness of people that, in turn, invigorates differences and animosities stretching or thought to stretch back deep into history.

Third, the processes of economic modernization and social change throughout the world are separating people from long-standing local identities. They also weaken the nation-state as a source of identity. In much of the world, religion has moved in to fill this gap, often in the form of movements that are labeled "fundamentalist." Such movements are found in Western Christianity, Judaism, Buddhism, and Hinduism, as well as in Islam. In most countries and most religions, the people active in fundamentalist movements are young, college-educated, middle-class technicians, professionals, and businesspersons. The "unsecularization of the world," George Weigel has remarked, "is one of the dominant social facts of life in the late twentieth century." The revival of religion, "la revanche de Dieu," as Gilles Kepel labeled it, provides a basis for identity and commitment that transcends national boundaries and unites civilizations.

Fourth, the growth of civilization-consciousness is enhanced by the dual role of the West. On the one hand, the West is at a peak of power. At the same time, however, and perhaps as a result, a return to the roots phenomenon is occurring among non-Western civilizations. Increasingly one hears references to trends toward a turning inward and "Asianization" in Japan, the end of the Nehru legacy and the "Hinduization" of India, the failure of Western ideas of socialism and nationalism and hence "re-Islamization" of the Middle East, and now a debate over Westernization versus Russianization in Boris Yeltsin's country. A West at the peak of its power confronts non-Wests that increasingly have the desire, the will, and the resources to shape the world in non-Western ways. . . .

Fifth, cultural characteristics and differences are less mutable and hence less easily compromised and resolved than political and economic ones. In the former Soviet Union, Communists can become Democrats, the rich can become poor and the poor rich, but Russians cannot become Estonians and Azeris cannot become Armenians. In class and ideological conflicts, the key question was "Which side are you on?" and people could and did choose sides and change sides. In conflicts between civilizations, the question is "What are you?" That is a given that cannot be changed. And as we know, from Bosnia to the Caucasus to the Sudan, the wrong answer to that question can mean a bullet in the head. Even more than ethnicity, religion discriminates sharply and exclusively among people. A person can be half-French and half-Arab and simultaneously even a citizen of two countries. It is more difficult to be half-Catholic and half-Muslim. . . .

As people define their identity in ethnic and religious terms, they are likely to see an "us" versus "them" relation existing between themselves and people of different ethnicity or religion. The end of ideologically defined states in Eastern Europe and the former Soviet Union permits traditional ethnic identities and animosities to come to the fore. Differences in culture and religion create differences over policy issues, ranging from human rights to immigration to trade and commerce to the environment. Geographical propinquity gives rise to conflicting territorial claims from Bosnia to Mindanao. Most important, the efforts of the West to promote its values of democracy and liberalism as universal values, to maintain its military predominance and to advance its economic interests, engender countering responses from other civilizations. Decreasingly able to mobilize support and form coalitions on the basis of ideology, governments and groups will increasingly attempt to mobilize support by appealing to common religion and civilization identity.

The clash of civilizations thus occurs at two levels. At the microlevel, adjacent groups along the fault lines between civilizations struggle, often violently, over the control of territory and each other. At the macrolevel, states from different civilizations compete for relative military and economic power, struggle over the control of international institutions and third parties, and competitively promote their particular political and religious values.

THE FAULT LINES BETWEEN CIVILIZATIONS

The fault lines between civilizations are replacing the political and ideological boundaries of the Cold War as the flash points for crisis and bloodshed. The Cold War began when the Iron Curtain divided Europe politically and ideologically. The Cold War ended with the end of the Iron Curtain. As the ideological division of Europe has disappeared, the cultural division of Europe between Western Christianity, on the one hand, and Orthodox Christianity and Islam, on the other, has reemerged. . . .

Conflict along the fault line between Western and Islamic civilizations has been going on for 1,300 years. After the founding of Islam, the Arab and Moorish surge west and north only ended at Tours in 732. From the eleventh to the thirteenth century, the Crusaders attempted with temporary success to bring Christianity and Christian rule to the Holy Land. From the fourteenth to the seventeenth century, the Ottoman Turks reversed the balance, extended their sway over the Middle East and the Balkans, captured Constantinople, and twice laid siege to Vienna. In the nineteenth and early twentieth centuries, as Ottoman power declined, Britain, France, and Italy established Western control over most of North Africa and the Middle East.

After World War II, the West, in turn, began to retreat; the colonial empires disappeared; first Arab nationalism and then Islamic fundamentalism manifested themselves; the West became heavily dependent on the Persian Gulf countries for its energy; the oil-rich Muslim countries became money-rich and, when they wished to, weapons-rich. Several wars occurred between Arabs and Israel (created by the West). France fought a bloody and ruthless war in Algeria for most of the 1950s; British and French forces invaded Egypt in 1956; American forces went into Lebanon in 1958; subsequently American forces returned to Lebanon, attacked Libya, and engaged in various military encounters with Iran; Arab and Islamic terrorists, supported by at least three Middle Eastern governments, employed the weapon of the weak and bombed Western planes and installations and seized Western hostages. This warfare between Arabs and the West culminated in 1990, when the United States sent a massive army to the Persian Gulf to defend some Arab countries against aggression by another. In its aftermath nato planning is increasingly directed to potential threats and instability along its "southern tier."

This centuries-old military interaction between the West and Islam is unlikely to decline. It could become more virulent. The Gulf War left some Arabs feeling proud that Saddam Hussein had attacked Israel and stood up to the West. It also left many feeling humiliated and resentful of the West's military presence in the Persian Gulf, the West's overwhelming military dominance, and their apparent inability to shape their own destiny. Many Arab countries, in addition to the oil exporters, are reaching levels of economic and social development where autocratic forms of government become inappropriate and efforts to introduce democracy become stronger. Some openings in Arab political systems have already occurred. The principal beneficiaries of these openings have been Islamist movements. In the Arab world, in short, Western democracy strengthens anti-Western political forces. This may be a passing phenomenon, but it surely complicates relations between Islamic countries and the West.

Those relations are also complicated by demography. The spectacular population growth in Arab countries, particularly in North Africa, has led to increased migration to Western Europe. The movement within Western Europe toward minimizing internal boundaries has sharpened political sensitivities with respect to this development. In Italy, France, and Germany, racism is increasingly open, and political reactions and violence against Arab and Turkish migrants have become more intense and more widespread since 1990.

On both sides the interaction between Islam and the West is seen as a clash of civilizations. The West's "next confrontation," observes M. J. Akbar, an Indian Muslim author, "is definitely going to come from the Muslim world. It is in the sweep of the Islamic nations from the Maghreb to Pakistan that the struggle for a new world order will begin." Bernard Lewis comes to a similar conclusion:

We are facing a mood and a movement far transcending the level of issues and policies and the governments that pursue them. This is no less than a clash of civilizations—the perhaps irrational but surely historic reaction of an ancient rival against our Judeo-Christian heritage, our

secular present, and the worldwide expansion of both.[7]

. . . The interactions between civilizations vary greatly in the extent to which they are likely to be characterized by violence. Economic competition clearly predominates between the American and European subcivilizations of the West and between both of them and Japan. On the Eurasian continent, however, the proliferation of ethnic conflict, epitomized at the extreme in "ethnic cleansing," has not been totally random. It has been most frequent and most violent between groups belonging to different civilizations. In Eurasia the great historic fault lines between civilizations are once more aflame. This is particularly true along the boundaries of the crescent-shaped Islamic bloc of nations from the bulge of Africa to central Asia. Violence also occurs between Muslims, on the one hand, and Orthodox Serbs in the Balkans, Jews in Israel, Hindus in India, Buddhists in Burma, and Catholics in the Philippines. Islam has bloody borders. . . .

THE WEST VERSUS THE REST

The west West is now at an extraordinary peak of power in relation to other civilizations. Its superpower opponent has disappeared from the map. Military conflict among Western states is unthinkable, and Western military power is unrivaled. Apart from Japan, the West faces no economic challenge. It dominates international political and security institutions and with Japan international economic institutions. Global political and security issues are effectively settled by a directorate of the United States, Britain, and France; world economic issues, by a directorate of the United States, Germany, and Japan, all of which maintain extraordinarily close relations with each other to the exclusion of lesser and largely non-Western countries. Decisions made at the UN Security Council or in the International Monetary Fund that reflect the interests of the West are presented to the world as reflecting the desires of the world community. The very phrase "the world

---

[7] Bernard Lewis, "The Roots of Muslim Rage," *The Atlantic Monthly*, Vol. 266, September 1990, p. 60; *Time*, June 15, 1992, pp. 24–28.

community" has become the euphemistic collective noun (replacing "the Free World") to give global legitimacy to actions reflecting the interests of the United States and other Western powers.[8] Through the imf and other international economic institutions, the West promotes its economic interests and imposes on other nations the economic policies it thinks appropriate. In any poll of non-Western peoples, the imf undoubtedly would win the support of finance ministers and a few others but get an overwhelmingly unfavorable rating from just about everyone else, who would agree with Georgy Arbatov's characterization of imf officials as "neo-Bolsheviks who love expropriating other people's money, imposing undemocratic and alien rules of economic and political conduct and stifling economic freedom."

Western domination of the UN Security Council and its decisions, tempered only by occasional abstention by China, produced UN legitimation of the West's use of force to drive Iraq out of Kuwait and its elimination of Iraq's sophisticated weapons and capacity to produce such weapons. It also produced the quite unprecedented action by the United States, Britain, and France in getting the Security Council to demand that Libya hand over the Pan Am 103 bombing suspects and then to impose sanctions when Libya refused. After defeating the largest Arab army, the West did not hesitate to throw its weight around in the Arab world. The West in effect is using international institutions, military power, and economic resources to run the world in ways that will maintain Western predominance, protect Western interests, and promote Western political and economic values.

That at least is the way in which non-Westerners see the new world, and there is a significant element of truth in their view. Differences in power and struggles for military, economic, and institutional power are thus one source of conflict between the West and other civilizations. Differences in culture, that is, basic values and beliefs, are a second source of conflict. V. S. Naipaul has argued that Western civilization is the "universal civilization" that "fits all men." At a superficial level, much of Western culture has indeed permeated the rest of the world. At a more basic level, however, Western concepts differ fundamentally from those prevalent in other civilizations. Western ideas of individualism, liberalism, constitutionalism, human rights, equality, liberty, the rule of law, democracy, free markets, the separation of church and state, often have little resonance in Islamic, Confucian, Japanese, Hindu, Buddhist, or Orthodox cultures. Western efforts to propagate such ideas produce instead a reaction against "human rights imperialism" and a reaffirmation of indigenous values, as can be seen in the support for religious fundamentalism by the younger generation in non-Western cultures. The very notion that there could be a "universal civilization" is a Western idea, directly at odds with the particularism of most Asian societies and their emphasis on what distinguishes one people from another. Indeed, the author of a review of a hundred comparative studies of values in different societies concluded that "the values that are most important in the West are least important worldwide."[9] In the political realm, of course, these differences are most manifest in the efforts of the United States and other Western powers to induce other peoples to adopt Western ideas concerning democracy and human rights. Modern democratic government originated in the West. When it has developed in non-Western societies it has usually been the product of Western colonialism or imposition.

The central axis of world politics in the future is likely to be, in Kishore Mahbubani's phrase, the conflict between "the West and the Rest" and the responses of non-Western civilizations to Western power and values.[10] Those responses generally take

---

[8] Almost invariably, Western leaders claim they are acting on behalf of the "world community." One minor lapse occurred during the run-up to the Gulf War. In an interview on *Good Morning America*, December 21, 1990, British Prime Minister John Major referred to the actions "the West" was taking against Saddam Hussein. He quickly corrected himself and subsequently referred to "the world community." He was, however, right when he erred.

---

[9] Harry C. Triandis, *New York Times*, December 25, 1990, p. 41, and "Cross-Cultural Studies of Individualism and Collectivism," *Nebraska Symposium on Motivation*, Vol. 37, 1989, pp. 41–133.

[10] Kishore Mahbubani, "The West and the Rest," *National Interest*, Summer 1992, pp. 3–13.

one or a combination of three forms. At one extreme, non-Western states can, like Burma and North Korea, attempt to pursue a course of isolation, to insulate their societies from penetration or "corruption" by the West, and, in effect, to opt out of participation in the Western-dominated global community. The costs of this course, however, are high, and few states have pursued it exclusively. A second alternative, the equivalent of "bandwagoning" in international relations theory, is to attempt to join the West and accept its values and institutions. The third alternative is to attempt to "balance" the West by developing economic and military power and cooperating with other non-Western societies against the West, while preserving indigenous values and institutions; in short, to modernize but not to Westernize.

IMPLICATIONS FOR THE WEST

This article does not argue that civilization identities will replace all other identities, that nation-states will disappear, that each civilization will become a single coherent political entity, that groups within a civilization will not conflict with and even fight each other. This paper does set forth the hypotheses that differences between civilizations are real and important; civilization-consciousness is increasing; conflict between civilizations will supplant ideological and other forms of conflict as the dominant global form of conflict; international relations, historically a game played out within Western civilization, will increasingly be de-Westernized and become a game in which non-Western civilizations are actors and not simply objects; successful political, security, and economic international institutions are more likely to develop within civilizations than across civilizations; conflicts between groups in different civilizations will be more frequent, more sustained, and more violent than conflicts between groups in the same civilization; violent conflict between groups in different civilizations are the most likely and most dangerous source of escalation that could lead to global wars; the paramount axis of world politics will be the relations between "the West and the Rest"; the elites in some torn non-Western countries will try to make their countries part of the West, but in most cases face major obstacles to accomplishing this; a central focus

of conflict for the immediate future will be between the West and several Islamic-Confucian states.

This is not to advocate the desirability of conflicts between civilizations. It is to set forth descriptive hypotheses as to what the future may be like. If these are plausible hypotheses, however, it is necessary to consider their implications for Western policy. These implications should be divided between short-term advantage and long-term accommodation. In the short term it is clearly in the interest of the West to promote greater cooperation and unity within its own civilization, particularly between its European and North American components; to incorporate into the West societies in Eastern Europe and Latin America whose cultures are close to those of the West; to promote and maintain cooperative relations with Russia and Japan; to prevent escalation of local inter-civilization conflicts into major inter-civilization wars; to limit the expansion of the military strength of Confucian and Islamic states; to moderate the reduction of Western military capabilities and maintain military superiority in East and Southwest Asia; to exploit differences and conflicts among Confucian and Islamic states; to support in other civilizations groups sympathetic to Western values and interests; to strengthen international institutions that reflect and legitimate Western interests and values and to promote the involvement of non-Western states in those institutions.

In the longer term, other measures would be called for. Western civilization is both Western and modern. Non-Western civilizations have attempted to become modern without becoming Western. To date only Japan has fully succeeded in this quest. Non-Western civilizations will continue to attempt to acquire the wealth, technology, skills, machines, and weapons that are part of being modern. They will also attempt to reconcile this modernity with their traditional culture and values. Their economic and military strength relative to the West will increase. Hence the West will increasingly have to accommodate these non-Western modern civilizations whose power approaches that of the West but whose values and interests differ significantly from those of the West. This will require the West to maintain the economic and military power necessary to protect its interests in relation to these civilizations. It will also, however, require the West to develop a more profound understanding of the basic religious and philosophical assumptions underlying other civilizations and the ways in which people in those civilizations see their interests. It will require an effort to identify elements of commonality between Western and other civilizations. For the relevant future, there will be no universal civilization, but instead a world of different civilizations, each of which will have to learn to coexist with the others.

Michael T. Klare

RESOURCE COMPETITION IN THE 21ˢᵀ CENTURY

It is possible that in focusing on explanations for past wars, we give insufficient attention to the causes of future conflicts. (On the other hand, it seems likely that certain fundamental characteristics—of "human nature," social systems, and so on—are likely to survive relatively unchanged from one era to the next.) In this selection, we present an effort by a noted peace researcher to look ahead and anticipate "new global schisms" that may characterize violent conflict in the twenty-first century. Note especially the suggestion that *inter*state wars have been and will be replaced by *intra*state conflicts.

As in all previous epochs, the world of the 21ˢᵗ century faces a variety of political, economic, social, and ecological pressures that threaten stability in many parts of the globe and embody a potential for violent conflict. Many of these pressures are akin to those that have imperiled regional and international stability in the past: ethnic and religious antagonisms; the struggle for dominance between aspiring and established powers; territorial disputes; economic competition; and so forth. It is likely, however, that additional sources of friction and instability will arise in this century, emerging from the distinctive features of the current era. Among the most powerful of these will be global competition for access to and control over key sources of vital non-renewable resources: oil, water, natural gas, arable land, and various industrial minerals.

The significant role played by resource competition in sparking conflict is evident in many of the recent outbreaks of armed violence, such as those in Afghanistan, Chad, Chiapas, Colombia, Congo, Iraq, Liberia, Mali, the Philippines, Sierra Leone, Somalia, Sudan, Zimbabwe, and parts of India. Violence has also arisen in disputes over contested offshore territories, such as the East and South China Seas, the Caspian Sea, and the Persian Gulf. Like all human conflicts, these upheavals have more than one cause; all, however, are driven to a considerable extent by competition over vital or valuable resources: diamonds in the case of Liberia and Sierra Leone; oil in the case of Colombia, Iraq, and Sudan; timber and minerals in the Congo; arable land in Chiapas and Zimbabwe; and so on. Indeed, the United Nations Environment Programme (UNEP) reported in 2009 that 18 recent and ongoing civil conflicts—including many of those cited above—were fueled in large part by competition over resources like these.[11]

It is true, of course, that competition over scarce and vital materials has long been a source of conflict. Indeed, many of the earliest recorded wars—notably those occurring in ancient Mesopotamia, Egypt, and the Jordan River valley—were driven by struggles over the control of water supplies and arable land. Similarly, many of the wars of the sixteenth through the early twentieth centuries were sparked by competition among the major European powers for control over resource-rich colonies in Africa, Asia, the East Indies, and the New World—struggles that culminated in World War I. The rise of Nazism and the outbreak of the Cold War tended to overshadow (but did not eliminate) the importance of resource competition in the last century, but this factor emerged with its historic vigor at the end of the Cold War, as demonstrated by the conflicts identified above.[12]

One can argue, then, that the re-emergence of resource conflict in the current period is nothing more than a return to the status quo ante: to the long stretch of time during which resource competition was a dominant theme in world affairs. But it is the contention of this chapter that the situation we face today is not just more of the same, but is, in fact, the product of altered circumstances in which resource competition has assumed a more pivotal role in armed conflict than has been the case in the past. To appreciate this, it is necessary to consider both the importance of key resources to contemporary human endeavors and the unique pressures on the world's resource base as we move deeper into the 21st century.

Some resources are, of course, essential for human survival. All humans need a certain amount of food and water, plus access to shelter, clothing—and, in northern climates, heat. At a very primitive level of existence, human societies can function on relatively modest quantities of these materials, so long as their numbers remain few. As societies grow larger and more complex, however, they require more resources for their own purposes and to produce trade goods to exchange for the things they lack, including luxury items sought by their elites. Modern means of warfare also consume vast quantities of resources, especially petroleum to fuel the tanks, planes, helicopters and ships that have come to dominate the contemporary battlefield. The more developed, urbanized, and prosperous a society, the greater is its requirement for resources of all types.[13]

The dilemma that confronts us as we proceed deeper into the 21st century is the fact that human consumption of almost all types of commodities is growing at an ever-increasing rate, imposing growing and possibly intolerable pressures on the world's existing stockpile of natural resources. Until now, humans have been able to mitigate these pressures by developing new sources of supply—for example, by digging deeper into the earth for metals and oil—and by inventing alternative materials. No doubt human ingenuity and the power of the market will continue to generate solutions of this sort. At some point, however, the demand for certain vital resources will simply overwhelm the available supply, producing widespread shortages and driving up the price of what remains; in some cases, moreover, it may prove impossible to develop viable substitutes. (For example, there is no known substitute for fresh water.) As resource stocks dwindle and prices rise, the divide between those with access to adequate supplies and those without will widen, straining the social fabric and in some cases leading to violent conflict.[14]

It is apparent, then, that resource competition will play an increasingly significant role in world affairs as time proceeds. Just *how* substantial its impact will be will depend, to a considerable extent, on the evolution of human consumption patterns. The greater the pressure we bring to bear

[11] United Nations Environment Programme (UNEP), *From Conflict to Peacebuilding: The Role of Natural Resources and the Environment* (Nairobi, Kenya: UNEP, 2009), Table 1, p. 11.
[12] For background and discussion, see: Steven A. LeBlanc, *Constant Battles* (New York: St. Martin's Press, 2003); and Clive Ponting, *A New Green History of the World* (New York: Penguin Books, 2007).

[13] The author first advanced this argument in Michael T. Klare, *Resource Wars* (New York: Metropolitan Books, 2001).
[14] For an elaboration of this argument, see Michael T. Klare, *The Race for What's Left* (New York: Metropolitan Books, 2012).

on the world's existing resource base, the higher the risk of major social and environmental trauma. It is essential, then, to consider the implication of five key trends in contemporary human behavior: globalization, population growth, resource depletion, and climate change.

GLOBALIZATION

The growing internationalization of finance, manufacturing, and trade—the phenomenon we know of as globalization—is having a powerful effect on many aspects of human life, including the demand for and consumption of basic resources. Globalization increases the demand for resources in several ways. Most significant is the spread of industrialization to more and more areas of the world, producing a dramatic increase in the demand for energy, minerals, and other basic commodities.

The spurt in demand for energy is especially evident in the newly-industrialized countries of Asia, which are expected to continue growing at a rapid pace in the decades ahead. According to the U.S. Department of Energy, energy consumption in developing Asia (including China, India, South Korea, and Taiwan) will grow by an estimated 2.9 percent per year over the next quarter-century, jumping from 138 quadrillion British thermal units (BTUs) in 2008 to an estimated 299 quadrillion BTUs in 2035.[15] The growth in demand for petroleum will be especially pronounced, with total consumption in developing Asia climbing from 17 million barrels per day in 2008 to a projected 34 million barrels in 2035. A similar pattern is evident with respect to consumption of natural gas and coal—both of which are projected to experience a substantial increase in demand in the coming decades.[16] The rising consumption of energy, along with other materials needed to sustain economic growth in the newly-industrialized countries, will significantly increase the pressures already being placed on the global resource base.

Globalization is further adding to the pressure on resources by contributing to the emergence of a new middle class in many parts of the world. As families acquire additional income, they tend to acquire more goods and appliances, eat higher-end foods (such as beef, pork, and chicken), and to move into larger living quarters—all of which generates a steep increase in the consumption of basic materials. Most significant in this regard is the growing international demand for private vehicles, a process known as the "motorization" of society. According to one recent estimate from the Energy Forum of the Baker Institute of Rice University, automobile ownership in China will jump from 63 million in 2009 to 210 million in 2020 and an astonishing 770 million by 2040.[17] Just to produce all of these vehicles will entail the consumption of vast amounts of iron, aluminum, and other minerals; once in operation, they will consume millions of gallons of oil per day, year after year.

Finally, globalization affects the global resource equation by extending the worldwide reach of multinational companies (MNCs), generating significant economic benefits for many poor and isolated countries but also providing incentives for cash-starved governments to permit the extraction of raw materials beyond sustainable levels or to cut down forests in order to make way for export-oriented ranching and agriculture. This has resulted, for instance, in the continuing deforestation of the Amazon region and the large-scale deforestation of such countries as Indonesia, Malaysia, and the Philippines.[18]

POPULATION GROWTH

Rising population is further adding to the pressures on the world's resource base. According to the latest United Nations projections, total world population will rise from 6.9 billion people in 2010 to an estimated 9.3 billion in 2050, for an increase of

---

[15] U.S. Department of Energy, Energy Information Administration (DoE/EIA), *International Energy Outlook 2011* (Washington, D.C.: DoE/EIA, 2011), Table A1, p. 157.
[16] Ibid., Tables A5–A7, pp. 162–64.

[17] Energy Forum of the James A. Baker III Institute for Public Policy, Rice University, *The Rise of China and Its Energy Implications: Executive Summary* (Houston: Baker Institute, 2011), pp. 13–15.
[18] For discussion, see Klare, *The Race for What's Left*. On the dynamics of deforestation, see Michael Williams, *Deforesting the Earth*, abridged ed. (Chicago: University of Chicago Press, 2006). For data on worldwide deforestation, see Food and Agriculture Organization (FAO), *State of the World's Forests* (Rome: FAO, 2011), and earlier editions.

2.4 billion.[19] These additional people will need to be fed, housed, clothed, and otherwise provided with basic necessities—producing a corresponding requirement for food, water, wood, metals, fibers, and other materials. Although the earth can supply these materials—at least in the amounts needed for a relatively modest standard of living—it cannot continue to sustain an ever growing human population *and* satisfy the rising expectations of the world's middle and upper classes. At some point, significant shortages will occur, intensifying the competition for access to remaining supplies and producing severe hardship for those without the means to pay the higher prices thereby incurred.

Of all basic necessities, the one that is most likely to be affected by population growth is fresh water. Humans must have access to a certain amount of water every day, for drinking, personal hygiene, and food production. Fortunately, the world possesses sufficient renewable supplies of fresh water to satisfy current requirements and to sustain some increase in the human population. As population grows, however, the pressure on many key sources of supply will increase, suggesting that severe shortages will develop in some water-scarce areas over the next few decades.[20]

This is especially true in the Middle East and North Africa, where fresh water is already in short supply and population growth rates are among the highest in the world. For example, the number of people who will be relying on the Nile River, the Jordan River, and the Tigris-Euphrates system for all or most of their water supply will grow from approximately 325 million in 2000 to 740 million in 2050—without any appreciable increase in the net supply of water in the region. Unless the existing sources of supply are used more efficiently or the desalination of seawater proves more affordable, competition over access to water will become more intense in these areas and could lead to war.[21]

RESOURCE DEPLETION

The three factors described above—globalization, population growth, and urbanization—are combining to create a fourth: the irreversible depletion of many non-renewable resources. While the earth contains large amounts of many key materials, these supplies are not unlimited and can be exhausted through excessive extraction or utilization. And, in the case of some vital resources, humans have reached this point or are likely to do so in the early decades of the 21st century. For example, humans have harvested some species of fish (such as the once-prolific cod) so intensively that they have virtually disappeared from the world's oceans and are not expected to recover. Similarly, some valuable types of hardwood have largely disappeared from the world's forests.[22]

Of the resources that are facing depletion in the decades ahead, none is more important to human life and society than petroleum. Oil provides about one-third of the world's basic energy supply—more than any other source—and provides about 97 percent of the energy used for transportation. It is the chemical feedstock for a vast array of valuable products, including plastics, fertilizers, pesticides, asphalt, and many pharmaceuticals. Oil is also essential for the conduct of modern warfare, providing fuel for tanks, planes, missiles, and most warships.

Like many other materials we rely on, petroleum is a non-renewable resource: once we consume the existing world supply (produced by geological processes over many millennia), there will be none left for future generations. We humans have already consumed about half of the earth's conventional petroleum—approximately 1.2 trillion barrels out of the 2.4 trillion barrels that are thought to have existed in 1859, when commercial extraction began—and are exploiting what remains at such a rapid pace that much of the remaining supply could disappear

---

[19] United Nations, Department of Economic and Social Affairs, Population Division, "World Population Prospects: The 2010 Revision," online edition, retrieved at http://www.un.org/esa/population on August 4, 2012.

[20] For background and discussion, see Marq de Villiers, *Water* (New York: Houghton Mifflin, 2000).

[21] For background, see Klare, *Resource Wars*, pp. 138–89.

[22] For background, see Klare, *The Race for What's Left*, pp. 19–40. For an inventory of the world's depleted resources, see World Wildlife Fund (WWF), *Living Planet Report 1998* (Gland, Switzerland: WWF, 1998). Substantial information on the depletion of particular resources is available in the annual publications of the Worldwatch Institute of Washington, D.C., notably *The State of the World*, and *Vital Signs*.

in the next 30–40 years.[23] Additional supplies of so-called "unconventional" oil—Canadian tar sands, Venezuelan extra-heavy crude, Rocky Mountain oil shale, Arctic oil, and so on—can replace some of the depleted conventional supply, but extracting these fuels requires vast amounts of water and energy while emitting huge amounts of GHGs, so it is not clear that societies will permit their full-scale exploitation.[24]

GLOBAL CLIMATE CHANGE

All of these problems are bound to be exacerbated by the effects of global climate change. Although climate scientists cannot be certain about the future effects of climate change on any particular locale, they are increasingly convinced that large parts of the planet will suffer from persistent drought, diminished rainfall, and the invasion of coastal areas by a rise in the sea level. This will, in turn, jeopardize water supplies and food production in many tropical and temperate areas of the world, forcing millions of people—perhaps tens or even hundreds of millions—to abandon their ancestral lands and migrate to other, less-severely affected areas. The result could well be an increase in conflict over access to food, fresh water, and arable land.[25]

Climate change will affect many aspects of the global resource equation, but its greatest impact—at least initially—will be on the supply of food and water. "Climate change will alter rainfall patterns and further reduce available freshwater by as much as 20 to 30% in certain regions," a paper prepared by the European Union secretariat noted in 2008. This, in turn, will result in diminished food production

in these areas, accompanied by rising food prices—a likely trigger for social unrest and conflict. "Water shortage in particular has the potential to cause civil unrest and to lead to significant economic losses, even in robust economies," the EU study noted. The consequences will be even more intense in areas under strong demographic pressure. The overall effect is that climate change will fuel existing conflicts over depleting resources. . . . "[26]

Along with global food supplies, climate change will affect the planet's energy supply. An increase in severe storm activity, for example, will endanger oil and natural gas production in such key producing areas as the Gulf of Mexico, the North Sea, and the western Pacific. Because such a large share of America's energy production and refining capacity is concentrated in the Gulf of Mexico, intense hurricanes will have a devastating effect on the nation's oil output. Hence Hurricane Katrina, which swept through the Gulf in August 2005, destroyed 45 drilling platforms and crippled about one-fourth of America's production capacity; Hurricane Rita, coming one month later, destroyed another 66 platforms.[27] The reduced levels of rainfall expected from global warming in many parts of the world will also reduce the flow of water into many rivers that have been dammed for the purpose of generating electricity; with less rainfall, these hydro-electricity plants could sit idle for long stretches of time.

THE PROSPECTS FOR CONFLICT

Together, these factors are producing increasing pressures on the world's resource base—pressures that can only increase as we proceed deeper into the 21st century. The resulting shortages are likely to produce or magnify antagonisms between and within societies as governments and factions compete for access to or control over major sources of vital materials. In the extreme case, such antagonisms can lead to the outbreak of armed violence.

---

[23] For background, see Klare, *The Race for What's Left*, pp. 29–32. This assessment is largely based on data and analysis in International Energy Agency (IEA), *World Energy Outlook 2008* (Paris: IEA, 2008), pp. 221–48.

[24] For background and discussion, see Michael Klare, *The Race for What's Left* (New York: Metropolitan Books, 2012), pp. 41–127.

[25] The most comprehensive study of the impact of climate change on human societies is Martin Parry, et al., *Climate Change 2007: Impacts, Adaptation and Vulnerability*, Contribution of Working Group II to the Fourth Assessment Report of the Intergovernmental Panel on Climate Change (Cambridge: Cambridge University Press, 2007).

[26] European Commission (EC) and High Commissioner, *Climate Change and International Security: Paper to the European Council* (Brussels: EC, 2008), p. 3.

[27] National Commission on the BP *Deepwater Horizon* Oil Spill and Offshore Drilling, *Deep Water* (Washington: National Commission, 2011), p. 50.

In general, violent struggle over resources can take one of four forms: territorial disputes, access conflicts, allocation disputes, and revenue disputes. Most of the armed conflicts of the post–Cold War era embody aspects of one or another of these types.

Territorial Disputes

Conflicts arising from disputed claims to contested lands have been a source of friction and warfare throughout human history, and still occasionally provoke armed violence—the 1998–2000 war between Eritrea and Ethiopia is a conspicuous example—but have become less frequent in recent years as nations have slowly but surely resolved outstanding boundary disputes. However, conflicts over *offshore* territories appear to be growing more frequent as governments fight over contested maritime areas with valuable fisheries and undersea resources, such as oil and natural gas deposits. Typically, the parties to these disputes cite differing interpretations of the United Nations Convention on the Law of the Sea (UNCLOS) to justify their claims to substantial (but often overlapping) offshore territories. As resource deposits on land become progressively depleted, disputes over offshore resources are likely to become more pronounced.[28]

Two such areas exhibiting a particularly high risk of conflict are the East China Sea and the South China Sea. Both of these areas are claimed in total or in part by the surrounding countries—China, Japan, and Taiwan in the case of the former; Brunei, China, Malaysia, the Philippines, Taiwan, and Vietnam in the latter—and both are thought to harbor substantial undersea reserves of oil and gas. Efforts to resolve these territorial disputes through peaceful negotiations have, until now, met with failure, and most of the claimants have employed military force to demonstrate their resolve to protect their interests—on some occasions, producing armed violence. The growing tensions in these areas have triggered a naval buildup among the countries involved,

provoking international concern over the risk of future clashes at sea.[29]

Tensions of this sort have also arisen in the waters surrounding the Falkland Islands (called the Malvinas by the Argentineans) and in the Arctic region. As in the East and South China Seas, both of these areas are thought to possess large reserves of oil and natural gas, and both have been the subject of competing claims to vast offshore territories. Argentina and the United Kingdom fought a war over the Falklands/Malvinas in 1982, but have remained peaceful since then; now, however, efforts by UK-based oil firms to drill for oil in waters off the islands has led to renewed tensions, resulting in the deployment of additional British military units and various punitive measures by the Argentineans. Similar disputes have arisen in the Arctic, where the boundaries between the surrounding countries have yet to be determined and ownership of vast areas remains in dispute. Here, too, tensions have been raised by the deployment of additional military units and talk of military action to protect vital interests.[30]

Access Conflicts

Conflicts arising from efforts by a resource-importing nation to safeguard its ability to procure needed resources from a distant source and to transport them safely to its own territory. Many of the colonial wars of past centuries were sparked by such efforts, as was Germany's 1941 invasion of the Soviet Union (intended in part to seize control of the oil fields of the Caucasus region) and Japan's subsequent invasion of the Dutch East Indies (also sparked by the pursuit of oil). Great Britain's determined efforts to retain a presence in Iraq after World War II and to retain control of its refinery at Abadan in Iran after its nationalization by Prime Minister Mohammed Mossadegh in 1951 also fit this pattern.[31]

---

28 For background on this point, see Klare, *The Race for What's Left*, pp. 41–69.

29 See ibid., pp. 224–27. On the risk of conflict in the South China Sea, see International Crisis Group (ICG), *Stirring Up the South China Sea (I)*, Asia Report no. 223 (Brussels: ICG, 2012).

30 For background on these disputes, see Klare, *The Race for What's Left*, pp. 63–65, 70–99.

31 For background on these events, see Daniel Yergin, *The Prize* (New York: Simon and Schuster, 1991), pp. 305–42, 450–78.

For the United States, ensuring access to the oil supplies of the Persian Gulf has long been a major military objective. This was made an explicit strategic objective in the so-called "Carter Doctrine" of January 23, 1980. Asserting that "[a]n attempt by any outside force to gain control of the Persian Gulf region"—and thereby impede the flow of oil—"will be regarded as an assault on the vital interests of the United States of America," President Jimmy Carter warned that this country would repel such an assault "by any means necessary, including military force."[32] This basic principle was then cited by President George H. W. Bush as the justification for going to war against Iraq when it invaded Kuwait in 1990 (and, it was said, posed a threat to Saudi Arabia) as well as for the subsequent economic blockade of Iraq by Presidents George H. W. Bush and Bill Clinton; it can also be viewed as the impetus for the 2003 U.S. invasion of Iraq.[33]

Access conflicts of this sort are also likely to arise in the future as the competition for vital resources intensifies and the major consuming nations become increasingly reliant on supplies acquired from distant and unstable regions. To better ensure its access to the oil supplies of Africa, for example, the United States has beefed up its naval presence in the Gulf of Guinea, the source of substantial U.S. oil imports.[34] The Chinese are also expanding their naval capabilities so as to better ensure their access to overseas resource supplies. "With the expansion of the country's economic interests, the navy wants to better protect the country's transportation routes and the safety of our major sea lanes," declared Rear Admiral Zhang Huachen, deputy commander of the East Sea Fleet, in 2010. "In order to achieve this, the Chinese Navy needs to develop along the lines of bigger vessels and with more comprehensive capabilities."[35] While it is impossible to predict the outcome of these efforts, it is not hard to imagine a situation in which U.S. and Chinese naval forces clash with one another as a result of efforts to gain or protect access to an embattled supplier in Africa or the Middle East—a scenario envisioned by the National Intelligence Council in its 2008 study of the future strategic environment, *Global Trends 2025*.[36]

Allocation Disputes

Conflicts that arise when neighboring states jointly occupy or rely on a shared resource source—a river system, an underground aquifer, an oil field, or so on. In such cases, conflict can erupt from disagreements over the distribution of materials taken from the shared resource. For example, Iraq, Syria, and Turkey have been squabbling over the allocation of water from the Tigris-Euphrates river system, which originates in Turkey but travels for much of its length through Iraq and Syria. The Jordan and Nile Rivers have also provoked allocation disputes of this sort, both in ancient times and in the present. The extraction of petroleum from a shared underground reservoir can also be a source of conflict, as demonstrated by Iraq's dispute with Kuwait over the prolific Rumaila field.[37]

Allocation disputes of this sort—especially those over shared sources of water—are likely to grow more heated in the years ahead as a result of population growth and climate change. The countries that depend on the three river systems noted above—the Nile, the Jordan, and the Tigris-Euphrates—are experiencing very rapid population growth, and in some cases (Ethiopia, Sudan) are expected to see a two- or three-fold increase in population between now and 2050. At the same time, these rivers lie in areas of the world that are expected to see a significant decline in rainfall as a result of climate change, meaning that less water will be available for use by these growing populations. Given the history of animosity between the countries involved (including Israel and its neighbors), the possibility of friction

---

[32] Jimmy Carter, State of the Union Address, Washington, D.C., February 23, 1980, retrieved at www .jimmycarterlibrary.org on March 31, 2007. For background on these events, see Michael A. Palmer, *Guardians of the Gulf* (New York: Free Press, 1992), pp. 101–11.

[33] For discussion, see Michael T. Klare, *Blood and Oil* (New York: Metropolitan Books, 2004), pp. 96–101.

[34] For background, see ibid., pp. 142–45.

[35] Edward Wong, "Chinese Military Seeks to Extend Its Naval Power," *New York Times*, April 23, 2010.

[36] U.S. National Intelligence Council (NIC), *Global Trends 2025* (Washington, D.C.: NIC, 2008), pp. 77–79.

[37] For background on these disputes, see Klare, *Resource Wars*, pp. 52, 138–89.

and conflict over the distribution of these rivers' diminishing supply is bound to grow.[38]

Revenue Disputes

Conflicts arising in divided or failing states when the national government has lost control of part or most of its territory and competing factions—warlords, ethnic militias, separatist groups, and other such formations—fight for control over oilfields, copper mines, diamond fields, or other resource sites that represent a significant source of revenue. Conflicts of this sort may first arise as a means to an end—to secure the funds needed to pay for arms and ammunition—but often become an end in themselves, as a way or enriching the commanders of these factions. This is evident, for example, in the protracted wars in Angola and Sierra Leone, where rebel commanders reportedly accumulated substantial fortunes from the sales of diamonds.[39] Such conflicts often prove difficult to resolve, as the leaders involved see no incentive to end the fighting—and the accompanying accumulation of private resource wealth.[40]

Conflicts over the possession of valuable materials can also figure in attempts by minority groups in a multinational society to separate from the larger nation and create their own state based on the exploitation of a particular resource located in the sub-region where they form a majority—and the corresponding efforts of the central government to prevent such a move. This is evident, for example, in the Biafran War of 1967–70, in which the people of southeastern Nigeria sought to establish a separate state financed by oil revenues, and in a similar separatist drive by the inhabitants of Angola's oil-rich Cabinda province. In these, and other such cases, the central government invariably seeks to crush such

attempts as it is typically very dependent on the revenues from oil (or other resource) exports.[41]

Violence is not, of course, the only possible response to resource competition: as will be argued below, there are other plausible responses to scarcity. But the risk of violence is always latent when countries perceive the possession of certain materials as a matter of *national security*—that is, as something so vital to the survival and well-being of the state that it is prepared to employ military force when deemed necessary to ensure access to that resource. For some countries—notably those in very arid areas—water has long been portrayed as a national security matter. For example, Israel has declared that access to the waters of the Jordan River is vital to its survival, just as Egypt has long viewed the Nile River in this fashion. For other nations, especially the United States and China, oil has been viewed as a matter of national security—as exemplified, for example, in the "Carter Doctrine" of 1980. So long as resources are viewed through the lens of national security, governments periodically will respond with military force when possession of or access to critical sources of supply is deemed to be at risk. Only by posing an alternative perspective—one that posits the advantages of cooperative, non-violent outcomes to such disputes—will it be possible to avert recurring conflict over scarce and valuable resources. Devising such outcomes and promoting their benefits, therefore, is an essential precondition for lasting peace and stability in the 21st century.

AVERTING CONFLICT OVER SCARCE RESOURCES

Assuming that the necessary political will can be generated, friction arising from resource scarcity can be channeled into constructive, non-violent outcomes through four general forms of action: mediation, adjudication, and consultation; joint development

---

[38] See UNEP, *From Conflict to Peacebuilding*, Case Study 8, p. 18. See also Ref: Dyer: Climate Wars.

[39] For background on this problem, see UNEP, *From Conflict to Peacebuilding*, pp. 10–14. See also William Reno, *Warlord Politics and African States* (Boulder: Lynne Rienner, 1998).

[40] For discussion of this phenomenon, see David Keen, *The Economic Functions of Violence in Civil Wars*, Adelphi Papers no. 320, International Institute of Strategic Studies (IISS) (Oxford: Oxford University Press and IISS, 1998).

[41] For discussion of this phenomenon, see Terry Lynn Karl, *The Paradox of Plenty* (Berkeley: University of California Press, 1997).

of contested resources; technological innovation; and conservation and efficiency.

Mediation, Adjudication, and Consultation

Given the risky and costly nature of modern warfare, states and other parties often conclude that it is preferable to resolve resource disputes through mediation, adjudication, and cooperation. Boundary disputes are particularly well-suited to international mediation and adjudication, as it is often possible to identify the historical and geographic factors that lend weight to one outcome or another. In recent years, the International Court of Justice (ICJ) in The Hague has adjudicated boundary disputes between Bahrain and Qatar over Hawar Island and between Cameroon and Nigeria over the Bakassi Peninsula—both of which are thought to harbor valuable resource deposits—with minimum rancor on the part of the disputants. Mediation by trusted international actors can also help in the resolution of resources disputes. The World Bank, for example, played a key role in negotiating the Indus Waters Treaty of 1960, governing the allocation of shared river and canal systems in the Indus River basin between India and Pakistan—a treaty that has largely been honored by both sides despite their squabbling over Kashmir and other issues.[42]

The creation of consultative bodies to oversee the exploitation of shared resources is another approach that can help to forestall the outbreak of conflict. This can be particularly effective in the case of shared river systems, where the acts of upstream countries—such as the construction of dams or irrigation works—can jeopardize the water supplies of downstream countries. To minimize these effects, countries in a common river basin can participate in a consultative body aimed at promoting dialogue on proposed projects and, in an ideal situation, giving all members of the system some say over their nature and scope. Two endeavors of this sort are the Nile Basin Initiative and the Mekong River Commission; while neither enterprise gives member countries full veto power over the actions of their neighbors, they do allow for dialogue on proposed projects and conduct "confidence-building" activities aimed at gathering information and building trust,

thereby setting the stage for more inclusive decision-making in the future.[43]

Joint Development of Shared Resources

In cases where the rival claimants to a resource that spans their territories cannot reach agreement on its division or ownership, it is possible to conceive of schemes for joint development of the resource pending a final outcome—thus providing an incentive to settle the matter peacefully. In such cases, the parties involved can establish a joint development authority based on some mutually-acceptable formula to manage the exploitation of the resource and distribute any profits. In addition to producing good will, this creates the breathing room in which diplomats from the various sides can negotiate a final outcome to the dispute.

One such initiative is the Malaysia-Thailand Joint Development Area (JDA) established by the two countries in 1979 to manage the exploitation of oil and natural gas reserves in a contested area of the Gulf of Thailand claimed by both of them. The 1979 agreement allowed for mutual development of the JDA without prejudice regarding each side's claims to the disputed territory, and established the Malaysia-Thailand Joint Authority to oversee extraction of hydrocarbons from the JDA.[44] This approach was also used as a model by Nigeria and the island nation of São Tomé and Principe in addressing their offshore boundary dispute in the Gulf of Guinea. Joint efforts of this sort could help reduce the risk of friction in other contested offshore areas where two or more countries are fighting for control over undersea resources, such as the East and South China Seas.

Technological Innovation

Technology can go a long way toward reducing the threat of conflict over scarce resources by providing

---

[42] For background, see Klare, *Resource Wars*, pp. 182–89.

[43] Information on the activities of the Nile Basin Initiative can be viewed at www.nilebasin.org. Activities of the Mekong River Commission can be viewed at www .mrcmekong.org.

[44] See Nguyen Hong Thao, "Joint Development in the Gulf of Thailand," *IBRU Boundary and Security Bulletin*, International Boundaries Research Unit, University of Durham, Autumn 1999, pp. 79–88.

alternative materials and less resource-depleting industrial processes. So long as our economies depend so heavily on non-renewable resources such as oil, natural gas, uranium, and copper, the risk of conflict is bound to rise as the demand for these products grows and supplies contract. By switching to reliance on renewable materials, or substances that are relatively plentiful like silicon, economies can reduce their vulnerability to resource-related friction and conflict.

The greatest imperative here is to reduce the world's reliance on petroleum. At present, oil provides the single largest share of global energy and is expected to do so for the foreseeable future. But because oil is an especially vital resource and is not likely to be available in sufficient quantities to satisfy rising world demand in the years ahead, it is among the resources most likely to provoke conflict. It follows from this that finding substitutes for oil (or for oil-powered contrivances) could help reduce the risk of war. This could mean, for example, developing alternative fuels that are renewable or highly abundant, such as biofuels made from algae, or embracing new modes of personal transportation using electric batteries or hydrogen-powered fuel cells.[45]

Water is another resource that is not likely to be available in sufficient quantities to meet anticipated demand in many parts of the world in the years ahead, with an attendant risk of friction and conflict. Here, too, technology can play a helpful role. Improvements in desalination technology, for example, could make it possible to convert sea water into fresh water at an affordable cost—existing methods of desalination consume large amounts of energy and so are very costly, putting them out of reach for many poor countries. Improved methods of crop irrigation, such as drip irrigation, would minimize waste and reduce water demand in areas where irrigation is essential for food production.

Aside from the contributions of the technology itself, the prospects for peace would be further enhanced if nations cooperate in the development of new materials and devices that would benefit all simultaneously. The cooperative development of alternative energy supplies, for example, could help temper the intense competition among the major oil-importing countries for control over contested oil fields. This was, in fact, one of the hoped-for outcomes of the energy cooperation agreements signed by Presidents Barack Obama of the United States and Hu Jintao of China in Beijing on November 17, 2009. These included a U.S.-China Renewable Energy Partnership and a U.S.-.–China Electric Vehicles Initiative—agreements that were incorporated into a U.S.-China Joint Statement in which the two sides pledged to work together to "promote world peace, security, and prosperity."[46]

Conservation and Efficiency

Adjudication, joint development, and technology can help address some resource problems, but ultimately the best way to avert significant shortages of scarce or limited supplies is to consume less of what we now possess of these materials. Indeed, efficiency and conservation is often the most practical and least costly method of expanding the long-term supply of a resource, thereby reducing the risk of dangerous competition. The more efficient our cars, appliances, manufacturing systems, and so on, the less energy and other raw materials we will need to consume, and so the less pressure will be imposed on the world's contracting and contested resource stocks.

The pressure on global energy stocks, for example, would be greatly reduced if trucks and automobiles required far less fuel to travel the same distance as they do today. Some progress in this direction was achieved in 2009, when the Obama administration and Congress agreed to increase the required average fuel efficiency of American automobiles and light trucks, from 27.5 miles per gallon then to 35.5 mpg in 2016[47]—a move that will result in substantially reduced U.S. petroleum consumption. Many scientists agree, however, that is possible to improve automotive fuel efficiency by a far greater amount, with the right combination of mandates and incentives. By

---

[45] For an assessment of the alternatives to oil, see Scott L. Montgomery, *The Powers that Be* (Chicago: University of Chicago Press, 2010).

[46] The White House, Office of the Press Secretary, "U.S.-China Joint Statement," Beijing, November 17, 2009, retrieved at http://www.whitehouse.gov/the-press-office/us-china-joint-statement on August 25, 2012.

[47] See Juliet Eilperin, "Emissions Limits, Greater Fuel Efficiency for Cars, Light Trucks Made Official," *Washington Post*, April 2, 2010.

increasing the efficiency of electrical devices, moreover, it is possible to reduce electricity demand, thereby reducing the need for coal, natural gas, uranium, and other primary fuels. Likewise, improved kitchen and bathroom fixtures, and limits on water use, can significantly diminish the consumption of water.

These, and other such techniques can be employed to slow the consumption of vital resources and to channel conflict into productive, non-violent outcomes. Many scientists, economists, environmentalists, and government leaders perceive the urgent need for such efforts, and have advocated them in every possible setting. As a result, progress *is* being made in some critical areas.[48] But strong resistance to such efforts has been mounted by some companies

that benefit from existing modes of consumption and from politicians who view vital resources from a traditional national security perspective, with its zero-sum, all-for-us-and-nothing-for-them outlook. For example, the major U.S. oil companies have fought against any effort to limit their ability to drill in offshore areas or the Arctic. By the same token, many consumers, especially in the wealthier countries, are reluctant to reduce their consumption of water, petroleum, rare timber (like teak and mahogany), and other scarce or limited materials.

It is evident, therefore, that efforts to reduce the depletion of vital resources and to avert conflict over critical sources of supply will require a substantial change in attitude toward the utilization of these precious materials. Only by recognizing a shared human obligation to serve as stewards of the earth's precious bounty and to work in concert to preserve vital materials for future generations will we be able to take the necessary steps to avert resource shortages and the very real risk of rising bloodshed over diminishing sources of supply.

---

[48] For discussion, see UNEP, *From Conflict to Peacebuilding*, pp. 19–27, 34–37.

Peter W. Singer

BATTLEFIELDS OF THE FUTURE

In addition to well-founded concerns about the causes of wars, we must keep track of the physical locations in which organized armed conflicts occur and where they are liable to take place in the future. Increasingly, these areas involve not only traditional regions on the global map but also the deep oceans, outer space, and cyberspace. Moreover, modern weaponry has also been changing rapidly, with implications not only for who is likely to "win" and "lose," but also for the economic, social, and political structure of the participants, including the fundamental question of who decides when a country goes to war. In the next two linked selections, Peter W. Singer, director of the 21st Century Defense Initiative at the Brookings Institute, explores some of the issues raised by these new considerations, specifically as these factors apply to the United States.

When most leaders think about the locales of war, their eyes are drawn to the burning places on the map. They try to find which state is about to collapse (Pakistan, Yemen?) or become the next crisis (Iran, Korea?) Those who see themselves as latter day Bismarcks wrestle with broader grand strategy and tend to view the globe as more like connecting tectonic plates, with rising powers like China or India changing the geopolitical landscape. These strategists typically look for where the regional spheres of influence overlap, trying to find the seams from where the earthquakes of war might emanate. But those who step back from the map will notice something even more: there are even greater shifts occurring that will shape the where of war in new ways in the coming century.

From the very first pre-historic battles over new hunting grounds to the European wars over gold in the "New World" (and one might even argue the more recent conflicts over Middle East oil fields), whenever we humans have discovered a new locale of value, we usually then fight over it. As we filled out the blank spaces on the map, though, it was new technologies that then shaped new spaces in which we contended. For 5000 years of war, for example, humans only fought on the land and then on top of the sea. Then, at the turn of the last century, technologies that had only recently existed in Jules Verne novels allowed the combatants of World War I to fight under the water and in the air above. These entirely new domains of submarine and air warfare required new forces to fight there and then new laws of war to regulate them.

Today, a series of 21st century parallels are emerging. For example, the Arctic has long been a foreboding place that no one much cared about in policy circles. But through changes that our technologies have created upon the global climate, the waters are warming up. As a result, this once whited-out part of the world map is yielding new and valuable navigable trade routes, as well as potential drilling spots for energy and mineral resources (with some believing there may be as much oil and natural gas at stake as Saudi Arabia has).

But opening up a new part of the globe yields new security questions; indeed, there hasn't been a geographically as large an area to resolve sovereignty issues since 1493, when Pope Alexander VI tried to divide the New World between Spain and Portugal (which spurred wars by the powers left out of the deal). Today, while conflict is by no means inevitable, various players are preparing for a polar scramble. One advisor to Russia's Vladimir Putin declared, "The Arctic is ours." The Canadians, Norway, the United States, and even non-Arctic contiguous states like China don't seem to agree and have started to build up their capabilities to stake out their claims.

Outer space is a similar once inaccessible domain, now of rapidly growing commercial and military value. The realm of Fritz Lang and George Lucas movies is now populated by 947 operational satellites, sent up by over 60 nations, through which runs the lifeblood of global commerce and communication, as well as military operations (over 80% of U.S. communications travels over satellites). In an ironic echo of Clausewitz, US Air Force General Lance Lord described that "Space is the center of gravity now" and the Pentagon has carried out over 20 studies of space warfare.

Of course, as Dr. Yao Yunzhu of the Chinese Army's Academy of Military Science has warned, if the United States believes that it is going to be "a space superpower, its not going to be alone. . . . " The Chinese passed the United States in launch numbers last year and plan to add more than 100 civilian and military satellites in the next decade. More important, both nations have demonstrated kinetic anti-satellite capabilities repeatedly over the past several years, with Russia, India, Iran, and even non-state actors like the Tamil Tigers also at work in counter-space operations and satellite jamming.

Unlike underwater, in the air, the polar cold, or outer space, Cyberspace isn't merely a domain that used to be inaccessible, it literally didn't exist just a generation ago. Yet its current centrality to our entire global pattern of life is almost impossible to fathom, as the numbers involved are so high as to sound imaginary. The global Internet is made up of almost a quarter billion websites, while almost 90 *trillion* emails were sent last year. The military use is equally astounding. The Pentagon alone operates 15,000 computer networks across 4,000 installations in 88 countries.

But with so much of real value being located in this new virtual domain, it is also becoming a locale for crime, political and economic contestation, and even conflict. Symantec identified more than 240 million distinct new malicious programs sent out last year and more than 100 organizations have been reported as engaging in sophisticated military, intelligence, or terrorist cyber operations. Indeed, the FBI described cybersecurity as the 3rd most important global security threat, notable considering that its Director didn't even have a computer in his office ten years ago. In reaction, the US Cyber Command, for example, went from imaginary concept just a few years ago to an organization of 90,000 personnel that coordinates more than $3 billion in spending.

While the majority of the cyber discussion has been on mostly overblown scenarios of "electronic Pearl Harbors," Russian-Georgian-Estonian "cyberwars," and the wiki-leaking of embarrassing policy memos, the vast majority of these attacks remain nuisances for now, the equivalent of cyber-graffiti or cyber-leaks, not war. The real danger may actually lie in the less sexy, but gradual, long-term undermining of innovation and intellectual property, so key to economic and national security strategy in the West. It is estimated that US and European firms suffer approximately $1 trillion a year in lost business, wasted R&D investment, and added spending due to cyberattacks that appear to be directed by political, military, or intelligence entities. The multinational Joint Strike Fighter program, for instance, had several terabytes of data (a terabyte is 1,000,000,000,000 bytes, roughly the equivalent of the entire Internet's size just a decade ago) stolen by hackers emanating from a certain large East Asian land power. These trillions of stolen bytes represent not just billions of research dollars, but also 10–20 years of technologic edge lost in both the global marketplace and potential future battlefields.

The lesson we should take away from these trends is that as important as the concern over the next year in Afghanistan or the looming rise of China is, policymakers in security must also be mindful that there are even broader changes afoot. The 21st century is seeing immense value being created in locales that either were inaccessible or literally didn't exist before. But this also means that we are (yet again in history) gearing up to fight in new places off the map we've never previously fought. For those who care about peace, the same lessons hold. One can either ignore these new domains, the nonstrategy of merely hoping for the best, or stave off future conflict and crisis by establishing the norms and institutions needed to stabilize and regulate the new spaces shaping our world.

DO DRONES UNDERMINE DEMOCRACY?

In democracies like ours, there have always been deep bonds between the public and its wars. Citizens have historically participated in decisions to take military action, through their elected representatives, helping to ensure broad support for wars and a willingness to share the costs, both human and economic, of enduring them. In America, our Constitution explicitly divided the president's role as commander in chief in war from Congress's role in declaring war. Yet these links and this division of labor are now under siege as a result of a technology that our founding fathers never could have imagined.

Just 10 years ago, the idea of using armed robots in war was the stuff of Hollywood fantasy. Today, the United States military has more than 7,000 unmanned aerial systems, popularly called drones. There are 12,000 more on the ground. Last year, they carried out hundreds of strikes—both covert and overt—in six countries, transforming the way our democracy deliberates and engages in what we used to think of as war.

We don't have a draft anymore; less than 0.5 percent of Americans over 18 serve in the active-duty military. We do not declare war anymore; the last time Congress actually did so was in 1942—against Bulgaria, Hungary and Romania. We don't buy war bonds or pay war taxes anymore. During World War II, 85 million Americans purchased war bonds that brought the government $185 billion; in the last decade, we bought none and instead gave the richest 5 percent of Americans a tax break.

And now we possess a technology that removes the last political barriers to war. The strongest appeal of unmanned systems is that we don't have to send someone's son or daughter into harm's way.

But when politicians can avoid the political consequences of the condolence letter—and the impact
that military casualties have on voters and on the
news media—they no longer treat the previously
weighty matters of war and peace the same way.

For the first 200 years of American democracy, engaging in combat and bearing risk—both
personal and political—went hand in hand. In the
age of drones, that is no longer the case. Today's
unmanned systems are only the beginning. The
original Predator, which went into service in 1995,
lacked even GPS and was initially unarmed; newer
models can take off and land on their own, and
carry smart sensors that can detect a disruption in
the dirt a mile below the plane and trace footprints
back to an enemy hide-out.

There is not a single new manned combat aircraft under research and development at any major
Western aerospace company, and the Air Force is
training more operators of unmanned aerial systems
than fighter and bomber pilots combined. In 2011,
unmanned systems carried out strikes from Afghanistan to Yemen. The most notable of these continuing operations is the not-so-covert war in Pakistan,
where the United States has carried out more than
300 drone strikes since 2004.

Yet this operation has never been debated in
Congress; more than seven years after it began, there
has not even been a single vote for or against it. This
campaign is not carried out by the Air Force; it is
being conducted by the C.I.A. This shift affects everything from the strategy that guides it to the individuals who oversee it (civilian political appointees) and
the lawyers who advise them (civilians rather than
military officers).

It also affects how we and our politicians view
such operations. President Obama's decision to send
a small, brave Navy Seal team into Pakistan for 40
minutes was described by one of his advisers as "the
gutsiest call of any president in recent history." Yet
few even talk about the decision to carry out more
than 300 drone strikes in the very same country.

I do not condemn these strikes; I support most
of them. What troubles me, though, is how a new
technology is short-circuiting the decision-making
process for what used to be the most important
choice a democracy could make. Something that

would have previously been viewed as a war is
simply not being treated like a war.

The change is not limited to covert action. Last
spring, America launched airstrikes on Libya as part
of a NATO operation to prevent Col. Muammar
el-Qaddafi's government from massacring civilians.
In late March, the White House announced that the
American military was handing over combat operations to its European partners and would thereafter
play only a supporting role.

The distinction was crucial. The operation's
goals quickly evolved from a limited humanitarian
intervention into an air war supporting local insur-
gents' efforts at regime change. But it had limited
public support and no Congressional approval.

When the administration was asked to explain
why continuing military action would not be a violation of the War Powers Resolution—a Vietnam-
era law that requires notifying Congress of military
operations within 48 hours and getting its authorization after 60 days—the White House argued that
American operations did not "involve the presence
of U.S. ground troops, U.S. casualties or a serious
threat thereof." But they did involve something we
used to think of as war: blowing up stuff, lots of it.

Starting on April 23, American unmanned
systems were deployed over Libya. For the next six
months, they carried out at least 146 strikes on
their own. They also identified and pinpointed the
targets for most of NATO's manned strike jets. This
unmanned operation lasted well past the 60-day
deadline of the War Powers Resolution, extending
to the very last airstrike that hit Colonel Qaddafi's
convoy on Oct. 20 and led to his death.

Choosing to make the operation unmanned
proved critical to initiating it without Congressional
authorization and continuing it with minimal public
support. On June 21, when NATO's air war was lag-
ging, an American Navy helicopter was shot down
by pro-Qaddafi forces. This previously would have
been a disaster, with the risk of an American aircrew
being captured or even killed. But the downed helicopter was an unmanned Fire Scout, and the story
didn't even make the newspapers the next day.

Congress has not disappeared from all decisions about war, just the ones that matter. The same
week that American drones were carrying out their

145th unauthorized airstrike in Libya, the president notified Congress that he had deployed 100 Special Operations troops to a different part of Africa.

This small unit was sent to train and advise Ugandan forces battling the cultish Lord's Resistance Army and was explicitly ordered not to engage in combat. Congress applauded the president for notifying it about this small noncombat mission but did nothing about having its laws ignored in the much larger combat operation in Libya.

We must now accept that technologies that remove humans from the battlefield, from unmanned systems like the Predator to cyberweapons like the Stuxnet computer worm, are becoming the new normal in war.

And like it or not, the new standard we've established for them is that presidents need to seek approval only for operations that send people into harm's way—not for those that involve waging war by other means.

Without any actual political debate, we have set an enormous precedent, blurring the civilian and military roles in war and circumventing the Constitution's mandate for authorizing it. Freeing the executive branch to act as it chooses may be appealing to some now, but many future scenarios will be less clear-cut. And each political party will very likely have a different view, depending on who is in the White House.

Unmanned operations are not "costless," as they are too often described in the news media and government deliberations. Even worthy actions can sometimes have unintended consequences. Faisal Shahzad, the would-be Times Square bomber, was drawn into terrorism by the very Predator strikes in Pakistan meant to stop terrorism. Similarly, C.I.A. drone strikes outside of declared war zones are setting a troubling precedent that we might not want to see followed by the close to 50 other nations that now possess the same unmanned technology—including China, Russia, Pakistan and Iran.

A deep deliberation on war was something the framers of the Constitution sought to build into our system. Yet . . . Congress will have to admit that its role has been reduced to the same part it plays during the president's State of the Union speech. These days, when it comes to authorizing war, Congress generally sits there silently, except for the occasional clapping. And we do the same at home.

Last year, I met with senior Pentagon officials to discuss the many tough issues emerging from our growing use of robots in war. One of them asked, "So, who then is thinking about all this stuff?" America's founding fathers may not have been able to imagine robotic drones, but they did provide an answer. The Constitution did not leave war, no matter how it is waged, to the executive branch alone.

Andrew J. Bacevich

THE REVISIONIST IMPERATIVE: RETHINKING TWENTIETH CENTURY WARS

Thinking about war in the twenty-first century, two well-worn sayings come to mind: "Wars are too important to be left to the generals" and "Generals are always planning for the last war." At the risk of seeming unfairly critical of generals, these two sayings convey considerable wisdom, especially today. Although military planners are necessarily conservative, in that they are expected to make "worst case" assumptions to avoid being surprised, they also display a regrettable tendency to think narrowly about events, thus missing the larger picture. In this selection, historian and military veteran Andrew J. Bacevich asks historians and the rest of us to reconsider the "lessons of war" in the light of new events and realities.

Not long before his untimely death, the historian Tony Judt observed that "For many American commentators and policymakers the message of the twentieth century is that war works."[49] Judt might have gone even further. Well beyond the circle of experts and insiders, many ordinary Americans–even today at least tacitly share that view.

This reading of the twentieth century has had profound implications for U.S. policy in the twenty-first century. With the possible exception of Israel, the United States today is the only advanced democracy in which belief in war's efficacy continues to enjoy widespread acceptance. Others—the citizens of Great Britain and France, of Germany and Japan—took from the twentieth century a different lesson: War devastates. It impoverishes. It coarsens. Even when seemingly necessary or justified, it entails brutality, barbarism, and the killing of innocents. To choose war is to leap into the dark,

entrusting the nation's fate to forces beyond human control.

Americans persist in believing otherwise. That belief manifests itself in a number of ways, not least in a pronounced willingness to invest in, maintain, and employ military power. (The belief that war works has not made soldiering per se a popular vocation; Americans prefer war as a spectator sport rather than as a participatory one).

Why do Americans cling to a belief in war that other advanced nations have long since abandoned? The simple answer is that for a time, war *did* work or seemed to anyway—at least for the United States, even if not for others. After all, the vast conflagration we remember not altogether appropriately as "World War II" vaulted the United States to the very summit of global power. The onset of that conflict found Americans still struggling to cope with a decade-long economic crisis. Recall that the unemployment rate in 1939 was several percentage points above the highest point it has reached during our own Great Recession.

[49] Tony Judt, "What Have We Learned, If Anything?" *New York Review of Books*, 1 May 2008.

The Journal of Military History 76 (April 2012): 1033–1046. Copyright © 2012 by *The Society for Military History*, all rights reserved.

Notwithstanding the palliative effects of Franklin Roosevelt's New Deal, the long-term viability of liberal democratic capitalism during the 1930s remained an open question. Other ideological claimants, on the far left and far right, were advancing a strong case that *they* defined the future.

By 1945, when the conflict ended, almost all of that had changed. At home, war restored economic prosperity and set the stage for a decades-long boom. At least as important, the war reinvigorated confidence in American institutions. The challenges of war management had prodded Washington to get its act together. Prodigious feats of production in places like Cleveland, Detroit, and Pittsburgh had enabled the United States to raise vast air, sea, and land forces, which it then employed on a global scale with considerable effectiveness.

The American way of war implied a remarkable knack for doing big things in a big way, sweeping aside whatever obstacles might stand in the way. The bumptious wartime motto of the army corps of engineers testified to this approach: "The difficult we do at once; the impossible takes a little longer. "This wasn't empty bluster: the Manhattan Project, culminating in the development of the atomic bomb, testified to American technical prowess, but also implied broader claims of superiority. The United States was once again a country that did things— really big things—that no other country could do.

Meanwhile, with the gross domestic product doubling in barely half a decade, the American way of life once again signified levels of material abundance that made its citizens the envy of the world. Thanks in considerable part to war, in other words, the United States had become an economic, technological, political, military, and cultural juggernaut without peer.

This was the America into which I was born in 1947. I breathed in the war's vapors, which lingered long after the war itself had ended. Both of my parents had served, my father a signalman on a destroyer escort in the Atlantic, my mother an army nurse in the Pacific. For them, as for countless others, the war shaped perceptions of past and present. It shaped as well their expectations for the future and their understanding of the dangers and opportunities that lay ahead.

How well I remember as a very young boy watching *Victory at Sea* on television, with that stirring score by Richard Rodgers, the documentary series narrated by Leonard Graves, who as the theme music faded began each episode by announcing in his deep baritone, "And now. . . . "

Here was history: gripping, heroic, immediate, and filled with high drama. Here too was the cornerstone of a grand narrative, constructed around the momentous events of 1939–1945, with special emphasis on those in which the United States had played a notable hand. I couldn't get enough of it.

The history I absorbed then and carried into adulthood—the story that really mattered—divided neatly into three distinctive chapters. The tale commenced with a prelude recounting the events of a *prewar* era, a period of fecklessness and folly, even if for a youngster the details tended to be a bit vague. It concluded with what Americans were calling the *postwar* era, unfolding in the war's shadow, its course to be determined by how well the nation had absorbed the war's self-evident lessons. But constituting the heart of the story was the war itself: a slumbering America brutally awakened, rising up in righteous anger, smiting evildoers, and thereby saving the world. One might say that the account I imbibed adhered closely to Winston Churchill's, albeit shorn of any British accent.

Thanks in no small part to Churchill (though not him alone), the war became in Judt's words "a moral memory palace," a source of compelling, instantly recognizable parables.[50] Compressed into just a word or two—Munich, Pearl Harbor, Normandy, Auschwitz, Yalta, Hiroshima—each parable expressed permanent, self-contained, and universally valid truths. Here was instruction that demanded careful attention.

With millions of others I accepted this instruction as unquestioningly as I accepted the proposition that major league baseball should consist of two leagues with eight teams each, none of them situated in cities west of the Missouri River.

In the decades since, of course, baseball has changed dramatically—and not necessarily for the

---

[50] Ibid.

better, one might add. Meanwhile, our commonplace understanding of World War II has remained largely fixed. So too has the historical narrative within which that conflict occupies so prominent a place.

I submit that this poses a problem. For history to serve more than an ornamental function, it must speak to the present. The version of past formed by World War II and perpetuated since—the version persuading Americans that war works—has increasingly little to say. Yet even as the utility of that account dissipates, its grip on the American collective consciousness persists. The times, therefore, are ripe for revisionism. Replacing the canonical account of the twentieth century with something more germane to actually existing circumstances prevailing in the twenty-first century has become an imperative.

And that requires rethinking the role of war in contemporary history. In any such revisionist project, military historians should play a prominent part. Let me emphasize two preliminary points as strongly as I can.

First, when I speak of history I am not referring to the ongoing scholarly conversation promoted by organizations such as the American Historical Association, a conversation that only obliquely and intermittently affects our civic life. I refer instead to history as a widely shared and deeply internalized understanding of the past, fashioned less by academics than by politicians and purveyors of popular culture—an interpretation shaped in Washington and Hollywood rather than in Cambridge or Berkeley.

Second, I want to acknowledge that revisionism can be a morally hazardous undertaking. To overturn received wisdom is to create opportunities for mischief makers as well as for truth seekers. When the subject is World War II, the opportunities to make mischief are legion.

Yet the clout wielded by the Washington-Hollywood Axis of Illusions should not deter historians from accepting the revisionist challenge. Nor should the prospect of sharing a dais with someone (like me) who, while conceding that the so-called isolationists of the 1930s got some things wrong, will insist that they also got a whole lot right. And much of what they got right deserves respectful consideration today. So if someone like Charles Beard

may not merit three lusty cheers, he deserves at least one and perhaps even two.

To illustrate the possibilities of revisionist inquiry, let me advance the following broad proposition for your consideration: for citizens of the twenty-first century, the twentieth century actually has two quite different stories to tell. The first story is familiar, although imperfectly understood. The second is little known, with large implications that have gone almost entirely ignored.

Enshrined today as a story of freedom besieged, but ultimately triumphant, the familiar story began back in 1914 and continued until its (apparently) definitive conclusion in 1989. Call this the Short Twentieth Century.

The less familiar alternative recounts a story in which freedom as such has figured only intermittently. It has centered on the question of who will dominate the region that we today call the Greater Middle East. Also kicking into high gear in 1914, this story continues to unfold in the present day, with no end in sight. Call this the story of the Long Twentieth Century.

The Short Twentieth Century, geographically centered on Eurasia, pitted great powers against one another. Although alignments shifted depending on circumstance, the roster of major players remained fairly constant. That roster consisted of Great Britain, France, Germany, Russia, and Japan, with the United States biding its time before eventually picking up most of the marbles.

From time to time, the Long Twentieth Century has also pitted great powers against one another. Yet that struggle has always had a second element. It has been a contest between outsiders and insiders. Western intruders with large ambitions, preeminently Great Britain until succeeded by the United States, pursued their dreams of empire or hegemony, typically cloaked in professions of "benevolent assimilation," uplift, or the pursuit of world peace. The beneficiaries of imperial ministrations—from Arabs in North Africa to Moros in the southern Philippines along with sundry groups in between—seldom proved grateful and frequently resisted.

The Short Twentieth Century had a moral and ideological aspect. If not especially evident at first, this became clearer over time.

Viewed in retrospect, President Woodrow Wilson's effort to portray the cataclysm of 1914–1918 as a struggle of democracy versus militarism appears more than a little strained. The problem is not that Germany was innocent of the charge of militarism. It is, rather, that Western theories of democracy in those days left more than a little to be desired. After all, those who labored under the yoke of British, French, and American rule across large swathes of Africa, Asia, and the Middle East enjoyed precious little freedom.

Yet the advent of the Third German Reich produced a moral clarity hitherto more theoretical than real. The war against Nazi Germany was indubitably a war on behalf of liberal democracy against vile, murderous totalitarianism. Of course, sustaining that construct is easier if you survey the events of World War II with one eye covered.

The central event of the Short Twentieth Century loses some of its moral luster once you acknowledge the following:

- First, concern for the fate of European Jewry exercised no discernible influence on allied conduct of the war, allied forces failing to make any serious attempt to avert, halt, or even retard the Final Solution;
- Second, in both Europe and the Pacific, allied strategic bombing campaigns killed noncombatants indiscriminately on a scale dwarfing, say, the atrocity of 9/11;
- Third, the price of liberating western Europe included the enslavement of eastern Europeans, a direct consequence of allocating to Uncle Joe Stalin's Red Army primary responsibility for defeating the Wehrmacht;
- Fourth, at war's end, the victors sanctioned campaigns of ethnic cleansing on a scale not seen before or since, while offering employment to scientists, engineers, and intelligence operatives who had loyally served the Third Reich;
- Fifth, on the American home front, the war fought for freedom and democracy left intact a well-entrenched system of de facto apartheid, racial equality not numbering among Franklin Roosevelt's Four Freedoms.

None of these disturbing facts, it need hardly be said, made any significant impact on the way World War II became enshrined in American memory. I do not recall encountering any of them while watching *Victory at Sea*.

Yet these facts matter. They remind us that if the Short American Century was *sometimes* about values, it was *always* about politics and power. The allies who joined together to defeat the Axis (a righteous cause) did not hesitate to employ means that were anything but righteous. In pursuit of that righteous cause, they simultaneously connived and jockeyed against one another for relative advantage on matters related to oil, territory, markets, and the preservation of imperial privilege.

Whether out of conscience or expediency, the onset of the postwar era soon enough prompted Americans to rethink some (but not all) of the morally dubious practices that made it necessary to sanitize the narrative of World War II.

So after 1945, liberal democracies, the United States now in the vanguard, turned on the leftwing totalitarianism that had played such a crucial role in the fight against rightwing totalitarianism. No longer a valued ally, Stalin became the new Hitler. At home meanwhile, the United States also began to amend the pronounced defects in its own approach to democratic practice. However haltingly, for example, the modern civil rights movement commenced. Both of these facilitated efforts by Cold Warriors to infuse the anti-communist crusade, successor to the anti-Axis crusade, with an ennobling moral clarity. The ensuing struggle between an American-led West and a Soviet-led East, in their view, deserved to be seen as an extension of World War II.

As with World War II, therefore, so too with the Cold War: American leaders insistently framed the contest in ideological rather than in geopolitical terms. The Free World ostensibly asked nothing more than that freedom itself should survive. This served to camouflage the real stakes: rival powers, previous wars having reduced their ranks to two, were vying for primacy in Eurasia, that long contest now reaching its penultimate chapter.

This framing device had important implications when the era of bipolarity came to its abrupt and surprising end. I don't know about you, but recalling the events that unfolded between 1978 when

John Paul II became pope and 1989 when the Berlin Wall came down still makes me dizzy.

Right before our very eyes, history had seemingly handed down a conclusive verdict. The search for alternatives to liberal democratic capitalism had failed. That failure was definitive. The Short Twentieth Century was kaput. Born 1914. Died 1989. Finis.

During what turned out to be a very abbreviated post–Cold War era, American politicians and commentators vied with one another to devise a suitably grandiose conception of what the passing of the Short Twentieth Century signified.

Whatever the specifics, the results were sure to be very good and very long lasting. As the "sole superpower," America now stood in solitary splendor, recognized by all as the "indispensable nation," able to discern even as it simultaneously embodied "the right side of history."

My text encloses those phrases in quotes. But during the 1990s, ostensibly serious people issuing such pronouncements did not intend to be ironic. They were merely reciting what had become the conventional wisdom. As well they might. Expanding on or embroidering such themes got your books on bestseller lists, your columns in all the best newspapers, and your smiling face on the Sunday talk shows.

My favorite artifact of this era remains the *New York Times Magazine* dated 28 March 1999. The cover story excerpted *The Lexus and the Olive Tree*, Tom Friedman's just-released celebration of globalization-as-Americanization. The cover itself purported to illustrate "What the World Needs Now." Alongside a photograph of a clenched fist adorned with the Stars and Stripes in brilliant red, white, and blue appeared this text: "For globalism to work, America can't be afraid to act like the almighty superpower that it is."

This was the *New York Times*, mind you, not the *Weekly Standard* or the editorial pages of the *Wall Street Journal*.

More or less overlooked amidst all this triumphalism was the fact that the other twentieth century—the one in which promoting freedom had never figured as a priority—continued without interruption. In Egypt, Saudi Arabia, the West Bank, Iraq, Iran, and Afghanistan, the collapse of communism did not qualify as a cosmic event. In such places, the

competition to dominate Eurasia had been a sideshow, not the main event. So the *annus mirabilis* of 1989 notwithstanding, the Long Twentieth Century continued apace, drawing the almighty superpower ever more deeply into what was fast becoming one helluva mess.

For those with a taste for irony try this one: 1991 was the year in which the U.S.S.R. finally gave up the ghost; it was also the year of the First Persian Gulf War. One headache went away; another was about to become a migraine.

In making the case for war against Iraq, George H. W. Bush depicted Saddam Hussein as a Hitler-like menace—neither the first nor the last time the infamous Führer would play a walk-on role in climes far removed from Germany. Indeed, Adolf Hitler has enjoyed an impressive second career as a sort of stunt-double for Middle Eastern villains. Recall that back in 1956, to justify the reckless Anglo-French-Israeli assault on Egypt, Prime Minister Anthony Eden had fingered Colonel Nasser as another Hitler. Not long ago, Lindsey Graham, the reflexively hawkish Republican senator from South Carolina, likened Libya's Muammar Gaddafi to the Nazi leader.[51] More recently still, the journalist Max Boot, who has made a career out of promoting war, has discovered Hitler's spirit lurking in present-day Iran.[52]

However absurd such comparisons, the Nazi dictator's periodic guest appearances make an important point. They illustrate the persistent Western disinclination to see the struggle for the Greater Middle East on its own terms. Instead, to explain developments there, Western leaders import clichés or stock figures ripped from the more familiar and, from their perspective, more reassuring Short Twentieth Century. In doing so, they confuse themselves and us.

Alas, the elder Bush's effort to eliminate his Hitler came up short. Celebrated in its day as a great victory, Operation Desert Storm turned out to be anything but that. The First Persian Gulf War deserves to be

---

[51] Justin Elliott, "Lindsey Graham: Gadhafi Is Like Hitler," 6 July 2011, Salon.com, http://www.salon.com/news/politics/war_room/2011/07/06/lindsey_graham_gadhafi_hitler
[52] Max Boot, "The Iran Threat," *Los Angeles Times*, 1 December 2011.

remembered chiefly as a source of wildly inflated and pernicious illusions. More than any other event, this brief conflict persuaded Washington, now freed of constraints imposed by the Cold War, that the application of U.S. military power held the key to reordering the Greater Middle East in ways likely to serve American interests. Here, it seemed, was evidence that war still worked and worked handsomely indeed.

Flexing U.S. military muscle on the battlefields of Europe and the Pacific had once made America stronger and the world a better place. Why not count on American power to achieve similar results in the Persian Gulf and Central Asia? Why not take the means that had seemingly brought the Short Twentieth Century to such a happy conclusion and apply them to the problems of the Greater Middle East?

Throughout the 1990s, neoconservatives and other jingoists vigorously promoted this view. After 9/11, George W. Bush made it his own. So in explaining what had happened on 11 September 2001 and what needed to happen next, President Bush appropriated precepts from the Short Twentieth Century. It was going to be World War II and the Cold War all over again.

"We have seen their kind before," the president said of the terrorists who had assaulted America. The occasion was an address before a joint session of Congress barely more than a week after the attack on the World Trade Center. "They're the heirs of all the murderous ideologies of the 20th century," he continued.

> By sacrificing human life to serve their radical visions, by abandoning every value except the will to power, they follow in the path of fascism, Nazism and totalitarianism. And they will follow that path all the way to where it ends in history's unmarked grave of discarded lies.[53]

Lest there be any doubt of where Bush was situating himself historically, he made a point of warmly welcoming the British prime minister to the proceedings. "America has no truer friend than Great Britain," the president declared, adding that "once again, we are joined together in a great cause."

The implications were clear: the partnership of Tony and George revived the tradition of Winston and Franklin and of Maggie and Ron. Good once again stood firm against evil.

From his vantage point in the great beyond, Churchill must have lit a cigar and poured himself a brandy. Imagine his gratitude to President Bush for overlooking the role that he and his countrymen had played in bollixing up the Greater Middle East in the first place.

In reality, during the Long Twentieth Century, the United States had only intermittently viewed Great Britain as a friend. "Perfidious Albion" had instead been a recurring source of rapacious tomfoolery—making a mess of things and then walking away once staying on had become inconvenient. The former British Mandate for Palestine offers one notable example of Great Britain's contributions to the Long Twentieth Century. Kashmir, the nexus of an intractable dispute between India and Pakistan, offers a second.

Even so, many gullible (or cynical) observers endorsed President Bush's interpretation. September 2001 became December 1941 all over again. Once again World War II—unwelcome or inconvenient details excluded, as always—was pressed into service as "a moral memory palace." As the bellicose authors of a great agitprop classic published in 2004 put it, "There is no middle way for Americans: it is victory or holocaust."[54] And so a new crusade—preposterously dubbed World War IV in some quarters—commenced.[55]

Since then, more than a decade has elapsed. Although President Bush is gone, the war he declared continues. Once commonly referred to as the Global War on Terror (World War IV never really caught on), today we hardly know what to call the enterprise.

Bush's attempt to graft the putative rationale for war during the Short Twentieth Century onto the new wars in the Greater Middle East didn't take. His Freedom Agenda withered and died. Even so, with Bush's successor closing down some fronts,

---

[53] George W. Bush, "Address to a Joint Session of Congress," 20 September 2001, http://www.historyplace.com/speeches/gw-bush-9-11.htm

[54] David Frum and Richard Perle, *An End to Evil: How To Win the War on Terror* (New York: Random House, 2004), 7.
[55] Norman Podhoretz, *World War IV: The Long Struggle Against Islamofascism* (Garden City, N.Y.: Doubleday, 2007).

ratcheting up others, and opening up new ones in places like Pakistan, Yemen, and Libya, the conflict itself persists. It's become the Long War—a collection of nominally related "overseas contingency operations," defined chiefly by their duration. Once begun, campaigns continue indefinitely.

What then of the American conviction, drawn from the remembered experience of the Short Twentieth Century, that "war works"? What evidence exists to suggest that this proposition retains any validity? Others may differ, but I see little to indicate that our affinity for war is making the country more powerful or more prosperous. If anything, a plethora of socioeconomic indicators suggest that the reverse is true.

Whatever the United States is experiencing today, it's not a reprise of World War II. Newsmagazines may enthuse over today's Iraq and Afghanistan veterans as our "New Greatest Generation," but they overlook a rather large distinction.[56] In contrast to the opportunities that awaited the previous "Greatest Generation" when its members came home, the wars fought by today's veterans point toward a bleaker rather than a brighter future.

History—the version that privileges the Short Twentieth Century above all other possibilities—makes it difficult to grasp the quandary in which we find ourselves as a consequence of our penchant for using force. After all, that account instructs us that "war works" or at least ought to if we simply try hard enough.

Yet it's just possible that a more expansive and less self-congratulatory accounting of the recent past—one that treats the Long Twentieth Century with the respect it deserves—could potentially provide a way out. To put it another way, we need to kick down the doors of the moral memory palace. We need to let in some fresh air.

I am not thereby suggesting that the canonical lessons of the Short Twentieth Century have lost all relevance. Far from it. Yet it's past time to restock our storehouse of policy-relevant parables. This means according to the Sykes-Picot agreement and the Hussein-McMahon correspondence, FDR's tête-à-tête with King Ibn Saud and the killing of Count Bernadotte by Zionist assassins, the Anglo-American

conspiracy to depose Mohammed Mossadegh and the bizarre Suez crisis, the Iran-Contra affair and, yes, Operation Iraqi Freedom, pedagogical weight equal to that habitually accorded to Munich, Pearl Harbor, and Auschwitz.

We could do with just a bit less of the Churchill who stood defiantly alone against Hitler. We might permit a bit more of the Churchill who, seeking ways after World War I to police the Middle East on the cheap, pushed for "experimental work on gas bombs, especially mustard gas" as a way to "inflict punishment on recalcitrant natives."[57]

Implicit in the standard American account of the Short Twentieth Century is the conviction that history is purposeful, with the vigorous deployment of U.S. power the best way to hasten history's arrival at its intended destination. A sober appreciation of the surprises, miscalculations, and disappointments permeating the Long Twentieth Century, beginning with Great Britain's cavalier decision to dismember the Ottoman Empire and running all the way to George W. Bush's ill-fated attempt to transform the Greater Middle East, should temper any such expectations. What the Long Twentieth Century teaches above all is humility.

"Ideas are not mirrors, they are weapons." The words are George Santayana's, written back when the twentieth century was young. "[T]heir function," he continued, "is to prepare us to meet events, as future experience may unroll them. Those ideas that disappoint us are false ideas; those to which events are true are true themselves."[58]

The ideas, assumptions, and expectations embedded in the received account of the Short Twentieth Century may not be entirely false. But they are supremely inadequate to the present. As historians, our obligations to the students who pass through our classrooms include this one: to provide them with a usable past, preparing them as best we can to meet events as they unfold. Measured by that standard, military historians are falling short.

William Faulkner famously said of the past that "It's not dead. It's not even past." As a general

---

[56] Cover story, *Time*, 29 August 2011.

[57] Richard Toye, *Churchill's Empire: The World That Made Him and the World He Made* (New York: Henry Holt, 2010), 145.
[58] George Santayana, "The Genteel Tradition in American Philosophy" (1913).

proposition, there's something to be said for that view. Not in this case, however. The past that Americans know is worse than dead; it's become a cause of self-inflicted wounds. As historians, we need to do better. The means to do so are readily at hand.

STUDY QUESTIONS

1. Identify and describe several important causes of war that are not represented in this chapter.
2. Is there any fundamental sense in which the causes of war in the twenty-first century are likely to be different from those earlier in history?
3. Compare "war" among animals with war among human beings. Comment on both the advantages and dangers of looking at human war as a special case of a more general phenomenon found in other species.
4. Discuss the advantages and disadvantages of looking for the causes of "war" as opposed to looking for the causes of specific wars.
5. Is there any evidence for a *dis*inclination to kill? If people are "naturally" inclined to be peaceful, why are there so many wars? If people are "naturally" inclined to be war-like, is the hope for peace unrealistic and doomed to failure?
6. Compare the basic attitudes of the political "left" and "right" with respect to war.
7. Make an argument that students of peace studies should know more about the anthropology of war—that is, "war" among nontechnological societies; make an argument that this is not terribly relevant.
8. During the nineteenth century, many people felt that nationalism could be a potent force for peace. Was it? Could it still be?
9. Make a case for (or against) the proposition that poverty is a major cause of war; make similar arguments for population pressure, military spending and preparation, the role of leaders, the psychology of human decision making, religious and ethnic orientation, and technology as causes of war.
10. It is clear that nuclear war would differ from conventional war in terms of its consequences. In what ways might nuclear war likely differ from conventional war with respect to possible *causes*? In what ways might it be similar?

SUGGESTIONS FOR FURTHER READING

Barash, David P., and C. P. Webel. 2014. *Peace and Conflict Studies*, 3rd ed. Los Angeles: Sage.
Blainey, Geoffrey. 1988. *The Causes of War*. New York: Free Press.
Bramson, Leon, and George W. Goethals, eds. 1964. *War: Studies from Psychology, Sociology, Anthropology*. New York: Basic.
Bueno de Mesquita, Bruce. 1983. *The War Trap*. New Haven, CT: Yale University Press.

Cashman, Greg. 2007. *An Introduction to the Causes of War: Patterns of Interstate Conflict from World War I to Iraq.* Lanham, MD: Rowman & Littlefield.

Fox, Jonathan. 2005. *Religion, Civilization, and Civil War: 1945 through the New Millennium.* Lanham, MD: Lexington Books.

Frank, Jerome. 1982. *Sanity and Survival in the Nuclear Age.* New York: Random House.

Pick, Daniel. 1993. *War Machine: The Rationalisation of Slaughter in the Modern Age.* New Haven, CT: Yale University Press.

Scheff, Thomas J. 1994. *Bloody Revenge: Emotions, Nationalism, and War.* Boulder, CO: Westview Press.

Van Evera, Stephen. 2001. *Causes of War.* Ithaca, NY: Cornell University Press.

CHAPTER 2

Building "Negative Peace"

W e have looked briefly at some of the outstanding approaches to the causes of war. Now we turn to prevention.

Whether or not war is too important to be left to the generals, the prevention of war is too important to be left to the politicians. Similarly, study of war's prevention is too important to be left to specialists in international relations, political science, or experts in "strategic studies," especially because many of these scholars tend to be apologists for the "war system" as it has operated for centuries.

And yet, most of the world's religious and ethical traditions deplore war and profess a desire for peace. "My peace I give unto you," offers Jesus (John 14:27), along with "the peace of God, which passes all understanding" (Phil. 4:7). The Indian leader Gandhi, a devout Hindu, became perhaps the world's greatest crusader for nonviolence. The Chinese philosopher Lao Tse, founder of Taoism, emphasized that the way of war is not the "Tao," or the "Way," that human beings ought to follow.

Tennyson (who also wrote the pro-military ode "The Charge of the Light Brigade"!) expressed what is nonetheless a worldwide yearning:

> Ring out the old, ring in the new. Ring out the false, ring in the true . . .
> Ring out old shapes of foul disease, ring out the narrowing lust of gold.
> Ring out the thousand wars of old, ring in the thousand years of peace.[1]

Considering the positive connotations of "peace" as opposed to "war," it is only fair to ask why peace—even in its inadequate and negative form as the mere absence of war—has not yet been attained. After all, longing for a thousand years of peace when nothing like it has ever been experienced seems a bit like someone who has never attended a concert looking forward to a paradise in which he or she will spend eternity listening to some heavenly choir! Most people readily give lip service to peace, but perhaps at some level, they haven't really desired it as fervently as they claim.

---

[1] "In Memoriam."

For one thing, maybe peace is boring. There are lots of war movies but precious few "peace movies,"; lots of martial music but only a handful of peace songs, and so on. As with rubbernecking at the scene of a traffic accident, people's attention is drawn to extreme situations of violence, in which exciting things happen. Those who complain, for example, about a tendency for the news media to focus only on "bad news," must confront the fact that whereas people are likely to pay attention to a war or even a border clash between contending forces, they would be less than fascinated by a headline blaring, "France and Germany did not go to war today."

For another thing, many people—despite their announced abhorrence of war—make exceptions in particular cases, especially in the interest of a "greater good." Thomas Jefferson once wrote of the United States that "peace is our passion," yet he also suggested that "the tree of liberty must be refreshed from time to time with the blood of patriots and tyrants." Similarly, Benjamin Franklin wrote that "there never was a good war, or a bad peace." But Franklin also warned that "even peace can be purchased at too high a price." For all its protestations on behalf of peace, the truth is that the United States has not been especially peaceful, having intervened militarily in other countries more than a hundred times.

Theodore Roosevelt urged his fellow citizens to cherish "the great fighting masterful virtues" and to accept imperial responsibilities in Hawaii, Puerto Rico, the Philippines, and Cuba:

> I preach to you, then, my countrymen, that our country calls not for the life of ease but for the life of strenuous endeavor. . . . If we stand idly by, if we seek merely swollen, slothful ease and ignoble peace, if we shrink from the hard contests where men must win at hazard of their lives and at the risk of all they hold dear, then the bolder and stronger peoples will pass us by, and will win for themselves the domination of the world.[2]

It is interesting that an acknowledged embracing of war is rare in modern thinking . . . although war itself is not rare at all. Departments of War, common until the 1940s, have universally been replaced by Departments or Ministries of "Defense." Only ideological devotees on either extreme have embraced war as virtuous and desirable, with Chinese revolutionary leader Mao Ze-Dong, for example, having spoken for the far left when he announced that "political power grows out of the barrel of a gun. . . . All things grow out of the barrel of a gun . . . " and fascist Italian dictator Benito Mussolini, speaking for the far right when he said:

> War alone brings up to their highest tension all human energies and puts a stamp of nobility upon the people who have the courage to meet it. . . . A doctrine, therefore, which begins with a prejudice in favor of peace is foreign to Fascism.

Many have extolled the sheer intensity of confronting basic issues of life and death, exploring the boundaries of one's capacities, and often reveling in the bonding that is involved. (See especially Chris Hedges's essay in Chapter 1.) Shakespeare's Henry V rhapsodizes about the joy a forthcoming battle holds for "We we few, we happy few, we band

---

[2] Theodore Roosevelt, *The Strenuous Life and Other Essays* (New York: Review of Reviews Co., 1910).

of brothers; For he today that sheds his blood with me shall be my brother." And a combat veteran from World War II wrote,

> We are liberated from our individual impotence and are drunk with the power that union with our fellows brings. In moments like these many have a vague awareness of how isolated and separate their lives have hitherto been.[3]

It is said that the Inuit ("Eskimos") have about a dozen words for "snow" (distinguishing between wet, powder, icy, etc.) and that among the Bedouin there are more than a hundred words for "camel" (ornery, easy-to-ride, etc.). Similarly, in English—and most other languages—there are numerous terms referring to specific wars: the Iraq War, Vietnam War, Korean War, World War II, and so on. By contrast, there is only one word for "peace." Although the peace that obtained, say, between World Wars I and II was quite different from that between the Franco–Prussian War and World War I, we do not identify distinct "peaces." Maybe when—or if—peace becomes as important to English-speaking people as snow is to the Inuit or camels are to the Bedouin, we will distinguish as carefully among the different varieties of peace as we now do about among different wars. For now, it must be concluded that war—for all its horrors—holds a particular interest, and even, for many, a special appeal. Hence, the need for organized opposition and for "positive approaches to negative peace."

Based on the number of national states that have existed since 1815, there have been approximately 16,000 nation-years, and during this time, war has occupied "only" 600 of these nation-years, or somewhat less that than 4 percent of the possible total. The twentieth century was a comparatively warlike one, and yet modern warfare, even with its enormous capacity for devastation, was directly responsible for fewer than about 2 percent of all human deaths occurring during that time. Note, however, that there have also been many indirect casualties of war because war and preparation for war divert resources that might be directed against other causes of death, such as disease and starvation. In addition, war itself typically retards economic development, destroys existing infrastructure, devastates natural environments, renders agriculture dangerous or impossible, displaces huge numbers of people who become homeless and desperate refugees, and also creates long-lasting psychological and social wounds.

Between the years 1500 and 1942 there was an average of nearly 1 one formally declared war per year, not including armed revolutions, yet but between 1900 and 1965 there were approximately 350 wars were declared, for an average of more than 5 five per year. According to peace researcher Lewis Richardson, there were at least 59 million deaths from human violence between 1820 and 1946, of which fewer than 10 million were attributable to individual and small-group violence; the remainder were due to war.[4] It is also noteworthy that historically, deaths directly attributable to disease (notably influenza, cholera, and pneumonia) as well as exposure have exceeded battle losses. In 1632, during the Thirty Years' War, the armies of Gustavus and Wallenstein faced each other outside Nuremberg, losing 18,000 men to typhus and scurvy before separating, without a shot having been fired!

---

[3] Glen Gray, *The Warriors: Reflections on Men in Battle* (New York: Harper & Row, 1967).
[4] Lewis Richardson, *Statistics of Deadly Quarrels* (Pittsburgh, PA: Boxwood Press, 1960).

The sheer wastefulness of war has been appalling, even with in the absence of non-nuclear weapons. During the Battle of the Somme (1916) in World War I, for example, the British gained a mere 120 square miles at a cost of 420,000 men (3,500 deaths per square mile), while the Germans lost 445,000. During World War I alone, Europe lost virtually an entire generation of young men. Here is F. Scott Fitzgerald's description of the Somme battlefield, after the war:

> See that little stream—we could walk to it in two minutes. It took the British a month to walk to it—a whole empire walking very slowly, dying in front and pushing forward behind. And another empire walked very slowly backward, a few inches a day, leaving the dead like a million bloody rugs.[5]

Of the 2,900,000 men who served in the U.S. armed forces in Vietnam (average age, 19), 300,000 were wounded and 55,000 were killed, along with an unknown number of Vietnamese (estimated at about 2 million). Yet these figures convey very little of the Vietnam War's significance, destructiveness, or horror. Numbers can be numbing.

There is no shortage of proposed solutions to the problem of war. Perhaps the simplest can be derived from the so-called war on drugs, or efforts to promote celibacy: "Just say no." But once again, this turns out to be no solution at all. "What if they had a war," goes the perennial question, "and no one came?" The problem, however, is that "they" have had many a war, and nearly always, lots of people show up. Simple condemnation of war, and/or moral exhortation for peace do not, by themselves, do the job.

Fortunately, there have been voices of sanity . . . indeed, many of them. Perhaps these voices, and the suggestions they give, have not been sufficiently innovative, forward thinking, or—that bugaboo of attempts to move beyond the war consensus—"realistic." Perhaps the problem is that no one solution has been pushed hard or far enough, or perhaps war is still with us because these various solutions have not been attempted in the right combination or with the right nuance. Maybe war—like Jesus' observation about the poor—will always be with us. Perhaps, instead, the eventual prevention of war is already en route, so that peace (or rather, "negative peace") is—like Herbert Hoover's claim about prosperity during the Great Depression—just around the corner. Or perhaps something altogether new and different is needed. In any event, perhaps by reviewing some of the distilled wisdom of humanity's efforts to prevent war, we can help peacemakers of the future avoid repeating the errors of the past. And, maybe, we can inspire greater efforts and achieve greater success in the days to come.

"War is waged," wrote St. Augustine, "so that peace may prevail. . . . But it is a greater glory to slay war with a word than people with a sword, and to gain peace by means of peace and not by means of war." In the following chapter, we examine efforts to gain peace by means of peace instead of by war or by threatening war. It is no easy quest, and there may be many routes, some of them blind alleys, others leading into thickets of maze-like complexity, whereas others still may turn our to be downright dangerous. But in the interest of "realism," it should be noted that war itself is downright dangerous, too.

---

[5] F. Scott Fitzgerald, *Tender Is the Night* (New York: Scribners, 1934).

William James

THE MORAL EQUIVALENT OF WAR

Famed historian Will Durant was once asked if he could summarize the history of the world in about five minutes. Responding that he could do so in even less time, he then said,

> History books describe the history of the world as a river red with blood. Running fast, it is filled with the men and events that cause bloodshed: kings and princes, diplomats and politicians. They cause revolutions and wars, violations of territory and rights. But the real history of the world takes place on the riverbanks where ordinary people dwell. They are loving one another, bearing children, and providing homes, all the while trying to remain untouched by the swiftly flowing river.[6]

Much of peace studies is concerned with efforts to build dikes—or at least, place sandbags—to channel the warlike river and keep it from people's homes; eventually, perhaps, to dry it up altogether.

But Durant's vision may be a bit romantic; after all, even though human beings have long yearned for peace, on many occasions they have also jumped rather enthusiastically into the river of war. If, as some suggest, this is at least in part because war meets certain deep-seated human needs, then it seems only reasonable to seek other, less destructive ways of satisfying those needs. If war represents what psychologist Abraham Maslow called a "peak experience," then it should be possible to achieve such an experience without killing. Probably the most famous attempt to come to terms with this problem occurred in the following essay by psychologist and philosopher William James. James's suggestion has its modern counterpart in such endeavors as the Peace Corps, vista, and other national service programs, although its basic thrust is directed less toward social betterment per se than toward a peaceful rechanneling of human energy.

The war against war is going to be no holiday excursion or camping party. The military feelings are too deeply grounded to abdicate their place among our ideals until better substitutes are offered than the glory and shame that come to nations as well as to individuals from the ups and downs of politics and the vicissitudes of trade. There is something highly paradoxical in the modern man's relation to war. Ask all our millions, north and south, whether they would vote now (were such a thing possible) to have our war for the Union expunged from history and the record of a peaceful transition to the present time substituted for that of its marches and battles, and probably hardly a handful of eccentrics would say yes.

---

[6] Quoted in Kermit Johnson, *Realism and Hope in a Nuclear Age* (Atlanta, GA: John Kow Press, 1988).

"The Moral Equivalent of War" by William James. McClure's Magazine Volume XXXV May to October 1910. S.S. McClure Company, New York & London 1910. Copyright, 1910 by S.S. McClure Co. Pages 463–468.

Those ancestors, those efforts, those memories and legends, are the most ideal part of what we now own together, a sacred spiritual possession worth more than all the blood poured out. Yet ask those same people whether they would be willing in cold blood to start another civil war now to gain another similar possession, and not one man or woman would vote for the proposition. In modern eyes, precious though wars may be, they must not be waged solely for the sake of the ideal harvest. Only when forced upon one, only when an enemy's injustice leaves us no alternative, is a war now thought permissible.

It was not thus in ancient times. The earlier men were hunting men, and to hunt a neighboring tribe, kill the males, loot the village, and possess the females was the most profitable, as well as the most exciting, way of living. Thus were the more martial tribes selected, and in chiefs and peoples a pure pugnacity and love of glory came to mingle with the more fundamental appetite for plunder.

Modern war is so expensive that we feel trade to be a better avenue to plunder, but modern man inherits all the innate pugnacity and all the love of glory of his ancestors. Showing war's irrationality and horror is of no effect upon him. The horrors make the fascination. War is the *strong* life; it is life *in extremis*; war taxes are the only ones men never hesitate to pay, as the budgets of all nations show us.

History is a bath of blood. The *Iliad* is one long recital of how Diomedes and Ajax, Sarpedon and Hector, *killed*. No detail of the wounds they made is spared us, and the Greek mind fed upon the story. Greek history is a panorama of jingoism and imperialism—war for war's sake, all the citizens being warriors. It is horrible reading, because of the irrationality of it all—save for the purpose of making history—and the history is that of the utter ruin of a civilization in intellectual respects perhaps the highest the earth has ever seen. . . .

Alexander's career was piracy pure and simple, nothing but an orgy of power and plunder made romantic by the character of the hero. There was no rational principle in it, and the moment he died his generals and governors attacked one another. The cruelty of those times is incredible. When Rome finally conquered Greece, Paulus Aemilius was told by the Roman Senate to reward his soldiers for their

toil by "giving" them the old kingdom of Epirus. They sacked seventy cities and carried off one hundred and fifty thousand inhabitants as slaves. How many they killed I know not, but in Aetolia they killed all the senators, five hundred and fifty in number. Brutus was "the noblest Roman of them all," but, to reanimate his soldiers on the eve of Philippi, he similarly promises to give them the cities of Sparta and Thessalonica to ravage if they win the fight.

Such was the gory nurse that trained societies to cohesiveness. We inherit the warlike type, and, for most of the capacities of heroism that the human race is full of, we have to thank this cruel history. Dead men tell no tales, and, if there were any tribes of other type than this, they have left no survivors. Our ancestors have bred pugnacity into our bone and marrow, and thousands of years of peace won't breed it out of us. The popular imagination fairly fattens on the thought of wars. Let public opinion once reach a certain fighting pitch, and no ruler can withstand it. In the Boer War both governments began with bluff but couldn't stay there; the military tension was too much for them. In 1898 our people had read the word "war" in letters three inches high for three months in every newspaper. The pliant politician McKinley was swept away by their eagerness, and our squalid war with Spain became a necessity.

At the present day, civilized opinion is a curious mental mixture. The military instincts and ideals are as strong as ever, but are confronted by reflective criticisms which sorely curb their ancient freedom. Innumerable writers are showing up the bestial side of military service. Pure loot and mastery seem no longer morally avowable motives, and pretexts must be found for attributing them solely to the enemy. England and we, our army and navy authorities repeat without ceasing, arm solely for "peace"; Germany and Japan it is who are bent on loot and glory. "Peace" in military mouths today is a synonym for "war expected." The word has become a pure provocative, and no government wishing peace sincerely should allow it ever to be printed in a newspaper. Every up-to-date dictionary should say that "peace" and "war" mean the same thing, now *in posse*, now *in actu*. It may even reasonably be said that the intensely sharp competitive *preparation* for war by the nations *is the real war*, permanent, unceasing, and that the battles are only a sort of public verification of the mastery gained during the "peace" interval.

It is plain that on this subject civilized man has developed a sort of double personality. If we take European nations, no legitimate interest of any one of them would seem to justify the tremendous destructions which a war to compass it would necessarily entail. It would seem as though common sense and reason ought to find a way to reach agreement in every conflict of honest interests. I myself think it our bounden duty to believe in such international rationality as possible. But, as things stand, I see how desperately hard it is to bring the peace party and the war party together, and I believe that the difficulty is due to certain deficiencies in the program of pacificism which set the militarist imagination strongly, and, to a certain extent, justifiably, against it. In the whole discussion both sides are on imaginative and sentimental ground. It is but one utopia against another, and everything one says must be abstract and hypothetical. Subject to this criticism and caution, I will try to characterize in abstract strokes the opposite imaginative forces and point out what to my own very fallible mind seems the best utopian hypothesis, the most promising line of conciliation.

In my remarks, pacificist though I am, I will refuse to speak of the bestial side of the war regime (already done justice to by many writers) and consider only the higher aspects of militaristic sentiment. Patriotism no one thinks discreditable, nor does anyone deny that war is the romance of history. But inordinate ambitions are the soul of every patriotism, and the possibility of violent death the soul of all romance. The militarily patriotic and romantic-minded everywhere, and especially the professional military class, refuse to admit for a moment that war may be a transitory phenomenon in social evolution. The notion of a sheep's paradise like that revolts, they say, our higher imagination. Where then would be the steeps of life? If war had ever stopped, we should have to reinvent it, on this view, to redeem life from flat degeneration.

Reflective apologists for war at the present day all take it religiously. It is a sort of sacrament. Its profits are to the vanquished as well as to the victor, and, quite apart from any question of profit, it is an absolute good, we are told, for it is human nature at

its highest dynamic. Its "horrors" are a cheap price to pay for rescue from the only alternative supposed, of a world of clerks and teachers, of coeducation and zoophily, of consumer's leagues and associated charities, of industrialism unlimited, and feminism unabashed. No scorn, no hardness, no valor anymore! Fie upon such a cattle-yard of a planet!

So far as the central essence of this feeling goes, no healthy-minded person, it seems to me, can help to some degree partaking of it. Militarism is the great preserver of our ideals of hardihood, and human life with no use for hardihood would be contemptible. Without risks or prizes for the darer, history would be insipid indeed, and there is a type of military character which everyone feels that the race should never cease to breed, for everyone is sensitive to its superiority. The duty is incumbent on mankind of keeping military characters in stock—of keeping them, if not for use, then as ends in themselves and as pure pieces of perfection—so that Roosevelt's weaklings and mollycoddles may not end by making everything else disappear from the face of nature. . . .

The virtues that prevail, it must be noted, are virtues anyhow, superiorities that count in peaceful as well as in military competition; but the strain on them, being infinitely intenser in the latter case, makes war infinitely more searching as a trial. No ordeal is comparable to its winnowings. Its dread hammer is the welder of men into cohesive states, and nowhere but in such states can human nature adequately develop its capacity. The only alternative is degeneration.

. . . Mankind was nursed in pain and fear and that the transition to a pleasure economy may be fatal to a being wielding no powers of defense against its disintegrative influences. If we speak of the *fear of emancipation from the fear regime*, we put the whole situation into a single phrase, fear regarding ourselves now taking the place of the ancient fear of the enemy.

Turn the fear over as I will in my mind, it all seems to lead back to two unwillingnesses of the imagination, one aesthetic and the other moral; unwillingness, first, to envisage a future in which army life, with its many elements of charm, shall be forever impossible and in which the destinies of peoples shall nevermore be decided quickly, thrillingly, and tragically by force, but only gradually and insip-idly by evolution; and, second, unwillingness to see the supreme theater of human strenuousness closed and the splendid military aptitudes of men doomed to keep always in a state of latency and never show themselves in action. These insistent unwilling-nesses, no less than other aesthetic and ethical insis-tencies, have, it seems to me, to be listened to and respected. One cannot meet them effectively by mere counter-insistency on war's expensiveness and hor-ror. The horror makes the thrill, and, when the ques-tion is of getting the extremest and supremest out of human nature, talk of expense sounds ignominious. The weakness of so much merely negative criticism is evident—pacifism makes no converts from the military party. The military partly denies neither the bestiality nor the horror nor the expense; it only says that these things tell but half the story. It only says that war is *worth* them; that, taking human nature as a whole, its wars are its best protection against its weaker and more cowardly self and that mankind cannot *afford* to adopt a peace economy.

Pacifists ought to enter more deeply into the aesthetical and ethical point of view of their opponents. . . . So long as antimilitarists propose no substitute for war's disciplinary function, no *moral equivalent* of war, analogous, as one might say, to the mechanical equivalent of heat, so long they fail to realize the full inwardness of the situation. And as a rule they do fail. The duties, penalties, and sanctions pictured in the Utopias they paint are all too weak and tame to touch the military-minded. Tolstoi's pacifism is the only exception to this rule, for it is profoundly pessimistic as regards all this world's val-ues and makes the fear of the Lord furnish the moral spur provided elsewhere by the fear of the enemy. But our socialistic peace advocates all believe abso-lutely in this world's values, and, instead of the fear of the Lord and the fear of the enemy, the only fear they reckon with is the fear of poverty if one be lazy. This weakness pervades all the socialistic literature with which I am acquainted. . . . Meanwhile men at large still live as they always have lived, under a pain-and-fear economy—for those of us who live in an ease economy are but an island in the stormy ocean—and the whole atmosphere of present-day utopian literature tastes mawkish and dishwatery to people who still keep a sense for life's more bitter flavors. It suggests, in truth, ubiquitous inferiority.

Inferiority is always with us, and merciless scorn of it is the keynote of the military temper. "Dogs, would you live forever?" shouted Frederick the Great. "Yes," say our utopians, "let us live forever and raise our level gradually." The best thing about our "inferiors" today is that they are as tough as nails and physically and morally almost as insensitive. Utopianism would see them soft and squeamish, while militarism would keep their callousness, but transfigure it into a meritorious characteristic, needed by "the service" and redeemed by that from the suspicion of inferiority. All the qualities of a man acquire dignity when he knows that the service of the collectivity that owns him needs them. If proud of the collectivity, his own pride rises in propor-tion. No collectivity is like an army for nourishing such pride, but it has to be confessed that the only sentiment which the image of pacific cosmopolitan industrialism is capable of arousing in countless worthy breasts is shame at the idea of belonging to *such* a collectivity. . . . Where is the sharpness and precipitousness, the contempt for life, whether one's own, or another's? Where is the savage yes and no, the unconditional duty? Where is the conscription? Where is the blood tax? Where is anything that one feels honored by belonging to?

Having said thus much in preparation, I will now confess my own utopia. I devoutly believe in the reign of peace and in the gradual advent of some sort of a socialistic equilibrium. The fatalistic view of the war function is to me nonsense, for I know that war-making is due to definite motives and subject to pru-dential checks and reasonable criticisms, just like any other form of enterprise. And when whole nations are the armies and the science of destruction vies in intellectual refinement with the sciences of produc-tion, I see that war becomes absurd and impossible from its own monstrosity. Extravagant ambitions will have to be replaced by reasonable claims, and nations must make common cause against them. . . .

All these beliefs of mine put me squarely into the antimilitarist party. But I do not believe that peace either ought to be or will be permanent on this globe, unless the states pacifically organized pre-serve some of the old elements of army discipline. A permanently successful peace economy cannot be a simple pleasure economy. In the more-or-less socialistic future toward which mankind seems drifting, we must still subject ourselves collectively to those severities which answer to our real position upon this only partly hospitable globe. We must make new energies and hardihoods continue the manliness to which the military mind so faithfully clings. Martial virtues must be the enduring cement; intrepidity, contempt of softness, surrender of private interest, obedience to command must still remain the rock upon which states are built—unless, indeed, we wish for dangerous reactions against commonwealths fit only for contempt and liable to invite attack whenever a center of crystallization for military-minded enterprise gets formed anywhere in their neighborhood.

The war party is assuredly right in affirming and reaffirming that the martial virtues, although originally gained by the race through war, are absolute and permanent human goods. Patriotic pride and ambition in their military form are, after all, only specifications of a more general competitive passion. They are its first form, but that is no reason for supposing them to be its last form. Men now are proud of belonging to a conquering nation, and without a murmur they lay down their persons and their wealth, if by so doing they may fend off subjection. But who can be sure that *other aspects of one's country* may not, with time and education and suggestion enough, come to be regarded with similarly effective feelings of pride and shame? Why should men not someday feel that it is worth a blood tax to belong to a collectivity superior in *any* ideal respect? Why should they not blush with indignant shame if the community that owns them is vile in any way whatsoever? Individuals, daily more numerous, now feel this civic passion. It is only a question of blowing on the spark until the whole population gets incandescent and, on the ruins of the old morals of military honor, a stable system of morals of civic honor builds itself up. What the whole community comes to believe in grasps the individual as in a vise. The war function has grasped us so far, but constructive interests may someday seem no less imperative and impose on the individual a hardly lighter burden.

Let me illustrate my idea more concretely. There is nothing to make one indignant in the mere fact that life is hard, that men should toil and suffer pain. The planetary conditions once and for all are such, and we can stand it. But that so many men, by mere accidents of birth and opportunity, should have a life of *nothing else* but toil and pain and hardness and inferiority imposed upon them, should have *no* vacation, while others natively no more deserving never get any taste of this campaigning life at all—*this* is capable of arousing indignation in reflective minds. It may end by seeming shameful to all of us that some of us have nothing but campaigning and others nothing but unmanly ease. If now—and this is my idea—there were, instead of military conscription, a conscription of the whole youthful population to form for a certain number of years a part of the army enlisted against nature, the injustice would tend to be evened out, and numerous other goods to the commonwealth would follow. The military ideals of hardihood and discipline would be wrought into the growing fiber of the people; no one would remain blind, as the luxurious classes now are blind, to man's relations to the globe he lives on and to the permanently sour and hard foundations of his higher life. To coal and iron mines, to freight trains, to fishing fleets in December, to dishwashing, clothes-washing, and window-washing, to road-building and tunnel-making, to foundries and stokeholes, and to the frames of skyscrapers, would our gilded youths be drafted off, according to their choice, to get the childishness knocked out of them and to come back into society with healthier sympathies and soberer ideas. They would have paid their blood tax, done their own part in the immemorial human warfare against nature; they would tread the earth more proudly, the women would value them more highly, they would be better fathers and teachers of the following generation.

Such a conscription, with the state of public opinion that would have required it and the many moral fruits it would bear, would preserve in the midst of a pacific civilization the manly virtues which the military party is so afraid of seeing disappear in peace. We should get toughness without callousness, authority with as little criminal cruelty as possible, and painful work done cheerily because the duty is temporary and threatens not, as now, to degrade the whole remainder of one's life. I spoke of the moral equivalent of war. So far, war has been the only force that can discipline a whole community, and, until an equivalent discipline is organized, I believe that war must have its way. But I have no serious doubt that the ordinary prides and shames of social man, once developed to a certain intensity, are capable of organizing such a moral equivalent as I have sketched or some other just as effective for preserving manliness of type. It is but a question of time, of skillful propagandism, and of opinion-making men seizing historic opportunities.

The martial type of character can be bred without war. Strenuous honor and disinterestedness abound elsewhere. Priests and medical men are in a fashion educated to it, and we should all feel some degree of it imperative if we were conscious of our work as an obligatory service to the state. We should be *owned*, as soldiers are by the army, and our pride would rise accordingly. We could be poor, then, without humiliation, as army officers now are. The only thing needed henceforward is to inflame the civic temper as past history has inflamed the military temper.

Roger Fisher, William Ury, and Bruce Patton

GETTING TO YES

One way of gaining peace "by means of peace and not by means of war" is for the contending sides to reach a mutually acceptable agreement among themselves. Not surprisingly, this is easier said than done, although normal people negotiate their differences every day, typically without violence. One of the most pervasive and pernicious myths of our current culture of militarism is that war and preparation for war are natural and unavoidable, whereas peace and preparation for peace are hopelessly unrealistic. Peacemaking is often represented as an impossible dream, the stuff of saints or the hopelessly deluded, whereas only the making of war—or at best, deterrence—is the only reality. Hence, it is important to affirm and make visible the peacemaking that happens all around us, most of the time. The active field of nonviolent conflict resolution offers interesting examples of applying peace studies to interpersonal behavior as well as to international affairs.

Although ways of fighting have changed throughout history, the basic techniques of negotiation scarcely have. At their most contentious, negotiators have recourse only to threats or promises, and conflict resolution can be backed up by varying degrees of goodwill or ill will and based on a continuum from blind trust to ironclad verification and/or arm-twisting. Negotiations, however, can succeed only if there is a set of outcomes that each party prefers over reaching no agreement. Occasionally, participants in a dispute negotiate only to appear virtuous, but in most cases, it appears that a negotiated settlement is preferred over failure to agree and recourse to violence in order to force an outcome. The trick is to find a peaceful solution that will be acceptable to all sides.

There are several ways to facilitate this "trick." One is by the involvement of highly trained third parties, who may arbitrate disputes (that is, lay down a judgment that the contenders have previously pledged to accept) or serve as mediators, whose role is to help the disputants clarify the issues and come to agreement. Third parties can help resolve disputes in several ways. For example, they can make suggestions that both sides find acceptable but which neither would be willing to offer for fear of being seen as weak. They can also help disputants go beyond the traditional, adversarial procedure of "positional bargaining" to a more creative and mutually acceptable outcome, the result of so-called integrative or principled negotiations. The following selection, written by a highly respected team of professional negotiators, discusses this new and forward-looking approach, in which solving a problem takes precedence over "winning."

Like it or not, you are a negotiator. Negotiation is a fact of life. You discuss a raise with your boss. You try to agree with a stranger on a price for his house. Two lawyers try to settle a lawsuit arising from a car accident. A group of oil companies plan a joint venture exploring for offshore oil. A city official meets with union leaders to avert a transit strike. The United States secretary of state sits down with his Soviet counterpart to seek an agreement limiting nuclear arms. All these are negotiations.

Everyone negotiates something every day. Like Molière's Monsieur Jourdain, who was delighted to learn that he had been speaking prose all his life, people negotiate even when they don't think of themselves as doing so. A person negotiates with his spouse about where to go for dinner and with his child about when the lights go out. Negotiation is a basic means of getting what you want from others. It is back-and-forth communication designed to reach an agreement when you and the other side have some interests that are shared and others that are opposed.

More and more occasions require negotiation; conflict is a growth industry. Everyone wants to participate in decisions that affect them; fewer and fewer people will accept decisions dictated by someone else. People differ, and they use negotiation to handle their differences. Whether in business, government, or the family, people reach most decisions through negotiation. Even when they go to court, they almost always negotiate a settlement before trial.

Although negotiation takes place every day, it is not easy to do well. Standard strategies for negotiation often leave people dissatisfied, worn out, or alienated—and frequently all three.

People find themselves in a dilemma. They see two ways to negotiate: soft or hard. The soft negotiator wants to avoid personal conflict and so makes concessions readily in order to reach agreement. He wants an amicable resolution; yet he often ends up exploited and feeling bitter. The hard negotiator sees any situation as a contest of wills in which the side that takes the more extreme positions and holds out longer fares better. He wants to win; yet he often ends up producing an equally hard response which exhausts him and his resources and harms his relationship with the other side. Other standard negotiating strategies fall between hard and soft, but each involves an attempted trade-off between getting what you want and getting along with people.

There is a third way to negotiate, a way neither hard nor soft, but rather both hard *and* soft. The method of *principled negotiation* . . . is to decide issues on their merits rather than through a haggling process focused on what each side says it will and won't do. It suggests that you look for mutual gains wherever possible, and that where your interests conflict, you should insist that the result be based on some fair standards independent of the will of either side. The method of principled negotiation is hard on the merits, soft on the people. It employs no tricks and no posturing. Principled negotiation

Customer	*Shopkeeper*
How much do you want for this brass dish?	That is a beautiful antique, isn't it? I guess I could let it go for $75.
Oh come on, it's dented. I'll give you $15.	Really! I might consider a serious offer, but $15 certainly isn't serious.
Well, I could go to $20, but I would never pay anything like $75. Quote me a realistic price.	You drive a hard bargain, young lady. $60 cash, right now.
$25.	It cost me a great deal more than that. Make me a serious offer.
$37.50. That's the highest I will go.	Have you noticed the engraving on that dish? Next year pieces like that will be worth twice what you pay today.

shows you how to obtain what you are entitled to and still be decent. It enables you to be fair while protecting you against those who would take advantage of your fairness. . . .

Every negotiation is different, but the basic elements do not change. Principled negotiation can be used whether there is one issue or several; two parties or many; whether there is a prescribed ritual, as in collective bargaining, or an impromptu free-for-all, as in talking with hijackers. The method applies whether the other side is more experienced or less, a hard bargainer or a friendly one. Principled negotiation is an all-purpose strategy. Unlike almost all other strategies, if the other side learns this one, it does not become more difficult to use; it becomes easier. . . .

Whether a negotiation concerns a contract, a family quarrel, or a peace settlement among nations, people routinely engage in positional bargaining. Each side takes a position, argues for it, and makes concessions to reach a compromise. The classic example of this negotiating minuet is the haggling that takes place between a customer and the proprietor of a secondhand store:

And so it goes, on and on. Perhaps they will reach agreement; perhaps not.

Any method of negotiation may be fairly judged by three criteria: It should produce a wise agreement if agreement is possible. It should be efficient. And it should improve or at least not damage the relationship between the parties. (A wise agreement can be defined as one which meets the legitimate interests of each side to the extent possible, resolves conflicting interests fairly, is durable, and takes community interests into account.)

The most common form of negotiation, illustrated by the above example, depends upon successively taking—and then giving up—a sequence of positions.

Taking positions, as the customer and storekeeper do, serves some useful purposes in a negotiation. It tells the other side what you want; it provides an anchor in an uncertain and pressured situation; and it can eventually produce the terms of an acceptable agreement. But those purposes can be served in other ways. And positional bargaining fails to meet the basic criteria of producing a wise agreement, efficiently and amicably.

ARGUING OVER POSITIONS PRODUCES UNWISE AGREEMENTS

When negotiators bargain over positions, they tend to lock themselves into those positions. The more you clarify your position and defend it against attack, the more committed you become to it. The more you try to convince the other side of the impossibility of changing your opening position, the more difficult it becomes to do so. Your ego becomes identified with your position. You now have a new interest in "saving face"—in reconciling future action with past positions—making it less and less likely that any agreement will wisely reconcile the parties' original interests.

The danger that positional bargaining will impede a negotiation was well illustrated by the breakdown of the talks under President Kennedy for a comprehensive ban on nuclear testing. A critical question arose: How many on-site inspections per year should the Soviet Union and the United States be permitted to make within the other's territory to investigate suspicious seismic events? The Soviet Union finally agreed to three inspections. The United States insisted on no less than ten. And there the talks broke down—over positions—despite the fact that no one understood whether an "inspection" would involve one person looking around for one day, or a hundred people prying indiscriminately for a month. The parties had made little attempt to design an inspection procedure that would reconcile the United States's interest in verification with the desire of both countries for minimal intrusion.

As more attention is paid to positions, less attention is devoted to meeting the underlying concerns of the parties. Agreement becomes less likely. Any agreement reached may reflect a mechanical splitting of the difference between final positions rather than a solution carefully crafted to meet the legitimate interests of the parties. The result is frequently an agreement less satisfactory to each side than it could have been.

ARGUING OVER POSITIONS IS INEFFICIENT

The standard method of negotiation may produce either agreement, as with the price of a brass dish, or breakdown, as with the number of on-site inspections. In either event, the process takes a lot of time.

Bargaining over positions creates incentives that stall settlement. In positional bargaining you try to improve the chance that any settlement reached is favorable to you by starting with an extreme position, by stubbornly holding to it, by deceiving the other party as to your true views, and by making small concessions only as necessary to keep the negotiation going. The same is true for the other side. Each of those factors tends to interfere with reaching a settlement promptly. The more extreme the opening positions and the smaller the concessions, the more time and effort it will take to discover whether or not agreement is possible.

The standard minuet also requires a large number of individual decisions as each negotiator decides what to offer, what to reject, and how much of a concession to make. Decision making is difficult and time-consuming at best. Where each decision not only involves yielding to the other side but will likely produce pressure to yield further, a negotiator has little incentive to move quickly. Dragging one's feet, threatening to walk out, stonewalling, and other such tactics become commonplace. They all increase the time and costs of reaching agreement as well as the risk that no agreement will be reached at all.

ARGUING OVER POSITIONS ENDANGERS AN ONGOING RELATIONSHIP

Positional bargaining becomes a contest of will. Each negotiator asserts what he will and won't do. The task of jointly devising an acceptable solution tends to become a battle. Each side tries through sheer willpower to force the other to change its position. "I'm not going to give in. If you want to go to the movies with me, it's *The Maltese Falcon* or nothing." Anger and resentment often result as one side sees itself bending to the rigid will of the other while its own legitimate concerns go unaddressed. Positional bargaining thus strains and sometimes shatters the relationship between the parties. Commercial enterprises that have been doing business together for years may part company. Neighbors may stop speaking to each other. Bitter feelings generated by one such encounter may last a lifetime . . . .

BEING NICE IS NO ANSWER

Many people recognize the high costs of hard positional bargaining, particularly on the parties and their relationship. They hope to avoid them by following a more gentle style of negotiation. Instead of seeing the other side as adversaries, they prefer to see them as friends. Rather than emphasizing a goal of victory, they emphasize the necessity of reaching agreement. In a soft negotiating game the standard moves are to make offers and concessions, to trust the other side, to be friendly, and to yield as necessary to avoid confrontation.

The following table illustrates two styles of positional bargaining, soft and hard. Most people see their choice of negotiating strategies as between these two styles. Looking at the table as presenting a choice, should you be a soft or a hard positional bargainer? Or should you perhaps follow a strategy somewhere in between?

PROBLEM

Positional Bargaining: Which Game Should You Play?

SOFT	HARD
Participants are friends.	Participants are adversaries.
The goal is agreement.	The goal is victory.
Make concessions to cultivate the relationship.	Demand concessions as a condition of the relationship.
Be soft on the people and the problem.	Be hard on the problem and the people.
Trust others.	Distrust others.
Change your position easily.	Dig in to your position.
Make offers.	Make threats.
Disclose your bottom line.	Mislead as to your bottom line.
Accept one-sided losses to reach agreement.	Demand one-sided gains as the price of agreement.
Search for the single answer: the one *they* will accept.	Search for the single answer: the one *you* will accept.
Insist on agreement.	Insist on your position.
Try to avoid a contest of will.	Try to win a contest of will.
Yield to pressure.	Apply pressure.

The soft negotiating game emphasizes the importance of building and maintaining a relationship. Within families and among friends much negotiation takes place in this way. The process tends to be efficient, at least to the extent of producing results quickly. As each party competes with the other in being more generous and more forthcoming, an agreement becomes highly likely. But it may not be a wise one. The results may not be as tragic as in the O. Henry story about an impoverished couple in which the loving wife sells her hair in order to buy a handsome chain for her husband's watch, and the unknowing husband sells his watch in order to buy beautiful combs for his wife's hair. However, any negotiation primarily concerned with the relationship runs the risk of producing a sloppy agreement.

More seriously, pursuing a soft and friendly form of positional bargaining makes you vulnerable to someone who plays a hard game of positional bargaining. In positional bargaining, a hard game dominates a soft one. If the hard bargainer insists on concessions and makes threats while the soft bargainer yields in order to avoid confrontation and insists on agreement, the negotiating game is biased in favor of the hard player. The process will produce an agreement, although it may not be a wise one. It will certainly be more favorable to the hard positional bargainer than to the soft one. If your response to sustained, hard positional bargaining is soft positional bargaining, you will probably lose your shirt.

THERE IS AN ALTERNATIVE

If you do not like the choice between hard and soft positional bargaining, you can change the game.

The game of negotiation takes place at two levels. At one level, negotiation addresses the substance; at another, it focuses—usually implicitly—on the procedure for dealing with the substance. The first negotiation may concern your salary, the terms of a lease, or a price to be paid. The second negotiation concerns how you will negotiate the substantive question: by soft positional bargaining, by hard positional bargaining, or by some other method. This second negotiation is a game about a game—a "meta-game." Each move you make within a negotiation is not only a move that deals with rent, salary, or other substantive questions; it also helps structure the rules of the game you are playing. Your move may serve to keep the negotiations within an ongoing mode, or it may constitute a game-changing move.

This second negotiation by and large escapes notice because it seems to occur without conscious decision. Only when dealing with someone from another country, particularly someone with a markedly different cultural background, are you likely to see the necessity of establishing some accepted process for the substantive negotiations. But whether consciously or not, you are negotiating procedural rules with every move you make, even if those moves appear exclusively concerned with substance.

The answer to the question of whether to use soft positional bargaining or hard is "neither." Change the game. . . . We have been developing an alternative to positional bargaining: a method of negotiation explicitly designed to produce wise outcomes efficiently and amicably. This method, called *principled negotiation* or *negotiation on the merits*, can be boiled down to four basic points.

These four points define a straightforward method of negotiation that can be used under almost any circumstance. Each point deals with a basic element of negotiation, and suggests what you should do about it.

People: Separate the people from the problem.

Interests: Focus on interests, not positions.

Options: Generate a variety of possibilities before deciding what to do.

Criteria: Insist that the result be based on some objective standard.

The first point responds to the fact that human beings are not computers. We are creatures of strong emotions who often have radically different perceptions and have difficulty communicating clearly. Emotions typically become entangled with the objective merits of the problem. Taking positions just makes this worse because people's egos become identified with their positions. Hence, before working on the substantive problem, the "people problem" should be disentangled from it and dealt with separately. Figuratively if not literally, the participants should come to see themselves as working side by side, attacking the problem, not each other. Hence the first proposition: *Separate the people from the problem*.

The second point is designed to overcome the drawback of focusing on people's stated positions when the object of a negotiation is to satisfy their underlying interests. A negotiating position often obscures what you really want. Compromising between positions is not likely to produce an agreement which will effectively take care of the human needs that led people to adopt those positions. The second basic element of the method is: *Focus on interests, not positions*.

The third point responds to the difficulty of designing optimal solutions while under pressure. Trying to decide in the presence of an adversary narrows your vision. Having a lot at stake inhibits creativity. So does searching for the one right solution. You can offset these constraints by setting aside a designated time within which to think up a wide range of possible solutions that advance shared interests and creatively reconcile differing interests. Hence the third basic point: Before trying to reach agreement, *invent options for mutual gain*.

Where interests are directly opposed, a negotiator may be able to obtain a favorable result simply by being stubborn. That method tends to reward intransigence and produce arbitrary results. However, you can counter such a negotiator by insisting that his single say-so is not enough and that the agreement must reflect some fair standard independent of the naked will of either side. This does not mean insisting that the terms be based on the standard you select, but only that some fair standard such as market value, expert opinion, custom, or law determine the outcome. By discussing such criteria rather than what the parties are willing or unwilling to do, neither party need give in to the other; both can defer to a fair solution. Hence the fourth basic point: *Insist on objective criteria*.

The method of principled negotiation is contrasted with hard and soft positional bargaining in the table on the next page, which shows the four basic points of the method in boldface type . . . .

"WINNING"

In 1964 an American father and his twelve-year-old son were enjoying a beautiful Saturday in Hyde

Park, London, playing catch with a Frisbee. Few in England had seen a Frisbee at that time and a small group of strollers gathered to watch this strange sport. Finally, one Homburg-clad Britisher came over to the father: "Sorry to bother you. Been watching you a quarter of an hour. Who's *winning*?"

In most instances to ask a negotiator, "Who's winning?" is as inappropriate as to ask who's winning a marriage. If you ask that question about your marriage, you have already lost the more important negotiation—the one about what kind of game to play, about the way you deal with each other and your shared and differing interests.

. . . Both theory and experience suggest that the method of principled negotiation will produce over the long run substantive outcomes as good as or better than you are likely to obtain using any other negotiation strategy. In addition, it should prove more efficient and less costly to human relationships. We find the method comfortable to use and hope you will too.

That does not mean it is easy to change habits, to disentangle emotions from the merits, or to enlist

PROBLEM

Positional Bargaining: Which Game Should You Play?

SOLUTION

Change the Game—Negotiate on the Merits

SOFT	HARD	PRINCIPLED
Participants are friends.	Participants are adversaries.	Participants are problem-solvers.
The goal is agreement.	The goal is victory.	The goal is a wise outcome reached efficiently and amicably.
Make concessions to cultivate the relationship.	Demand concessions as a condition of the relationship.	**Separate the people from the problem.**
Be soft on the people and the problem.	Be hard on the problem and the people.	Be soft on the people, hard on the problem.
Trust others.	Distrust others.	Proceed independent of trust.
Change your position easily.	Dig in to your position.	**Focus on interests, not positions.**
Make offers.	Make threats.	Explore interests.
Disclose your bottom line.	Mislead as to your bottom line.	Avoid having a bottom line.
Accept one-sided losses to reach agreement.	Demand one-sided gains as the price of agreement.	**Invent options for mutual gain.**
Search for the single answer: the one they will accept.	Search for the single answer: the one you will accept.	Develop multiple options to choose from; decide later.
Insist on agreement.	Insist on your position.	**Insist on objective criteria.**
Try to avoid a contest of will.	Try to win a contest of will.	Try to reach a result based on standards independent of will.
Yield to pressure.	Apply pressure.	Reason and be open to reasons; yield to principle, not pressure.

others in the task of working out a wise solution to a shared problem. From time to time you may want to remind yourself that the first thing you are trying to win

is a better way to negotiate—a way that avoids your having to choose between the satisfactions of getting what you deserve and of being decent. You can have both.

Charles Osgood

DISARMAMENT DEMANDS GRIT

"You cannot simultaneously prevent and prepare for war," wrote Albert Einstein. This sentiment can be carried further, to a more positive assertion: you can prevent war by getting rid of the weapons with which war is carried out. But not everyone would agree. Indeed, no one—not even the most ardent advocate of disarmament—claims that doing away with weapons will solve the problem of war. So long as the underlying causes persist, and so long as people have the capacity and inclination to resort to violence—especially organized violence—under certain circumstances, war will continue to haunt us.

Nonetheless, the connection between weaponry and war, although complex, is well established and legitimate. The dream of disarmament is thus an ancient one, intimately connected with the yearning for peace itself: "And they shall beat their swords into plowshares, and their spears into pruning hooks; nation shall not lift up sword against nation, neither shall they learn war any more" (Micah 4:3). The actual history of disarmament, however, is not especially encouraging. All too often, disarmament proposals have been self-serving, in which one side urges elimination of those weapons in which the other has an advantage or that are obsolete, or both sides make proposals simply for their publicity value, confident that they will be rejected.

Although general and complete disarmament has thus far eluded our grasp, there have been a number of modest successes, including prohibitions on specific weapons (dumdum bullets, biological agents, antiballistic missiles) as well as mutual agreements to forego forgo arms races in particular places (e.g., Antarctica, the seabed). These and other accomplishments fall within the category of disarmament's "poor sister," arms control. Arms control is controversial; within the peace studies community, it is often seen as potentially pernicious, if it shifts attention from the ultimate goal of disarmament, while also seeming to legitimize various arms races and even sometimes to accelerate them in areas not explicitly prohibited. There is also a long and sorry history of using arms control negotiations as a smoke screen to build yet more weapons under the guise that one must be able to "negotiate from strength."

However, peace specialists acknowledge four potential benefits of well-constructed arms control agreements, even if they serve largely as stopgap measures: (1) reducing

From "Disarmament Demands GRIT" by Charles Osgood, in Donald Keys and Ervin Laszlo's *Disarmament: The Human Factor*. Pergamon Press, 1981.

the chances of war breaking out (if each side becomes less worried that its opponent is accumulating weapons that makes it likely to initiate an attack); (2) reducing the destructiveness of war if it does break out (say, by eliminating weapons of mass destruction or those conventional weapons that are especially brutal); (3) reducing the economic costs of preparing for war (by permitting the redirection of society's resources away from certain weapons); and (4) developing cooperation and confidence-building, which can lead to yet further agreements (assuming that the agreed-upon measures are in fact lived up to).

Most of all, it is important to recognize that disarmament is a *process*, not an *event*, more a way of progressing than a finished masterpiece to be unveiled to the admiring world with a grand "voila!" Like perfect grace, total disarmament may never be achieved, but that doesn't diminish its worth as a goal, or, rather, as a route toward possible salvation. In the twenty-first century, with the end of the Cold War, specific disarmament proposals have received considerably less attention than in the past, with the exception of some relating to nuclear weapons (taken up later in this chapter). There has been essentially no change, however, in the necessity for international communication, even as experts and ideologues disagree as to the preferred methods.

All too often, when two parties disagree, their communication is limited to threats and—more rarely—promises. Moreover, if the situation deteriorates, there can be a rapid escalation of anger and distrust—as a result of which, things can spiral out of control. But as social psychologist Charles Osgood points out, people also have other behaviors in their repertoire, by which tensions can be ratcheted down. Osgood originally presented his formulation in an influential book titled *An Alternative to War or Surrender*, and although it was especially developed with superpower tensions in mind, it is equally applicable to daily life and to nonnuclear conflicts.

. . . The focus of my own long-term concern at the inter-nation level has been the rationalization of a strategy . . . whose technical name is "Graduated and Reciprocated Initiatives in Tension-reduction." While doodling at a conference in the early 1960s, I discovered that the initials of this mind-boggling phrase spelled out GRIT, and although I generally take a dim view of acronyms, this one was not only easy for people to remember, but also suggested the kind of determination and patience required to successfully apply it. One of the aims of GRIT is to reduce and control international tension levels. Another is to create an atmosphere of mutual trust within which negotiations on critical military and political issues can have a better chance of succeeding; in other words, GRIT is not a substitute for the more familiar process of negotiation, but rather a parallel process designed to enable a nation to take the initiative in a situation where a dangerous "balance" of mutual fear exists—and, to the degree successful, GRIT smooths the path of negotiation.

However, being unconventional in international affairs, the GRIT strategy is open to suspicion abroad and resistance at home. Therefore, it is necessary to spell out the ground rules under which this particular "game" should be played, to demonstrate how national security can be maintained during the process, how the likelihood of reciprocation can be maximized, and how the genuineness of initiations and reciprocations can be evaluated. These "rules" are spelled out in detail in my "basic" pocketbook, *An Alternative to War or Surrender*. . . .

RULES FOR MAINTAINING SECURITY

Rule 1: Unilateral initiatives must not reduce one's capacity to inflict unacceptable nuclear retaliation should one be attacked at that level.

Nuclear capacity can serve rational foreign policy (a) if it is viewed not only as a deterrent, but also as a security base from which to take limited risks in the direction of reducing tensions; (b) if the retaliatory, second-strike nature of the capacity is made explicit; and (c) if only the minimum capacity required for effective deterrence is maintained and the arms race damped. Needless to say, none of these conditions have been met to date by the two nuclear superpowers. Not only are nuclear weapons ambiguous as to initiation or retaliation, but both strategic and tactical weapons are redundantly deployed and in oversupply as far as capacity for graded response to aggression is concerned. Therefore, at some stage in the GRIT process, graduated and reciprocated reductions in nuclear weapons, along with the men that are assigned to them, should be initiated.

Rule 2: Unilateral initiatives must not cripple one's capacity to meet conventional aggression with appropriately graded conventional response.

Conventional forces are the front line of deterrence, and they must be maintained at rough parity in regions of confrontation. But the absolute level at which the balance is maintained is variable. The general rule would be to initiate unilateral moves in the regions of least tension and gradually extend them to what were originally the most tense regions.

Rule 3: Unilateral initiatives must be graduated in risk according to the degree of reciprocation obtained from an opponent.

This is the self-regulating characteristic of GRIT that keeps the process within reasonable limits of security. If bona fide reciprocations of appropriate magnitude are obtained, the magnitude and significance of subsequent steps can be increased; if not, then the process continues with a diversity of steps of about the same magnitude of risk. The relative risk thus remains roughly constant throughout the process.

Rule 4: Unilateral initiatives should be diversified in nature, both as to sphere of action and as to geographical locus of application.

The reason for diversification is twofold. First, in maintaining security, diversification minimizes weakening one's position in any one sphere (such as in combat troops) or any one geographical locus. Second, in inducing reciprocation, diversification keeps applying the pressure of initiatives having a common tension-reducing intent (and, hopefully, effect), but does not "threaten" the opponent by pushing steadily in the same sphere or locus and thereby limiting his options in reciprocating.

RULES FOR INDUCING RECIPROCATION

Rule 5: Unilateral initiatives must be designed and communicated so as to emphasize a sincere intent to reduce tensions.

Escalation and deescalation strategies cannot be "mixed" in the sense that military men talk about the "optimum mix" of weapon systems. The reason is psychological: reactions to threats (aggressive impulses) are incompatible with reactions to promises (conciliatory impulses); each strategy thus destroys the credibility of the other. It is therefore essential that a complete shift in basic policy be clearly signaled at the beginning. The top leadership of the initiating power must establish the right atmosphere by stating the overall nature of the new policy and by emphasizing its tension-reducing intent. Early initiatives must be clearly perceived as tension reducing by the opponents in conflict situations, must be of such significance that they cannot be easily discounted as "propaganda," and they must be readily verifiable. . . .

Rule 6: Unilateral initiatives should be publicly announced at some reasonable interval prior to their execution and identified as part of a deliberate policy of reducing tensions.

Prior announcements minimize the potentially unstabilizing effect of unilateral acts and their identification with total GRIT strategy helps shape the opponent's interpretation of them. However, the GRIT process cannot *begin* with a large, precipitate, and potentially destabilizing unilateral action. . . .

Rule 7: Unilateral initiatives should include in their announcement an explicit invitation to reciprocation in some form.

The purpose of this "rule" is to increase pressure on an opponent by making it clear that reciprocation of appropriate form and magnitude is essential to the momentum of GRIT, and to bring to bear pressures of world opinion. However, exactly specifying the form or magnitude of reciprocation has several drawbacks: having the tone of a demand rather than an invitation, it carries an implied threat of retaliation if the demand is not met; furthermore, the specific reciprocation requested may be based on faulty perceptions of the other's situation and this may be the reason for failure to get reciprocation. It is the occurrence of reciprocation in any form, yet having the same tension-reducing intent, that is critical. Again speaking psychologically, the greatest conciliatory impact on an opponent in a conflict situation is produced by his own, voluntary act of reciprocating. Such behavior is incompatible with his Neanderthal beliefs about the unalterable hostility and aggressiveness of the initiators, and once he *has* committed a reciprocating action, all of the cognitive pressure is on modifying these beliefs.

RULES FOR DEMONSTRATING THE GENUINENESS OF INITIATIVES AND RECIPROCATIONS

Rule 8: Unilateral initiatives that have been announced must be executed on schedule regardless of any prior commitments to reciprocate by the opponent.

This is the best indication of the firmness and bona fides of one's own intent to reduce tensions. The control over what and how much is committed is the graduated nature of the process; at the point when each initiative is announced, the calculation has been made in terms of prior-reciprocation history that this step can be taken within reasonable limits of security. Failure to execute an announced step, however, would be a clear sign of ambivalence in intent. This is particularly important in the early stages, when announced initiatives are liable to the charge of "propaganda."

Rule 9: Unilateral initiatives should be continued over a considerable period, regardless of the degree or even absence of reciprocation.

Like the steady pounding on a nail, pressure toward reciprocating builds up as one announced act follows another announced act of a tension-reducing nature, even though the individual acts may be small in significance. It is this characteristic of GRIT which at once justifies the use of the acronym and which raises the hackles of most military men. But the essence of this strategy is the calculated manipulation of the intent component of the "perceived-threat-equals-capability-times-intent" equation. It is always difficult to read the intentions of an opponent in a conflict situation and they are usually very complex. In such a situation, GRIT can be applied to consistently encourage conciliatory intents and interpretations at the expense of aggressive ones.

Rule 10: Unilateral initiatives must be as unambiguous and as susceptible to verification as possible.

Although actions do speak louder than words, even overt deeds are liable to misinterpretation. Inviting opponent verification via direct, on-the-spot observation or via indirect media observation (such as televising the act in question), along with requested reciprocation in the verification of his actions, is ideal; what little might be lost in the way of secrecy by both sides might be more than made up in a reduced need for secrecy on both sides. . . . However, the strategy of GRIT can be directly applied to this problem. Particularly in the early stages, when the risk potentials are small, observers could be publicly invited to guarantee the verifiability of doing what was announced, and although entirely *without* explicit insistence on reciprocation by the opponent, the implication would be strong indeed. Initiatives whose validities are apparently very high should be designed (for example, initial pullbacks of forces from border confrontations), and they can operate to gradually reduce suspicion and resistance to verification procedures. This should accelerate as the GRIT process continues.

APPLICATIONS OF GRIT STRATEGY

Over the past fifteen years or so there has been considerable experimentation with the GRIT strategy, but mostly in the laboratory. There have been spo-radic GRIT-like moves in the real world; for exam-ple, the graduated and reciprocated pullback of American and Soviet tanks that had been lined up practically snout-to-snout at the height of the Berlin Crisis. But for the most part in recent history, these have been one-shot affairs, always tentatively made and never reflecting any genuine change in basic strategy.

The one exception to this dictum was "the Kennedy experiment," as documented in a signifi-cant paper by Amitai Etzioni. The real-world test of a strategy of calculated deescalation was conducted in the period from June 1962 to November of 1963. The first step was President Kennedy's speech at the American University on June 10, in which he out-lined what he called "a strategy of peace," praised the Russians for their accomplishments, noted that "our problems are man-made . . . and can be solved by man," and then announced the first unilateral initiative: the United States was stopping all nuclear tests in the atmosphere, and would not resume them unless another country did. Kennedy's speech was published *in full* in both *Izvestia* and *Pravda*, with a combined circulation of 10 million. On June 15 Premier Khrushchev reciprocated with a speech wel-coming the U.S. initiative, and he announced that he had ordered the production of strategic bombers to be halted.

The next step was a symbolic reduction in the trade barriers between East and West. On October 9, President Kennedy approved the sale of $250 mil-lion worth of wheat to the Soviet Union. Although the United States had proposed a direct America-Russia communication link (the "hotline") in 1962, it was not until June 20, 1963—after the "Kennedy experiment" had begun—that the Soviets agreed to this measure. Conclusion of a test-ban treaty, long stalled, was apparently the main goal of the experi-ment. Multilateral negotiators began in earnest in

July, and on August 5, 1963, the test-ban treaty was signed. The Kennedy experiment slowed down with the deepened involvement in Vietnam, and it came to an abrupt end in Dallas.

Had this real-world experiment in calculated de-escalation been a success? To most of the initia-tives taken by either side, the other reciprocated, and the reciprocations were roughly proportional in significance. What about psychological impact? I do not think that anyone who lived through that period will deny that there was a definite warming of American attitudes toward Russians, and the same is reported for Russian attitudes toward Americans. The Russians even coined their own name for the new strategy, "the policy of mutual example."

The novelty of GRIT raises shrieks of incredulity from hawks and clucks of worry even from doves. The question I am most often asked is this: Doesn't any novel approach like this involve too much risk? Anything we do in the nuclear age means tak-ing risks. To escalate conflicts that involve another nuclear power unquestionably carries the greatest risk. Simply doing nothing—remaining frozen in a status quo that is already at much too high a level of force and tension—is certainly not without risk over the long run. GRIT also involves risk. But the risking comes in small packages. Looked at in a broad perspective, the superpower confrontation has many positive elements in it and many motiva-tions on both sides that favor détente. It therefore offers itself as a potential proving ground for a strat-egy that is novel but yet appropriate to the nuclear age in which we are trying to survive. The assump-tion behind nuclear deterrence—that we can go spinning forever into eternity, poised for mutual annihilation and kept from it only by fragile bonds of mutual fear—is untenable. The ultimate goal must be to get out from under the nuclear sword of Damocles by eliminating such weapons from the human scene.

David Krieger and Angela McCracken

TEN NUCLEAR MYTHS

Nuclear weapons represent the greatest of all violent threats to life on earth. With the end of the Cold War, a problem that had seemed as intractable as it was immense now offers exciting possibilities for genuine progress, including perhaps that ancient dream: disarmament. Even in the straitjacket of nuclear arms racing, treaties were negotiated that banned above-ground nuclear tests and restricted competition in antiballistic missiles as well as restraining nuclear proliferation. In 1996 a Comprehensive Test Ban Treaty was signed—its future marred, however, in 1998, when India, and then Pakistan, engaged in nuclear testing, as well as by the failure of the United States to ratify it.

Not surprisingly, nuclear competition in South Asia raised the specter of nuclear proliferation generally, a danger that is especially worrisome given that unlike the United States and the former U.S.S.R., India and Pakistan share a common border and have already engaged in several wars. (This problem also applies to other potential proliferators, such as Brazil and Argentina, Israel and the Arab states, etc.) Ironically, small nuclear arsenals may also be *less* secure than large ones, because they may tempt an opponent to try a "preemptive strike"; whereas in contrast, if it possessed a large supply of nuclear weapons, a country could maintain a secure "second-strike capability," being able to absorb an initial attack and still retaliate. The result, at least in theory, would be "deterrence," or at least a degree of "crisis stability." It is also possible, however, that nuclear arsenals will make hostile countries more careful and thus less likely to initiate hostilities or—if they begin—to escalate them. On the other hand, the greatest crisis stability would seem to derive from nuclear disarmament, which would have the added benefit of allowing desperately poor countries to invest in their people instead of their weapons.

With the Cold War now history, the time seems right for dramatic progress toward undoing the current reliance on nuclear weapons altogether, especially given the emergence of a new, widely recognized nuclear threat: possible use of nuclear weapons by terrorists, who might well be immune to deterrence insofar as their motivation is not traditionally "rational." In any event, some suggest that despite the manifold dangers posed by nuclear weapons, combined with the opportunity offered by the end of the Cold War, we are actually moving backward on the antinuclear front. For progress to be made, it might well be necessary for leaders as well as the public to shed some widespread nuclear myths, as identified here by David Krieger and Angela McCracken.

1. *Nuclear weapons were needed to defeat Japan in World War II.* It is widely believed, particularly in the United States, that the use of nuclear weapons against the Japanese cities of Hiroshima and Nagasaki was necessary to defeat Japan in World War II. This is not, however, the opinion of the leading U.S. military figures in the war, including General Dwight Eisenhower, General Omar Bradley, General Hap Arnold, and Admiral William Leahy. General Eisenhower, for example, who was the supreme Supreme allied Allied commander Commander in Europe during World War II and later a U.S. president, wrote, "I had been conscious of a feeling of depression and so I voiced [to Secretary of War Stimson] my grave misgivings, first on the basis of my belief that Japan was already defeated and that dropping the bomb was completely unnecessary, and secondly because I thought that our country should avoid shocking world opinion by the use of a weapon whose employment was, I thought, no longer mandatory as a measure to save American lives. It was my belief that Japan was, at that very moment, seeking some way to surrender with a minimum loss of 'face.'" Not only was the use of nuclear force unnecessary, its destructive force was excessive, resulting in 220,000 deaths by the end of 1945.

2. *Nuclear weapons prevented a war between the United States and the Soviet Union.* Many people believe that the nuclear standoff during the Cold War prevented the two superpowers from going to war with each other for fear of mutually assured destruction. While it is true that the superpowers did not engage in nuclear warfare during the Cold War, there were many confrontations between them that came uncomfortably close to nuclear war, the most prominent being the 1962 Cuban Missile Crisis. There were also many deadly conflicts and "proxy" wars carried out by the superpowers in Asia, Africa, and Latin America. The Vietnam War, which took several million Vietnamese lives and the lives of more than 58,000 Americans, is a prominent example. These wars made the supposed nuclear peace very bloody and deadly. Lurking in the background was the constant danger of a nuclear exchange. The Cold War was an exceedingly dangerous time, with a massive nuclear arms race, and the human race was extremely fortunate to have survived it without suffering a nuclear war.

3. *Nuclear weapons prevent nuclear terrorismthreats have gone away since the end of the Cold War.* In light of the Cold War's end, many people believed that nuclear threats had gone away. While the nature of nuclear threats has changed since the end of the Cold War, these threats are far from having disappeared or even significantly diminished. During the Cold War, the greatest threat was that of a massive nuclear exchange between the United States and the Soviet Union. In the aftermath of the Cold War, a variety of new nuclear threats have emerged. Among these are the following dangers:

   • Increased possibilities of nuclear weapons falling into the hands of terrorists who would not hesitate to use them;
   • Nuclear war between India and Pakistan;
   • Policies of the U.S. government to make nuclear weapons smaller and more usable;
   • Use of nuclear weapons by accident, particularly by Russia, which has a substantially weakened early- warning system; and
   • Spread of nuclear weapons to other states, such as North Korea, that may perceive them to be an "equalizer" against a more powerful state.

4. *The United States needs nuclear weapons for its national security.* There is a widespread belief in the United States that nuclear weapons are necessary for the United States to defend against aggressor states. U.S. national security, however, would be far improved if the United States took a leadership role in seeking to eliminate nuclear weapons throughout the world. Nuclear weapons are the only weapons that could actually destroy the United States, and their existence and proliferation threaten U.S. security. Continued high-alert deployment of nuclear weapons and research on smaller and more usable nuclear weapons by the United

States, combined with a more aggressive foreign policy, makes many weaker nations feel threatened. Weaker states may think of nuclear weapons as an equalizer, giving them the ability to effectively neutralize the forces of a threatening nuclear weapons state. Thus, as in the case of North Korea, the U.S. threat may be instigating nuclear weapons proliferation. Continued reliance on nuclear weapons by the United States is setting the wrong example for the world and is further endangering the country rather than protecting it. The United States has strong conventional military forces and would be far more secure in a world in which no country had nuclear arms.

5. *Nuclear weapons make a country safer.* It is a common belief that nuclear weapons protect a country by deterring potential aggressors from attacking. By threatening massive retaliation, the argument goes, nuclear weapons prevent an attacker from starting a war. To the contrary, nuclear weapons are actually undermining the safety of the countries that possess them by providing a false sense of security. While deterrence can provide some psychological sense of security, there are no guarantees that the threat of retaliation will succeed in preventing an attack. There are many ways in which deterrence could fail, including misunderstandings, faulty communications, irrational leaders, miscalculations, and accidents. In addition, the possession of nuclear weapons enhances the risks of terrorism, proliferation, and ultimately nuclear annihilation.

6. *No leader would be crazy enough to actually use nuclear weapons.* Many people believe that the threat of using nuclear weapons can go on indefinitely as a means of deterring attacks, because no leader would be crazy enough to actually use them. Unfortunately, nuclear weapons have been used, and it is likely that most, if not all, leaders possessing these weapons would, under certain conditions, actually use them. U.S. leaders, considered by many to be highly rational, are the only ones who have ever actually used nuclear weapons in war, against Hiroshima and Nagasaki. Outside of these two bombings, the leaders of nuclear weapons states have repeatedly come close to using nuclear weapons. Nuclear deterrence is based upon a believable threat of nuclear retaliation, and the threat of nuclear weapons use has been constant during the post–World War II period. U.S. policy has only in the past few years ceased to include the threat to use nuclear weapons in response to an attack with chemical or biological weapons against the United States U.S., its troops, or its allies. One of the premises of the U.S. argument for preventive war is that other leaders would be willing to attack the United States with nuclear weapons. Threats of nuclear attack by India and Pakistan provide still another example of nuclear brinksmanship that could turn into a nuclear war. Globally and historically, leaders have done their best to prove that they would use nuclear weapons. Assuming that they would not do so is unwise.

7. *Nuclear weapons are a cost-effective method of national defense.* Some have argued that nuclear weapons, with their high yield of explosive power, offer the benefit of an effective defense for minimum investment. This is one reason behind ongoing research into lower-yield tactical nuclear weapons, which would be perceived as more usable. The cost of nuclear weapons research, development, testing, deployment, and maintenance of nuclear weapons and their delivery systems, however, exceeded $5.5 exceeds $7.5 trillion by 1996(in 2005 dollars), according to a study by the Brookings Institutionfor the U.S. alone. With advances in nuclear technology and power, the costs and consequences of a nuclear war would be immeasurable.

8. *Nuclear weapons are well protected, and there is little chance that terrorists could get their hands on one.* Many people believe that nuclear weapons are well protected and that the likelihood of terrorists' obtaining these weapons is low. In the aftermath of the Cold War, however, the ability of the Russians to protect their nuclear forces has declined precipitously. In addition, a coup in a country with nuclear weapons, such as Pakistan, could lead to a government's coming to power that was willing to provide

nuclear weapons to terrorists. In general, the more nuclear weapons there are in the world and the more nuclear weapons proliferate to additional countries, the greater the possibility that nuclear weapons will end up in the hands of terrorists. The best remedy for keeping nuclear weapons out of the hands of terrorists is to drastically reduce their numbers and institute strict international inspections and controls on all nuclear weapons and weapons-grade nuclear materials in all countries, until these weapons and the materials for making them can be eliminated.

9. *The United States is working to fulfill its nuclear disarmament obligations.* Most U.S. citizens believe that the United States is working to fulfill its nuclear disarmament obligations. In fact, the United States has failed to fulfill its obligations under Article VI of the Nuclear Non-Proliferation Treaty, requiring good faith negotiations to achieve nuclear disarmament, for more than forty years. The United States has failed to ratify the Comprehensive Test Ban Treaty and has withdrawn from the Anti-Ballistic Missile Treaty. The 2010 Strategic Arms Reduction Treaty (New START) between Russia and the United States reduces the number of deployed strategic nuclear weapons to 1,550 on each side, but allows for additional nuclear weapons to be held in reserve, and it fails to adhere to the principle of irreversibility agreed to at the 2000 Non-Proliferation Treaty Review Conference. The treaty allows maximum flexibility for rearmament rather than irreversible reductions in nuclear arms. Nuclear weapons taken off active deployment will be put in storage, where they will actually become more vulnerable in both the United StatesU.S. and Russia to theft by terrorists.

10. *Nuclear weapons are needed to combat threats from terrorists and "rogue states."* It has been argued that nuclear weapons are needed to protect against terrorists and "rogue states." Yet nuclear weapons, whether used for deterrence or as offensive weaponry, are not effective for this purpose. The threat of nuclear force cannot act as a deterrent against terrorists, because they do not have a territory to retaliate against. Thus, terrorists would not be prevented from attacking a country for fear of nuclear retaliation. Nuclear weapons also cannot be relied on as a deterrent against "rogue states," because their responses to a nuclear threat may be irrational and deterrence relies on rationality. If the leaders of a rogue state do not use the same calculus regarding their losses from retaliation, nuclear deterrence can fail. As offensive weaponry, nuclear force only promises tremendous destruction to troops, civilians, and the environment. It might work to annihilate a rogue state, but the amount of force entailed in using nuclear weaponry is indiscriminate, disproportionate, and highly immoral. It would not be useful against terrorists, because strategists could not be certain of locating an appropriate target for retaliation.

George P. Shultz, William J. Perry, Henry A. Kissinger, and Sam Nunn

A WORLD FREE OF NUCLEAR WEAPONS

Sometimes a message is less important than—or, more accurately, its impact is greatly enhanced by—the identity of the messengers. This is especially true in the case of the following article, which appeared in the *Wall Street Journal* (recognized as the leading conservative newspaper in the United States) and was written by four prominent, pro-military members of the U.S. national security "establishment." George P. Shultz was secretary of state under President Ronald Reagan; William J. Perry had been secretary of defense under President Bill Clinton; Henry A. Kissinger was national security advisor and secretary of state under Presidents Nixon and Ford; and Sam Nunn was a longtime U.S. senator and chair of the U.S. Senate Armed Services Committee. Their endorsement in 2007 of a world free of nuclear weapons has therefore been especially influential, giving added credibility to a goal long advocated by peace activists.

Nuclear weapons today present tremendous dangers, but also an historic opportunity. U.S. leadership will be required to take the world to the next stage—to a solid consensus for reversing reliance on nuclear weapons globally as a vital contribution to preventing their proliferation into potentially dangerous hands, and ultimately ending them as a threat to the world.

Nuclear weapons were essential to maintaining international security during the Cold War because they were a means of deterrence. The end of the Cold War made the doctrine of mutual Soviet-American deterrence obsolete. Deterrence continues to be a relevant consideration for many states with regard to threats from other states. But reliance on nuclear weapons for this purpose is becoming increasingly hazardous and decreasingly effective.

North Korea's recent nuclear test and Iran's refusal to stop its program to enrich uranium—potentially to weapons grade—highlight the fact that the world is now on the precipice of a new and dangerous nuclear era. Most alarmingly, the likelihood that nonstate terrorists will get their hands on nuclear weaponry is increasing. In today's war waged on world order by terrorists, nuclear weapons are the ultimate means of mass devastation. And nonstate terrorist groups with nuclear weapons are conceptually outside the bounds of a deterrent strategy and present difficult new security challenges.

Apart from the terrorist threat, unless urgent new actions are taken, the U.S. soon will be compelled to enter a new nuclear era that will be more precarious, psychologically disorienting, and economically even more costly than was Cold War deterrence. It is far from certain that we can successfully replicate the old Soviet-American "mutually assured destruction" with an increasing number of potential nuclear enemies worldwide without dramatically increasing the risk that nuclear weapons will be used. New nuclear states do not have the benefit of years of step-by-step safeguards put in effect during the Cold War to prevent nuclear accidents, misjudgments, or unauthorized launches. The United States and the Soviet Union learned from mistakes that were less than fatal. Both countries were diligent to ensure that no nuclear weapon was used during the Cold War by design or by accident. Will new nuclear nations and the world be as fortunate in the next fifty years as we were during the Cold War?

⌒

Leaders addressed this issue in earlier times. In his "Atoms for Peace" address to the United Nations in 1953, Dwight D. Eisenhower pledged America's "determination to help solve the fearful atomic dilemma—to devote its entire heart and mind to find the way by which the miraculous inventiveness of man shall not be dedicated to his death, but consecrated to his life." John F. Kennedy, seeking to break the logjam on nuclear disarmament, said, "The world was not meant to be a prison in which man awaits his execution."

Rajiv Gandhi, addressing the UN General Assembly on June 9, 1988, appealed, "Nuclear war will not mean the death of 100 million people. Or even 1,000 million. It will mean the extinction of 4,000 million: the end of life as we know it on our planet Earth. We come to the United Nations to seek your support. We seek your support to put a stop to this madness."

Ronald Reagan called for the abolishment of "all nuclear weapons," which he considered to be "totally irrational, totally inhumane, good for nothing but killing, possibly destructive of life on earth and civilization." Mikhail Gorbachev shared this vision, which had also been expressed by previous American presidents.

Although Reagan and Mr. Gorbachev failed at Reykjavik to achieve the goal of an agreement to get rid of all nuclear weapons, they did succeed in turning the arms race on its head. They initiated steps leading to significant reductions in deployed long- and intermediate-range nuclear forces, including the elimination of an entire class of threatening missiles.

What will it take to rekindle the vision shared by Reagan and Mr. Gorbachev? Can a worldwide consensus be forged that defines a series of practical steps leading to major reductions in the nuclear

danger? There is an urgent need to address the challenge posed by these two questions.

The Non-Proliferation Treaty (NPT) envisioned the end of all nuclear weapons. It provides (a) that states that did not possess nuclear weapons as of 1967 agree not to obtain them, and (b) that states that do possess them agree to divest themselves of these weapons over time. Every president of both parties since Richard Nixon has reaffirmed these treaty obligations, but nonnuclear weapon states have grown increasingly skeptical of the sincerity of the nuclear powers.

Strong nonproliferation efforts are under way. The Cooperative Threat Reduction program, the Global Threat Reduction Initiative, the Proliferation Security Initiative, and the Additional Protocols are innovative approaches that provide powerful new tools for detecting activities that violate the NPT and endanger world security. They deserve full implementation. The negotiations on proliferation of nuclear weapons by North Korea and Iran, involving all the permanent members of the Security Council plus Germany and Japan, are crucially important. They must be energetically pursued.

But by themselves, none of these steps [is] adequate to the danger. Reagan and General Secretary Gorbachev aspired to accomplish more at their meeting in Reykjavik twenty years ago—the elimination of nuclear weapons altogether. Their vision shocked experts in the doctrine of nuclear deterrence, but galvanized the hopes of people around the world. The leaders of the two countries with the largest arsenals of nuclear weapons discussed the abolition of their most powerful weapons.

⌒

What should be done? Can the promise of the NPT and the possibilities envisioned at Reykjavik be brought to fruition? We believe that a major effort should be launched by the United States to produce a positive answer through concrete stages.

First and foremost is intensive work with leaders of the countries in possession of nuclear weapons to turn the goal of a world without nuclear weapons into a joint enterprise. Such a joint enterprise, by involving changes in the disposition of the states possessing nuclear weapons, would lend additional weight to efforts already under way to avoid the emergence of a nuclear-armed North Korea and Iran.

The program on which agreements should be sought would constitute a series of agreed and urgent steps that would lay the groundwork for a world free of the nuclear threat. Steps would include:

- Changing the Cold War posture of deployed nuclear weapons to increase warning time and thereby reduce the danger of an accidental or unauthorized use of a nuclear weapon.
- Continuing to reduce substantially the size of nuclear forces in all states that possess them.
- Eliminating short-range nuclear weapons designed to be forward-deployed.
- Initiating a bipartisan process with the Senate, including understandings to increase confidence and provide for periodic review, to achieve ratification of the Comprehensive Test Ban Treaty, taking advantage of recent technical advances, and working to secure ratification by other key states.
- Providing the highest possible standards of security for all stocks of weapons, weapons-usable plutonium, and highly enriched uranium everywhere in the world.
- Getting control of the uranium enrichment process, combined with the guarantee that uranium for nuclear power reactors could be obtained at a reasonable price, first from the Nuclear Suppliers Group and then from the International Atomic Energy Agency (IAEA) or other controlled international reserves. It will also be necessary to deal with proliferation issues presented by spent fuel from reactors producing electricity.
- Halting the production of fissile material for weapons globally; phasing out the use of highly enriched uranium in civil commerce; and removing weapons-usable uranium from research facilities around the world and rendering the materials safe.
- Redoubling our efforts to resolve regional confrontations and conflicts that give rise to new nuclear powers.

Achieving the goal of a world free of nuclear weapons will also require effective measures to impede or counter any nuclear-related conduct that is potentially threatening to the security of any state or peoples.

Reassertion of the vision of a world free of nuclear weapons and practical measures toward achieving that goal would be, and would be perceived as, a bold initiative consistent with America's moral heritage. The effort could have a profoundly positive impact on the security of future generations. Without the bold vision, the actions will not be perceived as fair or urgent. Without the actions, the vision will not be perceived as realistic or possible.

We endorse setting the goal of a world free of nuclear weapons and working energetically on the actions required to achieve that goal, beginning with the measures outlined above.

Jonathan Schell

A POWERFUL PEACE

Jonathan Schell helped energize the antinuclear movement of the 1980s with *The Fate of the Earth*, his eloquent description of the consequences of nuclear war. In a subsequent book, *The Gift of Time*, Schell argued for a more activist antinuclear policy, distinguishing between "vertical" and "horizontal" nuclear weapons accumulation, with the former referring to increased weaponry on the part of countries already possessing them, and the latter, to the proliferation of nuclear weapons among countries not currently identified as "nuclear powers." Many opponents of nuclear proliferation do not acknowledge that to a large extent, horizontal expansion of nuclear weapons is a consequence of its vertical counterpart, with previously nonnuclear countries justifying their acquisition of nuclear weapons by the refusal of nuclear-armed states to give up theirs. The following selection provides a brief, step-by-step agenda for achieving a nonnuclear world.

With each year that passes, nuclear weapons provide their possessors with less safety while provoking more danger. Possession of nuclear arms provokes proliferation. Both nourish the global nuclear infrastructure, which in turn enlarges the possibility of acquisition by terrorist groups.

The step that is needed to break this cycle can be as little doubted as the source of the problem. The double standard of nuclear "haves" and "have-nots" must be replaced by a single standard, which can only be the goal of a world free of all nuclear weapons.

What is it that prevents sensible steps toward nuclear abolition from being taken? The answer cannot be in doubt, either. It is the resolve of the world's nuclear powers to hold on to their nuclear arsenals. Countries that already have nuclear arms cite proliferation as their reason for keeping them, and those lacking nuclear arms seek them in large measure because they feel menaced by those with them.

A double-standard regime is a study in futility—a divided house that cannot stand. Its advocates preach what they have no intention of practicing. It is up to the nuclear powers to take the first step.

Their nuclear arsenals would be the largest pile of bargaining chips ever brought to any negotiating table. More powerful as instruments of peace than they ever can be for war, they would likely be more than adequate for winning agreements from the nonnuclear powers that would choke off proliferation forever.

The art of the negotiation would be to pay for strict, inspectable, enforceable nonproliferation and nuclear-materials-control agreements in the coin of existing nuclear bombs. What would be the price to the nuclear powers, for example, of a surrender by the nuclear-weapons-free states of their rights to the troublesome nuclear fuel cycle, which stands at the heart of the proliferation dilemma? Perhaps reductions by Russia and the United States from two thousand to a few hundred weapons each plus ratification of the Comprehensive Test Ban Treaty?

Further reductions, now involving the other nuclear powers, might pay for establishment and

Reprinted from "Superpower? Get Over It," the Summer 2008 *YES! Magazine*, 284 Madrona Way NE Ste 116, Bainbridge Island, WA 98110. Subscriptions: 800/937–4451. Web: www.yesmagazine.org.

practice of inspections of ever-greater severity, and still further reductions might buy agreements on enforcement of the final ban on nuclear arms. When nuclear weapons holdings reached zero, former nuclear weapons states and nonnuclear weapons states, abolitionists all, would exercise a unanimous will to manage, control, roll back, and extirpate all nuclear weapon technology.

A world from which nuclear weapons had been banned would, of course, not be without its dangers, including nuclear ones. But we must ask how they would compare with those now approaching.

Let us suppose that the nuclear powers had agreed to move step by step toward eliminating their own arsenals. The iron chains of fear that link all the nuclear arsenals in the world would then be replaced by bonds of reassurance. Knowing that Russia and the United States were disarming, China could agree to disarm. Knowing that China was disarming, India could agree to disarm. Knowing that India was ready to disarm, Pakistan could agree to disarm as well. Any country that decided otherwise would find itself up against the sort of united global will so conspicuous by its absence today.

During the Cold War, the principal objection in the United States to a nuclear-weapon-free world was that you could not get there. That objection melted away with the Soviet Union, and today the principal objection is that even if you could get there, you would not want to be there. The arguments usually begin with the observation that nuclear weapons can never be disinvented, and that a world free of nuclear weapons is therefore at worst a mirage, at best a highly dangerous place to be. It is supposedly a mirage because, even if the hardware is removed, the know-how remains. It is said to be highly dangerous because the miscreant rearmer, now in possession of a nuclear monopoly, would be able to dictate terms to a helpless, terrorized world or, alternately, precipitate a helter-skelter, many-sided nuclear arms race.

This conclusion seems reasonable until you notice that history has taught an opposite lesson. Repeatedly, even the greatest nuclear powers have actually lost wars against tiny, backward nonnuclear adversaries without being able to extract the slightest

utility from their colossal arsenals. Think of the Soviet Union in Afghanistan, or the U.S. in Vietnam, or Britian in Suez.

If, in the sixty years of the nuclear age, no great power has won a war by making nuclear threats against even tiny, weak adversaries, then how could a nuclear monopoly by a small country enable it to coerce and bully the whole world? The danger cannot be wholly discounted, but it is surely greatly exaggerated.

If the nuclear powers wish to be safe from nuclear weapons, they must surrender their own. They should collectively offer the world's nonnuclear powers a deal of stunning simplicity, inarguable fairness, and patent common sense: we will get out of the nuclear weapon business if you stay out of it. Then we will all work together to assure that everyone abides by the commitment.

The united will of the human species to save itself from destruction would be a force to be reckoned with.

HOW WE CAN DO IT

The United States, as the owner of the biggest nuclear arsenal, must take the initiative and lead the world to take these steps:

DE-ALERT. Take nuclear weapons off high alert; separate warheads from missiles.

NO FIRST USE. Agree to binding bans on first use of nuclear weapons.

NO NEW WEAPONS. Ban research and development of all new nuclear weapons.

BAN NUCLEAR TESTING FOREVER. Bring into force the Comprehensive Test Ban Treaty.

CONTROL NUCLEAR MATERIAL. Create a verifiable treaty to bring all weapons-grade nuclear material and the technology to create it under strict international control.

NUCLEAR WEAPONS CONVENTION. Start negotiations, as required by the Non-Proliferation Treaty, for the phased, verifiable, and irreversible elimination of weapons.

RESOURCES FOR PEACE. Spend the tens of billions now spent for nuclear arms on national and global humanitarian projects.

Volha Charnysh

NUCLEAR PROLIFERATION: HISTORY AND LESSONS

For many years, the specter of nuclear war involved the so-called superpowers, the United States and the Soviet Union. The danger of worldwide thermonuclear war did not disappear with the collapse of the Soviet Union and the ensuing end of the Cold War. However, much of the public's anxiety did in fact dissipate at that time, only to be reawakened in the form of worry about nuclear weapons falling into the hands of terrorists, "failed states," or other entities (notably North Korea and Iran) widely perceived to be less responsible than the original nuclear states. In addition, the danger has arisen that various countries—especially Israel and/or the United States—might respond to the threat of nuclear proliferation by preemptively attacking a presumed would-be proliferator. In this selection, Volha Charnysh examines the history and status of nuclear proliferation, pointing out, among other things, that the acknowledged nuclear powers—particularly the United States—have not only an interest in reducing and/or preventing proliferation, but also the opportunity to do so.

In the last hundred years, life expectancy has doubled and many deadly illnesses have been eradicated. The world would be a better place to live had these and other astonishing scientific discoveries not been devalued by nuclear weapons—an invention that could destroy life on earth. Fredrick Soddy, who together with Ernest Rutherford discovered in 1901 that radioactivity involved the release of energy, described an atomic future in which humanity could "transform a desert continent, thaw the frozen poles, and make the whole Earth one smiling Garden of Eden."[7] Although the poles are indeed thawing, the Earth hardly looks like paradise.

Today, nine states have nuclear weapons and are estimated to be collectively spending approximately one hundred billion dollars on their nuclear programs.[8] Citizens of these countries are paying a heavy price in taxes—sometimes also in sanctions—and many have sacrificed opportunities for economic and educational development to build and maintain weapons that could destroy their lives. Another forty or more states have the technological capacity to acquire nuclear weapons if they wish.

Under the first Obama administration, a number of important landmarks were achieved. The 2010 US Nuclear Posture Review reduced the role of nuclear weapons in US policy. Washington signed a long-awaited strategic weapons reduction treaty (New START) with Russia. Several Nuclear Security Summits have been held. But larger issues remain unresolved: the Comprehensive Test Ban Treaty (CTBT) is no closer to ratification. The Fissile Material Cutoff

---

[7] Richard E. Sclove, "From Alchemy to Atomic War: Frederick Soddy's 'Technology Assessment' of Atomic Energy, 1900–1915," *Science, Technology, & Human Values*, Vol. 14, No. 2 (Spring 1989), pp. 163–194: 170.
[8] Global Zero, "World spending on nuclear weapons surpasses $1 trillion per decade" (2011), http://www.globalzero.org/en/page/cost-of-nukes. Accessed July 27, 2012.

Treaty (FMCT) negotiations reached an impasse. Even as the United States and Russia are reducing their nuclear arsenals, nuclear powers outside the Non-Proliferation Treaty (NPT), have built (North Korea) or appear to be building (Iran) their own, and a revived nuclear arms race—between India and Pakistan—is a possibility. These developments are occurring in an increasingly uncertain international environment—with the Israeli-Palestinian conflict ongoing, the "war on terrorism" unfinished, and the Middle East destabilized by anti-regime protests in the Arab states.

LESSONS FROM NUCLEAR PROLIFERATION HISTORY

Fear and Pride Motivated States to Build the Bomb

Few would openly dispute that nuclear weapons are extremely dangerous, that building a nuclear arsenal is costly, or that proliferation should be prevented, or at least minimized. But even though nearly everyone condemns the atomic bomb, moral considerations have failed to stop states from seeking nuclear weapons.

Examining proliferation history, one comes across decisions made in fear, on one hand, and pride, on the other.[9] In 1939, fearing that Hitler's Germany would acquire the atomic bomb first, the United States launched a secret nuclear program in cooperation with the United Kingdom. To catch up with the United States after the bomb's destructive power was demonstrated in Hiroshima and Nagasaki, the increasingly isolated Soviet Union launched a full-speed secret nuclear weapons program. The US and Soviet hydrogen bomb tests in 1952 and 1954, respectively, led the British government to launch an effort to develop its own thermonuclear weapons. Having suffered a crushing political defeat by a former colony (Egypt) in the Suez Crisis, and feeling rebuked by its nuclear-armed ally (the United

States), France decided to reinforce its global status by obtaining an independent nuclear deterrent in the 1950s.

China's nuclear program originated under threat from the Western arsenals. Its fear was not without grounds: Washington contemplated bombing Beijing during the Korean war and then later to prevent it from developing its own nuclear arsenal.[10] India's nuclear ambitions, in turn, were spurred by the fear of China's program, and its first nuclear test was also timed to boost its status vis-à-vis Pakistan. Pakistan's nuclear weapons were meant to counter India's: Ali Bhutto, who established the Pakistani nuclear program in 1972, remarked that his people would "eat grass" to keep up.[11]

Israel hoped its nuclear arsenal would deter its many enemies in the Middle East. Iran claims that it is threatened by Israel and the United States. North Korea invokes the danger emanating from South Korea (which had enriched uranium to levels near weapons grade but then stopped[12]), as well as from the United States and the West in general. Furthermore, it can be argued that the nuclear ambitions of North Korea and Iran were generated at least in part by the "lessons" their leaders learned by observing the U.S.-led invasion of Iraq: namely, that possessing nuclear weapons might protect them from the same fate. Similarly, the five nuclear members of the Security Council use fear of other states acquiring nuclear weapons to justify dragging their feet on nuclear disarmament required of them by Article VI of the NPT.

---

[9] Jacques Hymans provides an excellent research and analysis of proliferants' intentions by examining four nuclear proliferation cases in his book. Jacques Hymans, *Psychology of Nuclear Proliferation: Identity, Emotions and Foreign Policy*. Cambridge University Press (2006).

---

[10] Cited in Gordon H. Chang, "JFK, China, and the Bomb," *The Journal of American History*, Vol. 74, No. 4 (Mar. 1988), pp. 1287–1310: 1287.
[11] William Epstein, "Why States Go—and Don't Go—Nuclear," *Annals of the American Academy of Political and Social Science*, Vol. 430, *Nuclear Proliferation: Prospects, Problems, and Proposals* (Mar. 1977), pp. 16–28: 19.
[12] "The official position is that 'it was a one-time experiment conducted without government authorization and it was geared toward the country's nuclear energy program.' Ironically, 'without the authorization or knowledge of the government' was also an explanation offered by Pakistan in explaining the rogue activities of Dr A. Q. Khan in the realm of global nuclear proliferation." Ehsan Ahrari, "Nuclear Genie Out of S Korean Bottle," *Asia Times*, Sep. 8, 2004. http://www.atimes.com/atimes/Korea/FI08Dg05.html. Accessed July 5, 2009.

Nuclear weapons have always been a status symbol as well. The leaders of France and the UK launched the nuclear weapons program primarily in quest for national grandeur. Charles de Gaulle greeted the first French nuclear test with words "Hurray for France! From this morning she is stronger and prouder!"[13] A Bharatiya Janata (Hindu nationalist) Party spokesman expressed similar feelings about the Indian bomb: "Nuclear weapons will give us prestige, power, standing. An Indian will talk straight and walk straight when we have the bomb."[14] Pakistan prided itself on being the first Muslim state to build the bomb. As William Epstein notes, because of their nuclear weapons capability, the United Kingdom and France, who have fallen behind Japan and Germany in economic strength, are still regarded as great powers, and China and India are also treated as having achieved great power status.[15]

Since it divides the world into nuclear "haves" and "have-nots," the non-proliferation regime increases the pride and envy of the nuclear "have-nots." Many countries explain their decisions to go nuclear by the need to overcome nuclear apartheid, racism, or discrimination on religious grounds.[16] The reluctance of the nuclear powers to further reduce their own arsenals has raised the apparent value of nuclear weapons and has increased other states' desire to nuclearize.

Status Concerns Can Also Contribute to Nuclear Disarmament

Currently there is a strong stigma against using nuclear weapons, but very little against acquiring them.[17] Although being caught violating the NPT may lead to international isolation, those states that succeeded in developing nuclear weapons have been respected or at least feared.

Even so, more countries have abandoned their nuclear ambitions than have chosen to build and retain nuclear arsenals. Nuclear programs were dismantled by states that no longer faced existential threats and that saw a chance to improve their international status by adhering to the non-proliferation regime. For example, three post-Soviet states—Ukraine, Belarus, and Kazakhstan—gave up the arsenals they had inherited from the Soviet Union, in order to obtain Western recognition as responsible, independent states and join international institutions.[18] South Africa gave up its nuclear program because accession to the NPT was seen as a chance to end international isolation at the time when the security threats that led to building the weapons dissipated.[19] These experiences suggest that if keeping a nuclear arsenal becomes a political liability and undermines rather than raises international status, proliferation will stop or at least be limited to states that face existential threats.

Civilian and Military Uses of Nuclear Energy Are Too Close for Comfort

There is an inseparable link between civilian and military uses of nuclear energy. Most of the countries presenting proliferation challenges today got a foot in the door of the nuclear club by developing civilian nuclear programs with the assistance of a nuclear weapon state. In 1953 the United States introduced the Atoms for Peace program to share peaceful nuclear technology with states that renounced nuclear weapons. Its positive contribution notwithstanding, this program accelerated the global spread of nuclear weapons technology as the United States and the Soviet Union provided research reactors in order to establish strategic ties with developing countries.[20] The United States signed more than 40 such nuclear cooperation agreements, including treaties with apartheid South Africa and India (both

[13] Marcel Duval and Dominique Mongin, *Histoire des Forces Nucleaires Francaises depuis 1945* (Paris: Presses Universitaires de France, 1993), p. 46.

[14] George Perkovich, "Nuclear Proliferation," *Foreign Policy*, No. 112 (Fall 1998), pp. 12–23: 16.

[15] Epstein, 21.

[16] For example, India, South Africa, Argentina, Iran, and Brazil. Perkovich, 21.

[17] Nina Tannenwald, *The Nuclear Taboo: The United States and the Non-Use of Nuclear Weapons since 1945*. New York: Cambridge University Press (2007).

[18] Zaitseva, pp. 27–30.

[19] J. W. de Villiers, Roger Jardine and Mitchell Reiss. "Why South Africa Gave up the Bomb," *Foreign Affairs* (Nov./Dec. 1993).

[20] Zia Mian & Alexander Glaser, "A frightening Nuclear Legacy," *Bulletin of the Atomic Scientists*, Vol. 64, No. 4 (Sep./Oct. 2008), pp. 42–47: 42.

of which later built nuclear weapons).[21] The Soviet Union assisted China and North Korea (both nuclear powers today). Iran and Iraq also used the Atoms for Peace program and their NPT membership to receive technology useful for developing nuclear weapons.[22]

About 31 countries currently use nuclear reactors for electricity production, and more than 60 countries have expressed an interest in acquiring them.[23] The number of states developing or expanding nuclear power capacity is growing, although it appears that mostcountries that employ nuclear power do not intend to build nuclear weapons. However, the spread of civilian nuclear capabilities expands the potential for proliferation by significantly reducing the number of additional steps needed to build a bomb. The rise in demand for nuclear technology occurs at the time when the nuclear industry is incentivized to lobby for "denuclearization" of its activities—such as uranium trade—in order to obtain freedom from national and international oversight and earn higher profit.[24] The fewer activities are considered nuclear, the fewer restrictions on the industry, and the more likely that a sale of sensitive technology will be approved or that purchases on the uranium market will go unmonitored. These incentives to commercialize nuclear materials and equipment and sell them with little oversight, combined with the increasing complexity of transactions in nuclear trade, increase the probability that in the long run leaders of some new nuclear-capable states will succeed in acquiring the bomb.

Proliferation Hinges on Political Decisions that More and More States Are Able to Make

While virtually every state is guided by security and status considerations, only a few ended up building

the "ultimate weapon." In the end, the acquisition of nuclear weapons is a political choice. It is a political choice whether to adhere to the NPT and comply with the IAEA safeguards. It is political reverberations that are faced by any violator of international non-proliferation norms. Finally, it is changing internal political realities rather than external pressures or moral considerations that explain why the states that eventually rolled back their nuclear programs did so. Realizing this is important if we are to come up with adequate measures to curb proliferation.

Structuring political incentives correctly is increasingly relevant today when most technologically advanced nonnuclear weapon states with civilian nuclear capabilities can quickly assemble and deploy full-fledged nuclear arsenals if they choose to do so.[25] This was acknowledged by Mohamed El-Baradei, the outgoing director general of the International Atomic Energy Agency (IAEA), who predicted that the next wave of proliferation would involve "virtual nuclear weapon states"—those that can produce plutonium or highly enriched uranium and possess the know-how to make warheads, but stop just short of assembling a weapon, thereby remaining technically compliant with the NPT.[26]

The case of Japan is instructive in this regard. While Japan has not actually developed or manufactured nuclear weapons, its advanced technological infrastructure can likely overcome this limitation within a few months. Japan's long-standing plutonium program, its geopolitical position, and its geostrategic vulnerability to an attack from North Korea make it possible that the country will consider an independent deterrent.

With the inevitable spread of "dual-use" nuclear technologies (weapons and reactors), virtual arsenals are becoming a global phenomenon. Looking into the future, it may no longer be necessary to build actual nuclear weapons to rely on nuclear

[21] Leonard Weiss, "Atoms for Peace," *Bulletin of the Atomic Scientists*, Vol. 59, No. 6 (Nov./Dec. 2003), pp. 34–44.
[22] Weiss, 44.
[23] IAEA, "International Status and Prospects of Nuclear Power." Board of Governors General Conference, GOV/INF/2010/12-GC (54)/INF/5, (Sep. 2, 2011), http://www.iaea.org/Publications/Booklets/NuclearPower/np10.pdf. Accessed July 28, 2012.
[24] Gabrielle Hecht, "An Elemental Force: Uranium Production in Africa, and What It Means to Be Nuclear," *Bulletin of the Atomic Scientists*, Vol. 68, No. 2, pp. 22–33.

[25] Joseph F. Pilat, "Virtual Nuclear Weapons," U.S. Institute for Peace, http://www.osti.gov/bridge/servlets/purl/615627-yBBEOO/webviewable/615627.pdf. Accessed July 19, 2009.
[26] Julian Borger, "Mohamed ElBaradei Warns of New Nuclear Age," *Guardian*, May 24, 2009, http://www.guardian.co.uk/world/2009/may/14/elbaradei-nuclear-weapons-states-un. Accessed July 19, 2009.

deterrence. While this may provide incentives for the current nuclear weapons states to reduce their arsenals, a world in which most states deter each other with fully-formed weapons infrastructure instead of the capability to divert dual-use technologies toward building such infrastructure will hardly be safer. The more states have nuclear capabilities, the more complex and unstable the global web of rivalries and corresponding deterrence dyads becomes.[27]

Existing Treaties and Agencies Are a Necessary but Insufficient Proliferation Barrier

Anti-proliferation measures remain a step behind the ever-changing proliferation challenges. First, the existing non-proliferation controls are out of date: the major treaties (NPT, CTBT) reflect exclusively state-centric solutions to the problem and focus on the physical aspects of nuclear weapons.[28] Second, the agencies in charge of maintaining nuclear governance, notably the IAEA, are politicized and thus unable to perform their tasks effectively.

Today's proliferation risks are qualitatively different from those envisioned at the time the NPT was signed and the IAEA established. It is no longer enough to guard against the intentions of a pariah head of state. Nuclear capabilities and responsible leadership do not prevent states from failing. Weak nuclear weapon states present proliferation risks of their own, as the uncovering of A. Q. Khan's proliferation network showed; Dr. Khan was intimately involved in Pakistan's nuclear weapons program, and subsequently found to have sold nuclear "secrets" to other countries. Even in strong states, sophisticated technologies are increasingly transferred to private hands.[29] If espionage and state-to-state transactions were the means of acquiring nuclear materials a few decades ago, the private sector and the nuclear black market can help states seeking nuclear technology today.[30] Violations become harder to detect and the new types of violators are immune to deterrence, sanctions, and international condemnation.

Upholding non-proliferation norms is becoming secondary to the economic benefits of globalization, as recent nuclear cooperation agreements (US–India, France–Pakistan) demonstrate. The global financial crisis may have increased the proliferant opportunities as financially stressed but nuclear-capable states are more likely to sell sensitive technologies to third parties.

Although the malicious software, Stuxnet, was successfully used to stem proliferation by damaging Iran's nuclear facilities,[31] the impact was only temporary and advances in cyber space are presenting additional challenges to nuclear deterrence and security. The Internet is open to a wide range of actors and its relative anonymity allows actions free of reputational constraints and with relative impunity. Just between 2009 and 2011, computer attacks by criminal gangs, hackers and other nations on US infrastructure increased 17-fold.[32] Technological revolutions have democratized access to nuclear know-how and controlling knowledge is problematic, since it may mean infringing on scientific freedom. Unfortunately, the IAEA system of declarations and inspections aimed at identifying physical aspects of proliferation cannot detect the spread of dangerous nuclear knowledge and expertise.[33]

---

[27] See Christopher Ford, "Weapons Reconstitution and Strategic Stability," Remarks at the Oak Ridge National Laboratory, in Oak Ridge, Tennessee (May 17, 2011), http://www.hudson.org/index.cfm?fuseaction=publication_details&id=9056. Accessed July 28, 2012.

[28] See Pilat.

[29] E.g., Michel Berthélemy, "What drives innovation in nuclear reactors technologies? An empirical study based on patent counts," Working Paper 12-ME-01, Interdisciplinary Institute for Innovation (January 2012).

[30] See "Nuclear black markets: other countries and networks" (Chapter 2). In *Nuclear Black Markets: Pakistan, A.Q. Khan and the rise of proliferation networks: A net assessment*, International Institute of Strategic Studies, http://www.iiss.org/publications/strategic-dossiers/nbm/ Accessed July 30, 2012.

[31] Nazli Choucri and Daniel Goldsmith, "Lost in Cyberspace: Harnessing the Internet, International Relations, and Global Security," *Bulletin of the Atomic Scientists*, Vol. 68, No. 2, pp. 70–77.

[32] "Rise Is Seen in Cyberattacks Targeting U.S. Infrastructure," *The New York Times*, July 26, 2012, http://www.nytimes.com/2012/07/27/us/cyberattacks-are-up-national-security-chief-says.html?ref=world. Accessed July 28, 2012.

[33] Pilat.

Although the intentions of states choosing not to join the NPT are apparent (for example, India from the very beginning decided not to commit to a nonnuclear status), those of the 188 NPT members are less straightforward. Even the five members of the UN Security Council (not coincidentally, all nuclear states) are hardly abiding by the NPT to the letter. Whereas Article VI of the treaty commits nuclear states to "good faith" negotiation toward nuclear disarmament, progress in this regard has been notably slow. Moreover, as the case of North Korean withdrawal from the NPT demonstrates, NPT membership can be easily abrogated. If nuclear proliferation escalates, it will not take long for some parties to give notice of withdrawal. "I am not really thinking of nuclear arms," said the Shah of Iran in a 1975 interview with *The New York Times*. "But if 20 or 30 ridiculous little countries are going to develop nuclear weapons, then I may have to revise my policies."[34]

The current system of nuclear governance also suffers from politicization that results from differing views among the current nuclear weapons states. The decisions of the IAEA board of governors often conflict with decisions taken by the UN Security Council. Members of the Nuclear Suppliers Group (countries with nuclear energy capability, which are supposed to operate according to terms of the NPT), have been caught violating their own rules and thus undermining the organization's credibility.[35] The lack of a common approach to nonproliferation and disagreements among the United States, China and Russia stand in the way of resolving pressing nuclear issues with Iran, North Korea, and Syria.[36] Additional tensions arise between the advanced nuclear states and the nuclear newcomers, mostly developing states. Many of these are members of the Non-Aligned Movement who resent the biases built into the current nonproliferation regime.

MEASURES TO CURB NUCLEAR PROLIFERATION

Of the more than 40 states that are technologically capable of producing nuclear weapons, fewer than a quarter have done so. Acquiring nuclear weapons thus remains a deviation rather than the norm. However, it can be argued that one nuclear weapon state is already too many, and, moreover, risks increase with more "fingers on the button." The current pattern of nuclear proliferation will doubtless continue, however, unless some decisive measures are taken. Although we cannot completely eliminate fear and pride caused by the structure of the international system, we can certainly decrease their influence on decisionmaking by the following measures.

Supporting the Global Effort to Abolish Nuclear Weapons

Changing the political decisions of others involves making one's own bold political decisions. It is important to frame and pursue nonproliferation as a global effort for the abolition—not mere reduction—of nuclear weapons. When it comes to nuclear weapons, the difference between zero and a few is enormous. (Indeed, there are cogent theoretical reasons to think that a small, vulnerable arsenal is more destabilizing than a relatively large one, since the latter is less susceptible to a disarming first strike.) As long as nuclear arsenals continue to exist—no matter in whose hands and however many—the incentive to acquire nuclear capabilities remains. Nonproliferation goals can only be achieved if the current nuclear weapon states are unequivocal about moving toward the goal of "Global Zero," and not just in words, but in deeds.

Possessing the strongest conventional forces in the world, the United States only faces existential danger in a world with nuclear weapons.[37] Those

---

[34] John B. Oakes, "Shah Offers a New Aid Plan for Developing Nations," *New York Times*, Sep. 24, 1975.

[35] For example, in the last ten years Russia supplied India with more than $700 million worth of nuclear fuel in violation of the NSG rules (until in 2008 India was granted an exception from the rules). Russia denied violation by citing NSG safety exception, but the Western states disagreed. (See Fred McGoldrick, "The Road Ahead for Export Controls: Challenges for the Nuclear Suppliers Group," *Arms Control Today*, January/February 2011; Mark Hibbs, "Nuclear Energy 2011: A Watershed Year," *Bulletin of the Atomic Scientists*, Vol. 68, No. 1, pp. 10–19: 17.)

[36] Hibbs.

---

[37] Robert Nelson, "Three Reasons Why the US Senate Should Ratify the Test Ban Treaty," *Bulletin of the Atomic Scientists*, Vol. 65, No. 2 (Mar./Apr. 2009), pp. 52–58: 53, 54.

states that already have nuclear weapons must stop dodging their responsibilities under the NPT, and advance a serious effort to reduce their nuclear stockpiles to zero. Otherwise, their behavior only weakens the treaty they try to use as a proliferation remedy. Article VI of the NPT commits the parties in possession of nuclear arsenals to pursue negotiations "in good faith" to end the nuclear-arms race and to achieve "nuclear disarmament,"[38] but the five nuclear weapon states have been slow to fulfill their commitments and continue to put high value on their nuclear arsenals. No wonder the rest of the world cannot be convinced to forgo nuclear weapons! US President Barack Obama promised to seek a world free of nuclear weapons; the United States could lead in this effort by providing political and financial support, as well as by example.

Building Confidence in Destabilized Regions

Since the NPT took effect in 1970, nuclear proliferation has been occurring in conflicted and/or unstable states in the Middle East and Asia. These states' interest in nuclear weapons has been animated by fear of vulnerability in regional crises. Some experts believe that any government in the unstable Middle East would acquire nuclear arms if it had the capability.[39] It is widely thought, for example, that if Iran (a Shi'ite state) were to develop nuclear weapons, Saudi Arabia and Egypt (largely Sunni states) would be strongly pre-disposed to follow suit. A nuclear arms buildup is already underway in South Asia, between India and Pakistan.

Arms races result from escalating political tensions, so that effective disarmament is only possible when political problems are resolved. A concrete example of how reducing tension can lead to arms reductions is the START talks and ensuing treaties between the US and Russia at the end of the Cold War. A potentially dangerous nuclear competition between Brazil and Argentina was averted when political relations improved between these long-time South American rivals. By the same token, countering proliferation threats in the long term means trying to resolve the Kashmir issue, which inflames relations between India and Pakistan, achieving a peaceful solution in the Middle East, reducing tensions in the Persian Gulf, addressing antagonism between the two Koreas, and so on. By reducing incentives for conflict, fear and other incentives to acquire nuclear weapons capabilities are similarly reduced.

Strengthening the Non-Proliferation Regime

Improving compliance with existing export regulations, negotiating a reasonable cutoff of fissile materials production, ratifying the CTBT,[40] and increasing the price paid for NPT violations are four immediate steps to strengthen the current non-proliferation regime. Stricter standards are necessary to ensure that countries obtaining nuclear reactors do not contribute to nuclear weapons proliferation.[41] However, in the long-term, the current regime requires larger fixes: nuclear governance needs to become more equitable, with the same rules and restrictions applied to all states, and non-proliferation measures need to address challenges by non-state actors more directly. The latter problem could even become a solution for the former, if the presence of non-state (including cyber) threats compels states to resolve their differences and advances a new level of cooperation between them as equals.

One of the major frustrations with the current non-proliferation regime is its biases. For example, it is easy to understand the Arab states' frustration with Israel's refusal to reduce and eventually eliminate its semi-covert nuclear arsenal (Israel refuses to officially confirm its existence, although it is an "open secret.") Even new guidelines for enrichment and reprocessing transfers by the Nuclear Suppliers Group (NSG) are creating tensions because the recipient states view them as discriminatory. Developing nations outside of the NSG argue that these

---

[38] Nuclear Non-Proliferation Treaty, Article VI, http://www.un.org/events/npt2005/npttreaty.html Accessed July 28, 2012.

[39] "Iran's Nuclear Ambitions Seen as Adding to Tehran's Prestige in Region," *VOA*, Cairo, 06 August 2003.

[40] Nelson, p. 53.

[41] "Confronting Nuclear Energy's Proliferation Problem," *Bulletin of the Atomic Scientists*, Vol. 65, No. 2 (Mar. /Apr. 2009), pp 1–3: 3.

guidelines are imposed by the advanced states in order to perpetuate the divide between the nuclear "haves" and "have nots".[42] Efforts need to be made to design more equitable rules and not by expanding proliferation opportunities for the nuclear "have-nots," but by curtailing opportunities for the "haves." New commitments by the nuclear weapons states—for example, no-first use declarations of the sort recently announced by the Obama Administration—could enhance the credibility of the nonproliferation regime.

Establishing Nuclear-Weapon-Free-Zones (NWFZs)

Elimination of nuclear weapons region by region by means of establishing NWFZs is one of the most effective paths toward global nuclear disarmament.[43] NWFZs complement the NPT by preventing the deployment of nuclear weapons in non-nuclear weapon states. Such practice is currently followed by NATO: under NATO's nuclear sharing arrangements, US tactical nuclear weapons are deployed in European states that do not have their own nuclear arsenals.[44] NWFZs also foster regional cooperation and help build confidence among countries in the region by increasing transparency and strengthening verification measures.[45] Even more importantly, members of a NWFZ can effectively band together to press for greater progress on nuclear disarmament. NWFZs are also a means of preventing nuclear testing in the regions they cover as well as addressing the threat of global nuclear terrorism. Finally, NWFZ members set a strong example to the rest of the international community.

There are currently five NWFZs, involving a total of 133 states: in Latin America and the Caribbean (the Treaty of Tlatelolco, 1967); in the South Pacific (the Treaty of Rarotonga, 1985); in Southeast Asia (the Treaty of Bangkok, 1995), in Africa (the Treaty of Pelindaba, 1996), and in Central Asia (Central Asian Nuclear-Weapon-Free Zone Treaty, 2006).[46] The 1967 Treaty of Tlatelolco helped pave the way for the NPT itself. The NWFZs have been extraordinarily successful not only in ensuring the absence of nuclear weapons in their respective regions, but also in promoting regional openness and cooperation as approaches to state security. However, progress toward the establishment of NWFZs has stalled. States face enormous difficulties in their attempts to establish additional NWFZs, as shown by the current stalemate in efforts toward a Middle East NWFZ.

Part of the problem is that not all countries are taking the idea seriously. For example, the US has lacked commitment to a more generalized Weapons of Mass Destruction—free zone in the Middle East, which was first proposed by the Arab League more than 15 years ago. At the 2010 NPT Review Conference, certain basic initiatives were undertaken, but fundamental questions—such as the participation of Israel and Iran—remain unresolved.[47]

---

[42] Steven E. Miller, "Nuclear Weapons 2011: Momentum Slows, Reality Returns," *Bulletin of the Atomic Scientists,* Vol. 68, No. 1, pp. 20–28.

[43] "A nuclear-weapon-free zone (NWFZ) is a specified region in which countries commit themselves not to manufacture, acquire, test, or possess nuclear weapons. [. . .] Article VII of the nuclear Nonproliferation Treaty (NPT), which entered into force in 1970, affirms the right of countries to establish specified zones free of nuclear weapons. The UN General Assembly reaffirmed that right in 1975 and outlined the criteria for such zones. Within these nuclear-weapon-free zones, countries may use nuclear energy for peaceful purposes." Nuclear-Weapon-Free Zones (NWFZ) at a Glance, Arms Control Association, Fact Sheet, November 2007. http://www.armscontrol.org/factsheets/nwfz. Accessed August 3, 2009.

[44] In 2009, the German government asked for the withdrawal of the U.S. nuclear weapons from Germany, starting a larger debate on NATO's nuclear posture. See Oliver Meier and Paul Ingram, "The NATO Summit: Recasting the Debate Over U.S. Nuclear Weapons in Europe," *Arms Control Today*, Vol. 42 (May 2012).

[45] In 2003, the UN General Assembly adopted a resolution "Nuclear Weapon Free Southern Hemisphere and Adjacent Areas," in which the members of the existing NWFZ pledged to work together to "pursue common goals," and "to explore and implement further ways and means of cooperation among themselves." "Nuclear Weapon Free Southern Hemisphere and Adjacent Areas," UN General Assembly Resolution 58/49, December 8, 2003.

[46] In addition to NWFZs, treaties ban the deployment of nuclear weapons in Antarctica, Mongolia, on the seabed, and in outer space.

[47] Steven E. Miller, "Nuclear Weapons 2011: Momentum Slows, Reality Returns," *Bulletin of the Atomic Scientists*, Vol. 68, No. 1, pp. 20–28.

Despite difficulties of implementation, the concept of NWFZs seems essential to addressing the crucial nonproliferation challenges on the Korean peninsula and in the Middle East.[48]

Reducing the Risks of the Global Nuclear Power Spread

The need to meet growing energy needs and limit carbon dioxide emissions has increased global interest in nuclear power and generates further threats to the nuclear non-proliferation regime. The disaster at the Fukushima Daiichi Nuclear Power Station in Japan in 2011 did not slow the spread of the civilian nuclear technology worldwide, and dozens of new states interested in mastering the atom have since approached the IAEA, despite the fact that Japan itself has moved away from reliance on nuclear energy after its recent, painful experience. Stricter controls on exports of enrichment technology are one measure to discourage states from acquiring nuclear weapon capabilities. Using "multinational enrichment facilities as an alternative to nationally controlled plants" is another.[49] Such facilities are cheaper and have been effective thus far.[50] It is also important to realize that new nuclear power plants are not a safe, long-term solution for a country's energy needs and that investment in renewable energy offers a safer, more cost-effective and practical alternative.

Preventing Nuclear Terrorism

There are approximately 1,440 tons of highly enriched uranium (HEU) in the world today—ready to be stolen by terrorists seeking to build a nuclear weapon. Low-enriched uranium (LEU) can be used in virtually all civilian applications and no technical impediments to the conversion of HEU into LEU

remain.[51] However, about 700 kilograms of HEU continues to be annually used in civilian research reactors, and 40 to 50 kilograms in civilian isotope production.[52] At the same time, there have been many illicit attempts to buy fissile materials.[53] The risks are growing exponentially with the emergence of every new nuclear state and the weakening of controls in the existing nuclear states.

It is important to continue assisting states that currently lack sufficient financial controls, adequate border security, and up-to-date export controls.[54] The lessons of cooperative non-proliferation programs in the former Soviet Union suggest that such assistance is most effective when security and developmental goals are combined. Threat reduction programs in post-Soviet states can serve as models to create new, peaceful jobs for North Korea's cadre of nuclear scientists and bomb makers. More than simply removing nuclear material and infrastructure, it is vital to provide the North's nuclear workers with alternative civilian jobs, since they could presumably resume their country's nuclear activities in the future or hire themselves out to help others build nuclear weapons. An approach similar to the Cooperative Threat Reduction (CTR) program between the United States and former Soviet states could be the best way to prevent future clandestine North Korean nuclear activities. The CTR program, established in 1991, has made a positive contribution, helping to destroy excess nuclear,

[48] Scott Parrish and Jean du Preez, "Nuclear-Weapon-Free Zones: Still a Useful Disarmament and Nonproliferation Tool?" Report for Weapons of Mass Destruction Commission, 2006.

[49] James, Goodby and Fred McGoldrick, "Reducing the Risks of Nuclear Power's Global Spread," *Bulletin of the Atomic Scientists*, Vol. 65, No. 3 (May 2009), pp. 40–47: 44.

[50] Ibid., 46.

[51] So far, nearly 450 tons of HEU have been converted. Corey Hinderstein, Andrew Newman, and Ole Reistad, "From HEU Minimization to Elimination: Time to Change the Vocabulary," *Bulletin of the Atomic Scientists*, Vol. 68, No. 4, pp. 83–95.

[52] Ole Reistad and Styrkaar Hustveit. "HEU Fuel Cycle Inventories and Progress on Global Minimization," *Nonproliferation Review*, Vol. 15, No. 2, (2008), pp. 265–287.

[53] For example, in 2011, Moldovan officials arrested six people for nuclear smuggling. Andrew E. Kramer, "Arrests in Moldova Over Possible Uranium Smuggling," *The New York Times*, June 29, 2011. Also see Center for Nonproliferation Studies, "Confirmed Proliferation-Significant Incidents of Fissile Material Trafficking in the Newly Independent States (NIS), 1991–2001," November 30, 2001. http:// cns.miis.edu/reports/traff.htm. Accessed July 30, 2012.

[54] Brian Finlay and Elizabeth Turpen, "The Next 100 Project: Leveraging National Security Assistance to Meet Developing World Needs," *Stanley Foundation*, Feb. 2009.

chemical, and biological weapons and to support related non-proliferation objectives in Russia, Kazakhstan, Belarus, and Ukraine.[55]

CONCLUSION

The hand of "The Doomsday Clock," maintained since 1947 by the *Bulletin of the Atomic Scientists*

to represent the threat of global nuclear war, currently stands at five minutes to midnight. Half-measures will not turn the world back from the brink. Although one state, no matter how powerful, cannot make political decisions on behalf of another, it can contribute to structuring appropriate incentives in the international system and affecting these decisions indirectly. It is up to the nuclear weapon states of today to shape the incentives of other states so as to help create a safer world.

---

[55] Jungmin Kang, "Redirecting North Korea's Nuclear Workers," *Bulletin of the Atomic Scientists*, Vol. 65, No. 1 (Jan./Feb. 2009), pp. 48–55: 48.

Lloyd J. Dumas

TRANSFORMING THE WAR ECONOMY INTO THE PEACEKEEPING ECONOMY: USING ECONOMIC RELATIONSHIPS TO BUILD A MORE PEACEFUL, PROSPEROUS AND SECURE WORLD

During the Cold War, it was routinely acknowledged that about 85 to 90 percent of the U.S. military budget was driven by competition with communism generally, and with the Soviet Union in particular. Now that the Soviet Union and the Cold War are both defunct and only remnant Communist regimes are still in power (in Cuba, Vietnam, and North Korea), the U.S. military budget has declined as a percentage of GDP, but is enormous in objective terms.. Clearly, any "peace dividend" has been elusive, which is troublesome for many reasons. For one thing, a militarized economy distorts and ultimately weakens any society. "Every gun that is made," said President Dwight D. Eisenhower in his 1961 Farewell Address, "every warship launched, every rocket fired signifies, in the final sense, a theft from those who hunger and are not fed, those who are cold and are not clothed."

These costs are devastating enough to warrant "economic conversion" as part of any peace-oriented future. But additionally, a war-oriented economy is probably more likely to be war-prone, so that the prevention of war may well require a reorientation of priorities away from the military and toward the domestic economy. This point has been made by many serious thinkers, including economist Joseph Schumpeter, who wrote that "the orientation toward war is mainly fostered by the domestic interests of ruling classes, but also by the influence of all those who tend to gain individually from a war policy, whether economically or socially."[56] Following World War I, concern focused increasingly on the role of the armaments industry, the so-called merchants of death, in fostering wars.

Interestingly, however, it was President Eisenhower once again—no starry-eyed idealist or softheaded pacifist—who gave voice to the most influential, critical, and regrettably accurate description of this problem when he warned in his Farewell Address that

> we have been compelled to create a permanent armaments industry of vast proportions. . . . The total influence—economic, political, even spiritual—is felt in every city, every statehouse, every office of the federal government. . . . In the councils of government, we must guard against the acquisition of unwarranted influence . . . by the military-industrial complex.

This alliance of military and industrial sectors that Eisenhower so decried has now become a military-industrial-labor-science-governmental complex, and it has shown itself to be firmly entrenched indeed. But, we presume, not entrenched permanently. The stage may now be set for "economic conversion," whose long-term advantages would go beyond the immediately economic to embrace the prospect of a society, an economy, and a politics oriented toward meeting human needs. As Lloyd Dumas emphasizes in the following selection, peace-related aspects of economic transformation can also go beyond simply redirecting financial resournces.

On a personal note, the editor of this book lives part-time in Costa Rica, which is the only independent country that has abolished its military: by constitutional mandate, Costa Rica has no army, navy or air force. It is probably not coincidental that on various international surveys, Costa Ricans typically rank as the happiest people on the planet!

INTRODUCTION

In the hard-nosed realities of this world, security is primarily a matter of relationships, not military power. That is easy enough to demonstrate. During the whole of the Cold War, the American military spent a great deal of effort and trillions of dollars building weapons and structuring forces to deter the Soviet Union from attacking the U.S. or its major allies with nuclear weapons. During much of that time, both France and Britain had enough nuclear capability to deliver a devastating, perhaps terminal attack against the U.S. Yet we spent little or no time

or resources worrying about or preparing for a British or French attack. The reason for that difference is obvious. The relationship between the U.S. and the Soviet Union was hostile, while the relationship between the U.S. and Britain or France was friendly.

Furthermore the U.S has never been all that concerned about the nuclear arsenal of Israel, a nation with which we have close ties, but went to war in Iraq in 2003 citing what turned out to be mistaken fears that the hostile Iraqi government was trying to develop weapons of mass destruction. Today the U.S. is very worried about the possibility that a hostile Iran may be trying to build a nuclear arsenal. Clearly, security is primarily a matter of relationships.

---

[56] Joseph Schumpeter, *Imperialism and Social Classes* (New York: Meridian, 1955).

Many specialists in international relations tend to think of force or the threat of force as the most effective way to provide security because they believe it is ultimately the most effective way of influencing behavior. But economists tend to think of influencing behavior primarily through incentives. There is no particular reason why this basic approach cannot be applied to influencing the behavior of nations. The problem is to define a set of conditions that will generate stronger positive incentives for nations to keep the peace.

BASIC PRINCIPLES OF A PEACEKEEPING ECONOMY[57]

A handful of basic principles define the character of peacekeeping economic relationships:

Principle I: Establish Balanced Relationships

There has been a longstanding debate in the political science literature as to whether economic relationships prevent or provoke war. The "liberals" claim that higher levels of international economic activity help keep the peace; the "realists" claim that they create conflict and war. These perspectives seem utterly contradictory, but I believe they are both right. Economic activity can make war either more or less likely. Which it actually does depends crucially on the nature of the relationship, not just the extent of the activity. Unbalanced, exploitative relationships tend to increase the number and severity of conflicts; balanced mutually beneficial relationships tend to reduce them.

A relationship is "balanced and mutually beneficial" if its benefits flow to every participant and there is a rough equality between contribution to the relationship and benefits received.[58] A balance

of benefit implies that the gains of those who participate reflect the value of their contribution rather than differences in their bargaining power. In unbalanced exploitative relationships, the flow of benefit is overwhelmingly in one direction, and does not correspond to relative contribution.

If any party to an unbalanced relationship is suffering a net loss, that party will certainly feel ill used and hostile. But even if everyone is gaining, the fact that the vast majority of benefit flows elsewhere is likely to irritate those who receive less value than they contribute. There is little or no incentive for them to work at resolving whatever conflicts might occur, economic or otherwise. If they come to see disrupting the relationship as key to rebalancing it or replacing it with a different, more beneficial relationship, they will be ready to raise the intensity of those conflicts—in extreme cases, even to the point of war. The revolution that gave birth to the United States is an important example of the power of economic exploitation to provoke antagonisms that can lead to war.

Balanced economic relationships have the opposite effect. Since everyone gains benefit at least equal to their contribution, out of pure self-interest no one wants to disrupt the relationship, let alone take deliberate action to disrupt it themselves. When conflicts occur, they will try hard to settle them amicably. If their partners come under external stress, they have an incentive to help relieve, rather than exacerbate, the pressure. In this situation, everyone in the relationship will feel more secure, and no one will need to expend extra effort and expense just to keep it going.

Unbalanced, exploitative economic relationships are something like a zero sum game (such as poker), where the gains of one party are achieved at the expense of another. But balanced, mutually beneficial relationships do not simply divide up a fixed pie of benefit; they help the pie to grow. Balanced relationships distribute the gains of the larger pie in ways that tend to create a "virtuous circle," a positive feedback loop that keeps the pie growing. The advantages of balanced relationships grow over time.

Beyond this, when two nations are engaged in an expanding web of balanced mutually beneficial

---

[57] These principles, along with strategies for implementation and supporting institutional changes are discussed in much greater detail in Dumas, Lloyd J., *The Peacekeeping Economy: Using Economic Relationships to Build a More Peaceful, Prosperous, and Secure World* (Yale University Press, 2011).

[58] This concept of balance and benefit is consistent with Aristotle's dictum that "the well-being of every polis depends on each of its elements rendering to others an amount equivalent to what it received from them," though in a very different context. (See Aristotle, *Politics*, translated by Earnest Barker. London: Oxford University Press, 1958, p.41).

economic interactions, more and more people in both countries have increasing contact as a natural consequence of engaging in economic activity together. They need to exchange emails, talk on the telephone, and even have face-to-face meetings simply to co-ordinate their activities. At first these contacts may be stilted, formal and focused on the business at hand. But people are people, and eventually their social interactions will lead them to begin to know each other better. They will spend more time in each other's country and almost inevitably become more familiar with each other's life circumstances. Sometimes they won't like each other. But more often than not, this increased contact will melt away at least any stereotypical images they may have had of each other and lead to a greater understanding and empathy. Some friendships will be made, and long-held suspicions—even enmities—are likely to slowly disappear.

Even when gains are balanced, if the process involved in making key decisions relative to a relationship is unbalanced, those with less input and control are likely to feel less secure. When decision power is balanced, all participants have a sense of security because they know that they will be directly involved in any decision to change the rules or character of the relationship.[59] This will not necessarily prevent all changes that at least temporarily reduce their gains or increase their costs. But it will assure them that no changes will occur without their input, and perhaps their consent. It is easier for anyone who has been a full partner in deciding to make a change to accept it without undue hostility, even if it hurts. Painful change that is coerced or imposed is an entirely different thing. (The famous slogan of the American Revolution was not "No taxation," but rather "No taxation without representation.")

There are thus two aspects of balance in international economic relationships that are key: 1) balance of benefits; and 2) balance of decision power. When economic relationships are balanced in both these senses, current gains and the prospect of greater

gains in the future create strong self-interested incentives to settle the conflicts that inevitably arise more peacefully.[60] As those conflicts are successfully resolved time after time, the idea of allowing them to fester to the point of violent confrontation comes to seem more and more absurd, and war itself ultimately comes to be seen as unnecessary, undesirable, and inherently counterproductive.

The European Union. The effectiveness of mutually beneficial, balanced economic relationships in keeping the peace is illustrated by today's European Union (EU). The EU began as the European Coal and Steel Community formed by six nations shortly after World War II (1952), with the purpose of trying to build economic bonds (especially between France and Germany) to make the outbreak of war among them less likely.[61] By the mid-1980s, the dozen nations that belonged to the European Economic Community included Belgium, France, Germany, Great Britain, Italy, the Netherlands, Portugal and Spain. These nations fought countless wars with each other over the centuries (including World Wars I and II), and were also major colonial powers that militarily dominated and exploited much of the rest of the world. Yet today, if you were to ask the leaders (or the citizens) of any of these countries the odds of their countries fighting a war with each other over the next fifty years, they wouldn't even consider it a sensible question.

It is not as if these countries no longer have conflicts with each other. They have many, economic and otherwise, some of them very serious. There have been major disagreements recently over whether economic growth or austerity was called for

---

[59] The sole exception, of course, is that any party to a purely voluntary relationship, unconstrained by contractual requirements to the contrary, is free to end their participation without anyone else's consent.

[60] The strength of that incentive depends on the salience of that relationship to the parties involved. Even if a relationship is balanced, if it is of little significance to either party, the incentive it creates to avoid conflict arising from other causes will be weak.

[61] The formation of the ECSC was the result of a proposal by Robert Schuman, the Minister for Foreign Affairs of France. This proposal was based on provisions in the Marshall Plan, the American plan for the postwar economic reconstruction of Europe. Rittberger, B. "Which Institutions for Post-War Europe? Explaining the Institutional Design of Europe's First Community," *Journal of European Public Policy* (2001: 8(5)), pp. 673–708.

in the face of severe financial crisis (especially in the eurozone); and earlier over the "mad cow" related banning of British beef by other EU states and the U.S.-led 2003 invasion of Iraq.

But the EU nations understand that the network of balanced, mutually beneficial economic relationships they have created gives them a strong stake in finding ways to manage, if not to resolve, the conflicts they have with each other. They have too much to lose to let their disagreements get out of control. So they debate, they argue, they shout. But they no longer threaten, or even think about threatening each other militarily, let alone actually going to war. With all of its problems, the EU is a clear piece of evidence that using properly structured economic relationships to build and keep the peace between former enemies is an eminently practical and achievable enterprise.

Principle II: Emphasize Development

The poverty and frustration of so many of the world's people is a fertile breeding ground for violent conflict. There have been well more than 120 wars since the end of World War II, taking more than twenty million human lives. Nearly all of them have been fought in developing countries. People in desperate economic straits tend to reach for extreme solutions. They are much more easily manipulated by demagogues. Violent disruption is more threatening to people in good economic condition because they have a lot more to lose. Therefore, emphasizing inclusive and widespread development is important to inhibiting the outbreak of war.

Emphasizing development is also a useful counter-terrorist strategy, despite the fact that many terrorists are neither poverty stricken nor uneducated. All but the craziest, most isolated terrorists depend on support, at least for their cause if not their tactics. They have to recruit operatives. They also have to be able to move around, coordinate activities, take care of logistics, and find secure places to train and to store materiel. This is much, much easier to do the wider their base of support.

To recruit reliable operatives and build support networks, terrorist groups must have a cause that can convince "normal" people to engage in or support acts of horrific violence they would not otherwise condone. If people can be made to feel that by engaging in (or supporting) terrorism they become the avengers of a great wrong done to "their people," they can be made not only ready but eager to perpetrate or support terrible acts of violence against innocent people who have never directly done them any harm.

Development can be an effective counter-terrorist approach, *not* because terrorists or their financial supporters are necessarily economically desperate, but because raising the economic wellbeing and political status of the larger group of which the terrorists and their supporters feel part makes it harder to recruit operatives and weakens support. Development can help dry up both the pool of potential terrorists and the wider support for terrorist groups that is vital to their operation.

Principle III: Minimize Ecological Stress

There is no question that competition for depletable resources generates conflict. The desire to gain (and if possible monopolize) access to raw materials and fuels was one of the driving forces behind the colonization of much of the world by the more economically and militarily advanced nations in centuries past. This competition continues to bring nations and groups within nations into dangerous conflicts in which at least one party believes that the continued economic wellbeing, political sovereignty or even survival of its people is at stake.

There is little doubt that Middle East conflicts would be much less likely to lead to military action by the major powers if it were not for oil. The considerable difference among the reactions of those powers to slaughter in Cambodia, genocide in Rwanda, war in Liberia, hostility in Iraq, revolution in Libya, and brutality in Syria may have a variety of causes, but the presence or absence of oil is certainly one of them. In the 20th and early 21st century the most contentious resource conflicts might have been over oil, but in the mid to late 21st century it may be that the most stress-generating resource conflicts will be over water.

Furthermore, the air and the water do not recognize the artificial lines that we have drawn on the earth to separate ourselves from each other. Trans-border pollution itself may not lead to war, but it has already generated considerable conflict and has the prospect of generating a great deal more. Widespread international hostility to the U.S. decision to abandon the Kyoto accords, for example, is in no small measure due to the dramatic effect that continued trans-border pollution by "greenhouse gases" is likely to have on climate change, imposing potentially enormous long run costs on the world economy. Every additional source of tension contributes to the strain on the international system and therefore to the likelihood that other sources of conflict will lead to the eruption of violence.

Some argue that the expansion of economic activity itself is inconsistent with maintaining environmental quality, that modern production techniques and consumption activities generate an unavoidable degree of ecological stress. While there is some truth to this, the levels of economic well-being to which the people of the developed countries have become accustomed can be maintained, improved and extended to the people of the developing nations without even generating current levels of environmental damage. Accomplishing this feat requires: 1) a great deal more attention to the efficient use of natural resources; 2) the development and extensive use of pollution-abating technologies and procedures; and 3) a substantial shift toward qualitative, rather than quantitative economic growth, particularly on the part of the developed countries.

Using natural resources more efficiently requires more intensive and widespread recycling, improving the design and operation of energy-using systems, and greater reliance on ecologically benign, renewable energy and material resources. The development and use of improved pollution-abating technologies and procedures means better filtration, waste treatment and other after-the-fact cleanup. But it also means the development and use of less environmentally damaging production and consumption technologies. Finally, continuing to think of economic growth mainly in quantitative terms is foolish and unnecessary. Standards of living are also raised by improvements in the quality of goods and services. Shifting attention to qualitative growth will allow the developed nations to reduce their appetite for nonrenewable resources, helping to make their continued growth indefinitely sustainable. It will also reduce environmental pollution and create space for the quantitative expansion of goods and services still required in many developing nations.

If we insist on continuing to think about security primarily in narrow military-oriented terms, we will be stuck with the enormous expense of equipping and maintaining very large military forces that have in recent years proven less than completely effective, if not counterproductive, in furthering our national interests and thus our national political and economic security. Even if we are doing the best we can under existing circumstances, we will miss the chance to realize the enormous security gains that could be achieved at dramatically lower cost by using economic peacekeeping to change those circumstances for the better. We simply cannot allow ourselves to be trapped by an unwillingness to think broadly and act boldly.

By learning to put aside the idea that force and threat of force is ultimately the most effective means of affecting international behavior and adopt instead the economist's perspective that behavior is best influenced by creating incentives and opportunities for mutual gain, we can create a web of international economic relationships that not only serves our material needs, but also provides strong positive incentives to make and keep the peace. And rather than a world of deepening inequality and growing insecurity, we can build a world that is at once more equitable, peaceful, prosperous and secure.

REMOVING BARRIERS TO DEMILITARIZED SECURITY

One of the most important benefits of adopting economic peacekeeping or any other less militarized approach to security is that it permits substantial reductions in the currently heavy military burden on the domestic and global economies.[62] This realignment of security strategy will go a long way to freeing up the resources needed to repair the considerable economic damage that has resulted from decades of

---

[62] Dumas, Lloyd J., *The Peacekeeping Economy*, Chapter 7.

bearing that burden, provided those resources are efficiently redirected to a viable mix of productive economic activities. As it turns out, this redirection is not as simple or straightforward as it might seem.

It is necessary to overcome political resistance to the change that is rooted in the vested interests of those workers, businesses and communities who believe their economic success—in terms of jobs, profits and tax base—is tightly tied to the military-oriented security system. In the U.S. for example, since the early 1950s the so-called "jobs argument" ("thousands of jobs will be lost if this military project is cut") has been a powerful political obstacle to serious cutbacks in any sizeable weapons program, no matter how ill conceived or unnecessary. This has been even truer of across-the-board reductions in military spending. Politicians have found it extraordinarily difficult to vote against military programs when that vote would cost their own constituents large numbers of jobs, even in the short run.

If there were comparable alternative economically productive jobs available for those who would be displaced by the transition—and smooth and effective ways of getting them from here to there—their representatives in the Congress would be freer to cast their votes on particular military projects and the military budget as a whole on the basis of legitimate national security needs rather than vested economic interests.

There is actually a remarkable precedent for making this kind of large-scale military-to-civilian transition successfully. At the end of World War II, the U.S. was faced with shifting an enormous amount of the nation's output from military to civilian production. The challenge was met with room to spare by a combination of corporate planning and federal, state, and local government planning. Roughly thirty percent of U.S. output was transferred in one year without the unemployment rate ever rising above three percent.[63] With the right approach, it is possible to smoothly and efficiently redirect even

very large amounts of productive resources from military to civilian activity without unbearable economic disruption. Yet this is an experience that must be interpreted carefully.

Nearly all the companies that produced equipment for the military during WWII were civilian enterprises that shifted temporarily to military production. Their normal business was making civilian products. All of their workers, including their managers, engineers and scientists, knew how to operate in a civilian commercial market environment. Some modifications had been made to their production facilities and equipment to better support the war effort, but most of it had originally been designed and configured for efficient civilian production. For these workers and the firms that employed them, this was "reconversion": They had converted from civilian to military production during the war, and now they were going back to business as usual.

The situation is very different today. Nearly 70 years after World War II, there are whole generations of military sector managers, engineers, scientists, production and maintenance workers whose experience includes little or nothing except military-oriented work. Many of today's military-industrial firms never competed in the civilian commercial marketplace. Even large firms that manufacture both military and civilian products have typically kept their military and civilian divisions operationally separate.

During the Second World War, both the production processes and the technologies embodied in military goods were still fairly similar to those in the World War II vintage civilian economy. But over the past half-century, the physical plant, machinery and processes involved in producing military and civilian goods have sharply diverged. The technologies built into the products themselves have become even more different. For example, the design of a World War II era bomber was not all that different from the design of a civilian aircraft of the day. But the design of a B-2 Stealth bomber of today could scarcely be more different from that of a modern airliner or civilian cargo plane. For the major military producers, moving into civilian commercial markets is no longer a matter of returning to business-as-usual. It is a movement into new and unexplored territory. It is conversion, not reconversion.

---

[63] Boulding, Kenneth E., in Foreword to Dumas, L.J., ed., *The Political Economy of Arms Reduction: Reversing Economic Decay* (Boulder, Colorado: The American Association for the Advancement of Science and Westview Press, 1982), p. xiii.

The Nature of the Transition Problem

Military industry is fundamentally government-oriented, performance-driven and insensitive to cost. The perception that every increment of performance may be crucial to the outcome in battle creates enormous pressure to squeeze out every ounce of performance possible in the design and manufacture of weapons and related systems. Though there are cost constraints, the high priority (and associated funding) given to the military sector in the U.S. and most other arms-producing countries makes those constraints so loose that the cost of the product is no more than a secondary consideration.

Civilian industry may be oriented to the government or to the private sector, but it tends to be much more sensitive to cost. That is especially true if it is operating in a competitive commercial marketplace. There the customer is not a high priority government department with very deep pockets and an output ("national security") that is essentially unmeasurable, but an ordinary consumer with relatively limited income or a firm that must sell to such a consumer. If a company servicing ordinary civilian customers in a competitive marketplace is not attentive to keeping cost down, it will eventually be forced out of business by its more astute competitors.

At the same time, while product performance is clearly important to civilian customers, it is nowhere near as much of a driving force for most civilian products as it routinely is in military industry. These differences turn the two sectors into two very different worlds: an extreme performance, cost-insensitive military-oriented world; and a good performance, extremely cost-sensitive civilian world.

Transitioning Engineers and Scientists

Engineers and scientists play a critical role in driving the productivity gains that are so important to keeping the economy healthy and strong over the long run. The prospect of being able to undo the military drain of these technological resources and re-invigorate the industrial economy is exciting. But the difference between the military and civilian-oriented worlds makes an enormous difference to the daily functioning of engineers and scientists. Because of the emphasis on maximizing the technical capability of weapons

and related systems, and the relative looseness of cost constraints, large teams of technologists are assembled to design, develop and produce these extremely complex and sophisticated products. The engineers, scientists and technicians that make up such teams tend to be highly specialized within very limited areas of expertise, so they can do the difficult detailed work necessary to squeeze every increment of performance out of the resulting product. Since cost is of much less importance, they are also relatively ignorant about the impact of the research and design choices they make on the ultimate cost of the product.

Because successful design for the civilian marketplace requires careful attention to keeping cost down, engineers and scientists in the civilian sector must be well versed in the implications of all aspects of what they do for product cost. Among other things, designers should not be extremely specialized, because they need to understand the overall design of the product and the interactions of its components so that they can trade off changes in one part of the design against changes in another to achieve good product performance at the lowest possible cost. Keeping production costs down enables the firm to increase its sales and profits by keeping its prices at a level that makes its products attractive to ordinary civilian customers.

Because of these differences, the engineers and scientists of military industry must be both retrained (given some different skills) and re-oriented (taught to look at what they do from a different perspective) before they are likely to be successful in civilian research and development. A degree of de-specialization and a strong dose of learning to pay careful attention to cost, along with the skills necessary to do that successfully, are required to connect them firmly with the realities of civilian design.

Converting Management

In practice, military weapons producing firms have only one customer—the nation's armed services. They cannot directly sell their products to civilian customers, and in most cases, even the weapons that they sell to foreign governments were originally designed, developed and produced for sale to their own government. This one-customer orientation produces a very different sales and marketing situation from that faced by civilian firms. Managers of civilian commercial firms must typically know how to advertise effectively in a mass market, how to survey markets for acceptability of new product lines, how to price a product for penetration of a new market or expansion of an existing one, etc., most of which is entirely irrelevant to operating in the military sector. Military industry managers, on the other hand, have to know the minute detail of government procurement regulations, how to develop good working relationships with key government procurement personnel, and how to lobby effectively with the legislature and the administration, much of which is irrelevant to operating in the civilian sector. Beyond this, the military industry firm typically sells its product before it is produced, putting the firm in a much better financing situation from that faced by most civilian manufacturers.

It is not reasonable to expect managers accustomed to operating in a situation in which there is little financial risk, high costs can become a path to higher revenues and only one well-funded customer needs to be serviced, to operate successfully in risky, cost-sensitive, multi-customer civilian markets without substantial retraining and re-orientation. The dismal performance of unconverted military industry managements in producing civilian products is frequently cited as evidence that military-oriented enterprises cannot really be converted and must instead simply lay off workers and shrink the company. Aside from the fact that downsizing leaves unsolved the basic economic problem of making productive use of what is, after all, a highly skilled work force, this is an excessively superficial reading of the record. These enterprises never really reshaped themselves to fit civilian requirements. They simply began making something civilian essentially the same way they had always made military products in the past. This is not conversion. And there is little ground in theory or experience for believing this approach would ever work.

In addition, the management organization will almost certainly need to be reshaped.[64] The special requirements of the military sector (including a high degree of secrecy, which leads to a high degree of compartmentalization) typically result in managerial structures that are top heavy and poorly organized for civilian operations. Re-orientation to the standards of work efficiency required to minimize cost is likely to be necessary for production workers with long experience in the military sector, and may be required for administrative staff as well. It is also possible that some of the more highly skilled workers, being more specialized, may require some retraining to convert successfully to civilian work, though that will tend to be minimal compared to what is required for converting engineers, scientists, and managers. This level of retraining and re-orientation can probably be handled on the job.

Conversion of Capital Equipment and Facilities

Some of the industrial equipment and facilities currently employed in military industry and at military bases are sufficiently general purpose to be directly usable in civilian-oriented work. But some, such as certain types of machine tools with extreme performance capabilities, are not directly transferable. The transferability of some machinery and equipment with excessive capabilities suffers mainly from its high cost. Those industrial facilities that do not so much possess excess capabilities as the wrong capabilities have to be reconstructed or abandoned. Preparing capital equipment and facilities for the military-to-civilian transition requires a detailed assessment of what changes in layout, direct equipment and facilities and support equipment and facilities are implied by the chosen civilian alternative products. Given such an assessment, it is not difficult to estimate both financing requirements and the time needed from start to finish for the actual physical conversion. This, in turn, enables development of a financial plan, as well as effective coordination of this phase of the transition process with others.

Internal vs. External Conversion

"Internal" conversion involves the transition of workforce, facilities and equipment to civilian-oriented activities inside a formerly military-oriented

---

[64] See Mehring, George, "Restructuring the Organization: The Importance of Strategic Learning in Conversion", in L. J. Dumas, ed., *The Socio-Economics of Conversion: From War to Peace* (Armonk, New York: M. E. Sharpe Publishers, 1995).

firm (or division of a firm) that is transitioning to the civilian market. "External" conversion involves finding new, civilian-oriented uses elsewhere for workers, facilities and equipment that are released by a downsizing military-oriented firm (or a closing military base). Since it retains as much of the workforce intact as is economically sensible, internal conversion minimizes the disruption of the lives of workers and their families. It minimizes disruption of the surrounding community as well by maintaining the tax base and the geographic patterns of living, spending and commuting. Generally speaking, there will be less on-the-job adjustment for the affected workforce, because they will continue to work within the setting of a firm and workplace with which they are familiar.

But some external conversion is unavoidable. Even if all military contractors moving to civilian markets were committed to planning for internal conversion, at least some of their workforce would have to be externally converted. The engineering intensity and management staff size common in military industry are simply unsupportable in any economically viable, unsubsidized civilian firm.[65] An efficient transition almost inevitably requires some paring of the workforce. External conversion would therefore be needed both to retrain the engineers, scientists and managers laid off from converting military enterprises and to reconnect them to civilian firms.

One of the great technical advantages of internal conversion is that job retraining programs are much more effective if they are targeted to specific job opportunities. With internal conversion, the nature of the job any given worker will be doing after the transition is known nearly as well as the nature of their present job. No matter what kind of employees we are dealing with, from scientists and engineers to clerical or administrative workers, with this knowledge in hand it is much easier to develop a successful program for whatever retraining and/or re-orientation might be necessary.

---

[65] One striking anecdotal example was the B1 bomber plant in El Segundo, California, which at the height of its operation had 14,000 workers: 5,000 production workers; 5,000 engineers; and 4,000 managers. Very few if any civilian manufacturers, low tech or high tech, could survive supporting one engineer and close to one manager per production worker.

Choosing Alternative Products

It is best to generate the most comprehensive list possible of alternative products that the company is capable of producing, and then choose among them those that make the most economic sense. This process should begin by analyzing the "core competencies" of the firm, its workforce and equipment—looking in detail at what particular things they are best at doing. For example, the firm may be expert at integrating electronic and mechanical controls, or it might have considerable experience designing products to operate in highly corrosive environments. Once they have been clearly identified, these core competencies can then be matched with civilian applications that will result in products with a strong and profitable market. It could easily turn out, for example, that the best civilian alternative product for an enterprise currently manufacturing components for fighter aircraft is industrial control equipment, rather than components for civilian aircraft. Looking only for the closest matches to existing product lines is not the best way to find the civilian product lines likely to be the most successful.

It is extremely important to distinguish between that which is merely technically feasible, and that which is actually economically viable. It has been a common mistake to think of alternative products as appropriate as long as it was technically possible to make them with the workforce, equipment and facilities available. But successful conversion requires that the new range of civilian products have a sufficient market to be sold at prices higher than their costs of manufacture. If the products are not economically viable, the firms will either go bankrupt or need continuing and burdensome public subsidy, neither one of which is a necessary or acceptable alternative.

Public/Private Sector Responsibilities

The military-to-civilian transition will work best if it is a real public sector–private sector partnership, specialized according to comparative advantage. It is very helpful to have the coordination and assistance that the national government can provide, but the conversion process is not likely to work well unless it is highly decentralized. The managements of the enterprises involved in conversion have a strong comparative advantage in looking for and finding productive and profitable civilian activities to replace the previous military mission. Plans for the reshaping of capital and labor that the new activities chosen imply must be tailored to the details of each particular facility and workplace. This is one case where a "one-size-fits-all" approach is a virtual guarantee that nothing will fit well. Because no one knows details and capability of the workforce and facility better then those who work there and those who manage the enterprise, they have an enormous advantage in working out transition plans as compared to some distant government employee. It would therefore be a serious mistake for the federal government to try to blueprint facility and workforce conversion. Even close oversight of plant and firm-level conversion by the federal government is unlikely to improve the effectiveness of conversion plans and very likely to be inefficient and expensive.

A more appropriate role for the national government is to use its leverage as customer to pressure military-industrial firms to begin transition planning in advance of need. Serious corporate planning for the post–World War II military-to-civilian transition began fully two years before the war ended. So did a parallel process of preparations by the state, local and national government. Following the precedent of other federal legislation, such as equal employment opportunity laws that set requirements for eligibility for federal contracts, the national government could, for example, require military contractors to set up independently funded labor-management "alternative use committees" as a condition of eligibility for any future federal contract, military or civilian. While it cannot be guaranteed that this planning would be taken seriously and done well, with independent funding and both labor and management participating, the probability of triggering an effective internal conversion planning process in most military industrial facilities is high.[66]

Coping with Demobilization

Generally speaking, the economic and social re-absorption of former soldiers into civilian life that would be associated with movement toward a peacekeeping economy is not likely to be much of a problem in countries with well-developed, relatively intact economies and well-integrated societies.[67] The more developed countries, especially those not engaged one way or another in large-scale active warfare, should be able to handle this aspect of the transition without a huge public effort. The shift of money from military budgets to more economically productive forms of public and/or private expenditure enabled by the change in security strategy will provide a stimulus to the economy through the market just when that stimulus is most needed to ease the transition. That will help a great deal.

With a handful of notable exceptions, only a few less developed countries have any sizable military industrial sector and therefore any substantial conversion problem. Demobilization, not conversion, will be the first order transition problem for most developing countries. The smaller size and relative weakness of their economies complicates the absorption of a sudden bulge in the workforce. This is especially true of those developing countries that are emerging from long civil wars or long periods of brutal political and economic oppression.

If demobilization is not handled properly, the potential economic benefits of demilitarization will fail to be achieved and new problems may be created that will further disrupt economic and political development efforts. In demobilization, as in economic conversion, retraining and reorientation of the personnel involved is a critical matter. People lacking useful civilian-oriented economic skills—as many long-time soldiers in the developing world will be—must be retrained so that they can take advantage of whatever current or newly created economic opportunities may exist. They must also learn to replace the military way of thinking with a way of

---

[66] The basic specifications for proposed national legislation that would set up such requirements, along with an explanation of the reasoning behind its provisions, appear as "Model Specifications for a National Economic Adjustment Act" in Dumas, Lloyd J., *The Overburdened Economy: Uncovering the Causes of Chronic Unemployment, Inflation and National Decline* (Berkeley, CA: University of California Press, 1986), Appendix, pp. 261–271.

---

[67] The psychological readjustment of returning soldiers, especially those who as active combatants or prisoners of war have suffered severe psychological and/or physical trauma, is an entirely different and much more difficult problem.

thinking that is more compatible with success in the very different context of civilian life. In demobilization, this means changing from a military mindset in which unquestioned obedience is expected and extreme violence is an acceptable means of achieving the mission at hand, to a mindset that is oriented to individual creativity, initiative, and achieving results by peaceful cooperation. In the end, both conversion and demobilization require a major shift in perspective that is critical to success, a shift that cannot be safely assumed to be automatic.

CONCLUSION

Psychologists tell us that transitions—even good transitions—are among the most stressful life events. They are movements from the known into the as yet unknown. On a societal scale, the transition from a security strategy centered on the threat or use of military force to one that relies primarily on economic peacekeeping has much to recommend it. But it would be foolish to simply ignore stresses that even contemplating such a structural shift can create, if for no other reason than because failing to address them adequately may prevent us from building the political will to make the change in the first place.

It is ironic, but nevertheless true, that one of the most important sources of stress produced by what would be a greatly beneficial economic change is the uncertainty it creates for those who believe their economic present and future to be tied to the continuation of the current military security system. In this as in many situations of progressive social change, the vastly greater but more diffuse benefit the change will produce for a majority of the population can be held hostage to the much smaller pain it will produce for a concentrated but politically influential minority. Economists often talk of overcoming this kind of roadblock by having the gainers directly compensate the losers. In this case, it makes more sense to put a mechanism into place that will reassure those who fear loss that they will be protected from that loss, not by a handout but by help in moving efficiently through the change and reconnecting to productive economic activity. Such a mechanism is not only valuable in overcoming political barriers to moving toward a peacekeeping economy, it is crucial to assuring that we realize the enormous potential economic gains of reconnecting the resources diverted to the economically deadweight military sector to productive economic activity.

Many economists argue that no such mechanism is necessary to facilitate conversion. The unaided market is fully capable of handling any necessary transition that might result from the decision to move to a new and structurally different security system. In one sense, they are right. Given that decision, market forces will eventually lead us to a new allocation of resources in which military-serving activity accounts for a much smaller share of business. But market forces will not prevent or even mitigate the degree of economic pain inflicted during that unaided transition. More importantly, without some means of smoothing this transition, it will be much more difficult to overcome the politically powerful vested interests that are arrayed against it. Preparing in advance for military-to-civilian conversion will prevent us from getting stuck in the past, and therefore from failing to realize the reinforcing cycle of prosperity and security that a peacekeeping economy is capable of delivering.

David P. Barash

INTERNATIONAL LAW

For some people, international law is one of the great hopes of humanity, offering the prospect of subjecting the often chaotic interactions of countries to the same reason and order that—at least in theory—governs the interactions of individuals. For others, international law is laughably inadequate, primarily because it has no clear-cut enforcement mechanism. Nevertheless, in the aftermath of genocidal cruelty in Bosnia and Rwanda, many of the perpetrators were declared international outlaws, and at least some have been brought before the International Court of Justice (ICJ). This is a pattern that may become increasingly common in the future, especially with the inception of the comparatively new International Criminal Court (ICC). Unlike the ICJ, the ICC is legally independent from the United Nations, although it cannot respond to events that occurred prior to its establishment in 2002.

International law may be held to an unfairly strict standard. Breaches of international law, for example, are sometimes thought to show the absurdity of international law itself, perhaps because such offenses (genocide, torture, etc.) are often so egregious. But by contrast, violations of national or local law are virtually never taken as reasons to disavow legal systems. Presumably, this is because nearly everyone recognizes the need for law, even if existing laws are not perfect or perfectly complied with. The "law of nations" is and will be what we make it. Depending on our choice, international law offers the prospect of restraining, or possibly ending, war and promoting a more lawful world, which may also be more predictable, just, and peaceful.

———————————— ✑ ————————————

The international community should support a system of laws to regularize international relations and maintain the peace in the same manner that law governs national order.
—Pope John Paul II

Schemes for ending war—for creating negative peace and, ultimately, positive peace as well—often founder at the level of states. By zealously guarding their sovereignty, states undermine, or at best diminish, the authority and effectiveness of international organizations such as the United Nations. Even when these organizations operate in a manner that recognizes the primacy of state sovereignty, an unavoidable tension arises between a state-centered world system and one organized around different fundamental values. By providing a unit around which dangerous and misleading notions such as peace through strength can congeal, nationalism and state-centeredness legitimize the use of violence in settling disputes. By emphasizing the similarities and often suggesting some kind of superiority on the part of each group of people, and cutting them off from others, the current political divisions of our planet make prospects for disarmament seem terribly difficult, perhaps impossible. By rewarding those who behave violently—so long as such violence, or the threat of violence, is successful—our current world system works strongly against peaceful ethical or religious resolutions of conflict. And by fractionating the people of the world, our current political organization makes it very difficult to deal effectively with problems that cross traditional borders and that require global solutions....

In short, many people are becoming increasingly aware that our current state-centric system is part of the problem, and that we must move beyond the nation-state to find the solution....All governments operate by laws, the rules of behavior that specify what is permissible and, more commonly, what is not. Even in our current system of separate states, a legal framework undergirds the relationship of states to one another. It is known as international law....

THE SOURCES OF INTERNATIONAL LAW

We are all familiar with domestic law, with its prohibitions against violent crimes such as murder, robbery, and assault, as well as with the way it regulates the nonviolent conduct of daily living, from the flow of traffic to the affairs of business and the standards of acceptable conduct in private and public life. Less familiar, by contrast, is international law, the acknowledged principles that guide the interactions between states, and that set limits upon what is and what is not permissible. People live within societies, not between them, so we have done far more to encourage *intra*national law than *inter*national law. And yet, international law does exist; in fact, the current body of international law is very large. Just as most daily life among individuals within a society is peaceful, most interactions among states on the world scene is also peaceful, in accord with expectations, and thus, in a sense, "legal."

Unlike domestic law, which in the United States is codified in constitutions and amendments, as well as in the specific laws passed by federal, state, and municipal lawmaking bodies, the body of

international law is relatively chaotic, spread over history and generated in many different ways. There are four major sources of international law: (1) classical writings that have become widely accepted, (2) custom, (3) treaties, and (4) the rulings of international courts.

Classical Writings

In the sixteenth century, the Spanish legal scholar Francisco de Victoria developed the thesis that war must be morally justifiable, and could not simply be fought over differences of religion or for the glory of a ruler. He also maintained that soldiers were not obliged to fight in unjust wars, even if so commanded by their king. But the best-known and most influential example of classical international law is found in the work of the Dutch legal scholar Hugo Grotius. In his treatise *On the Law of War and Peace* (1625), Grotius maintained that there was a fundamental "natural law," which transcended that of nations, and which emanated from the fact that people were ultimately members of the same community. Grotius argued strongly for the sovereignty of individual states, within their own realms. From this, he concluded that states must avoid interference in the internal affairs of other states. Grotius pointed to the agreements that states have made among themselves, and that have proved to be durable: peace treaties, decisions as to the allocation of fishing and navigation rights, commonly accepted boundaries, and so on. The Grotian tradition thus derives the legitimacy of international law from the legitimacy of states themselves. But it goes further in seeking to derive principles whereby the behavior of one state toward another can be regulated, arguing that "natural right" must govern the interactions among states, and that this supercedes the authority of the states themselves. As Grotius saw it (and subsequent international law has affirmed), international "society" exists, which requires certain norms of conduct among states, including rules governing what is acceptable during war itself. For Grotius, war was not a breakdown in the law of nations, but rather a special condition to which law still applied....

The term *international law* first appeared in 1783, with the publication of Jeremy Bentham's

Principles of International Law. Accordingly, it is worth emphasizing that, whatever its shortcomings, nearly all our progress in international law has taken place in just a few hundred years; in fact, things have really gathered steam in the last fifty years. We might therefore be on the threshold of dramatic new developments.

Custom

Custom is one of the most important and least appreciated sources of international law. For example, consider the "rules of diplomatic protocol," whereby diplomats from one country are considered immune to arrest or detention in another. Clearly, these "rules" are in the interest of all countries, since, if the representatives of opposing states could legally be harassed, communication between states could quickly cease, to the disadvantage of all sides. Diplomats occasionally are expelled from a host country, usually for "activities incompatible with their diplomatic status" (that is, for spying), in which case some of the other side's diplomats typically are expelled in retaliation. But normally—that is, customarily, and thus by international law—diplomats are allowed substantial leeway, including the ability to communicate freely and secretly with their home government, as well as guarantees of their safety. (The strength of this presumption is shown by the outrage when it is violated, as when U.S. diplomats were held hostage in Iran in 1979–1980.)...

Treaties

International treaties are analogous to contracts among individuals. And of course, there have been many treaties, covering not only the termination of wars, but also agreements about boundaries, fishing and navigation rights, and mutually agreed restrictions as to permissible actions during war. Treaties are not always honored, but in the vast majority of cases, they have been. Backing away from treaty obligations results in a substantial loss of face, and once branded a treaty-breaker, a state may not be able to establish useful, reliable relationships with other states. Through treaties as well as customary practice, international law provides "rules of the road" by which international interaction, beneficial to

each side, can be conducted. As a result, states have a strong interest in abiding by them.

Courts

Finally, international law—just like domestic law—requires courts to hear disputed cases and render decisions. The first example of an international court was the Central American Court of Justice, established by treaty in 1908 by five Central American republics....

Best known and most important, however, has been the International Court of Justice (formerly the Permanent Court of International Justice, during its tenure under the League of Nations), located at The Hague, Netherlands, and administered by the UN. Also known as the World Court, this institution consists of a rotating membership of world jurists. It issues decisions about international law that are generally considered authoritative, although typically unenforceable. More recently, the ICJ has been joined by the International Criminal Court (ICC), which is officially independent of the UN, and which the United States has refused to acknowledge, claiming that it might "unlawfully" subject U.S. citizens (including soldiers) to "foreign" codes of law.

The verdict on international courts (or, alternatively, on the world's countries) is thus mixed. On the one hand, states are gradually becoming accustomed to letting go of enough sovereignty to settle disputes in court instead of in combat. On the other, adherence to the dictates of the World Court is entirely "consensual"—it is up to the consent of those involved—whereas adherence to domestic law is obligatory. Imagine a community in which accused lawbreakers could only be brought to trial if they agreed that the laws applied to them; further, imagine that they could then decide whether or not to abide by the ruling of the courts! As of the second decade of the 21st century, the United States remains one of the very few countries that has not.

ENFORCEMENT OF INTERNATIONAL LAW

The major problem with international law, therefore, aside from its diffuseness, is enforcement. Because enforcement provisions are generally lacking, some people contend that international "law" is not, strictly speaking, law at all, but rather, a set of acknowledged customs, or norms of behavior. The importance of norms alone should not be underestimated; in fact, most human behavior is conducted according to widely shared norms, not law itself. Nonetheless, domestic law is the last resort (short of violence, which domestic law typically prohibits), and law is effective at least in part because if worse comes to worst, and a lawbreaker is apprehended and found guilty of violating the law, he or she can be held accountable, suffering fines, prison terms, and the like. In the case of domestic law, individuals acknowledge (whether overtly or not) that they are subordinate to the state and its machinery of enforcement: the police, court bailiffs, the national guard, and so on. When it comes to relations among states, by contrast, the "individuals" insist on their sovereignty; they most emphatically do not recognize that any authority supercedes their own. If individual people behaved this way, domestic law could not effectively regulate their behavior. The major problem with international law, therefore, is that individual states insist on a kind of latitude that they would never allow their own citizens.

Let us briefly consider the role of sanctions (punishments for noncompliance) in law more generally. There are three primary incentives for obeying any law, domestic or international: self-interest, duty, and coercion. For example, most individuals stop at red lights not because they fear getting a traffic ticket, but rather because they know that otherwise, they are more likely to have an accident. Rules may therefore be followed out of purely utilitarian concerns, in this case, interest in one's own personal safety. Laws provide a way of regulating human conduct, for the benefit of all: You can proceed with reasonable safety through an intersection when your light is green, because you know that opposing traffic has a red light, and you have some confidence that other drivers will respect this law, just as you do.

In addition, individuals may follow the law because they feel themselves duty-bound to contribute toward an orderly society that functions with respect for authority. As members of society, who benefit from it, individuals assume a responsibility toward it. That is, some are influenced by normative considerations, or a kind of Kantian categorical imperative to do what is right and good for its own sake. And finally, some people are induced to be law-abiding by fear that "violators may be prosecuted" and forced to succumb to the state's authority if they are found guilty. Although the role of such coercive factors cannot be denied, coercion is not the only reason why most people obey the law. And similarly, the absence of such coercion does not invalidate international law, or render it toothless.

States have numerous incentives, both positive and negative, for abiding by their legal obligations to other states. If a state defects from its legal obligations, adversaries may well retaliate, one's friends and allies are liable to disapprove, and world opinion is likely to be strongly negative, leading to ostracism and possible economic, political, and cultural sanctions. Moreover, governments themselves have a strong stake in their own legitimacy, and—even in totalitarian states—adherence to law is fundamental to such legitimacy....

THE CONFLICT WITH STATE SOVEREIGNTY

It simply isn't true that all is anarchy in the international arena, any more than it is true that all is peaceful in the domestic sphere: More than one quarter of all wars, for example, are civil wars. States generally obey the law—out of a combined sense of duty and self-interest—even though coercive sanctions, as understood in domestic law, are absent. States engage in nonviolent commerce—exchange of tourists, diplomats, ideas, trade—according to certain regulations, and usually with goodwill and amity. Moreover, states usually do not enter into treaties unless they intend to abide by them, and they only acquiesce with customary norms of behavior when they anticipate that over the long run, they will benefit by doing so. At the same time, however, they typically cling to various aspects of sovereignty. Most treaties—notably those involving nuclear weapons—include a provision permitting signatories to withdraw within a set period of time, typically three or six months, if their "supreme national interests" are jeopardized. And who makes this decision? The state itself.

We have defined states as those political entities that are granted a monopoly of legitimate violence within their borders. When they engage in what they claim is lawful violence outside their borders, states typically maintain that (1) they are acting in self-defense (the U.S.S.R. in World War II, Israel in the Six Day War), (2) they are fulfilling treaty obligations (France and Britain in World War II), (3) they are intervening on the side of legitimate authority (the United States in Vietnam, the U.S.S.R. in Afghanistan), (4) the situation is anarchic and lacks a legitimate authority (the UN in the Congo), or (5) the conflict is within the realm of international obligations (the UN in Korea). In short, state sovereignty continues to reign, although a semblance of international law is generally invoked as well. States have been especially hesitant, however, to circumscribe their day-to-day authority. It is significant that whereas the Hague Conferences produced a few halting restrictions on the waging of war, they were unable to establish any significant binding rules for peace.

States are also selective when it comes to accepting the jurisdiction of the International Court of Justice, a process known as "adjudication." Adjudication is similar to arbitration in that the decision of the third party is binding. The only difference is that in adjudication, the decision is based on international law, rather than made by an arbitrator. The Soviet Union, for example, has historically refused to submit disputes to this body, although...the United States has been no better, despite the fact that in 1946, it formally agreed to submit all of its international disputes to the International Court of Justice. At that time, the U.S. Senate attached an amendment, known as the Connally Reservation, stipulating that the Court would not have authority over any disputes that "are essentially within the domestic jurisdiction of the United States of America as determined by the United States of America." With this loophole, the United States is free to "determine" that any dispute is essentially within its domestic jurisdiction, thereby avoiding international adjudication whenever it wishes....

Law is an important part of modern human life; some would even say that it is crucial to civilization. Despite concerns about enforcement—and anxiety when, as in the case of international law, enforcement powers are lacking—law is in many ways the antithesis of rule by brute force. Might does not make right; law does (or better yet, it reflects what is right). As a result, most good, decent people are presumed to be "law-abiding," and in fact, rule by law is almost inevitably seen as preferable to rule by force. We should also be aware, however, that law can be an instrument of oppression. Laws are made by those in power, and as such, they serve to perpetuate that power, and to prevent change. Thus, laws—international as well as domestic—serve best in a conservative environment. Third world and revolutionary states often point out that international laws were established by Western powers in support of their domination. The clearest example might well be the Treaty of Tordesillas (1494), following Columbus's "discovery" of the New World, whereby the pope "legally" divided that world into Spanish and Portuguese domains...without any regard for the people already living there....

International law must be flexible, if only because of the march of technology. For several centuries, for example, ever since a Dutch ruling in 1737, "territorial waters" have been considered to extend three miles from shore; this distance was based on the effective range of shore-based cannons. Now, new guidelines are being sought, with controversy fueled by disagreement among states, especially between the exploiters and the exploited. The former, particularly the developed industrialized states with relatively little shoreline (such as Britain and Japan) argue for narrow territorial waters, while those with extensive coastal waters (like Brazil and Burma), which seek to protect their fishing industry from foreign fleets, argue for a 200-mile limit.

These issues were partly resolved by the Law of the Sea Treaty, completed after decades of wrangling. This treaty also arranged for mechanisms of dispute resolution, waste disposal, and navigation procedures, but under the Reagan administration, the United States refused to sign, maintaining that the treaty's call for an intergovernmental body to supervise mining on the deep-sea bed constituted "international socialism." This also highlights once again the susceptibility of international law to asserted claims of state sovereignty, as well as the growing pressure of north/south cleavages.

HIDDEN STRENGTHS
OF INTERNATIONAL LAW

Governmental Respect for Law

Yet, governments do not routinely flout the law, not even their own domestic statutes, over which they have complete control. In most democratic countries, governments accede to legal decisions, even those that go against them. Citizens of the United States, for example, often take for granted the fact that in many cases, they can, if they wish, bring legal action against their own government. And if the courts—which are themselves organs of the government—rule against the government, citizens can receive compensation or other redress for their grievances, even though governments, not the courts, have the strong-arm potential of enforcing their will. This emphasizes the primacy of law over force. For example, following a strike during the Korean War—an action that supposedly threatened U.S. war production at a critical time—President Truman sought to nationalize the U.S. steel industry. The Supreme Court, however, overruled this action, whereupon the government obeyed the law, albeit reluctantly. Because democratic governments have a long-range interest in settling disputes amicably that supercedes any short-term interest in winning a given dispute, they tend to abide by legal rulings, even those that they dislike.

In international affairs, as we have seen, major powers are less likely to abide by international laws...unless the opponents are so balanced that the potential costs of losing a case are less than those of further wrangling, and possibly war....

International law often appears weaker than it really is, however. This is because violations, when they occur, are often sensational and dramatic, whereas compliance is taken for granted. When domestic law is broken by individuals, only rarely are we moved to question the appropriateness of the law itself, and never to doubt the existence of such law. But a different standard seems to be applied to international law. When states violate international law, they may or may not be condemned by public opinion, but almost invariably, the law itself is called into question, and the purported weakness of international law is once again lamented. Just as we

are not told about the vast majority of people who obey domestic law every day, we do not see news stories proclaiming that "Paraguay today complied with its treaty obligations regarding its border with Bolivia, and therefore, no invasion took place."

Virtually the entire civilized world was shocked, by contrast, when Chancellor Theobald von Bethmann-Hollweg justified the German invasion of Belgium in the early days of World War I by describing the international guarantee of Belgian neutrality as a "mere scrap of paper" that could readily be torn up. On the one hand, this announcement—and even more so, the brutal invasion itself—showed the truth of the chancellor's assertion: Belgian neutrality was in fact "only" an international agreement, lacking any guarantee and incapable, by itself, of keeping the invading German divisions out. On the other hand, the level of international outrage showed that international law, even when it lacks explicit means of enforcement, has undeniable effects on public perception. (In addition, we should note that the immediate reason for Britain entering the war against Germany was the German violation of Belgian neutrality; so, in a sense, international treaty law was ultimately enforced in this case. Had Germany respected the law, it might have won the war.)

The Law of War

War—the violent resolution of conflict—can be seen as the antithesis of law, whose goal after all is the ordering of relations without recourse to violence. Cicero first wrote that *inter arma silent legis* ("in war the law is silent"). This is taken to mean that the justifiability of any given war is outside the purview of international law, since states are sovereign authorities unto themselves, and free to make war or not, as they choose. Under this view, since there is no higher authority than a state, no one can claim that a state is making war unlawfully....

Nonetheless, a body of law is widely thought to apply to states under conditions of war. War itself can even be defined as "the legal condition which equally permits two or more hostile groups to carry on a conflict by armed force." Therefore—at least according to some experts—war represents a highly formalized interval during which violence may legitimately be practiced between two opposing groups. Enough agreement exists within the community of nations that belligerents and neutrals alike recognize the existence of certain accepted standards: "Although war manifests the weakness of the community of nations, it also manifests the existence of that community."

THE NUREMBERG PRINCIPLES

States that are party to international treaties may find themselves subject, even against their will, to the legal restraints of these treaties. The losers in World War II, for example, were tried—and many were convicted—for having waged aggressive war in defiance of their obligations under the Kellogg-Briand Treaty. These trials, conducted in the German city of Nuremberg, were unique in developing the legal doctrine that individuals are personally liable to criminal prosecution for crimes against international law. This includes illegal resort to war as well as violations of accepted restraints as to appropriate conduct during war, notably the treatment of prisoners and the waging of genocide. Thus, the chief Allied prosecutor at Nuremberg wrote that

> war consists largely of acts that would be criminal if performed in time of peace—killing, wounding, kidnapping, destroying or carrying off other people's property. Such conduct is not regarded as criminal if it takes place in the course of war, because the state of war lays a blanket of immunity over the warriors.... But the area of immunity is not unlimited and its boundaries are marked by the laws of war.

It should also be pointed out, however, that critics objected to these proceedings, claiming that the Nuremberg Trials were simply examples of "victors' justice," and not concerned with genuine international law. Nevertheless, the so-called Nuremberg Principles have served as a benchmark in efforts to introduce humane and reasoned limits to acceptable wartime behavior. Thus, the international military tribunal that convened in Nuremberg specified a series of international crimes. Article 6 of the Nuremberg Charter identified the following:

1. Crimes against the peace, namely planning, preparation, initiation or waging of a war of aggression, or a war in violation of international treaties....
2. Crimes against humanity, namely, murder, extermination, enslavement, deportation, and other inhumane acts committed against any civilian population....
3. War crimes, namely, violations of the laws or customs of war. Such violations shall include, but not be limited to, murder, ill-treatment or deportation to slave labor or for any other purpose of civilian population of or in occupied territory, murder or ill-treatment of prisoners of war or persons on the seas, killing of hostages, plunder of public or private property, wanton destruction of cities, towns or villages, or devastation not justified by military necessity.

Article 7 specified that "the official position of defendants, whether as Heads of State or responsible officials of Government departments, shall not be considered as freeing them from their responsibility or mitigating their punishment." And according to Article 8, "the fact that the defendant acted pursuant to orders of this Government or of a superior shall not free him from responsibility."

Whereas the German defendants at Nuremberg were tried for crimes they had committed in violation of international law, a series of lesser-known trials were also conducted in Tokyo, of Japanese officials accused in large part of crimes of *omission*—that is, illegal failure to act.

...Several decades later, when U.S. army lieutenant William Calley was tried and found guilty for his role in the My Lai massacre during the Vietnam War, it marked the first time a state had accused one of its own soldiers of war crimes. Calley's highest-ranking commanding officers were not tried, however....

So again, whereas international laws exist, and have been enforced, such enforcement has been highly selective.

The treaties that were violated by the Nuremberg defendants, originating from the Geneva and Hague Conventions, specified limitations on such actions as naval or aerial bombardment. But they also made allowances for "military necessity," which can be stretched to permit nearly any act in wartime, however outrageous. Similarly, even the toothless Kellogg-Briand Treaty was interpreted by many as permitting "wars of self-defense," as does the current UN Charter: Article 51 grants states the "inherent right of individual or collective self-defense." Self-defense would clearly justify Poland's short-lived response in seeking to resist the German invasion in 1939, but what about France's response, namely, declaring war on Germany (France was treaty-bound to help defend Poland)? And what about the Israeli invasion of Egypt in 1967, in which Israel clearly struck first, but in which it was argued that Egyptian behavior constituted a real provocation as well as an imminent threat that justified a "pre-emptive" attack by Israel? Similarly, the "Brezhnev Doctrine," by which the U.S.S.R. justified its invasion of Czechoslovakia, was described as laudable pan-socialist self-defense against Western-inspired counterrevolutionaries. And the "Reagan Doctrine," under which the United States assisted right-wing revolutionaries in Marxist states such as Angola or Afghanistan, has been described by its supporters as providing aid to people seeking to defend themselves. Apologists for wars of self-defense and self-determination have thus far always been able to find loopholes in international treaties large enough to drive an army through. . . .

A FINAL NOTE ON INTERNATIONAL LAW

International law has many imperfections. It appears to have exerted some useful restraints in some cases, while being woefully inadequate in others. The major powers give it less credence than do the lesser states, in part because the former have recourse to their military strength, whereas the latter must depend on the rule of law to offer them the possibility of a "level playing field" in contests with larger, stronger opponents. Some authorities recommend only a modest role for international law in the future, avoiding "the Charybdis of subservience to state ambitions and the Scylla of excessive pretensions of restraint," and recognizing that "it is in the interest of international law itself to put states' consciences neither to sleep nor to torture." Another view holds that international law is a beginning, something on which to build a world without boundaries, or at least, one in which the sanctity of state sovereignty is greatly curtailed in the interest of human survival as well as quality of life.

JUST WAR DOCTRINE

Military action—whether a formally declared war or some other violent response, such as to terrorism—involves one of the most drastic actions that can be undertaken. Killing another human being—except by accident, as self-defense, or out of insanity—is universally condemned . . . except during war, in which time it is not only permitted, but applauded. Nonetheless, such applause is not universal, and even when it occurs, it is rarely unequivocal. Advocates of peace have often derived strength, inspiration, and even specific suggestions for action or inaction from moral and ethical teaching, although to be sure, such teachings have not been unilaterally antiwar. There have been concerted and influential efforts to support the ethical legitimacy of war under certain circumstances. Indeed, even though violence is perhaps the most frequent target of the world's moral systems, and although war in general is widely criticized, it is debatable whether such systems have been more likely to oppose or to support *specific* wars.

Perhaps it avails nothing if moralists condemn war in general but lend their approval to each particular war as it comes along. But this conclusion omits a potentially important characteristic of moral thought: a continuing predisposition *against* violence and killing. There is little room, after all, to criticize the horrors of Auschwitz or the bombing of Hiroshima from an engineering standpoint—these events were technical triumphs! It is only by applying moral judgments that outrage—and from such outrage, a determination to change—can be developed.

The most carefully enunciated and influential moral approach to war in the Western tradition, the so-called "just war doctrine," is largely the result of Catholic teaching, derived especially from the writings of St. Augustine. This approach, sometimes called "Christian realism," can be criticized as unacceptably apologetic when it comes to war-making. Certainly, the doctrine cannot by itself be counted on as a bulwark against war, if only because just war doctrine is specifically concerned with identifying circumstances under which war is permissible. It is no coincidence that this way of thinking developed in the immediate aftermath of the conversion of the Roman emperor Constantine to Christianity, which meant that Roman Christians were faced with the responsibility of dealing with practical political and military realities—namely, the defense of the Roman Empire—as contrasted with their previous situation as prophetic outsiders.

In general, just war doctrine is nuanced and, if anything, biased *against* war, except under specifically defined conditions and when conducted in carefully restricted ways. Thus, it offers some potential assistance in preventing war, or at least making it less destructive and possibly even less likely.

The following selection is a good representation of a Christian—specifically, Roman Catholic—elaboration of just war doctrine.

THE ROOTS OF JUST WAR DOCTRINE

In the Beatitudes, Jesus tells us "blessed are the peacemakers" (Matt. 5:9). Elsewhere in the Sermon on the Mount he tells us "if any one strikes you on the right cheek, turn to him the other also" (Matt. 5:39). From such verses some have concluded that Christianity is a pacifist religion and that violence is never permitted.

But the same Jesus elsewhere acknowledges the legitimate use of force, telling the apostles, "let him who has no sword sell his mantle and buy one" (Luke 22:36). How are these passages to be reconciled?

In broad terms, Christians must not love violence. They must promote peace whenever possible and be slow to resort to the use of arms. But they must not be afraid to do so when it is called for. Evil must not be allowed to remain unchecked.

Added weight is given to this realization when one recognizes that Scripture—all of Scripture—is inspired by God (2 Tim. 3:16). This means that the Old Testament is just as inspired as the New Testament and thus an expression of the will of Christ.

The Old Testament acknowledges frankly that there is "a time to kill" (Eccles. 3:3). At various times in the Old Testament, God commanded the Israelites to defend their nation by force of arms. Yet it was always with the recognition that peace is the goal to be worked for. Thus the psalmist exclaims, "how good and pleasant it is when brothers dwell in unity!" (Ps. 133:1). Peace is the goal, but when it cannot be achieved without force, force must be used.

In the same way, the New Testament sets forth the goal of peace but acknowledges the legitimate use of force. It does so by John the Baptist's acknowledgment that Roman soldiers, whose job it was to enforce the *Pax Romana*, or "Peace of Rome," could keep their jobs (Luke 3:14) and by Paul's observation that the state "does not bear the sword in vain" but is "God's servant for your good" (Rom. 13:4).

As long as Christianity remained a minority religion in the Roman Empire, it was not forced to put these insights together into a formal theory of when warfare could be used. But as Christianity grew predominant, more attention had to be devoted to this subject. By the time of Augustine (A.D. 354–430)

the need for a theory of when warfare was just was keen, and Augustine provided one, crystallizing biblical principles into what is now known as just war doctrine. In the intervening centuries the theory has been refined, but its framework remains as he gave it.

JUST WAR DOCTRINE TODAY

The most authoritative and up-to-date expression of just war doctrine is found in paragraph 2309 of the *Catechism of the Catholic Church*. It says:

> The strict conditions for legitimate defense by military force require rigorous consideration. The gravity of such a decision makes it subject to rigorous conditions of moral legitimacy. At one and the same time:
>
> - the damage inflicted by the aggressor on the nation or community of nations must be lasting, grave, and certain;
> - all other means of putting an end to it must have been shown to be impractical or ineffective;
> - there must be serious prospects of success;
> - the use of arms must not produce evils and disorders graver than the evil to be eliminated. The power of modern means of destruction weighs very heavily in evaluating this condition.

These are the traditional elements enumerated in what is called the "just war" doctrine. The evaluation of these conditions for moral legitimacy belongs to the prudential judgment of those who have responsibility for the common good.

Let us take a closer look at each of the elements in the Church's just war doctrine.

Strict Conditions

> The strict conditions for legitimate defense by military force require rigorous consideration. The gravity of such a decision makes it subject to rigorous conditions of moral legitimacy. At one and the same time . . .

Here the Catechism indicates the gravity of the decision to go to war. Before this can be done "rigorous consideration" must be given to whether the following conditions are met. It is not enough for just some of them to be met. Instead, all must be met "at one and the same time."

Lasting, Grave, and Certain Damage

The damage inflicted by the aggressor on the nation or community of nations must be lasting, grave, and certain.

The first condition indicates that there must be an aggressor who is harming the nation or the community of nations. One cannot go to war simply to expand one's sphere of influence, conquer new territory, subjugate peoples, or obtain wealth. One only can go to war to counter aggression.

In recent wars, the aggressor often has been a nation-state, such as Germany was in the First and Second World Wars. But nation-states are relatively new in world history. Throughout much of history the aggressors were much smaller and more loosely organized. Even today many small wars are fought between tribes. In recent years they have been fought between national armies and drug cartels. And in the war on terrorism a principal aggressor has been the terrorist organization al Qaeda.

The damage inflicted by the aggressor must be "lasting, grave, and certain." An aggression that is temporary and mild would not meet this condition. It must be foreseen to have effects that are both lasting and grave.

It also must be foreseen with moral certainty, moral certainty being the highest kind of assurance that is possible in geo-political matters. If this is present—and if the other conditions are met—then it is lawful to resort to war.

This means that it is not necessary for the aggressor to strike first. A moral certainty that the aggression will occur is sufficient. Such certainty might be present, for instance, if a party with a history of aggression began amassing troops or munitions.

In a world where it is possible for an aggressor to strike at a distance, with little or no warning, and to cause mass casualties, it is important to identify a potential aggressor early and determine whether he poses a morally certain danger.

Other Means Impractical or Ineffective

All other means of putting an end to it must have been shown to be impractical or ineffective.

The second condition establishes war as a last resort. If there are other practical and effective means of stopping the aggressor, they must be used.

Alternatives include one-to-one diplomacy; international pressure; economic sanctions; and such tools as blockades, quarantines, covert actions, and small-scale raids that do not amount to a full-scale war effort. It is not necessary to employ all such methods before going to war. It is sufficient if rigorous consideration reveals them to be impractical or ineffective.

They would be shown to be impractical if rigorous consideration revealed that, even though they might work in theory, they were not practically possible.

They would be shown to be ineffective if they had little or no chance of stopping the aggression and preventing the damage that it will bring.

Prospects of Success

There must be serious prospects of success.

The third condition is that the war must have "serious prospects of success."

It is not possible to have a guarantee of success. Even nations with overwhelming military force can lose wars to less well-armed nations, as happened to the U.S. in the Vietnam War. This may be caused by a loss of public will, by lack of expertise in fighting a particular conflict, the intervention of other nations, the outbreak of side conflicts, or other factors.

Because it is impossible to guarantee the outcome of an event as chaotic and destabilizing as war, all that is required for this condition is that there be a substantial possibility of success.

Greater Evils?

The use of arms must not produce evils and disorders graver than the evil to be eliminated. The power of modern means of destruction weighs very heavily in evaluating this condition.

The final condition has to do with the foreseen consequences of the war. Even if a victory can be foreseen, the damage that is done by the war itself must be taken into account.

As the Catechism notes, the weapons of mass destruction that are available to many nations play a large part in evaluating whether this condition is met. Armed with these weapons, it would be possible for nations to use excessive destructive force when stopping an aggressor, resulting in more casualties than would have occurred if the aggression had been allowed to run its course. In some measure, the evaluation of this condition pertains to the question of how the war is conducted, which will be dealt with below.

Wars inescapably cause damage. This includes the collateral damage they produce in civilian casualties. They also can create other evils, such as destabilizing neighboring countries, changing international alliances in harmful ways, and creating economic burdens.

It is incumbent on those making the decision to go to war to attempt to the best of their ability to foresee both what damage will result if the war is conducted and what damage will result if it is not. The former must not clearly outweigh the latter.

Who Decides?

> The evaluation of these conditions for moral legitimacy belongs to the prudential judgment of those who have responsibility for the common good.

Finally, the Catechism identifies those who have the burden of evaluating the conditions for whether a particular war is just: "those who have responsibility for the common good." In modern nation-states, this means the government.

Governments are privy to information gathered by intelligence services and other means that the general public does not possess. Because the public is not in possession of this information, the public is not in as advantaged a position to determine whether the conditions are met. As a result, the public must in significant measure be prepared to trust its leaders to make the right decision.

There may not be a guarantee that the government will do so, but, except in the case of fundamentally evil regimes, it is more likely that the government would arrive at an appropriate course of action than would the general public.

This is not to say that the public has no voice in such matters. Particularly in democracies, it does. The public elects its leaders and, through public debate, helps guide its leaders' decisions. Nevertheless, the general public does not bear ultimate responsibility for the decision to go to war. That belongs "to the prudential judgment" of its political leaders. They must evaluate the situation and make their best judgment whether the conditions for just war have been fulfilled.

JUSTICE IN WAR

Once the decision to go to war has been reached, a new set of issues is placed in focus. These have to do with how the war is conducted. Thus the Catechism states:

> The Church and human reason both assert the permanent validity of the moral law during armed conflict. The mere fact that war has regrettably broken out does not mean that everything becomes licit between the warring parties (CCC 2312).

A particular danger in wartime is brutality toward those not engaged in combat. Frequently in the history of warfare, soldiers have maimed, raped, and even killed those who did not pose a physical threat to them. Sometimes this has escalated into genocide. The Catechism is at pains to stress the moral illegitimacy of all of these:

> Non-combatants, wounded soldiers, and prisoners must be respected and treated humanely. Actions deliberately contrary to the law of nations and to its universal principles are crimes, as are the orders that command such actions. Blind obedience does not suffice to excuse those who carry them out. Thus the extermination of a people, nation, or ethnic minority must be condemned as a mortal sin. One is morally bound to resist orders that command genocide (CCC 2313).

Unlike many countries, America has a strong commitment to this principle. The U.S. is famous for its humane treatment of non-combatants, wounded soldiers, and prisoners of war. Indeed, America is renowned for turning former wartime enemies—such as Germany, Japan, and Italy—into friends.

The treatment of non-hostile individuals in wartime is not the only consideration involved in the just prosecution of a war. The existence of weapons of mass destruction poses special moral challenges. In this regard the Catechism states:

> Every act of war directed to the indiscriminate destruction of whole cities or vast areas with their inhabitants is a crime against God and man, which merits firm and unequivocal condemnation. A danger of modern warfare is that it provides the opportunity to those who possess modern scientific weapons—especially atomic, biological, or chemical weapons—to commit such crimes (CCC 2314).

The U.S. has not always been committed to this principle. In the Civil War, World War I, and World War II the United States violated it. Grave violations during World War II included the firebombing of Dresden and the atomic bombings of Hiroshima and Nagasaki.

These were not attacks designed to destroy targets of military value while sparing civilian populations. They were deliberate attempts to put pressure on enemy governments by attacking non-combatants. As a result, they were grave violations of God's law, according to which, "the direct and voluntary killing of an innocent human being is always gravely immoral" (John Paul II, Evangelium Vitae 57).

It is important to recognize what this principle does and does not require. While it does require strenuous efforts to avoid harming innocents, it does not require the result of no innocents being harmed. Such a result is impossible to guarantee. Even with the smartest of smart munitions, it is not possible to ensure that no non-combatants will be harmed in wartime. As tragic as it is, collateral damage to innocents is an inescapable consequence of war. Catholic theology recognizes this. It applies to such situations a well-established principle known as the law of double-effect. According to this law it is permissible to undertake an action which has two effects, one good and one evil, provided that certain conditions are met.

Although these conditions can be formulated in different ways, they may be enumerated as follows: (1) the action itself must not be intrinsically evil; (2) the evil effect must not be an end in itself or a means to accomplishing the good effect (in other words, it must be a foreseen but undesired side-effect of the action); and (3) the evil effect must not outweigh the good effect. If these three conditions are met, the action may be taken in spite of the foreseen damage it will do.

The law of double-effect would not have applied to the cases of Dresden, Hiroshima, and Nagasaki. In these situations though the act (dropping bombs) was not intrinsically evil and though it is arguable that in the long run more lives were saved than lost, the second condition was violated because the death of innocents was used as a means to achieve the good of the war's end.

Fortunately, despite these past, grave transgressions, the United States is now committed to the principle of sparing innocent life during military actions. It has repeatedly and sincerely expressed its intent to minimize civilian casualties and to serve as a liberator of captive populations in the War on Terrorism. The U.S. is now committed to the principles of the just war.

CONCLUSION

As the Second Vatican Council noted, "insofar as men are sinful, the threat of war hangs over them, and hang over them it will until the return of Christ" (Gaudium et Spes 78). The danger of war will never be completely removed prior to the Second Coming.

Christ's followers must be willing to meet this challenge. They must be willing to wage war when it is just and they must be willing to wage it in a just manner.

Simultaneously, they must work to establish a just and peaceful order among the nations. In so doing they seek to fulfill the words of the prophet, according to which the nations "shall beat their swords into plowshares, and their spears into pruning hooks; nation shall not lift up sword against nation, neither shall they learn war any more" (Is. 2:4).

Linda Fasulo

AN INSIDER'S GUIDE TO THE UN

Conflict situations can be resolved in two basic ways: "associative" and "disassociative." The latter relies on military strength and political separation, and is based on the notion that "good fences make good neighbors." Associative solutions, by contrast, involve tearing down walls and joining together. As we have seen, prominent among the causes of war is the existence of feisty, sovereign states that are, by definition, disassociative relative to each other. Associative solutions include heightened reliance on international law, shared ethical norms, and the joining together of otherwise independent countries to form international organizations. As with the other "solutions" considered in this chapter, international organizations are not perfect or foolproof. Although their record is mixed, there is much to applaud in the activities of various international organizations, especially the United Nations, which offers a way of ameliorating—although not eliminating—the often troublesome role of states.

When considering the UN, it is important to recognize what it is *not*: it is not a world government, because its members retain their sovereignty. Also, it has not proven effective in preventing conflicts among the major powers, because these powers were granted vetoes over any UN-led enforcement activities. However, the UN has been occasionally effective in peacekeeping, and in monitoring compliance with cease-fires and other negotiated settlements, and, often, in mediating disputes that might otherwise have turned violent. The UN also provides a valuable forum for debates in addition to the contribution of its various "functional" agencies (such as the Food and Agriculture Organization, the World Health Organization, UNESCO, UNICEF, etc.), which not only help alleviate much human misery but also help creatively undermine reliance on states as the sole unit of political/economic/social recourse.

Thus, the benefits of the United Nations go beyond simply contributing to "negative peace." It may also represent a partial step in the progression from individualism through to tribalism, to nationalism and then to globalism, a transition that may well be essential if we are ever to give peace a realistic chance. As might be expected, the United Nations is regularly criticized, especially by right-wing militarists and ardent nationalists...which in itself suggests that it may have a major role to play in preventing war!

Regrettably, the UN has been especially unsuccessful in quelling civil wars, such as in Libya or Syria. It also has been notably reluctant – or unable – to intevene in wars of would-be separation, especially when the major powers are directly involved. On the other hand, UN peacekeeping operations, which are the primary focus of the next selection, have in fact achieved far more than is widely appreciated; after all, just as news reports are unlikely to announce, "War did *not* break out today between countries X and Y," people are far more aware of any failures to prevent war than of the numerous successes.

Article 43

All Members of the United Nations, in order to contribute to the maintenance of international peace and security, undertake to make available to the Security Council, on its call and in accordance with a special agreement or agreements, armed forces, assistance, and facilities, including rights of passage, necessary for the purpose of maintaining international peace and security.

—*UN Charter*

Although peacekeeping is one of the quintessential UN functions, it is mentioned only briefly in the Charter. Its full scope and nature have gradually emerged, through need, as a middle ground between mere arbitration of disputes, on the one hand, and use of armed force, on the other. The Security Council's first peacekeeping resolution set important precedents, establishing the United Nations Truce Supervision Organization (UNTSO) in 1948 to oversee the truce between Arabs and Jews when the United Kingdom left Palestine. Like peacekeepers today, the UNTSO troops were provided by member states. The troopers wore the blue helmets that have marked UN peacekeepers ever since. UNTSO also set the model for nomenclature: it is invariably referred to by its acronym rather than its full name. That decades-old practice has led to a roster of past and current operations that read like a chapter out of Genesis, with names that sound like the biblical Gog and Magog—actually, MOONUC and UNOMIG. UNTSO is still in operation, with an expanded mandate that includes supervising the implementation and observance of the general agreements between Israel and its four Arab neighbors.

Once the Security Council authorizes the deployment of an operation, defines its mission, and recommends how it should be carried out, the secretary general appoints a force commander and through the Secretariat's Department of Peacekeeping Operations (DPKO) arranges for management and logistics. Member states are asked to provide personnel, equipment, and logistics. The UN pays member states at the rate of $1,100 per peacekeeper per month, and the governments pay the troops according to their own scales. Member states retain control over their units. Peacekeeping personnel rely less on their arms than on their international authority and their reputation for impartiality. They wear their country's uniform and are identified as peacekeepers by a UN blue helmet or a beret and a badge.

Some UN peacekeeping operations consist of military observers charged with monitoring truces, troop withdrawals, and borders or demilitarized zones. Other operations involve military formations capable of acting as buffers between hostile forces. More recently, some peacekeeping operations have combined military and police or civilian functions and personnel, with the aim of creating or strengthening political institutions, providing emergency aid, clearing land mines, or administering and monitoring free elections.

Peace-related issues have always been central to Security Council deliberations, but in the past decade they have become especially numerous and demanding of time and resources. The decade of the 1990s saw the UN launch more peace-related operations than in all the previous four decades. During the year ending June 2003, there were 14 peacekeeping missions, employing 45,000 personnel at a cost of $2.6 billion.

And the nature of the disputes has largely changed. The norm used to be that wars occurred between nation-states, which fought with field armies that were supposed to target combatants and not civilians—that was the theory, anyway. But these days nation-states have been remarkably well behaved toward one another, and in some places, like Europe, they have even forged close political ties. Instead, conflicts tend to occur within nations, in the form of civil wars (as in Rwanda, Congo, and the former Yugoslavia) or national resistance movements (like the East Timorese against Indonesian occupation, the Islamic separatists in the Philippines, the independence fighters in Kosovo, or the Palestinians against the Israelis).

A PEACE GLOSSARY

Just as Eskimos have many words to describe the various kinds of snow, the UN has developed words and phrases for the making and keeping of peace. Here are just a few.

Preventive diplomacy

As its name suggest, preventive diplomacy seeks to head off disputes before they become full-blown conflicts. The UN prefers this kind of diplomacy but is able to apply it in only some instances. The UN employs its extensive contacts and offices around the world to detect early signs of potential threats to international peace and security.

Peacemaking

Peacemaking involves the use of diplomacy to persuade belligerents to stop fighting and negotiate an end to their dispute.

Peace enforcement

Peace enforcement involves the use of force against one of the belligerents to enforce an end to the fighting.

Peacebuilding

Peacebuilding involves helping nations promote peace before, during, or after a conflict. Broadly defined, it employs a wide range of political, humanitarian, and human rights activities and programs.

Many parts of the UN system may join in a peacebuilding effort, as well as private bodies like nongovernmental organizations (NGOs). The secretary general often appoints representatives to coordinate the activities through special peacebuilding support offices, such as those established in Liberia, Guinea-Bissau, and the Central African Republic.

The responsibility to protect

The Charter gives the UN the right to intervene in a nation's affairs to prevent egregious human rights violations, but in recent years there has been talk about a variant on this, called the responsibility to protect. A recent international commission stated in its report that "the responsibility to protect implies an evaluation of the issues from the point of view of those seeking or needing support, rather than those who may be considering intervention."

THE TALKING CURE

Today, the council has to address so many requests for making or keeping peace that it usually begins by looking for a solution that does not involve a UN deployment. It starts with behind-the-scenes diplomacy, escalating to open diplomacy as needed.

A good example is the conflict between Ethiopia and its breakaway province of Eritrea, which began in the 1990s and has only recently been resolved, largely through UN and regional efforts. During the early 1980s, Ethiopia, a landlocked country, unilaterally annexed Eritrea, which gave it a port on the Red Sea; but the Eritreans resisted and finally secured their independence after a long war. Then, on May 6, 1998, the Eritrean government ordered its armed forces to occupy a slice of disputed territory on the border with Ethiopia. A regional body, the Organization of African Unity (OAU), worked out an agreement for settling the dispute, but neither side would commit to it.

In February 1999, the Security Council stepped in and urged the disputants to accept the OAU's plan.

When they refused and began fighting, the council moved to its next stage of action, which was to tell the combatants to stop fighting, start talking, and arrange a cease-fire. The U.S. also joined the cease-fire efforts, and in February and March OAU special envoy Ahmed Ouyahia (of Algeria) and former U.S. national security advisor Anthony Lake visited Asmara and Addis Ababa. Algeria then brought the two parties together for talks, which broke down.

The fighting had by then stopped but seemed on the verge of resuming when, in April, the council reiterated its demand for a cease-fire and implementation of the OAU's plan. In June the council again asked the two parties to negotiate, citing a looming humanitarian crisis as drought and unrest threatened massive starvation. The U.S. sent more then 700,000 metric tons of food assistance to Ethiopia and 100,000 to Eritrea. A UN Security Council mission to Congo, led by U.S. permanent representative Richard Holbrooke, began shuttle diplomacy during several days early in May, with Holbrooke leaning on both sides not to renew the fighting.

The shuttle talks failed, the mission left, and on May 12, 2000, Ethiopia sent its forces deep into Eritrea. The Security Council passed a resolution demanding an end to military action, but the next day Ethiopia's forces made a major breakthrough and eventually advanced to within 100 kilometers of the Eritrean capital. Then the Ethiopian government, apparently satisfied it had acquired a good bargaining position, stated it was ending the war. Meanwhile, the Security Council passed another resolution, 1298, requiring that member states enforce an arms sales embargo on both combatants. Eritrea then declared that it would move its troops back to the border that existed in May 1998.

As each combatant backed off, the OAU, UN, and other parties arranged for new talks in Algiers, which led to an agreement on June 18 for a cease-fire. Once the fighting ended, the council created the UN Mission in Ethiopia and Eritrea (UNMEE), charged with monitoring the border and ensuring that the provisions of the cease-fire were honored. The council authorized the mission at a strength of more than 4,200 military and other personnel.

By then, Ethiopia and Eritrea had been fighting or at least glaring at each other for more than two years. Why did the council wait so long? The answer is that UN peacekeepers maintain peace once it is agreed to by the combatants, but they do not create peace through military action. The main purpose of peacekeeping is simply to help prevent fighting from erupting and to give negotiators a chance to find a permanent resolution to the dispute.

A resolution seems to have been found in the Ethiopia–Eritrea border dispute. In fall 2000, the OAU envoy and Anthony Lake pursued shuttle diplomacy while members of the Security Council urged the disputants to negotiate a complete solution. At Algiers in December 2000, the two nations signed a final accord in the presence of secretary general Kofi Annan and U.S. secretary of state Madeleine Albright. The end is in sight but not quite achieved. UNMEE is expected to remain deployed until the final border between the two nations is demarcated, and until the two governments establish sufficient dialogue to ensure that they can peacefully resolve any disagreements or misunderstandings that might arise between them.

UN SANCTIONS

Sanctions are nonlethal, noninvasive mechanisms aimed at preventing a state from interacting with the outside world in certain ways, such as engaging in trade or acquiring arms. Travel bans and financial or diplomatic restrictions are also types of sanction. Although sanctions are intended to pressure governments, they may also unintentionally harm civilians too. Sometimes it is the poorest or most vulnerable members of society who are most harmed when their nation is placed under a sanction, especially one that affects trade and commerce. Consider the case of Saddam Hussein's regime in Iraq, after the Gulf War.

When Iraq invaded Kuwait in 1990, the UN imposed sweeping sanctions intended to bar the aggressor from all trade and financial dealings, except for humanitarian purposes, with the rest of the world. After the U.S. and its allies, with the blessing of the UN, routed the Iraqi armed forces and arranged a cease-fire (which the UN monitored) in 1991, the UN left the sanctions in place while stipulating that Iraq divest itself of weapons of mass destruction. Because the Iraqi government was not fully cooperating with inspections, the UN continued the sanctions throughout the years of the Saddam Hussein regime.

The Iraqi government, meanwhile, was able to partly evade the sanctions while complaining noisily that its citizens were being deprived of access to vital medicines, food, and other necessities. This effective campaign influenced the Security Council to create the Oil for Food program, which permitted the Iraqi government the option of exporting specified amounts of crude oil, under UN scrutiny, in order to pay for "humanitarian goods." Terms of the program were liberalized in 1998 and 1999, and finally in 2002, to give Iraq access to most civilian goods. The last liberalization was done through a Security Council resolution offered by the U.S. in May 2002. The idea behind the resolution was to replace typical UN sanctions with "smart sanctions" that would enable Iraqi citizens to get necessities more easily while making it more difficult for Saddam Hussein's regime to use trade in order to obtain arms and other forbidden items. On May 22, 2003, two months after the U.S.-led invasion of Iraq, the Security Council lifted sanctions, except for the sale of weapons and related materiel.

RETHINKING PEACEKEEPING

Although traditional peacekeeping remains important, it is increasingly regarded as merely the first step in a process of moving from armed conflict to political dialogue and engagement. The new approach tries to engage all stakeholders in dialogue, which means governments, of course, but also nongovernmental organizations and other groups. Among the pioneers of the new approach is Kofi Annan, who spent four years in charge of peacekeeping operations when he was undersecretary general, and one of his top aides, Shashi Tharoor. As Tharoor says of his experiences during the 1990s, when the new approach emerged, in addition to doing the usual peacekeeping tasks, they were experimenting with "all sorts of new things, everything from delivering humanitarian aid under fire, hunting down warlords, and of course monitoring no-fly zones. It was very much like fixing the engine of a moving car."

One of the places where the UN has applied its new thinking about peacekeeping is East Timor, which recently gained national independence from Indonesia. The Security Council hosted the negotiations that led in 1999 to a popular referendum in which the Timorese rejected autonomy within Indonesia and opted for complete independence. But the council had to authorize a multinational security force after Indonesian-backed militants unleashed a campaign of systematic destruction and violence in response to the Timorese referendum. Many East Timorese were killed and more than 200,000 were forced to flee, most of them to West Timor.

In October 1999, acting under Chapter VII of the UN Charter, the Security Council established the UN Transitional Administration in East Timor (UNTAET) to restore order and provide administrative services as East Timor prepared for independence. The council appointed Sergio Vieira de Mello of Brazil as the transitional administrator for East Timor. UNTAET began a program of "Timorization" of key government posts to prepare for transition to full independence. In July UNTAET established the East Timor Transitional Administration (ETTA), with a cabinet of nine ministries, five headed by East Timorese. Then UNTAET appointed a thirty-six-member National Council representing a wide spectrum of Timorese society. UNTAET began preparations for elections in late summer 2001 for a national assembly, which drew up and adopted a constitution. In 2002 the Timorese elected a president and became a new nation.

The UN's nation-building has succeeded in launching East Timor on its new path, but interestingly the effort has gotten mixed reviews. David Malone praises its director: "To make good things happen at the UN requires particular skills and qualities that may not be required in running a major corporation or running a major government. They are particular skills of endurance and determination that I think find expression in Sergio Vieira de Mello, who pulled off the East Timor operation in spite of tremendous problems on the ground and enormous bureaucratic inertia within the UN. He just has the sheer determination to get things done and they did get done." Shepard Forman concedes that the effort went fairly well but questions whether it was appropriate: "The UN as a government in Kosovo and East Timor is questionable. Few of the people that went out to govern had any more experience than any of the East Timorese. That's an example of where it [the UN] took on a role to prove itself, and it did an all right job, but we lost a year or so in terms of the Timoreses' own capacity to develop, to reconstruct."

Good, bad, or inappropriate, the UN's mission to East Timor shows that new ideas are floating about and being acted on, which is crucial if the world body is going to adapt and remain vital. Which opens up another area of change: the faces under those blue helmets.

NEW PEACEKEEPERS, NEW FACES

A relic of the colonial era, which didn't end until the 1970s, is that the Western media tend to present the European-American nations as militarily superior. This is increasingly an outdated notion. David Malone says, "It's just assumed that the West, because it is so well equipped when it goes into the peacekeeping field, is the only region providing qualified peacekeepers." Not so, he asserts. The Indians and the Pakistanis are "excellent peacekeepers," and the Bangladeshis and the Kenyans "have proved very good in the field." As proof he cites the case of the UN peacekeeping mission established in Rwanda in 1993, the same mission that was unable to stop the genocide between Hutus and Tutsis. The commander, the Canadian general Romeo Dallaire, led a mixed force of Europeans and Ghanaians, who were outnumbered by the killers and suffered casualties as they tried to protect specific groups of victims. The Ghanaian peacekeepers saved the most lives, according to Malone, under their own brigadier general, Dallaire's deputy. "About 500 of them stayed behind and they saved at least 25,000 lives in the Kigali stadium and elsewhere," he says. "They never received any attention at all, and this tells us something about the way that peacekeeping is covered by the media. Dallaire has constantly tried to draw attention to the heroic behavior of the Ghanaians, but never with any success whatsoever."

Malone's own solution is to combine the technical prowess of the West with the commitment and courage of the Africans and other peacekeepers. "What is important in peacekeeping is that some of the Western militaries have the high-tech capacities that, say, the Ghanaian army doesn't have. So ideally a peacekeeping force in Africa will be composed of a mix of developing-country contingents and Western contingents."

Equally needed, as Malone and other insiders would agree, is a basic overhaul of how the UN constitutes and funds its peacekeeping missions. Imagine having to conduct potentially risky and difficult military operations when you don't have a standing army and lack the right to levy taxes. Understandably,

the attempt to enlarge the peacekeeping concept along lines described above has stretched the peacekeeping effort sometimes beyond what it can handle. Some have likened UN peacekeeping to a volunteer fire department—but it's not that well organized, according to Kofi Annan, because for every mission it is necessary to scrounge up the fire engines and the money to pay for them "before we can start dousing any flames."

The Security Council commissioned a study led by Lakhdar Brahimi, the former foreign minister of Algeria, to examine the main shortcomings of the current operation and offer solutions for change. This so-called Brahimi report, submitted in August 2000, has become a blueprint for such efforts. The report recommends that the UN make fundamental changes in its policies and practices of peacekeeping and that it provide more financial backing. It urges an updating of the concept of peacekeeping to address modern situations where the combatants may be heavily armed and not always obedient to commanders or political leaders. In such highly charged scenarios the peacekeepers may have to choose sides, at least temporarily, in order to protect the innocent. The Security Council must therefore provide peacekeeping missions with precise instructions on how to act in a variety of possible circumstances. Equally important, according to the report, is the integration of military functions with historically civil concerns such as human rights, policing, and food, shelter, and medical services. The UN has begun acting on the report, beginning with the Security Council's acceptance of the report's recommendations. Questions now are whether the General Assembly will deliver adequate financial support and whether the council and the secretariat have the will to follow through on the report over the long term.

David P. Barash

WORLD GOVERNMENT?

The dream of world government has been around for a long time and is often derided as just that: a noble but impossible dream, taken seriously only by fuzzy-headed, unrealistic idealists. However, it is worth noting that the current arrangement of nation-states was not God-given and thus, immutable; rather, it was created by human beings, in historical time, and is not necessarily the only way for humanity to organize itself. Certainly, a system of international anarchy (also called "state sovereignty") has not proved especially conducive to peace and happiness! As for "realism," one might ask whether it is "realistic" to expect that the world can or should continue under its current system of international relationships, and whether an alternative system would not be possible as well as preferable.

Nothing will ever be attempted if all possible objections must be first overcome.

—*Samuel Johnson*

It is increasingly clear that most of the problems afflicting our planet and our species transcend the boundaries of the nation-state. The notable exception, war, is itself largely a *product* of the nation-state, which leads to the question: What about world government? Many informed people have long sought for alternatives to the nation-state system; not surprisingly, in an age of diminishing resources, shrinking distances, and ever-more-devastating weaponry, advocates of world government speak with a particular urgency.

Ever since the Tower of Babel, people have been plagued by their own political disunity. A potential solution, proposed in one form or another for literally thousands of years, has been to erase the existing political boundaries and to replace them with government structures at the largest, most inclusive level. This suggestion has been raised most urgently with regard to war and its prevention, since when it comes to war, nation-states have been only haltingly part of the solution; in the eyes of many, they are much of the problem. War making has fractured the human community along ideological, social, and geopolitical lines. The prevention of war, accordingly, may well require that this community be reforged on a global scale.

PRE- AND POST-WESTPHALIAN WORLDS

In medieval times, most Europeans owed their allegiance to a feudal lord, who in turn may have been subject to the secular authority of the Holy Roman Emperor and the religious power of the Pope. Then came the so-called Wars of Religion, culminating with the Thirty Years' War and the signing, in 1648, of the Treaty of Westphalia, which inaugurated the European state system that was eventually extended into the modern network of nation-states. For citizens in pre-Westphalian, medieval times, concerns were overwhelmingly bounded by day-to-day events taking place in local surroundings, nearby towns, and the closest castle with its protector (or oppressor) nobility. The Westphalian world expanded the

From *Peace and Conflict Studies*, Third Edition, 2014. Sage Publications: Thousand Oaks, CA.

allegiance of state and national subjects to include lands and people more distant than one's immediate surroundings. In addition, technological advances, especially in transportation and communication, made it unavoidable that individuals became involved with other places and people beyond their closest neighbors.

It can be argued that we now live in a post-Westphalian world, one in which the state or nation-state system is as obsolete as its feudal antecedents. Our mounting problems—notably pollution, poverty, resource depletion, and the destructive effects of war—supersede the old, traditional political boundaries, making it imperative that we think as planetary citizens. The world, in short, has become functionally integrated, even while it remains politically fragmented.

AN IDEA WHOSE TIME HAS COME?

The appeal of world government is basically that political and legal authorities ought to be able to force quarreling subordinates to refrain from violence; to respect larger, common interests; and to solve their disputes peacefully. When two individuals disagree about something, they are expected to resolve the issue in a law-abiding manner; they are not permitted to start shooting each other. Settling disputes by a duel, popular in previous centuries, is analogous to nation-states "settling" today's disputes by war. The former has been universally outlawed; the latter has not—or rather, to put it idealistically, not yet. Similarly, individual households are not "sovereign." They do not have the right to dump toxic chemicals into "their" stream, thereby poisoning their neighbors' water supplies; why, then, should "sovereign" states be permitted to do this?

International organizations, such as the UN, offer frameworks for transcending political boundaries, but they operate within the present system of sovereign states, which are free to disagree, overrule, or simply ignore these organizations if they choose, because there is no larger authority that can impose restraint on the states themselves. In modern times, the parts (states) claim to be greater than the whole (humanity and the planet Earth). With a just and globally recognized world government,

this would likely change: States would be prohibited from imposing themselves on their neighbors, whether economically, ecologically, or militarily, just as domestic governments now prevent individuals from overstepping their bounds and as federal governments keep the peace among their smaller, constituent parts.

A BRIEF HISTORY OF PLANS FOR WORLD GOVERNMENT

By the 17th and 18th centuries, there had been many proposals designed to establish worldwide political restraints on war making. William Penn, in 1693, wrote *An Essay Towards the Present and Future Peace of Europe*, which included a general parliament with military force to compel observance of its decrees. In 1713, the Abbé de Saint-Pierre, in his *Project for Perpetual Peace*, called for a "Senate of Europe" consisting of one representative from each European state, a plan that received much attention—and criticism. Voltaire, for example, noted that the states in question would overwhelmingly be monarchies and maintained that for peace to be preserved, democracy was necessary . . . and, at that time, democracy was unthinkable as a practical matter, just like world government.

Notable among such proposals, in addition to Jeremy Bentham's *Plan for an Universal and Perpetual Peace* (1789), was one advanced by the philosopher Jean-Jacques Rousseau (1712–1778). In his *Discourse on the Origin of Inequality*, Rousseau claimed that ownership of private property was the underlying cause of war and that to achieve world peace, it would therefore be necessary to abolish private property worldwide. His work, in turn, leads to an interesting—if currently unanswerable—question: If war is a result of a specific form of social organization, is this reason to condemn the society or to justify certain wars? Thus, many political theorists have argued that the defense of property is a legitimate reason for war.

In *The Spirit of Laws* (1748), the French political philosopher Montesquieu maintained that war was not caused by human nature but by flaws inherent in the system of political states: "As soon as man enters a state of society . . . each particular society begins to feel its strength, whence arises a state of war between different nations."[68] Like Montesquieu, Rousseau argued that war could be prevented by severing the bonds by which the state held people together: "It is only after he is a citizen," noted Rousseau in *The Social Contract*, "that he becomes a soldier." Rousseau also maintained that "conquering princes make war at least as much on their subjects as on their enemies" and that "all the business of kings . . . is concerned with two objects alone; to extend their rule abroad or make it more absolute at home."

Probably the most ambitious design for a potentially workable form of world government was put forth by the great German philosopher Immanuel Kant. In *Perpetual Peace* (1795), Kant made the first major effort to focus specifically on the dangers of arms races and armaments, rather than just proposing yet another kind of world parliament. He also argued strongly for "republican" governments—that is, democracies—as being most likely to keep the peace and that people would necessarily act upon a rational understanding of what is in their shared best interest.

Kant's views should be contrasted with those of Thomas Hobbes, who, 150 years earlier, had emphasized that sense perceptions are individual and personal, rather than universal, and that, because of this, individual viewpoints are bound to diverge. Accordingly, agreement among different and contending agents requires enforcement by fear of and obedience to an overarching power. Whereas Hobbes's emphasis on conflicting interests served to justify the existence of a powerful political state (the "Leviathan"), Kant was concerned with preventing the excesses of state power, especially when states interact violently with one another. Kant proposed a worldwide organization that would be bound by international law and composed of a federation of free states. His work represented a tendency toward what may be called "optimistic internationalism" among peace theorists and devotees of world government. Rather than focusing on the problem posed by the state's very existence, Kant identified the cause of the problem in what he called the "lawlessness" of

how states interact with one another. For Kant, some form of "external coercion" is therefore necessary to establish peace between states. (Shortly after Kant's book appeared, the Napoléonic Wars convulsed Europe. For some, this showed the impossibility of peace; for others, it emphasized its necessity.)

The Early 20th Century

The 19th century was not notable for important proposals concerning world government, at least in part because the post-Napoléonic Concert of Europe did a reasonably good job at keeping the fragile peace. After World War I, however, and the subsequent failure of the League of Nations, there was a flurry of renewed interest in world union, led by such groups as the United World Federalists. In fact, some tension arose between supporters of the United Nations and world federalists, who believe that international organizations of this sort tend to enhance state authority rather than transcend it. Some argue that so long as international organizations are structured around the preservation of state sovereignty, they are not so much steppingstones to world government as threats and impediments to its implementation.

The Clark-Sohn Plan

The most elaborate and detailed scheme for world government was developed in 1966 by the legal scholars Grenville Clark and Louis Sohn.[69] It called for transforming the UN into a world peacekeeping unit, whereby states would retain their sovereignty *except* in matters of disarmament (which would be mandatory) and war (which would be prohibited). Clark and Sohn proposed to increase the power of the General Assembly and to change its voting procedures, making decision-making largely proportional to population. Under the Clark-Sohn Plan, the four largest countries (China, India, the USSR, and the United States) would have 30 votes each, the next eight largest would have 15 votes each, and so on. An Executive Council would be authorized to intervene militarily worldwide, so as to prevent

---

[68] Charles L. de Montesquieu. 1949. The Spirit of Laws. New York: Hafner.

[69] Grenville Clark and Louis Sohn. 1960. World Peace through World Law. Cambridge, MA: Harvard University Press.

war. Unlike the present UN Security Council, however, there would be no veto, although a clear majority (12 of 17 members) would have to approve any armed action, and this vote would have to include a majority of the largest states. An Inspection Commission would ensure that disarmament is total; after a 2-year census of each country's military forces, it would supervise 10% annual reductions, across the board. A World Peace Force, under UN auspices, would consist of 200,000 to 600,000 professional volunteers, initially using supplies and weapons obtained as the member states disarmed themselves. Nuclear weapons would not be supplied to this force, but they could be accumulated if needed—from a Nuclear Energy Authority—to deter the use or threatened use of nuclear weapons by any state that kept a small cache.

The Clark-Sohn Plan, although very detailed and specific, does not offer any suggestions as to the means of achieving its major goal, of getting from "here" to "there." It does illustrate, however, that there is no shortage of precise ideas about possible future world governments. Whatever the strengths or weaknesses of any particular plan, the point is that world government has not been stymied by a shortage of good ideas but rather by a lack of political will.

THE MAINTENANCE OF PEACE

The argument for peacefulness under world government is derived largely from analogy: Since domestic governments enforce peace (e.g., between New York and Pennsylvania in the United States) or attempt to do so (Armenia and Azerbaijan in the former USSR), a world government would presumably do the same, treating nation-states much as municipal governments now treat their citizens or as federal governments now treat their subordinate provinces or constituent republics. But analogies do not always hold. Moreover, federal governments do not always create or maintain peace: Civil wars are common and often highly destructive. Europe during the 19th century, for example, was composed of feisty, sovereign states, while the United States was a single, ostensibly united country. Yet, the war casualties suffered by the "United" States during its civil

war (about 600,000) were almost precisely equal in number to the casualties suffered by Europe during the entire period between 1815 and 1913.

Perhaps if they were not held forcibly within a larger state, independent republics would be freer to work out their ethnic conflicts in peace. Alternatively, maybe they would go to war: Ethnic antagonisms within the former Yugoslavia, for example, were kept from erupting into violence because of the inhibiting and unifying influence of the central government in Belgrade, under a widely respected leader, Josip Tito (a Croatian). With that central force removed, the constituent republics (notably Serbia, Croatia, and Bosnia) were vulnerable to violence appeals to previously submerged nationalistic passions. A similar situation appears to have developed in post–Saddam Hussein Iraq, with Shiites, Sunnis, and Kurds resisting a transnational identity as Iraqis.

PROS AND CONS: THE DANGER OF OPPRESSION

To some people, the prospect of a world government is truly frightening. These include many persons—notably in the United States—associated with various self-styled "militia" and "patriot" movements, who believe that an oppressive world government, most likely under the auspices of the United Nations, is ready to swoop down in fleets of black helicopters and deprive them of their civil liberties (notably, their guns). Such delusions aside, the claim that, as a cure, world government might be worse than the disease (state anarchy) needs to be taken seriously.

If large political units tend to be unresponsive to the needs of their citizens and are sometimes oppressive, imagine the danger inherent in government by a worldwide "super state" with the power to enforce its decrees on everyone. (The Clark-Sohn Plan carefully envisioned that the armed forces of several countries, combined, would exceed those of the world force, thereby hedging against centralized despotism.) But why, critics ask, should we expect better government from a world authority than we now get from national governments? And, it is worth noting, only a minority of states today enjoy functioning representative democracies. So what, if anything, guarantees that a world government would not be a worldwide tyranny? Most of us want to have our cake and eat it too: peace *and* freedom, international order *and* national sovereignty. But perhaps these goals are conflicting. If so, and if we have to choose, which is preferable? Or perhaps we can hope for a compromise, maybe along the lines of the Clark-Sohn Plan, something that offers restrictions on the state's ability to make war, without impinging on other aspects of domestic life.

This may be easier said than done, however. For one thing, powerful states are usually not just uninterested but often vigorously opposed to world government, since it would require that they give up some of the influence and power that they exercise today. It might also make them subject to certain basic principles of equality and fairness, from which they are at present largely exempt. In some cases— notably that of the United States—state sovereignty combined with military/economic/scientific/political might has been a means of achieving and maintaining what many people believe to be inequitable access to the world's riches. What if, having surrendered its military autonomy, the United States is faced with a demand from the economically less developed states that it cease consuming scarce resources and polluting the planet out of proportion to its population or that it redistribute its wealth? Would world government mean a responsibility to share? If so, many in the wealthy West might prefer autonomy and gluttony, even at the risk of occasional war.

Critics of world government also point to what they see as an inconsistency. World government is supposed to be necessary because the ferocious Hobbesian world of independent nation-states is simply too violent and irresponsible to continue unchecked. But what supports the assertion that fierce competitors and vicious inclinations can be rendered peaceful by a kind of world government modeled after the ideals of John Locke and other Euro-American liberals: a limited, mild, and democratic authority that is based largely on mutual consent? Such a "Lockean" government might indeed be more palatable than its Hobbesian alternative, but if the problem is so grave, it might simply be inadequate. In short, a Hobbesian world may require a Hobbesian

government. The problem is that a Hobbesian government is likely to be very unpleasant. And it might be even more unpleasant—and more difficult to reform—if its resources and authority were global rather than merely national.

On the other hand, there is no reason why a functioning world government could not allow current national governments to continue exercising autonomy and sovereignty in their internal affairs. But rather than worrying about what national governments would have to surrender, perhaps we should focus on what they would be gaining. World government could then be viewed not so much as requiring us to give up something that we now have (state sovereignty and the ability to threaten and wage offensive war) but rather as offering the opportunity to gain something now lacking and desperately needed: extending the peaceful rule of law to international affairs and, with it, a massive increase in genuine national security.

As to criticism that world government would deprive states of one of the most important perquisites of state sovereignty—deciding whether or not to go to war—it is sobering to realize that such independence as the nation-states now cherish is in part illusory. The Soviet Union, for example, had no choice about entering World War II; when it was attacked by Germany in June 1941, it was forced to respond. Similarly, the United States was propelled into World War II not so much by a declaration of war by the U.S. House of Representatives as by decisions made by the Imperial War Council in Tokyo.

Advocates of world government emphasize that any viable world authority would have clear enforcement powers but that these powers would also be carefully circumscribed and limited. As with the U.S. federal government, rights not specifically granted to a world authority would be reserved for its constituent states. Similarly, in our private lives, we cherish certain personal rights while also accepting restrictions on them: One person's freedom to swing his or her arm ends, for example, where someone else's nose begins. Under minimalist world government, nation-states would have to accept just two restrictions circumscribing their freedom: They would be obliged (1) not to maintain armed forces and (2) not to behave aggressively against other states.

Similarly, there need be no anxiety that world government would necessarily mean the homogenization of national identities. Within the United States, Florida is still recognizably distinct from Alaska, and Maine from Arizona, just as national cultures within Russia range from urban Muscovites to tundra-dwelling indigenous people of Siberia and from industrialism to seminomadic Islamic pastoralism. As Israeli Prime Minister Golda Meir once pointed out: "Internationalism doesn't mean the end of individual nations. Orchestras don't mean the end of violins."

THE DREAM OF WORLD GOVERNMENT: A WASTE OF TIME?

There is one other potential problem of world government: By focusing on it, devotees may lose touch with the world and its serious problems as they now exist. Or these problems may simply be ignored by the self-styled "realists" who run today's states and, by extension, the world. Lost in dreams of utopia, hungering after what may turn out to be nothing more than "globaloney," proponents of world government run the risk of being marginalized, considered irrelevant to "serious" discourse on issues of war and peace. If advocates of peace studies withdraw into musings over ideal but impractical solutions to real problems, they essentially give over the reins of power to those willing to deal instead with current reality. And time itself is critical, since world government will certainly not happen tomorrow, while wars are happening today. Even Freud, who supported the idea of world government, also warned (in his famous correspondence with Albert Einstein) about unrealistic dreams that "conjure up an ugly picture of mills which grind so slowly that, before the flour is ready, men are dead of hunger."

But no serious student of peace or devotee of world government recommends putting all of one's eggs in the one distant basket of global political union. It is not necessary to choose between nuclear arms reduction and world government, between peace in the Middle East and global disarmament, or between ecological harmony and transnational thinking and acting. In addition, even while addressing immediate, practical, pressing issues, isn't there also a need to focus on ultimate goals, even if they seem—at the moment—to exceed our grasp? As General Omar Bradley once pointed out, "It is time we steered by the stars and not by the lights of each passing ship."

Accordingly, we might ask the self-styled realists—the practical, hardheaded men (and they largely are *men*) - if it is truly realistic to believe that the state system, with its divisions and contradictions and its history of repetitive warfare and state-centered selfishness, can be relied on to keep the peace and create a decent and humane planet into the indefinite future? Clearly, world government is unlikely to be perfect, but in view of the current state system's imperfections, it seems unlikely to be worse, or more dangerous, than our current plight. The dangers of a world with some form of centralized, war-suppressing government seem to pale in contrast to the dangers of a world without it.

THE PROSPECTS FOR WORLD GOVERNMENT: A PENCHANT FOR SEPARATING?

Despite the attractiveness of the idea of world government, the fact is that most people—once organized into relatively large units—show far more eagerness for splitting off than for joining together. There have been virtually no examples of the successful merging of states. The union of North and South Vietnam might be one such case, although it was only achieved via appalling violence—and despite substantial resistance from many of the South Vietnamese themselves. Moreover, Vietnam had previously been a single country, so the outcome was not so much the merging of different states as the reunification of a state that had been artificially separated. The same can be said of the reunification of Germany in 1989 after its post–World War II separation into West and East.

At one time, Egypt and Syria attempted a peaceful merger, establishing the United Arab Republic, but that union was quickly disbanded. The former Yugoslavia now consists of separate, independent states: Slovenia, Croatia, Bosnia, Serbia, Montenegro, and Macedonia (with a distinct Kosovo likely to emerge as well). The former Czechoslovakia broke up into Slovakia and the Czech Republic, and of course, what had been the Soviet Union now consists of numerous independent states, ranging from the Baltic republics of Latvia, Lithuania, and Estonia to the "stans" (Kazakhstan, Turkmenistan, and so forth) of central Asia.

When consolidation has occurred, a smaller unit is typically swallowed up by a larger one, often against its will: Tibet was forcibly incorporated into China, Goa into India, and the Baltic states into the USSR after World War I. A major reason, indeed, for the breakup of the USSR was the fact that it was an artificial entity, composed of numerous republics, many of which maintained a national, ethnic identity that resisted decades of domination and efforts to subordinate local loyalty to a larger Soviet whole. Furthermore, much of the tension in the world today is generated specifically by regions desiring not to submerge their identities but rather to *separate* themselves from control by a larger whole: Catholics in Northern Ireland, Basques in Spain, Tamils in Sri Lanka, Kurds in Iraq (as well as in Turkey, Iran, and Syria), and so on.

Despite its flaws, dangers, or difficulties, world government may well be essential. However, just because something is desirable—even necessary—does not mean that it will come to pass. Thus, it is not sufficient simply to state that world government ought to emerge because it is a prerequisite for survival. Maybe we will not survive with or without a world government. But given the current and likely future tensions among nuclear-armed states, it is hard to imagine a world government doing any worse!

THE PROSPECTS FOR WOLRD GOVERNMENT: COMMITMENT TO STATES

The pressures against world government are strong. People retain a deep loyalty to their nation-states and also a powerful distrust of large, centralized systems. In addition, like so many proposals for dramatic reform (for example, disarmament), the "devil is in the details." How do we get from here to there?

In 1712, the French Abbé de Saint-Pierre proposed his pan-European Union, complete with a Senate of Peace, which would have authority over military forces sufficient to compel any recalcitrant ruler to submit to the will of the larger unit. Interestingly, the French Foreign Minister at the time, André Hercule de Fleury, did not question the desirability of such a system, but he pointed out to Saint-Pierre: "You have forgotten an essential article, that of dispatching missionaries to touch the hearts of princes and to persuade them to enter into your views."

It might seem that state leaders agreeing to world government would be as unlikely as slaveholders banding together to outlaw slavery. But slavery has in fact been outlawed worldwide, sometimes (as in the United States) only after much bloodshed. It might also be worthwhile to examine in greater detail how certain nation-states (e.g., Sweden, Holland, Portugal, Spain) have made a seemingly healthy transition from world power to secondary status in international politics. This might serve not only to prepare the United States for the possibility of future decline in a world of continuing nation-states but also perhaps to suggest how the state system itself might be afforded lesser prominence and perhaps eventually eased out of existence.

At present, no powerful country seems prone to relinquish sovereignty and embrace world government; in most respects, such states remain fiercely independent. Western capitalist nations in particular tend to be particularly jealous about guarding political autonomy. And whereas Marxist theory calls for the eventual "withering away" of the state, the former Soviet Union and its allies were equally unreceptive to world government—unless it were under Soviet control!

When the state is taken to embody the needs and aspirations of its citizens, there is little reason to surrender the state's power. Even "peace groups" were described as unnecessary in most Soviet bloc states, since the state itself was purported to be everybody's collective "peace group." (*It* was not the problem; *other* states were the problem!) Traditionally, the political right wing has engaged in relatively more militaristic flag-waving patriotism, while accusing the left of being part of, or duped by, various "international conspiracies," generally communist inspired. However, the heyday of socialist internationalism, as we have seen, was in the late 19th and early 20th centuries; in recent decades, many leftists have shown as much adherence to their own nation-state as have partisans of the political right. And in much of the developing world, militant nationalism is even more pronounced than in the industrialized North.

THE PROSPECTS FOR WORLD GOVERNMENT: EXAMPLES OF A WIDER IDENTITY

Although we do not know whether people are capable of acting as part of a united planet, the prospects may not be all that bleak. The United States of America, for example, is a very diverse country, made up of Caucasians, African Americans, Native Americans, Asian Americans, Catholics, Protestants, Jews, and Muslims—and yet, the country as a whole enjoys a reasonable degree of coherence despite longstanding prejudices, ethnocentrism, and racial enmities. Although some may say that U.S. citizens are united by shared fear of "the other"—Chinese or North Korean communists, Islamic terrorists, international Mafia-style gangsters—the United States also has achieved its unity from a shared cultural and social identity, a shared history, and shared ideals. Certainly, the human species is capable of establishing even wider affiliations than those between Maine and Hawaii, if feelings of connection are encouraged from birth and are reinforced by teaching, symbols, slogans, and a range of appeals, to emotion as well as reason. We are all subjected to vast amounts of pronational and prostate propaganda. Even more desirable would be education for a psychology of world citizenship.

Take another example: People calling themselves "Germans" and "French" have long been at each other's throats, via their respective governments, the nation-states we identify as Germany and France. Yet, quite near these perennially warring states, several million very "French" people live—and have lived for centuries—peacefully with about three times as many equally "German" people. The difference is that in the former case, a sovereign state of Germany has confronted an equally sovereign France, whereas in the latter, "French" and "German" have submerged war-making authority in the sovereignty of a third shared entity, known as Switzerland

(which also contains a third large subpopulation that is Italian-speaking). Similarly, English and Irish, Italians and Austrians, Vietnamese and Chinese, and Arabs and Jews all have waged brutal wars across the globe . . . but when they become citizens of the United States of America, they submit themselves to a common identity and live together peaceably, at least for the most part. Clearly, it can be done.

The Prospects for World Government: The Case of the United States of America

Consider again the United States of America as it is now constituted: When California, for example, has a dispute with Arizona regarding water rights, the two governments do not call up their militias and fight it out. The "law of force" is subordinated to the "force of law," and both sides submit arguments, if need be, to the U.S. Supreme Court. Then, they abide by the ruling. The states of the United States do not walk about like gunslingers from the Wild West, revolvers on their hips, ready to settle disputes by the fastest draw.

Following the Revolutionary War, the United States under the Articles of Confederation was a loose amalgamation of states, headed toward disaster because of its virtual anarchy. Maryland and Delaware fought an undeclared "oyster war" over fishing rights to the Potomac River; nine states had navies of their own; state militias were separate and distinct armies; seven of the states even printed their own currency; New York placed a tariff on wood from Connecticut and on butter from New Jersey; Boston was boycotting grain from Rhode Island; various states imposed taxes on shipping from other states; and so on. Things were a mess, just as they are in the world today.

With the writing of the U.S. Constitution, however, a strong federal system was created, out of whole cloth. Advocates of world government point to this transition from pluralism to unity that gave birth to the United States of America as "the great rehearsal" for world federalism, a transition that the world system can also make if and when the need is widely recognized. Just as some people today fear a potential world "super state," the delegates to the Constitutional Convention also feared to establish a potential despotic dictatorship. Yet, the framers of the Constitution recognized that the semi-independent 13 states were threatened with war and chaos, so they successfully designed a workable federal union, one that preserved the rights of states in regulating their internal affairs while establishing a strong federal system capable of providing unity and ensuring the peace. They did this by establishing a careful, democratic system of checks and balances. At present, the politically independent nation-states of Europe, with all their similarities and all the benefits of federation, have moved haltingly but with increasing confidence toward a limited and fragile form of economic and legal union.

Most European states recognize the euro as a common currency; furthermore, within most countries of Europe, passports and visas are now entirely unnecessary, and passage through international borders—previously heavily controlled and guarded—is now usually very fast and no more consequential than going from Texas to Oklahoma, despite a history of major wars and a present reality of numerous distinct and cherished linguistic and cultural traditions.

The reality of what the United States accomplished—in the face of grave doubts—suggests the magnitude of what can be achieved. The problem in 1787 was for people to learn to think nationally about the United States, rather than locally. Now, the problem is for people to learn to think internationally, about the planet, rather than nationally.

Must world government then wait until humanity has achieved a higher level of spiritual development? It is true that the "founding fathers" are currently revered in the United States, but they were human beings, just like us. It is also true that the U.S. Constitution was not perfect (although it was certainly better than what preceded it). Moreover, no one in the late 18th century claimed that a strong federal government could not be enacted until all the inhabitants of North America had first become saints.

TOWARD WORLD GOVERNMENT?

Several transgovernmental movements have sought to go beyond the current state system by establishing links that intentionally defy present political boundaries. Thus, a number of international tribunals have worked toward delegitimizing certain warlike actions of states, trying to apply principles of international law, even though such proceedings have lacked enforcement capability. For example, the Russell Tribunal in the 1960s excoriated the U.S. wars in Vietnam and the rest of the former Indochina; in 1982, at a meeting held in Nuremberg, another tribunal of international legal experts heard testimony and condemned the existing nuclear weapons regime. The MacBride Commission in Britain investigated Israel's 1982 invasion of Lebanon and pronounced it a violation of international law. Such tribunals and peace movements generally are unpopular with the governments of affected nation-states, because they seek to restrict war-making capacity and also because they represent a budding transnational sensitivity, which might one day undermine state authority more generally.

If these activities truly threaten the current system of state sovereignty, it is an example of the important sociological principle that "if people define situations as real, they are real in their consequences." If we define ourselves as bound irreparably to the current state system, we are so bound, by a kind of self-fulfilling prophecy. But the more we look beyond the states—and the more we find when we do so—the more we may find ourselves liberated from our customary allegiances.

Indeed, one of the things that keeps us prisoners of the state system is our difficulty in envisioning alternatives to it. Few people, as recently as 1990, would have predicted a 21st-century world in which South Africa had become a democratic, multiracial state or in which the Soviet Union has dissolved and, with it, the Cold War. Two futures are easy to imagine: this world ending with the "bang" of nuclear war or with the "whimper" of continued degradation (ecological, social) plus ongoing conventional wars. Both of these are plausible but undesirable extrapolations of the *status quo*. World government—in whatever specific form—offers a potential third way.

Recently, there has been a proliferation of planetary gatherings, reflecting and dramatizing the fact that as advances in communication and transportation make the world smaller, the costs and responsibilities of technology—no less than its benefits—require attention on a global scale. Such conferences include those on world population, women's rights, food, pollution, the status of indigenous people, the fights against racism and against AIDS, the linkages between disarmament and development, the problems of global warming, ozone depletion, destruction of the world's rainforests, and the need to protect biodiversity. With or without world government, it is clear that worldwide problems cannot be solved if governments remain stiffly within their traditional state boundaries.

Not surprisingly, the new social movements tend to be either local, community based, or region centered (and thus below the level of the state) or transnational and global (above the level of the state). Moreover, states themselves have already begun to surrender some aspects of sovereignty, as in the case of certain international organizations, as well as the general acknowledgment of—if not universal obedience to—international law. Perhaps this is a foot in the door. Or perhaps it simply reflects a defensive strategy by the states themselves: make a few trivial concessions to "the common good" while at the same time remaining as unwilling as ever to permit any meaningful challenge to their authority. But more subtly, many nation-states have already surrendered some aspects of their autonomy: The United States government, for example, is not politically "free" to declare war on Canada. A kind of *de facto* (in fact) restriction of state sovereignty has thus already come into effect, even though it is not yet *de jure* (in law). War is currently extremely unlikely between such historical rivals as Britain and France,

Finland or Turkey and Russia, France and Germany, and Japan and the United States.

Interest in world government tends to increase after major world wars—notably, immediately following World Wars I and II. Then, just as predictably, when memories of the horrors of the last war fade, so do impassioned cries of "Never Again! No More War!" So, unfortunately, perhaps another major war, or a close brush with nuclear obliteration, will be necessary for people to rise up and demand a dramatic reworking—if not a surrender—of state sovereignty. Meanwhile, it should be emphasized that "futurism" need not be limited to technological panaceas and derring-do, a world of genetic engineering, cyborgs, and Star Wars. It can also include moving beyond the state and national security to global human security.

It is also important not to discount the role of vision and visionaries. Before we can ever establish a better world, we must first imagine it. This is not to deny the importance of dealing with the world as it is. It simply emphasizes that to "accept" current realities is not necessarily to accept them as god-given, engraved in stone, or immune to challenge and change. The world system of states, no matter how firmly entrenched, is nothing more than a human creation—and a relatively recent one at that. There is no reason to think that it is so perfect, or so powerful, as to be a permanent part of the human condition. "The dogmas of the quiet past," wrote Abraham Lincoln, "are inadequate to the stormy present. We must think anew and act anew." Only if we think, plan, dream, and act for a future world that is better than today's or yesterday's can we have any hope of attaining such a future.

Steven Pinker

VIOLENCE VANQUISHED

One of the biggest obstacles to establishing a solid regime of negative peace (that is, one that prevents war) is widespread pessimism that such a situation is possible. Many people have glumly concluded that human beings are naturally aggressive and violent creatures who cannot be expected to live peacefully with their fellows. The result, ironically, can be a "self-fulfilling prophecy" in which a state of affairs becomes true simply because people believe it to be so. In the next selection, a summary of his influential book *The Better Angels of our Nature*, psychologist Steven Pinker argues that although "human nature" hasn't changed in hundreds or even thousands of years, there has been a distinct reduction in violence that is attributable to a number of cultural changes. This observation leads to the important conclusion that even though we cannot change our basic, biological nature, evolution has bequeathed to *Homo sapiens* a set of basic responses and inclinations that are sufficiently flexible to assure us that there is every reason to hope, *realistically*, for a future that is considerably more peaceful than our past.

⁂

On the day this manuscript appears, you will read about a shocking act of violence. Somewhere in the world there will be a terrorist bombing, a senseless murder, a bloody insurrection. It's impossible to learn about these catastrophes without thinking, "What is the world coming to?" But a better question may be, "How bad was the world in the past?"

Believe it or not, the world of the past was *much* worse. Violence has been in decline for thousands of years, and today we may be living in the most peaceable era in the existence of our species. The decline, to be sure, has not been smooth. It has not brought violence down to zero, and it is not guaranteed to continue. But it is a persistent historical development, visible on scales from millennia to years, from the waging of wars to the spanking of children.

This claim, I know, invites skepticism, incredulity, and sometimes anger. We tend to estimate the probability of an event from the ease with which we can recall examples, and scenes of carnage are more likely to be beamed into our homes and burned into our memories than footage of people dying of old age. There will always be enough violent deaths to fill the evening news, so people's impressions of violence will be disconnected from its actual likelihood.

Evidence of our bloody history is not hard to find. Consider the genocides in the Old Testament and the crucifixions in the New, the gory mutilations in Shakespeare's tragedies and Grimm's fairy tales, the British monarchs who beheaded their relatives and the American founders who dueled with their rivals. Today the decline in these brutal practices can be quantified. A look at the numbers shows that over the course of our history, humankind has been blessed with six major declines of violence. The first was a process of pacification: the transition from the anarchy of the hunting, gathering and horticultural societies in which our species spent most of its evolutionary history to the first agricultural civilizations, with cities and governments, starting about 5,000 years ago.

For centuries, social theorists like Hobbes and Rousseau speculated from their armchairs about what life was like in a "state of nature." Nowadays we can do better. Forensic archeology—a kind of "CSI: Paleolithic"—can estimate rates of violence from the proportion of skeletons in ancient sites with bashed-in skulls, decapitations or arrowheads embedded in bones. And ethnographers can tally the causes of death in tribal peoples that have recently lived outside of state control.

These investigations show that, on average, about 15% of people in prestate eras died violently, compared to about 3% of the citizens of the earliest states. Tribal violence commonly subsides when a state or empire imposes control over a territory, leading to the various "paxes" (Romana, Islamica, Brittanica and so on) that are familiar to readers of history.

It's not that the first kings had a benevolent interest in the welfare of their citizens. Just as a farmer tries to prevent his livestock from killing one another, so a ruler will try to keep his subjects from cycles of raiding and feuding. From his point of view, such squabbling is a dead loss—forgone opportunities to extract taxes, tributes, soldiers and slaves.

The second decline of violence was a civilizing process that is best documented in Europe. Historical records show that between the late Middle Ages and the 20th century, European countries saw a 10- to 50-fold decline in their rates of homicide.

The numbers are consistent with narrative histories of the brutality of life in the Middle Ages, when highwaymen made travel a risk to life and limb and dinners were commonly enlivened by dagger attacks. So many people had their noses cut off that medieval medical textbooks speculated about techniques for growing them back.

Historians attribute this decline to the consolidation of a patchwork of feudal territories into large kingdoms with centralized authority and an infrastructure of commerce. Criminal justice was nationalized, and zero-sum plunder gave way to positive-sum trade. People increasingly controlled their impulses and sought to cooperate with their neighbors.

The third transition, sometimes called the Humanitarian Revolution, took off with the Enlightenment. Governments and churches had long maintained order by punishing nonconformists with mutilation, torture and gruesome forms of execution, such as burning, breaking, disembowelment, impalement and sawing in half. The 18th century saw the widespread abolition of judicial torture, including the famous prohibition of "cruel and unusual punishment" in the eighth amendment of the U.S. Constitution.

At the same time, many nations began to whittle down their list of capital crimes from the hundreds (including poaching, sodomy, witchcraft and counterfeiting) to just murder and treason. And a growing wave of countries abolished blood sports, dueling, witch hunts, religious persecution, absolute despotism and slavery.

The fourth major transition is the respite from major interstate war that we have seen since the end of World War II. Historians sometimes refer to it as the Long Peace.

Today we take it for granted that Italy and Austria will not come to blows, nor will Britain and Russia. But centuries ago, the great powers were almost always at war, and until quite recently, Western European countries tended to initiate two or three new wars every year. The cliché that the 20th century was "the most violent in history" ignores the second half of the century (and may not even be true of the first half, if one calculates violent deaths as a proportion of the world's population).

Though it's tempting to attribute the Long Peace to nuclear deterrence, non-nuclear developed states have stopped fighting each other as well. Political scientists point instead to the growth of democracy, trade and international organizations—all of which, the statistical evidence shows, reduce the likelihood of conflict. They also credit the rising valuation of human life over national grandeur—a hard-won lesson of two world wars.

The fifth trend, which I call the New Peace, involves war in the world as a whole, including developing nations. Since 1946, several organizations have tracked the number of armed conflicts and their human toll world-wide. The bad news is that for several decades, the decline of interstate wars was accompanied by a bulge of civil wars, as newly independent countries were led by inept governments, challenged by insurgencies and armed by the cold war superpowers.

The less bad news is that civil wars tend to kill far fewer people than wars between states. And the best news is that, since the peak of the cold war in the 1970s and '80s, organized conflicts of all kinds—civil wars, genocides, repression by autocratic governments, terrorist attacks—have declined throughout the world, and their death tolls have declined even more precipitously.

The rate of documented direct deaths from political violence (war, terrorism, genocide and warlord militias) in the past decade is an unprecedented few hundredths of a percentage point. Even if we multiplied that rate to account for unrecorded deaths and the victims of war-caused disease and famine, it would not exceed 1%.

The most immediate cause of this New Peace was the demise of communism, which ended the proxy wars in the developing world stoked by the superpowers and also discredited genocidal ideologies that had justified the sacrifice of vast numbers of eggs to make a utopian omelet. Another contributor was the expansion of international peacekeeping forces, which really do keep the peace—not always, but far more often than when adversaries are left to fight to the bitter end.

Finally, the postwar era has seen a cascade of "rights revolutions"—a growing revulsion against aggression on smaller scales. In the developed world, the civil rights movement obliterated lynchings and lethal pogroms, and the women's-rights movement has helped to shrink the incidence of rape and the beating and killing of wives and girlfriends.

In recent decades, the movement for children's rights has significantly reduced rates of spanking, bullying, paddling in schools, and physical and sexual abuse. And the campaign for gay rights has forced governments in the developed world to repeal laws criminalizing homosexuality and has had some success in reducing hate crimes against gay people.

Why has violence declined so dramatically for so long? Is it because violence has literally been bred out of us, leaving us more peaceful by nature?

This seems unlikely. Evolution has a speed limit measured in generations, and many of these declines have unfolded over decades or even years. Toddlers continue to kick, bite and hit; little boys continue to play-fight; people of all ages continue to snipe and bicker, and most of them continue to harbor violent fantasies and to enjoy violent entertainment.

It's more likely that human nature has always comprised inclinations toward violence and inclinations that counteract them—such as self-control, empathy, fairness and reason—what Abraham Lincoln called "the better angels of our nature." Violence has declined because historical circumstances have increasingly favored our better angels.

The most obvious of these pacifying forces has been the state, with its monopoly on the legitimate use of force. A disinterested judiciary and police can defuse the temptation of exploitative attack, inhibit the impulse for revenge and circumvent the self-serving biases that make all parties to a dispute believe that they are on the side of the angels.

We see evidence of the pacifying effects of government in the way that rates of killing declined following the expansion and consolidation of states in tribal societies and in medieval Europe. And we can watch the movie in reverse when violence erupts in zones of anarchy, such as the Wild West, failed states and neighborhoods controlled by mafias and street gangs, who can't call 911 or file a lawsuit to resolve their disputes but have to administer their own rough justice.

Another pacifying force has been commerce, a game in which everybody can win. As technological progress allows the exchange of goods and ideas over longer distances and among larger groups of trading partners, other people become more valuable alive than dead. They switch from being targets of demonization and dehumanization to potential partners in reciprocal altruism.

For example, though the relationship today between America and China is far from warm, we are unlikely to declare war on them or vice versa. Morality aside, they make too much of our stuff, and we owe them too much money.

A third peacemaker has been cosmopolitanism—the expansion of people's parochial little worlds through literacy, mobility, education, science, history, journalism and mass media. These forms of virtual reality can prompt people to take the perspective of people unlike themselves and to expand their circle of sympathy to embrace them.

These technologies have also powered an expansion of rationality and objectivity in human affairs. People are now less likely to privilege their own interests over those of others. They reflect more on the way they live and consider how they could be better off. Violence is often reframed as a problem to be solved rather than as a contest to be won. We devote ever more of our brainpower to guiding our better angels. It is probably no coincidence that the Humanitarian Revolution came on the heels of the Age of Reason and the Enlightenment, that the Long Peace and rights revolutions coincided with the electronic global village.

Whatever its causes, the implications of the historical decline of violence are profound. So much depends on whether we see our era as a nightmare of crime, terrorism, genocide and war or as a period that, in the light of the historical and statistical facts, is blessed by unprecedented levels of peaceful coexistence.

Bearers of good news are often advised to keep their mouths shut, lest they lull people into complacency. But this prescription may be backward. The discovery that fewer people are victims of violence can thwart cynicism among compassion-fatigued news readers who might otherwise think that the dangerous parts of the world are irredeemable hell holes. And a better understanding of what drove the numbers down can steer us toward doing things that make people better off rather than congratulating ourselves on how moral we are.

As one becomes aware of the historical decline of violence, the world begins to look different. The past seems less innocent, the present less sinister. One starts to appreciate the small gifts of coexistence that would have seemed utopian to our ancestors: the interracial family playing in the park, the comedian who lands a zinger on the commander in chief, the countries that quietly back away from a crisis instead of escalating to war.

For all the tribulations in our lives, for all the troubles that remain in the world, the decline of violence is an accomplishment that we can savor—and an impetus to cherish the forces of civilization and enlightenment that made it possible.

Douglas P. Fry

LIFE WITHOUT WAR

Anthropologists have long been interested in pretechnologic societies, not only for their own sake, but also because of possible insights they might offer into the ancestral human condition. Clearly, all currently existing human beings are "modern," in the sense that none are directly ancestral to current, mainstream civilizations. Current hunter-gatherer people from Africa or the high arctic, for example, are not the ancestors of today's computer geniuses or Siberian reindeer herders. Nonetheless, by examining a diversity of lifestyles and cultures, it is possible to learn something of the range of human potential. Attention has often focused on groups that are especially violent and prone to "primitive war," such as the Yanomamo of the upper Amazon or the Inuit

("Eskimos"), among whom war is unknown. In this selection, anthropologist Douglas Fry examines several human societies in which warfare is either nonexistent or has effectively been eliminated, pointing out certain common factors that appear to predispose to "life without war."

War—a group activity involving lethal aggression between communities—and other forms of violent conflict occur all too regularly in the 21st century and contribute substantially to human suffering. At the same time, most daily human behavior, within and across societies, is nonviolent. Conflict—defined generally as perceived divergence of interests—occurs regularly within and between societies and can be handled in many ways, only a few of which involve any physical violence.[70,71] With variation from one culture to the next, disputants, for example, may seek the help of an impartial mediator to resolve their disagreements, appear in court, negotiate the payment of compensation, or practice avoidance.

A NEW PERSPECTIVE

A dominant evolutionary perspective, as captured in Tennyson's famous phrase "nature, red in tooth and claw," has proposed that competition, often in the form of violence, is the evolutionary norm.[72-76] It appears, however, that this perspective may be shifting toward a new understanding that, although not totally dismissive of self-interested competition and conflict, nonetheless draws on recent advances in evolutionary theory[72-74] and a substantial body of human and nonhuman animal data[76,77] to show that cooperation, sharing, helping, and reconciliation also have a solid evolutionary basis.[72-80]

Traditionally, warfare has been seen as ancient,[81-83] but this view is also being reconsidered.[71,84] Chimpanzee intergroup killings have been used to make inferences about past hominid behavior,[82] but ancestral hominid conflict behavior may have been more bonobo-like—that is, nonlethal—than chimp-like,[72] as perhaps reflected in the small, nonprojecting canines and minimal sexual dimorphism of 4.4-millionold *Ardipithecus ramidus*.[85] Likewise, humans and their predecessors have long been characterized as hunters, but recently a reconsideration of several types of evidence suggests that they might more accurately have been considered prey.[79]

Similarly, a much-discussed suggestion based on Yanomamö data, that warriors have higher reproductive success than nonwarriors,[86] has been reevaluated theoretically, mathematically, and empirically with the conclusion that the opposite may actually be the

[70] J. Rubin, D. Pruitt, S. H. Kim, *Social Conflict* (McGraw-Hill, New York, ed. 2, 1994).

[71] D. P. Fry, *The Human Potential for Peace* (Oxford Univ. Press, New York, 2006).

[72] F. de Waal, *The Age of Empathy* (Harmony Books, New York, 2009).

[73] M. A. Nowak, with R. Highfield, *SuperCooperators* (Free Press, New York, 2011).

[74] R. W. Sussman, C. R. Cloninger, Eds., *Origins of Altruism and Cooperation* (Springer, New York, 2011).

[75] S. Bowles, H. Gintis, *A Cooperative Species* (Princeton Univ. Press, Princeton, NJ, 2011).

[76] M. Bekoff, J. Pierce, *Wild Justice* (Univ. of Chicago Press, Chicago, 2009).

[77] F. de Waal, *Peacemaking among Primates* (Harvard Univ. Press, Cambridge, MA, 1989).

[78] P. Verbeek, *Behaviour* 145, 1497 (2008).

[79] D. Hart, R. W. Sussman, in *Origins of Altruism and Cooperation*, R. W. Sussman, C. R. Cloninger, Eds. (Springer, New York, 2011), pp. 19–40.

[80] K. Weiss, A. Buchanan, *The Mermaid's Tale* (Harvard Univ. Press, Cambridge, MA, 2009).

[81] C. Ember, *Ethnology* 17, 439 (1978).

[82] R. Wrangham, D. Peterson, *Demonic Males* (Houghton Mifflin, Boston, 1996).

[83] S. Pinker, *The Better Angels of Our Nature* (Viking, New York, 2011).

[84] R. B. Ferguson, in *Origins of Altruism and Cooperation*, R. W. Sussman, C. R. Cloninger, Eds. (Springer, New York, 2011), pp. 248–270.

[85] T. D. White et al., *Science* 326, 64 (2009).

[86] N. A. Chagnon, *Science* 239, 985 (1988).

case.[71,84,87,88] First, in terms of theory, computer simulations indicate that unrestrained, escalated forms of aggression do not fare as well as strategies of limited agonism.[89,90] Second, a mathematical reanalysis of the data on the Yanomamö men in the original study revealed that those reported to have killed averaged more offspring in part because they were more than 10 years older than the men who had never killed.[71] Third, attempted replications using data on the Cheyenne and the Waorani failed to support the original findings; to the contrary, fitness was found to be negatively correlated with killing.[71,87]

The evidence for a new orientation that gives cooperation and peacefulness a seat at the evolutionary table comes from a variety of sources. From ethology, studies document cooperation, empathy, and conflict resolution in various animal.[72,76-78] Mammalian patterns of intraspecific agonism correspond with game theoretic simulations,[89] namely, escalated fighting among rival conspecifics is very rare compared with the widespread use of noncontact displays and ritualized contests (wherein serious injuries or death are unlikely), and similar patterns of restraint characterize much human conflict as well.[72,90,91] Primates, including humans, readily cooperate and reconcile after aggression, especially within social groups when partners are mutually dependent on each other (e.g., as allies in dominance struggles).[72,76,78,92] A reevaluation of nomadic forager data—such as on the Yahgan of South America, the Saulteaux and Paiute of North America, the Semang and Vedda of Asia, and the Ju/'hoansi and Mbuti of Africa—shows that warfare is most often absent at this ancestral level of social organization,[71] whereas cooperating and helping (e.g., the sharing of meat) occur without exception in nomadic band societies.[71,93,94] Furthermore,

neurobiological research shows that humans receive an immediate biochemical reward in oxytocin for cooperating,[95] and this may be part of an evolved brain-reward system in humans related to cooperation, trust, and altruism.[95] Finally, research from military science suggests that it is more difficult to get soldiers to kill in combat than commonly assumed. The resistance by soldiers to killing the enemy has been documented across various battlefield settings, for instance, among French officers in the 1860s, the battle of Gettysburg in the U.S. Civil War, soldiers from Argentina in the Falklands War, and U.S. troops during World War II (where it has been estimated that at most 25% of the combat soldiers shot at the enemy).[88,96] The relevant point, as General S. L. A. Marshall, who studied firing rates during World War II, concluded, is that "the average and normally healthy individual . . . [has] an inner and usually unrealized resistance toward killing."[97] Subsequently, this reluctance to kill has been largely overcome by the U.S. military through intense training in reflexive firing.[96]

In sum, the traditional focus in the evolutionary sciences has been on competition and violent conflict[74,76]; however, this perspective is shifting toward one that is more appreciative of cooperation, peacemaking, empathy, and sharing. Obviously, humans have the capacity to engage in war, but a growing body of studies on animals and humans suggests that nature is less violent than commonly has been assumed.[71-74,76-78]

NONWARRING SOCIETIES

Ethnographically, most societies engage in warfare, but there are some that do not.[71,98] Considering

[87] S. Beckerman et al., *Proc. Natl. Acad. Sci. U.S.A.* 106, 8134 (2009).

[88] M. Miklikowska, D. P. Fry, in *Nonkilling Psychology*, D. J. Christie, J. E. Pim, Eds. (Center for Global Nonkilling, Honolulu, 2012), pp. 43–70.

[89] J. Maynard Smith, G. Price, *Nature* 246, 15 (1973).

[90] D. P. Fry, G. Schober, K. Björkqvist, in *Nonkilling Societies*, J. E. Pim, Ed. (Center for Global Nonkilling, Honolulu, 2010), pp. 101–128.

[91] P. Roscoe, *Am. Anthropol.* 109, 485 (2007).

[92] J. B. Silk et al., *Proc. Biol. Sci.* 276, 3099 (2009).

[93] S. Hrdy, *Mothers and Others* (Harvard Univ. Press, Cambridge, MA, 2009).

[94] D. P. Fry, in *Origins of Altruism and Cooperation*, R. W. Sussman, C. R. Cloninger, Eds. (Springer, New York, 2011), pp. 227–247.

[95] J. Rilling, in *Origins of Altruism and Cooperation*, R. W. Sussman, C. R. Cloninger, Eds. (Springer, New York, 2011), pp. 295–306.

[96] D. Grossman, *On Killing* (Little Brown, New York, Rev. ed., 2009).

[97] S. Marshall, *Men Against Fire* (Univ. of Oklahoma Press, Norman, 2000).

[98] Q. Wright, *A Study of War* (Univ. of Chicago Press, Chicago, 1942).

the existence of nonwarring societies is important because it demonstrates that humans are capable of living without war. Nonwarring societies can be found in various locations around the globe, for example, the Machiguenga swidden farmers of Peru[99] and the Batek of Malaysia.[100] Among the Batek, core values, as evident in everyday social interaction, include helping anyone in need, respecting others, being noncompetitive and nonviolent, and sharing food.[100] The Mardu Aborigines of Australia's Great Western Desert, who were studied by Tonkinson beginning in the 1960s, had remained up until that time relatively isolated and unaffected by outside influences. The Mardu and neighboring Aborigines do not practice warfare; even the concept is alien to the Mardu because their language lacks words for feud and war.[101] The types of conflicts that arise, for instance elopements or sorcery accusations, tend to be interpersonal, and the Mardu routinely resolve such grievances when several bands gather together.[101] Many additional cases of nonwarring societies have been described from the Pemon and Piaroa of South America, the Kawaiisu and Karok of North America, the Central and Copper Inuit of the Arctic, and the Ladakhi and Lepcha of Asia, to nearly all Australian Aborigine societies.[71] It is also worth noting that some nations (for example, Iceland, Switzerland, and Sweden) have avoided wars for generations. Thus, war is not always and everywhere present.

One robust anthropological finding is that complexity of social organization correlates positively with warfare. Hierarchical societies such as chiefdoms, kingdoms, states, and empires are more likely to engage in war and practice more severe forms of warfare than are comparatively egalitarian tribes or highly egalitarian nomadic forager bands.[71] In bands, especially, numerous factors protect against war. For example, individuals have close relatives in neighboring bands, lethal disputes generally have very personal, not political, causes (e.g., due to sexual jealousy, an insult, or revenge-seeking by a homicide victim's family), there are no caches of stored food or other goods to plunder, no one possesses the authority to command other band members to fight, and population densities tend to be very low with adequate resources spread over wide areas.[71,94]

PEACE SYSTEMS

As reflected in Table 2-1, peace systems—groups of neighboring societies that do not make war on each other and sometimes not with outsiders either—have been documented on different continents.[102-104] Some peace systems are strictly nonwarring, whereas other peace systems are only nonwarring within the system itself. For example, the Batek, Btsisi, Chewong, Jahai, Semai and other nearby Malaysian societies constitute a peace system comprised of cultures that totally shun war.[100]

In addition to ethnographic cases, peace systems are reflected in the archaeological record. For example, very complete archaeological data exist for the prehistoric Anasazi of the southwestern United States, which clearly shows the time periods when war was either absent or present. War leaves tell-tale marks such as habitation sites protected by stockades, evidence of widespread fire or destruction, high percentages of violent death reflected in burials, and so forth.[71] The archaeological record across the Anasazi cultural area from before 700 CE until almost 1200 CE shows no evidence of war.[105] At the end of this period, as the climate changed to drought conditions, war appears. By the mid-13th century, in marked contrast to the preceding centuries, the evidence for war is unmistakable. Village destruction is evident, settlements have shifted to

[99] A. Johnson, in *Adaptive Responses of Native Amazonians*, R. Hames, W. Vickers, Eds. (Academic Press, New York, 1983), pp. 61–63.

[100] K. Endicott, K. Endicott, *The Headman Was a Woman* (Waveland, Long Grove, IL, 2008).

[101] R. Tonkinson, in *Keeping the Peace*, G. Kemp, D. P. Fry, Eds. (Routledge, New York, 2004), pp. 89–104.

[102] D. P. Fry, B. Bonta, K. Baszarkiewicz, in *Handbook on Building Cultures of Peace*, Joseph de Rivera, Ed. (Springer, New York, 2009).

[103] D. P. Fry, *J. Aggression, Conflict, Peace Res.* 1, 4 (2009).

[104] M. Miklikowska, D. P. Fry, *Beliefs and Values* 2, 124 (2010).

[105] J. Haas, in *Ancient Warfare*, J. Carman, A. Harding, Eds. (Sutton, Gloucestershire, UK, 1999), pp. 11–24.

TABLE 2-1 Examples of peace systems. Peace systems are groups of neighboring societies that do not make war on each other (and sometimes not with outsiders either). Peace systems can be found in various parts of the globe.

Geographical location	Peace system
Australia	Peoples of the Great Western Desert (e.g., the Mardudjara/Mardu, Gugadji, Walmadjeri, and Pintupi, among numerous others)
Canada	Montagnais-Naskapi and East Main Cree of the Labrador Peninsula
India	Nilgiri Plateau/Hills societies (Toda, Kota, Badaga, and Kurumbas)
Malaysia	Central Peninsular Orang Asli societies (e.g., Batek, Jahai, Semai, Chewong, and Btsisi)
Greenland	Native Inuit populations
United States and Canada	Iroquois Great League of Peace (Cayuga, Mohawk, Oneida, Onondaga, Seneca, and Tuscarora)
Brazil	Ten tribes of the Upper Xingu River basin (Kuikuru, Kalapolo, Nafukuá, Matipú, Mehinaku, Wauja, Yawalapití/Yaulapití, Kamayura/Kamaiyura, Aultí, and Trumaí)
Europe	European Union (27 member countries and growing)

defensive locations, and lethal trauma is endemic in the skeletal population.[105] After a successful 500-year run, the Anasazi peace system broke down, likely under the pressure of demographic and environmental stress.

An examination of existing peace systems can provide insights for creating peace in other settings.[103] Preliminary comparisons suggest that, for some peaceful groups, nonwarring may be simply the behavioral default (passive systems), perhaps because war is traditionally unknown among the member societies, as seen in the Malaysian case mentioned previously, whereas other peace systems are more actively created and maintained (active systems).

A comparison of active peace systems suggests that common features that can be hypothesized to be important include (i) an overarching social identity, (ii) interconnections among subgroups, (iii) interdependence (ecological, economic, and/or defensive), (iv) nonwarring values, (v) symbolism and ceremonies that reinforce peace, and (vi) superordinate institutions and conflict management. Each of these features will be briefly considered using ethnographic examples from various cultures, but with

a primary focus on three examples of active peace systems, the Upper Xingu River basin tribes in Brazil, the Iroquois Confederacy, and the European Union (EU) (Table 2-2).

All three of these peace systems have eliminated warfare within the system, but not necessarily against outsiders. The 10 Upper Xingu River basin tribes protected themselves if attacked by aggressive outsiders.[106] Additionally, and as in many societies, homicide occasionally occurred, but homicide is not war. Among the original Iroquoians—the Mohawk, Oneida, Onondaga, Cayuga, and Seneca nations—archaeology and ethnohistory clearly document chronic feuding, warring, and cannibalism before the creation of the peace system put an end to the carnage within the new confederacy.[107,108] Since its beginning in the second half of the

---

[106] T. Gregor, in *The Anthropology of Peace and Nonviolence*, L. Sponsel, T. Gregor, Eds. (Lynne Rienner, Boulder, CO, 1994).
[107] M. Dennis, *Creating a Landscape of Peace* (Cornell Univ. Press, Ithaca, 1993).
[108] C. Kupchan, *How Enemies Become Friends* (Princeton Univ. Press, Princeton, NJ, 2010).

TABLE 2-2 Features of five peace systems compared. Additional information on the three active peace systems is provided in the text. Information on the two passive peace systems is presented here for comparative purposes.

Feature	Active peace systems			Passive peace systems	
	Upper Xingu River basin	Iroquois Great League of Peace	European Union	Central Malaysia Orang Asli	Montagnais-Naskapi and East Main Cree
Overarching social identity	Yes	Yes	Growing	No	No
Interconnections among subgroups	Yes	Yes	Yes	?	?
Interdependence	Augmented	Augmented	Pivotal	No	No
Values for peace	Yes	Yes	Yes	Yes (nonviolence)	Not reported
Symbols, rituals, ceremonies for peace	Yes (chiefly ceremonies, peace myths)	Yes (Tree of Peace, rituals of condolence)	Yes (flag, anthem, Euro currency)	No	No
Intergroup conflict management	Weak: harangues, wrestling	Strong: Great Council of Chiefs, compensation	Intermediate: EU Court, Commission, Parliament	Weak: avoidance and toleration	Weak: avoidance, toleration, public opinion
Overarching governance	No	Yes (Council of Chiefs)	Yes (e.g., EU Parliament, Commission)	No	No

15th century, the Iroquois Confederacy, also known as the League of Peace, "proved remarkably durable, maintaining the peace among the Iroquois for over three hundred years."[108] EU member nations have contributed troops to recent wars outside the EU borders, but the use of military force within the EU has not occurred for more than 60 years. In post–World War II Europe, as the horrific memories of widespread death, bombings, blackouts, food rationing, hunger, concentration camps, and mass graves were still fresh in the minds of the survivors, the motivation was very strong to devise a way to prevent future European wars. Thus, creating a sustainable peace was the primary driving force behind European integration. These three cases do not show a total abstention from war, but rather they illustrate how clusters of neighboring societies have successfully created peace systems among themselves.

IDENTITY: EXPANDING THE US

The promotion of an "us-versus-them" mentality can facilitate intergroup hostility[70,109]; however, at least some successful peace systems form a common identity that helps to promote peace. For example, among the 10 tribes of the Upper Xingu River basin, which represent four different language groups, identities go beyond individual tribal membership.[103,106,110] The societies have "expanded the us" to encompass a common identity with the other tribes.

The Iroquois also expanded the us and metaphorically referred to their confederacy as a longhouse,

---

[109] M. Sherif et al., *The Robbers Cave Experiment: Intergroup Conflict and Cooperation* (Wesleyan Univ. Press, Middletown, CT, 1988).
[110] T. Gregor, in *The Anthropology of War*, J. Haas, Ed. (Cambridge Univ. Press, Cambridge, 1990), pp. 105–124.

symbolically denoting an extended family living together in peace.[111] "They sought to expand their League of Peace, and to embrace ever more people as kinsmen who would share the peace, prosperity, and security of the Iroquois Longhouse."[107] An evolving pan-Iroquois identity is reflected in many ways. As the peace system developed, the previous practice of exacting blood revenge over a homicide was replaced by the payment of compensation; the former practice of cannibalism within the system became obsolete as outsiders became insiders; the distinct pottery styles of past eras became progressively uniform across the region, reflecting a common identity; intermarriage increased, being simultaneously a cause and a result of the expanding Iroquois social identification; ritualized adoptions turned nonkin into relatives, and importantly, the use of kinship imagery and terminology supported the unifying view of all Iroquoians as relatives.[107,108]

Within the EU, a new overarching identity is emerging.[108] This is evident in the issuance of EU passports, EU automobile license plates, the Euro as a common currency (in most member countries), the free movement of EU citizens across borders, democratic elections for EU parliamentarians, and an EU flag and anthem.[103] In short, the trend is toward a new pan-European identity that parallels how the Upper Xingu and the Iroquois peoples developed additional overarching social identities. Expanding the us is a powerful force in the service of peace.[102,108]

INTERGROUP TIES

Intergroup bonds of friendship and kinship discourage violence.[70,102] For example, as we have seen, the Mardu of Australia do not feud or war. The Mardu bands are interlinked with each other and also with bands from neighboring societies as part of a larger kinship system, and cross-cutting ties help to promote peaceful relations among the groups.[104] The intergroup ties are diverse. This is due in part to the numerous interconnections (shared values, norms, religion, cosmology, friendship, kinship, and marriage alliances) that link all Mardu bands with each other. Such commonalities and linkages greatly facilitate the resolution of disputes.[101] Similarly, among

the nonwarring Ju/'hoansi of Africa, everybody has kin and trade partners in other groups and, as among the Mardu, intergroup connections discourage intergroup hostility.[71] Intermarriage also served a similar peace-sustaining function for the Iroquois and Upper Xingu River peace systems.[102,106,107,110] The emergence of a pan-Iroquois material culture reflects the progressive social integration across the confederacy.[107] The general principle is that the existence of cross-cutting ties such as ceremonial unions, fictive and consanguineal kinship, economic partnerships, and friendships, decreases the chances that conflicts will result in war.

INTERDEPENDENCE AS A KEY FACTOR

Interestingly, data from disciplines as diverse as primatology, anthropology, social psychology, and political science converge on showing the importance of interdependence for promoting cooperation to achieve a superordinate goal,[71,101,109,112] although economic interdependence may play a more important role later in the process.[108] In turn, engaging in cooperation is beneficial for relationships and thus can contribute to peaceful intergroup relations.[71,103,109,112] There are various types of interdependence, some imposed by circumstance and some purposefully created. The harshness of the physical environment can be a unifying force. The solution in Africa's Kalahari Desert or Australia's Great Western Desert is for local groups to reciprocally allow each other access to water and food resources.[71,102] To let disputes harden into feuding or warfare under such conditions of ecological interdependence would be suicidal.[71,101]

The tribes of the Upper Xingu peace system enhance interdependence by specializing in the production of particular trade goods, such as pottery, hardwood bows, or salt, and this type of specialization creates multiple economic interdependencies among them.[106] The founders of the EU augmented interdependence as part of a deliberate plan to create a new level of governance. An explicit impetus behind

---

[111] P. Wallace, *White Roots of Peace* (Clear Light, Santa Fe, NM, 1994).

[112] J. D. Sachs, *Common Wealth* (Penguin, New York, 2008).

European integration was to eliminate the threat of war in the region.[103,113] The creative approach was to build economic and political interdependence by incrementally integrating the national economies.[103] The first step, taken in the 1950s, was placing coal and steel—critical resources in times of peace and war—under supranational control. Thus began an agenda of cooperation and unification.[113] Current economic challenges within the EU, such as high unemployment and debt burden in some countries, in no way diminish the success of European integration and unification in creating a continent safe from war. In Europe today, less than 70 years since World War II ravaged the continent, war among EU member nations has become highly unlikely.[103] Using interdependence to deliberately create a regional peace system is a remarkable achievement.

VALUES FOR PEACE

Some value orientations are more conducive to peace than others.[104] In the value system of the Upper Xingu tribes, the warrior role is shunned—peace is moral, but war is not.[106,110] In that values become internalized within the minds of people and serve as guidelines for behavior, the promotion of antiwar values in society has a role to play in sustaining the peace.[71,104] The Iroquois made their value of peace within their confederacy explicit: "Thus we bury all the weapons of war out of sight, and establish the 'Great Peace.' Hostilities shall not be seen nor heard of any more among you, but 'Peace' shall be preserved among the Confederated Nations."[107]

The EU was founded with the explicit goal of bringing peace and prosperity to Europe. Peace related values such as democracy, social equality, human rights, and respect for the law serve as the EU's moral compass, as explicitly stated: "Promoting these values, as well as peace and the well-being of the Union's peoples are now the main objectives of the Union."[114] The actualization of these values

in the EU is reflected in numerous ways, including health care provided for all people, inexpensive (sometimes free) university education, a high standard of living, effective public transportation, strong democratic institutions, sufficient retirement security, affordable child care, paid parental leave, and so on.[115] Rates of violent crime are much lower in the EU nations than in the United States.[71] In short, a strong argument can be made that Europeans have successfully devised social institutions that promote not only peace but also respect for the law, justice, democracy, equality, and human rights among EU nations.

SYMBOLISM AND CEREMONIES FOR PEACE

Symbols and ceremonies reinforce unity and commitment to peace. All the Upper Xingu tribes participate in ceremonies to mourn the deaths of deceased chiefs and to inaugurate new ones. Joint ceremonies help to unify the tribes and reinforce their expanded shared identity as members of the same broader peaceful society. One Xinguano expressed the intention in this way: "We don't make war; we have festivals for the chiefs to which all of the villages come. We sing, dance, trade and wrestle."[110] Like the longhouse that symbolically represented the Iroquois Confederacy as one family, the Tree of Peace was a powerful symbol for peace and unity (Fig. 1). According to an often-recounted legend, at the formation of the League of Peace, the weapons of war were buried beneath the tree and then washed away into a subterranean cavern. Symbolically, the white roots of the Tree of Peace represent the desire for peace to spread beyond the confederacy to embrace neighboring societies in all directions.[111] The eagle perched atop the Tree of Peace was a reminder that one must remain vigilant to threats to the peace. The legends and symbols of peace were regularly recounted at the meetings of the Council of Chiefs.[107,111] Whereas the Iroquois still engaged in external warfare after the confederacy was formed, the main goal was to maintain peace, security, and unity within the confederacy.[108] They expressed the hope that someday the League of Peace would be extended to include all their neighbors.[107,111]

---

[113] A. Staab, *The European Union Explained* (Indiana Univ. Press, Bloomington, IN, 2008).

[114] Europa, Treaty of Lisbon: A Europe of Rights and Values. Accessed Feb. 15, 2012 at http://europa.eu/lisbon_treaty/glance/rights_values/index_en.htm.

FIGURE 2-1 The Tree of Peace. The insignia on the flag of the Oneida Nation, one of the original five member societies of the Iroquois Confederacy, depicts the Tree of Peace. The Cayuga, Mohawk, Oneida, Onondaga, and Seneca (later joined by the Tuscarora) brought an end to the chronic warfare among themselves, represented ritualistically as they interred their war hatchets and war clubs under the Tree of Peace. An underground river washed all their weapons away, making them irretrievable, thus reflecting symbolically the five nations' commitment to unity and peace. The eagle of vigilance is shown, as are the white roots for peace, the latter symbolizing the Iroquois desire to spread peace to all the peoples of the world. The legendary prophet Deganawidah proclaimed as the weapons of war were eliminated, "We have rid the earth of these things of an Evil Mind. . . . Thus . . . shall the Great Peace be established, and hostilities shall no longer be known between the Five Nations, but peace to the United People."[III]

SUPERORDINATE INSTITUTIONS AND CONFLICT MANAGEMENT

Conflicts within or between groups can be addressed in different ways, most of which do not entail the use of violence, for instance, negotiation, mediation, and adjudication (Fig. 2). Moreover, higher levels of governance can be created with the effect that conflict management among constituent social units becomes more effective and less belligerent.[71] The creation of the Iroquois Confederacy established a higher level of governance consisting of a Council of Chiefs representing all five nations (and later six when the Tuscarora joined) that assembled

to resolve disputes and address other political issues. In terms of structure, the Iroquois employed the same model of village and tribal councils, but scaled up to the supratribal level.[108] The governing approach was built on discussion and consensus formation. Although there were places on the council for 50 chiefs from major villages across all the nations, each of the nations had only one vote. The Iroquois core value of peace within their confederacy was personified in the decorum and actions of the Council of Chiefs, who reenacted the legend of how the prophet Deganawidah had originally shown the people of the five nations the path away from feuding and warring among themselves and toward peace, unity, and security under their Tree of Peace.[107, 111]

In 1946, Winston Churchill proposed that a pan-European peace could be forged through the creation of strong trade relations and called for the creation of the United States of Europe.[115, 116] Likewise, Jean Monnet realized that the centuries of warfare in Europe fundamentally stemmed from a nation-state system and, therefore, to abolish warfare in Europe, a new order with centralized, supranational institutions must be established. A number of leaders, such as Robert Schuman and Konrad Adenauer, adopted the vision of an interdependent and united Europe that would put an end to war in the region once and for all.[114, 116] The EU has added a higher level of governance that includes new institutions for dealing with conflict, such as the European Court of Justice, to accomplish the superordinate goals of preventing war and promoting prosperity within the union.[113, 114] In both the Iroquois and EU cases, the key was to create a higher-order level of governance, along with a new common identity and a new unity of purpose, to bring about an end to war and to guarantee peace and security within the system. In fact, the same process has taken place in the formation of the United States from 13 original colonies each initially having their own social identities. In the United States today, it is taken for granted that crimes and disputes

[115] S. Hill, *Europe's Promise* (Univ. of California Press, Berkeley, 2010).
[116] T. Reid, *The United States of Europe* (Penguin, New York, 2004).

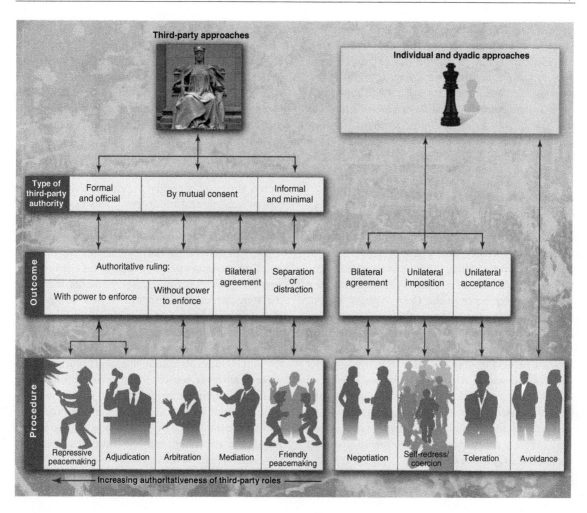

FIGURE 2–2 Approaches to conflict management. Approaches to conflict can entail individual, dyadic, or triadic forms. This typology shows five kinds of third-party assisted procedures (on the left) and four individual or dyad approaches (on the right). Self redress/ coercion may involve purely verbal arguments or threats but sometimes entails the use of physical violence (e.g., assault, homicide, feud, or war). Most conflict management approaches do not involve the use of physical violence. Negotiation, for example, is a dyadic procedure wherein parties use techniques like problem-solving and compromising in an attempt to reach an agreement or a resolution of the dispute. In the triadic approaches of adjudication and arbitration, for example, third parties render formal decisions, but adjudication and arbitration differ in that judges have the authority to enforce their rulings, whereas arbitrators do not. Different approaches to conflict management are favored in different cultures, but every society, even where self redress/coercion regularly occurs, has various alternative ways to managing conflict without physical violence.[118–120] [Photo credit: David Dye]

---

[117] T. Hudgens, *We Need Law* (BILC Corporation, Denver, 1986).

[118] K.-F. Koch, *War and Peace in Jalemo* (Harvard Univ. Press, Cambridge, MA, 1974).

[119] D. Black, *The Social Structure of Right and Wrong* (Academic Press, San Diego, 1993).

[120] D. P. Fry, in *Natural Conflict Resolution*, F. Aureli, F. de Waal, Eds. (Univ. of California Press, Berkeley, 2000), pp. 334–351.

will be handled though a hierarchy of courts that range from the municipal, state, and district level to the Supreme Court. President Harry Truman once observed, "When Kansas and Colorado have a quarrel over the water in the Arkansas River, they don't call out the National Guard in each state and go to war over it. They bring suit in the Supreme Court of the United States and abide by the decision. There isn't a reason in the world why we cannot do that internationally."[117]

CONCLUSION

Can humanity exist without war? Some completely nonwarring societies and peace systems, such as the tribes of India's Nilgiri and Wynaad plateaus, the Orang Asli societies of mainland Malaysia, and the Australian Aborigines of the Great Western Desert, suggest that this is possible. Furthermore, the Upper Xingu peoples, Iroquois Confederacy, and EU are not mere utopian fantasies; they represent real-world clusters of neighboring societies that live together without war within their peace systems. They have found similar multifaceted paths to successfully keep the peace. These peace systems represent new perspectives and possibilities for living without war that play on the necessity for cooperation under conditions of interdependence.

Could a global peace system be created to abolish war from the planet? Theoretically, this could be done. The people of the earth today face some of the same challenges that Europeans successfully addressed after World War II. Specifically, how can we create security, peace, and prosperity among former enemies and nations with different languages, customs, and cultural traditions? In the 21st century, humanity must determine how to live without war and work together to solve shared challenges like global warming, oceanic pollution, deforestation, desertification, and biodiversity loss that not only threaten particular regions but ultimately endanger human survival overall. When it comes to such threats, all peoples on Earth are interdependent.

Constructing a peace system for the entire planet would involve many synergistic elements, including the transformative vision that a new peace-based global system is in fact possible, the understanding that interdependence and common challenges require cooperation, an added level of social identity that includes all human beings and encompasses more than mere national patriotism, the creation of effective democratic and judicial procedures at a supranational level, and the development of values and symbols that not only sustain peace and justice for all but also relegate the institution of war, like slavery before it, to the pages of history.

STUDY QUESTIONS

1. Identify and discuss some ways of preventing war that were *not* touched upon in this chapter but deserve consideration. Look specifically at whether the phenomenon of "asymmetric conflict" introduces qualitatively new issues, or simply a different slant on the same problem.

2. Choose one or more of the selections in this chapter and disagree with their main argument, pointing out, for example, how it is unrealistic, undesirable, or even counterproductive.

3. Take a current source of conflict and describe how "principled negotiation" might help both sides reach an acceptable agreement.

4. With the Cold War receding into distant memory, is arms control still important? If yes, where would you like to see it be concentrated? If no, why not?

5. Look into the current status of international organizations *other* than the United Nations. Which of these seem especially promising? Do any seem liable to be especially troublesome? Why?

6. Are there any weaknesses in international law other than the problem of enforcement? Describe them and suggest improvements.

7. What are some reasons for thinking that the current system of sovereign states is inappropriate for meeting the problems of the twenty-first century? Are there any reasons to think that this system is weakening? If so, what benefits and dangers might this shift pose?

8. An earlier edition of this book included a famous suggestion for world government by philosopher Immanuel Kant. Look into other schemes for world government that have been proposed since then. Are they necessarily as unrealistic as some critics suggest? (In other words, was it wise to delete consideration of world government from this chapter?)

9. Describe ways in which Osgood's strategy of GRIT might be applied to a current conflict situation. Be specific.

10. What similarities exist between attempts to achieve negative peace on the international level and similar attempts on the personal level? Differences?

SUGGESTIONS FOR FURTHER READING

Benton, Barbara, ed. 1996. *Soldiers for Peace: Fifty Years of United Nations Peacekeeping.* New York: Facts On File.

Blix, Hans. 2008. *Why Nuclear Disarmament Matters.* Cambridge, MA: MIT Press.

Cassidy, Kevin J., and Gregory A. Bischak. 1993. *Real Security: Converting the Defense Economy and Building Peace.* Albany: State University of New York Press.

Clark, Grenville, and Louis Sohn. 1966. *World Peace through World Law: Two Alternative Plans.* Cambridge, MA: Harvard University Press.

Crocker, Chester A, Fen Osler Hampson, and Pamela R. Aall, eds. 2001. *Turbulent Peace: The Challenges of Managing International Conflict.* Washington, DC: United States Institute of Peace Press.

Findlay, Trevor, ed. 1996. *Challenges for the New Peacekeepers.* New York: Oxford University Press.

Gittings, John. 2012. *The Glorious Art of Peace: From the Iliad to Iraq.* Oxford: Oxford University Press.

Goldman, Ralph Morris, and Willard M. Hardman.1997 *Building Trust: An Introduction to Peacekeeping and Arms Control.* Brookfield, VT: Ashgate.

Horgan, John. 2012. *The End of War.* New York: McSweeney's.

Mason, David T., and James D. Meernik, eds. 2006. *Conflict Prevention and Peacebuilding in Post-War Societies: Sustaining the Peace.* New York: Routledge.

Schell, Jonathan. 2007. *The Seventh Decade: The New Shape of Nuclear Danger.* New York: Metropolitan.

Sidhu, Waheguru Pal Singh, and Ramesh Chandra Thakur. 2006. *Arms Control After Iraq: Normative and Operational Challenges.* New York: United Nations University Press.

Shaw, Malcolm. 2008. *International Law.* London: Cambridge University Press.

CHAPTER 3

Responding to Terrorism

For most Americans, terrorism suddenly emerged as a major concern immediately following the terrorist attacks of 9/11. However, for many other people, terrorism has been an ever-present reality—not only terrorism perpetrated by nonstate actors (what can be designated "terrorism from below") but also terrorism brought about by the actions of states themselves ("terrorism from above"). This distinction may be jarring for readers whose understanding of terrorism is limited to the former designation: the use of violence or the threat of violence against civilians by unofficial entities seeking to influence the action of governments. But it is worth noting that official entities—namely, governments themselves—have not been reluctant to employ violence or the threat of violence against civilians in the hope of influencing the actions of governments or of the civilian population: this is the essence of nuclear deterrence and, traditionally, of most counterinsurgency campaigns.

A further, potentially jarring and controversial suggestion is embodied in the saying, "One person's terrorist is another's freedom fighter." Thus, in the late eighteenth century, American revolutionaries were frequently described by the British as "terrorists," just as in the twentieth century, the Irish Republican Army—substantially funded by Irish émigrés to the United States—has long been reviled, especially in England, as a terrorist organization. Even more dramatically, perhaps, a prominent "terrorist" organization (the *Irgun*), which that fought on behalf of Israeli independence from British rule, subsequently contributed to the post-independence political leadership of Israel, just as the Palestinian Liberation Organization, once reviled as "terrorist," has become the recognized government on the occupied West Bank.

These issues are not raised here in order to minimize the horror derived from terrorist attacks but simply to emphasize that even such a seemingly open-and-shut case as "terrorism" is best understood as a nuanced concept, not usefully categorized as a simple matter of "us" (the good guys, who are moral and law-abiding) versus "them" (the bad guys, who are immoral, unprincipled and uniquely disrespectful of human life). Moreover, terrorism's history is much older and broader than most Americans assume and is not defined or constrained by considerations of religion.

This chapter is focused especially on terrorism as embodied by Islamic fundamentalism because it is largely intended for an American audience. However, it also seeks to widen the reader's perspective on this enormous and complex problem.

RAND Corporation

TERRORISM PAST AND PRESENT

Concern about future conflicts in the twenty-first century has increasingly focused on the phenomenon of "asymmetrical conflicts," among which terrorism and counterterrorism loom large. The RAND Corporation was originally formed as a semi-independent "think tank" to advise the United States Air Force ("RAND" originally stood for "research and development"). Its involvement in matters of terrorism speaks to this shift in emphasis. At the same time, the following RAND report, commissioned by the nonpartisan and highly respected League of Women Voters, provides a useful, mainstream, and comparatively uncontroversial introduction to terrorism past and present.

A BRIEF OVERVIEW OF TERRORISM

Depending on how it is defined, terrorism, both in practice and in name, dates back hundreds, even thousands, of years. In the realm of political action, the word "terrorism" was a product of the French Revolution's *régime de la terreur* (1793–1794). Ironically, "terror" initially had a positive connotation because it was associated with a struggle for democracy and a more virtuous society. That was not to last in the face of the generalized fear induced by the ever-present guillotine, and *terrorism* came to be associated with abuse of power, especially by the state.

During the nineteenth and early twentieth centuries, there was an increase in both Europe and America of the use of terror-inducing violence to promote antistate outcomes or to achieve independent statehood. Anarchists carried out a series of bombings and assassinations, the best known of which were the murders of Czar Alexander II in Russia (1881), President William McKinley in the United States (1901), and Archduke Franz Ferdinand in Sarajevo (1914). Irish, Armenian, and Bosnian insurrectionists were among the ethnoseparatist groups fighting against alien regimes. Labor uprisings in many countries were bitter and often bloody.

Beginning in about the 1930s, terrorism was turned on its head when "revolutionary" violence directed against heads of state and other persons in authority began to be replaced by "repressive" violence applied by dictators such as Adolf Hitler,

Benito Mussolini, and Joseph Stalin against their own citizenry. This kind of state-directed terror, used by those in power against their own citizens, later had many counterparts in third world countries, especially in Central and South America.

Following World War II, terrorism again assumed its revolutionary connotation, most notably through the nationalist or anticolonial revolts carried out in Asia, Africa, and the Middle East in opposition to European rule. In the 1980s, there was a further expansion of the concept of terrorism in the form of state-sponsored, covert violence against other nations—such as that sponsored by Iran, Iraq, Libya, and Syria—which allowed weaker regimes to confront more powerful countries without risking large-scale retaliation.

It was primarily the activities of the Palestinian Liberation Organization (PLO) that put terrorism in the international spotlight. Although the PLO's 1968 hijacking of an Israeli El Al commercial aircraft and the 1972 attack on the Israeli Olympic team in Munich did not achieve their objectives, they did succeed in drawing world attention to their cause, which was the plight of Palestinian refugees who had either voluntarily left or had been driven from Israel and were living in overcrowded camps in neighboring countries. The PLO served as an example to other aggrieved groups, and "within the decade, the number of terrorist groups either operating internationally or committing attacks against foreign targets in their own country in order to attract international attention had more than quadrupled."[1]

Given the substantial changes that have occurred over time in the notion of what constitutes terrorism, it is important to try to pin down a definition that can act as an anchor. Bruce Hoffman, an internationally recognized authority on the subject of terrorism, suggests the following:

[Terrorism is] the deliberate creation and exploitation of fear through violence or the threat of violence in the pursuit of political change. All terrorist acts involve violence or the threat of violence. Terrorism is specifically designed to have far-reaching psychological effects beyond the immediate victim(s) or object of the terrorist attack. It is meant to instill fear within, and thereby intimidate, a wider "target audience" that might include a rival ethnic or religious group, an entire country, a national government or political party, or public opinion in general. Terrorism is designed to create power where there is none or to consolidate power where there is very little. Through the publicity generated by their violence, terrorists seek to obtain the leverage, influence, and power they otherwise lack to effect political change on either a local or an international scale.[2]

TERRORISM AS A RELIGIOUS IMPERATIVE

Terrorism motivated by religious belief is a centuries-old phenomenon, and scores of examples can be found in all major religions in all parts of the world. However, in the modern consciousness, the resurgence of religious terrorism is often linked to the 1979 revolution that transformed Iran into an Islamic republic. The Ayatollah Khomeini had long condemned the growing influence of the West under the government of Mohammad Reza Shah, and had called on Muslims to reject secular government in favor of the restoration of fundamental Islamic law. Moreover, Khomeini sought to extend the revolution to other Muslim countries. Violence in the service of this goal was promoted not as a tactic but, under certain conditions, as an obligation.

One of the central tenets of Islam is the duty of Muslims to engage in jihad. As Rudolph Peters, an expert on the Middle East, has explained,

The Arabic word jihad means to strive, to exert oneself, to struggle. The word has a basic connotation of an endeavour towards a praiseworthy

---

[1] Bruce Hoffman, *Inside Terrorism*, 2d ed. (New York: Columbia University Press, 2006), p. 70. Hoffman goes on to say that "according to the RAND Terrorism Incident Database, the number of organizations engaged in *international* terrorism grew from only eleven in 1968 . . . to an astonishing fifty-five in 1978. Of this total, more than half (thirty, or 54 percent) were ethno-nationalist separatist movements, all seeking to copy or capitalize on the PLO's success."

[2] Hoffman, pp. 40–41.

aim. In a religious context it may express a struggle against one's evil inclinations or an exertion for the sake of Islam and the umma [Muslim community], e.g., trying to convert unbelievers or working for the moral betterment of Islamic society ("jihad of the tongue" and "jihad of the sword"). In the books on Islamic law, the word means armed struggle against the unbelievers, which is also a common meaning in the Koran.[3]

The Soviet invasion of Afghanistan further stimulated jihad and was critical to the later formation of Al Qaeda. Its leader, Osama bin Laden, has been clear and consistent in his condemnation of the West—the new Crusaders—and his desire to protect Islam from Christian aggression. Although his overarching goal is to create a worldwide, totalitarian theocracy, he has turned jihadis against the United States in particular by exploiting resentments over its military presence in the Arabian Peninsula, the war in Iraq, and American support of Israel. Bin Laden has been extremely skillful in capitalizing on the belief that engaging in defensive jihad is an individual obligation when Islam is under assault, and he has succeeded in building a broad base of support that assures a steady flow of recruits to his cause.

One of the things that make religious terrorists so formidable is their willingness to carry out operations that are far more deadly and destructive than those conducted by their secular counterparts.[4] The attacks by nineteen Al Qaeda airplane hijackers on the World Trade Center and the Pentagon are the most dramatic case in point. Including the deaths on the fourth aircraft that crashed in Pennsylvania, nearly three thousand people were killed. Until that time, no terrorist operation had killed more than five hundred.[5]

Suicide terrorism is a particularly effective and lethal form of attack. It has advantages in timing, access, and flexibility if plans have to be changed at the last minute. It is inexpensive to carry out. It results in higher death and casualty rates than other methods.[6] Since the perpetrator is not expected to survive, there is no need for a complicated getaway plan. Broad media coverage is assured; thus, the psychological, fear-inducing effects are widespread and profound.

Robert Pape argues in his study of suicide terrorism, *Dying to Win*, that contrary to what many Westerners believe, there is little connection between this phenomenon and Islamic fundamentalism or any other world religion. "Rather, what nearly all suicide terrorist attacks have in common is a specific secular and strategic goal: to compel modern democracies to withdraw military forces from territory that the terrorists consider to be their homeland."[7]

However, many terrorism specialists acknowledge a link between religion and terrorism. For example, Bruce Hoffman points to the growth in the number of religious terrorist groups during the past two decades and asserts that a major challenge facing those charged with developing effective countermeasures is to understand "why mainstream religious traditions become radicalized and co-opted by violent extremists and why '"fringe'" movements or hitherto peaceful religious cults sud-

---

[3] Rudolph Peters, *Jihad in Classical and Modern Islam: A Reader*, 2d ed. (Princeton, NJ: Markus Wiener Publishers, 2005), p. 1.

[4] "Although religious terrorists committed only 6 percent of recorded terrorist incidents between 1998 and 2004, their acts were responsible for 30 percent of the total number of fatalities recorded during that time period. . . . While Al Qaeda perpetrated only 0.1 percent of all terrorist attacks between 1998 and 2004, it was responsible for nearly 19 percent of total fatalities during that time period" (Hoffman, p. 88).

[5] Hoffman, pp. 18–19.

[6] Hoffman, pp. 132–133. "According to one estimate, the total cost of a typical Palestinian suicide operation, for example, is about one hundred fifty dollars. Yet this modest sum yields a very attractive return: on average, suicide operations worldwide kill about four times as many people as other kinds of terrorist attacks. In Israel the average is even higher, inflicting six times the number of deaths and roughly twenty-six times more casualties than other acts of terrorism" (p. 133).

[7] Robert A. Pape, *Dying to Win: The Strategic Logic of Suicide Terrorism* (New York: Random House, 2005), p. 4. Pape's study of all suicide bombings and attacks worldwide from 1980 through 2003 shows that "the leading instigators of suicide attacks are the Tamil Tigers in Sri Lanka, a Marxist-Leninist group whose members are from Hindu families but who are adamantly opposed to religion. This group committed 76 of the 315 incidents, more suicide attacks than Hamas . . . [and] 301 could have their roots traced to large, coherent political or military campaigns."

denly embark on lethal campaigns of indiscriminate terrorism."[8]

TRENDS IN TERRORISM

Just as the definitions of what constitutes terrorism have changed over time, so have the ways that terrorists operate. Several of the apparent trends are described below.[9]

Terrorism has become bloodier, and suicide terrorism is now the most deadly form. In the period 1980–2003, suicide attacks comprised only 3 percent of all terrorist incidents but accounted for 48 percent of the fatalities.[10]

Terrorists have evolved new models of organization. In place of the hierarchies of the past, terrorist groups now employ flat organizational structures and operate independent, scattered cells. They use modern communications techniques for networking across regions, and their compartmentalization makes it difficult for their enemies to penetrate their operations.

Terrorists have developed financial resources that make them less dependent on state sponsors. Terrorists have become skilled in raising money, moving it, and blocking detection of their financial operations. They have direct contributors, and many groups receive financial contributions through the Internet as well. Islamic nongovernmental charity organizations are another source of funds, sometimes knowingly and sometimes not. Certain terrorist groups also engage in kidnapping for ransom, extortion, protection rackets, and drug trafficking. Others have very substantial legitimate investments that are difficult to trace.[11]

Terrorists have learned to effectively exploit modern communication technologies. To reach their target audiences, terrorists no longer need to rely on underground publications and radio stations. A full range of video equipment, computers, e-mail, mass-marketed CDs and DVDs—all of the advances represented by the latest information revolution are available to them, and they are taking full advantage. They can now shape, produce, and disseminate sophisticated messages via the high-speed Internet and World Wide Web without concern for censorship and very little fear of discovery.[12]

Terrorists have increased their mobility and expanded their operational theater. As a result of widespread exodus from zones of conflict, terrorists are able, on their own and through networked contact with migrating populations, to operate more extensively and effectively across borders. In addition, modern communication has also enabled transnational connectivity among terrorist groups who may not share the same ideology but do share expertise, tactics, and even technology.

---

[8] Hoffman, p. 127. Hoffman points out that "in 1994, a third (sixteen) of the forty-nine identifiable international terrorist groups active that year could be classified as religious in character and/or motivation. . . . " By 2004, that number had risen to nearly half (fifty-two, or 46 percent), "while thirty-two (28 percent) were left-wing groups, and twenty-four (21 percent) were ethno-nationalist/separatist organizations" (p. 86).

[9] Material for this discussion has been drawn primarily from four sources: Rohan Gunaratna, ed., *The Changing Face of Terrorism* (Singapore: Marshall Cavendish Academic, 2004), pp. 18–30; Bruce Hoffman, *Inside Terrorism*; Brian Michael Jenkins, "The New Age of Terrorism" in *Homeland Security Handbook* (New York: McGraw Hill, 2006), pp. 117–128; and Michael Scheuer, *Through Our Enemies' Eyes: Osama bin Laden, Radical Islam, and the Future of America*, 2d ed. (Washington, DC: Potomac Books, 2006).

[10] Pape, p. 6.

[11] Cindy Combs, *Terrorism in the Twenty-First Century*, 4th ed. (Upper Saddle River, NJ: Prentice Hall, 2005), p. 12. Combs states that "if the PLO [Palestinian Liberation Organization] were an American corporation, it would have been on the list of Fortune 500 companies." In the mid-1980s the organization's financial empire was estimated to be worth $5 billion. Return on investments brought in about $1 billion a year. Most of the PLO's assets were held by private individuals or in numbered bank accounts. Its financial advisers invested money in the European market and on Wall Street. "The PLO also held large amounts of lucrative money certificates in the United States. These and other investments were said to provide as much as 20 percent of all the group's revenues." Like many multinational corporations, the PLO was generally involved in business ventures designed to earn money, but in some cases their purpose was primarily to generate goodwill and political support (Combs, pp. 90–91).

[12] See "The New Media, Terrorism, and the Shaping of Global Opinion" in Hoffman, pp. 197–228.

THE FUTURE TERRORIST THREAT

Most people in the United States were blindsided by the September 11 attacks. Being geographically distant from most of the places in the world that foster terrorism, we did not expect such a brutal and catastrophic assault on our homeland. Perhaps that was naïve. As Michael Scheuer emphasizes in *Through Our Enemies' Eyes*, in its entire history America has rarely had an enemy that made his plans clearer or repeated them so often:

> Osama bin Laden publicly declared war on the United States on 2 September 1996; for good measure, he did so again on 23 February 1998. Since 1996, bin Laden has repeatedly warned Americans—again always in public—that he would incrementally increase the lethality of his attacks on U.S. interests until we stopped supporting Israel, withdrew our military forces from Saudi Arabia, and ended the embargo on Iraq. During this period, he was true to his word; his forces and those he incited attacked us with steadily increasing skill, lethality, and audacity in Somalia, Saudi Arabia, Kenya, Tanzania, and Yemen. He warned that if the United States did not yield to his demands, he would bring the war he was waging into the continental United States.[13]

The fight against Al Qaeda has been called the defining conflict of the early twenty-first century.

How, then, should we respond as a nation? Scheuer suggests this for a start:

> Until Americans begin to see that some of their values and goals are neither accepted or acceptable to all races, nations, and creeds, they will not begin to understand the appeal of a person like bin Laden or be able to defend their interests against him. Indeed, they will need to go another step and recognize that, for many Muslims, U.S. foreign policy is seen as an attack on Islam . . . and is drawing an armed response as a matter of self-defense and scriptural requirement.[14]

It is also important to recognize that the rise of radical Islam is not confined to the Middle East. The phenomenon that we in the West associate with A1 Queda Qaeda has metastasized throughout the world. Muslim minorities in many countries consider themselves marginalized within their societies, and their resentment is increasingly being directed against the United States and its allies. In *The Next Attack*, Daniel Benjamin and Steven Simon observe that the "churn of local conflicts is providing soldiers for the global jihad. It may not be long before substantially more extremists from these five regions—Europe, Chechnya, Saudi Arabia, Pakistan, and Southeast Asia—are participating directly in the war against America."[15]

---

[13] Scheuer, p. xvi.

[14] Scheuer, p. 29.

[15] Daniel Benjamin and Steven Simon, *The Next Attack: The Failure of the War on Terror and a Strategy for Getting It Right* (New York: Henry Holt and Company, 2005), p. 81.

Noam Chomsky

THE EVIL SCOURGE OF TERRORISM: REALITY, CONSTRUCTION, REMEDY

Terrorism, it has been said, is the warfare of the poor, while war is the terrorism of the rich. Not surprisingly, citizens of the wealthy North are more accustomed to criticizing the former while taking the latter for granted. There is, however, a striking and often ignored similarity between the terrorism precipitated by comparatively weak, unorganized, non-state actors and that conducted by powerful, officially sanctioned governments themselves. The former is (rightly) condemned by nearly everyone in the West; only rarely is the latter placed in the same category. To do so, however, is to experience a potentially valuable shift in perspective, helping us to, as the poet Robert Burns put it, "see ourselves as others see us." The result may be troubling . . . but then again, so is terrorism itself, regardless of its source.

In the following selection, famed linguist and political activist Noam Chomsky points out the need for wealthy "developed" countries (especially the United States) to take responsibility for their own actions, not only to expand political and social awareness, but in hopes of eventually modifying international affairs to ensure that no one is either a terrorist or a victim.

The president could not have been more justified when he condemned "the evil scourge of terrorism." I am quoting Ronald Reagan, who came into office in 1981 declaring that a focus of his foreign policy would be state-directed international terrorism, "the plague of the modern age" and "a return to barbarism in our time," to sample some of the rhetoric of his administration. When George W. Bush declared a "war on terror" 20 years later, he was *re*-declaring the war, an important fact that is worth exhuming from Orwell's memory hole if we hope to understand the nature of the evil scourge of terrorism, or more importantly, if we hope to understand ourselves. We do not need the famous Delphi inscription to recognize that there can be no more important task. . . .

The reasons why Reagan's war on terror has been dispatched to the repository of unwelcome facts are understandable and informative—about ourselves. Instantly, Reagan's war on terror became a savage terrorist war, leaving hundreds of thousands of tortured and mutilated corpses in the wreckage of Central America, tens of thousands more in the Middle East, and an estimated 1.5 million killed by South African terror that was strongly supported by the Reagan administration in violation of congressional sanctions. All of these murderous exercises of course had pretexts. The resort to violence always does. In the Middle East, Reagan's decisive support for Israel's 1982 invasion of Lebanon, which killed some 15–20,000 people and destroyed much of southern Lebanon and Beirut, was based on the pretense that it was in self-defense against PLO rocketing of the Galilee, a brazen fabrication: Israel recognized at once that the threat was PLO diplomacy, which might have undermined Israel's illegal takeover of the occupied territories. In Africa, support for the marauding of the apartheid state was officially justified within the framework of the war on terror: it was necessary to protect white South Africa from one of the world's "more notorious terrorist groups," Nelson Mandela's African National Congress, so Washington determined in 1988. The pretexts in the other cases were no more impressive.

For the most part, the victims of Reaganite terror were defenseless civilians, but in one case the victim was a state, Nicaragua, which could respond through legal channels. Nicaragua brought its charges to the World Court, which condemned the US for "unlawful use of force"—in lay terms, international terrorism—in its attack on Nicaragua from its Honduran bases, and ordered the US to terminate the assault and pay substantial reparations. The aftermath is instructive.

Congress responded to the Court judgment by increasing aid to the US-run mercenary army attacking Nicaragua, while the press condemned the Court as a "hostile forum" and therefore irrelevant. The same Court had been highly relevant a few years earlier when it ruled in favor of the US against Iran. Washington dismissed the Court judgment with contempt. In doing so, it joined the distinguished company of Libya's Qaddafi and Albania's Enver Hoxha. Libya and Albania have since joined the world of law-abiding states in this respect, so now the US stands in splendid isolation. Nicaragua then brought the matter to the UN Security Council, which passed two resolutions calling on all states to observe international law. The resolutions were vetoed by the US, with the assistance of Britain and France, which abstained. All of this passed virtually without notice, and has been expunged from history.

Also forgotten—or rather, never noticed—is the fact that the "hostile forum" had bent over backwards to accommodate Washington. The Court rejected almost all of Nicaragua's case, presented by a distinguished Harvard University international lawyer, on the grounds that when the US had accepted World Court jurisdiction in 1946, it added a reservation exempting itself from charges under international treaties, specifically the Charters of the United Nations and the Organization of American States. . . . Such thoughts as these should be uppermost in our minds when we consider the evil scourge of terrorism. We should also recall that although the Reagan years do constitute a chapter of unusual extremism in the annals of terrorism, they are not some strange departure from the norm. We find much the same at the opposite end of the political spectrum as well: the Kennedy administration. One illustration is Cuba. According to long-standing myth, thoroughly dismantled by recent scholarship, the US intervened in Cuba in 1898 to secure its liberation from Spain. In reality, the intervention was designed to *prevent* Cuba's imminent liberation from Spain, turning it into a virtual colony of the United States. In 1959, Cuba finally did liberate itself, causing consternation in Washington. Within months, the Eisenhower administration planned in secret to overthrow the government, and initiated bombing and economic sanctions. The basic thinking was expressed by a high State Department official: Castro would be removed "through disenchantment and disaffection based on economic dissatisfaction and hardship [so] every possible means should be undertaken promptly to weaken the economic life of Cuba [in order to] bring about hunger, desperation and [the] overthrow of the government."

The incoming Kennedy administration took over and escalated these programs. The reasons are frankly explained in the internal record, since declassified. Violence and economic strangulation were undertaken in response to Cuba's "successful defiance" of US policies going back 150 years; no Russians, but rather the Monroe Doctrine, which established Washington's right to dominate the hemisphere. The concerns of the Kennedy administration went beyond the need to punish successful defiance. The administration feared that the Cuban example might infect others with the thought of "taking matters into their own hands," an idea with great appeal throughout the continent because "the distribution of land and other forms of national wealth greatly favors the propertied classes and the poor and underprivileged, stimulated by the example of the Cuban revolution, are now demanding opportunities for a decent living." That was the warning conveyed to incoming President Kennedy by his Latin America advisor, liberal historian Arthur Schlesinger. The analysis was soon confirmed by the CIA, which observed that "Castro's shadow looms large because social and economic conditions throughout Latin America invite opposition to ruling authority and encourage agitation for radical change," for which Castro's Cuba might provide a model.

Ongoing plans for invasion were soon implemented. When the invasion failed at the Bay of Pigs, Washington turned to a major terrorist war. The president assigned responsibility for the war to his brother, Robert Kennedy, whose highest priority was to bring "the terrors of the earth" to Cuba, in the words of his biographer, Arthur Schlesinger. . . . Commentators are polite enough not to recall the Bush doctrine declared when he attacked Afghanistan: those who harbor terrorists are as guilty as the terrorists themselves, and must be treated accordingly, by bombing and invasion. Perhaps this is enough to illustrate that state-directed international terrorism is considered an appropriate tool of diplomacy across the political spectrum. Nevertheless, Reagan was the first modern president to employ the audacious device of concealing his resort to "the evil scourge of terrorism" under the cloak of a "war on terror." . . .

Apart from Cuba, the plague of state terror in the Western hemisphere was initiated with the Brazilian coup in 1964, installing the first of a series of neo-Nazi National Security States and initiating a plague of repression without precedent in the hemisphere, always strongly backed by Washington, hence a particularly violent form of state-directed international terrorism. The campaign was in substantial measure a war against the Church. It was more than symbolic that it culminated in the assassination of six leading Latin American intellectuals, Jesuit priests, in November 1989, a few days after the fall of the Berlin wall. They were murdered by an elite Salvadoran battalion, fresh from renewed training at the John F. Kennedy Special Forces School in North Carolina. . . . The murder of the Jesuit priests was a crushing blow to liberation theology, the remarkable revival of Christianity initiated by Pope John

XXIII at Vatican II, which he opened in 1962, an event that "ushered in a new era in the history of the Catholic Church," in the words of the distinguished theologian and historian of Christianity Hans Küng. Inspired by Vatican II, Latin American Bishops adopted "the preferential option for the poor," renewing the radical pacifism of the Gospels that had been put to rest when the Emperor Constantine established Christianity as the religion of the Roman Empire—"a revolution" that converted "the persecuted church" to a "persecuting church," in Küng's words. In the post-Vatican II attempt to revive the Christianity of the pre-Constantine period, priests, nuns, and laypersons took the message of the Gospels to the poor and the persecuted, brought them together in "base communities," and encouraged them to take their fate into their own hands and to work together to overcome the misery of survival in brutal realms of US power.

The reaction to this grave heresy was not long in coming. The first salvo was Kennedy's military coup in Brazil in 1964, overthrowing a mildly social democratic government and instituting a reign of torture and violence. The campaign ended with the murder of the Jesuit intellectuals 20 years ago. There has been much debate about who deserves credit for the fall of the Berlin wall, but there is none about the responsibility for the brutal demolition of the attempt to revive the church of the Gospels. Washington's School of the Americas, famous for its training of Latin American killers, proudly announced as one of its "talking points" that liberation theology was "defeated with the assistance of the US army"—given a helping hand, to be sure by the Vatican, using the gentler means of expulsion and suppression.

. . . At Stanford University's prestigious Hoover Institution Reagan is revered as a colossus whose "spirit seems to stride the country, watching us like a warm and friendly ghost." We arrive by plane in Washington at Reagan international airport—or if we prefer, at John Foster Dulles international airport, honoring another prominent terrorist commander, whose exploits include overthrowing Iranian and Guatemalan democracy, installing the terror and torture state of the Shah and the most vicious of the terrorist states of Central America. The terrorist exploits of Washington's Guatemalan clients reached true genocide in the highlands in the 1980s while Reagan praised the worst of the killers, Rioss Montt, as "a man of great personal integrity" who was "totally dedicated to democracy" and was receiving a "bum rap" from human rights organizations.

I have been writing about international terrorism ever since Reagan declared a war on terror in 1981. In doing so, I have kept to the official definitions of "terrorism" in US and British law and in army manuals, all approximately the same. To take one succinct official definition, terrorism is "the calculated use of violence or threat of violence to attain goals that are political, religious, or ideological in nature . . . through intimidation, coercion, or instilling fear." Everything I have just described, and a great deal more like it, falls within the category of terrorism, in fact state-directed international terrorism, in the technical sense of US-British law.

For exactly that reason, the official definitions are unusable. They fail to make a crucial distinction: the concept of "terrorism" must somehow be crafted to include *their* terrorism against *us*, while excluding *our* terrorism against *them*, often far more extreme. To devise such a definition is a challenging task. Accordingly, from the 1980s there have been many scholarly conferences, academic publications, and international symposia devoted to the task of defining "terrorism." In public discourse the problem does not arise. Well-educated circles have internalized the special sense of "terrorism" required for justification of state action and control of domestic populations, and departure from the canon is generally ignored, or if noticed, elicits impressive tantrums.

Let us keep, then, to convention, and restrict attention to the terror *they* commit against *us*. It is no laughing matter, and sometimes reaches extreme levels. Probably the most egregious single crime of international terrorism in the modern era was the destruction of the World Trade Center on 9/11, killing almost 3000 people, a "crime against humanity" carried out with "wickedness and awesome cruelty," as Robert Fisk reported. It is widely agreed that 9/11 changed the world.

Awful as the crime was, one can imagine worse. Suppose that al-Qaeda had been supported by an awesome superpower intent on overthrowing the government of the United States. Suppose that the attack had succeeded: al-Qaeda had bombed the White House, killed the president, and installed a vicious military dictatorship, which killed some 50–100,000 people, brutally tortured 700,000, set up a major center of terror and subversion that carried out assassinations throughout the world and helped establish "National Security States" elsewhere that tortured and murdered with abandon. Suppose further that the dictator brought in economic advisers who within a few years drove the economy to one of the worst disasters in its history while their proud mentors collected Nobel Prizes and received other accolades. That would have been vastly more horrendous even than 9/11.

And as we all should know, it is not necessary to imagine, because it in fact did happen: in Chile, on the date that Latin Americans sometimes call "the first 9/11," 11 September 1973. The only change I have made is to per capita equivalents, an appropriate measure. But the first 9/11 did not change history, for good reasons: the events were too normal. In fact the installation of the Pinochet regime was just one event in the plague that began with the military coup in Brazil in 1964, spreading with similar or even worse horrors in other countries and reaching Central America in the 1980s under Reagan— whose South American favorite was the regime of the Argentine generals, the most savage of them all, consistent with his general stance on state violence.

Putting all of this inconvenient reality aside, let us continue to follow convention and imagine that the war on terror re-declared by George W. Bush on 9/11 2001 was directed to ending the plague of international terrorism, properly restricted in scope to satisfy doctrinal needs. There were sensible steps that could have been undertaken to achieve that goal. The murderous acts of 9/11 were bitterly condemned even within the jihadi movements. One constructive step would have been to isolate al-Qaeda, and unify opposition to it even among those attracted to its project. Nothing of the sort ever seems to have been considered. Instead, the Bush administration and its allies chose to unify the jihadi movement in support of Bin Laden and to mobilize many others to his cause by confirming his charge that the West is at war with Islam: invading Afghanistan and then Iraq, resorting to torture and rendition, and in general, choosing violence for the purposes of state power. . . .

The attack on Afghanistan in October 2001 is called "the good war," no questions asked, a justifiable act of self-defense with the noble aim of protecting human rights from the evil Taliban. . . . Three weeks after the bombing began, war aims shifted to overthrow of the regime. British Admiral Sir Michael Boyce announced that the bombing would continue until "the people of the country . . . get the leadership changed"—a textbook case of international terrorism.

It is also not true that there were no objections to the attack. With virtual unanimity, international aid organizations vociferously objected because it terminated their aid efforts, which were desperately needed. At the time it was estimated that some 5 million people were relying on aid for survival, and that an additional 2.5 million would be put at risk of starvation by the US–UK attack. The bombing was therefore an example of extreme criminality, whether or not the anticipated consequences took place.

Furthermore, the bombing was bitterly condemned by leading anti-Taliban Afghans, including the US favorite, Abdul Haq, who was given special praise as a martyr after the war by President Hamid Karzai. Just before he entered Afghanistan, and was captured and killed, he condemned the bombing that was then underway and criticized the US for refusing to support efforts of his and others "to create a revolt within the Taliban." The bombing was "a big setback for these efforts," he said, outlining them and calling on the US to assist them with funding and other support instead of undermining them with bombs. The US, he said, "is trying to show its muscle, score a victory and scare everyone in the world. They don't care about the suffering of the Afghans or how many people we will lose."

Shortly after, 1000 Afghan leaders gathered in Peshawar, some of them exiles, some coming from within Afghanistan, all committed to overthrowing the Taliban regime. It was "a rare display of unity among tribal elders, Islamic scholars, fractious politicians, and former guerrilla commanders," the press reported. They had many disagreements, but unanimously "urged the US to stop the air raids" and appealed to the international media to call for

an end to the "bombing of innocent people." They urged that other means be adopted to overthrow the hated Taliban regime, a goal they believed could be achieved without further death and destruction. The bombing was also harshly condemned by the prominent women's organization RAWA—which received some belated recognition when it became ideologically serviceable to express concern (briefly) about the fate of women in Afghanistan. . . .

It should not be necessary to tarry on the invasion of Iraq. Keeping solely to the effect on jihadi terror, the invasion was undertaken with the expectation that it would lead to an increase in terrorism, as it did, far beyond what was anticipated. It caused a seven-fold increase in terror, according to analyses by US terrorism experts. One may ask why these attacks were undertaken, but it is reasonably clear that confronting the evil scourge of terrorism was not a high priority, if it was even a consideration.

If that had been the goal, there were options to pursue. Some I have already mentioned. More generally, the US and Britain could have followed the proper procedures for dealing with a major crime: determine who is responsible, apprehend the suspects (with international cooperation if necessary, easy to obtain), and bring them to a fair trial. Furthermore, attention would be paid to the roots of terror. That can be extremely effective, as the US and UK had just learned in Northern Ireland. IRA terror was a very serious matter. As long as London reacted by violence, terror, and torture, it was the "indispensable ally" of the more violent elements of the IRA, and the cycle of terror escalated. By the late '90s, London began to attend to the grievances that lay at the roots of the terror, and to deal with those that were legitimate—as should be done irrespective of terror. Within a few years terror virtually disappeared. . . . Even without this experience we should know that violence engenders violence, while sympathy and concern cool passions and can evoke cooperation and empathy.

If we seriously want to end the plague of terrorism, we know how to do it. First, end our own role as perpetrators. That alone will have a substantial effect. Second, attend to the grievances that are typically in the background, and if they are legitimate, do something about them. Third, if an act of terror occurs, deal with it as a criminal act: identify and apprehend the suspects and carry out an honest judicial process. That actually works. In contrast, the techniques that are employed enhance the threat of terror. . . . This is not the only case where the approaches that might well reduce a serious threat are systematically avoided, and those that are unlikely to do so are adopted instead. One such case is the so-called "war on drugs." Over almost 40 years, the war has failed to curtail drug use or even street price of drugs. It has been established by many studies, including those of the US government, that by far the most cost-effective approach to drug abuse is prevention and treatment. But that approach is consistently avoided in state policy, which prefers far more expensive violent measures that have barely any impact on drug use, though they have other consistent consequences.

In cases like these, the only rational conclusion is that the declared goals are not the real ones, and that if we want to learn about the real goals, we should adopt an approach that is familiar in the law: relying on predictable outcome as evidence for intent. I think the approach leads to quite plausible conclusions, for the "war on drugs," the "war on terror," and much else. That, however, is work for another day.

Eqbal Ahmad

TERRORISM: THEIRS AND OURS

Islamic voices are rarely heard in the West. An exception has been Eqbal Ahmad, a noted Pakistani writer and antiwar activist. In his work, Ahmad was equally critical of fundamentalist nationalism and religion in the Middle East and throughout the Islamic world, and of what he saw as the imperial policy of the West, notably the United States. The following material—a transcribed lecture—was written several years before the terrorist attacks of 2001; it is offered not only for its useful geopolitical and demographic perspective but also to emphasize the relevance of terrorism as a concern independent of the U.S. experience on 9/11.

In the 1930s and 1940s, the Jewish underground in Palestine was described as "terrorist." Then new things happened.

By 1942, the Holocaust was occurring, and a certain liberal sympathy with the Jewish people had built up in the Western world. At that point, the terrorists of Palestine, who were Zionists, suddenly started to be described, by 1944–1945, as "freedom fighters." At least two Israeli prime ministers, including Menachem Begin, you can find in books and posters with pictures, saying "Terrorists, Reward This Much." The highest reward I have noted so far was 100,000 British pounds on the head of Menachem Begin, the terrorist.

Then from 1969 to 1990, the PLO, the Palestine Liberation Organization, occupied the center stage as the terrorist organization. Yasir Arafat has been described repeatedly by the great sage of American journalism, William Safire of the *New York Times*, as the "chief of terrorism." That's Yasir Arafat.

Now, on September 29, 1998, I was rather amused to notice a picture of Yasir Arafat to the right of President Bill Clinton. To his left is Israeli Prime Minister Benjamin Netanyahu. Clinton is looking toward Arafat and Arafat is looking literally like a meek mouse. Just a few years earlier he used to appear with this very menacing look around him, with a gun appearing menacing from his belt.

You remember those pictures, and you remember the next one.

In 1985 President Ronald Reagan received a group of bearded men. They were very ferocious, with turbans, looking like they came from another century. President Reagan received them in the White House. After receiving them, he spoke to the press. He pointed toward them, I'm sure some of you will recall that moment, and said, "These are the moral equivalent of America's founding fathers." These were the Afghan Mujahiddin. They were at the time, guns in hand, battling the Evil Empire. They were the moral equivalent of our founding fathers!

In August 1998, another American president ordered missile strikes from the American navy based in the Indian Ocean to kill Osama bin Laden and his men in the camps in Afghanistan. I do not wish to embarrass you with the reminder that Mr. bin Laden, whom fifteen American missiles were fired to hit in Afghanistan, was only a few years ago the moral equivalent of George Washington and Thomas Jefferson! He got angry over the fact that he has been demoted from "moral equivalent" of your "founding fathers." So he is taking out his anger in different ways. I'll come back to that subject more seriously in a moment.

You see, I have recalled all these stories to point out to you that the matter of terrorism is rather complicated. Terrorists change. The terrorist of yesterday is the hero of today, and the hero of yesterday becomes the terrorist of today. This is a serious matter of the constantly changing world of images in which we have to keep our heads straight to know what is terrorism and what is not. But more importantly, to know what causes it and how to stop it.

The next point about our terrorism is that [a] posture of inconsistency necessarily evades definition. If you are not going to be consistent, you're not going to define. I have examined at least twenty official documents on terrorism. Not one defines the word. All of them explain it, express it emotively, polemically, to arouse our emotions rather than exercise our intelligence. I give you only one example, which is representative. October 25, 1984, George Shultz, then secretary of state of the U.S., is speaking at the New York Park Avenue Synagogue. It's a long speech on terrorism. In the State Department Bulletin of seven single-spaced pages, there is not a single definition of terrorism. What we get is the following:

Definition number one: "Terrorism is a modern barbarism that we call terrorism."

Definition number two is even more brilliant: "Terrorism is a form of political violence." Aren't you surprised? It is a form of political violence, says George Shultz, secretary of state of the U.S.

Number three: "Terrorism is a threat to Western civilization."

Number four: "Terrorism is a menace to Western moral values."

Did you notice, does it tell you anything other than arouse your emotions?

This is typical. They don't define terrorism, because definitions involve a commitment to analysis, comprehension, and adherence to some norms of consistency. That's the second characteristic of the official literature on terrorism.

The third characteristic is that the absence of [a] definition does not prevent officials from being globalistic. We may not define terrorism, but it is a menace to the moral values of Western civilization. It is a menace also to mankind. It's a menace to good order. Therefore, you must stamp it out worldwide. Our reach has to be global. You need a global reach to kill it. Antiterrorist policies therefore have to be global. Same speech of George Shultz: "There is no question about our ability to use force where and when it is needed to counter terrorism." There is no geographical limit. On a single day the missiles hit Afghanistan and Sudan. Those two countries are 2,300 miles apart, and they were hit by missiles belonging to a country roughly 8,000 miles away. Reach is global.

A fourth characteristic: claims of power are not only globalist, they are also omniscient. We know where they are; therefore we know where to hit. We have the means to know. We have the instruments of knowledge. We are omniscient. Shultz: "We know the difference between terrorists and freedom fighters, and as we look around, we have no trouble telling one from the other."

Only, Osama bin Laden doesn't know that he was an ally one day and an enemy another. That's very confusing for Osama bin Laden. I'll come back to his story toward the end. It's a real story.

Five. The official approach eschews causation. You don't look at the causes of anybody is becoming a terrorist. Cause? What cause? They ask us to be looking, to be sympathetic to these people.

Another example. The *New York Times*, December 18, 1985, reported that the foreign minister of Yugoslavia, you remember the days when there was a Yugoslavia, requested the secretary of state of the U.S. to consider the causes of Palestinian terrorism. The secretary of state, George Shultz, and I am quoting from the *New York Times*, "went a bit red in the face. He pounded the table and told the visiting foreign minister, there is no connection with any cause. Period." Why look for causes?

Number six. The moral revulsion that we must feel against terrorism is selective. We are to feel the terror of those groups, which are officially disapproved. We are to applaud the terror of those groups of whom officials do approve. Hence, President Reagan, "I am a Contra." He actually said that. We know the Contras of Nicaragua [weren't] anything, by any definition, but terrorists. The media, to move away from the officials, heed the dominant view of terrorism.

The dominant approach also excludes from consideration, more importantly to me, the terror of friendly governments. To that question I will return because it excused among others the terror of Pinochet (who killed one of my closest friends) and Orlando Letelier; and it excused the terror of Zia ul-Haq, who killed many of my friends in Pakistan. All I want to tell you is that according to my ignorant calculations, the ratio of people killed by the state terror of Zia ul-Haq, Pinochet, Argentinian, Brazilian, Indonesian types, versus the killing of the PLO and other terrorist types is literally, conservatively, one to one hundred thousand. That's the ratio.

History unfortunately recognizes and accords visibility to power and not to weakness. Therefore, visibility has been accorded historically to dominant groups. In our time, the time that began with this day, Columbus Day.

The time that begins with Columbus Day is a time of extraordinary unrecorded holocausts. Great civilizations have been wiped out. The Mayas, the Incas, the Aztecs, the American Indians, the Canadian Indians were all wiped out. Their voices have not been heard, even to this day fully. Now they are beginning to be heard, but not fully. They are heard, yes, but only when the dominant power suffers, only when resistance has a semblance of costing, of exacting a price. When a Custer is killed or when a Gordon is besieged. That's when you know that they were Indians fighting, Arabs fighting and dying.

My last point of this section—U.S. policy in the Cold War period has sponsored terrorist regimes one after another. Somoza, Batista, all kinds of tyrants have been America's friends. You know that. There was a reason for that. I or you are not guilty. Nicaragua, Contra. Afghanistan, Mujahiddin. El Salvador, etc.

Now the second side. You've suffered enough. So suffer more.

There ain't much good on the other side either. You shouldn't imagine that I have come to praise the other side. But keep the balance in mind. Keep the imbalance in mind and first ask ourselves, What is terrorism?

Our first job should be to define the damn thing, name it, give it a description of some kind, other than "moral equivalent of [the] founding fathers" or "a moral outrage to Western civilization." *Webster's Collegiate Dictionary*: "Terror is an intense, overpowering fear." [One] uses terrorizing, terrorism, "the use of terrorizing methods of governing or resisting a government." This simple definition has one great virtue, that of fairness. It's fair. It focuses on the use of coercive violence, violence that is used illegally, extra-constitutionally, to coerce. And this definition is correct because it treats terror for what it is, whether the government or private people commit it.

Have you noticed something? Motivation is left out of it. We're not talking about whether the cause is just or unjust. We're talking about consensus, consent, absence of consent, legality, absence of legality, constitutionality, absence of constitutionality. Why do we keep motives out? Because motives differ. Motives differ and make no difference.

I have identified in my work five types of terrorism.

First, state terrorism. Second, religious terrorism; terrorism inspired by religion, Catholics killing Protestants, Sunnis killing Shiites, Shiites killing Sunnis, God, religion, sacred terror, you can call it if you wish. State, church. [Third,] crime. Mafia. All kinds of crimes commit terror. [Fourth,] there is pathology. You're pathological. You're sick. You want the attention of the whole world. You've got to kill a president. You will. You terrorize. You hold up a bus. Fifth, there is political terror of the private group; be they Indian, Vietnamese, Algerian, Palestinian, Baader-Meinhof, the Red Brigade. Political terror of the private group. Oppositional terror.

Keep these five in mind. Keep in mind one more thing. Sometimes these five can converge on each other. You start with protest terror. You go crazy. You become pathological. You continue. They converge. State terror can take the form of private terror. For example, we're all familiar with the death squads in Latin America or in Pakistan. Government has employed private people to kill its opponents. It's not quite official. It's privatized. Convergence. Or the political terrorist who goes crazy and becomes pathological. Or the criminal who joins politics. In Afghanistan, in Central America, the CIA employed in its covert operations drug pushers. Drugs and guns often go together. Smuggling of all things often go together.

Of the five types of terror, the focus is on only one, the least important in terms of cost to human lives and human property [political terror of those who want to be heard]. The highest cost is state terror. The second highest cost is religious terror, although in the twentieth century religious terror has, relatively speaking, declined. If you are looking historically, massive costs. The next highest cost is crime. Next highest, pathology. A RAND Corporation study by Brian Jenkins, for a ten-year period up

to 1988, showed [that] 50 percent of terror was committed without any political cause at all. No politics. Simply crime and pathology.

So the focus is on only one, the political terrorist, the PLO, the bin Laden, whoever you want to take. Why do they do it? What makes the terrorist tick?

I would like to knock them out quickly to you. First, the need to be heard. Imagine, we are dealing with a minority group, the political, private terrorist. First, the need to be heard. Normally, and there are exceptions, there is an effort to be heard, to get your grievances heard by people. They're not hearing it. A minority acts. The majority applauds.

The Palestinians, for example, the superterrorists of our time, were dispossessed in 1948. From 1948 to 1968 they went to every court in the world. They knocked at every door in the world. They were told that they became dispossessed because some radio told them to go away—an Arab radio, which was a lie. Nobody was listening to the truth. Finally, they invented a new form of terror, literally their invention: the airplane hijacking. Between 1968 and 1975 they pulled the world up by its ears. They dragged us out and said, Listen, Listen. We listened. We still haven't done them justice, but at least we all know. Even the Israelis acknowledge. Remember Golda Meir, prime minister of Israel, saying in 1970, "There are no Palestinians. They do not exist." They damn well exist now. We are cheating them at Oslo. At least there are some people to cheat now. We can't just push them out. The need to be heard is essential. One motivation there.

[A] mix of anger and helplessness produces an urge to strike out. You are angry. You are feeling helpless. You want retribution. You want to wreak retributive justice. The experience of violence by a stronger party has historically turned victims into terrorists. Battered children are known to become abusive parents and violent adults. You know that. That's what happens to peoples and nations. When they are battered, they hit back. State terror very often breeds collective terror.

Do you recall the fact that the Jews were never terrorists? By and large Jews were not known to commit terror except during and after the Holocaust. Most studies show that the majority of members of the worst terrorist groups in Israel or in Palestine, the Stern and the *Irgun* gangs, were people who were immigrants from the most anti-Semitic countries of Eastern Europe and Germany. Similarly, the young Shiites of Lebanon or the Palestinians from the refugee camps are battered people. They become very violent. The ghettos are violent internally. They become violent externally when there is a clear, identifiable external target, an enemy where you can say, "Yes, this one did it to me." Then they can strike back.

Example is a bad thing. Example spreads. There was a highly publicized Beirut hijacking of a TWA plane. After that hijacking, there were hijacking attempts at nine different American airports. Pathological groups or individuals modeling on the others. Even more serious are examples [were] set by governments. When governments engage in terror, they set very large examples. When they engage in supporting terror, they engage in other sets of examples.

Absence of revolutionary ideology is central to victim terrorism. Revolutionaries do not commit unthinking terror. Those of you who are familiar with revolutionary theory know the debates, the disputes, the quarrels, the fights within revolutionary groups of Europe, the fight between anarchists and Marxists, for example. But the Marxists have always argued that revolutionary terror, if ever engaged in, must be sociologically and psychologically selective. Don't hijack a plane. Don't hold hostages. Don't kill children, for God's sake. Have you recalled also that the great revolutions, the Chinese, the Vietnamese, the Algerian, the Cuban, never engaged in hijacking? They did engage in terrorism, but it was highly selective, highly sociological, still deplorable, but there was an organized, highly limited, selective character to it. So [the] absence of revolutionary ideology that begins more or less in the post–World War II period has been central to this phenomenon.

My final question is—these conditions have existed for a long time. But why, then, this flurry of private political terrorism? Why now so much of it and so visible? The answer is modern technology. You have a cause. You can communicate it through radio and television. They will all come swarming if you have taken an aircraft and are holding 150 Americans hostage. They will all hear your cause. You have a modern weapon through which you can shoot a mile away. They can't reach you. And you

have the modern means of communicating. When you put together the cause, the instrument of coercion, and the instrument of communication, politics is made. A new kind of politics becomes possible.

To this challenge, rulers from one country after another have been responding with traditional methods. The traditional method of shooting it out, whether it's missiles or some other means. The Israelis are very proud of it. The Americans are very proud of it. The French became very proud of it. Now the Pakistanis are very proud of it. The Pakistanis say, "Our commandos are the best." Frankly, it won't work. A central problem of our time, political minds, rooted in the past, and modern times, producing new realities. Therefore, in conclusion, what is my recommendation to America?

Quickly. First, avoid extremes of double standards. If you're going to practice double standards, you will be paid with double standards. Don't use it. Don't condone Israeli terror, Pakistani terror, Nicaraguan terror, El Salvadoran terror, on the one hand, and then complain about Afghan terror or Palestinian terror. It doesn't work. Try to be evenhanded. A superpower cannot promote terror in one place and reasonably expect to discourage terrorism in another place. It won't work in this shrunken world.

Do not condone the terror of your allies. Condemn them. Fight them. Punish them. Please eschew, avoid covert operations and low-intensity warfare. These are breeding grounds of terror and drugs. Violence and drugs are bred there. The structure of covert operations—I've made a film about it, which has been very popular in Europe, called *Dealing with the Demon*. I have shown that wherever covert operations have been, there has been the central drug problem. That has been also the center of the drug trade. Because the structure of covert operations, Afghanistan, Vietnam, Nicaragua, Central America, is very hospitable to drug trade. Avoid it. Give it up. It doesn't help.

Please focus on causes and help ameliorate causes. Try to look at causes and solve problems. Do not concentrate on military solutions. Do not seek military solutions. Terrorism is a political problem. Seek political solutions. Diplomacy works.

Take the example of the last attack on bin Laden. You don't know what you're attacking. They say they know, but they don't know. They were trying to kill

Qadaffi. They killed his four-year-old daughter. The poor baby hadn't done anything. . . . They tried to kill Saddam Hussein. They killed Laila Bin Attar, a prominent artist, an innocent woman. They tried to kill bin Laden and his men. Not one but twenty-five other people died. They tried to destroy a chemical factory in Sudan. Now they are admitting that they destroyed an innocent factory, one-half of the production of medicine in Sudan has been destroyed, not a chemical factory. You don't know. You think you know.

Four of your missiles fell in Pakistan. One was slightly damaged. Two were totally damaged. One was totally intact. For ten years the American government has kept an embargo on Pakistan because Pakistan is trying, stupidly, to build nuclear weapons and missiles. So we have a technology embargo on my country. One of the missiles was intact. What do you think a Pakistani official told the *Washington Post*? He said it was a gift from Allah. We wanted U.S. technology. Now we have got the technology, and our scientists are examining this missile very carefully. It fell into the wrong hands. So don't do that. Look for political solutions. Do not look for military solutions. They cause more problems than they solve.

Please help reinforce, strengthen the framework of international law. There was a criminal court in Rome. Why didn't they go to it first to get their warrant against bin Laden, if they have some evidence? Get a warrant, then go after him. Internationally. Enforce the UN. Enforce the International Court of Justice. This unilateralism makes us look very stupid and them relatively larger.

Haviland Smith

THE U.S. RESPONSE TO TERRORISM

Sometimes, as an academic or even a concerned citizen, it is all too easy to sit back and criticize national policies without being responsible either for carrying them out or for their consequences. In the next selection, a retired CIA station chief offers his perspective on how the challenges of foreign policy have changed between the Cold War and the current "war on terrorism." In the process, he makes an especially important distinction between recommended antiterrorism tactics and long-term strategy.

During the Cold War, American foreign policy was built on the twin bases of containment and alliances: containment of the Soviet Union and her allies and alliances with our friends in support of that containment. The critical element in the success of that policy was acceptance by both sides that the nuclear weaponry of the day would preclude any preemptive strike of one against the other. We called that MAD, or Mutual Assured Destruction. An additional important element in that policy was the fact that our allies, and to a somewhat lesser extent the allies of the Soviet Union, were able to exercise constraints on the policies and activities of both of the principals. Say what you will, even with a couple of very close calls, that policy prevailed and the Cold War never turned hot.

The role of the intelligence community during the Cold War, as it is (or should be) at any given time, was to provide policy makers with finished intelligence designed to help with the decision making process. Whether or not the collection and analytical processes succeed, all the intelligence-producing organizations in the intelligence community are designed to provide that product.

The demise of the Soviet Union and the end of the accompanying threat of Soviet nuclear weaponry brought a close to that era. The events of 9/11 set us on a completely different path. Since that horrible moment, we have embarked on a totally new foreign policy of preemptive unilateralism and an equally new domestic policy of intolerance for dissent and of creating and maintaining fear and anxiety in the American public. The question for examination is whether or not those changes and these new policies serve us well in the ongoing struggle with radical Muslim terrorism.

A RADICAL REVOLUTION IN FOREIGN POLICY

Preemptive unilateralism represents a radical revolution in foreign policy. After a whole string of "reasons" for the attack on Iraq, we are now told that we needed to preemptively attack Iraq because they had the "intellectual capability" to create a nuclear weapon. Is that to be the basis for future foreign preemptions? The constraints placed on previous administrations by our Cold War alliances have gone completely out the window. The "unilateral" part of this new policy, as mirrored in our established refusal to listen to anyone about our plans for invading Iraq, has ruled out moderating counsel from any of our former friends and allies, leaving us almost friendless in today's world. As we saw in the run-up to the Iraq invasion, it has been more important to the Bush administration to go ahead with its plans than to listen to its (former) friends and allies.

Although it is extremely difficult to sort out the true motivation behind that policy, what we have learned from the "kiss and tell" revelations

of former members of this administration is that the decision to invade Iraq had been made well before 9/11. Given the fact that none of the litany of "justifications" (WMD, Iraqi ties to Al-Qaida, bringing democracy to the Arabs, etc.) for the invasion has held up to scrutiny, that decision would now appear to be based primarily on ideological imperatives.

For intelligence professionals, both active and retired, that raises the question of the role, if any, for finished intelligence in today's foreign policy deliberations. The Bush administration's disinclination to listen to counsel from the State Department, the unprecedented visits of the Vice President to CIA analysts, the creation of the Office for Special Plans in the Pentagon to "relook" old intelligence, and the willingness to listen to "Curveball," a known fabricator, and Ahmed Chalabi of the Iraq National Congress, whose goal of overthrowing the Baathists in Iraq could only be achieved through misleading the United States into war, give a clear picture of an administration that was only interested in seeing intelligence that supported an already settled policy decision. The only conceivably worse basis for action would be if someone in the administration were listening to extraterrestrial voices!

Many past administrations, both Republican and Democrat, have made foreign policy decisions not only on the basis of the objective facts in the area under consideration, but also on the basis of their domestic political needs. It is difficult, however, to recall an administration that has so blatantly ignored objective realities as this one. As long as this is the way foreign policy is formulated, there will be little to no role for input from the intelligence community. However imperfect intelligence may be at any given moment or on any given issue, it does have a potentially constructive role to play in support of foreign policy. At minimum, intelligence deserves to be heard, not summarily dismissed.

DOMESTIC POLICY PROBLEMS

The administration's domestic policy during this same period has been based solely on ensuring the "security of the American people." That has brought us the Patriot Acts, wireless wiretapping, the abrogation of habeas corpus, torture, rendition, Abu Ghraib, Guantanamo, etc. And those are only the things we know about! We have been given a color coded terrorist threat warning system and daily hammering on what constitutional rights Americans have to give up to be "safe." Most importantly, this administration and its supporters in the Congress, the media, and the public have resorted to the worst kinds of character assassination and name calling to maintain the atmosphere of fear and anxiety they have so adroitly created. If you disagree with the policy they support, you are "soft on terror," "unpatriotic," or, even worse, a traitor. In short, dissent is intimidated—a process never approved by our founding fathers.

These are results that must gladden the heart of Osama bin Laden. He has to know that without our inadvertent complicity in the Middle East and at home in America, he would not have come out looking nearly as successful as has been the case. The facts are that we are on the verge of creating chaos in the Middle East, and that we can hardly look like a "shining city on the hill" to people who once admired us. What more could he possibly ask, and how much of the result stems directly from our own policies?

THE TERRORIST WORLD TODAY

Our preoccupation with fundamentalist Muslim terrorism will probably last a generation or more. That gives us plenty of time to continue to make mistakes, or to get it right. Certainly today we have got it wrong, probably because, as a result of 9/11, which was essentially a paramilitary operation, this administration concluded that we needed a military response. Afghanistan was the first response. In many respects, it satisfied America's domestic emotional and political needs as well as our regional Middle East and general foreign policy needs. Our big mistake was in not carrying it through to a more favorable conclusion when we shifted our attention to Iraq.

Unfortunately, the threat from this kind of terrorism cannot be successfully challenged militarily. There can be no conventional war with these people. Our military might is not mighty. The real struggle is for minds, and we are hardly addressing that issue.

Because with our remaining allies we have focused on Al Qaida, much of the leadership of that organization has been killed or captured. This has weakened the "center," and power has flowed outward to the more dispersed elements of fundamentalist Muslim terrorism. There has almost been a McDonald's type franchising of the movement. This has meant that more recruiting, planning, and implementation has devolved to local organizations. There is less central control and probably less central knowledge of what is going on around the world. That changes the target for us.

All organizations change as they age. In the 1940s and 50s Soviets were hardly ever seen outside their embassies, and when they were, they were clannish and seldom mixed with foreigners. As time went on and Soviet goals and personnel changed, they became more approachable and engageable. The dispersal of Al Qaida has hastened this same process for that organization. Now, absent continuing central control, attitudes are changing. There is increasing friction between the "old hands" and the young Turks about what sort of activity is appropriate. This is reportedly true in Yemen, and it presents us with some opportunities wherever it obtains. It was at this stage of ageing that the Soviet system, for a variety of human reasons, produced "flawed" citizens who were susceptible to blandishments from the United States.

Muslims range from brown-eyed, black-skinned straight through to blond, fair-skinned and blue-eyed. They are everywhere in East Asia, the Subcontinent, Central Asia, the Middle East, and Africa. Not only do they look different from each other, they are different. In the world of terrorism, they range from types like Al Qaida, who really are terrorists in the truest sense of the word, to groups who use unconventional warfare (terrorist tactics) in pursuit of their own freedom from repressive rulers. It is important to keep them separately in mind and not equate Chechens with Al Qaida. When we do that, we create all kinds of credibility problems for ourselves.

STRATEGIC GOALS

Al Qaida has very simple strategic goals. They want to push us and our influence out of the Middle East and replace repressive secular Muslim regimes with theocracies.

American strategic goals are far more difficult to identify. It is simply too easy (and inaccurate) to say that our strategy is about oil. Sadly, we have lost our way in Afghanistan. Where our surge in Iraq seems predictably successful, our "strategy" of bringing harmony and democracy to a historically fractious "country" is daily more precarious. Our occupation of Iraq looks like a war on Islam and catalyzes Muslims against us, daily creating new terrorists. In fact, to say we have no clear-cut strategic goals may be more accurate.

Fundamentalist Muslim terrorists attack us wherever they can find us. At this moment they are working to kill us mostly on their turf or in adjacent parts of the world. The events of 9/11 notwithstanding, repeating that sort of operation here in the United States is no easy task. That is not to say that it will not happen, but the odds are not in their favor.

America's tactics are different. Our public face to the world is a direct reflection of what we do and say. We are seen as cocky and arrogant: "Bring 'em on!" The puerile braggadocio with which we alternately dehumanize and belittle the Muslims may make some of us feel better, but is directly counterproductive to our goals for dealing with terrorism. Equating all Muslims with terrorism is not only inaccurate, but also demeaning and infuriating for mainstream, moderate Muslims.

We are viewed as hypocritical, duplicitous, and self-serving. When we push for democratic elections in the Islamic world and Hamas wins in Palestine, our emotional rejection of the results proves our hypocrisy to the moderate Muslim. The point here is that it matters what you say and how you say it, particularly when, through injudicious behavior, the only cause you hurt is your own.

A STRATEGY FOR AMERICA

At home, we need to stop the policies that lead to anxiety over terrorism and security. Perhaps we might even consider reinstating our civil liberties in the knowledge that doing so might invite another attack here. In this regard, we need to foster civil discourse by ceasing to label those with divergent ideas as "unpatriotic" or "soft on terrorism." There are a lot of very smart Americans who know a great deal about terrorism and Islam. We might do well to hear what they have to say in a climate that doesn't intimidate them. Personal attacks and defamation serve only to impoverish our search for the best alternatives.

Right now, we are sitting here in America pointing our finger at the Iraqis, Afghanis, Turks, Syrians, Pakistanis, and Central Asians and telling them what they have to do, while in many cases, we have lost the moral credibility to make such pronouncements. While we preach democratization abroad, we diminish democracy at home. As long as the world associates us with torture and renditions, we will have little credibility abroad. However, we do have the potential to once again become that shining city on the hill—a place that leads by example, by what it does and is, not by what it blusteringly says.

Our foreign policy today is not helping us. The key to success against fundamentalist Muslim terrorism is to minimize our enemies and maximize our friends. To do that we have to reestablish and strengthen our traditional alliances. The price for that will be to give them a say in what we do. That makes sense when their problem is identical with ours.

In this regard, we need to strengthen our intelligence liaison relationships. The best people to work against this target are the intelligence services of the countries in which they are operating. That is their home turf, and in the new "franchised" terrorist environment they are potentially far and away the most effective organizations to address those targets.

We need to soften the appeal of Muslim fundamentalism. To do that, we have to diminish the level of moderate Muslim indifference to that phenomenon. There are nearly 1.5 billion Muslims in the world. It takes only a tiny percentage of them to make major problems for us. The key to keeping those numbers down lies in the attitudes of moderate Islam.

In summary, it seems that just about everything we are doing in the so-called "Global War on Terrorism" is not helping. It is constantly claimed by Bush administration representatives that the techniques and tools to which so many Americans object (waterboarding, renditions, etc.) and which diminish our civil liberties, have spared us numerous terrorist attacks here in the homeland. Let's just arbitrarily stipulate that that is true. Even if it is, it is only a tactical response to the threat. Optimally, it may stop the occasional attack, but it won't solve the fundamental problem. We need a new strategy that deals with the weaknesses in this terrorist threat with a view to stopping the movement, not just the attacks. Without such a strategy, there will be no foreseeable end to this problem.

Robert Pape

DYING TO WIN: THE STRATEGIC LOGIC OF SUICIDE TERRORISM

Concern about terrorism as a general phenomenon has typically eclipsed interest in the actual motivations of individual terrorists, who, after all, are human beings with their own goals, hopes, fears, angers, and other driving forces. Just as peace activists like to ask, "What if they had a war and no one came?" we might inquire, "What if they called for a terrorist attack and no one volunteered?" Or, similarly, "What makes individuals ' "volunteer' "—not only to engage in lethal violence toward presumably innocent victims but also to willingly give up their lives in the process?" Discussion of the causes of war often revolves around a presumed tension between causation at the level of individuals (the role of personal aggressiveness, frustration, anger, greed, obedience to authority, etc.) and causation at the level of states (realpolitik, institutionalized decision making, the influence of history, socioeconomic or geopolitical considerations, etc.) The following selection represents one of the more notable efforts to rectify this omission and to introduce a personalized interpretive level into what is otherwise a diffuse geopolitical and ideological debate.

Suicide terrorism is rising around the world, but there is great confusion as to why. Since many such attacks—including, of course, those of September 11, 2001—have been perpetrated by Muslim terrorists professing religious motives, it might seem obvious that Islamic fundamentalism is the central cause. This presumption has fueled the belief that future 9/11s can be avoided only by a wholesale transformation of Muslim societies, a core reason for broad public support in the United States for the recent conquest of Iraq.

However, the presumed connection between suicide terrorism and Islamic fundamentalism is misleading and may be encouraging domestic and foreign policies likely to worsen America's situation and needlessly harm many Muslims.

I have compiled a database of every suicide bombing and attack around the globe from 1980 through 2003—315 attacks in all. It includes every attack in which at least one terrorist killed himself or herself while attempting to kill others; it excludes attacks authorized by a national government, for example by North Korea against the South. This database is the first complete universe of suicide terrorist attacks worldwide. I have amassed and independently verified all the relevant information that could be found in English and other languages (for example, Arabic, Hebrew, Russian, and Tamil) in print and online. The information is drawn from suicide terrorist groups themselves, from the main organizations that collect such data in target countries, and from news media around the world. More than a "list of lists," this database probably represents the most comprehensive and reliable survey of suicide terrorist attacks that is now available.

The data show that there is little connection between suicide terrorism and Islamic fundamentalism, or any one of the world's religions. In fact, the leading instigators of suicide attacks were the liberation tigers of Tamil Eelam (the "Tamil Tigers") in Sri Lanka, a Marxist-Leninist group whose members are from Hindu families but who are adamantly opposed to religion. This group committed 76 of the 315 incidents, more suicide attacks than Hamas.

Rather, what nearly all suicide terrorist attacks have in common is a specific secular and strategic goal: to compel modern democracies to withdraw military forces from territory that the terrorists consider to be their homeland. Religion is rarely the root cause, although it is often used as a tool by terrorist organizations in recruiting and in other efforts in service of the broader strategic objective.

Three general patterns in the data support my conclusions. First, nearly all suicide terrorist attacks occur as part of organized campaigns, not as isolated or random incidents. Of the 315 separate attacks in the period I studied, 301 could have their roots traced to large, coherent political or military campaigns.

Second, democratic states are uniquely vulnerable to suicide terrorists. The United States, France, India, Israel, Russia, Sri Lanka, and Turkey have been the targets of almost every suicide attack of the past

two decades, and each country has been a democracy at the time of the incidents.

Third, suicide terrorist campaigns are directed toward a strategic objective. From Lebanon to Israel to Sri Lanka to Kashmir to Chechnya, the sponsors of every campaign have been terrorist groups trying to establish or maintain political self-determination by compelling a democratic power to withdraw from the territories it claims. Even Al Qaeda fits this pattern: although Saudi Arabia is not under American military occupation per se, a principal objective of Osama bin Laden is the expulsion of American troops from the Persian Gulf and the reduction of Washington's power and influence in the region.

Understanding suicide terrorism is essential for the promotion of American security and international peace after September 11, 2001. On that day, nineteen Al Qaeda terrorists hijacked four airlines and destroyed the World Trade Center towers and part of the Pentagon, killing nearly three thousand innocent people. This episode awakened Americans and the world to a new fear that previously we had barely imagined: that even at home in the United States, we were vulnerable to devastating attack by determined terrorists, willing to die to kill us.

What made the September 11 attack possible—and so unexpected and terrifying—was that willingness to die to accomplish the mission. The final instructions found in the luggage of several hijackers leave little doubt about their intentions, telling them to make

> an oath to die. . . . When the confrontation begins, strike like champions who do not want to go back to this world. . . . Check your weapons long before you leave; . . . you must make your knife sharp and must not discomfort your animal during the slaughter. . . . Afterwards, we will all meet in the highest heaven. . . .

The hijackers' suicide was essential to the terrible lethality of the attack, making it possible to crash airplanes into populated buildings. It also created an element of surprise, allowing the hijackers to exploit the counterterrorism measures and mind-set that had evolved to deal with ordinary terrorist threats. Perhaps most jarring, the readiness of the terrorists to die in order to kill Americans amplified our sense of vulnerability. After September 11, Americans knew that we must expect that future Al Qaeda or other anti-American terrorists may be equally willing to die, and so not deterred by fear of punishment or of anything else. Such attackers would not hesitate to kill more Americans, and could succeed in carrying out equally devastating attacks—or worse—despite our best efforts to stop them.

September 11 was monstrous and shocking in scale, but it was not fundamentally unique. For more than twenty years, terrorist groups have been increasingly relying on suicide attacks to achieve major political objectives. From 1980 to 2003, terrorists across the globe waged seventeen separate campaigns of suicide terrorism, including those by Hezbollah to drive the United States, French, and Israeli forces out of Lebanon; by Palestinian terrorist groups to force Israel to abandon the West Bank and Gaza; by the Tamil Tigers to compel the Sri Lankan government to accept an independent Tamil homeland; by Al Qaeda to pressure the United States to withdraw from the Persian Gulf region. Since August of 2003, an eighteenth campaign has begun, aimed at driving the United States out of Iraq; as of this writing, it is not yet clear how much this effort owes to indigenous forces and how much to foreigners, possibly including Al Qaeda.

More worrying, the raw number of suicide terrorist attacks is climbing. At the same time that terrorist incidents of all types have declined by nearly half, from a peak of 666 in 1987 to 348 in 2001, suicide terrorism has grown, and the trend is continuing. Suicide terrorist attacks have risen from an average of 3 per year in the 1980s to about 10 per year in the 1990s to more than 40 each year in 2001 and 2002, and nearly 50 in 2003. These include continuing campaigns by Palestinian groups against Israel and by Al Qaeda and Taliban-related forces in Saudi Arabia and Afghanistan, as well as at least 20 attacks in Iraq against U.S. troops, the United Nations, and Iraqis collaborating with the American occupation.

Although many Americans have hoped that Al Qaeda has been badly weakened by U.S. counterterrorism efforts since September 11, 2001, the data show otherwise. In 2002 and 2003, Al Qaeda

conducted 15 suicide terrorist attacks, more than in all the years before September 11 combined, killing 439 people.

Perhaps most worrying of all, suicide terrorism has become the most deadly form of terrorism. Suicide attacks amount to just 3 percent of all terrorist incidents from 1980 through 2003, but account for 48 percent of all fatalities, making the average suicide terrorist attack twelve times deadlier than other forms of terrorism—even if the immense losses of September 11 are not counted. If a terrorist group does get its hands on a nuclear weapon, suicide attack is the best way to ensure the bomb will go off and the most troublesome scenario for its use.

Since September 11, 2001, the United States has responded to the growing threat of suicide terrorism by embarking on a policy to conquer Muslim countries—not simply rooting out existing havens for terrorists in Afghanistan but going further to remake Muslim societies in the Persian Gulf. To be sure, the United States must be ready to use force to protect Americans and their allies, and must do so when necessary. However, the close association between foreign military occupations and the growth of suicide terrorist movements in the occupied regions should make us hesitate over any strategy centering on the transformation of Muslim societies by means of heavy military power. Although there may still be good reasons for such a strategy, we should recognize that the sustained presence of heavy American combat forces in Muslim countries is likely to increase the odds of the next 9/11.

To win the war on terrorism, we must have a new conception of victory. The key to lasting security lies not only in rooting out today's generation of terrorists who are actively planning to kill Americans, but also in preventing the next, potentially larger generation from rising up. America's overarching purpose must be to achieve the first goal without failing at the second. To achieve that purpose, it is essential that we understand the strategic, social, and individual logic of suicide terrorism.

Our enemies have been studying suicide terrorism for over twenty years. Now is the time to level the playing field.

Ali Gomaa

CLARIFYING THE MEANING OF JIHAD

Like all great religious traditions, Islam is complex and multifaceted when it comes to questions of peace and war, violence and nonviolence. Although many critics claim that violence is intrinsic to Islam, others argue that Islam is essentially a religion of peace. Indeed, similar arguments arise with respect to Judaism, Christianity, and Hinduism, leaving unsettled whether religious sanction of violence is essential to each religion in question or whether it constitutes a departure from its primary message.

In any event, in the aftermath of the terrorist attacks of September 11, 2001, unusual attention has been directed to the teachings of Islam, especially the concept of "jihad," readily translated as "holy war" but, as argued in the following piece by an influential Muslim cleric, just as readily misunderstood.

Within Islam the term "jihad" refers to a large category of meanings. Today, however, there are attempts to isolate this term to only one form of jihad to the exclusion of all others. This includes a conception of jihad that at best refers only to armed struggle, and at worst to a barbaric form of warfare that seeks to destroy whatever peace may still remain in the world. This could not be further from the concept of jihad as understood by Muslims throughout history and the world over. For Muslims, jihad is much more than armed struggle against an enemy from the outside, for it includes constant struggles within both oneself and one's own society. When jihad actually does take the form of armed struggle, Muslims are aware that it can only be done for the sake of a just cause.

Once, upon returning from a battle, the Prophet Muhammad said to his companions, "We have returned from the lesser jihad to the greater jihad; the jihad of the soul." Here the term "jihad" refers to the spiritual exercise of opposing the lower self. This is referred to as the "greater" jihad, since people spend their entire lives struggling against the base desires within them that can harm both themselves and those around them.

Jihad is also used to refer to the pilgrimage to Mecca. When Aishah, the wife of the Prophet, was asked about the jihad of women, she said, "Your jihad is to make the pilgrimage." Here the pilgrimage is the lesser jihad of women and the elderly, who are not members of the armies that fight in defense of the country, so pilgrimage, which is a journey that is comprised of great difficulties due to the crowds and the physically demanding nature of its practices, is called jihad. The term "jihad" is also used to refer to speaking truth to those in power, so in Islam government oversight is a form of jihad.

In addition to these meanings, the term "jihad" refers to the defense of a nation or a just cause. This is what jihad was legislated for, and it must be differentiated from indiscriminate killing by the condition that it be "in the way of God," meaning to struggle in self-defense, to alleviate tyranny, or to prevent aggression. These are the characteristics that differentiate jihad from killing, which is a crime. These characteristics that amount to "in the way of God" are summed up in the Quran, "Fight in the way of God against those who wage war against you, but do not commit aggression—for, verily, God does not love aggressors" (Quran 2:190). This verse summarizes everything that has been agreed upon concerning guidelines of warfare, including the first and second Geneva Conventions.

As for suicide bombing, Islam forbids suicide; it forbids the taking of one's own life. In addition, Islam forbids aggression against others. Attacking civilians, women, children, and the elderly by blowing oneself up is absolutely forbidden in Islam. No excuse can be made for the crimes committed in New York, Spain, and London, and anyone who tries to make excuses for these acts is ignorant of Islamic law (shari'ah), and their excuses are a result of extremism and ignorance.

STUDY QUESTIONS

1. In what ways does twenty-first-century terrorism confront the world with issues that are historically unique? In what ways is it essentially a continuation of the past?
2. Familiarize yourself with the "just war" tradition, especially as developed by Christian ethicists. To what extent do these considerations apply to terrorism?
3. Make a case that terrorism is best confronted by international police work and law enforcement rather than by military action. Make the opposite case.
4. It has sometimes been claimed that terrorists are simply "evil," and/or that they are motivated by hatred of "our freedom." Agree or disagree with these statements.
5. Are there other potential "clashes of civilizations" beyond those enumerated by Samuel Huntington? Does his approach provide insight into terrorism specifically, as distinct from other conflicts? Discuss some issues that might be misrepresented by Huntington's argument.
6. Make a case for (or against) the idea that "terrorism from above" is in any way connected to "terrorism from below."
7. What are some consequences of analyzing the motivations of individual terrorists as opposed to looking at "terrorism" more generally?
8. Develop a range of possible nonviolent responses to the problem of terrorism.
9. It has been said that the Bush administration's "war on terror" is merely an excuse for a never-ending militarization of U.S. foreign policy. Agree or disagree with this statement.
10. Does the struggle against terrorism require policies that differ from those used in the struggle against other forms of violence? Be specific.

SUGGESTIONS FOR FURTHER READING

Allison, Graham. 2005. *Nuclear Terrorism: The Ultimate Preventable Catastrophe*. New York: Holt.
Bobbitt, Philip. 2008. *Terror and Consent: The Wars for the Twenty-First Century*. New York: Alfred A. Knopf.

Chaliand, Gérard, and Arnaud Blin, eds. 2007. *The History of Terrorism: From Antiquity to al Qaeda.* Berkeley: University of California Press.

Chomsky, Noam. 2003. *Pirates and Emperors, Old and New: International Terrorism in the Real World.* Boston: South End Press.

Coll, Steven. 2004. *Ghost Wars: The Secret History of the CIA, Afghanistan, and Bin Laden, from the Soviet Invasion to September 10, 2001.* New York: Penguin Books.

Cronin, Audrey K. 2011. *How Terrorism Ends.* Princeton, NJ: Princeton University Press.

Keefer, Philip, and Norman Loayza, eds. 2008. *Terrorism, Economic Development, and Political Openness.* New York: Cambridge University Press.

Laqueur, Walter. 2004. *No End to War: Terrorism in the Twenty-First Century.* New York: Continuum.

Miller, Seamus. 2008. *Terrorism and Counter-Terrorism: Ethics and Liberal Democracy.* New York: Wiley-Blackwell.

Nacos, Brigitte L. 2011. *Terrorism and Counterterrorism.* Englewood Cliffs, NJ: Prentice-Hall.

Scheuer, Michael, and Bruce Hoffman. 2007. *Through Our Enemies' Eyes: Osama bin Laden, Radical Islam, and the Future of America.* Washington, DC: Potomac Books.

Smelser, Neil J. 2007. *The Faces of Terrorism: Social and Psychological Dimensions.* Princeton, NJ: Princeton University Press.

CHAPTER 4

Building "Positive Peace"

I t is important to be against war. But it is not enough. We also need to be in favor of something—something positive and affirming: namely, peace. Peace studies is unique not only because it is multidisciplinary and forth-rightly proclaims its adherence to "values" but also because it identifies positive visions of peace as being greater than the absence of war.

The "positive peace" toward which peace studies strives may be, if anything, even more challenging than the prevention of war. It is a variation on what has been called the "dog–car problem." Imagine a dog that has spent years barking and running after cars. Then, one day, he catches one. What does he *do* with it? What would devotees of peace *do* with the world if they had the opportunity?

This is not a useless exercise, since before any future can be established, it must first be imagined. And moreover, unlike our hypothetical car-chasing dog, the establishment of positive peace is not an all-or-nothing proposition. The movement toward positive peace is likely to be halting and fragmentary, with substantial success along certain dimensions, and likely failures along others. On balance, the project is formidable, nothing less than a fundamental effort to rethink the relationship of human beings to each other and to their shared planet. If war and its causes are difficult to define—and this is assuredly the case—positive peace is even more elusive. (It can even be dangerous, because disagreements over what constitutes a desirable "peace" can lead to war.)

Earlier, we briefly considered "just war" doctrine. The conditions for a "just peace" are no less strenuous stringent or important. The relevant issues include—but are not limited to—aspirations for human rights, economic fairness and opportunity, democratization, and environmental well-being and sustainability. Nonetheless, there is no agreement as to what, specifically, is desired or how much emphasis to place on each goal.

The pursuit of positive peace nonetheless leads to certain agreed principles, one of which is a minimization of violence, —not only the overt violence of war, but also what has been called "structural violence," a condition that is typically built into many social and cultural institutions. A slaveholding society may be at "peace" in that it is not literally at war, but it is also rife with structural violence. Structural violence has the effect of denying people important rights such as economic opportunity, social and political equality, a sense of fulfillment and self-worth, and access to a healthy, natural environment. When people starve to death, or even go hungry, a kind of violence is taking place. Similarly, when human beings suffer from diseases that are preventable, when they are denied a decent education, housing, an opportunity to play, to grow, to work, to raise a family, to express themselves freely, to organize peacefully, or to participate in their own governance, a kind of violence is occurring, even if bullets or clubs are not being used. Society visits violence on human rights and dignity when it forcibly stunts the optimum development of each human being, whether because of race, religion, sex, sexual preference, age, ideology, or some other reason. In short, structural violence is another way kind of identifying oppression, and positive peace would be a situation in which structural violence and oppression are minimized.

In addition, social injustice is important not only in its contribution to structural violence but also as a major contributor to war, often in unexpected ways. For many citizens of the United States and Europe, as well as privileged people worldwide, current lifestyles are fundamentally acceptable. Hence, peace for them has come to mean the continuation of things as they are, with the additional hope that overt violence will be prevented. For others—perhaps the majority on our planet—change of one sort or another is desired. And for a small minority, peace is something to fight for! A Central American peasant was quoted in the *New York Times* as saying, "I am for peace, but not peace with hunger." By the same token, many Israelis are more or less satisfied with what they see as a condition of relative "peace" – since as of 2013, there have been very few cases of lethal violence directed by Palestinians toward Israelis – yet, at the same time, the majority of Palestinians do not consider their own situation to be an acceptable state of "peace."

There is a long tradition suggesting that injustice is a primary cause of war. The French philosopher Denis Diderot, for example, was convinced that a world of justice and plenty would mean a world free of tyranny and war. Hence, in his eighteenth-century treatise, the *Encyclopedia*, Diderot sought to establish peace by disseminating all the world's technical information, from beekeeping to iron forging. And, of course, similar efforts continue today, although few advocates of economic and social development claim that the problem of violence can be solved simply by spreading knowledge or even by keeping everyone's belly full.

The troubling relationship of human beings to their natural environment must also be reworked, perhaps in fundamental ways. A world at peace must be one in which environmental, human rights, and economic issues all cohere to foster maximum well-being; ecological harmony cannot realistically be separated from questions of human rights or economic justice (or, for that matter, from the issues of democratization and demilitarization).

In relation to the environment, political or economic ideology do not appear to be significant. Environmental degradation is, to be sure, intimately connected to poverty: wealthy states often export their most odious environmental abuses, and impoverished states are often forced by their poverty to accept the situation. Moreover, within any given

state, wealthy people are able to purchase certain amenities, while the poor find themselves living in degraded, and often downright dangerous, surroundings. But in general,
left-leaning governments have not shown themselves to be more environmentally sensitive than their right-leaning counterparts. In avowedly Socialist socialist or Communist
communist societies, for example, "production goals" typically replaced the capitalist
pursuit of "profit" as the "bottom line" to which environmental values were are all too
frequently sacrificed.

A very important shift in human consciousness—intimately related to the agenda of
peace studies—is the realization that "national security" must be defined in ways that go
far beyond military strength and that as our planet becomes increasingly interconnected
politically, economically, and socially, and also as our global environment is increasingly
endangered, the health, well-being, and security of every individual becomes inseparable
from the health, well-being, and security of the Earth itself.

Aldo Leopold

THE LAND ETHIC

An ecological perspective demands that we recognize the reality of connectedness, which,
as the poet Francis Thompson put it, "all things . . . / near and far, / hiddenly / to each
other, connected are, / that thou canst not stir a flower / without the troubling of a star."
This is true not only for biology, but also for social, political, and economic systems.
Thus, not only do wars ruin the environment, but environmental destruction—and its
threat—can lead to wars. Millions of refugees regularly flee environmental disasters such
as drought, floods, famine, and disease. These refugees, who constitute a humanitarian
disaster in themselves, can also raise international tensions.

The destruction of rain forests, for example, is not only a deeply troubling environmental issue with worldwide implications, but it also arises from particular economic
systems (notably a free- market free-for-all), with no small dose of racism (notably,
devaluing the rights of indigenous peoples). The poverty resulting from deforestation
and displacement leads to land degradation and the growing problem of desertification
as hungry, desperate people clear and cultivate regions that should be left untouched.
This in turn leads to yet more poverty and social unrest. Intensive farming of highly erod-
ible land permanently destroys soil; large-scale intrusions into wildlife habitat (which
contribute to species extinction) are in large part responses to land hunger in rural,
developing countries, where a small minority of wealthy people own most of the arable

land, thereby pushing others to engage in environmentally abusive behavior. Worldwide, the burning of fossil fuels produces greenhouse gases; resulting global climate warming may increase food insecurity by reducing agricultural productivity. All of these factors—plus many others—are intertwined in complex ways with the exponential growth of the human population.

There is an enormous and growing literature on specific solutions to environmental problems, such as mass transportation; improved energy efficiency and cogeneration; "soft" energy paths such as solar, wind, and tidal power; organic agriculture; enhanced recycling; eating "lower on the food chain"; and an enlightened population policy that encourages family planning, especially by empowering women.

The word "ecology" derives from the Greek *oikos,* meaning house. It refers to the interrelations between living things and their environment, with the latter including other living things (plants, animals, microorganisms) as well as inanimate objects and processes such as climate, rock, water, and air. Despite dreams of space travel and the colonization of other planets, the fact remains that human beings have only one home, and good planets are hard to find.

In the final analysis, a world at peace must be one in which all living things experience themselves as being "at home." In recent times, some of the crucial relationships among the world's species, and between those species and their environments, have become increasingly tenuous, which in turn has begun to threaten the quality of life, and even its continuation. At risk is nothing less than the integrity of various life-support systems: the air we breathe, the water we drink, the food we eat, as well as the diverse fabric of life that provides emotional and spiritual sustenance.

The following selection—written by one of the great figures in ecology, and the founder of "wildlife management"—attempts to look broadly at the problem and to suggest the beginning of a solution: notably, a code of environmental ethics.

When godlike Odysseus returned from the wars in Troy, he hanged all on one rope a dozen slave-girls of his household whom he suspected of misbehavior dur-ing his absence.

This hanging involved no question of propriety. The girls were property. The disposal of property was then, as now, a matter of expedience, not of right and wrong.

Concepts of right and wrong were not lacking from Odysseus' Greece: witness the fidelity of his wife through the long years before at last his black-prowed galleys clove the wine-dark seas for home. The ethical structure of that day covered wives, but had not yet been extended to human chattels.

During the three thousand years which have since elapsed, ethical criteria have been extended to many fields of conduct, with corresponding shrinkages in those judged by expediency only.

THE ETHICAL SEQUENCE

This extension of ethics, so far studied only by philosophers, is actually a process in ecological evolution. Its sequences may be described in ecological as well as in philosophical terms. An ethic, ecologically, is a limitation on freedom of action in the struggle for existence. An ethic, philosophically, is a differentiation of social from antisocial conduct. These are two definitions of one thing. The thing has its origin in the tendency of interdependent individuals or groups to evolve modes of cooperation. The ecologist calls these symbioses. Politics and economics are advanced symbioses in which the original free-for-all competition has been replaced, in part, by cooperative mechanisms with an ethical content.

The complexity of cooperative mechanisms has increased with population density, and with the efficiency of tools. It was simpler, for example, to define the anti-social uses of sticks and stones in the days of the mastodons than of bullets and billboards in the age of motors.

The first ethics dealt with the relation between individuals; the Mosaic Decalogue is an example. Later accretions dealt with the relation between the individual and society. The Golden Rule tries to integrate the individual to society; democracy to integrate social organization to the individual.

There is as yet no ethic dealing with man's relation to land and to the animals and plants which grow upon it. Land, like Odysseus' slave-girls, is still property. The land-relation is still strictly economic, entailing privileges but not obligations.

The extension of ethics to this third element in human environment is, if I read the evidence correctly, an evolutionary possibility and an ecological necessity. It is the third step in a sequence. The first two have already been taken. Individual thinkers since the days of Ezekiel and Isaiah have asserted that the despoliation of land is not only inexpedient but wrong. Society, however, has not yet affirmed their belief. I regard the present conservation movement as the embryo of such an affirmation.

An ethic may be regarded as a mode of guidance for meeting ecological situations so new or intricate, or involving such deferred reactions, that the path of social expediency is not discernible to the average individual. Animal instincts are modes of guidance for the individual in meeting such situations. Ethics are possibly a kind of community instinct in-the-making.

THE COMMUNITY CONCEPT

All ethics so far evolved rest upon a single premise: that the individual is a member of a community of interdependent parts. His instincts prompt him to compete for his place in that community, but his ethics prompt him also to cooperate (perhaps in order that there may be a place to compete for).

The land ethic simply enlarges the boundaries of the community to include soils, waters, plants, and animals, or collectively: the land.

This sounds simple: do we not already sing our love for and obligation to the land of the free and the home of the brave? Yes, but just what and whom do we love? Certainly not the soil, which we are sending helter-skelter downriver. Certainly not the waters, which we assume have no function except to turn turbines, float barges, and carry off sewage. Certainly not the plants, of which we exterminate whole communities without batting an eye. Certainly not the animals, of which we have already extirpated many of the largest and most beautiful species. A land ethic of course cannot prevent the alteration, management, and use of these "resources," but it does affirm their right to continued existence, and, at least in spots, their continued existence in a natural state.

In short, a land ethic changes the role of *Homo sapiens* from conqueror of the land-community to plain member and citizen of it. It implies respect for his fellow-members, and also respect for the community as such.

In human history, we have learned (I hope) that the conqueror role is eventually self-defeating. Why? Because it is implicit in such a role that the conqueror knows, *ex cathedra*, just what makes the community clock tick, and just what and who is valuable, and what and who is worthless, in community life. It always turns out that he knows neither, and this is why his conquests eventually defeat themselves.

In the biotic community, a parallel situation exists. Abraham knew exactly what the land was for: it was to drip milk and honey into Abraham's mouth. At the present moment, the assurance with which we regard this assumption is inverse to the degree of our education.

The ordinary citizen today assumes that science knows what makes the community clock tick; the scientist is equally sure that he does not. He knows that the biotic mechanism is so complex that its workings may never be fully understood . . . .

THE ECOLOGICAL CONSCIENCE

Conservation is a state of harmony between men and land. Despite nearly a century of propaganda, conservation still proceeds at a snail's pace; progress still consists largely of letterhead pieties and convention oratory. On the back forty we still slip two steps backward for each forward stride.

The usual answer to this dilemma is "more conservation education." No one will debate this, but is it certain that only the *volume* of education needs stepping up? Is something lacking in the *content* as well?

It is difficult to give a fair summary of its content in brief form, but, as I understand it, the content is substantially this: obey the law, vote right, join some organizations, and practice what conservation is profitable on your own land; the government will do the rest.

Is not this formula too easy to accomplish anything worthwhile? It defines no right or wrong, assigns no obligation, calls for no sacrifice, implies no change in the current philosophy of values. In respect of land-use, it urges only enlightened self-interest. Just how far will such education take us?

No important change in ethics was ever accomplished without an internal change in our intellectual emphasis, loyalties, affections, and convictions. The proof that conservation has not yet touched these foundations of conduct lies in the fact that philosophy and religion have not yet heard of it. In our attempt to make conservation easy, we have made it trivial.

SUBSTITUTES FOR A LAND ETHIC

When the logic of history hungers for bread and we hand out a stone, we are at pains to explain how much the stone resembles bread. I now describe some of the stones which serve in lieu of a land ethic.

One basic weakness in a conservation system based wholly on economic motives is that most members of the land community have no economic value. Wildflowers and songbirds are examples. Of the 22,000 higher plants and animals native to Wisconsin, it is doubtful whether more than 5 percent can be sold, fed, eaten, or otherwise put to economic use. Yet these creatures are members of the biotic community, and if (as I believe) its

stability depends on its integrity, they are entitled to continuance.

When one of these non-economic categories is threatened, and if we happen to love it, we invent subterfuges to give it economic importance. At the beginning of the century songbirds were supposed to be disappearing. Ornithologists jumped to the rescue with some distinctly shaky evidence to the effect that insects would eat us up if birds failed to control them. The evidence had to be economic in order to be valid.

It is painful to read these circumlocutions today. We have no land ethic yet, but we have at least drawn nearer the point of admitting that birds should continue as a matter of biotic right, regardless of the presence or absence of economic advantage to us.

A parallel situation exists in respect of predatory mammals, raptorial birds, and fish-eating birds. Time was when biologists somewhat overworked the evidence that these creatures preserve the health of game by killing weaklings, or that they control rodents for the farmer, or that they prey only on "worthless" species. Here again, the evidence had to be economic in order to be valid. It is only in recent years that we hear the more honest argument that predators are members of the community, and that no special interest has the right to exterminate them for the sake of a benefit, real or fancied, to itself. . . .

Lack of economic value is sometimes a character not only of species or groups, but of entire biotic communities: marshes, bogs, dunes, and "deserts" are examples. Our formula in such cases is to relegate their conservation to government as refuges, monuments, or parks. The difficulty is that these communities are usually interspersed with more valuable private lands; the government cannot possibly own or control such scattered parcels. The net effect is that we have relegated some of them to ultimate extinction over large areas. . . .

Industrial landowners and users, especially lumbermen and stockmen, are inclined to wail long and loudly about the extension of government ownership and regulation to land, but (with notable exceptions) they show little disposition to develop the only visible alternative: the voluntary practice of conservation on their own lands.

When the private landowner is asked to perform some unprofitable act for the good of the community, he today assents only with outstretched palm. If the act costs him cash this is fair and proper, but when it costs only forethought, open-mindedness, or time, the issue is at least debatable. The overwhelming growth of land-use subsidies in recent years must be ascribed, in large part, to the government's own agencies for conservation education: the land bureaus, the agricultural colleges, and the extension services. As far as I can detect, no ethical obligation toward land is taught in these institutions.

To sum up: a system of conservation based solely on economic self-interest is hopelessly lopsided. It tends to ignore, and thus eventually to eliminate, many elements in the land community that lack commercial value, but that are (as far as we know) essential to its healthy functioning. It assumes, falsely, I think, that the economic parts of the biotic clock will function without the uneconomic parts. It tends to relegate to government many functions eventually too large, too complex, or too widely dispersed to be performed by government.

An ethical obligation on the part of the private owner is the only visible remedy for these situations.

THE LAND PYRAMID

An ethic to supplement and guide the economic relation to land presupposes the existence of some mental image of land as a biotic mechanism. We can be ethical only in relation to something we can see, feel, understand, love, or otherwise have faith in.

The image commonly employed in conservation education is "the balance of nature." For reasons too lengthy to detail here, this figure of speech fails to describe accurately what little we know about the land mechanism. A much truer image is the one employed in ecology: the biotic pyramid. I shall first sketch the pyramid as a symbol of land, and later develop some of its implications in terms of land-use.

Plants absorb energy from the sun. This energy flows through a circuit called the biota, which may be represented by a pyramid consisting of layers. The bottom layer is the soil. A plant layer rests on the soil, an insect layer on the plants, a bird and rodent layer on the insects, and so on up through various animal groups to the apex layer, which consists of the larger carnivores.

The species of a layer are alike not in where they came from, or in what they look like, but rather in what they eat. Each successive layer depends on those below it for food and often for other services, and each in turn furnishes food and services to those above. Proceeding upward, each successive layer decreases in numerical abundance. Thus, for every carnivore there are hundreds of his prey, thousands of their prey, millions of insects, uncountable plants. The pyramidal form of the system reflects this numerical progression from apex to base. Man shares an intermediate layer with the bears, raccoons, and squirrels which eat both meat and vegetables.

The lines of dependency for food and other services are called food chains. Thus soil-oak-deer-Indian is a chain that has now been largely converted to soil-corn-cow-farmer. Each species, including ourselves, is a link in many chains. The deer eats a hundred plants other than oak, and the cow a hundred plants other than corn. Both, then, are links in a hundred chains. The pyramid is a tangle of chains so complex as to seem disorderly, yet the stability of the system proves it to be a highly organized structure. Its functioning depends on the cooperation and competition of its diverse parts.

In the beginning, the pyramid of life was low and squat; the food chains short and simple. Evolution has added layer after layer, link after link. Man is one of thousands of accretions to the height and complexity of the pyramid. Science has given us many doubts, but it has given us at least one certainty: the trend of evolution is to elaborate and diversify the biota.

Land, then, is not merely soil; it is a fountain of energy flowing through a circuit of soils, plants, and animals. Food chains are the living channels which conduct energy upward; death and decay return it to the soil. The circuit is not closed; some energy is dissipated in decay, some is added by absorption from the air, some is stored in soils, peats, and long-lived forests; but it is a sustained circuit, like a slowly augmented revolving fund of life. There is always a net loss by downhill wash, but this is normally small and offset by the decay of rocks. It is deposited in the ocean and, in the course of geological time, raised to form new lands and new pyramids.

The velocity and character of the upward flow of energy depend on the complex structure of the plant and animal community, much as the upward flow of sap in a tree depends on its complex cellular organization. Without this complexity, normal circulation would presumably not occur. Structure means the characteristic numbers, as well as the characteristic kinds and functions, of the component species. This interdependence between the complex structure of the land and its smooth functioning as an energy unit is one of its basic attributes.

When a change occurs in one part of the circuit, many other parts must adjust themselves to it. Change does not necessarily obstruct or divert the flow of energy; evolution is a long series of self-induced changes, the net result of which has been to elaborate the flow mechanism and to lengthen the circuit. Evolutionary changes, however, are usually slow and local. Man's invention of tools has enabled him to make changes of unprecedented violence, rapidity, and scope.

One change is in the composition of floras and faunas. The larger predators are lopped off the apex of the pyramid; food chains, for the first time in history, become shorter rather than longer. Domesticated species from other lands are substituted for wild ones, and wild ones are moved to new habitats. In this worldwide pooling of faunas and floras, some species get out of bounds as pests and diseases, others are extinguished. Such effects are seldom intended or foreseen; they represent unpredicted and often untraceable readjustments in the structure. Agricultural science is largely a race between the emergence of new pests and the emergence of new techniques for their control.

Another change touches the flow of energy through plants and animals and its return to the soil. Fertility is the ability of soil to receive, store, and release energy. Agriculture, by overdrafts on the soil, or by too radical a substitution of domestic for native species in the superstructure, may derange the channels of flow or deplete storage. Soils depleted of their storage, or of the organic matter which anchors it, wash away faster than they form. This is erosion.

Waters, like soil, are part of the energy circuit. Industry, by polluting waters or obstructing them with dams, may exclude the plants and animals necessary to keep energy in circulation.

Transportation brings about another basic change: the plants or animals grown in one region are now consumed and returned to the soil in another. Transportation taps the energy stored in rocks, and in the air, and uses it elsewhere; thus we fertilize the garden with nitrogen gleaned by the guano birds from the fishes of seas on the other side of the Equator. Thus the formerly localized and self-contained circuits are pooled on a worldwide scale.

The process of altering the pyramid for human occupation releases stored energy, and this often gives rise, during the pioneering period, to a deceptive exuberance of plant and animal life, both wild and tame. These releases of biotic capital tend to becloud or postpone the penalties of violence.

This thumbnail sketch of land as an energy circuit conveys three basic ideas:

1. That land is not merely soil.
2. That the native plants and animals kept the energy circuit open; others may or may not.
3. That man-made changes are of a different order than evolutionary changes, and have effects more comprehensive than is intended or foreseen.

These ideas, collectively, raise two basic issues: Can the land adjust itself to the new order? Can the desired alterations be accomplished with less violence? . . .

The combined evidence of history and ecology seems to support one general deduction: the less violent the man-made changes, the greater the probability of successful readjustment in the pyramid. Violence, in turn, varies with human population density; a dense population requires a more violent conversion. In this respect, North America has a better chance for permanence than Europe, if she can contrive to limit her density.

This deduction runs counter to our current philosophy, which assumes that because a small increase in density enriched human life, that an indefinite increase will enrich it indefinitely. Ecology knows of no density relationship that holds for indefinitely wide limits. All gains from density are subject to a law of diminishing returns.

Whatever may be the equation for men and land, it is improbable that we as yet know all its terms. Recent discoveries in mineral and vitamin nutrition reveal unsuspected dependencies in the up-circuit: incredibly minute quantities of certain substances determine the value of soils to plants, of plants to animals. What of the down-circuit? What of the vanishing species, the preservation of which we now regard as an esthetic luxury? They helped build the soil; in what unsuspected ways may they be essential to its maintenance? [It has been proposed] . . . that we use prairie flowers to reflocculate the wasting soils of the dust bowl; who knows for what purpose cranes and condors, otters and grizzlies may some day be used?

LAND HEALTH AND THE A-B CLEAVAGE

A land ethic, then, reflects the existence of an ecological conscience, and this in turn reflects a conviction of individual responsibility for the health of the land. Health is the capacity of the land for self-renewal. Conservation is our effort to understand and preserve this capacity.

Conservationists are notorious for their dissensions. Superficially these seem to add up to mere confusion, but a more careful scrutiny reveals a single plane of cleavage common to many specialized fields. In each field one group (A) regards the land as soil, and its function as commodity-production; another group (B) regards the land as a biota, and its function as something broader. How much broader is admittedly in a state of doubt and confusion.

In my own field, forestry, Group A is quite content to grow trees like cabbages, with cellulose as the basic forest commodity. It feels no inhibition against violence; its ideology is agronomic. Group B, on the other hand, sees forestry as fundamentally different from agronomy because it employs natural species, and manages a natural environment rather than creating an artificial one. Group B prefers natural reproduction on principle. It worries on biotic as well as economic grounds about the loss of species like chestnut, and the threatened loss of the white pines. It worries about a whole series of secondary forest functions: wildlife, recreation, watersheds, wilderness areas. To my mind, Group B feels the stirrings of an ecological conscience.

In the wildlife field, a parallel cleavage exists. For Group A the basic commodities are sport and meat; the yardsticks of production are ciphers of take in pheasants and trout. Artificial propagation is acceptable as a permanent as well as a temporary recourse—if its unit costs permit. Group B, on the other hand, worries about a whole series of biotic side-issues. What is the cost in predators of producing a game crop? Should we have further recourse to exotics? How can management restore the shrinking species, like prairie grouse, already hopeless as shootable game? How can management restore the threatened rarities, like trumpeter swan and whooping crane? Can management principles be extended to wildflowers? Here again it is clear to me that we have the same A-B cleavage as in forestry. . . .

The ecological fundamentals of agriculture are just as poorly known to the public as in other fields of land-use. For example, few educated people realize that the marvelous advances in technique made during recent decades are improvements in the pump, rather than the well. Acre for acre, they have barely sufficed to offset the sinking level of fertility.

In all of these cleavages, we see repeated the same basic paradoxes: man the conqueror *versus* man the biotic citizen; science the sharpener of his sword *versus* science the searchlight on his universe; land the slave and servant *versus* land the collective organism. Robinson's injunction to Tristram may well be applied, at this juncture, to *Homo sapiens* as a species in geological time:

> Whether you will or not
> You are a King, Tristram, for you are one
> Of the time-tested few that leave the world,
> When they are gone, not the same place it was.
> Mark what you leave.

THE OUTLOOK

It is inconceivable to me that an ethical relation to land can exist without love, respect, and admiration for land, and a high regard for its value. By value,

I of course mean something far broader than mere economic value; I mean value in the philosophical sense.

Perhaps the most serious obstacle impeding the evolution of a land ethic is the fact that our educational and economic system is headed away from, rather than toward, an intense consciousness of land. Your true modern is separated from the land by many middlemen, and by innumerable physical gadgets. He has no vital relation to it; to him it is the space between cities on which crops grow. Turn him loose for a day on the land, and if the spot does not happen to be a golf links or a "scenic" area, he is bored stiff. If crops could be raised by hydroponics instead of farming, it would suit him very well. Synthetic substitutes for wood, leather, wool, and other natural land products suit him better than the originals. In short, land is something he has "outgrown."

Almost equally serious as an obstacle to a land ethic is the attitude of the farmer for whom the land is still an adversary, or a taskmaster that keeps him in slavery. Theoretically, the mechanization of farming ought to cut the farmer's chains, but whether it really does is debatable.

One of the requisites for an ecological comprehension of land is an understanding of ecology, and this is by no means co-extensive with "education"; in fact, much higher education seems deliberately to avoid ecological concepts. An understanding of ecology does not necessarily originate in courses bearing ecological labels; it is quite as likely to be labeled geography, botany, agronomy, history, or economics. This is as it should be, but whatever the label, ecological training is scarce.

The case for a land ethic would appear hopeless but for the minority which is in obvious revolt against these "modern" trends.

The "key-log" which must be moved to release the evolutionary process for an ethic is simply this: quit thinking about decent land-use as solely an economic problem. Examine each question in terms of what is ethically and esthetically right, as well as what is economically expedient. A thing is right when it tends to preserve the integrity, stability, and beauty of the biotic community. It is wrong when it tends otherwise.

It of course goes without saying that economic feasibility limits the tether of what can or cannot be done for land. It always has and it always will. The fallacy the economic determinists have tied around our collective neck, and which we now need to cast off, is the belief that economics determines *all* land-use. This is simply not true. An innumerable host of actions and attitudes, comprising perhaps the bulk of all land relations, is determined by the land-user's tastes and predilections, rather than by his purse. The bulk of all land relations hinges on investments of time, forethought, skill, and faith rather than on investments of cash. As a land-user thinketh, so is he.

I have purposely presented the land ethic as a product of social evolution because nothing so important as an ethic is ever "written." Only the most superficial student of history supposes that Moses "wrote" the Decalogue; it evolved in the minds of a thinking community, and Moses wrote a tentative summary of it for a "seminar." I say tentative because evolution never stops.

The evolution of a land ethic is an intellectual as well as emotional process. Conservation is paved with good intentions which prove to be futile, or even dangerous, because they are devoid of critical understanding either of the land, or of economic land-use. I think it is a truism that as the ethical frontier advances from the individual to the community, its intellectual content increases.

The mechanism of operation is the same for any ethic: social approbation for right actions: social disapproval for wrong actions.

By and large, our present problem is one of attitudes and implements. We are remodeling the Alhambra with a steam shovel, and we are proud of our yardage. We shall hardly relinquish the shovel, which after all has many good points, but we are in need of gentler and more objective criteria for its successful use.

Al Gore

NOBEL PRIZE ACCEPTANCE SPEECH

To be sure, global warming isn't the only environmental issue that must be confronted by advocates of positive peace: the world also faces a dramatic and potentially catastrophic reduction in biodiversity, the variety and abundance of living species. Economic exploitation of nature is becoming increasingly unsustainable, especially given the incontrovertible fact that many resources are finite and not renewable. Energy in particular poses thorny problems, especially insofar as use patterns remain tethered to fossil fuels. Population pressure seems unrelenting and, paradoxically, is most concentrated in third world countries, that which are least capable of absorbing its social and economic impact, not to mention the its environmental costs. And the aforementioned is but a small sample, beyond the general perspective advocated by Aldo Leopold.

Looming above these issues, however, is the increasingly evident fact that human beings are dramatically and perhaps irreversibly changing the climate of planet Earth. And responsible for many of the warnings about this potential catastrophe has been Al Gore, former vice president of the United States, whose efforts in this regard earned him a Nobel Peace Prize in 2007. The following selection is Mr. Gore's Nobel Prize acceptance speech, delivered on December 10, 2007, in Oslo, Norway.

We, the human species, are confronting a planetary emergency—a threat to the survival of our civilization that is gathering ominous and destructive potential even as we gather here. But there is hopeful news as well: we have the ability to solve this crisis and avoid the worst—though not all—of its consequences, if we act boldly, decisively, and quickly.

However, despite a growing number of honorable exceptions, too many of the world's leaders are still best described in the words Winston Churchill applied to those who ignored Adolf Hitler's threat: "They go on in strange paradox, decided only to be undecided, resolved to be irresolute, adamant for drift, solid for fluidity, all powerful to be impotent."

So today, we dumped another 70 million tons of global-warming pollution into the thin shell of atmosphere surrounding our planet, as if it were an open sewer. And tomorrow we will dump a slightly larger amount, with the cumulative concentrations now trapping more and more heat from the sun.

As a result, the earth has a fever. And the fever is rising. The experts have told us it is not a passing affliction that will heal by itself. We asked for a second opinion. And a third. And a fourth. And the consistent conclusion, restated with increasing alarm, is that something basic is wrong.

We are what is wrong, and we must make it right.

Last September 21, as the Northern Hemisphere tilted away from the sun, scientists reported with unprecedented distress that the North Polar ice cap is "falling off a cliff." One study estimated that it could be completely gone during summer in less than twenty-two years. Another new study, to be presented by U.S. Navy researchers later this week, warns it could happen in as little as seven years.

Seven years from now.

In the last few months, it has been harder and harder to misinterpret the signs that our world is spinning out of kilter. Major cities in North and South America, Asia, and Australia are nearly out of water due to massive droughts and melting glaciers. Desperate farmers are losing their livelihoods. Peoples in the frozen Arctic and on low-lying Pacific islands are planning evacuations of places they have long called home. Unprecedented wildfires have forced a half million people from their homes in one country and caused a national emergency that almost brought down the government in another. Climate refugees have migrated into areas already inhabited by people with different cultures, religions, and traditions, increasing the potential for conflict. Stronger storms in the Pacific and Atlantic have threatened whole cities. Millions have been displaced by massive flooding in South Asia, Mexico, and eighteen countries in Africa. As temperature extremes have increased, tens of thousands have lost their lives. We are recklessly burning and clearing our forests and driving more and more species into extinction. The very web of life on which we depend is being ripped and frayed.

We never intended to cause all this destruction, just as Alfred Nobel never intended that dynamite be used for waging war. He had hoped his invention would promote human progress. We shared that same worthy goal when we began burning massive quantities of coal, then oil and methane.

Even in Nobel's time, there were a few warnings of the likely consequences. One of the very first winners of the prize in chemistry worried that, "We are evaporating our coal mines into the air." After performing ten thousand equations by hand, Svante Arrhenius calculated that the earth's average temperature would increase by many degrees if we doubled the amount of CO_2 in the atmosphere.

Seventy years later, my teacher, Roger Revelle, and his colleague, Dave Keeling, began to precisely document the increasing CO_2 levels day by day.

But unlike most other forms of pollution, CO_2 is invisible, tasteless, and odorless—which has helped keep the truth about what it is doing to our climate out of sight and out of mind. Moreover, the catastrophe now threatening us is unprecedented—and we often confuse the unprecedented with the improbable.

We also find it hard to imagine making the massive changes that are now necessary to solve the crisis. And when large truths are genuinely inconvenient, whole societies can, at least for a time, ignore them. Yet as George Orwell reminds us: "Sooner or later a false belief bumps up against solid reality, usually on a battlefield."

In the years since this prize was first awarded, the entire relationship between humankind and the earth has been radically transformed. And still, we have remained largely oblivious to the impact of our cumulative actions.

Indeed, without realizing it, we have begun to wage war on the earth itself. Now, we and the earth's climate are locked in a relationship familiar to war planners: "Mutually assured destruction."

More than two decades ago, scientists calculated that nuclear war could throw so much debris and smoke into the air that it would block life-giving sunlight from our atmosphere, causing a "nuclear winter." Their eloquent warnings here in Oslo helped galvanize the world's resolve to halt the nuclear arms race.

Now science is warning us that if we do not quickly reduce the global warming pollution that is trapping so much of the heat our planet normally radiates back out of the atmosphere, we are in danger of creating a permanent "carbon summer."

As the American poet Robert Frost wrote, "Some say the world will end in fire; some say in ice." Either, he notes, "would suffice."

But neither need be our fate. It is time to make peace with the planet.

We must quickly mobilize our civilization with the urgency and resolve that has previously been seen only when nations mobilized for war. These prior struggles for survival were won when leaders found words at the eleventh hour that released a mighty surge of courage, hope, and readiness to sacrifice for a protracted and mortal challenge.

These were not comforting and misleading assurances that the threat was not real or imminent;

that it would affect others but not ourselves; that ordinary life might be lived even in the presence of extraordinary threat; that Providence could be trusted to do for us what we would not do for ourselves.

No, these were calls to come to the defense of the common future. They were calls upon the courage, generosity, and strength of entire peoples, citizens of every class and condition who were ready to stand against the threat once asked to do so. Our enemies in those times calculated that free people would not rise to the challenge; they were, of course, catastrophically wrong.

Now comes the threat of climate crisis—a threat that is real, rising, imminent, and universal. Once again, it is the eleventh hour. The penalties for ignoring this challenge are immense and growing, and at some near point would be unsustainable and unrecoverable. For now, we still have the power to choose our fate, and the remaining question is only this: Have we the will to act vigorously and in time, or will we remain imprisoned by a dangerous illusion?

Mahatma Gandhi awakened the largest democracy on earth and forged a shared resolve with what he called "Satyagraha"—or "truth force."

In every land, the truth—once known—has the power to set us free.

Truth also has the power to unite us and bridge the distance between "me" and "we," creating the basis for common effort and shared responsibility.

There is an African proverb that says, "If you want to go quickly, go alone. If you want to go far, go together." We need to go far, quickly.

We must abandon the conceit that individual, isolated, private actions are the answer. They can and do help. But they will not take us far enough without collective action. At the same time, we must ensure that in mobilizing globally, we do not invite the establishment of ideological conformity and a new lockstep "ism."

That means adopting principles, values, laws, and treaties that release creativity and initiative at every level of society in multifold responses originating concurrently and spontaneously.

This new consciousness requires expanding the possibilities inherent in all humanity. The innovators who will devise a new way to harness the sun's energy for pennies or invent an engine that's carbon

negative may live in Lagos or Mumbai or Montevideo. We must ensure that entrepreneurs and inventors everywhere on the globe have the chance to change the world.

When we unite for a moral purpose that is manifestly good and true, the spiritual energy unleashed can transform us. The generation that defeated fascism throughout the world in the 1940s found, in rising to meet their awesome challenge, that they had gained the moral authority and long-term vision to launch the Marshall Plan, the United Nations, and a new level of global cooperation and foresight that unified Europe and facilitated the emergence of democracy and prosperity in Germany, Japan, Italy, and much of the world. One of their visionary leaders said, "It is time we steered by the stars and not by the lights of every passing ship."

In the last year of that war, you gave the Peace Prize to a man from my hometown of two thousand people, Carthage, Tennessee. Cordell Hull was described by Franklin Roosevelt as the "Father of the United Nations." He was an inspiration and hero to my own father, who followed Hull in the Congress and the U.S. Senate and in his commitment to world peace and global cooperation.

My parents spoke often of Hull, always in tones of reverence and admiration. Eight weeks ago, when you announced this prize, the deepest emotion I felt was when I saw the headline in my hometown paper that simply noted I had won the same prize that Cordell Hull had won. In that moment, I knew what my father and mother would have felt were they alive.

Just as Hull's generation found moral authority in rising to solve the world crisis caused by fascism, so too can we find our greatest opportunity in rising to solve the climate crisis. In the Kanji characters used in both Chinese and Japanese, "crisis" is written with two symbols, the first meaning "danger," the second "opportunity." By facing and removing the danger of the climate crisis, we have the opportunity to gain the moral authority and vision to vastly increase our own capacity to solve other crises that have been too long ignored.

We must understand the connections between the climate crisis and the afflictions of poverty, hunger, HIV-AIDS, and other pandemics. As these problems are linked, so too must be their solutions. We must begin by making the common rescue of the global environment the central organizing principle of the world community.

Fifteen years ago, I made that case at the "Earth Summit" in Rio de Janeiro. Ten years ago, I presented it in Kyoto. This week, I will urge the delegates in Bali to adopt a bold mandate for a treaty that establishes a universal global cap on emissions and uses the market in emissions trading to efficiently allocate resources to the most effective opportunities for speedy reductions.

This treaty should be ratified and brought into effect everywhere in the world by the beginning of 2010—two years sooner than presently contemplated. The pace of our response must be accelerated to match the accelerating pace of the crisis itself.

Heads of state should meet early next year to review what was accomplished in Bali and take personal responsibility for addressing this crisis. It is not unreasonable to ask, given the gravity of our circumstances, that these heads of state meet every three months until the treaty is completed.

We also need a moratorium on the construction of any new generating facility that burns coal without the capacity to safely trap and store carbon dioxide.

And most important of all, we need to put a price on carbon—with a CO_2 tax that is then rebated back to the people, progressively, according to the laws of each nation, in ways that shift the burden of taxation from employment to pollution. This is by far the most effective and simplest way to accelerate solutions to this crisis.

The world needs an alliance—especially of those nations that weigh heaviest in the scales where earth is in the balance. I salute Europe and Japan for the steps they've taken in recent years to meet the challenge, and the new government in Australia, which has made solving the climate crisis its first priority.

But the outcome will be decisively influenced by two nations that are now failing to do enough: the United States and China. While India is also growing fast in importance, it should be absolutely clear that it is the two largest CO_2 emitters—most

of all, my own country—that will need to make the boldest moves, or stand accountable before history for their failure to act.

Both countries should stop using the other's behavior as an excuse for stalemate and instead develop an agenda for mutual survival in a shared global environment.

These are the last few years of decision, but they can be the first years of a bright and hopeful future if we do what we must. No one should believe a solution will be found without effort, without cost, without change. Let us acknowledge that if we wish to redeem squandered time and speak again with moral authority, then these are the hard truths:

The way ahead is difficult. The outer boundary of what we currently believe is feasible is still far short of what we actually must do. Moreover, between here and there, across the unknown, falls the shadow.

That is just another way of saying that we have to expand the boundaries of what is possible. In the words of the Spanish poet Antonio Machado, "Pathwalker, there is no path. You must make the path as you walk."

We are standing at the most fateful fork in that path. So I want to end as I began, with a vision of two futures—each a palpable possibility—and with a prayer that we will see with vivid clarity the necessity of choosing between those two futures, and the urgency of making the right choice now.

The great Norwegian playwright Henrik Ibsen wrote, "One of these days, the younger generation will come knocking at my door."

The future is knocking at our door right now. Make no mistake, the next generation will ask us one of two questions. Either they will ask, "What were you thinking; why didn't you act?"

Or they will ask instead, "How did you find the moral courage to rise and successfully resolve a crisis that so many said was impossible to solve?"

We have everything we need to get started, save perhaps political will, but political will is a renewable resource.

So let us renew it, and say together, "We have a purpose. We are many. For this purpose we will rise, and we will act."

Paulo Freire

THE PEDAGOGY OF THE OPPRESSED

Peace implies a state of satisfaction. But it is very difficult to be satisfied when denied basics such as food, clothing, shelter, education, medical care, and hope. Not surprisingly, therefore, there is little peace in a world characterized by painful differences between the rich and poor, between the haves and the have-nots. Poverty and social oppression may not lead directly to war, but they certainly are not conducive to peace. Indeed, a substantial motivation for military expenditures may well be concern on the part of the "haves" with preventing any fundamental reorganization in the worldwide distribution of power and wealth.

And yet, fundamental changes have begun. With the end of the Cold War, the primary division among the world's inhabitants has shifted from an East-West to a North-South axis. The search for peace must therefore include a search for economic and social betterment.

Measured by life expectancy, calories consumed, years of education, per capita gross domestic product, and so forth, there are extraordinary disparities in wealth, both within and between countries. Especially in so-called third world countries, grinding poverty is persistent, degrading, miserable, life shortening, life threatening, and life denying. Although "development" has long been the preferred solution for poverty among Western elites, others have criticized such approaches as mere masks for continued oppression. Thus, "dependencia" theory—based on the Spanish word for "dependency"—suggests that indigenous peoples and resources are simply being exploited by the wealthier, industrialized states of the North and that poor people and poor countries are not so much underdeveloped as overexploited, such that poverty results not from neglect but from altogether too much attention! Dependencia theorists point out, for example, that Indonesia, Brazil, and Sudan are rich; only their people are poor.

Poverty is fundamental to the appeal long exerted by communism. Once again, however, our focus is less on specific, ideological proposals than on understanding some of the background issues. One of the most stimulating (and radical) approaches to the issue of poverty is found in the work of revolutionary Brazilian educator and social theorist Paulo Freire, who has long been concerned with those who are oppressed. Freire explores how to break down the wall between the oppressed and their oppressors, between theory and practice, between teacher and those taught—to achieve true "dialogue," with the goal of moving toward a more egalitarian society.

While the problem of humanization has always, from an axiological point of view, been humankind's central problem, it now takes on the character of an inescapable concern.[1] Concern for humanization leads at once to the recognition of dehumanization, not only as an ontological possibility but as an historical reality. And as an individual perceives the extent of dehumanization, he or she may ask if humanization is a viable possibility. Within history, in concrete, objective contexts, both humanization and dehumanization are possibilities for a person as an uncompleted being conscious of their incompletion.

But while both humanization and dehumanization are real alternatives, only the first is the people's vocation. This vocation is constantly negated, yet it is affirmed by that very negation. It is thwarted by injustice, exploitation, oppression, and the violence of the oppressors; it is affirmed by the yearning of the oppressed for freedom and justice, and by their struggle to recover their lost humanity.

Dehumanization, which marks not only those whose humanity has been stolen, but also (though in a different way) those who have stolen it, is a *distortion* of the vocation of becoming more fully human. This distortion occurs within history; but it is not an historical vocation. Indeed, to admit of dehumanization as an historical vocation would lead either to cynicism or total despair. The struggle for humanization, for the emancipation of labor, for the overcoming of alienation, for the affirmation of men and women as persons would be meaningless. This struggle is possible only because dehumanization, although a concrete historical fact, is *not* a given destiny but the result of an unjust order that engenders violence in the oppressors, which in turn dehumanizes the oppressed.

Because it is a distortion of being more fully human, sooner or later being less human leads the oppressed to struggle against those who made them so. In order for this struggle to have meaning, the oppressed must not, in seeking to regain their humanity (which is a way to create it), become in turn oppressors of the oppressors, but rather restorers of the humanity of both.

This, then, is the great humanistic and historical task of the oppressed: to liberate themselves and their oppressors as well. The oppressors, who oppress, exploit, and rape by virtue of their power, cannot find in this power the strength to liberate either the oppressed or themselves. Only power that springs from the weakness of the oppressed will be sufficiently strong to free both. Any attempt to "soften" the power of the oppressor in deference to the weakness of the oppressed almost always manifests itself in the form of false generosity; indeed, the attempt never goes beyond this. In order to have the continued opportunity to express their "generosity," the oppressors must perpetuate injustice as well. An unjust social order is the permanent fount of this "generosity," which is nourished by death, despair, and poverty. That is why the dispensers of false generosity become desperate at the slightest threat to its source.

True generosity consists precisely in fighting to destroy the causes which nourish false charity. False charity constrains the fearful and subdued, the "rejects of life," to extend their trembling hands. True generosity lies in striving so that these hands—whether of individuals or entire peoples—need be extended less and less in supplication, so that more and more they become human hands which work and, working, transform the world.

This lesson and this apprenticeship must come, however, from the oppressed themselves and from those who are truly in solidarity with them. As individuals or as peoples, by fighting for the restoration of their humanity they will be attempting the restoration of true generosity. Who is better prepared than

---

[1] The current movements of rebellion, especially those of youth, while they necessarily reflect the peculiarities of their respective settings, manifest in their essence this preoccupation with people as beings in the world and with the world—preoccupation with *what* and *how* they are "being." As they place consumer civilization in judgment, denounce bureaucracies of all types, demand the transformation of the universities (changing the rigid nature of the teacher-student relationship and placing that relationship within the context of reality), propose the transformation of reality itself so that universities can be renewed, attack old orders and established institutions in the attempt to affirm human beings as the Subjects of decision, all these movements reflect the style of our age, which is more anthropological than anthropocentric.

the oppressed to understand the terrible significance of an oppressive society? Who suffers the effects of oppression more than the oppressed? Who can better understand the necessity of liberation? They will not gain this liberation by chance but through the praxis of their quest for it, through their recognition of the necessity to fight for it. And this fight, because of the purpose given it by the oppressed, will actually constitute an act of love opposing the lovelessness which lies at the heart of the oppressors' violence, lovelessness even when clothed in false generosity.

But almost always, during the initial stage of the struggle, the oppressed, instead of striving for liberation, tend themselves to become oppressors, or "sub-oppressors." The very structure of their thought has been conditioned by the contradictions of the concrete, existential situation by which they were shaped. Their ideal is to be men; but for them, to be men is to be oppressors. This is their model of humanity. This phenomenon derives from the fact that the oppressed, at a certain moment of their existential experience, adopt an attitude of "adhesion" to the oppressor. Under these circumstances they cannot "consider" him sufficiently clearly to objectivize him—to discover him "outside" themselves. This does not necessarily mean that the oppressed are unaware that they are downtrodden. But their perception of themselves as oppressed is impaired by their submersion in the reality of oppression. At this level, their perception of themselves as opposites of the oppressor does not yet signify engagement in a struggle to overcome the contradiction;[2]; the one pole aspires not to liberation, but to identification with its opposite pole.

In this situation the oppressed do not see the "new man" as the person to be born from the resolution of this contradiction, as oppression gives way to liberation. For them, the new man and woman themselves become oppressors. Their vision of the new man or woman is individualistic; because of their identification with the oppressor, they have no consciousness of themselves as persons or as members of an oppressed class. It is not to become free that they want agrarian reform, but in order to acquire land and thus become landowners—or, more precisely, bosses over other workers. It is a rare peasant who, once "promoted" to overseer, does not

become more of a tyrant toward his former comrades than the owner himself. This is because the context of the peasant's situation, that is, oppression, remains unchanged. In this example, the overseer, in order to make sure of his job, must be as tough as the owner—and more so. Thus is illustrated our previous assertion that during the initial stage of their struggle the oppressed find in the oppressor their model of "manhood."

Even revolution, which transforms a concrete situation of oppression by establishing the process of liberation, must confront this phenomenon. Many of the oppressed who directly or indirectly participate in revolution intend—conditioned by the myths of the old order—to make it their private revolution. The shadow of their former oppressor is still cast over them.

The "fear of freedom" which afflicts the oppressed,[3] a fear which may equally well lead them to desire the role of oppressor or bind them to the role of oppressed, should be examined. One of the basic elements of the relationship between oppressor and oppressed is *prescription*. Every prescription represents the imposition of one individual's choice upon another, transforming the consciousness of the person prescribed to into one that conforms with the prescriber's consciousness. Thus, the behavior of the oppressed is a prescribed behavior, following as it does the guidelines of the oppressor.

The oppressed, having internalized the image of the oppressor and adopted his guidelines, are fearful of freedom. Freedom would require them to eject this image and replace it with autonomy and responsibility. Freedom is acquired by conquest, not by gift. It must be pursued constantly and responsibly. Freedom is not an ideal located outside of man; nor is it an idea which becomes myth. It is rather the indispensable condition for the quest for human completion.

To surmount the situation of oppression, people must first critically recognize its causes, so that

---

[2] The term "contradiction" denotes the dialectical conflict between opposing social forces.—Translator's note.
[3] This fear of freedom is also to be found in the oppressors, though, obviously, in a different form. The oppressed are afraid to embrace freedom; the oppressors are afraid of losing the "freedom" to oppress.

through transforming action they can create a new situation, one which makes possible the pursuit of a fuller humanity. But the struggle to be more fully human has already begun in the authentic struggle to transform the situation. Although the situation of oppression is a dehumanized and dehumanizing totality affecting both the oppressors and those whom they oppress, it is the latter who must, from their stifled humanity, wage for both the struggle for a fuller humanity; the oppressor, who is himself dehumanized because he dehumanizes others, is unable to lead this struggle.

However, the oppressed, who have adapted to the structure of domination in which they are immersed, and have become resigned to it, are inhibited from waging the struggle for freedom so long as they feel incapable of running the risks it requires. Moreover, their struggle for freedom threatens not only the oppressor, but also their own oppressed comrades who are fearful of still greater repression. When they discover within themselves the yearning to be free, they perceive that this yearning can be transformed into reality only when the same yearning is aroused in their comrades. But while dominated by the fear of freedom they refuse to appeal to others, or to listen to the appeals of others, or even to the appeals of their own conscience. They prefer gregariousness to authentic comradeship; they prefer the security of conformity with their state of unfreedom to the creative communion produced by freedom and even the very pursuit of freedom.

The oppressed suffer from the duality which has established itself in their innermost being. They discover that without freedom they cannot exist authentically. Yet, although they desire authentic existence, they fear it. They are at one and the same time themselves and the oppressor whose consciousness they have internalized. The conflict lies in the choice between being wholly themselves or being divided; between ejecting the oppressor within or not ejecting them; between human solidarity or alienation; between following prescriptions or having choices; between being spectators or actors; between acting or having the illusion of acting through the action of the oppressors; between speaking out or being silent, castrated in their power to create and

re-create, in their power to transform the world. This is the tragic dilemma of the oppressed which their education must take into account. . . .

The central problem is this: How can the oppressed, as divided, unauthentic beings, participate in developing the pedagogy of their liberation? Only as they discover themselves to be "hosts" of the oppressor can they contribute to the midwifery of their liberating pedagogy. As long as they live in the duality in which *to be* is *to be like*, and *to be like* is *to be like the oppressor*, this contribution is impossible. The pedagogy of the oppressed is an instrument for their critical discovery that both they and their oppressors are manifestations of dehumanization. . . .

Any situation in which "A" objectively exploits "B" or hinders his or her pursuit of self-affirmation as a responsible person is one of oppression. Such a situation in itself constitutes violence, even when sweetened by false generosity, because it interferes with the individual's ontological and historical vocation to be more fully human. With the establishment of a relationship of oppression, violence has *already* begun. Never in history has violence been initiated by the oppressed. How could they be the initiators, if they themselves are the result of violence? How could they be the sponsors of something whose objective inauguration called forth their existence as oppressed? There would be no oppressed had there been no prior situation of violence to establish their subjugation.

Violence is initiated by those who oppress, who exploit, who fail to recognize others as persons—not by those who are oppressed, exploited, and unrecognized. It is not the unloved who initiate disaffection, but those who cannot love because they love only themselves. It is not the helpless, subject to terror, who initiate terror, but the violent, who with their power create the concrete situation which begets the "rejects of life." It is not the tyrannized who initiate despotism, but the tyrants. It is not the despised who initiate hatred, but those who despise. It is not those whose humanity is denied them who negate humankind, but those who denied that humanity (thus negating their own as well). Force is used not by those who have become weak under the preponderance of the strong, but by the strong who have emasculated them.

For the oppressors, however, it is always the oppressed (whom they obviously never call "the oppressed" but—depending on whether they are fellow countrymen or not—"those people" or "the blind and envious masses" or "savages" or "natives" or "subversives") who are disaffected, who are "violent," "barbaric," "wicked," or "ferocious" when they react to the violence of the oppressors.

Yet it is—paradoxical though it may seem—precisely in the response of the oppressed to the violence of their oppressors that a gesture of love may be found. Consciously or unconsciously, the act of rebellion by the oppressed (an act which is always, or nearly always, as violent as the initial violence of the oppressors) can initiate love. Whereas the violence of the oppressors prevents the oppressed from being fully human, the response of the latter to this violence is grounded in the desire to pursue the right to be human. As the oppressors dehumanize others and violate their rights, they themselves also become dehumanized. As the oppressed, fighting to be human, take away the oppressors' power to dominate and suppress, they restore to the oppressors the humanity they had lost in the exercise of oppression.

It is only the oppressed who, by freeing themselves, can free their oppressors. The latter, as an oppressive class, can free neither others nor themselves. It is therefore essential that the oppressed wage the struggle to resolve the contradiction in which they are caught; and the contradiction will be resolved by the appearance of the new man: neither oppressor nor oppressed, but man in the process of liberation. If the goal of the oppressed is to become fully human, they will not achieve their goal by merely reversing the terms of the contradiction, by simply changing poles.

. . . An act is oppressive only when it prevents people from being more fully human. Accordingly, these necessary restraints do not *in themselves* signify that yesterday's oppressed have become today's oppressors. Acts which prevent the restoration of the oppressive regime cannot be compared with those which create and maintain it, cannot be compared with those by which a few men and women deny the majority their right to be human.

However, the moment the new regime hardens into a dominating "bureaucracy" the humanist

dimension of the struggle is lost and it is no longer possible to speak of liberation. Hence our insistence that the authentic solution of the oppressor-oppressed contradiction does not lie in a mere reversal of position, in moving from one pole to the other. Nor does it lie in the replacement of the former oppressors with new ones who continue to subjugate the oppressed—all in the name of their liberation. . . .

A careful analysis of the teacher-student relationship at any level, inside or outside the school, reveals its fundamentally *narrative* character. This relationship involves a narrating Subject (the teacher) and patient, listening objects (the students). The contents, whether values or empirical dimensions of reality, tend in the process of being narrated to become lifeless and petrified. Education is suffering from narration sickness.

The teacher talks about reality as if it were motionless, static, compartmentalized, and predictable. Or else he expounds on a topic completely alien to the existential experience of the students. His task is to "fill" the students with the contents of his narration—contents which are detached from reality, disconnected from the totality that engendered them and could give them significance. Words are emptied of their concreteness and become a hollow, alienated, and alienating verbosity.

The outstanding characteristic of this narrative education, then, is the sonority of words, not their transforming power. "Four times four is sixteen; the capital of Pará is Belém." The student records, memorizes, and repeats these phrases without perceiving what four times four really means, or realizing the true significance of "capital" in the affirmation "the capital of Pará is Belém," that is, what Belém means for Pará and what Pará means for Brazil.

Narration (with the teacher as narrator) leads the students to memorize mechanically the narrated content. Worse yet, it turns them into "containers," into "receptacles" to be "filled" by the teacher. The more completely she fills the receptacles, the better a teacher she is. The more meekly the receptacles permit themselves to be filled, the better students they are.

Education thus becomes an act of depositing, in which the students are the depositories and the teacher is the depositor. Instead of communicating, the teacher issues communiqués and makes deposits which the students patiently receive, memorize, and repeat. This is the "banking" concept of education, in which the scope of action allowed to the students extends only as far as receiving, filing, and storing the deposits. They do, it is true, have the opportunity to become collectors or cataloguers of the things they store. But in the last analysis, it is the people themselves who are filed away through the lack of creativity, transformation, and knowledge in this (at best) misguided system. For apart from inquiry, apart from the praxis, individuals cannot be truly human. Knowledge emerges only through invention and re-invention, through the restless, impatient, continuing, hopeful inquiry human beings pursue in the world, with the world, and with each other.

In the banking concept of education, knowledge is a gift bestowed by those who consider themselves knowledgeable upon those whom they consider to know nothing. Projecting an absolute ignorance onto others, a characteristic of the ideology of oppression, negates education and knowledge as processes of inquiry. The teacher presents himself to his students as their necessary opposite; by considering their ignorance absolute, he justifies his own existence. The students, alienated like the slave in the Hegelian dialectic, accept their ignorance as justifying the teacher's existence—but, unlike the slave, they never discover that they educate the teacher.

The *raison d'être* of libertarian education, on the other hand, lies in its drive toward reconciliation. Education must begin with the solution of the teacher-student contradiction, by reconciling the poles of the contradiction so that both are simultaneously teachers *and* students. . . .

Dialogue cannot exist, . . . in the absence of a profound love for the world and for people. The naming of the world, which is an act of creation and re-creation, is not possible if it is not infused with love. Love is at the same time the foundation of dialogue and dialogue itself. It is thus necessarily the task of responsible Subjects and cannot exist in a relation of domination. Domination reveals the pathology of love: sadism in the dominator and masochism in the dominated. Because love is an act of courage, not of fear, love is commitment to others. No matter where the oppressed are found, the act of love is commitment to their cause—the cause of liberation. And this commitment, because it is loving, is dialogical. As an act of bravery, love cannot be sentimental; as an act of freedom, it must not serve as a pretext for manipulation. It must generate other acts of freedom; otherwise, it is not love. Only by abolishing the situation of oppression is it possible to restore the love which that situation made impossible. If I do not love the world—if I do not love life—if I do not love people—I cannot enter into dialogue.

On the other hand, dialogue cannot exist without humility. The naming of the world, through which people constantly re-create that world, cannot be an act of arrogance. Dialogue, as the encounter of those addressed to the common task of learning and acting, is broken if the parties (or one of them) lack humility. How can I dialogue if I always project ignorance onto others and never perceive my own? How can I dialogue if I regard myself as a case apart from others—mere "its" in whom I cannot recognize other "I"s? How can I dialogue if I consider myself a member of the in-group of "pure" men, the owners of truth and knowledge, for whom all non-members are "these people" or "the great unwashed"? How can I dialogue if I start from the premise that naming the world is the task of an elite and that the presence of the people in history is a sign of deterioration, thus to be avoided? How can I dialogue if I am closed to—and even offended by—the contribution of others? How can I dialogue if I am afraid of being displaced, the mere possibility causing me torment and weakness? Self-sufficiency is incompatible with dialogue. Men and women who lack humility (or have lost it) cannot come to the people, cannot be their partners in naming the world. Someone who cannot acknowledge himself to be as mortal as everyone else still has a long way to go before he can reach the point of encounter. At the point of encounter there are neither utter ignoramuses nor perfect sages; there are only people who are attempting, together, to learn more than they now know.

Dialogue further requires an intense faith in humankind, faith in their power to make and remake, to create and re-create, faith in their vocation to be more fully human (which is not the privilege of an elite, but the birthright of all). Faith in people is an *a priori* requirement for dialogue; the "dialogical man" believes in others even before he meets them face-to-face. His faith, however, is not naïve. The "dialogical man" is critical and knows that although it is within the power of humans to create and transform, in a concrete situation of alienation individuals may be impaired in the use of that power. Far from destroying his faith in the people, however, this possibility strikes him as a challenge to which he must respond. He is convinced that the power to create and transform, even when thwarted in concrete situations, tends to be reborn. And that rebirth can occur—not gratuitously, but in and through the struggle for liberation—in the supersedence of slave labor by emancipated labor which gives zest to life. Without this faith in people, dialogue is a farce which inevitably degenerates into paternalistic manipulation.

Founding itself upon love, humility, and faith, dialogue becomes a horizontal relationship of which mutual trust between the dialoguers is the logical consequence. It would be a contradiction in terms if dialogue—loving, humble, and full of faith—did not produce this climate of mutual trust, which leads the dialoguers into ever closer partnership in the naming of the world. Conversely, such trust is obviously absent in the anti-dialogics of the banking method of education. Whereas faith in humankind is an *a priori* requirement for dialogue, trust is established by dialogue. Should it founder, it will be seen that the preconditions were lacking. False love, false humility, and feeble faith in others cannot create trust. Trust is contingent on the evidence which one party provides the others of his true, concrete intentions; it cannot exist if that party's words do not coincide with their actions. To say one thing and do another—to take one's own word lightly—cannot inspire trust. To glorify democracy and to silence the people is a farce; to discourse on humanism and to negate people is a lie.

Nor yet can dialogue exist without hope. Hope is rooted in men's incompletion, from which they move out in constant search—a search which can be carried out only in communion with others. Hopelessness is a form of silence, of denying the world and fleeing from it. The dehumanization resulting from an unjust order is not a cause for despair but for hope, leading to the incessant pursuit of the humanity denied by injustice. Hope, however, does not consist in crossing one's arms and waiting. As long as I fight, I am moved by hope; and if I fight with hope, then I can wait.

Jeffrey Sachs

GLOBAL ECONOMIC SOLIDARITY

Poverty persists as an underlying cause as well as an effect of structural violence. It also lurks behind much of the world's overt violence and is, in any event, a constant rebuke to any conception of human dignity and positive peace. Although the world as a whole is, in a sense, wealthy, great disparities exist, and in some places, those disparities have been increasing. Many factors contribute to this, including (but not limited to) population pressure, environmental degradation, governmental corruption, traditions of helplessness and hopelessness, and exploitation by local socioeconomic systems as well as by foreign countries and multinational corporations.

The struggle against world poverty and economic injustice is intimately connected with efforts toward positive peace and has been undertaken not only by nongovernmental organizations but also by increasing numbers of prominent economists. Among them, one of the most effective and influential is Columbia University Jeffrey Sachs. Here is an excerpt from a one of his lectures.

⟨⟩

The end of poverty—by the year 2025. It's seems like an outlandish claim, an impossible dream. But it's within reach. It is a scientifically sound objective. And it is the most urgent challenge of our generation.

In fact, if we in the rich world fail to take up this challenge, we will imperil ourselves and the world. A crowded world, one that is "bursting at the seams," cannot afford to leave millions to die each year of extreme poverty without imperiling all the rest.

John F. Kennedy . . . put it this way in his inaugural address in 1961:

To those peoples in the huts and villages across the globe struggling to break the bonds of mass misery, we pledge our best efforts to help them help themselves, for whatever period is required—not because the Communists may be doing it, not because we seek their votes, but because it is right. If a free society cannot help

the many who are poor, it cannot save the few who are rich.

In my last lecture, in New York, I talked about war and peace and about our extremely dangerous tendency to define the world as "us versus them." Because of that tendency, war can erupt as a self-fulfilling prophecy of conflict between mutually suspicious groups.

. . . War can . . . erupt as a result of the collapse of an impoverished society, one suffering the scourges of drought, hunger, lack of jobs, and lack of hope. Ending poverty is therefore a basic matter of our own security.

Darfur, Somalia, Afghanistan. These are all, at their core, wars of extreme poverty. So too, quite obviously, were the recent wars of Liberia, Sierra Leone, Haiti, and many others. The U.S. has just established a new military command in Africa, declaring Africa to pose new security threats to the U.S. But even as the U.S. spends more than $600 billion on the military, and even as U.S. counterinsurgency forces spread out across the impoverished stretches of the Sahel, the U.S. will never achieve peace if it continues to spend less than one hundredth of the military budget on Africa's economic development. An army can never pacify a hungry, disease-ridden, and impoverished population.

We need to understand the challenge of extreme poverty not only as a matter of ethics and politics, but also as a matter of science. We can and must achieve a much clearer understanding of how to end poverty, based on the best scientific evidence. We have powerful technologies that can be mobilized, and which can make a remarkable difference at a remarkable speed.

We can usefully start our diagnosis by understanding the progress that has been made. When John Kennedy spoke of the bonds of mass misery in 1961, close to half the planet was in extreme poverty, measured by the traditional standard of living of $1 per day or less. Today, the proportion of the world's population in extreme poverty is down to around one-sixth, approximately 1 billion of the world's 6.6 billion people. The absolute numbers of the poor are declining, and their proportion is declining even faster. Globalization has, on balance, helped the poor, especially in Asia, where economic growth and poverty reduction are proceeding at historically unprecedented rates. We have the wind in our sails, since world markets give a powerful impetus to the spread of technologies and the rise of income. Once countries get on to the ladder of development—exporting manufactures and services in world markets, and linked to the world in networks of production, trade, finance, and technology—they tend to make continued progress up the ladder. Market forces, based on saving, investment, trade, and technological advance take hold. The crisis of extreme poverty is centered in those regions not yet on the development ladder, stuck in extreme poverty and hunger, with only the weakest of links to global production—through primary agricultural goods and mineral resources.

Poverty is not yet declining in tropical Africa and a few other places. Africa has not so much been harmed by globalization, as bypassed by it.

The basic challenge is to help Africa and other still-impoverished regions onto the development ladder.

Consider some recent data, this time using the metrics of life and death rather than dollars. Life expectancy at birth is probably the best single indicator of overall human well-being that we have. Life expectancy is not only a crucially important goal in its own right, but is also an excellent indicator of overall social organization—for example, the quality of the health system, the presence or absence of war, the reach of infrastructure, and the extent of food insecurity. Life expectancy at birth is also relatively easy to measure and to compare across countries.

The worldwide improvements in life expectancy on the planet have been dramatic. In 1960, 105 countries, with two-thirds of the world's population, had a life expectancy at birth of less than 60 years. By 2004, that list had shrunk to only 47 countries, with a mere 12 percent of the world's population. And virtually all of those 47 countries are in Africa (with the exceptions being Afghanistan, Cambodia, Haiti, Laos, and Papua New Guinea).

Why does Africa lag? Here is where the scientific evidence on extreme poverty is vital. The overwhelming nonscientific assumption held in our societies is that Africa suffers mainly from the corruption and mismanagement of its leaders. With the viciousness and despotism of Robert Mugabe in Zimbabwe, it's an understandable view. Yet this seemingly self-evident view is wrong as a generalization. Zimbabwe may get the headlines, but there are many countries in Africa, like Tanzania and Mozambique just nearby, that have talented and freely elected governments struggling against poverty. But they too face great obstacles, and their people too continue to suffer from extreme deprivation.

Consider the fact that nine developing countries—with two in Africa—were tied with exactly the same corruption score in this year's Transparency International index. Specifically, Ghana and Senegal were assessed to be at the same level of corruption as Brazil, China, Egypt, India, Mexico, Peru, and Saudi Arabia. Yet the two African countries have life expectancies of around fifty-six years, while all but one of the other countries have life expectancies of more than seventy years. On average, for countries with comparable corruption levels, Africa's life expectancy rates are nearly twenty years below the rest of the world's.

Africa's problems are not due mainly to corruption, but to its ecology, history, weak infrastructure, and burgeoning population growth. Moreover, once those underlying sources of extreme poverty and disease are scientifically identified, we can also identify the practical technologies and strategies needed to solve these problems, and thereby enable Africa like the rest of the world to break free of the poverty trap.

Africa, compared with other poor regions of the world, suffers from four enormous burdens, all of which are solvable with proven and relatively low-cost technologies.

The first is low food production. Africa is a hungry continent, with grain yields roughly one-third of other developing regions of the planet. Part of the problem is Africa's age-old dependence on rain-fed agriculture in a savanna climate, where the risks of drought are ever present. Sub-Saharan Africa lacks the river-based irrigation systems of South and East Asia. Another urgent problem with Africa's agriculture is that Africa's soils have been depleted of nutrients because impoverished farmers have been unable to afford fertilizers to replenish their soils. Older techniques for replenishing soil nutrients, such as the rotation of farmlands, allowing the replenishment of nutrients on land left fallow for ten or twenty years, are no longer feasible. Rising land scarcity because of Africa's burgeoning population means that scarce arable land can no longer be left fallow even for one year, much less a generation.

The second challenge is Africa's disease ecology, which leads to uniquely high burdens of tropical diseases, especially malaria. This again is a matter of ecology. Africa has a climate and species of disease vectors that contribute to its unique burden of tropical infectious diseases. These are controllable, but at much greater effort than is needed in other parts of the world.

The third challenge is Africa's miserably deficient infrastructure, with the world's poorest network of roads, power, rail, and fiber-optic cables for Internet. For many historical and geographical reasons, Africa's colonial powers did not build the roads, rail, and power grids that they did in other parts of the world.

The fourth challenge is the continuing surge of population, in which poor families are still having six or more children in rural areas. Fertility rates are still so high in rural Africa that populations are doubling each generation.

These challenges—food production, disease control, weak infrastructure, burgeoning populations—are not caused by corruption but by ecology, by history, and by the vicious cycle of extreme poverty itself. Each of these challenges is susceptible to utterly practical solutions, and in short order, but they require public-sector investments beyond the levels that impoverished African countries can afford.

African countries, in short, face a poverty trap. They can overcome impoverishment through identifiable and proven public investments, but these countries are simply too poor to undertake those investments out of their own resources. Nor are they creditworthy enough to borrow those resources from global capital markets, though these markets can help.

This litany of problems may seem overwhelming. Left alone, they will be. But each is actually solvable, and much more easily than is typically imagined. We've seen what can be done, for example, in our own Millennium Villages, a project that applies proven techniques to these very challenges in villages across a dozen countries of Africa. Here is what can be accomplished.

Powerful technologies, as simple as insecticide-treated bed nets and a new generation of anti-malaria medicines, can control malaria by 90 percent or more. Antiretroviral medicines can make AIDS a chronic rather than fatal disease, and one with reduced stigma and much more chance of prevention. These successes, and many like them, have been accomplished in countless specific projects where donor funds have been made available, but not on a country scale or regional scale.

Current agronomic technologies can triple food production. The key in that case is to get smallholder farms the vital inputs of high-yield seeds, fertilizers, and small-scale water management techniques that can dramatically boost farm yields. Africa can and must have a "green revolution" as India initiated nearly forty years ago. Malawi has started this year, with a program to guarantee vital inputs for the poorest farmers. Food yields have soared in a neighborhood of acute food shortages. And we should certainly remember that India's green revolution also depended on international aid in its early years. Virtually every country has needed a helping hand at some point. It's a rule of life.

Current technologies can extend roads, rail, power, and the Internet even to the most remote regions. A satellite dish, or a mobile phone tower, can end isolation that might have seemed irremediable a generation ago.

The fourth challenge, excessive population growth, is similarly susceptible to practical and proven solutions. Fertility rates in rural Africa are still around six children or more. This is understandable, if disastrous. Poor families are worried about the high rates of child mortality, and compensate by having large families. Poor families lack access to contraception and family planning. Girls often are deprived of even a basic education, because the family cannot afford it, and are instead forced into early marriage rather than encouraged to stay in school. And the value placed on mothers' time is very low, in part because agricultural productivity is itself so low. With few opportunities to earn remunerative income, mothers are pushed—often by their husbands or the community—to have more children.

Yet, as shown by countless countries around the world, fertility rates will fall rapidly, and on a voluntary basis, if an orderly effort is led by government with adequate resources. Investments in child survival, contraceptive availability, schooling of children—especially girls—and higher farm productivity can result in a voluntary decline in total fertility from around six to perhaps three or lower within a single decade. But these things will not happen by themselves. They require resources, which impoverished Africa lacks.

The world has committed, time and again, to help Africa accomplish these development objectives. We are pledged, all countries on the planet, to support the Millennium Development Goals (MDGs), the internationally agreed goals set in the year 2000 to cut poverty, hunger, and disease decisively by the year 2015. We are halfway to 2015, but

still far off the mark. Our governments talk, and they even begin to act, but they fail to act with the urgency and decisiveness required by the circumstances, and commensurate with our promises. And the urgency will grow as climate stresses multiply. The longer we wait, the greater is the suffering and the larger are the long-term risks and costs.

Success in the MDGs will require stronger actions on all fronts—by civil society, by businesses, by African governments and communities. . . . But success will also require finance, at a scale that can only be provided by official development assistance by rich country governments. Our governments have long promised to deliver 0.7 percent of rich-world GNP as official aid, but so far have consistently failed to do so.

The situation is absurd in many ways—at least 10 million people dying each year because the rich world refuses to spend 0.7 percent of GNP on aid! For Africa specifically, we would need around $70 billion per year to enable Africa to get onto the ladder of development. That's $70 per person per year from each of us in the rich countries. It's about 0.2 per cent of our annual income. It's well under the annual cost of the Iraq War. Indeed, it's about 2 percent of the estimated wealth of the world's 1,000 billionaires. And consider that Wall Street and the City of London together took home Christmas bonuses of some $40 billion this past holiday season.

The deep question is why the rich countries, with so much wealth, are so irresponsibly and relentlessly neglectful, when the amounts needed are so small and the consequences of inaction are so catastrophic for all. Is this the fate of modern societies? Are our politicians inevitably distracted by local concerns, or by the illusions of war? Are our populations so jaded and cynical and uncaring as to make this neglect inevitable? The answer, thankfully, is no. Let's not overgeneralize. Several of the world's wealthiest countries do honor their commitments. The key for us is to understand why they do, while the rest do not.

Five countries of Northern Europe have long met the 0.7 percent of GNP commitment. These are Denmark, Luxembourg, the Netherlands, Norway, and Sweden. The European Union has now promised, once again, to do so by 2015. Yet the European Union obviously agonizes in this promise. The U.S.

doesn't even agonize. It doesn't even try. The U.S. will spend $600 billion on the military this year, but only $4 billion on African development. Moreover, senior U.S. officials vigorously reject the global standard of 0.7 percent in aid, even though the U.S. government signed on to that international target.

The striking thing about the aid performance is the very strong correlation between a country's international aid and its care for the poor at home. Countries that take care of their own poor also tend to help the world's poor. Countries that neglect their own poor tend to walk away from their international responsibilities as well.

In brief, the social welfare model of Northern Europe helps the poor both at home and abroad. The U.S. model, alas, leaves the poor to suffer their fate, both at home and abroad. Americans, as a result, are fearful of their economic future, as they are left to fend for themselves. They have little time for others. The world is seen as filled with threats, and of "us versus them," rather than with opportunities in an interconnected global society. The Nordic countries, by contrast, have the domestic security of social protection, which they then seek to extend to the world.

The successes of the Nordic system are crucial for us to understand. Many on the political left admire the Nordic social welfare state, as do I. Yet they mistakenly believe that the Nordic countries are somehow antimarket and antiglobalization. Nothing could be further from the truth. Denmark, Finland, the Netherlands, Norway, and Sweden are all market-based economies, competing fiercely in world markets. They believe in open trade and invest heavily in high technology and in R&D to keep their international competitiveness. But they have discovered that it is possible to combine market efficiency and open trade with strong social services and social protection. They have achieved, in short, a system of "economic solidarity" within a market economy. Rather than compromising their economic well-being, these institutions of economic solidarity have strengthened the market system itself. The Nordic countries have not only eliminated poverty in their midst and achieved the best health outcomes in the world, they have also fostered the confidence to extend such solidarity to the rest of the world.

No doubt, the Nordic successes have depended, in part, on their relatively small size and social homogeneity. Their levels of internal social trust are very high. Migration is putting that social trust under challenge. But even if their social homogeneity is not replicable elsewhere, their social trust can be. Perhaps the key to success, after all, in the twenty-first century will be building trust across ethnic and cultural lines within our own societies, as well as across societies.

We can end poverty, at home and abroad, with the technologies and tools that we have, if we trust each other sufficiently, at home and abroad. As John F. Kennedy said in the context of war and peace, we need not talk about blind trust, a naïve trust, a trust of dreamers or fanatics. We must seek a practical trust, built on specific institutions and specific ways of delivering help for the poor. Our economic solidarity must rely on scientific evidence and rigorous audits as much as on trust. But at the core of such institutions is the trust that we are all in this together, that our fates, economic and otherwise, are shared, and that the defeat of poverty will be a victory of security for all on the planet.

My suggestions on economic solidarity therefore are the following:

First, let us embrace market economics—yes—but also recognize that free-market economics are passé. We need an active role of the state, to help the poorest to break free of the poverty trap, and to help narrow the inequalities of a high-income market society.

Let us understand that economic solidarity is insurance for all, the poor and the rich. Our societies can be both productive and safe. If we invest in solidarity, we will also end up with a more caring society. It's not our poor versus the poor abroad. It is help and solidarity with both.

Let us resolve to honor our commitments in the fight against poverty, hunger, and disease. Our commitments are small compared with our vast wealth, and the benefits will be vast. We have the power to save millions of lives each year, to help slow a burgeoning population growth in the poorest countries, and to reduce, if not end, the conflicts and wars caused by extreme poverty, which threaten peace everywhere. This, truly, is the work of our generation.

Martin Luther King, Jr.

LETTER FROM A BIRMINGHAM JAIL

Martin Luther King, Jr., was especially concerned with racial prejudice and the absence of civil rights for African Americans in the United States. (As time went on, he expanded this focus to include the problems of poverty and the war in Vietnam.) His "Letter from a Birmingham Jail," one of the signal documents of the U.S. civil rights movement, was originally written on the margins of a local newspaper that had published a statement by a number of Southern ministers denouncing the civil rights campaign in which Reverend King, and many others, had been engaged. This selection could also have been placed in the next chapter on nonviolence. As a passionate and influential call for social justice, it seems equally appropriate to any consideration of positive peace.

My Dear Fellow Clergymen:

. . . I am in Birmingham because injustice is here. Just as the prophets of the eighth century BC left their villages and carried their "thus saith the Lord" far beyond the boundaries of their home towns, and just as the apostle Paul left his village of Tarsus and carried the gospel of Jesus Christ to the far corners of the Greco-Roman world, so am I compelled to carry the gospel of freedom beyond my own hometown. Like Paul, I must constantly respond to the Macedonian call for aid.

Moreover, I am cognizant of the interrelatedness of all communities and states. I cannot sit idly by in Atlanta and not be concerned about what happens in Birmingham. Injustice anywhere is a threat to justice everywhere. We are caught in an inescapable network of mutuality, tied in a single garment of destiny. Whatever affects one directly affects all indirectly. Never again can we afford to live with the narrow, provincial "outside agitator" idea. Anyone who lives inside the United States can never be considered an outsider anywhere within its bounds.

. . . You may well ask, "Why direct action? Why sit-ins, marches and so forth? Isn't negotiation a better path?" You are quite right in calling for negotiation. Indeed, this is the very purpose of direct action. Nonviolent direct action seeks to create such a crisis and foster such a tension that a community which has constantly refused to negotiate is forced to confront the issue. It seeks so to dramatize the issue that it can no longer be ignored. My citing the creation of tension as part of the work of the nonviolent-resister may sound rather shocking. But I must confess that I am not afraid of the word "tension." I have earnestly opposed violent tension, but there is a type of constructive, nonviolent tension which is necessary for growth. Just as Socrates felt that it was necessary to create a tension in the mind so that individuals could rise from the bondage of myths and half-truths to the unfettered realm of creative analysis and objective appraisal, so must we see the need for nonviolent gadflies to create the kind of tension in society that will help men rise from the dark depths of prejudice and racism to the majestic heights of understanding and brotherhood. . . .

Lamentably, it is an historical fact that privileged groups seldom give up their privileges voluntarily. Individuals may see the moral light and voluntarily give up their unjust posture; but, as Reinhold Niebuhr has reminded us, groups tend to be more immoral than individuals.

We know through painful experience that freedom is never voluntarily given by the oppressor; it must be demanded by the oppressed. Frankly, I have yet to engage in a direct-action campaign that was "well timed" in the view of those who have not suffered unduly from the disease of segregation. For years now I have heard the word "Wait!" It rings in the ear of every Negro with piercing familiarity. This "Wait" has almost always meant "Never." We must come to see, with one of our distinguished jurists, that "justice too long delayed is justice denied."

We have waited for more than 340 years for our constitutional and God-given rights. The nations of Asia and Africa are moving with jetlike speed toward gaining political independence, but we still creep at horse-and-buggy pace toward gaining a cup of coffee at a lunch counter. Perhaps it is easy for those who have never felt the stinging darts of segregation to say, "Wait." But when you have seen vicious mobs lynch your mothers and fathers at will and drown your sisters and brothers at whim; when you have seen hate-filled policemen curse, kick, and even kill your black brothers and sisters; when you see the vast majority of your 20 million Negro brothers smothering in an airtight cage of poverty in the midst of an affluent society; when you suddenly find your tongue twisted and your speech stammering as you seek to explain to your six-year-old daughter why she can't go to the public amusement park that has just been advertised on television, and see tears welling up in her eyes when she is told that Funtown is closed to colored children, and see ominous clouds of inferiority beginning to form in her little mental sky, and see her beginning to distort her personality by developing an unconscious bitterness toward white people; when you have to concoct an answer for a five-year-old son who is asking, "Daddy, why do white people treat colored people so mean?"; when you take a cross-country drive and find it necessary to sleep night after night in the uncomfortable corners of your automobile because no motel will accept you; when you are humiliated day in and day out by nagging signs reading "white" and "colored"; when your first name becomes "nigger,"

your middle name becomes "boy" (however old you are) and your last name becomes "John," and your wife and mother are never given the respected title "Mrs."; when you are harried by day and haunted by night by the fact that you are a Negro, living constantly at tiptoe stance, never quite knowing what to expect next, and are plagued with inner fears and outer resentments; when you are forever fighting a degenerating sense of "nobodiness"—then you will understand why we find it difficult to wait. There comes a time when the cup of endurance runs over, and men are no longer willing to be plunged into the abyss of despair. I hope, sirs, you can understand our legitimate and unavoidable impatience.

You express a great deal of anxiety over our willingness to break laws. This is certainly a legitimate concern. Since we so diligently urge people to obey the Supreme Court's decision of 1954 outlawing segregation in the public schools, at first glance it may seem rather paradoxical for us consciously to break laws. One may well ask, "How can you advocate breaking some laws and obeying others?" The answer lies in the fact that there are two types of laws: just and unjust. I would be the first to advocate obeying just laws. One has not only a legal but a moral responsibility to obey just laws. Conversely, one has a moral responsibility to disobey unjust laws. I would agree with St. Augustine that "an unjust law is no law at all."

Now, what is the difference between the two? How does one determine whether a law is just or unjust? A just law is a man-made code that squares with the moral law or the law of God. An unjust law is a code that is out of harmony with the moral law. To put it in the terms of St. Thomas Aquinas: An unjust law is a human law that is not rooted in eternal law and natural law. Any law that uplifts human personality is just. Any law that degrades human personality is unjust. All segregation statutes are unjust because segregation distorts the soul and damages the personality. It gives the segregator a false sense of superiority and the segregated a false sense of inferiority. Segregation, to use the terminology of the Jewish philosopher Martin Buber, substitutes an "I–it" relationship for an "I–thou" relationship and ends up relegating persons to the status of things. Hence segregation is not only politically, economically, and sociologically unsound, it is morally wrong and sinful. Paul Tillich has said that sin is separation. Is not segregation an existential expression of man's tragic separation, his awful estrangement, his terrible sinfulness? Thus it is that I can urge men to obey the 1954 decision of the Supreme Court, for it is morally right; and I can urge them to disobey segregation ordinances, for they are morally wrong.

Let us consider a more concrete example of just and unjust laws. An unjust law is a code that a numerical or power majority group compels a minority group to obey but does not make binding on itself. This is *difference* made legal. By the same token, a just law is a code that a majority compels a minority to follow and that it is willing to follow itself. This is *sameness* made legal.

Let me give another explanation. A law is unjust if it is inflicted on a minority that, as a result of being denied the right to vote, had no part in enacting or devising the law. Who can say that the legislature of Alabama which set up that state's segregation laws was democratically elected? Throughout Alabama all sorts of devious methods are used to prevent Negroes from becoming registered voters, and there are some counties in which, even though Negroes constitute a majority of the population, not a single Negro is registered. Can any law enacted under such circumstances be considered democratically structured? . . .

We should never forget that everything Adolf Hitler did in Germany was "legal," and everything the Hungarian freedom fighters did in Hungary was "illegal." It was "illegal" to aid and comfort a Jew in Hitler's Germany. Even so, I am sure that, had I lived in Germany at the time, I would have aided and comforted my Jewish brothers. If today I lived in a Communist country where certain principles dear to the Christian faith are suppressed, I would openly advocate disobeying that country's anti-religious laws. . . .

I had hoped that the white moderate would understand that law and order exist for the purpose of establishing justice and that when they fail in this purpose they become the dangerously structured dams that block the flow of social progress. I had hoped that the white moderate would understand that the present tension in the South is a necessary phase of the transition from an obnoxious negative

peace, in which the Negro passively accepted his unjust plight, to a substantive and positive peace, in which all men will respect the dignity and worth of human personality. Actually, we who engage in nonviolent direct action are not the creators of tension. We merely bring to the surface the hidden tension that is already alive. We bring it out in the open, where it can be seen and dealt with. Like a boil that can never be cured so long as it is covered up but must be opened with all its ugliness to the natural medicines of air and light, injustice must be exposed, with all the tension its exposure creates, to the light of human conscience and the air of national opinion before it can be cured.

. . . Human progress never rolls in on wheels of inevitability; it comes through the tireless efforts of men willing to be co-workers with God, and without this hard work, time itself becomes an ally of the forces of social stagnation. We must use time creatively, in the knowledge that the time is always ripe to do right. Now is the time to make real the promise of democracy and transform our pending national elegy into a creative psalm of brotherhood. Now is the time to lift our national policy from the quicksand of racial injustice to the solid rock of human dignity. . . .

Oppressed people cannot remain oppressed forever. The yearning for freedom eventually manifests itself, and that is what has happened to the American Negro. Something within has reminded him of his birthright of freedom, and something without has reminded him that it can be gained. Consciously or unconsciously, he has been caught up by the *Zeitgeist*, and with his black brothers of Africa and his brown and yellow brothers of Asia, South America, and the Caribbean, the United States Negro is moving with a sense of great urgency toward the promised land of racial justice. If one recognizes this vital urge that has engulfed the Negro community, one should readily understand why public demonstrations are taking place. The Negro has many pent-up resentments and latent frustrations, and he must release them. So let him march; let him make prayer pilgrimages to the city hall; let him go on freedom rides—and try to understand why he must do so. If his repressed emotions are not released in nonviolent ways, they will seek expression through violence; this is not a threat but a fact of history. So I have not said to my people, "Get rid of your discontent." Rather, I have tried to say that this normal and healthy discontent can be channeled into the creative outlet of nonviolent direct action. And now this approach is being termed extremist.

But though I was initially disappointed at being categorized as an extremist, as I continued to think about the matter I gradually gained a measure of satisfaction from the label. Was not Jesus an extremist for love: "Love your enemies, bless them that curse you, do good to them that hate you, and pray for them which despitefully use you, and persecute you." Was not Amos an extremist for justice: "Let justice roll down like waters and righteousness like an ever-flowing stream." Was not Paul an extremist for the Christian gospel: "I bear in my body the marks of the Lord Jesus." Was not Martin Luther an extremist: "Here I stand; I cannot do otherwise, so help me God." And John Bunyan: "I will stay in jail to the end of my days before I make a butchery of my conscience." And Abraham Lincoln: "This nation cannot survive half slave and half free." And Thomas Jefferson: "We hold these truths to be self-evident, that all men are created equal. . . . " So the question is not whether we will be extremists, but what kind of extremists we will be. Will we be extremists for hate or for love? Will we be extremists for the preservation of injustice or for the extension of justice? In that dramatic scene on Calvary's hill three men were crucified. We must never forget that all three were crucified for the same crime—the crime of extremism. Two were extremists for immorality, and thus fell below their environment. The other, Jesus Christ, was an extremist for love, truth and goodness, and thereby rose above his environment. Perhaps the South, the nation, and the world are in dire need of creative extremists.

I had hoped that the white moderate would see this need. Perhaps I was too optimistic; perhaps I expected too much. I suppose I should have realized that few members of the oppressor race can understand the deep groans and passionate yearnings of the oppressed race, and still fewer have the vision to see that injustice must be rooted out by strong, persistent, and determined action. I am thankful, however, that some of our white brothers in the South have grasped the meaning of this social revolution and committed themselves to it.

. . . I hope the church as a whole will meet the challenge of this decisive hour. But even if the church does not come to the aid of justice, I have no despair about the future. I have no fear about the outcome of our struggle in Birmingham, even if our motives are at present misunderstood. We will reach the goal of freedom in Birmingham and all over the nation, because the goal of America is freedom. Abused and scorned though we may be, our destiny is tied up with America's destiny. Before the pilgrims landed at Plymouth, we were here. Before the pen of Jefferson etched the majestic words of the Declaration of Independence across the pages of history, we were here. For more than two centuries our forebears labored in this country without wages; they made cotton king; they built the homes of their masters while suffering gross injustice and shameful humiliation—and yet out of a bottomless vitality they continued to thrive and develop. If the inexpressible cruelties of slavery could not stop us, the opposition we now face will surely fail. We will win our freedom because the sacred heritage of our nation and the eternal will of God are embodied in our echoing demands.

. . . One day the South will recognize its real heroes. They will be the James Merediths, with the noble sense of purpose that enables them to face jeering and hostile mobs, and with the agonizing loneliness that characterizes the life of the pioneer. They will be old, oppressed, battered Negro women, symbolized in a seventy-two-year-old woman in Montgomery, Alabama, who rose up with a sense of dignity and with her people decided not to ride segregated buses, and who responded with ungrammatical profundity to one who inquired about her weariness: "My feets is tired, but my soul is at rest." They will be the young high school and college students, the young ministers of the gospel and a host of their elders, courageously and nonviolently sitting in at lunch counters and willingly going to jail for conscience' sake. One day the South will know that when these disinherited children of God sat down at lunch counters, they were in reality standing up for what is best in the American dream and for the most sacred values in our Judaeo-Christian heritage, thereby bringing our nation back to those great wells of democracy which were dug deep by the founding fathers in their formulation of the Constitution and the Declaration of Independence.

Never before have I written so long a letter. I'm afraid it is much too long to take your precious time. I can assure you that it would have been much shorter if I had been writing from a comfortable desk, but what else can one do when he is alone in a narrow jail cell, other than write long letters, think long thoughts, and pray long prayers?

If I have said anything in this letter that overstates the truth and indicates an unreasonable impatience, I beg you to forgive me. If I have said anything that understates the truth and indicates my having a patience that allows me to settle for anything less than brotherhood, I beg God to forgive me.

I hope this letter finds you strong in the faith. I also hope that circumstances will soon make it possible for me to meet each of you, not as an integrationist or a civil-rights leader but as a fellow clergyman and a Christian brother. Let us all hope that the dark clouds of racial prejudice will soon pass away and the deep fog of misunderstanding will be lifted from our fear-drenched communities, and in some not too distant tomorrow the radiant stars of love and brotherhood will shine over our great nation with all their scintillating beauty.

Yours for the cause of Peace and Brotherhood,
Martin Luther King, Jr.

David P. Barash

HUMAN RIGHTS

Like Mark Twain's celebrated remark about the weather, it sometimes appears that everyone talks about human rights, but no one does anything about it. The truth, fortunately, is otherwise. To some extent, moreover, talking about human rights *is* doing something about it, because in many cases a focused attention to human rights, combined with the power of the international community's approval or disapproval, can be surprisingly effective.

The situation, however, is rather grim: nearly half the world's people are denied democratic freedoms and participation; more than half of Asia and black Africa do not have access to safe water; jails are filled with political prisoners, many of them held without trial and victimized by torture; child labor is widespread; women are often deprived of the economic, social, and political rights that men take for granted; many workers are not only unionized but prohibited even from forming unions; the right of conscientious objection to military service is not recognized in most countries; censorship is widespread; many millions of people are illiterate, chronically sick, without adequate shelter, and just plain hungry; the basic rights of homosexuals, indigenous people, the elderly, and the deviant are routinely trampled. And yet, concern with human rights has been growing, and real progress is being made, with more anticipated.

From *Introduction to Peace Studies* by David P. Barash. 1991. Belmont, CA: Wadsworth. Used by permission.

A BRIEF HISTORY OF HUMAN RIGHTS

It is tempting to claim that human rights are as old as the human species, but in truth, this is not so. Even if human rights themselves are God-given, inalienable, and fundamental, the conception of human rights as such—and respect for them—is relatively new. Individuals may possess rights and privileges, but these have traditionally been considered the province of society, to be bestowed or revoked by the larger unit (band, tribe, village, city, state) at will. In virtually all societies, for virtually all of human history, ultimate value derived from the social order, not the individual. Hence, an individual human being could not claim entitlement to very much, if anything, simply because he or she existed as a human being. . . .

It was not until the Enlightenment, particularly in Europe, that the concept of universal human rights for all people first gained prominence. It had existed before, but primarily as a smattering of isolated thought rather than a consistent, widespread trend.

According to this new perspective, a body of human rights exists that are intrinsic and not provable; they stem ultimately from the natural order of things, not from the laws of society or from human logic. Hence, this approach derives human rights from what is called "natural law," with its implication that such rights are established by an authority even higher than that of governments. Heraclitus (about 500 b.c.) wrote that "all human laws are nourished by one, which is divine. For it governs as far as it will, and is sufficient for all, and more than enough." And Aristotle, in his *Ethics,* advanced the notion that "of political justice, part is natural, part legal—natural, that which everywhere has the same force and does not exist by people's thinking this or that." When the natural law viewpoint reappeared during the Enlightenment, it was used especially to counter claims that kings ruled with absolute authority and by divine right. Finally, by the seventeenth and eighteenth centuries, the concept crystalized that people possess inherent rights, and that it is society's job to *recognize* these preexisting rights, not to create them.

The idea of human rights as currently understood . . . is largely a Western tradition, deriving especially from the work of John Locke and John Stuart Mill. Locke maintained that the fundamental human right was the right to property, the primary one being the right to the secure ownership of one's own body; civil and political rights flowed, in his view, from this. And Mill strove to identify a set of rights not covered by the state. Thus, there is some truth to the criticism that Western human rights advocates may occasionally be guilty of moral arrogance, seeking to export their own rather culture-bound ideas, especially their emphasis on civil/political freedom.

It should also be emphasized that Western political thought is not limited to individualism and human rights; rather, it coexists with respect for—and often, virtual worship of—the state. According to influential theorists such as Hegel and Herder, rights are enlarged and created for individuals only through the actions of the state. And for orthodox Marxists, value derives only from the social order; in Marxist analysis, individual rights do not exist unless they are explicitly granted by society. Although Communist societies are supposedly designed to maximize the benefits of every person, the "rights" of each individual come to naught if they run counter to the greater good of society as a whole. Individuals can expect to receive benefits from a community only insofar as they participate in it, and further its goals. And as we shall see, even today—with ever-increasing agreement on the meaning and desirability of human rights—there continues to be substantial disagreement as to priorities.

Human Rights in the Twentieth Century

Internationally, there was very little concern with human rights until quite recently, after World War II. Despite the Enlightenment, despite capitalism's emphasis on individual property rights, and despite democracy's emphasis on individual political rights, as a practical matter, state sovereignty has long superseded human rights. When the worldwide state system was established in the mid-seventeenth century, governments agreed—ostensibly in the interest of world peace—not to concern themselves very much with how other governments treated their own citizens. Within its own boundaries, each state was supreme and could do as it wished.

Gradually, however, human rights law developed, initially out of concern for protecting persons during armed conflict. The Geneva Convention of 1864, for example, sought to establish standards for treatment of wounded soldiers and of prisoners. (It is ironic that war—the most inhumane of situations—should have led to the first organized recognition of shared humanitarian values.) The International Committee of the Red Cross is a notable nongovernmental organization long concerned with international human rights; it was organized by a group of Swiss citizens, involved in the 1864 Geneva Conference. . . .

Following World War I, there was widespread recognition that one cause of that conflict had been the denial of national rights within large empires such as Austria's. Hence, human rights received explicit attention from the League of Nations, which emphasized that the rights of minorities must be respected by larger federal governments. Labor rights—the right to organize and to decent working conditions and wages, and restrictions on child labor—were the focus of the International Labor Organization, which later functioned within the United Nations. Opposition to slavery catalyzed numerous early human rights organizations, such as the Anti-Slavery League. (Most Americans do not realize that in many countries, slavery was only abolished during the 1950s; some claim that it is still being practiced today, in Mauritania and Pakistan.)

Organized, worldwide concern for human rights did not really coalesce until after World War II, perhaps in part as a reaction to the devastating denials of rights that occurred in association with that conflict. In the aftermath of the Nazi Holocaust most especially, the world's conscience was finally activated—partly out of regret for those who had suffered, and partly, too, out of enlightened self-interest. Martin Niemoeller put it memorably:

> First they came for the Jews and I did not speak out—because I was not a Jew. Then they came for the Communists and I did not speak out—because I was not a Communist. Then they came for the trade unionists and I did not speak out—because I was not a trade unionist. Then they came for me—and there was no one left to speak out for me.[4]

_____
[4] In fact, Pastor Niemoeller himself became a victim of the Nazis.

In recent decades, the world's people have begun to speak out for themselves and for human rights of every sort. Before we review some of the legal protections, conventions, and treaties that have resulted, let us consider the question of what is meant by human rights, and how they have come to be asserted.

THE POLITICAL PHILOSOPHY OF HUMAN RIGHTS

Human rights implies a new way of viewing the relationship of governments and their peoples, whereby governance is intended to enhance the dignity of human beings, not exploit them. With this in mind, let us examine three major political philosophies of human rights, each of which is divisible into two branches.

Liberalism

In traditional liberal thought, human rights exist not only because of their contribution to human dignity, but also because human beings, themselves, naturally possess such rights. "The object of any obligation," wrote the philosopher Simone Weil,

> in the realm of human affairs, is always the human being as such. There exists an obligation towards every human being for the sole reason that he or she is a human being, ...

In Jefferson's phrase, people have certain "inalienable rights" that may not be denied. The liberal view of human rights thus corresponds to the "natural law" perspective. One of the great classical liberals, John Locke, argued that civil law, to be valid, must be tested against this "natural law," which is the ultimate arbiter of justice. And when the framers of the Declaration of Independence complained of a "long train of abuses and usurpations" on the part of King George III, it was precisely natural law that they believed was being abused and usurped.

Another liberal theory of human rights derives from "utilitarianism," especially the works of John Stuart Mill and Jeremy Bentham. The idea here is that society should value whatever is utilitarian, or useful, in maximizing human happiness and freedom. The best-known motto of utilitarianism is "the greatest good for the greatest number," although individual freedom and equality are recognized as well, so as to prevent tyranny by the majority. Social betterment is to be achieved through equality and maximum personal liberty. . . .

Conservatism

Traditional conservatism is rarely articulated today with respect to human rights, because it is in large part a philosophy of unequal rights and privileges, and as such, difficult to defend in an avowedly egalitarian age. But the unspoken tenets of conservatism are nonetheless influential in actual practice. Classical conservatism can be said to have originated with Plato, who argued in *The Republic* that all people are not equal, and that the best form of government is therefore not democracy, but rule by a philosopher–king. This belief in unequal rights underpins many right-wing governments, from the "classical conservatism" of the military juntas that ruled Brazil and Greece, as well as the various U.S.-sponsored Central American governments (Guatemala, Honduras, Panama), to the neo-fascist dictatorships that arose in Chile and Paraguay, where rights were reserved only for the most powerful. More recently–especially in the United States–conservatives have been especially concerned with the denial of religious freedom in certain countries, notably China, which, despite its embrace of state-supported capitalism, remains officially communist and thus, atheist.

Group-oriented Oriented Philosophies

Finally, there is a third branch of human rights philosophy, which, for want of a better term, might be called "group oriented." It can be subdivided into two branches, Marxist and nationalist. For Karl Marx, individuals were not independent actors; rather, they were controlled by economic forces, pawns in a relentless class struggle. In the Marxist view, the liberal emphasis on individual rights is therefore misplaced, a bourgeois luxury, form without substance. Instead, rights are conferred by society, and they should belong exclusively to the proletariat (the working class). Such an approach leads automatically to an embrace of socioeconomic rights and material equality, with a downplaying of civil/political rights. Thus, in Marxist societies, freedom of speech and opinion are permitted insofar as they do not conflict with the stated goals of group advancement and welfare. The state, and not the working class, typically becomes paramount. . . .

The second version of group-oriented human rights has a leftist flavor, but is not, strictly speaking, Marxist. It originates instead in the experience of national liberation movements, and places special emphasis on the right to national self-determination and economic development, from which all other rights are then derived. Believers in the human right to national self-determination downplay the individual as well as the social class, although they remain committed to equal rights. Emphasis instead is on the rights of a national grouping. This approach lay behind the "Universal Declaration of the Rights of Peoples," which grew out of a meeting of highly regarded, nongovernmental third world spokespersons in 1976. The first three articles in this thirty-article document read as follows:

1. Every people has the right to existence.
2. Every people has the right to the respect of its national and cultural identity.
3. Every people has the right to retain peaceful possession of its territory and to return to it if it is expelled.

. . . The emphasis on "people's rights" clearly distinguishes this approach from the Western focus on "individual rights."

Nationalist group-oriented regimes are found in many third world states, such as Algeria and Zimbabwe, which are often leftist, but rarely Communist. Tanzanian president Julius Nyerere was one of the most articulate spokespersons for the nationalist group-oriented point of view:

For what do we mean when we talk of freedom? First, there is national freedom; that is, the ability of the citizens of Tanzania to determine their own future, and to govern themselves without interference from non-Tanzanians. Second, there is freedom from hunger, disease, and poverty. And third, there is personal freedom for the individual; that is, his right to live in dignity and equality with all others, his right to freedom of speech.

The difference between this viewpoint and the others (classical and egalitarian liberal, classical and neofascist conservative, Marxist group-oriented) is more one of emphasis than of absolutes. But the "rights" associated with individual competition—so dear to the liberal conception of human rights—are devalued. "The important thing for us," explains Nyerere, "is the extent to which we succeed in preventing the exploitation of one man by another, and in spreading the concept of working together cooperatively for the common good instead of competitively for individual private gain." . . .

On balance, capitalist democracies give insufficient attention to socioeconomic rights, while socialist governments take inadequate account of civil/political ones. Recent evidence suggests that economic development is more rapid under capitalism: but relatively little benefit from such development actually reaches the poorest citizens. . . .

Those who are wealthy and privileged characteristically favor maximum freedom (especially, freedom of economic competition) and a minimal role for government, which, at least in the United States, often leads in turn to opposition to the "welfare state" or resistance to affirmative action plans. Those lacking in wealth and power are typically more in need of laws and specified rights, to be assured by society. Hence, Western governments tend to describe socioeconomic rights as not really "human rights" at all, but rather, goals or aspirations for society.

As we shall see, human rights can be characterized in many ways, although a global consensus has been developing that incorporates not only the traditional American concern with political liberty, but also the second and third world concern with socioeconomic rights, as well as additional values that are difficult to pigeonhole. Many other rights are also asserted—states' rights, consumer rights— but to suggest that something is a "human right" is to claim something particularly fundamental and weighty, and should not be done lightly. . . .

Citizens of the United States need to recognize the importance that large numbers of people, especially in the second and third worlds, attribute to

socioeconomic rights. In the words of Leopold Senghor, former president of Senegal, "human rights begin with breakfast." Without such an awareness, relatively well-off Westerners too quickly sneer at the poor "rights" records of other countries, oblivious to their own shortcomings in the eyes of others. In addition, once we recognize the validity of socioeconomic rights, then governments such as Libya under Qaddafi or Cuba under Castro—which to many in the West are failures in the civil/political sphere because of their lack of representative government, widespread censorship, and torture and abuse of political prisoners—can be recognized as effective, even admirable, in other domains, such as public health or literacy. (This is not to claim that success in some dimensions of human rights cancels outrages in another; rather, it helps permit a more balanced perception of systems that might otherwise seem unidimensionally evil, and whose high level of domestic acceptance would otherwise be difficult for Americans to understand.) Thus, in an effort to identify basic human rights, Richard Falk has proposed the following:

1. *Basic human needs*: the rights of individuals and groups to food, housing, health, and education; the duty of governments to satisfy these rights. . . .
2. *Basic decencies*: the rights of individuals and groups to be protected against genocide, torture, arbitrary arrest, detention, and execution, or their threat; . . .
3. *Participatory rights*: the rights of individuals and groups to participate in the processes that control their lives, including choice of political leadership, of job, of place of residence, or cultural activity and orientation; . . .
4. *Security rights*: the rights of individuals and groups (including those of unborn generations) to be reasonably secure about their prospects of minimal physical well-being and survival; the duty of governments and peoples to uphold this right by working to achieve sustainable forms of national and ecological security . . . .

The Rights of Categories of People

We have thus far focused on the various rights themselves (civil, political, social, economic, and so on), rather than on the categories of people in whom such rights are supposed to inhere. But these categories are in many cases so important that, by themselves, they constitute major areas of concern. Women's rights is one example. Women comprise more than 50 percent of the world's population, and yet they are without doubt an oppressed group. For centuries, women have suffered from patriarchal social structures that devalue their personhood and deny many of their basic human rights. This includes a diverse array of abuses, such as footbinding in pre-Communist China, the forced seclusion and isolation of women in certain modern-day Hindu and Moslem societies, sexual mutilation as currently practiced on millions of young women in several African societies, polygamy, restricted or nonexistent choice as to marriage, and—even in ostensibly "liberated" societies such as those of the United States and Great Britain—greatly restricted economic and professional opportunities along with underrepresentation in political life.

Other groups also deserve attention. There are about 200 million indigenous people worldwide, representing national majorities in such states as Guatemala and Bolivia, and small minorities in such states as Brazil, Australia, and the United States. Regardless of their numbers, indigenous people are generally in dire straits, sometimes—as in Guatemala or Brazil—being subjected to outright genocide. In other cases, they are severely maltreated, and/or they enjoy dramatically fewer opportunities and privileges than their nonnative counterparts. Australian aborigines are the most imprisoned people on Earth, with an incarceration rate sixteen times that of the Caucasian population; the life expectancy of Mayan Indians in Guatemala is eleven years shorter than that of the nonindigenous population; the average per capita income of native Americans is one-half that of the rest of the U.S. population; large dams have devastated the homelands of indigenous peoples in Canada, Brazil, Norway, the Philippines, and India, depriving them of an arguably crucial human right: to live in their ancestral homelands. And this is but a partial list.

Other groups can also be identified as having particular human rights claims and vulnerabilities: the mentally ill, children, the homeless, racial minorities, the handicapped, convicts, unskilled workers, migrant laborers, refugees, political dissidents, the elderly, and so on. Ideally, human rights such as civil freedoms, economic opportunity, protection from mass destruction, and the right to a safe and clean environment will be equally shared by all people. In practice, these rights must often be defended most vigilantly for those groups that have thus far been the most victimized. . . .

It seems unavoidable that various rights will conflict. In a famous opinion, U.S. Supreme Court justice Oliver Wendell Holmes concluded that the right to free speech did not extend to yelling "Fire" in a crowded theater. The "right" to a drug-free environment may conflict with the "rights" to privacy, just as the "right" of third world people to healthy babies has already been found to conflict with the "right" of the Nestlé company to market substandard infant formula. In Islamic states, women's "rights" are often subordinated to the "rights" of people to practice the religion of their choice. A woman's "right" to control her own body, including an abortion if she desires, runs contrary to a fetus's "right" to life; the "right" of religious freedom can conflict with a child's "right" to necessary medical care, as when fundamentalist parents refuse lifesaving treatment for their child; the public's "right" to safe air travel appears to have triumphed over individual "rights" not to be searched without a warrant; and the list goes on. . . .

However they are sliced, many human rights are essentially claims against the authority of governments. As such, they are freedoms *from*—guarantees that governments will refrain from behaving badly toward their own people. These can be distinguished from freedoms *to*—the asserted obligations of society to help its members to achieve a better life. This distinction somewhat parallels the one between negative and positive peace—between those rights asserted *against* governments (no war, no intrusions into personal freedom) and those expected *of* them (establish positive peace, provide for basic human needs). In most cases, the first category (negative rights) seems easier for governments to achieve; certain states may simply lack the resources to make substantial improvements in socioeconomic conditions, but they all can stop torturing, murdering, and otherwise oppressing their people. . . .

UN-Related Agreements

In assessing the legal status of human rights, the UN Charter represents a useful starting point. Its major reference to human rights appears in Article 55:

With a view to the creation of conditions of stability and well-being which are necessary for peaceful and friendly relations among nations based on respect for the principle of equal rights and self-determination of peoples, the United Nations shall promote: a. higher standards of living, full employment, and conditions of economic and social progress and development; b. solutions of international economic, social, health, and related problems, and international cultural and educational cooperation; and c. universal respect for, and observance of, human rights and fundamental freedoms for all without distinction as to race, sex, language, or religion.

But if the UN Charter serves as a constitution, it lacks a bill of rights, specifying which human rights are to be "respected" and "observed." This was accomplished largely by the UN-sponsored Universal Declaration of Human Rights (UDHR), passed unanimously in 1948. Thus, after the UN Charter endorsed human rights, the Universal Declaration went ahead and enumerated them. The United States was a major contributor to the UDHR; much of its impetus came from Eleanor Roosevelt, widow of the late U.S. president. The UDHR consists of thirty articles, of which the first twenty-one are primarily civil/political, prohibiting torture and arbitrary arrest, and guaranteeing freedom of assembly, religion, speech, emigration, and even the right to vote by secret ballot. The remaining articles are concerned with socioeconomic and cultural rights, including the right to work, to an "adequate" standard of living, to an education, and to some form of social security, and even specifying the right to vacations with pay.

The Universal Declaration is not technically binding in the sense of an international treaty; it is a recommendation only, and makes no provisions for enforcement. Nonetheless, it has had substantial impact on thinking worldwide. The UDHR is widely respected, and has legitimated concern with human rights; it has even been incorporated into many national constitutions. To some degree, it has become part of customary international law; accordingly, many judicial scholars argue that it has the literal force of law, although it is often violated. (It

should be noted that customary law is more universal and more durable than treaty law.) . . .

People dispute precisely what obligations member states undertake when, in the UN Charter, they agree to "promote universal respect for and observance" of human rights. Nonetheless, an underlying consensus has emerged. The accepted phrase is that governments have no business engaging in a "consistent pattern of gross violations of human rights." Thus, isolated incidents are unlikely to generate worldwide outrage. By contrast, "gross violations"— that is, serious, recurring acts—merit condemnation and, ultimately, such actions as censure, economic boycott, and possibly even military intervention. Abuses of this sort could include widespread torture, mass arrests and imprisonment without trial, genocide, and vicious policies of racial segregation and debasement. . . .

The Problem of Enforcement

Faced with the awesome, sovereign power of states, the international human rights regime can seem woefully inadequate, based as it is on mere legalisms or exhortations, and devoid of enforcement mechanisms. But legal systems always have difficulty controlling powerful actors—labor unions in Britain, for example, or large corporations in the United States. And ultimately, most of them rely on voluntary compliance. Some states have in fact complied voluntarily with international human rights norms, largely to achieve international legitimacy as well as to avoid ostracism.

Frustration with the rights-denying policies of states occasionally spills over into efforts to transcend the authority of states. Although lacking in legal authority, individuals of high moral and international standing have on occasion gathered together to fill what they see as a vacuum in the protection of human rights. So-called people's tribunals have periodically convened to draw attention to various human rights abuses. Most notable of these was the Russell Tribunal, which roundly criticized U.S. policy during the Vietnam War. The League for the Rights of Peoples, established in Rome in 1976, has held numerous sessions, evaluating repression under Marcos in the Philippines, offering a retrospective on Turkish genocide against Armenians from 1915 to 1916, and criticizing Brazil's behavior toward its indigenous Amazonian population, Indonesia's strong-arm tactics in East Timor, U.S. intervention in Central America, and Soviet intervention in Afghanistan, as well as questioning the legitimacy of nuclear weapons. Such actions are of uncertain effectiveness, but they do attract a degree of public attention, while also serving to undercut the presumption that only state-centered approaches are relevant in dealing with violations of human rights. . . .

An approach that emphasizes human rights represents a fundamentally new way of thinking about human dignity and world politics, reflecting as it does the determination that states must meet certain standards, both in their own domestic affairs and in their international relations. Even today, after several decades of vigorous pro–human rights advocacy, states typically act with primary regard to their power and perceived national interests, rather than according to the ideals of human rights. There is, as a result, the constant danger that concern for human rights will be sacrificed on the altar of state sovereignty, expediency, and realpolitik.

Human rights advocacy involves a different perspective from which to view the human condition and the goals of society and politics—as citizens of a larger community than individual states or nation-states. As opposed to the relatively narrow focus of states, concern with superordinate human rights requires that political barriers be transcended, in the search for human dignity on the widest possible scale. . . .

HUMAN RIGHTS AND PEACE

Human rights and peace are inextricably connected, in several ways. First, the denial of human rights is itself a denial of peace. A world in which there is no armed conflict, but in which fundamental human rights are thwarted, could not in any meaningful sense be considered peaceful. Speaking at the United Nations, Pope John Paul II explicitly linked human rights and war:

> The Universal Declaration of Human Rights has struck a real blow against the many deep roots of war since the spirit of war in its basic primordial meaning springs up . . . where the inalienable rights of men are violated. This is a new and

deeply relevant vision of the cause of peace. One that goes deeper and is more radical.

The pope's perspective applies to socioeconomic rights no less than civil/political ones. As one Scandinavian peace researcher has noted, "Whether a child dies in infancy due to poverty and consequent malnutrition and lack of hygiene, or if it grows up and at a later stage is executed as a political opponent, the society in which this happens must be considered hostile to human rights." And, we might add, to peace as well.

Second, there appears to be a connection between the way a state treats its own population and its inclinations toward other states. As Franklin Roosevelt put it, "We in this nation still believe that it [self-determination] should be predicated on certain freedoms which we think are essential everywhere. We know that we ourselves will never be wholly safe at home unless other governments recognize such freedoms." . . .

Third, a denial of human rights can provoke breaches of the peace, if other states become involved. Humanitarian intervention of this sort may be legal; certainly, there is ample precedent in the classical writings of international law. . . .

On the other hand, claims of humanitarian intervention have often been used as an excuse for aggression (of which the Spanish–American War may well be an example). Hitler claimed that dismemberment of Czechoslovakia and, later, the invasion of Poland were warranted to stop the persecution of both countries' German-speaking minorities. Vietnam invaded Cambodia ostensibly to oust the genocidal Khmer Rouge regime, and the United States explained its invasion of Grenada at least partly as a response to human rights violations on that Caribbean island. . . . (No comparable justifications were ever used by the United States to overthrow rightist regimes, including the Somoza dictatorship, which was far more abusive of human rights, or the government of El Salvador. . . .)

Finally, one of the widely recognized human rights—specified in the first articles of both 1966 human rights conventions—is that of national self-determination. Abuses of this right often lead directly to war, especially civil war . . . which makes this issue a difficult one. The pursuit of human rights may in fact lead more to violence than to peace, since human rights often are won by struggle and confrontation. Furthermore, it is not obvious whether all claims for national self-determination are worthy of success. Should there be independent states for . . . Basques, Welsh, Scots, Quebecois, and Native Americans? For its part, the UN Security Council has determined that, at least in certain cases, such as anticolonial struggles, a continuing denial of human rights constitutes a formal threat to international peace (this was applied to Zimbabwe, Namibia, and South Africa).

In summary, the connection between human rights and peace is complex and multifaceted. It is useful to claim that human rights contribute to peace, but the most fundamental connection may well be that such claims encourage adherence to human rights, for their own sake, regardless of whether this actually promotes peace as narrowly defined.

THE FUTURE

What of the future? Several things can be said with confidence. The first is that the question of human rights will continue to demand attention on the international agenda. . . .

A second safe conclusion is that the question of human rights will continue to be controversial, with different conceptions competing with one another, while the very notion of human rights competes with the basic inclination of states to engage in amoral, realpolitik maneuverings. The dilemma may be profound. Consider these realpolitik questions, for example, from the perspective of a government leader. What should a state do when confronted with this choice it desires a particular strategic relationship with another state, but that other state engages in human rights abuses. ? Which should be sacrificed, national strategy or a commitment to human rights? . . .

Perhaps, on the other hand, the "natural law" school is correct, and support of human rights is simply the right thing to do, period, regardless of its practical consequences. . . .

There is yet another possibility, a way station between the amorality of realpolitik and the

absolutism of morality for its own sake. Some argue that power (or at least, security) can readily be reconciled with human rights. . . . Former secretary of state Cyrus Vance echoed this sentiment when he observed: "We pursue our human rights objectives, not only because they are right, but because we have a stake in the stability that comes when people can express their hopes and find their futures freely. Our ideals and our interests coincide."

Promoting Human Rights

It is difficult to imagine exactly what a U.S. foreign policy would be if it was organized primarily around the promotion of human rights worldwide. However, the following specific actions, which have already been taken at different times in support of human rights, suggest the benefits to be gained from a continuation, to say nothing of an expansion, of such policies:

- *Subtle diplomacy.* Quiet, persistent pressure raised with offending governments has the advantage that the government in question need not worry about losing face if and when abuses are corrected. A disadvantage, beyond the high chance of being ignored, is that a government may claim that it is employing subtle diplomacy while it is actually doing nothing.
- *Public statements.* This involves drawing world attention to specific abuses and to governments that violate human rights. It may involve publicly dissociating one's own government from the unacceptable behavior of another. Human rights compliance can be promoted by publicizing violations through the publication of reports conducted by respected, impartial investigative commissions; especially in a world climate committed to human rights, most governments seek to avoid the embarrassment that comes with being branded a violator of these rights.
- *Symbolic acts.* Sending support to dissidents, either by words, by contact with opposition figures, or by otherwise indicating disapproval of abuses, is a way of emphasizing to both the offending government and its people that human rights violations are noticed and rejected.
- *Cultural penalties.* By isolating offenders at international cultural events, including athletic

contests and other exchanges, such governments are made to feel like pariahs. Although it is easy to scoff at such minimal "penalties," pride and the universal desire to be accepted enhance the impact of such actions.

- *Economic penalties.* Applying trade embargoes, renouncing investment in the offending country, refusing development loans and other forms of foreign aid—these actions can hurt the economy of offending countries, thereby putting pressure (often on the more wealthy and influential citizens) to modify policies and/or oust the government. . . .
- *Immigration.* Human rights activists, dissidents, and those being deprived of their human rights can be permitted to enter the United States. In the recent past, the "right" of immigration has been applied quite selectively, facilitating immigration by people fleeing leftist countries whose human rights policies the United States wishes to criticize, while making it very difficult for refugees from rightist countries that are allied to the United States, and whose human rights policies it is inclined to ignore or whitewash.
- *Legal approaches.* International law can be applied more vigorously, by indicting violators of human rights overseas, just as people involved in the international drug trade have occasionally been indicted and, when possible, extradited for trial.
- *Multilateral approaches.* The United States can commit itself to the various human rights organizations now ac-tiveactive worldwide, especially the United Nations Commission on Human Rights. . . .
- *Destabilization and belligerency.* The United States has actively sought to destabilize the governments of certain countries—for example, Nicaragua—at least in part, we are told, for their human rights abuses. This remains an option,

although of questionable legality or morality, unless the abuses are sufficiently flagrant, and unless the policy is applied evenhandedly to all regimes, regardless of ideology. Certainly, the human rights abuses of Nazi Germany and imperial Japan were influential in the U.S. decision to make war upon them, although these abuses actually became more serious after war was declared. The Tanzanian invasion of Uganda, which ultimately toppled the government of Idi Amin, won widespread support because that regime's human rights record was particularly atrocious. . . .

I conclude this discussion of human rights with an account by Jerome Shestack, a longtime human rights activist. Shestack recognizes the extraordinarily difficult and seemingly hopeless task of securing human rights worldwide, in the face of human cruelty, frailty, misunderstandings, and the power of states. He conjures up the Greek myth of Sisyphus, who was condemned to spend eternity pushing a boulder up a hill, only to have it roll back again just as he reached the top. Sisyphus' task is absurd, and yet—echoing the existential philosopher Albert Camus—Shestack points out that

> Sisyphus may turn out to be a more enduring hero than Hercules. For if, as Camus taught, life itself is absurd, Sisyphus represents the only triumph possible over that absurdity. In his constancy to reach that summit, even with failure preordained, Sisyphus demonstrated that the human spirit is indomitable and that dedication to a higher goal is in itself man's reason for living. . . . The realities of the world may foredoom a great part of the struggle and make most of the effort seem abysmal. Yet, the very struggle itself takes on symbolic meaning, enhancing human dignity. And when all is said and done, there is no other humane course to pursue.

STUDY QUESTIONS

1. Discuss the connections among overpopulation, poverty, and environmental destruction.
2. In some ways, "human rights" is like Mom and apple pie: everyone is in favor. But in fact, the question of human rights can be enormously controversial. Explain why.
3. Martin Luther King, Jr., once said that "injustice anywhere is an affront to justice everywhere." The merits of this statement are—or should be—obvious. But is there any sense in which this idea could be troublesome?
4. Agree or disagree with the notion that human rights are a Western concept that should not be applied to other societies. Take "female circumcision" as an example.
5. Look into the question of whether ecological stability and sustainability conflict with economic growth and development.
6. It is often said that one cannot make omelets without breaking eggs. Propose some guidelines to determine how many eggs, and of what sort, might legitimately be "broken" in order to establish positive peace.
7. Positive peace is as much a matter of national security as is negative peace. Agree or disagree with this argument, trying to be specific and "hard-headed" in your response.
8. Compare and contrast differences in wealth within a country with differences in wealth between countries; is the solution to such differences simply a matter of "development"?
9. When peace becomes a positive goal (as opposed to mere war prevention), then people feel inclined to fight for it; hence, it is better to aim "lower." Agree or disagree with this statement, using historical examples and/or plausible future scenarios.
10. Describe some successes in achieving positive peace. What can we learn from them? Do the same with some failures.

SUGGESTIONS FOR FURTHER READING

Barry, Brian. 2005. *Why Social Justice Matters*. New York: Polity Press.

Collier, Paul. 2008. *The Bottom Billion: Why the Poorest Countries are Failing and What Can Be Done about It*. New York: Oxford University Press.

Donnelly, Jack. 2002. *Universal Human Rights in Theory and Practice*. Ithaca, NY: Cornell University Press.

Hunt, Lynn. 2008. *Inventing Human Rights: A History*. New York: W. W. Norton.

Lockwood, Bert B., ed. 2006. *Women's Rights: A Human Rights Quarterly Reader*. Baltimore: Johns Hopkins University Press.

Philander, S. George. 2008. *Encyclopedia of Global Warming and Climate Change*. Los Angeles: Sage.

Pojman, Louis P., and Paul Pojman. 2007. *Environmental Ethics: Readings in Theory and Application*. Belmont, CA: Wadsworth.

Renner, Michael. 1996. *Fighting for Survival: Environmental Decline, Social Conflict, and the New Age of Insecurity*. New York: Norton.

Tietenberg, Tom. 2006. *Environmental Economics and Policy*. Boston: Addison Wesley.

Todaro, Michael P., and Stephen C. Smith. 2008. *Economic Development*. Boston: Addison Wesley.

CHAPTER 5

Nonviolence

M uch of the human world is structured by violence—the international political and military system perhaps most of all. Hence, a commitment to nonviolence is necessarily radical. Nonviolence is not limited to tactics for overcoming any one oppressive system—whether colonial domination, denial of civil rights, and so forth—but rather it seeks to overthrow all relationships based on violence, oppression, and the unfair domination of some by others. Thus, nonviolence is directly relevant not only to the prevention of war but also to the establishment of social justice, environmental protection, and the securing of human rights. Nonviolence seeks to change the terms whereby on which individuals and groups interact: , not only with each other, but even with planet Earth.

It can be argued, for example, that the destructive patterns whereby that people and states follow in interacting violently with one another are also reflected in the destructive style that characterizes so much of the interaction of people with their environment: the burning of rain forests, the clear-cutting of temperate woodlands, the gouging of the earth during strip mining, the pollution of water and air, the extinction of plant and animal species. All these can be seen as deriving from a lack of what Gandhi called *ahiṃsā*, best translated into English, perhaps, as "nonviolent love." This is not love of the sloppy, sentimental kind but is closer to the Christian concept of *agape*, a transcending love of connection and mutual commitment. It is also similar to Albert Schweitzer's concept of "reverence for life."

The poet Walt Whitman had this love in mind when he wrote the following:

Were you looking to be held together by lawyers?
Or by an agreement on paper? Or by arms?
Nay, nor the world, nor any living thing, will so cohere.
Only those who love each other shall become indivisible.

It must be emphasized that nonviolence has emerged as a definite, defiant, hard-headed strategy of social transformation. The very word "nonviolence" is thus unfortunate because it evokes images of passivity, especially in its regrettable counterpart, "passive resistance." This is akin to translating *light* as "nondarkness" or defining *good* as merely the absence of evil. Mohandas Gandhi, the greatest twentieth-century apostle of nonviolence, coined the word *satyagraha*, which can be translated literally from the Sanskrit as "soul-force" or "soul-truth." It This term incorporates such positive traits as courage, directness, friendly civility, absolute honesty, respect for other living creatures, and willingness to suffer in pursuit of deeply felt goals.

Traditionally, when conflicts are resolved by violence, they simply involve the triumph of one protagonist over the other. Such a "resolution" may occur via threat, persuasion, or compulsion by naked force, but, in any event, the presumption is that one side wins and the other loses: what mathematicians call a "zero-sum game." (In most competitive sports, for example, for every winner there is a loser, so the sum total of wins and losses equals zero.) By contrast, devotees of nonviolence seek to resolve the conflict at its source rather than to defeat or annihilate the opponent. The goal is to persuade the adversary that all parties have more to gain by acting in harmony and love than by persevering in discord and violence: —that is, that the parties are not really adversaries at all!

As we shall see, there have been numerous spokespeople for nonviolence and for creative nonviolent resistance. It was Gandhi, however, who most closely wedded theory to practice, employing nonviolence as a coherent approach to peace. For nonviolent activists in the Gandhian mold, violence itself is the enemy, and, thus, there is no room for violence in the arsenal of those who would effect creative, peaceful change. If the goal is a genuine social revolution, then the more violence, the less revolution: . "The practice of violence, like all action, changes the world," wrote social philosopher Hannah Arendt. "But the most probable change is to a more violent world."[1]

For practitioners of nonviolence, therefore, it is crucially important to recognize the interdependence of means and ends: a goal of peace can only be achieved by the use of nonviolence. For example, by using violent methods, revolutions (even the most well-meaning ones) and even antiwar movements can build up reservoirs of resentment and hatred, thereby laying the foundations for additional injustice and yet more violence. Political activists of the far left and far right are generally prone to make compromises with violence, convinced that their vision of the world-as-it-should-be justifies virtually any means of attaining it. Lenin announced, for example, that "to achieve our ends, we will unite even with the Devil."

Similarly, ideologues of the far right did not hesitate to make common cause with oppressive dictatorships—such as Somoza in Nicaragua, Marcos in the Philippines, Chun doo Hwan in South Korea, Pinochet in Chile, Duvalier in Haiti, the Shah in Iran, Suharto in Indonesia, Botha in South Africa—in the interest of a presumed greater good, the defeat or containment of international communism.

Cicero, in *The Letters to His Friends*, asks, "What can be done against force, without force?" Students of nonviolence would answer, "Plenty." They would, in fact, question whether anything effective, lasting, or ultimately worthwhile can be done against force,

---

[1] Hannah Arendt, *On Violence* (New York: Harcourt, Brace and World, 1969).

with force. The Rev. Martin Luther King, Jr., nonviolent leader of the civil rights movement in the United States—and a visionary who, like Gandhi, was also intensely practical and result-oriented—wrote that "returning violence for violence multiplies violence, adding deeper darkness to a night already devoid of stars. Darkness cannot drive out darkness; only light can do that. Hate cannot drive out hate; only love can do that." This does not mean that the practitioner of nonviolence is forbidden anger, even hate; rather, these feelings must be redirected creatively against various *systems* of evil rather than individuals.

What, then, does nonviolence look like in practice? It takes many forms: marches; boycotts; picketing; leafleting; strikes; civil disobedience; the peaceful occupation of various government facilities; vigils and fasts; mass imprisonment; tax resistance; and a willingness to be abused by the authorities and yet to respond nonviolently, with courage and determination, even politeness. Thus, the nonviolent struggle is if anything more intense and difficult than its violent counterpart. It is not an alternative to fighting, but, rather, a different (nonviolent and loving) way of doing so.

When a victim responds to violence with yet more violence, he or she is reacting in predictable, perhaps even instinctive ways. Violent responses validate the original attacker, even, in a way, vindicating the original violence as far as the attacker is concerned: because the opponent is so violent, then presumably he or she "deserved it." Thus, there is a widespread expectation of countervailing power analogous in the social sphere to Newton's first law, which states that for every action there is an equal and opposite reaction. Accustomed to counter-violence—and even, perhaps, hoping for it—the violent person who encounters a nonviolent opponent who is courageous and respectful, even loving, becomes a "victim" of a kind of moral judo in which the attacker's own energy is redirected, knocking him or her off balance.

It is said of some people and some nations that "they only understand force," and, therefore, they cannot be moved by anything other than force or the threat of force. The truth, however, may be precisely the opposite: those who understand and expect force can generally deal with it effectively. By contrast, the British authorities in India, like supporters of segregation laws in the U.S. South, were consistently thrown off balance and left flustered by the creative nonviolent tactics employed against their regime.

Historically, violent governmental overreaction has often worked to the ultimate detriment of the perpetrators, transforming victims into martyrs who became symbols of their regime's callous wrongheadedness. In 1819, for example, a nonviolent crowd in Manchester, England, was attacked by soldiers while listening to speeches calling for the repeal of the Corn Laws; this so-called Peterloo Massacre became a rallying cry for radicals who eventually succeeded in having their demands met. The slaughter of participants in the Paris Commune of 1871 led to greater solidarity among the French working class. In 1905, a large gathering of nonviolent Russian peasants in St. Petersburg, led by Father Gapon, attempted to submit a petition to Czar Nicholas, whose troops responded by slaughtering hundreds of unarmed people. This led to a general strike, which ushered in some limited democratic reforms but, more important, also signaled the beginning of the end for czarist tyranny. When the Russian Revolution finally took place, thirteen years later, it was in many ways the culmination of mounting popular revulsion at the czar's wanton violence toward his own people.

The arrest and beating of U.S. civil rights protesters during the 1950s and early 1960s, along with the murder of civil rights workers and innocent bystanders (including children), was instrumental in bringing about desegregation and the passing of the subsequent Civil Rights and Voting Rights Acts. The "police riot" at the 1968 Democratic Party Convention in Chicago led to widespread condemnation of the political system, just as the killing of four unarmed students at Kent State University in 1970 galvanized sentiment against the Vietnam War. The 1988 Israeli policy of beating Palestinian protesters who sought an end to Israeli occupation of the West Bank led to solidification of Palestinian sentiment and subjected the Israeli government to greater pressure for a negotiated agreement. In 1989, when nonviolent protesters—mostly students—occupied Tiananmen Square and demanded political reforms, the Chinese government responded with tanks and the slaughter of hundreds, perhaps thousands of protesters. Although the Chinese government has thus far survived this episode, it seems clear that when nonviolent protesters are abused, the world's conscience is aroused, and significant changes are often set in motion.

Nonviolent protest has accomplished much more than the creation of martyrs. In 1986, for example, the corrupt dictatorship of Ferdinand Marcos in the Philippines was toppled, largely due to "people power," the persistent nonviolence of Filipino civilians. Strongly supported by the Catholic church, crowds of unarmed Filipinos at one point interposed themselves between a small number of dissident troops and those ostensibly loyal to Marcos, who had been ordered to suppress their opponents. When it became evident that his own military would not fire on the nonviolent, unarmed populace, it was clear that the end of the Marcos regime had come. Similar campaigns caused the ouster of the long-lasting Duvalier regime in Haiti and produced the first ever democratic government in South Korea. And the prodemocracy movement in Eastern Europe succeeded in throwing off Communist domination with through essentially nonviolent techniques (except in Romania). It is also notable that in many countries, this "Velvet Revolution"—so named because of the virtual absence of bloodshed—was hastened by instances in which the repressive government reacted violently to nonviolent protesters . . . which in turn served to delegitimate the government itself.

This pattern continued into the 21st twenty-first century as well, with initially, the so-called Rose Revolution in Georgia, the Orange Revolution in Ukraine, and the Tulip Revolution in Kyrgyzstan, among others. More recently, the pro-democracy "Arab Spring" of 2010 and 2011 was largely nonviolent (at least on the part of the protestors in Tunisia, Egypt and Bahrain); its outcome surprised most observers who had concluded that change in these societies would come only–if at all–with considerable lethal violence.

This is but a small and but highly selective sampling of nonviolent protest. It is noteworthy that examples of "successful" violence are far better known—although not necessarily more numerous or important—than their successful nonviolent counterparts. The argument can in fact be made that violent outcomes are, by definition, failures and that nonviolence represents the best in our politics and in human potential.

Henry David Thoreau

CIVIL DISOBEDIENCE

Henry David Thoreau was not, strictly speaking, an advocate of nonviolence. However, he was deeply troubled by government misbehavior, notably the institution of slavery and the Mexican–American War, which he saw as a blatant act of imperialist aggression by the United States. Thoreau protested by famously refusing to pay taxes and was imprisoned as a result. He was influential in developing the concept of civil disobedience and had a powerful effect on the thinking of Leo Tolstoy and Mohandas Gandhi, among many others. Thoreau, in turn himself—like Gandhi after him—had been influenced by the Bhagavad Gita, the great Hindu epic that emphasized the importance of renouncing personal possessiveness and striving in pursuit of greater aims.

Advocates of civil disobedience have long been considered unpatriotic, not only because they recommend a less bellicose stand toward proclaimed national "enemies" but also because their efforts are in some ways subversive of accepted national values. When, in the 1960s, Black Power advocate H. Rap Brown pointed out that violence was "as American as cherry pie," he spoke a part of the truth. So did theologian and peace activist Thomas Merton, when he warned that the sources of violence can be found

> not in esoteric groups but in the very culture itself, its mass media, its extreme individualism and competitiveness, its inflated myths of virility and toughness, and its overwhelming preoccupation [with means of destruction].[2]

Thoreau's call for civil disobedience and for the priority of conscience, combined with the image of him living in relative isolation by the shores of Walden Pond, challenge us to consider the position of the peace activist as principled outsider. Thus, pacifism and tax resistance, for example, are warily tolerated in the United States so long as they are performed by small and uninfluential groups. But, as Thomas Merton pointed out,

> There is also an implication that any minority stand against war on grounds of conscience is *ipso facto* a kind of deviant and morally eccentric position, to be tolerated only because there are always a few religious half-wits around in any case, and one has to humor them in order to preserve the nation's reputation for respecting individual liberty.[3]

The following selection is from Thoreau's essay "Civil Disobedience."

───────────── ❀ ─────────────

[2] Thomas Merton, *The Non-Violent Alternative* (New York: Farrar, Straus & Giroux, 1980).
[3] Merton, *Non-Violent Alternative.*

From *Civil Disobedience: Theory and Practice* by Henry David Thoreau.

I heartily accept the motto—"That government is best which governs least"; and I should like to see it acted up to more rapidly and systematically. Carried out, it finally amounts to this, which also I believe—"That government is best which governs not at all"; and when men are prepared for it, that will be the kind of government which they will have. Government is at best but an expedient; but most governments are usually, and all governments are sometimes, inexpedient. The objections which have been brought against a standing army, and they are many and weighty, and deserve to prevail, may also at last be brought against a standing government. The standing army is only an arm of the standing government. The government itself, which is only the mode which the people have chosen to execute their will, is equally liable to be abused and perverted before the people can act through it. Witness the present Mexican war, the work of comparatively a few individuals using the standing government as their tool; for, in the outset, the people would not have consented to this measure.

This American government—what is it but a tradition, though a recent one, endeavoring to transmit itself unimpaired to posterity, but each instant losing some of its integrity? It has not the vitality and force of a single living man; for a single man can bend it to his will. It is a sort of wooden gun to the people themselves. But it is not the less necessary for this; for the people must have some complicated machinery or other, and hear its din, to satisfy that idea of government which they have. Governments show thus how successfully men can be imposed on, even impose on themselves, for their own advantage. It is excellent, we must all allow. Yet this government never of itself furthered any enterprise, but by the alacrity with which it got out of its way. *It* does not keep the country free. *It* does not settle the West. *It* does not educate. The character inherent in the American people has done all that has been accomplished; and it would have done somewhat more, if the government had not sometimes got in its way. For government is an expedient by which men would fain succeed in letting one another alone; and, as has been said, when it is most expedient, the governed are most let alone by it. . . .

But, to speak practically and as a citizen, unlike those who call themselves no-government men, I ask for, not at once no government, but *at once* a better government. Let every man make known what kind of government would command his respect, and that will be one step toward obtaining it.

. . . I think that we should be men first, and subjects afterward. It is not desirable to cultivate a respect for the law, so much as for the right. The only obligation which I have a right to assume, is to do at any time what I think right. It is truly enough said, that a corporation has no conscience; but a corporation of conscientious men is a corporation *with* a conscience. Law never made men a whit more just; and, by means of their respect for it, even the well-disposed are daily made the agents of injustice. A common and natural result of an undue respect for law is, that you may see a file of soldiers, colonel, captain, corporal, privates, powder monkeys, and all, marching in admirable order over hill and dale to the wars, against their wills, ay, against their common sense and consciences, which makes it very steep marching indeed, and produces a palpitation of the heart. They have no doubt that it is a damnable business in which they are concerned; they are all peaceably inclined. Now, what are they? Men at all? or small movable forts and magazines, at the service of some unscrupulous man in power? . . .

The mass of men serve the state thus, not as men mainly, but as machines, with their bodies. They are the standing army, and the militia, jailers, constables, posse comitatus, & c. In most cases there is no free exercise whatever of the judgment or of the moral sense; but they put themselves on a level with wood and earth and stones; and wooden men can perhaps be manufactured that will serve the purpose as well. Such command no more respect than men of straw or a lump of dirt. They have the same sort of worth only as horses and dogs. Yet such as these even are commonly esteemed good citizens. Others—as most legislators, politicians, lawyers, ministers, and officeholders—serve the state chiefly with their heads; and, as they rarely make any moral distinctions, they are as likely to serve the Devil, without *intending* it, as God. A very few, as heroes, patriots, martyrs, reformers in the great sense, and *men*, serve the state with the consciences also, and so necessarily resist it for the most part; and they are commonly treated as enemies by it. . . .

How does it become a man to behave toward this American government to-day? I answer, that he cannot without disgrace be associated with it. I cannot for an instant recognize the political organization as *my* government which is the *slave's* government also.

All men recognize the right of revolution; that is, the right to refuse allegiance to, and to resist, the government, when its tyranny or its inefficiency are great and unendurable. But almost all say that such is not the case now. But such was the case, they think, in the Revolution of '75. If one were to tell me that this was a bad government because it taxed certain foreign commodities brought to its ports, it is most probable that I should not make an ado about it, for I can do without them. All machines have their friction; and possibly this does enough good to counterbalance the evil. At any rate, it is a great evil to make a stir about it. But when the friction comes to have its machine, and oppression and robbery are organized, I say, let us not have such a machine any longer. In other words, when a sixth of the population of a nation which has undertaken to be the refuge of liberty are slaves, and a whole country is unjustly overrun and conquered by a foreign army, and subjected to military law, I think that it is not too soon for honest men to rebel and revolutionize. What makes this duty the more urgent is the fact, that the country so overrun is not our own, but ours is the invading army.

. . . I quarrel not with far-off foes, but with those who, near at home, cooperate with, and do the bidding of, those far away, and without whom the latter would be harmless. We are accustomed to say, that the mass of men are unprepared; but improvement is slow, because the few are not materially wiser or better than the many. It is not so important that many should be as good as you, as that there be some absolute goodness somewhere; for that will leaven the whole lump. There are thousands who are *in opinion* opposed to slavery and to the war, who yet in effect do nothing to put an end to them; who, esteeming themselves children of Washington and Franklin, sit down with their hands in their pockets, and say that they know not what to do, and do nothing; who even postpone the question of freedom to the question of free-trade, and quietly read the prices-current along with the latest advices from Mexico, after dinner, and, it may be, fall asleep over them both. What is the price-current of an honest man and patriot to-day? They hesitate, and they regret, and sometimes they petition; but they do nothing in earnest and with effect. They will wait, well disposed, for others to remedy the evil, that they may no longer have it to regret. . . .

It is not a man's duty, as a matter of course, to devote himself to the eradication of any, even the most enormous wrong; he may still properly have other concerns to engage him; but it is his duty, at least, to wash his hands of it, and, if he gives it no thought longer, not to give it practically his support. If I devote myself to other pursuits and contemplations, I must first see, at least, that I do not pursue them sitting upon another man's shoulders. I must get off him first, that he may pursue his contemplations too. See what gross inconsistency is tolerated. I have heard some of my townsmen say, "I should like to have them order me out to help put down an insurrection of the slaves, or to march to Mexico—see if I would go"; and yet these very men have each, directly by their allegiance, and so indirectly, at least, by their money, furnished a substitute. . . .

How can a man be satisfied to entertain an opinion merely, and enjoy *it*? Is there any enjoyment in it, if his opinion is that he is aggrieved? If you are cheated out of a single dollar by your neighbor, you do not rest satisfied with knowing that you are cheated, or with saying that you are cheated, or even with petitioning him to pay you your due; but you take effectual steps at once to obtain the full amount, and see that you are never cheated again. Action from principle, the perception and the performance of right, changes things and relations; it is essentially revolutionary, and does not consist wholly with anything which was. It not only divides states and churches, it divides families; ay, it divides the *individual*, separating the diabolical in him from the divine.

Unjust laws exist: shall we be content to obey them, or shall we endeavor to amend them, and obey them until we have succeeded, or shall we transgress them at once? Men generally, under such a government as this, think that they ought to wait until they have persuaded the majority to alter them. They think that, if they should resist, the remedy would be worse than the evil. But it is the fault of the government itself that the remedy *is* worse than the evil. *It* makes it worse. Why is it not more apt to anticipate and provide for reform? Why does it not cherish its wise minority? Why does it cry and resist before it is hurt? Why does it not encourage its citizens to be on the alert to point out its faults, and *do* better than it would have them? Why does it always crucify Christ, and excommunicate Copernicus and Luther, and pronounce Washington and Franklin rebels? . . .

If the injustice is part of the necessary friction of the machine of government, let it go, let it go: perchance it will wear smooth—certainly the machine will wear out. If the injustice has a spring, or a pulley, or a rope, or a crank, exclusively for itself, then perhaps you may consider whether the remedy will not be worse than the evil; but if it is of such a nature that it requires you to be the agent of injustice to another, then, I say, break the law. Let your life be a counter friction to stop the machine. What I have to do is to see, at any rate, that I do not lend myself to the wrong which I condemn. . . .

I do not hesitate to say, that those who call themselves Abolitionists should at once effectually withdraw their support, both in person and property, from the government of Massachusetts, and not wait till they constitute a majority of one, before they suffer the right to prevail through them. I think that it is enough if they have God on their side, without waiting for that other one. Moreover, any man more right than his neighbors constitutes a majority of one already.

. . . I know this well, that if one thousand, if one hundred, if ten men whom I could name—if ten *honest* men only—ay, if *one* honest man, in this State of Massachusetts, *ceasing to hold slaves*, were actually to withdraw from this copartnership, and be locked up in the county jail therefore, it would be the abolition of slavery in America. For it matters not how small the beginning may seem to be: what is once well done is done forever. . . .

Under a government which imprisons any unjustly, the true place for a just man is also a prison. The proper place to-day, the only place which Massachusetts has provided for her freer and less desponding spirits, is in her prisons, to be put out and locked out of the State by her own act, as they have already put themselves out by their principles. It is there that the fugitive slave, and the Mexican prisoner on parole, and the Indian come to plead the wrongs of his race, should find them; on that separate, but more free and honorable ground, where the State places those who are not *with* her, but *against* her—the only house in a slave State in which a free man can abide with honor. If any think that their influence would be lost there, and their voices no longer afflict the ear of the State, that they would not be as an enemy within its walls, they do not know by how much truth is stronger than error, nor how much more eloquently and effectively he can combat injustice who has experienced a little in his own person. Cast your whole vote, not a strip of paper merely, but your whole influence. A minority is powerless while it conforms to the majority; it is not even a minority then; but it is irresistible when it clogs by its whole weight. If the alternative is to keep all just men in prison, or give up war and slavery, the State will not hesitate which to choose. If a thousand men were not to pay their tax-bills this year, that would not be a violent and bloody measure, as it would be to pay them, and enable the State to commit violence and shed innocent blood. This is, in fact, the definition of a peaceable revolution, if any such is possible. If the tax-gatherer, or any other public officer, asks me, as one has done, "But what shall I do?" my answer is, "If you really wish to do anything, resign your office." When the subject has refused allegiance, and the officer has resigned his office, then the revolution is accomplished. But even suppose blood should flow. Is there not a sort of bloodshed when the conscience is wounded? Through this wound a man's real manhood and immortality flow out, and he bleeds to an everlasting death. I see this blood flowing now. . . .

I have paid no poll-tax for six years. I was put into a jail once on this account, for one night; and, as I stood considering the walls of solid stone, two or three feet thick, the door of wood and iron, a foot thick, and the iron grating which strained the light, I could not help being struck with the foolishness of that institution which treated me as if I were mere flesh and blood and bones, to be locked up. I wondered that it should have concluded at length that this was the best use it could put me to, and had never thought to avail itself of my services in some way. I saw that, if there was a wall of stone between me and my townsmen, there was a still more difficult one to climb or break through, before they could get to be as free as I was. I did not for a moment feel confined, and the walls seemed a great waste of stone and mortar. I felt as if I alone of all my townsmen had paid my tax. They plainly did not know how to treat me, but behaved like persons who are underbred. In every threat and in every compliment there was a blunder; for they thought that my chief desire was to stand the other side of that stone wall. I could not but smile to see how industriously they locked the door on my meditations, which followed them out again without let or hindrance, and *they* were really all that was dangerous. As they could not reach me, they had resolved to punish my body; just as boys, if they cannot come at some person against whom they have a spite, will abuse his dog. I saw that the State was half-witted, that it was timid as a lone woman with her silver spoons, and that it did not know its friends from its foes, and I lost all my remaining respect for it, and pitied it.

Thus the State never intentionally confronts a man's sense, intellectual or moral, but only his body, his senses. It is not armed with superior wit or honesty, but with superior physical strength. I was not born to be forced. I will breathe after my own fashion. Let us see who is the strongest. What force has a multitude? They can only force me who obey a higher law than I. They force me to become like themselves. I do not hear of *men* being *forced* to live this way or that by masses of men. What sort of life were that to live? When I meet a government which says to me, "Your money or your life," why should I be in haste to give it my money? It may be in a great strait, and not know what to do: I cannot help that. It must help itself; do as I do. It is not worth the while to snivel about it. I am not responsible for the successful working of the machinery of society. I am not the son of the engineer. I perceive that, when an acorn and a chestnut fall side by side, the one does not remain inert to make way for the other, but

both obey their own laws, and spring and grow and flourish as best they can, till one, perchance, overshadows and destroys the other. If a plant cannot live according to its nature, it dies; and so a man.

. . . I have never declined paying the highway tax, because I am as desirous of being a good neighbor as I am of being a bad subject; and, as for supporting schools, I am doing my part to educate my fellow-countrymen now. It is for no particular item in the tax-bill that I refuse to pay it. I simply wish to refuse allegiance to the State, to withdraw and stand aloof from it effectually. I do not care to trace the course of my dollar, if I could, till it buys a man or a musket to shoot one with—the dollar is innocent—but I am concerned to trace the effects of my allegiance. In fact, I quietly declare war with the State, after my fashion, though I will still make what use and get what advantage of her I can, as is usual in such cases.

. . . I sometimes say to myself, When many millions of men, without heat, without ill will, without personal feeling of any kind, demand of you a few shillings only, without the possibility, such is their constitution, of retracting or altering their present demand, and without the possibility, on your side, of appeal to any other millions, why expose yourself to this overwhelming brute force? You do not resist cold and hunger, the winds and the waves, thus obstinately; you quietly submit to a thousand similar necessities. You do not put your head into the fire. But just in proportion as I regard this as not wholly a brute force, but partly a human force, and consider that I have relations to those millions as to so many millions of men, and not of mere brute or inanimate things, I see that appeal is possible, first and instantaneously, from them to the Maker of them, and secondly, from them to themselves. But, if I put my head deliberately into the fire, there is no appeal to fire or to the Maker of fire, and I have only myself to blame. . . .

I do not wish to quarrel with any man or nation. I do not wish to split hairs, to make fine distinctions, or set myself up as better than my neighbors. I seek rather, I may say, even an excuse for conforming to the laws of the land. I am but too ready to conform to them. Indeed, I have reason to suspect myself on this head; and each year, as the tax-gatherer comes round, I find myself disposed to review the acts and position of the general and State governments, and the spirit of the people, to discover a pretext for conformity. . . .

The authority of government, even such as I am willing to submit to—for I will cheerfully obey those who know and can do better than I, and in many things even those who neither know nor can do so well—is still an impure one: to be strictly just, it must have the sanction and consent of the governed. It can have no pure right over my person and property but what I concede to it. The progress from an absolute to a limited monarchy, from a limited monarchy to a democracy, is a progress toward a true respect for the individual. Even the Chinese philosopher was wise enough to regard the individual as the basis of the empire. Is a democracy, such as we know it, the last improvement possible in government? Is it not possible to take a step further toward recognizing and organizing the rights of man? There will never be a really free and enlightened State, until the State comes to recognize the individual as a higher and independent power, from which all its own power and authority are derived, and treats him accordingly. I please myself with imagining a State at last which can afford to be just to all men, and to treat the individual with respect as a neighbor; which even would not think it inconsistent with its own repose, if a few were to live aloof from it, not meddling with it, nor embraced by it, who fulfilled all the duties of neighbors and fellow-men. A State which bore this kind of fruit, and suffered it to drop off as fast as it ripened, would prepare the way for a still more perfect and glorious State, which also I have imagined, but not yet anywhere seen.

Leo Tolstoy

LETTER TO ERNEST HOWARD CROSBY

As a young man, Leo Tolstoy served in the Russian army during the Crimean War. In his later years, however, Tolstoy increasingly adopted a unique brand of Christianity, embracing personal nonviolence and especially the first commandment, "Thou shalt not kill," so vigorously that he was widely hailed as the "thirteenth apostle." Tolstoy was especially concerned about personal compliance with war, which he denounced as nothing less than murder. As such, his writings stand in marked contrast to the "Christian realist" tradition, which sought to elaborate situations under which recourse to war was acceptable (see the introduction to Just War doctrine in Chapter 2).

Tolstoy maintained a kind of principled anarchism, opposing not only participation in war but the very workings of government, whose institutionalized violence he considered inimical to peace and to religious conscience. In his "Letter on the Peace Conference," Tolstoy wrote,

Armies can be reduced and abolished only in opposition to the will, but never by the will, of government. Armies will only be diminished and abolished when people cease

From "Letter to Ernest Howard Crosby" by Leo Tolstoy.

to trust governments, and themselves seek salvation from the miseries that oppress them, and seek that safety, not by the complicated and delicate combinations of diplomats, but in the simple fulfillment of that law, binding upon every man, inscribed in all religious teachings, and present in every heart, not to do to others what you wish them not to do to you—above all, not to slay your neighbors.

Armies will first diminish, and then disappear, only when public opinion brands with contempt those who, whether from fear, or for advantage, sell their liberty and enter the ranks of those murderers, called soldiers; and when the men now ignored and even blamed—who, in despite of all the persecution and suffering they have borne—have refused to yield the control of their actions into the hands of others, and become the tools of murder—are recognized by public opinion to be the foremost champions and benefactors of mankind. Only then will armies first diminish and then quite disappear, and a new era in the life of mankind will commence. And that time is near.

Tolstoy was convinced that the common people are as responsible for war as their leaders. This, in turn, contributed to his determination that individuals have the opportunity—indeed, the responsibility—to take things into their own hands and refuse to fight.

In the following selection, the influence of Eastern thought can be seen in Tolstoy's embrace of nonviolence, notably his rejection of ethical egoism and even utilitarianism: "the The greatest good for the greatest number."

"What would happen if people were all obliged to obey the law of nonresistance?"

But, in the first place, it is impossible to oblige every one to accept the law of nonresistance. Secondly, if it were possible to do so, such compulsion would in itself be a direct negation of the very principle set up. Oblige all men to refrain from violence? Who then should enforce the decision? Thirdly, and this is the chief point, the question, as put by Christ, is not at all, "Can nonresistance become a general law for humanity?" but, "How much each man act to fulfil his allotted task, to save his soul, and to do the will of God, three things which are really one and the same thing?" . . .

Tradition—the collective wisdom of my greatest forerunners—tells me that I should do unto others as I would that they should do unto me. My reason shows me that only by all men acting thus is the highest happiness for all men attainable. Only when I yield myself to that intuition of love which demands obedience to this law is my own heart happy and at rest. And not only can I then know how to act, but I can and do discern that work, to cooperate in which my activity was designed and is required. I cannot fathom God's whole design, for the sake of which the universe exists and lives; but the divine work which is being accomplished in this world, and in which I participate by living, is comprehensible to me.

This work is the annihilation of discord and strife among men, and among all creatures; and the establishment of the highest unity, concord, and love. It is the fulfillment of the promises of the Hebrew prophets, who foretold a time when all men should be taught by truth, when spears should be turned into reaping-hooks, swords be beaten to plowshares, and the lion lie down with the lamb. So that a man of Christian intelligence not only knows what he has to do, but he also understands the work he is doing. He has to act so as to cooperate toward the establishment of the kingdom of God on earth. For this, a man must obey his intuition of God's will, i.e., he must act lovingly toward others, as he would that others should act toward him. Thus the intuitive demands of man's soul coincide with the external aim of life which he sees before him. . . .

And yet, in spite of such a twofold indication, clear and indubitable to a man of Christian understanding of what is the real aim and meaning of human life, and of what men should do and should not do, we find people (and people calling themselves Christians) who decide that in such and such circumstances men ought to abandon God's law and reason's guidance, and act in opposition to them; because, according to their conception, the effects of actions performed in submission to God's law may be detrimental or inconvenient.

According to the law, contained alike in tradition, in our reason, and in our hearts, man should always do unto others as he would that they should do unto him; he should always cooperate in the development of love and union among created beings. But on the contrary, in the judgment of these people who look ahead, as long as it is premature, in their opinion, to obey this law, man should do violence, imprison or kill people, and thereby evoke anger and venom instead of loving union in the hearts of men. It is as if a bricklayer, set to do a particular task, and knowing that he was cooperating with others to build a house, after receiving clear and precise instructions from the master himself how to build a certain wall, should receive from some fellow bricklayers (who like himself knew neither the plan of the house nor what would fit in with it) orders to cease building his wall, and instead rather to pull down a wall which other workmen had erected.

Astonishing delusion! A being who breathes one day and vanishes the next receives one definite, indubitable law to guide him through the brief term of his life; but instead of obeying that law he prefers to fancy that he knows what is necessary, advantageous, and well-timed for men, for all the world— this world which continually shifts and evolves; and for the sake of some advantage (which each man pictures after his own fancy) he decides that he and other people should temporarily abandon the indubitable law given to one and to all, and should act, not as they would that others should act toward them, bringing love into the world, but instead do violence, imprison, kill, and bring into the world enmity whenever it seems profitable to do so. And he decides to act thus, though he knows that the most horrible cruelties, martyrdoms, and murders—from

the inquisitions, and the murders, and horrors of all the revolutions, down to the violences of contemporary anarchists, and their slaughter by the established authorities—have only occurred because people will imagine that they know what is necessary for mankind and for the world. But are there not always, at any given moment, two opposite parties, each of which declares that it is necessary to use force against the other—the "law and order" party against the "anarchist"; the "anarchist" against the "law and order" men; English against Americans, and Americans against English, and English against Germans; and so forth in all possible combinations and rearrangements?

A man enlightened by Christianity sees that he has no reason to abandon the law of God, given to enable him to walk with sure foot through life, in order to follow the chance, inconstant, and often contradictory demands of men. But besides this, if he has lived a Christian life for some time, and has developed in himself a Christian moral sensibility, he literally cannot act as people demand of him. Not this reason only, but his feeling also, makes it impossible. To many people of our society it would be impossible to torture or kill a baby, even if they were told that by so doing they could save hundreds of people. And in the same way a man, when he has developed a Christian sensibility of heart, finds a whole series of actions are become impossible for him. For instance, a Christian who is obliged to take part in judicial proceedings in which a man may be sentenced to death, or who is obliged to take part in evictions, or in debating a proposal leading to war, or to participate in preparations for war (not to mention war itself), is in a position parallel to that of a kindly man called on to torture or to kill a baby. It is not reason alone that forbids him to do what is demanded of him; he feels instinctively that he cannot do it. For certain actions are morally impossible, just as others are physically impossible. As a man cannot lift a mountain, and as a kindly man cannot kill an infant, so a man living the Christian life cannot take part in deeds of violence. Of what value then to him are arguments about the imaginary advantages of doing what is morally impossible for him to do?

But how is a man to act when he sees clearly an evil in following the law of love and its corollary law of nonresistance? How (to use the stock example) is a man to act when he sees a criminal killing or outraging a child, and he can only save the child by killing the criminal? When such a case is put, it is generally assumed that the only possible reply is that one should kill the assailant to save the child. But this answer is given so quickly and decidedly only because we are all so accustomed to the use of violence, not only to save a child, but even to prevent a neighboring government altering its frontier at the expense of ours, or to prevent some one from smuggling lace across that frontier, or even to defend our garden fruit from a passerby. It is assumed that to save the child, the assailant should be killed.

But it is only necessary to consider the question, "On what grounds ought a man, whether he be or be not a Christian, to act so?" in order to come to the conclusion that such action has no reasonable foundation, and only seems to us necessary because up to two thousand years ago such conduct was considered right, and a habit of acting so had been formed. Why should a non-Christian, not acknowledging God, and not regarding the fulfillment of His will as the aim of life, decide to kill the criminal in order to defend the child? By killing the former he kills for certain; whereas he cannot know positively whether the criminal would have killed the child or not. But letting that pass, who shall say whether the child's life was more needed, was better, than the other's life? Surely, if the non-Christian knows not God, and does not see life's meaning to be in the performance of His will, the only rule for his actions must be a reckoning, a conception, of which is more profitable for him and for all men, a continuation of the criminal's life or of the child's. To decide that, he needs to know what would become of the child whom he saves, and what, had he not killed him, would have been the future of the assailant. And as he cannot know this, the non-Christian has no sufficient rational ground for killing a robber to save a child.

If a man be a Christian, and consequently acknowledges God, and sees the meaning of life in fulfilling His will, then, however ferocious the assailant, however innocent and lovely the child, he has even less ground to abandon the God-given law, and

to do to the criminal as the criminal wishes to do to the child. He may plead with the assailant, may interpose his own body between the assailant and the victim; but there is one thing he cannot do—he cannot deliberately abandon the law he has received from God, the fulfillment of which alone gives meaning to his life. Very probably bad education, or his animal nature, may cause a man, Christian or non-Christian, to kill an assailant, not to save a child, but even to save himself or to save his purse. But it does not follow that he is right in acting thus, or that he should accustom himself or others to think such conduct right. What it does show is that, notwithstanding a coating of education and of Christianity, the habits of the stone age are yet so strong in man that he still commits actions long since condemned by his reasonable conscience.

I see a criminal killing a child, and I can save the child by killing the assailant—therefore, in certain cases, violence must be used to resist evil. A man's life is in danger, and can be saved only by my telling a lie—therefore, in certain cases, one must lie. A man is starving, and I can only save him by stealing—therefore, in certain cases, one must steal. . . . There is no moral law concerning which one might not devise a case in which it is difficult to decide which is more moral, to disobey the law or to obey it? But all such devices fail to prove that the laws, "Thou shalt not lie, steal, or kill," are invalid.

It is thus with the law of nonresistance. People know it is wrong to use violence, but they are so anxious to continue to live a life secured by "the strong arm of the law," that, instead of devoting their intellects to the elucidation of the evils which have flowed, and are still flowing, from admitting that man has a right to use violence to his fellowmen, they prefer to exert their mental powers in defense of that error. *Fais ce que dois, advienne que pourra*—"Do what's right, come what may"—is an expression of profound wisdom. We each can know indubitably what we ought to do, but what results will follow from our actions we none of us either do or can know. Therefore it follows that, besides feeling the call of duty, we are further driven to act as duty bids us by the consideration that we have no other guidance, but are totally ignorant of what will result from our action.

Christian teaching indicates what a man should do to perform the will of Him who sent him into life; and discussion as to what results we anticipate from such or such human actions have nothing to do with Christianity, but are just an example of the error which Christianity eliminates. None of us has ever yet met the imaginary criminal with the imaginary child, but all the horrors which fill the annals of history and of our own times came, and come, from this one thing, namely, that people will believe they really foresee speculative future results of actions.

The case is this. People once lived an animal life, and violated or killed whom they thought well to violate or to kill. They even ate one another, and public opinion approved of it. Thousands of years ago, as far back as the times of Moses, a day came when people had realized that to violate or kill one another is bad. But there were people for whom the reign of force was advantageous, and these did not approve of the change, but assured themselves and others that to do deeds of violence and to kill people is not always bad, but that there are circumstances when it is necessary and even moral. And violence and slaughter, though not so frequent or so cruel as before, continued, only with this difference, that those who committed or commended such acts excused themselves by pleading that they did it for the benefit of humanity.

It was just this sophistical justification of violence that Christ denounced. When two enemies fight, each may think his own conduct justified by the circumstances. Excuses can be made for every use of violence, and no infallible standard has ever been discovered by which to measure the worth of these excuses. Therefore Christ taught us to disbelieve in any excuse for violence, and (contrary to what had been taught by them of old times) never to use violence. One would have thought that those

who have professed Christianity would be indefatigable in exposing deception in this matter; for in such exposure lay one of the chief manifestations of Christianity. What really happened was just the reverse. People who profited by violence, and who did not wish to give up their advantages, took on themselves a monopoly of Christian preaching, and declared that, as cases can be found in which non-resistance causes more harm than the use of violence (the imaginary criminal killing the imaginary child), therefore Christ's doctrine of non-resistance need not always be followed; and that one may deviate from His teaching to defend one's life or the life of others; or to defend one's country, to save society from lunatics or criminals, and in many other cases.

The decision of the question in what cases Christ's teaching should be set aside was left to the very people who employed violence. So that it ended by Christ's teaching on the subject of not resisting evil by violence being completely annulled. . . . The real question is not whether it will be good or bad for a certain human society that people should follow the law of love and the consequent law of nonresistance. But it is this: Do you, who today live and tomorrow will die, you who are indeed tending deathward every moment, do you wish now, immediately and entirely, to obey the law of Him who sent you into life, and who clearly showed you His will, alike in tradition and in your mind and heart; or do you prefer to resist His will? And as soon as the question is put thus, only one reply is possible: I wish now, this moment, without delay or hesitation, to the very utmost of my strength, neither waiting for one or counting the cost, to do that which alone is clearly demanded by Him who sent me into the world; and on no account, and under no conditions, do I wish to, or can I, act otherwise—for herein lies my only possibility of a rational and unharassed life.

Edna St. Vincent Millay

CONSCIENTIOUS OBJECTOR

Nonviolent antiwar protest takes many forms. Much has been written by way of specific advice for individuals contemplating tax resistance, draft resistance, organized opposition to various government policies, and so forth. Consistent with the goal of this book, however, which is to focus on general principles and to provide lasting food for thought, we present "Conscientious Objector," a remarkable and timeless poem by Edna St. Vincent Millay.

I shall die, but that is all that I shall do for Death.

I hear him leading his horse out of the stall; I hear the clatter on
    the barn-floor.
He is in haste; he has business in Cuba, business in the Balkans,
    many calls to make this morning.
But I will not hold the bridle while he cinches the girth.
And he may mount by himself: I will not give him a leg up.

Though he flick my shoulders with his whip, I will not tell him
    which way the fox ran.
With his hoof on my breast, I will not tell him where the black
    boy hides in the swamp.
I shall die, but that is all that I shall do for Death; I am not on
    his pay-roll.

I will not tell him the whereabouts of my friends nor of my ene-
    mies either.
Though he promise me much, I will not map him the route to
    any man's door.
Am I a spy in the land of the living, that I should deliver men to
    Death?
Brother, the password and the plans of our city are safe with me;
    never through me
Shall you be overcome.

Albert Camus

NEITHER VICTIMS NOR EXECUTIONERS

Personal commitment to nonviolence takes many forms. To complement Millay's statement in poetry, and Tolstoy's Christian-based faith, next comes a prose, secular selection,
from a renowned essay by French philosopher-novelist-playwright Albert Camus. Ironically, "Neither Victims nor Nor Executioners" first appeared in a magazine titled *Combat*,
which was edited by Camus on behalf of the anti-Nazi French Resistance during World War
II. Somewhat like Tolstoy—although without the latter's religious motivation—Camus
eventually committed himself to nonviolence. He was especially concerned with denying
the legitimacy of violence on behalf of political ideologies of any persuasion.

The seventeenth century was the century of mathematics, the eighteenth that of the physical
sciences, and the nineteenth that of biology. Our
twentieth century is the century of fear. I will be told
that fear is not a science. But science must be somewhat involved since its latest theoretical advances
have brought it to the point of negating itself while its
perfected technology threatens the globe itself with
destruction. Moreover, although fear itself cannot be
considered a science, it is certainly a technique.

The most striking feature of the world we live in
is that most of its inhabitants—with the exception of
pietists of various kinds—are cut off from the future.
Life has no validity unless it can project itself toward
the future, can ripen and progress. Living against a
wall is a dog's life.

. . . I once said that, after the experiences of
the last two years, I could no longer hold to any
truth which might oblige me, directly or indirectly,
to demand a man's life. Certain friends whom I
respected retorted that I was living in Utopia, that
there was no political truth which could not one day
reduce us to such an extremity, and that we must
therefore either run the risk of this extremity or else
simply put up with the world as it is.

They argued the point most forcefully. But I
think they were able to put such force into it only
because they were unable to really *imagine* other
people's death. It is a freak of the times. We make
love by telephone, we work not on matter but on
machines, and we kill and are killed by proxy. We
gain in cleanliness, but lose in understanding.

But the argument has another, indirect meaning: it poses the question of utopia. People like
myself want not a world in which murder no longer
exists (we are not so crazy as that!) but rather one in
which murder is not legitimate. Here indeed we are
utopian—and contradictory. For we do live, it is true,
in a world where murder is legitimate, and we ought
to change it if we do not like it. But it appears that
we cannot change it without risking murder. Murder
thus throws us back on murder, and we will continue to live in terror whether we accept the fact with
resignation or wish to abolish it by means which
merely replace one terror with another.

It seems to me every one should think this over.
For what strikes me, in the midst of polemics, threats,
and outbursts of violence, is the fundamental good
will of every one. From Right to Left, every one, with
the exception of a few swindlers, believes that his

particular truth is the one to make men happy. And yet the combination of all these good intentions has produced the present infernal world, where men are killed, threatened, and deported, where war is prepared, where one cannot speak freely without being insulted or betrayed. . . .

Little is to be expected from present-day governments, since these live and act according to a murderous code. Hope remains only in the most difficult task of all: to reconsider everything from the ground up, so as to shape a living society inside a dying society. Men must therefore, as individuals, draw up among themselves, within frontiers and across them, a new social contract which will unite them according to more reasonable principles.

More precisely, the latter's task would be to speak out clearly against the confusions of the Terror and at the same time to define the values by which a peaceful world may live. The first objectives might be the drawing up of an international code of justice whose Article No. 1 would be the abolition of the death penalty, and an exposition of the basic principles of a sociable culture (*"civilisation du dialogue"*). Such an undertaking would answer the needs of an era which has found no philosophical justification for that thirst for fraternity which today burns in Western man. There is no idea, naturally, of constructing a new ideology, but rather of discovering a style of life.

Let us suppose that certain individuals resolve that they will consistently oppose to power the force of example; to authority, exhortation; to insult, friendly reasoning; to trickery, simple honor. Let us suppose they refuse all the advantages of present-day society and accept only the duties and obligations which bind them to other men. Let us suppose they devote themselves to orienting education, the press, and public opinion toward the principles outlined here. Then I say that such men would be acting not as utopians but as honest realists. They would be preparing the future and at the same time knocking down a few of the walls which imprison us today. If realism be the art of taking into account both the present and the future, of gaining the most while sacrificing the least, then who can fail to see the positively dazzling realism of such behavior?

Whether these men will arise or not I do not know. It is probable that most of them are even now thinking things over, and that is good. But one thing is sure: their efforts will be effective only to the degree they have the courage to give up, for the present, some of their dreams, so as to grasp the more firmly the essential point on which our very lives depend. Once there, it will perhaps turn out to be necessary, before they are done, to raise their voices. . . .

To save what can be saved so as to open up some kind of future—that is the prime mover, the passion and the sacrifice that is required. It demands only that we reflect and then decide, clearly, whether humanity's lot must be made still more miserable in order to achieve far-off and shadowy ends, whether we should accept a world bristling with arms where brother kills brother; or whether, on the contrary, we should avoid bloodshed and misery as much as possible so that we give a chance for survival to later generations better equipped than we are.

For my part, I am fairly sure that I have made the choice. And, having chosen, I think that I must speak out, that I must state that I will never again be one of those, whoever they be, who compromise with murder, and that I must take the consequences of such a decision. . . .

We are asked to love or to hate such and such a country and such and such a people. But some of us feel too strongly our common humanity to make such a choice. Those who really love the Russian people, in gratitude for what they have never ceased to be—that world leaven which Tolstoy and Gorky speak of—do not wish for them success in power-politics, but rather want to spare them, after the ordeals of the past, a new and even more terrible bloodletting. So, too, with the American people, and with the peoples of unhappy Europe. This is the kind of elementary truth we are liable to forget amidst the furious passions of our time.

Yes, it is fear and silence and the spiritual isolation they cause that must be fought today. And it is sociability (*"le dialogue"*) and the universal intercommunication of men that must be defended. Slavery, injustice, and lies destroy this intercourse and forbid this sociability; and so we must reject them. But these evils are today the very stuff of history, so that many consider them necessary evils. It is true that we cannot "escape history," since we are in it up to our necks. But one may propose to fight within history to preserve from history that part of man which is not its proper province. That is all I have tried to say here. The "point" of this article may be summed up as follows:

Modern nations are driven by powerful forces along the roads of power and domination. I will not say that these forces should be furthered or that they should be obstructed. They hardly need our help and, for the moment, they laugh at attempts to hinder them. They will, then, continue. But I will ask only this simple question: what if these forces wind up in a dead end, what if that logic of history on which so many now rely turns out to be a will-o'-the-wisp? What if, despite two or three world wars, despite the sacrifice of several generations and a whole system of values, our grandchildren—supposing they survive—find themselves no closer to a world society? It may well be that the survivors of such an experience will be too weak to understand their own sufferings. Since these forces are working themselves out and since it is inevitable that they continue to do so, there is no reason why some of us should not take on the job of keeping alive, through the apocalyptic historical vista that stretches before us, a modest

thoughtfulness which, without pretending to solve everything, will constantly be prepared to give some human meaning to everyday life. The essential thing is that people should carefully weigh the price they must pay.

To conclude: all I ask is that, in the midst of a murderous world, we agree to reflect on murder and to make a choice. After that, we can distinguish those who accept the consequences of being murderers themselves or the accomplices of murderers, and those who refuse to do so with all their force and being. Since this terrible dividing line does actually exist, it will be a gain if it be clearly marked. Over the expanse of five continents throughout the coming years an endless struggle is going to be pursued between violence and friendly persuasion, a struggle in which, granted, the former has a thousand times the chances of success than that of the latter. But I have always held that, if he who bases his hopes on human nature is a fool, he who gives up in the face of circumstances is a coward. And henceforth, the only honorable course will be to stake everything on a formidable gamble: that words are more powerful than munitions.

Mohandas Gandhi

AHIMSĀ, OR THE WAY OF NONVIOLENCE

Mohandas Gandhi is the preeminent figure of nonviolence, at least in the twentieth century, if not for future centuries. (The word "Mahatma" is an honorific title in the Hindi language, meaning "great soul.") Gandhi may have been the first person—certainly, he was the most effective and influential—to extend nonviolence from a principle of individual behavior to a concerted strategy grounded in a wider search for political and social justice.

Gandhi's teachings—as well as his practical example—have been carefully studied by many nonviolent leaders, including the Rev. Martin Luther King, Jr., who patterned his leadership of the civil rights struggle in the United States after Gandhi's decades-long efforts in South Africa and then India. (Gandhian thought and practice has also influenced human rights crusaders in China, Burma, Indonesia, and, indeed, around the globe.)

From *All Men Are Brothers* by Mohandas Gandhi.

"With the increased velocity of modern changes we do not know what the world will be a hundred years hence," wrote S. Radhakrishnan, vice president and later president of India, in the introduction to Gandhi's book of autobiographical reflections, *All Men Are Brothers.*

> We cannot anticipate the future currents of thought and feeling. But years may go their way, yet the great principles of *satya* and *ahiṃsā*, truth and nonviolence, are there to guide us. They are the silent stars keeping holy vigil above a tired and turbulent world. Like Gandhi we may be firm in our conviction that the sun shines above the drifting clouds.
>
> We live in an age which is aware of its own defeat and moral coarsening, an age in which old certainties are breaking down, the familiar patterns are tilting and cracking. There is increasing intolerance and embitterment. . . . It is our pride that one of the greatest figures of history lived in our generation, walked with us, spoke to us, taught us the way of civilized living. He who wrongs no one fears no one. He has nothing to hide and so is fearless. He looks everyone in the face. His step is firm, his body upright, and his words are direct and straight. Plato said long ago: "There always are in the world a few inspired men whose acquaintance is beyond price."

Gandhi explained that *ahiṃsā* "does not mean meek submission to the will of the evildoer, but it means pitting of one's whole soul against the will of the tyrant. Working under this law of our being, it is possible for a single individual to defy the whole might of an unjust empire. . . . " In addition to *ahiṃsā* and *satya* (or *satyagraha*), another Gandhian term is crucially important: *tapasya*, a willingness to undergo suffering oneself and not to shift it onto another—including the opponent—as a consequence of one's commitment to the truth of nonviolence.

Although *tapasya* may be especially difficult for many people to accept or understand (not to mention, to practice!), it should not be especially foreign, especially if one substitutes "courage" for "willingness to suffer," which has the added benefit of helping dispel the frequent misunderstanding that practitioners of nonviolence are lazy or cowardly, seeking an easy way out of conflict.

The courage and commitment of *satyagrahis* come at a price, as revealed in this eyewitness account of the famous "salt *satyagraha*" of 1930. Gandhi and twenty-five hundred peaceful marchers arrived at a police stockade near the Dharasana Salt Works, in defiance of law and in complete silence, approaching and in turn being battered on the head with steel-shod clubs, while no one even raised an arm in self-protection: "From where I stood I heard the sickening whack of the clubs on unprotected skulls. . . . The survivors, without breaking ranks, silently and doggedly marched on until struck down."[4] In the long run, such techniques have in fact been overwhelmingly successful, in no small part because of their powerful appeal to shared human conscience. (Once, when visiting England, Gandhi was asked his impression of Western civilization, to which he replied, "It would be a good idea.")

---

[4] Quoted in Erik Erikson, *Gandhi's Truth* (New York: W. W. Norton, 1969).

It may be that—as is frequently pointed out—Gandhian nonviolence would not have succeeded against, say, a nuclear-armed Hitler. Perhaps it requires a degree of underlying humanity and goodwill on the other side. But it is also true that the British empire Empire had not been especially gentle or humane in its treatment of colonial subjects, and, in the end, persistent nonviolent tactics succeeded in liberating a nation of (at that time) more than 400 million people, without firing a shot.

Gandhi himself pointed out that nonviolence is more pervasive in ordinary human life than most of us realize and is far more frequently (and successfully) employed than is violence.

It is hoped that the following selections will help acquaint the reader with the remarkable, inspired person Gandhi was, and, in the process, reveal the potential for nonviolence as an approach to peace.

Nonviolence is the greatest force at the disposal of mankind. It is mightier than the mightiest weapon of destruction devised by the ingenuity of man. Destruction is not the law of the humans. Man lives freely by his readiness to die, if need be, at the hands of his brother, never by killing him. Every murder or other injury, no matter for what cause, committed or inflicted on another is a crime against humanity.

Harijan, July 20, 1931

The first condition of nonviolence is justice all round in every department of life. Perhaps, it is too much to expect of human nature. I do not, however, think so. No one should dogmatize about the capacity of human nature for degradation or exaltation.

Mahatma, V, April, 1940

Just as one must learn the art of killing in the training for violence, so one must learn the art of dying in the training for nonviolence. Violence does not mean emancipation from fear, but discovering the means of combating the cause of fear. Nonviolence, on the other hand, has no cause for fear. The votary of nonviolence has to cultivate the capacity for sacrifice of the highest type in order to be free from fear. He recks not if he should lose his land, his wealth, his life. He who has not overcome all fear cannot practice *ahiṃsā* to perfection. The votary of *ahiṃsā* has

only one fear, that is of God. He who seeks refuge in God ought to have a glimpse of the *Atma* that transcends the body; and the moment one has a glimpse of the imperishable *Atma* one sheds the love of the perishable body. Training in nonviolence is thus diametrically opposed to training in violence. Violence is needed for the protection of things external, nonviolence is needed for the protection of the *Atma*, for the protection of one's honour.

Harijan, September 1, 1940

It is no nonviolence if we merely love those that love us. It is nonviolence only when we love those that hate us. I know how difficult it is to follow this grand law of love. But are not all great and good things difficult to do? Love of the hater is the most difficult of all. But by the grace of God even this most difficult thing becomes easy to accomplish if we want to do it.

Letter of December 31, 1934

I have found that life persists in the midst of destruction and therefore there must be a higher law than that of destruction. . . .

It is not that I am incapable of anger, for instance, but I succeed on almost all occasions to keep my feelings under control. Whatever may be the result, there is always in me conscious struggle for following the law of nonviolence deliberately and ceaselessly.

Such a struggle leaves one stronger for it. The more I work at this law, the more I feel the delight in my life, the delight in the scheme of the universe. It gives me a peace and a meaning of the mysteries of nature that I have no power to describe.

Young India, October 1, 1931

If we turn our eyes to the time of which history has any record down to our own time, we shall find that man has been steadily progressing towards *ahiṃsā*. Our remote ancestors were cannibals. Then came a time when they were fed up with cannibalism and they began to live on chase. Next came a stage when man was ashamed of leading the life of a wandering hunter. He therefore took to agriculture and depended principally on mother earth for his food. Thus from being a nomad he settled down to civilized stable life, founded villages and towns, and from member of a family he became member of a community and a nation. All these are signs of progressive *ahiṃsā* and diminishing *hiṃsā*. Had it been otherwise, the human species should have been extinct by now, even as many of the lower species have disappeared.

Prophets and *avatārs* have also taught the lesson of *ahiṃsā* more or less. Not one of them has professed to teach *hiṃsā*. And how should it be otherwise? *Hiṃsā* does not need to be taught. Man as animal is violent, but as Spirit is nonviolent. The moment he awakes to the Spirit within, he cannot remain violent. Either he progresses towards *ahiṃsā* or rushes to his doom. That is why the prophets and *avatārs* have taught the lesson of truth, harmony, brotherhood, justice, etc. all attributes of *ahiṃsā*.

Harijan, August 11, 1940

I have never claimed to present the complete science of nonviolence. It does not lend itself to such treatment. So far as I know, no single physical science does, not even the very exact science of mathematics. I am but a seeker.

Harijan, February 22, 1942

In the application of *Satyāgraha*, I discovered in the earliest stages that pursuit of truth did not admit of violence being inflicted on one's opponent but that he must be weaned from error by patience and

sympathy. For, what appears to be truth to the one may appear to be error to another. And patience means self-suffering. So the doctrine came to mean vindication of truth, not by infliction of suffering on the opponent, but on one's self.

Young India, November, 1919

In this age of wonders no one will say that a thing or idea is worthless because it is new. To say it is impossible because it is difficult, is again not in consonance with the spirit of the age. Things undreamt of are daily being seen, the impossible is ever becoming possible. We are constantly being astonished these days at the amazing discoveries in the field of violence. But I maintain that far more undreamt of and seemingly impossible discoveries will be made in the field of nonviolence.

Harijan, August 25, 1940

Nonviolence is a universal principle and its operation is not limited by a hostile environment. Indeed, its efficacy can be tested only when it acts in the midst of and in spite of opposition. Our nonviolence would be a hollow thing and worth nothing, if it depended for its success on the goodwill of the authorities.

Harijan, November 12, 1938

No man could be actively nonviolent and not rise against social injustice no matter where it occurred.

Harijan, April 20, 1940

Passive resistance is a method of securing rights by personal suffering; it is the reverse of resistance by arms. When I refuse to do a thing that is repugnant to my conscience, I use soul-force. For instance, the government of the day has passed a law which is applicable to me. I do not like it. If by using violence I force the government to repeal the law, I am employing what may be termed body-force. If I do not obey the law and accept the penalty for its breach, I use soul-force. It involves sacrifice of self.

Everybody admits that sacrifice of self is infinitely superior to sacrifice of others. Moreover, if this kind of force is used in a cause that is unjust, only the person using it suffers. He does not make others suffer for his mistakes. Men have before now done many things which were subsequently found to have been wrong. No man can claim that he is absolutely in the right or that a particular thing is wrong because he thinks so, but it is wrong for him so long as that is his deliberate judgement. It is therefore meet that he should not do that which he knows to be wrong, and suffer the consequence whatever it may be. This is the key to the use of soul-force.

Indian Home Rule, 1909

You might of course say that there can be no nonviolent rebellion and there has been none known to history. Well, it is my ambition to provide an instance, and it is my dream that my country may win its freedom through nonviolence. And, I would like to repeat to the world times without number, that I will not purchase my country's freedom at the cost of nonviolence. My marriage to nonviolence is such an absolute thing that I would rather commit suicide than be deflected from my position. I have not mentioned truth in this connexion, simply because truth cannot be expressed except by nonviolence.

Young India, November 12, 1931

The conviction has been growing upon me, that things of fundamental importance to the people are not secured by reason alone but have to be purchased with their suffering. Suffering is the law of human beings; war is the law of the jungle. But suffering is infinitely more powerful than the law of the jungle for converting the opponent and opening his ears, which are otherwise shut, to the voice of reason. Nobody has probably drawn up more petitions or espoused more forlorn causes than I and I have come to this fundamental conclusion that if you want something really important to be done you must not merely satisfy the reason, you must move the heart also. The appeal of reason is more to the head but the penetration of the heart comes from suffering. It opens up the inner understanding in man. Suffering is the badge of the human race, not the sword.

Young India, November 4, 1931

Nonviolence is a power which can be wielded equally by all—children, young men and women, or grown up people—provided they have a living faith in the God of Love and have therefore equal love for all mankind. When nonviolence is accepted as the law of life it must pervade the whole being and not be applied to isolated acts.

Harijan, September 5, 1936

Perfect nonviolence is impossible so long as we exist physically, for we would want some space at least to occupy. Perfect nonviolence whilst you are inhabiting the body is only a theory like Euclid's point or straight line, but we have to endeavour every moment of our lives.

Harijan, July 21, 1940

Taking life may be a duty. We do destroy as much life as we think necessary for sustaining our body. Thus for food we take life, vegetable and other, and for health we destroy mosquitoes and the like by the use of disinfectants, etc., and we do not think that we are guilty of irreligion in doing so . . . for the benefit of the species, we kill carnivorous beasts. . . . Even manslaughter may be necessary in certain cases. Suppose a man runs amuck and goes furiously about, sword in hand, and killing anyone that comes in his way, and no one dares to capture him alive. Anyone who despatches this lunatic will earn the gratitude of the community and be regarded as a benevolent man.

Young India, November 4, 1926

A man cannot practise *ahiṃsā* and be a coward at the same time. The practice of *ahiṃsā* calls forth the greatest courage.

Speeches and Writings of Mahatma Gandhi,
no date given

Nonviolence is "not a resignation from all real fighting against wickedness." On the contrary, the nonviolence of my conception is a more active and real fight against wickedness than retaliation whose very nature is to increase wickedness. I contemplate a mental and therefore a moral opposition to immoralities. I seek entirely to blunt the edge of the tyrant's sword, not by putting up against it a sharper-edged weapon, but by disappointing his expectation that I would be offering physical resistance. The resistance of the soul that I should offer would elude him. It would at first dazzle him and at last compel recognition from him, which recognition would not humiliate but would uplift him. It may be urged that this is an ideal state. And so it is.

Young India, October 8, 1925

I object to violence because when it appears to do good, the good is only temporary; the evil it does is permanent. I do not believe that the killing of even every Englishman can do the slightest good to India. The millions will be just as badly off as they are today, if someone made it possible to kill off every Englishman tomorrow. The responsibility is more ours than that of the English for the present state of things. The English will be powerless to do evil if we will but be good. Hence my incessant emphasis on reform from within.

Young India, May 21, 1925

History teaches one that those who have, no doubt with honest motives, ousted the greedy by using brute force against them, have in their turn become a prey to the disease of the conquered.

Young India, May 6, 1926

It is to me a matter of perennial satisfaction that I retain generally the affection and trust of those whose principles and policies I oppose. The South Africans gave me personally their confidence and extended their friendship. In spite of my denunciation of British policy and system I enjoy the affection of thousands of Englishmen and women, and in spite of unqualified condemnation of modern materialistic civilization, the circle of European and American friends is ever widening. It is again a triumph of nonviolence.

Young India, March 17, 1927

My experience, daily growing stronger and richer, tells me that there is no peace for individuals or for nations without practising truth and nonviolence to the uttermost extent possible for man. The policy of retaliation has never succeeded.

Young India, December 15, 1927

I have been practising with scientific precision nonviolence and its possibilities for an unbroken period of over fifty years. I have applied it in every walk of life—domestic, institutional, economic and political. I know of no single case in which it has failed. Where it has seemed sometimes to have failed, I have ascribed it to my imperfections. I claim no perfection for myself. But I do claim to be a passionate seeker after Truth, which is but another name for God. In the course of that search the discovery of nonviolence came to me. Its spread is my life mission. I have no interest in living except for the prosecution of that mission.

Harijan, July 6, 1940

I do not want to live at the cost of the life even of a snake. I should let him bite me to death rather than kill him. But it is likely that if God puts me to that cruel test and permits a snake to assault me, I may not have the courage to die, but that the beast in me may assert itself and I may seek to kill the snake in defending this perishable body. I admit that my belief has not become so incarnate in me as to warrant my stating emphatically that I have shed all fear of snakes so as to befriend them as I would like to be able to.

An Autobiography

Ahiṃsā is soul-force and the soul is imperishable, changeless, and eternal. The atom bomb is the acme of physical force and, as such, subject to the law of dissipation, decay, and death that governs the physical universe. Our scriptures bear witness that when soul-force is fully awakened in us, it becomes irresistible. But the test and condition of full awakening is that it must permeate every pore of our being and emanate with every breath that we breathe.

But no institution can be made nonviolent by compulsion. Nonviolence and truth cannot be written into a constitution. They have to be adopted of one's own free will. They must sit naturally upon us like next-to-skin garments or else they become a contradiction in terms.

Mahatma Gandhi, The Last Phase, II, circa 1947

My creed of nonviolence is an extremely active force. It has no room for cowardice or even weakness.

There is hope for a violent man to be some day nonviolent, but there is none for a coward. I have therefore said more than once in these pages that if we do not know how to defend ourselves, our women, and our places of worship by the force of suffering, i.e., nonviolence, we must, if we are men, be at least able to defend all these by fighting.

Young India, June 16, 1927

In life, it is impossible to eschew violence completely. Now the question arises, where is one to draw the line? The line cannot be the same for everyone. For, although, essentially the principle is the same, yet everyone applies it in his or her own way. What is one man's food can be another's poison. Meat-eating is a sin for me. Yet, for another person, who has always lived on meat and never seen anything wrong in it, to give it up, simply in order to copy me, will be a sin.

If I wish to be an agriculturist and stay in a jungle, I will have to use the minimum unavoidable violence, in order to protect my fields. I will have to kill monkeys, birds, and insects, which eat up my crops. If I do not wish to do so myself, I will have to engage someone to do it for me. There is not much difference between the two. To allow crops to be eaten up by animals, in the name of *ahiṃsā*, *ahim.sa⁻*, while there is a famine in the land, is certainly a sin. Evil and good are relative terms. What is good under certain conditions can become an evil or a sin, under a different set of conditions. . . .

Mahatma, VII, 1946

The people of a village near Bettia told me that they had run away whilst the police were looting their houses and molesting their womenfolk. When they said that they had run away because I had told them to be nonviolent, I hung my head in shame. I assured them that such was not the meaning of my nonviolence. I expected them to intercept the mightiest power that might be in the act of harming those who were under their protection, and draw without retaliation all harm upon their own heads even to the point of death, but never to run away from the storm centre. It was manly enough to defend one's property, honour, or religion at the point of the sword. It was manlier and nobler to

defend them without seeking to injure the wrongdoer. But it was unmanly, unnatural, and dishonourable to forsake the post of duty and, in order to save one's skin, to leave property, honour, or religion to the mercy of the wrongdoer. I could see my way of delivering *ahiṃsā* to those who knew how to die, not to those who were afraid of death.

Gandhiji in Indian Villages, published in 1927

My nonviolence does not admit of running away from danger and leaving dear ones unprotected. Between violence and cowardly flight, I can only prefer violence to cowardice. I can no more preach nonviolence to a coward than I can tempt a blind man to enjoy healthy scenes. Nonviolence is the summit of bravery. And in my own experience, I have had no difficulty in demonstrating to men trained in the school of violence the superiority of nonviolence. As a coward, which I was for years, I harboured violence. I began to prize nonviolence only when I began to shed cowardice.

Young India, May 28, 1924

Nonviolence cannot be taught to a person who fears to die and has no power of resistance. A helpless mouse is not nonviolent because he is always eaten by pussy. He would gladly eat the murderess if he could, but he ever tries to flee from her. We do not call him a coward, because he is made by nature to behave no better than he does. But a man who, when faced by danger, behaves like a mouse, is rightly called a coward. He harbours violence and hatred in his heart and would kill his enemy if he could without hurting himself. He is a stranger to nonviolence. All sermonizing on it will be lost on him. Bravery is foreign to his nature. Before he can understand nonviolence he has to be taught to stand his ground and even suffer death, in the attempt to defend himself against the aggressor who bids fair to overwhelm him. To do otherwise would be to confirm his cowardice and take him farther away from nonviolence. Whilst I may not actually help anyone to retaliate, I must not let a coward seek shelter behind nonviolence so-called. Not knowing the stuff of which nonviolence is made, many have honestly believed that running away from danger every time was a virtue compared to offering resistance, especially when it was fraught with danger to one's life. As a teacher of nonviolence I must, so far as it is possible for me, guard against such an unmanly belief.

Harijan, July 20, 1935

I am not a visionary. I claim to be a practical idealist. Religion of nonviolence is not meant merely for the *rishis* and saints. It is meant for the common people as well. Nonviolence is the law of our species as violence is the law of the brute. The spirit lies dormant in the brute, and he knows no law but that of physical might. The dignity of man requires obedience to a higher law, to the strength of the spirit.

I have ventured to place before India the ancient law of self-sacrifice. For *Satyāgraha* and its offshoots, noncooperation and civil resistance are nothing but new names for the law of suffering. The *rishis*, who discovered the law of nonviolence in the midst of violence, were greater geniuses than Newton. They were themselves greater warriors than Wellington. Having themselves known the use of arms, they realized their uselessness and taught a weary world that its salvation lay not through violence but through nonviolence.

Nonviolence in its dynamic condition means conscious suffering. It does not mean meek submission to the will of the evildoer, but it means putting of one's whole soul against the will of the tyrant. Working under this law of our being, it is possible for a single individual to defy the whole might of an unjust empire to save his honour, his religion, his soul, and lay the foundation for that empire's fall or its regeneration.

And so I am not pleading for India to practice nonviolence because it is weak. I want her to practice nonviolence being conscious of her strength and power. No training in arms is required for realization of her strength. We seem to need it, because we seem to think that we are but a lump of flesh. I want to recognize that she has a soul that cannot perish and that can rise triumphant above every physical weakness and defy the physical combination of a whole world. . . . If India takes up the doctrine of the sword, she may gain momentary victory. Then India will cease to be the pride of my heart. I am wedded to India because I owe my all to her.

I believe absolutely that she has a mission for the world. She is not to copy Europe blindly. India's acceptance of the doctrine of the sword will be the hour of my trial. I hope I shall not be found wanting. My religion has no geographical limits. If I have a living faith in it, it will transcend my love for India herself. My life is dedicated to the service of India through the religion of nonviolence which I believe to be the root of Hinduism.

Mahatma, II, Young India, August 11, 1920

I must continue to argue till I convert opponents or I own defeat. For my mission is to convert every Indian, even Englishmen, and finally the world to nonviolence for regulating mutual relations whether political, economic, social, or religious. If I am accused of being too ambitious, I should plead guilty. If I am told that my dream can never materialize, I would answer, "That is possible," and go my way. I am a seasoned soldier of nonviolence, and I have evidence enough to sustain my faith. Whether, therefore, I have one comrade or more or none, I must continue my experiment.

Mahatma, V, Harijan, January 13, 1940

It has been suggested by American friends that the atom bomb will bring in *ahiṃsā, ahiṃsā,* as nothing else can. It will, if it is meant that its destructive power will so disgust the world, that it will turn it away from violence for the time being. And this is very like a man glutting himself with the dainties to the point of nausea, and turning away from them only to return with redoubled zeal after the effect of nausea is well over. Precisely in the same manner will the world return to violence with renewed zeal, after the effect of disgust is worn out.

Often does good come out of evil. But that is God's, not man's plan. Man knows that only evil can come out of evil, as good out of good. . . . The moral to be legitimately drawn from the supreme tragedy of the atom bomb is that it will not be destroyed by counter bombs, even as violence cannot be by counter violence. Mankind has to go out of violence only through nonviolence. Hatred can be overcome only by love. Counter hatred only increases the surface, as well as the depth of hatred. . . .

Mahatma, VII, Harijan, July 1946

Gene Sharp

SEEKING A SOLUTION TO THE PROBLEM OF WAR

Could nonviolence be applied, as a practical matter, to the defense strategy of modern governments? One of the most seriously considered applications involves civilian-based defense, or CBD, which embraces a variety of nonviolent techniques intended to make it very difficult, if not impossible, for a conquering state to govern another and to gain any benefit from its "victory." CBD must be distinguished from "civil defense," the much less realistic government plan for protecting citizenry in the event of nuclear war, widely derided as neither civil nor defense. CBD is also different from so-called nonprovocative defense (NPD), which emphasizes "defensive defense" via such armaments as antitank devices, antiaircraft munitions, and mobile infantry, as opposed to potentially provocative, offensive weaponry such as bombers, tanks, and other "power-projecting" technology. NPD is a potential way of helping countries avoid the "security dilemma," whereby the pursuit of military security by one country induces insecurity on the part of others. Nonetheless, it clearly fails the test of true nonviolence.

The major theorist of CBD, Gene Sharp, has identified numerous specific tactics of nonviolent action. His writings were especially influential in providing direct, practical suggestions that were followed by nonviolent protesters during the "Arab Spring" of 2010 and 2011. When applied to international affairs, civilian defenders would not violently resist the occupation of their country and would in fact willingly expose themselves to the possibility of substantial hardship, suffering, and even death. But traditional military defenders, too, must anticipate great hardship, suffering, and sometimes death, even in a "successful" violent war. Advocates of CBD emphasize that substantial training of committed citizens would be required. But again, traditional military training in the ways of violence also requires time, effort, and sacrifice as well as commitment. Moreover, most efforts at nonviolent resistance—Hungary in the mid-nineteenth century, Norway in World War II, Eastern Europe in 1989—were spontaneous, unplanned, and largely leaderless movements. Serious CBD, well rehearsed and supported by material resources, has never been tried. Given its impressive track record as a form of resistance when it was essentially extemporized, the future of CBD might be bright indeed if it were ever actually carried out by a well-trained populace. Certainly, the prospect of facing a determined and highly disciplined citizenry committed to denying the invader virtually all fruits of conquest might deter invasion no less effectively than the amassing of military forces—and at it might do so at substantially less cost and risk of provocation.

As weapons become ever more destructive, doctrines of national security based on traditional military techniques offer fewer and fewer prospects of defense. During the Vietnam War, for example, a U.S. major claimed that the village of Ben Tre "had to be destroyed

This chapter is excerpted from: *Social Power and Political Freedom*, by Gene Sharp. Boston: Extending Horizons Books, Porter Sargent Publishers, 1980. To order copies of this publication, or for more information, please contact: The Albert Einstein Institution, P.O. Box 455, East Boston, MA 02128, USA. Tel: USA + 617-247-4882. Fax: USA + 617-247-4035. Email: einstein@igc.org. Website: www.aeinstein.org.

in order for us to save it." Gene Sharp has pointed out that by contrast, CBD alters this dynamic in a crucial way, because it would seek nonviolently to "deny the attackers their objectives and to make society politically indigestible and ungovernable."[5]

A reexamination of the problem of war and the possible means for its solution must begin with a recognition of the failure of past movements and proposals for the abolition of war. These have failed despite the widespread understanding of the destructiveness of modern war. Hardly anyone believes that we are on the way to end war. Military technology stands at its highest stage of development ever. During this decade and the past, military institutions in many countries have been, for a period which is not one of world war, the most powerful ever in comparison to civil branches of government and to the rest of society. Except for world wars, a higher proportion of resources has been devoted in this period to military purposes than ever before. A larger number of lives can now be threatened and destroyed more quickly than earlier imagined.

Defenders of the status quo are not the only practitioners and supporters of war and other political violence. Political movements, parties, and governments which espouse change are often equally committed to military means—as was the case in the war in Vietnam. Nor are we on the verge of a popular rebellion against war as such. The time when the general public might have been capable of significant shock and revulsion at the nature of modern weaponry to rebel against it—as in its early atomic and thermonuclear forms in the late 1940s and the 1950s—has gone.

True, there are antiwar groups. For example, some people object to all war, perhaps even more now do so than previously: the perpetually small minority which witnesses against all war by a refusal to participate in it. Many other people may oppose a *particular* war, as that in Vietnam, when it is perceived as especially unjust or inhuman.[6] (Some of the opponents of the United States' actions in Vietnam were, however, silent about, or even supported, the war effort of the other side.) Still other people, and even governments, support more limited measures and seek to limit the development, manufacture, spread, and use of certain military weapons while accepting that serious disarmament is outside the realm of reality.

But, with very few exceptions, the dream in which many people only a few decades ago firmly believed—that war, along with certain other objectionable aspects of society, could and would be abolished—is for the most part no longer even dreamed. The few persons who still believe in and voice that dream are perceived as out of touch with political reality. If ever in world history awareness of the destructiveness and brutality of war and of the relative power of military systems might have been expected to increase efforts to abolish the military system and to enhance the prospects for doing so, it should have been by now. Instead, we have witnessed the demise of even major efforts to end war.

REEXAMINING THE PROBLEM

It is, of course, possible that one or several of the previously proposed solutions to the problem of war have been partially or largely valid. In any case, those more orthodox approaches will continue to receive attention, as they generally should. However, our further examination of the problem of war should not be limited to those past approaches. It is not reasonable to presume that the answer to it must lie

---

[5] Gene Sharp, *Making Europe Unconquerable: The Potential of Civilian-Based Deterrence and Defense* (Cambridge, MA: Ballinger, 1985). from Gene Sharp, "Seeking a Solution to the Problem of War"

[6] On the varieties of pacifism and on selective nonviolence, see Gene Sharp, *Gandhi as a Political Strategist, with Essays on Ethics and Politics* (Boston: Porter Sargent Publishers, 1979), Chapter Ten, "The Types of Principled Nonviolence."

in an existing proposal, or course, or system, which has not yet moved us perceptibly closer to the resolution of that problem. A careful and critical reexamination of those earlier proposals to ensure peace and to abolish war is impossible here, although it is important that it be done. Since the past proposals have not yet worked, we shall here instead concentrate on developing a different analysis of the nature of the problem of war which will point the direction toward a possible alternative policy and solution. We are unlikely to find a solution to the problem of war if we do not adequately understand the nature of that problem. We need to examine afresh whether war might be abolished for particular societies, or generally—and, if so, how this might be done.

DISTASTEFUL "GIVENS"

A new effort to abolish war requires a prior rejection of any romantic illusions we may have about such abolition; the effort also requires a willingness to recognize certain facts which are often distasteful to exponents of peace. It is assumed here:

- that there will always be intra-societal and inter-societal conflicts;
- that in any such conflict, some type of power will always be present and needed, on both sides;
- that what is crudely called "human nature" need not, and most likely will not, be changed;
- that people and governments will not, and should not be asked to, sacrifice either freedom or justice for the sake of peace;
- that peace is not identical with maintenance of the status quo, nor with revolution;
- that individual conversions to pacifism are not going to happen by the hundreds of millions, and world peace will have to come in a different way;
- that there is no break in the spiral of military technology within the context of military technology and military assumptions;
- that there have been, and are, brutal dictatorships and oppressive systems in the world, which may continue and recur, use new forms of control, and may expand against other countries in various ways;

- that the abolition of capitalism does not produce the abolition of war (the military system is more powerful now in noncapitalist States than before the change, and military action is threatened and used by noncapitalist States against each other);
- that negotiation is not a substitute for the capacity to wage conflict and wield sanctions (a capacity which itself is a crucial factor in negotiations);
- that unilateral "disarmament" (understood as the major reduction or abandonment of defense capacity) is not possible (for reasons which will be discussed);
- that major multilateral disarmament is nearly as unlikely because of the fear of every country to be at a relative disadvantage, and also because of the constantly changing nature of the international situation;
- that national independence is *not* the origin of war, but instead reliance on military means as the ultimate sanction of the independent State;
- that peace through world government is either a dangerous illusion because it is unrealizable, or, if achievable, would constitute a severe danger to world peace (likely to produce a world civil war), to freedom (if capable of preventing war it would be capable of tyranny), and to justice (who would control, to what ends, and how could shifts of control and ends be prevented?).

Other such factors may also need to be recognized. Our search for an understanding of the problem of war, and for a solution to it, must not rest on utopian illusions. Neither must our search be naive concerning the political intentions of protagonists to international conflicts.

Nor can we neglect the role of the basic nature of certain social and political systems. The recognition of this role does not require agreement that any particular system be identified as the "devil." Critical analyses of any and all such systems are desirable; but it is unnecessary and dangerous to gloss over their unsatisfactory characteristics in order to contribute to peace. However, this attention to social and political systems should not lead us to neglect the military system itself. It has its own major requirements and structural consequences; without elimination of reliance on military means, structural or systemic change is unlikely to be very significant, and the new system is likely to find itself distorted or controlled by the military system it has accepted.[7]

FUNCTIONAL ALTERNATIVES

One possible approach to the problem of war has rarely been applied: analysis of the military system's capacity to wage war in terms of its function of providing defense (either in reality, or belief that it does), and exploration of whether or not defense could be provided in some other way. Functional analysis is sometimes dismissed as a status quo approach, but it is utilized here as a tool precisely because it may provide insights making possible fundamental change which may otherwise not be possible. Here the sociological terminology of "function" and "structure" will be used, which might instead be called "need" or "task" and "instrument" or "institution" for the particular purposes of this discussion.[8]

A.R. Radcliffe-Brown defined function as "the part it plays in the social life as a whole and therefore the contribution it makes to the maintenance of the structural continuity."[9] John Bennett and Melvin Tumin wrote that to ask the function of something is to ask "What does it 'do for' people and groups."[10] The recognition that human institutions have functions and perform certain jobs for society in no way blocks the way to change, even fundamental change. Instead, examination of the existence and possibilities of "functional substitutes," or "functional equivalents," or "functional alternatives" opens the way

for basic change. Functional substitutes have been referred to by various analysts and theorists, including Theodor Newcomb,[11] Talcott Parsons,[12] Parsons and Edward A. Shils,[13] Lewis Coser,[14] and especially Robert K. Merton.[15]

Merton pointed out in 1949 that the existing social structures—that is, patterns of action, institutions, instruments, or "means" to a social goal—are not the only possible ones. There also exist other ways of fulfilling the function served by the present structure. The specific existing social structures, he insisted, are *not* functionally indispensable. Merton offered "as a major theorem of analysis": *". . . the same function [may] be diversely fulfilled by alternative items.* Functional needs are here taken to be permissive, rather than determinant, of specific social structures."[16] In fact, alternative social structures have served the functions necessary for groups to continue to exist.[17] This, he wrote, "unfreezes the identity of the existent and the inevitable."[18] Since there may be a range of ways in which a particular functional need may be fulfilled, we should look for functional alternatives. He insisted that this was relevant to conscious efforts to produce social change, and offered also as "a basic theorem":

> *. . . any attempt to eliminate an existing social structure without providing adequate alternative structures for fulfilling the functions previously fulfilled by the abolished organization is doomed to failure.*[19]

---

[7] See Chapter Eleven, "The Societal Imperative," and Chapter Twelve, "Popular Empowerment, subchapter Sanctions and Society.

[8] Here I will in part repeat and enlarge upon a portion of the discussion in Chapter Nine, "'The Political Equivalent of War'—Civilian-Based Defense." See also the discussion on functions and structures in Chapter Twelve, "Popular Empowerment."

[9] A. R. Radcliffe-Brown, *Structure and Function in Primitive Society* (Glencoe, Ill.: The Free Press, 1952), p. 180.

[10] John Bennett and Melvin Tumin, *Social Life: Structure and Function* (New York: Alfred A. Knopf, 1948), p. 245.

[11] Theodor Newcom, *Social Psychology* (New York: Dryden Press, 1950), p. 351.

[12] Talcott Parsons, *Essays in Sociological Theory, Pure and Applied* (Glencoe, Ill.: The Free Press, 1949), p. 58. Also, Parsons, *The Social System* (Glencoe, Ill.: The Press, 1951), p. 210.

[13] T. Parsons and Edward A. Shils, *Toward a General Theory of Action* (Cambridge, Mass.: Harvard University Press, 1951), p. 5.

[14] Lewis Coser, *The Functions of Social Conflict* (London: Collier-Macmillan, and New York: The Free Press, 1956), p. 50.

[15] Robert K. Merton, *Social Theory and Social Structure* (Glencoe, Ill.: The Free Press, 1949), pp. 35–36, 52 and 79.

[16] Ibid., p. 35. Italics are Merton's.

[17] Ibid.

[18] Ibid., p. 52.

[19] Ibid., p. 79. Italics are Merton's.

Parsons similarly wrote: "There must be a development of 'functional alternatives' to the structures which have been eliminated."[20] And Coser, too, argued:

> In realistic conflict, there exist functional alternatives as to means . . . . [T]here are always possibilities of choice between various forms of contention, such choice depending . . . on an assessment of their instrumental adequacy.[21]

FUNCTIONS OF WAR

War is such a prominent institution of modern society that if these theoretical views are valid they must apply to the military system which wages war. Let us therefore explore the application of this functional substitute theory to war.

Such a complex and diverse structure as the military system has doubtless served many purposes or functions. A careful analysis of *all* of them is needed (a task which is not attempted here), including examinations of alternative ways of fulfilling those functions which seem lasting, and exploration of whether some of the functions of the military—especially those deemed undesirable—may be required only under specific conditions and not universally, and may hence be removed, reduced, or dealt with in some other way.

We shall here identify four functions of a military capacity which are primarily political and are associated with national policy of the governments:

Attack: especially international aggression, motivated or justified variously, including the desire for: economic benefit, power expansion, egocentric aggrandizement of rulers, "liberation," extending "civilization," seizure of territory, and extermination of "inferiors." Sometimes the attack is internal, against the governmental system of that very country, or against another part of the society, as in a coup d'etat or civil war.

Domination: control and oppression of the home population, or foreign populations and countries, or both, also with diverse motivations remarkably similar to those just listed.

Deterrent: that is, prevention of attack by possession of sufficient capacity to cause the potential attacker to anticipate greater losses than gains, or that the attack will fail, and hence to decide against initiating the venture.

Defense: that is, "defense" in the literal sense of the term, as warding off, protection, resistance against attack, denial of the objective of the attacker, and upholding or maintaining one's own objectives against the attacker. This includes both defense against genuine attack and preparations to defend in case of attack. Also at times the excuse of "defense" is used to assist in internal domination or is used to disguise for the home population what is in fact an attack on another country. (This last point is very important, and the following analysis is by implication relevant to it, although that specific kind of situation requires separate analysis.)

The relative importance of each of the several functions of war may vary from case to case, culture to culture, and time to time, although certain ones may be both far more persistent and perceived to be more generally justifiable than others. Let us now look at these four functions more closely, in two groups.

FUNCTIONS OF ATTACK AND DOMINATION

It appears that the functions of attack and domination may be dealt with in other ways than by providing substitute nonmilitary means of attacking and dominating, functions which are in any case undesirable. These functions might be removed, or attempts to carry them out might be frustrated, and thus the functions in practice are finally drastically reduced in two ways:

1. Changes may be carried out in the society which is, or potentially is, the origin of an attack, to reduce or eliminate both motives and ability to attack, by changes in its social institutions, distribution of power, economic system, beliefs and attitudes as to legitimacy, acceptable policies, and the like. Those social

---

[20] Parsons, *The Social System,* p. 167.
[21] Coser, *The Functions of Social Conflict,* p. 50

changes require separate attention, which unfortunately is not possible here.[22] If attacks can be reduced or eliminated by social changes which remove the "need," functional alternatives are not required here.

2. The capacity of the attacked society to defend itself by some means might be increased, so as effectively to deter attacks, to defeat attacks if they occur, or to liberate itself from the oppression caused by past attacks. Successful and repeated defense (and liberation) to such internal or external attacks, denying the objectives to the attackers is likely to reduce the frequency with which military systems are used to attack, *provided that* the defense is by means which do not confirm the attacker's belief in the omnipotence of the military system to gain ends. In other words, in the case of this function, it may not be a functional substitute means of *attack* which may be required, but a functional substitute means of *defeating* the attack. There are very important reasons (which are developed elsewhere) why such deterrence and struggle against internal or external attacks may be more advantageously and effectively achieved by means *other than* the military forms of conflict.[23]

FUNCTIONS OF DETERRENCE AND DEFENSE

Military systems also are widely used to deter and to defend. The reasons offered by most people, policymakers, and government spokesmen for keeping and relying upon the military system even today are that a strong military capacity can, better than anything else, deter an attack, and defend against an attack. In the face of these perceived functions of military systems, pleas to abandon military capacity on moral, religious, humanitarian, or political grounds have historically been accepted by only a small minority, while the general population has, with few exceptions, rejected the antimilitary pleadings. War may be brutal, immoral, and even suicidal, but people have perceived that it provided an ultimate sanction and means of struggle for which they have perceived no alternative. Even where deterrence and defense are *not* the real motives for military systems, popular support for those systems and war efforts will be forthcoming even for aggressive purposes, as long as people believe they have no alternative means of defense.

Whether to be held in reserve to back up one's position in international negotiations, to deter attack by adequate preparations, or to defend in case of attack, military systems have been believed necessary since no other way to fulfill those functions of deterrence and defense has been believed to exist. It has been commonly assumed that the alternative to war is impotence, cowardice, and passive submission, and that perception of "ordinary" people has been shared by statesmen, policymakers, intellectuals, and academics. Even nuclear and similar weapons have not changed this, for people believe that, although nuclear weapons normally ought not to be launched, their existence will prevent attack, and thus provide safety and avoid helplessness.

All of this analysis is fully compatible with the application of Merton's "basic theorem" to the

---

[22] However, the view that institutional or systemic changes (with or without accompanying attitude changes) will lead to the abandonment of the military system without specific attention to that abandonment is rejected here. In fact, social changes and social revolution may *increase* the military system, and popular support for it, because of a perceived greater need to defend the changes against counterrevolutionary threats (domestic or foreign), or because the society is perceived to be more worthy of defense, and the like. If violent struggle has produced the social revolution, the relative role of the military system in comparison to civil branches of the government and other institutions is likely to increase. If the struggle was largely nonviolent but with confidence remaining in military means for defense, an increase in the military system is also likely, only to a lesser degree. Almost without exceptions, countries which have undergone avowed social revolutions possess stronger military systems after the revolution than they did under the old order. Attention is therefore needed to other means of abolishing war than changes in the social system unaccompanied by abandonment of the military system. See the fuller discussion of these points in Chapter Twelve, "Popular Empowerment," subchapter Sanctions and Society.

[23] See Chapter Nine, "'The Political Equivalent of War'— Civilian-Based Defense."

problem of war, for Merton postulated that efforts to remove a basic structure without providing an alternative structure for fulfilling its function would be doomed to failure.[24] The need for defense of a society, its populace, its institutions, way of life and the like, is such a basic societal need that in conditions of perceived and actual threats of attack, the military system will not be abandoned when it is understood that this will leave the society helpless and defenseless in meeting real or imagined dangers. This is, however, precisely what proposals for abandonment of war and the military system have almost always meant or been perceived to mean.

SEPARATING STRUCTURE AND FUNCTION

Peace movements and most peace proposals have in their assumptions and analyses often confused structure and function, or, putting it in other ways, confused institution and job, or instrument and task. Exponents of peace have largely accepted the identity of the structure (the military system and war) with its perceived most justified functions (deterrence and defense), just as have the exponents and practitioners of the war system itself. It has been assumed that effective defense and strong military capacity are synonymous. Whether judged by Merton's theorem, by statements of political officials, or by the views of "ordinary" people, it was predictable and inevitable that past efforts to abolish war would fail. This also explains why present and future efforts which are primarily antimilitary and antiwar cannot succeed.

The simple distinction between structure and function, or instrument and task, applied to war and defense may free us from the axiomatic presumption of the identity of defense with the military system. The distinction between defense and the military system enables us to ask whether there can be alternative means of defense which are not military—a question which to most people has been inconceivable.

This ought not to be as ludicrous a question as it might appear to others, since, even with present policies, defense and military capacity are not identical. First, the growth and development of military technology means that in its extreme forms the actual use of military means can in some cases provide only vast destruction and death, *not* actual defense. Second, in some cases, the advance perception of such possible destruction, or of overwhelming military capacity by the attacker, may lead to a realization that military resistance for defense is futile and hence to a decision not to attempt it. Third, and most important, in some international conflicts, nonmilitary means of resistance have already been improvised and used for national defense purposes. Also, such nonviolent means of struggle, in crude and undeveloped forms, have been widely used and often highly important in internal conflicts.

The analysis in this section of the chapter has pointed in this direction:

> *The path to the abolition of war may lie through the substitution of nonmilitary means of defense, if these exist, can be created or refined, and if they are, or can be made to be, at least as instrumentally effective as military means of defense have been and now are.*

NONVIOLENT STRUGGLE

The world, much less politics, is not divided neatly into categories of "violence" and "nonviolence." There are many intermediary phenomena which are neither violent nor nonviolent. But in terms of ultimate sanctions and means of struggle, which are used when milder means are judged inadequate or have failed, there do appear to be two broad techniques, one violent action—which includes several types of violent conflict, among them conventional and nuclear war—the other, nonviolent action—which is also a broad and diverse technique. It is to the nature and potential of this nonviolent technique of struggle that our attention now turns.

Our awareness and understanding of the nonviolent counterpart of violent struggle is generally sharply limited and filled with many serious distortions and errors of fact. Therefore, an initial effort is usually required to free our minds from inaccurate perceptions of this type of struggle which we have accumulated from a culture in which belief in violence as the ultimate form of power and as the most

---

[24] A longer discussion of some aspects of this exploration is contained in Gene Sharp, "The Need of a Functional Substitute for War," *International Relations* (London), vol. III, no. 3 (April 1967), pp. 187–207.

significant single fact in history—both of which are now challenged—are fundamental axioms. This belief in the omnipotence of violence, and ignorance of the power of popular nonviolent struggle, may have also been compatible with the interests of past dominating elites who did not want people to realize their power potential.

Because of preconceptions, it is necessary to indicate some of the things that nonviolent action is *not*. This technique is the opposite of passivity, submissiveness, and cowardice. Nonviolent action uses social, economic, psychological, and political power in the matching of forces in conflict, and is not to be equated with verbal or purely psychological persuasion. This means of struggle does not assume that humans are inherently "good." This is not "pacifism"; in fact, this technique has been predominantly used by "ordinary" people who never became pacifists, and also some pacifists find it offensive. Nonviolent conflict may operate even in cases of extreme social distance between contending groups. The technique may be more "Western" than "Eastern," and certainly is not the reverse. It is designed to combat a violent opponent, and does not presume a nonviolent response to the nonviolent challenge. This technique may be used for both "good" and "bad" causes, though the social consequences of its use for "bad" causes differs sharply from those of violence.[25] While violence is believed to work fast, and nonviolent action slowly, often violence takes a great length of time and nonviolent struggle may operate extremely quickly. Finally, and most importantly for this chapter, nonviolent action is not limited to domestic conflicts within a democratic system; it has been used widely against dictatorial regimes, foreign occupations, and even totalitarian systems,[26] and it has already been applied without advance preparations internationally, even in improvised national defense struggles.

Our recent studies of this technique have revealed it to be infinitely richer, more variable and powerful than hitherto dreamed.[27] It has been widely thought that, for the most part, politically significant nonviolent struggle began with Gandhi. We now know that it has a rich and vast history which we are only beginning to piece together which goes back at least to several centuries B.C., and ranges over many cultures, continents, countries, historical periods, issues, types of groups, and opponents. Instead of the list of specific methods, or forms of action included within this technique being relatively few (a dozen or so as was once thought) we now know that even with a partial listing the number is at least 198, arranged in three main classes of nonviolent protest and persuasion (the milder forms), noncooperation (including boycotts of social relations, economic boycotts, strikes, and political noncooperation), and nonviolent intervention.

It was thought by some that conversion of the opponent by the sufferings of the nonviolent actionists was the only, or at least the best, way in which nonviolent action produced change. We now know that this is not true, and that nonviolent struggle can also be coercive, possibly even more so than violence against an obstinate opponent. This is because nonviolent struggle is capable of severing the various sources of the opponent's power, as by massive civil disobedience of the population as a whole paralyzing the political system, strikes by workers and noncooperation by management paralyzing the economic system, noncooperation by civil servants paralyzing the governmental structure, mutiny by soldiers destroying the repressive capacity, and in many other equally important but more subtle ways.

COMPARISON WITH VIOLENT STRUGGLE

A survey of the knowledge we now have of the history of nonviolent action would facilitate our

---

[25] See the discussion on this point in Chapter Twelve, "Popular Empowerment."

[26] See Chapter Four, "Facing Dictatorships with Confidence."

[27] See esp. Gene Sharp, *The Politics of Nonviolent Action* (Boston: Porter Sargent Publisher, 1973). This is a comprehensive presentation and analysis of the nature of nonviolent struggle. Discussion in this chapter of that technique is documented in that book. It does not contain, however, discussion of the "civilian-based defense policy," although it provides the necessary groundwork to that policy. On Gandhi, see Gene Sharp, *Gandhi as a Political Strategist, with Essays on Ethics and Politics* (Boston: Porter Sargent Publishers, 1979), esp. Chapters One, Two, and Three.

consideration of this largely neglected socio-political technique, but that is not possible within the scope of this chapter. Suffice it to say that it is a remarkable history which when more fully revealed will require and produce major reexaminations of not only social but political history, and fundamental reinterpretations of very significant historical cases where violence is widely presumed to have been the only form of struggle, or the only possible successful one. In this, the American Revolution,[28] the Russian Revolution, and struggles against Nazism are only three of the more dramatic such cases.

This new understanding and information about the nature, history, dynamics, and existing capacities of nonviolent struggle is of a magnitude to require major reevaluation of the judgements which have been made or assumed about its effectiveness and potential in comparison with violence. That is but the beginning, however.

Nonviolent action has almost always been improvised without significant awareness of the history of this type of struggle. It has usually been waged without qualified leadership, or without compensating wide popular understanding of the technique, without thorough comprehension of its requirements for effectiveness, without preparations and training, without analyses of past conflicts, without studies of strategy and tactics, without conscious development of its "weaponry," and often without a consciousness among the actionists that they were waging a special type of struggle. In short, the most unfavorable circumstances possible have accompanied the use of this technique. It is amazing that the significant number of victories for nonviolent struggle exists at all, for these conditions of the lack of knowledge, skill, and preparations have been to the highest degree unfavorable. In contrast, for many centuries military struggle has benefited from conscious efforts to improve its effectiveness in all the ways which nonviolent action has lacked.

---

[28] See Walter Conser, Ronald McCarthy, Gene Sharp, David Toscano, and Kenneth Wadoski, eds., *To Bid Defiance to Tyranny: Nonviolent Action and the American Independence Movement 1765–1775* (Boston: Porter Sargent Publishers, 1981).

INTERNATIONAL RELEVANCE

Some people assume that means of conflict which have predominantly been used in domestic conflicts—as nonviolent action—are intrinsically limited to that range of conflict situations, while military struggle is the means obviously appropriate to the international level. On closer reflection it becomes obvious that this distinction is by no means as clear-cut as is often assumed. Violent action, of course, is also widely used internally—in repression, resistance, coups d'etat, revolution, guerrilla war, civil war, and the like. Also, certain forms of nonviolent action are used internationally far more frequently than is usually recognized—such as embargoes, freezing the assets of another country, economic boycotts, cancellation of planned conferences and diplomatic visits, and refusal of diplomatic recognition. Other forms—which are far more relevant to our analysis—are the cases of widespread civilian resistance against invasion forces and occupation regimes.

The reality may be that whether a given technique is applicable to domestic or international conflicts is not determined by whether it does or does not use physical violence but by whether people have tried to adapt it as effectively as possible to that particular type of conflict situation. The presumption that nonviolent struggle is only appropriate to domestic conflicts is not valid.

Nonviolent struggle has already been applied in international politics *without planning or preparations and at times even without advice decision* (all of which are regarded as essential for maximum effectiveness). These international struggles do not refer to international economic boycotts and embargoes. Contrary to Thomas Jefferson, who saw those economic weapons as the basis for a substitute for war, they are probably not models, or even primitive prototypes, upon which to build a nonviolent functional substitute for war. Other cases exist which, although not models, might be early prototypes upon which to build more successful prepared and trained nonviolent defense capacities.

The resistance of Czechoslovakia in 1968–69 is the closest to what is envisaged. This was a nonviolent war of resistance to invasion and occupation, a war which in the end was lost. We learn from lost military wars, however, and we can learn from lost nonviolent wars. According to some reports, the Russians anticipated military resistance from the able Czechoslovak army, and expected they could overcome it and install a puppet government within four days. Despite very considerable Czechoslovak military capacity based on years of preparations and training, the obvious futility of military resistance in face of five invading armies, including that of the Soviet Union, produced a decision not to resist with military force.

Instead, an unprepared, improvised nonviolent resistance occurred. Despite serious problems, and apparent major strategic errors, and sometimes without adequate assistance from the official leadership, this resistance managed initially to frustrate completely the Russian efforts to install a puppet government in spite of the distribution of troops throughout the country. This resistance also forced the Soviet Union to negotiate with Czechoslovak leaders (some of whom, as Dubcek, already had been arrested and kidnapped). All this was produced by people whose country was already totally occupied and whose army had never entered the field, conditions under which negotiations should not—by conventional views—have been required or expected!

Even after those negotiations, such resistance in less dramatic forms in fact maintained the Dubcek regime, so hated by the Russians, in power (after their release from arrest and imprisonment) until April of 1969—eight months! Even then, it can be argued, the demise resulted more from the collapse of resistance by the Government and Party at a time of anti-Russian riots (a break in the nonviolent discipline, possibly caused by *agents provocateurs*) than it did from any intrinsic weakness in the means of resistance.

That initial week of unified nonviolent resistance and complete denial of political victory to the Russians, and the eight-month life of the very regime which was the stimulus for the Russian invasion, are achievements of immense proportions. This is especially true considering that this nonviolent resistance capacity was *unprepared*, and hence probably less effectual and certainly less reliable than if it had

been adequately prepared. Had unprepared military struggle against such odds held off the Russians for eight months it would have been hailed as victory even in defeat, with courage and historical significance comparable to Thermopylae.

There have been other cases, such as the struggle in the Ruhr against the French and Belgian occupation in 1923 in which nonviolent resistance was launched as offical German Government policy. (The situation became mixed with sabotage later with detrimental effects for the German cause.) This case is widely regarded as a complete German defeat. Nevertheless, it led to an end of the occupation, and disastrous economic consequences for France (as well as Germany), and the French people's revulsion against the French Government's repression policies of their former enemies. This revulsion is said to have contributed to the unexpected electoral defeat of Prime Minister Poincaré's Government in the next election—achievements which Germany was militarily unable even to *attempt* at the time.

Significant other cases of nonviolent resistance can be classed as nonviolent struggle for national defense. These include the Hungarian struggle against Austria for home rule from 1850 to 1867, and Finland's struggles against Russification, especially from 1898 to 1905. Even the Gandhian struggles in India against British rule were those of an occupied country seeking restoration of independence—surely an international conflict. (Gandhi was far from the first Indian nationalist to advocate or organize nonviolent struggle for independence.) During the Second World War, Norwegian, Danish, and Dutch resistance against the Nazi occupations and certain other anti-Nazi struggles, including limited efforts to save Jews, produced some modest but significant victories. Some of these actions had the support of, or were even initiated by, the Government-in-exile.

A BASIS FOR A SUBSTITUTE FOR WAR?

Nonviolent action generally, and its use for national defense purposes specifically, has never even yet received systematic efforts to develop its capacity, to increase its effectiveness, and to expand the areas of its utility. The nonviolent technique is thus an underdeveloped political technique, probably at the stage comparable to violent group conflict several thousand years ago. Hence, nonviolent struggle as waged to date may only have revealed a small fraction of its potential fighting power and effectiveness.

The challenge now is to bring to nonviolent struggle research, analysis, experimentation, planning, preparations, and training, with the objective of attaining greater knowledge and understanding, facilitating our ability to evaluate it fairly, increasing the effectiveness of this technique, and, finally, exploring its progressive extension to serious conflict situations where most people have presumed that only military, or other violent, conflict was adequate.

Specifically, the question is this: can a national defense policy, for both small and large countries, be created by the capacity of the civilian population, trained, prepared, knowledgeable, to wield nonviolent struggle? Can this policy make the consolidation and maintenance of control by an invading force or a coup d'état impossible? Even cursory examination of strategies for civilian-based defense lies outside this chapter. We note only that they are diverse, and flexible, and always need to be related to the specific situation and the objectives of the attacker in order to defeat his specific aims as effectively and efficiently as possible.

Also, the question arises as to whether such preparations can be perceived as sufficiently effective to deter invasions and coups. Finally, can this policy be relevant to the present nuclear powers? Would such a country which (1) had gradually built up its capacity to wage civilian-based defense, and then (2) had by unilateral action or negotiated agreements gradually phased down and dispensed with its military weaponry, including its nuclear capacity, as unneeded, be likely to be threatened or attacked with nuclear weapons? (This needs careful attention even though today it is generally the nuclear powers that fear attack, while the nonnuclear powers generally do not expect it.)

In comparing nonviolent struggle with military struggle for defense capacity the same criteria must be used in evaluating both, in terms of the degree of risk, what is risked, the costs if it comes to an open clash, the nature of failure and success in such a clash, and the possible gains in case of success.

IS IT POSSIBLE?

This type of policy is called "civilian defense," in some countries, "social defense" in Germany and the Netherlands, and increasingly "civilian-based defense" in the United States. It is direct defense of the society, its principles, people, way of life, chosen institutions, right to maintain or change itself, by action of the civilian population as a whole, and their institutions, using civilian (nonmilitary, nonviolent) means of struggle. It should go without saying that this is not a panacea and other diverse programs are needed to help meet many other needs.

This approach on a serious policy level began only in 1957. it has thus far received the most respectful attention from people regarded as hard-headed realists, strategists, defense analysts, planners, and military officers, as well as others interested in social change and world peace. The response is as yet small, but it includes limited governmental interest in several European countries. Books and other publications now exist on the subject in several European languages and Japanese. Thus in the relatively few years since 1957 this idea has been transformed from a vague conception into a strategic proposal receiving serious thought from the most unlikely people.

Some people still see this as a romantic conception unassociated with the real and the possible. Yet, there is profound truth contained in what Kenneth Boulding calls "Boulding's First Law"; "What exists, is possible."[29] Nonviolent action exists. It has occurred in human history on a scale, seriousness, and with a degree of success (nothing is ever always successful) which has hitherto been unrealized (despite the noted lack of understanding). Nonviolent struggle has even been applied against ruthless tyrants, and as we observed has already been used for national defense. Social science research, policy development, and strategic analysis also exist and can be applied to this phenomenon. We have more evidence today that a civilian-based defense policy is possible, and, if adequately prepared, could work

---

[29] Kenneth Boulding, quoted in Jerome D. Frank, *Sanity and Survival: Psychological Aspects of War and Peace* (New York: Vintage Books, Random House, 1968), p. 270.

more effectively than military means for real defense at this stage of history, than there was in August 1939 that atomic bombs were possible. That was the date when Dr. Einstein wrote the famous letter to President Roosevelt saying that *maybe* a new highly explosive bomb could be made from atoms.

It is popular today to pronounce that war is inevitable because of the aggressive nature of human beings, and hence some people conclude that this nonviolent "thing" is all nonsense. That is not the view of significant writers on human aggressiveness. Konrad Lorenz has insisted that: "modern war has become an institution and . . . being an institution war can be abolished."[30] Robert Ardrey, no less, has asserted: "We must be nonviolent. Yes, we can do it—but are we going to have to work at it."[31]

Civilian-based defense is set forth for study and research as a possible functional substitute for war, as a means of abolishing war while providing real defense by nonviolent means against tyrants and aggressors. If it could be made to work at least as well as military means, it would be possible for individual countries, alone or in groups, without waiting on others, to "transarm," that is to change over to this defense system. This would be possible (in contrast to disarmament) because if it does work, civilian-based defense will maintain or increase defense capacity while making possible abandonment of military means as unneeded. It would thus by-pass the most serious blockage to disarmament proposals, fear of reduced fighting capacity, or an unfavorable relative fighting capacity for providing defense against attack.

FOUR TASKS

A vast amount of research, analysis, and problem-oriented investigation is required to examine whether this approach to provide a functional substitute for

the military system and defensive military warfare is indeed a fruitful one, and whether, and if so how, the multitude of difficult problems associated with it can be solved. These problems include such questions as the means of training and preparations, how to handle the transarmament period, ways to meet the particular defense needs of individual countries, and the potential of this policy (compared with violence) in confronting successfully the most extreme and ruthless regimes.

Four tasks now urgently need to be tackled simultaneously to determine whether the approach to the problem of war presented in this chapter contains the basis for its solution.

First, a major program of research, analysis, and problem-oriented investigation, involving thousands of scholars of many disciplines, analysts, and other specialists. Outlines of some general research areas which might be tackled have been already proposed,[32] and others are needed. Dozens of research centers and programs are required.

Second, public and private discussion and evaluation of this substitute-for-war-policy, the problems with which it attempts to deal, existing knowledge relevant to whether it could work, and the difficulties which must be overcome if the policy is to be viable, and its potentialities and possible consequences.

Third, serious investigation and evaluation of this policy by civilian governmental bodies, defense departments, private institutions and groups, organizations, institutions, and individuals.

Fourth, high school, college, university, and general public education courses on the nature of nonviolent action, its potential as an alternative to domestic violence, and on the potential and problems of civilian-based defense as a substitute for war.

Each of these four tasks will require major resources and personnel. Considering the seriousness of our problems, this is a very modest proposal.

[30] Konrad Lorenz, *On Aggression* (New York: Harcourt, Brace and World, 1963), p. 284.

[31] Louis S. B. Leakey and Robert Ardrey, in a dialogue, on "Man, the Killer," *Psychology Today*, vol. 6, no. 4 (September 1972), p. 85

[32] Gene Sharp, *Exploring Nonviolent Alternatives* (Boston: Porter Sargent Publisher, 1970), pp. 73–114, and Gene Sharp, "Research Areas on the Nature, Problems, and Potentialities of Civilian Defense," in S. C. Biswas, ed., *Gandhi: Theory and Practice, Social Impact and Contemporary Relevance: Proceedings of a Conference* (Simla: Indian Institute of Advanced Studies, 1969), pp. 393–414.

Joseph S. Nye, Jr.

SOFT POWER

It goes without saying that when self-styled "realists" consider the question of international "power," they mean military power or, occasionally, economic power. Partisans of realpolitik also consider, that the goal of a country's international relations is to maximize its power—as defined above—and thus its ability to orchestrate international affairs for its own benefit. Rarely considered is the notion that a country's benefit may be ultimately achieved in the context of "win-win solutions" in which the payoff to each participant, rather than requiring a negative outcome for others, actually derives from maximizing the payoff for all, and that unlike a military confrontation, relations among countries need not involve a loss for one in order for others to gain. Moreover, there has been a growing undercurrent of recognition that our conception of "power" itself needs to be reconsidered, with special attention given to the role of what scholar/diplomat Joseph Nye calls "soft power."

Power is a contested concept. No one definition is accepted by all who use the word, and people's choice of definition reflects their interests and values. Some define power as the ability to make or resist change. Others say it is the ability to get what we want. This broad definition includes power over nature as well as power over other people. For an interest in politics and policies, a commonsense place to start is the dictionary, which tells us that power is the capacity to do things, but that more specifically, in social situations, we are interested in the ability to affect others to get the outcomes we want. Some people call this influence, and they distinguish power from influence, but that is confusing, because the dictionary defines the two terms interchangeably.

Many factors affect our ability to get what we want. We live in a web of inherited social forces, some of which are visible and others of which are indirect and sometimes called "structural." We tend to identify and focus on some of these constraints and forces rather than others, depending on our interests. For example, in his work on civilizations, the political scientist Peter Katzenstein argues that "the power of civilizations is different from power in civilizations. Actors in civilizations command hard and soft power. . . . Social power operates beneath the behavioral level by shaping underlying social structures, knowledge systems and general environment." While such structural social forces are important, for policy purposes, we also want to understand what actors or agents can do within given situations. Civilizations and societies are not immutable, and effective leaders can try to shape larger social forces with varying degrees of success. As Max Weber put it in his *The Theory of Social and Economic Organization*, we want to know the probability that an actor in a social relationship can carry out his own will.

Even when we focus primarily on particular agents or actors, we cannot say that an actor "has power" without specifying power "to do what" (Nagel 14). One must specify *who* is involved in the

Used by permission of Joseph S. Nye, University Distinguished Service Professor at Harvard and author of The Future of Power.

power relationship (the scope of power) as well as *what* topics are involved (the domain of power). For example, the pope has power over some Christians but not others (such as Protestants). Even among Catholics, he may wish to have power over all their moral decisions, but some adherents may reject his power on some issues (such as birth control or marriage outside the church). Thus, to say that the pope has power requires us to specify the context (scope and domain) of the relationship.

A psychopath may have the power to kill and destroy random strangers but not the power to persuade them. Some actions that affect others and obtain preferred outcomes can be purely destructive and not depend on what the victim thinks. For example, Pol Pot oversaw the killing of millions of Cambodians. Some say such use of force is not power, because there was no two-way relationship involved, but that depends on context and motive. If the actor's motive is pure sadism or terror, the use of force fits within the definition of power as affecting others to get what one wants. Most power relationships, however, depend very much on what the victim thinks. A dictator who wishes to punish a dissident may be misled in thinking he exercised power if the dissident really sought martyrdom to advance her cause. On the other hand, if the dictator simply wanted to destroy the dissident, her intentions did not matter to his power.

THE THREE FACES OF POWER

It is useful to distinguish three different aspects of relational power. The ability to compel others to change their behavior against their initial preferences is one important dimension, but it is not the only important aspect of relational power. One can also affect others' preferences so that they need not be compelled to change them. Former U.S. President (and General) Dwight D. Eisenhower referred to this as getting people to do something "not only because you tell them to do so, but because they instinctively want to do it for you." This co-optive power contrasts with and complements command power. It is a mistake to think that power consists of just ordering others to change. You can affect others' behavior by shaping their preferences in ways that produce

what you want rather than relying on carrots and sticks to change their behavior "when push comes to shove." Sometimes you can get the outcomes you want without pushing or shoving.

The first aspect, or "face," of power was defined by the Yale political scientist Robert Dahl in studies of New Haven in the 1950s, and it is widely used in comparative politics today even though it covers only part of power behavior. It focuses on the ability to get others to act in ways that are contrary to their initial preferences and strategies. To measure or judge power, you have to know how strong another person or nation's initial preferences were and how much they were changed by your efforts. Coercion is quite clear, even when there appears to be some degree of choice. If a gunman says, "your money or your life," you have some choice, but it is small and not consistent with your initial preferences (unless they included suicide or martyrdom).

Economic measures are somewhat more complex. Negative sanctions (taking away economic benefit) are clearly felt as coercive. Payment or economic inducement to do what you initially did not want to may seem more attractive to the subject, but any payment can easily be turned into a negative sanction by the implicit or explicit threat of its removal. A year-end bonus is a reward, but its removal is felt as a penalty. Moreover, in unequal bargaining relationships, say between a millionaire landowner and a starving peasant, a paltry "take-it-or-leave-it" payment may give the peasant little sense of choice. The important point is that someone has the capacity to make others act against their initial preferences and strategies, and both sides feel that power.

In the 1960s, shortly after Dahl developed his widely accepted definition, the political scientists Peter Bachrach and Morton Baratz pointed out that Dahl's definition missed what they called the "second face of power." Dahl ignored the dimension of framing and agenda setting. If one can use ideas and institutions to frame the agenda for action in a way that makes others' preferences seem irrelevant or out of bounds, then it may never be necessary to push or shove them. In other words, it may be possible to shape others' preferences by affecting their expectations of what is legitimate or feasible. Agenda framing focuses on the ability to keep issues off the table, or as Sherlock Holmes might put it, dogs that fail to bark.

Powerful actors can make sure that the less powerful are never invited to the table, or that if they get there, the rules of the game have already been set by those who arrived first. Those who are subject to this second face of power may or may not be aware of it. If they accept the legitimacy of the institutions or the social discourse that framed the agenda, they may not feel unduly constrained by the second face of power. On the other hand, if the agenda of action is constrained by threats of coercion or promises of payments, then it is just an instance of the first face of power. The target's acquiescence in the legitimacy of the agenda is what makes it co-optive and a part of soft power.

Still later, in the 1970s, the sociologist Steven Lukes pointed out that ideas and beliefs also help shape others' *initial* preferences. In Dahl's approach, I can exercise power over you by getting you to do what you would otherwise not want to do—in other words, by changing your situation, I can make you change your preferred strategy. I can also, however, exercise power over you by determining your very wants. I can shape your basic or initial preferences, not merely change the situation in a way that makes you change your strategy for achieving your preferences.

This dimension of power is missed in Dahl's definition. A teenage boy may carefully choose a fashionable shirt to wear to school to attract a girl, but the teenager may not be aware that the reason the shirt is so fashionable is that a national retailer recently launched a major advertising campaign for it. Both his preference and that of the other teenagers have been formed by an unseen actor who has shaped the structure of preferences. If you can get others to want the same outcomes that you want, it will not be necessary to override their initial desires. Lukes called this "the third face of power."

There are critical questions of voluntarism in determining how freely people chose their preferences. Not all soft power looks so soft to outside critics. In some extreme cases, it is difficult to ascertain what constitutes voluntary formation of preferences. For instance, in the "Stockholm syndrome," victims of kidnapping who suffered traumatic stress begin to identify with their abductors. Captors sometimes try to "brainwash" their captives and, sometimes, to win them over with kindnesses. In some situations, however, it is more difficult to be certain of others' interests. Sometimes it is difficult to know the extent of voluntarism from mere outward appearances. Dictators like Hitler and Stalin tried to create an aura of invincibility to attract followers. To the extent that force creates a sense of awe that attracts others, it can be an indirect source of co-optive power, but if the force is directly coercive, then it is simply an instance of the first face of power.

SOFT POWER

Soft power is the ability to get what you want by the co-optive means of framing the agenda, persuasion, and positive attraction. Both soft power and hard power fit all three faces or aspects of power behavior discussed above, though soft power is more often associated with the second and third faces.

Thus, the three faces of power behavior are:

1. First Face (Dahl: make others do what they otherwise would not do). Hard A uses force/payment to change B's existing strategies or preferences. Soft A uses attraction/persuasion to change B's existing preferences.
2. Second Face (Bachrach and Baratz: agenda setting). Hard A uses force/pay to truncate B's agenda (whether B likes it or not). Soft A uses attraction or institutions so that B sees the agenda as legitimate.
3. Third Face (Lukes: shape others' preferences). Hard A uses force/pay to shape B's preferences ("Stockholm syndrome"). Soft A uses attraction and/or institutions to shape B's initial preferences.

For example, suppose a school principal does not want a teenager to smoke. Under the first dimension of power, the principal could threaten the student with fines or expulsion to change her desire to smoke (hard power) or spend hours persuading her to change her existing preference about smoking (soft power). Under the second dimension, the principal could ban cigarette vending machines (a hard aspect of agenda setting) or use public-service advertisements about cancer and yellow teeth to create a climate in which smoking becomes unpopular and unthinkable (soft power). Under the third dimension of power behavior, the principal could hold a school assembly in which students discuss smoking and vow not to smoke (soft power), or go further and threaten to ostracize the minority who smoke (hard power). In other words, the principal can use her hard power to stop smoking or use the soft power of framing, persuasion, and attraction. The success of her soft-power efforts will depend upon her ability to attract and create credibility and trust.

Attraction is more complex than it first appears. It can refer to drawing attention—whether positive or negative—as well as creating alluring or positive magnetic effects. Attention may be welcome or unwelcome. Lawyers refer to some things as an "attractive nuisance." If attraction is asymmetrical and leads to a hard-power response, it produces vulnerability rather than power. Soft power relies on positive attraction in the sense of "alluring."

What generates positive attraction? Alexander Vuving usefully suggests that three clusters of qualities of the agent and action are central to attraction: benignity, competence, and charisma. *Benignity* is an aspect of how an agent relates to others. Being perceived as benign tends to generate sympathy, trust, credibility, and acquiescence. Competence, refers to how an agent does things, and it produces admiration, respect, and emulation. Charisma, is an aspect of an agent's relation to ideals, values and vision, and it tends to produce inspiration and adherence.

Without such perceived qualities, a given resource may produce indifference or even revulsion—the opposite of soft power. The production of soft power by attraction depends upon both the qualities of the agent and how those qualities are perceived by the target. What produces attraction for one target may produce revulsion for another. When an actor or action is perceived as malign, manipulative, incompetent, or ugly, it is likely to produce revulsion. Thus, a given cultural artifact, such as a Hollywood movie that portrays liberated women acting independently, may produce positive attraction in Rio but revulsion in Riyadh.

Persuasion is closely related to attraction. It is the use of argument to influence the beliefs and actions of others without the threat of force or promise of payment. Persuasion almost always involves some degree of manipulation, with some points being emphasized and others neglected. Dishonest persuasion may go so far as to involve fraud. Rational argument—appealing to facts— along with beliefs about causality and also normative premises are mixed with the framing of issues in attractive ways and the use of emotional appeals. That is why attraction, trust, and persuasion are closely related. Some rational arguments are self-executing. A theorem in pure math can convince on its own internal merit even if propounded by an enemy. Most arguments, however, involve assertions about facts, values, and framing that depend upon some degree of attraction and trust that the source is credible.

In turn, framing is closely related to persuasion. An argument that is framed in an attractive way that is seen as legitimate by the target is more likely to be persuasive. Much persuasion is indirect, mediated through mass audiences rather than elites. Perceptions of legitimacy can also involve third-party audiences. Indirect attempts at persuasion often involve efforts to persuade third parties with emotional appeals and narratives rather than pure logic. Narratives are particularly important in framing issues in persuasive ways so that some "facts" become important and others fall by the wayside. Yet, if a narrative is too transparently manipulative and discounted as propaganda, it loses persuasive power. Again, it is not just the influence effort by the agent but also the perceptions by the targets that are critical for the creation of soft power.

SOFT POWER IN PRACTICE

Police power, financial power, and the ability to hire and fire are examples of tangible "hard" power that can be used to get others to change their positions. Hard power rests on inducements ("carrots") and threats ("sticks"). Soft power rests on the ability to shape the preferences of others to want what you want. At the personal level, we all know the power of attraction and seduction. Power in a relationship or a marriage does not necessarily reside with the larger partner. Smart executives know that leadership is not just a matter of issuing commands but that it also involves leading by example and attracting others to do what you want. It is difficult to run a large organization by commands alone unless you can get others to buy into your values.

Community-based police work relies on making the police friendly and attractive enough that a community wants to help them achieve their shared objectives. Military theories of counterinsurgency stress the importance of winning the hearts and minds of the population, not merely killing the enemy. Similarly, political leaders have long understood the power that comes from setting the agenda and determining the framework of a debate. While leaders in authoritarian countries can use coercion and issue commands, politicians in democracies must rely more on a combination of inducement and attraction.

Of course, in many real-world situations, peoples' motives are mixed. Moreover, the distinction between hard and soft power is one of degree, both in the nature of the behavior and in the tangibility of the resources. In real-world situations, hard and soft power are often combined, sometimes with a soft layer of attraction overlaid upon underlying relationships that rest on coercion or payment. A lobbyist may first try to persuade a legislator, but the lobbyist may also make a legal and well-timed campaign contribution. A government may try to persuade young people to forgo drugs with an advertisement campaign featuring attractive celebrities, but if this soft power fails, the hard power of law enforcement remains.

In institutions with flat hierarchies, such as universities and nonprofit organizations, soft power is often the major asset available to a leader. Once that soft power has eroded, little else is left. People just say no. Even in the American presidency, as Richard Neustadt argues, power is mostly the ability to persuade others that they want to do in their own interests what you want them to do. As Dwight Eisenhower put the case for soft power, "You don't lead by hitting people over the head; that's assault, not leadership." Democratic politics would be impossible without the soft power of agenda setting, attraction and persuasion.

Conclusions: Although I developed the concept in the context of a debate over American power at the end of the 20th century, soft power is not restricted to states or to international relations. Leaders in democratic societies are constantly relying on their power of attraction to get elected, and presidents of universities and other non-profit organizations often find that their soft power is far greater than their hard power. For example, the importance of soft power is now widely accepted in the analysis of international affairs, and it is interesting to see it used as well by practical politicians such as Chinese President Hu Jintao.

Soft power is not necessarily a path to peace. Like any form of power it can be used for immoral purposes. Charismatic leaders have soft power and some use it for bellicose purposes. For instance, Osama bin Laden had a good deal of soft power in the eyes of his followers. He did not coerce or pay his followers who flew civil aircraft into the World Trade Center and killed thousands of civilians. Other charismatic leaders like Ghandi or Mandela have used their soft power for more pacific transformations.

It is in the dimension of means that one can construct a normative preference for greater use of soft power, even if international relations cannot be based solely on reasoned persuasion. Ethical judgments have three dimensions: intentions, means and consequences. While soft power can be used with bad intentions and wreak horrible consequences, it does differ in terms of means. Power defined in behavioral terms is a relationship, and soft power depends more upon the subject's role in that relationship than does hard power. Attraction depends upon what is happening in the mind of the subject. While there may be instances of coercive verbal manipulation, there are more degrees of freedom for the subject when the means involve soft power. I may have few degrees of freedom if the person with the gun demands my money or my life. I have even fewer degrees of freedom if he kills me and simply takes my wallet from my pocket. But to persuade me that he is a guru to whom I should donate my money leaves open a number of degrees of freedom as well as the possibility of other outside influences arising and influencing the power relationship. After all, minds can change over time while the dead cannot be revived.

Soft power is a form of power and can be used for good or bad purposes. It is not always better to twist minds than to twist arms. In international relations, leaders will need to combine various soft power skills with Machiavellian hard power skills, but an ethical case can be made that leaders should have a general preference for soft power options when possible.

BIBLIOGRAPHY

Bachrach, Peter and Morton Baratz. "Decisions and Nondecisions: An Analytical Framework," *American Political Science Review* 57, no. 3 (1963): 632–642.

Dahl, Robert A. *Who Governs: Democracy and Power in an American City.* (New Haven, 1961).

Katzenstein, Peter J., ed. *Civilizations in World Politics: Plural and Pluralist Perspectives.* (New York, 2009).

Lukes, Steven. *Power: A Radical View*, 2nd ed. (London, 2005).

Nagel, Jack. *The Descriptive Analysis of Power.* (New Haven, 1975), p. 14.

Neustadt, Richard. *Presidential Power and the Modern Presidents: The Politics of Leadership from Roosevelt to Reagan.* (New York, 1990).

Weber, Max. *The Theory of Social and Economic Organizations.* (New York, Oxford University Press, 1947), p. 152.

STUDY QUESTIONS

1. What is meant by Gandhi's insistence that *satyāgraha* must be done by the strong, rather than the weak?

2. Suggest nonreligious bases for nonviolence, both as a social practice and as a way of life.

3. Black power advocate H. Rap Brown once wrote that violence was "as American as cherry pie." Agree or disagree with this statement.

4. "Let no man pull you so low," wrote Martin Luther King, Jr., "as to make you hate him." Analyze and interpret this observation.

5. "My creed of nonviolence is an extremely active force," wrote Gandhi. "It has no room for cowardice or even weakness. There is hope for a violent man to be some day nonviolent, but there is none for a coward." Why not?

6. According to Victor Hugo (and many others), "No army can withstand the force of an idea whose time has come." Is there any evidence that nonviolence is such an idea? Or is this simply wishful thinking? What about "selective nonviolence," that is, using violence in some circumstances and nonviolence in others?

7. Can you find any examples of nonviolence among animals? Can we learn from it?

8. What about the oft-cited problem of how nonviolence (Gandhian or otherwise) would fare if it had to face, for example, a nuclear-armed Hitler? Similarly, is there anything in the events and issues of the twenty-first century that render nonviolence especially compelling, or, alternatively, less appropriate than in the past?

9. Compare the nonviolent conceptions of Gandhi, Tolstoy, King, and one or more modern leaders.

SUGGESTIONS FOR FURTHER READING

Ackerman, Peter, and Christopher Kruegler. 1994. *Strategic Nonviolent Conflict: the Dynamics of People Power in the Twentieth Century*. Westport, CT: Praeger.

Burrowes, Robert J. 1996. *The Strategy of Nonviolent Defense: A Gandhian Approach*. Albany: State University of New York Press.

Hanigan, James P. 1984. *Martin Luther King, Jr. and the Foundations of Nonviolence*. Lanham, MD: University Press of America.

Kurlansky, Mark. 2008. *Nonviolence: The History of a Dangerous Idea*. New York: Modern Library.

Lakey, George. 1987. *Powerful Peacemaking: A Strategy for a Living Revolution*. Philadelphia: New Society Publishers.

Merton, Thomas. 1980. *The Nonviolent Alternative*. New York: Farrar, Straus & Giroux.

Moses, Greg. 1997. *Revolution of Conscience: Martin Luther King, Jr., and the Philosophy of Nonviolence*. New York: Guilford Press.

Schell, Jonathan. 2004. *The Unconquerable World: Power, Nonviolence, and the Will of the People*. New York: Henry Holt.

Sharp, Gene, and Joshua Paulson. 2005. *Waging Nonviolent Struggle: 20th Century Practice and 21st Century Potential*. Manchester, NH: Extending Horizons Books.

Zinn, Howard. 2002. *The Power of Nonviolence: Writings by Advocates of Peace*. Boston: Beacon Press.

CHAPTER 6

Peace Movements, Transformation, and the Future

The Cold War generated much of the momentum for recent peace movements, in part because the simmering antagonism between the United States and the former Soviet Union gave rise to numerous "proxy wars," fueled by the U.S.–Soviet rivalry. (Of these, the Vietnam War is perhaps the most dramatic for Americans, although residents of the Korean peninsula, Cambodia, Angola, Mozambique, the Dominican Republic, Afghanistan, and others all have their own stories to tell.) In addition, Cold War fears contributed to a tendency for both sides to prop up dictatorial, unrepresentative governments, thereby foisting painful conditions of "structural violence" upon local populations. Notably, this applies to the role of the United States in supporting right-wing despotisms in Spain, Portugal, Cuba, most of Central and South America, Zaire, South Africa, Iran, Pakistan, South Korea, Indonesia, and so on. A similar dynamic describes the actions of the U.S.S.R. in Eastern Europe, which essentially suffered under Soviet domination from the end of World War II until roughly 1989/1990.

Most of all, perhaps, the Cold War threat of nuclear holocaust gave special energy and urgency to people deeply worried about personal survival as well as the prospect of global extinction. Along the way, numerous other concerns surfaced, for varying lengths of time and with varying intensity: for example, chemical and biological warfare, apartheid in South Africa, land reform in Central America, opposition to specific weapons (e.g., landmines, chemical and biological warfare), weapons testing, forcible impressment of child soldiers, and the military draft generally.

A variety of other peace movements were successful, such as independence for India and of other victims of colonialism, the civil rights movement in the United States, and the passage of treaties banning biological weapons and genocide, and so forth. The long-term effects of the Cold War's end remain to be seen, although one unfortunate consequence has been a diminution in antinuclear activism. There has also been less opposition to specific weapons systems, even though new weapons are regularly developed and deployed. The international arms trade continues in high gear, and within the United States, the military budget has grown, not shrunk, to the point that it currently exceeds that of the rest of the world combined.

Overall, there has been a decrease in warfare between states but no decrease in wars generally, as most wars currently take place within a given country. Ethnic, nationalist, and religion-based passions are as intense as ever, sometimes erupting into genocide. Proliferation of nuclear weapons has been less rampant than had been feared during the 1960s and 1970s, but an increase may be imminent. At the same time, the United States and Russia have signed a series of nuclear arms reduction treaties, and a worldwide Comprehensive Test Ban regime, although shaky, is currently in place.

There has been a welcome increase in democratization, notably in South and Central America, although Africa, the Middle East, and much of mainland Asia retain governments that are substantially less representative than most citizens would prefer. Human rights—especially religious freedom—are under attack in many places, although overall there seems to be progress. Women's rights and population policy policies are just beginning to receive their due. Economic fairness seems to be diminishing, as the gap between rich and poor continues to grow. Ecological issues are "all over the map." There have been improvements in air and water quality, for example, in certain parts of the "developed world," but if anything, air and water quality have generally gotten worse in most developing countries. Species extinction, global warming, and ozone depletion are, if anything, more severe than ever, while the earth's population continues to expand (albeit at a decreasing rate). On the positive side, there is more worldwide environmental awareness than ever before, an essential prerequisite for any significant and lasting progress. (But there is also a growing anti-environment backlash, largely sponsored by right-wing political organizations and industries such as coal, oil, etc., that profit from environmental destruction.

In summary, movement toward a more peaceful world has been, at best, uneven and painfully slow. And yet, in some ways, the world has changed remarkably: —not just with the end of the Cold War, but also because of the breakup of the former Soviet Union itself, the transition to capitalism and at least a semblance of democracy in many countries where such change had previously been unimaginable, the end of apartheid in South Africa and the dramatic success of black African rule there, and the end of numerous insurrections and government repressions in Central and South America. There is still abundant room for peace movements in the future, and, indeed, immense need for them. It seems likely, however, that in many cases these movements will focus on issues different from those of the past.

Nonetheless, certain things still have not changed. Militarism, violence, and the misdirection of national resources call for opposition. Denial of human rights, of economic fairness, and of ecological sustainability all demand redress. There is need for creative and empathic efforts to envision and promote a peaceful world. People must strive for both negative and positive peace.

It is a cliche for graduation speakers to announce that we have reached a crossroads and that the present time is uniquely consequential . . . not just for individuals making their personal life decisions but for society in general, and even for the world. But in fact, there truly may be unique opportunities as well as risks at this time in world history, when it often seems that we have been, as Matthew Arnold put it, "Wandering wandering between two worlds, one dead, the other powerless to be born."[1]

The special hope of peace movements is that they might serve as midwives for that newer world, providing it with the impetus and power to be born at last. Just as birth may be difficult, often painful, and even dangerous, the course of peace movements has not run altogether smoothly, nor have peace movements been unidimensional or universally welcomed. But just as birth is natural and necessary if life is to continue, it seems equally certain that peace is necessary (whether or not it is "natural") and that peace movements may contribute mightily toward success. Pope John Paul II once said that "it is only through a conscious choice and through a deliberate policy that humanity can survive." Peace movements and peace studies both strive to help establish such a policy and to represent such a choice.

---

[1] Matthew Arnold, "Stanzas from the Grande Chartreuse," *Essays and Poems of Matthew Arnold* (New York: Harcourt Brace Jovanovich, 1934).

Richard Falk

ON HUMANE GOVERNANCE

Long before President George H. W. Bush spoke of a "new world order" in 1990, peace advocates were concerned with remaking the world political system to be responsive to social justice, environmental protection, human rights, democratization, and the demilitarization of international relations. One of the leaders in this effort has been Richard Falk, an active participant in the decades-long World Order Models Project, affectionately known as WOMP. The following selection is from the last chapter of Falk's book *On Humane Governance: Toward a New Global Politics*, a superb overall introduction to socially responsible, hardheaded, yet visionary futurism, informed by a deep commitment to all dimensions of peace.

What is most revealing in this world is not where we are, but where we are going.

　　　　　　　　　　　—Anonymous saying

Every child is born with the message that God is not yet discouraged with humanity.

　　　　　　　　　　　—Rabindranath Tagore

The contemporary quest for humane governance builds on kindred efforts in the past, while being rooted in an unfolding present, and above all aspiring to achieve an imagined future. The idea of humane governance is itself a way of expressing this process that is sensitive to the shortcomings, achievements, and gropings toward human betterment on this planet. What shapes the orientation and gives it substantive content in diverse settings is this normative underpinning, a blend of legal, moral, and spiritual perspectives.

To endow this underpinning with greater concreteness and sense of direction, this chapter briefly depicts ten dimensions of this world-encompassing normative project, acknowledging its historical depth yet also identifying its inspirational and prophetic assumptions about the future. Such a depiction should not be regarded as a listing of attributes or an inventory, and far less as a program. Each aspect that is rendered as distinct touches and influences the others in countless ways. . . .

The normative project posits an imagined community for the whole of humanity which overcomes the most problematic aspects of the present world scene: the part (whether as individual, group, nation, religion, civilization) and the whole (species, world, universe) are connected; difference and uniformities across space and through time are subsumed beneath an overall commitment to world order values in the provisional shape of peace, economic well-being, social and political justice, and environmental sustainability. As such, the normative project partakes of shared values and aspirations, trends, fears and expectations about the future, rooted hopes, visions of the possible. The framing of this project acknowledges primarily the efforts of movements and peoples at the grass roots, but also takes note of the participation of prominent leaders, governments, and other institutions, as well as the specificity of opportunities and challenges arising in the aftermath of the Cold War. The normative project has ten dimensions.

TAMING WAR

The contemporary normative project has its roots in the reaction to the barbarity of warfare. It was Grotius's horrified response to the Thirty Years War in Europe that gave birth to international law in the seventeenth century and to the specific regulatory urge to put limits on what states could do in the midst of war. This impulse ripened through time, leading to the Hague Conferences of 1899 and 1907 which brought together the leaders of the dominant states of the day, purporting to be the managers of the global order. For the first time a series of international law treaties were drafted and adopted to regulate the tactics and weaponry of warfare to some degree, incorporating some customary principles of behavior embodied at high levels of abstraction in religion and morality: the requirement that tactics and weaponry distinguish between civilian and military targets, sparing the former; that force be used in a proportionate manner; that cruelty be avoided, including unnecessary suffering for those wounded or captured, even if part of the opposing military forces.

This endeavor to tame the conduct of war has persisted to the present. After World War II the Geneva Conventions of 1949 placed great stress on specific duties to protect the victims of war, including civilians and those military personnel wounded or captured in battle. These protections were later extended to the circumstances of intervention and civil war by the Geneva Protocols of 1977. Much current attention at the grassroots and governmental levels is being devoted to regimes of prohibition associated with weaponry of mass destruction: nuclear, chemical, and biological. At present, with respect to nuclear weaponry, the governmental emphasis has been on maintaining a partial regime (nonproliferation) as opposed to the efforts of transnational democratic initiatives to achieve a comprehensive regime of prohibition (delegitimizing nuclear weapons as such and arranging for their phased elimination from arsenals, thereby treating these weapons as chemical and biological weapons have been treated).

Whether this enterprise has been successful, on balance, remains controversial. Advocates claim that the suffering of war has been mitigated for millions of participants. Skeptics believe that the law of war is a hypocritical and deceptive misnomer which deflects reformist energy from war itself. At the root of the difficulty is the subordination of the principle of restraint to the achievement of victory in war by whatever means it takes. The supremacy of "military necessity" has tended to overwhelm the normative pressures of law, morality, and religion. This supremacy has been abetted by continuous innovation in the weaponry of war, the search by states for military superiority, and the development, reliance, and use of ultimate weapons and tactics in the course of winning World War II. Evidence of civilian devastation rarely inhibits tactics or weaponry. The current movement to prohibit land mines is illustrative. Despite the evidence of overwhelming civilian injury, much of it long after hostilities have ceased, governments seem reluctant to ban land mines, partly because of their cost–benefit advantages compared to other weapons. The debate itself confirms that nothing significant will happen until civil initiatives mount strong pressures.

Although the results are disappointing, the struggle to tame war continues alongside the wider, more dramatic series of efforts to abolish war itself as a hideous and outmoded social institution.

ABOLISHING WAR

The more fundamental struggle, at the very center of the normative project, is to challenge war itself, the social and political process of mass, intentional killing in the name of the state, for the sake of wealth and power, in defense of ideology and a way of life, allegedly on behalf of security in self-defense, but also to satisfy expansionist ambitions. This challenge directed against war is often analogized to the struggle against slavery, the divine right of kings, colonialism, each a social institution that like war was once generally accepted, at least by elites, as necessary and inevitable. Arguably, all advances in the human condition have involved challenging institutions and practices treated as necessary and inevitable.

The real and imagined carnage of war has been the principal impetus to abolitionist efforts, as have certain pacifist traditions of religious and secular thought. After World War I, in particular, antiwar sentiments flourished, taking aim at the legality of so-called "aggressive war" and at "the merchants of death" (those who made profits from arms sales).

Public pressures were so great that leading countries subscribed to the Kellogg-Briand Pact of 1928 (also known as the Pact of Paris) that renounced war as an instrument of national policy, authorizing war only as a response to aggression, in a posture of self-defense. This new ground rule was invoked after World War II as a principal basis for convicting German and Japanese leaders of crimes against the peace for their role in planning and waging aggressive warfare. This prohibition is reproduced in the UN Charter in the form of Article 2(4), which prohibits altogether the use of force, although it is qualified by Article 51 which preserves the "inherent right of self-defense." The Charter seeks to restrict the scope of self-defense by requiring that only in situations of "prior armed attack" is self-defense permitted, and even then the claimant state is required to seek immediate approval from the Security Council.

As with the efforts to tame war, those to abolish war remain controversial and are not implemented to any great extent. States interpret for themselves what self-defense means, and have ignored the requirement of armed attack. The mobilization of response against aggression has been inconsistent and often halfhearted. Preparation for war, the tactics, secrecy, and weaponry have made war an integral part of the global landscape, especially in the South where more than 125 wars have been fought in the last 50 years. In the North, fear of catastrophic war, reinforced by deterrence and containment, avoided direct war during the Cold War, but added to the frequency and intensity of warfare in the South.

With the Cold War over, there is at present no strategic rivalry of the sort likely to produce warfare, but the war system seems as rooted as ever in the operational code of statecraft, expressed by way of large military establishments, expensive weapons innovations, huge arms sales, and interventionary diplomacy. What is also discouraging, especially during this period of geopolitical moderation, is the absence of moves from above or below that challenge seriously the war system, or even move toward large reductions of spending and embark upon ambitious types of disarmament. Yet the abolition of war remains a centerpiece of the normative project, and its political relevance is embedded in each and every dimension.

The intractability of war as a social institution suggests that unlike slavery and the other analogies relied upon by the new abolitionists, war is different: it presupposes shifts in the structures of power and authority, or at least in their normative foundations. Those who argue on the basis of structure generally regard world government as the precondition for disarmament; those who emphasize normative foundations tend either to insist upon democratizing the world (on the presumption that democracies don't go to war against one another and hence that if the foundations of authority in all states become democratic, there will be no political will to engage in war and the war system will wither away) or to disseminate the ethos of nonviolence throughout the whole gamut of social relations so widely that it undermines support for military approaches to conflict, displacing the war system in time by pacifism.

MAKING INDIVIDUALS ACCOUNTABLE

. . . One dimension of the normative project has been to make those in authority accountable for their transgressions, especially with respect to war and in relation to severe abuses of human rights. The essence of this approach has been to criminalize *aggressive* war, while not challenging rights of self-defense or military preparations. The Nuremberg and Tokyo War Crimes Tribunals at the end of World War II were the foundation of this struggle to impose individual accountability, and the decisions reached rejected defenses based on reason of state or superior orders. It was also notable that secondary trials were held to assess the individual responsibility of doctors, judges, business leaders, local military commanders, and local officials, expanding the reach of accountability to encompass those who variously implemented the policies of the regime or carried out independent atrocities of their own.

This Nuremberg experience, now being widely reassessed during the fiftieth anniversary year of the main judgment, has been criticized as "victors' justice." The crimes of the victorious powers, most notably the use of atomic bombs and the excesses of strategic bombing, were exempted from any scrutiny. The prosecutors at Nuremberg did pledge that the

principles being laid down to judge the defendants would become binding international law that would henceforth be made applicable to the whole world and its leaders. Indeed, the UN General Assembly by unanimous vote endorsed the Nuremberg principles, seeking their authoritative formulation by the International Law Commission, the expert body at the UN, which in 1950 provided the text of these principles that is relied upon to this day to identify the nature of individual accountability.

Governments have not implemented the Nuremberg principles. Indeed, the victorious powers in World War II, the countries which provided the judges, have each engaged subsequently in aggressive war. Further, these leading states have opposed efforts to institutionalize Nuremberg through the creation of procedures and some sort of international criminal court. The Nuremberg idea has been kept alive by two major developments: first, by activists who relied on the Nuremberg idea to challenge the supremacy of the state in the war/peace area, validating the emergence of civil resistance as a step beyond what Thoreau and others had in mind by "civil disobedience"; secondly, after the Cold War, by moves toward convening war crimes tribunals to address allegations of genocidal behavior in Bosnia and Rwanda (even prior to this, issues of accountability emerged in various countries in South America as the transitions were made from the authoritarian rule of the 1960s to some sort of constitutional governance).

The importance of individual accountability to the establishment of global governance is evident. Crimes of states need to be deterred and, once committed, dealt with effectively if confidence in the emergence of wider regional communities of participation is to arise and if the formation of an eventual global community is to be encouraged. At this point, all the contradictions of world order are present: powerful states enjoy the full prerogatives of territorial supremacy and sovereignty, exempting leaders from accountability, especially if an authoritarian political order prevails; further, the diplomacy of reconciliation and peace often sharply conflicts with the impulse to impose individual responsibility—without surrender or defeat, the accused leadership is elusive and may well prolong its period of rule, fearing what the Argentinean human rights activist Jacopo Timmermann referred to in the 1970s as "the ghosts of Nuremberg."

COLLECTIVE SECURITY

. . . One important strand of the normative project for a reformed world was to replace balance-of-power geopolitics with a rule-governed global security system that protected states threatened by aggressive war. Woodrow Wilson championed such an approach and advocated the creation of the League of Nations to achieve collective security. These efforts have persisted in various forms. The League was created but the United States refused to join, and when aggressive war occurred in Asia and Europe the response was ineffectual. Yet the idea of collective security persisted, and was embodied in a more detailed form in Chapter VII of the UN Charter. Again the experience of the Cold War confirmed the inadequacy of existing mechanisms of collective security, highlighted by the bipolarity of the period and the inability of the opposed blocs of states to agree upon the identity of an aggressor in most situations involving the outbreak of war. The defense of South Korea in 1950 was nominally a UN operation, but was substantively controlled by the United States, receiving a UN mandate only because the Soviet Union deprived itself of its veto by temporarily boycotting the Security Council in protest against the unrelated failure to seat representatives from the People's Republic of China.

The Gulf crisis of 1990 presented a renewed, neo-Wilsonian opportunity to establish collective security. The conditions were finally right: clear aggression against a UN member; a political consensus of the permanent members of the Security Council; a threat to the strategic interests of leading countries; and the political will to provide the capabilities to perform effectively. The Gulf War that resulted in 1991 has had an ambiguous impact. It certainly established the possibility of UN effectiveness since Kuwait's sovereignty was restored and aggression was reversed. Yet the undertaking was again essentially geopolitical in motivation and character, the decisions being made in Washington, not at the Security Council in New York. When the

challenge of Serbian aggression and ethnic cleansing in Bosnia arose a year later, the old circumstance of ineffectuality was again evident. Without both political consensus and a strategic stake of magnitude, leading states are not willing to pay the price for maintaining collective security. It was clear that countries without strategic relevance were on their own; the case of East Timor is exemplary, with Indonesia's aggression and crimes against humanity being neglected almost totally in the setting of collective security.

Not only is geopolitical practice discouraging, but leading states oppose the creation of independent UN capabilities by way of a peace force of volunteers and a reliable means to finance collective security. Perhaps collective security will take hold on a regional level during the decade ahead. In any event, the time has come to rethink collective security within the UN setting, associating UN uses of force with ideas of policing and reconciliation, not as a species of war-making. Such a reorientation would also greatly constrain uses of force that could not be focused on the elite responsible for aggression or genocide. The Wilsonian impulse survives. Without collective security as an interim mechanism to deter and resist aggression, the prospects of abolishing war in the near future seem severely diminished.

RULE OF LAW

The legal mind-set has exerted considerable influence on shaping the priorities of the normative project for a reformed world order. In particular, U.S. reformist energies since the Wilsonian era have stressed the importance of judicial procedures for the settlement of disputes. The establishment of a World Court in The Hague, initially in 1920, has epitomized this logic of world peace through law, although isolationist tendencies within the United States have polarized opinion on the desirability of enhancing the role and prestige of the judicial arm of the UN.

This manifested itself strongly during the controversy with the Sandinista government in Nicaragua in the 1980s. The Court decided in favor of Nicaragua with respect to the basic contention as to whether the U.S. was illegally sponsoring Contra violence against an established state. This outcome so angered the White House that it withdrew the U.S. from full participation, limiting its role to ad hoc arrangements to appear before the Court if it specifically agreed to do so. Additionally, the U.S. government refused to abide by the 1986 decision, and the Security Council did not fulfill its Charter responsibility to implement World Court decisions. Surprisingly perhaps, the Non-Aligned Movement picked up the dropped baton, impressed by the objectivity of the World Court and its willingness to decide in favor of Nicaragua. It is highlighting the importance of obliging all countries to resolve their disputes by recourse to the World Court if diplomacy fails, and setting as a goal the year 1999, the hundredth anniversary of the initial Hague peace conference.

So far the reliance on judicial solutions has not been very successful in relation to fundamental conflicts involving core interests of states. The World Court has effectively resolved potentially troubling, long-festering, marginal disputes, especially involving disputed frontiers and maritime boundaries, as well as other technical matters. The regional role of judicial institutions in Europe is suggestive of how far the rule of law can be carried in crucial matters of economic policy and the protection of human rights, according precedence to supranational authority and subordinating in the event of conflict the highest expressions of judicial and legislative authority at the level of the sovereign state. The structuring of global governance on the basis of enhanced judicial roles within the various regional settings and for the world as a whole would be a major step in averting both civil and international warfare, being expressive of the disposition of well-governed political communities to entrust even the most serious disputes to third party procedures.

NONVIOLENT REVOLUTIONARY POLITICS

. . . The thrust of Mahatma Gandhi's courageous and brilliantly managed nonviolent anticolonial struggle against British rule in India introduced a radical new dimension into many subsequent political struggles for freedom, dignity, independence, and well-being that have been at the center of numerous historical narratives of the last half century. Martin Luther King, Jr., imaginatively and powerfully carried a nonviolent orientation into the domain of race relations, specifically on behalf of civil rights for black Americans. Such victories were until recently viewed as special cases, and nonviolence was not widely regarded as capable of challenging major structures of oppression around the world. Then came a series of developments in the 1980s that gave a great potency to nonviolent political strategies, although with outcomes that were sometimes disappointing in various ways: the Khomeini-led revolutionary movement against the Shah in Iran; the People Power movement of Corazon Aquino in the Philippines; the various emancipatory struggles in East Europe against Communist rule; the *intifada* in occupied Palestine; the prodemocracy movement in China and other Asian countries, including Burma, Nepal, and South Korea; the negotiated settlements of long-lasting and seemingly perpetual armed struggles in South Africa, El Salvador, possibly Cambodia—and most recently even the struggle in Northern Ireland appears to be moving on to a political plane. (It has to be realized that these and other manifestations of nonviolence were never pure, and that recourse to nonviolent tactics often seemed to be for opportunistic and temporary reasons, and sometimes merely done as a clever adjustment to the lack of weaponry.)

This sense that nonviolence can challenge formidable power systems is indispensable in relation to the central struggles against war, militarism, and civic abuse of all types. It represents the countertradition to the persisting dominance of violence at all levels of social organization, and underpins the various approaches to the construction of a global civil society that both constitutes and is constituted by cosmopolitan democracy. Yet to achieve enduring results in relation to governance the commitment to nonviolence must be constantly deepened and extended to the most private spheres of human existence, including the socializing of the young, the reconceiving of "manhood," the aims of education, and the "pleasures" nurtured in the marketplace. The theory and practice of nonviolence involves the reconstruction of society, culture, and even consciousness, challenging many current practices, beliefs, and worldviews in various civilizational spaces. Yet without the substantial displacement of violence in all its forms, humane governance is not attainable, especially given the global character of interaction that is becoming standard. Rwanda and Bosnia are neighborhood events for the entire world, and as such are not capable of being cordoned off even in a physical sense: refugees and disease flow across borders and reach distant shores by boat and plane.

HUMAN RIGHTS

. . . Sovereignty and democracy are profoundly affected by the realization of human rights. The European idea of past centuries that the governing authority of a territorial state is supreme and unaccountable is challenged to the extent that the standards of human rights are effectively superimposed by either citizen initiative or external intervention. Sovereignty is subverted from without and diluted from within, giving rise to interventionary and resistance claims and prerogatives on behalf of the victims of abuse. In particular, the citizenry is morally and legally empowered to the extent it appreciates that its leaders can be challenged when they transgress the restraints on power as contained in the international law of human rights. In these regards, the protection of human rights represents a radical tendency in our historical period, but the potency of this effort depends on education (human rights need to be far better understood as empowering by those most victimized if they are to function even more widely as a political instrument of resistance and transformation) and a focus of conviction (human rights must appear consistent with cultural values, or at least these values must themselves be reassessed from within).

Recourse to genocidal practice by any government is increasingly regarded as a forfeiture of its claim to sovereign authority within territory. Other breakdowns of authority in terms of minimal provision of food, shelter, and medicine are being perceived as calling for a response by the wider regional and global communities. The extension of human rights from their civil and political character in liberal democracies to the economic and social concerns of the poor is a crucial transition in thought.

The socialist challenge to capitalism and the individualist ethic were responsible for the broad, earlier acceptance that every person has the material entitlement to the necessities of life, a ground rule for humane governance already present in the seminal document, the Universal Declaration of Human Rights in 1948. With the market ascendant since the late 1980s, international competitiveness has been elevated as a criterion for policy choice and socialist concerns have been discredited. As matters now stand, the unmet challenge of economic and social rights is greater than ever. Ground has been lost in recent years. The only hope now is that globalization from below, with the many initiatives of transnational democracy and the emergence of global civil society, will re-articulate human solidarity in a manner that gives political weight to a renewed movement to achieve social and economic rights.

In the end, the struggle for human rights is the struggle against all forms of abuse, neglect, humiliation, and vulnerability. As Upendra Baxi has so eloquently argued in the setting of India, human rights in the end is a matter of taking suffering seriously. Looking back on this century of world wars and weaponry of mass destruction, it may well be that the gradual development of a human rights framework will be the centerpiece of a more hopeful narration of the experience of the period. Of course, the evolution of human rights is itself a source of suspicion, emanating from the West, reeking of hypocrisy, selective application, and contradictory implications. A wider process of creation and application is unfolding, and is essential, bringing into the domain of human rights the interplay of diverse tendencies within and between cultures, combining the educative imperative to know with the religious imperative to listen, to be humble in the face of the claims of the other, and above all, to refrain from linking the right of self-determination to claims of ethnic exclusivity.

STEWARDSHIP OF NATURE

A recent addition to the normative agenda has been the rediscovery of human dependence on natural surroundings. Ancient peoples, of course, were acutely sensitive to their vulnerability to the severities of nature, especially cycles of drought and flooding. The modern scientific illusion supposed that technological ingenuity could enable human society to master nature, ignore limitations on resource availability, and expand indefinitely both resource-consuming lifestyles and the population of the planet. An emergent environmental consciousness over the last several decades, while still subordinate to market pressures and an ideology of growth, is emphasizing anew ideas of sustainability and limits. What these limits should be is a matter of fundamental political controversy, raising issues of conditions of survival at one end of the debate and matters of the conditions of human happiness and relations to the animal kingdom at the other end.

The distinctive challenge in the establishment of humane governance is to connect development with the stewardship of nature in a manner that realizes economic and social rights for all peoples, adjusting for unevenness of circumstance. . . . At the same time, the enjoyment of the beauty of nature is the foundation of spirituality and creativity, and thus stewardship cannot be conceived of merely in materialist terms.

POSITIVE CITIZENSHIP

The foundations of community reflect the contours of individual and group identity, and more specifically in relation to governance, the quality of participation. In the West, positive participation has been associated with the shift from the status of "subject" (slave, vassal, serf) to "citizen." The modern media--shaped political life threatens individuals with a new type of postmodern serfdom, in which elections, political campaigns, and political parties provide rituals without substance, a politics of sound bytes and manipulative images, reducing the citizen to a mechanical object to be controlled, rather than being the legitimating source of legitimate authority.

What forms of political participation can combine rootedness in the circumstances of a given place (the grassroots test of integrity and relevance) with the connections and aspirations of an emergent global civil society is an essential, variable challenge. Empowerment from below as an alternative to the

ritualization of politics at the level of the state and to subordination to those types of globalization that express market priorities is at the core of the evolving normative project. The projection of a global identity, without the conditions of community, and the claim now to be "world citizens" express striving for humane governance, but they also arouse serious suspicions that the necessary struggles associated with transformation are being evaded by the sentimental, New Age pretense that a reorientation of personal energy will suffice.

Positive citizenship, stressing this interplay between the concreteness of situation and the imagined community that represents humane governance, will mean various things in different societies. The idea of citizenship is being promoted, also, as extending beyond state/society relations and involving all relationships of a participatory nature, that is, institutions and practices that invoke authority. Positive citizenship also draws on nonviolence and human rights as inspirational sources. The greatest challenge, at present, is to reconcile the territorial dimensions of citizenship with the temporal dimensions: acting in the present for the sake of the future, establishing zones of humane governance as building blocks.

COSMOPOLITAN DEMOCRACY

This is the binding idea of democracy encompassing all relationships, providing the grounds of institutional legitimacy, and establishing the basis for procedures and practices linking individuals and groups with institutions. It is becoming the pervasive underpinning that has been evolving along several tracks for several centuries, and now, in tandem with technology and high finance, is necessarily operative across statist boundaries as well as within them. Of course, leadership styles based on hierarchy and soft authoritarianism remain potent realities, especially in the Asian/Pacific region and in Islamic countries; elsewhere, a democratic facade is fashioned to hide the persistence of authoritarian institutional controls. But what gives promise to the vision of cosmopolitan democracy is the legitimation of democratic ideas of governance on a universal basis, the embodiment of these ideas in human rights as specified in global instruments, the democratic implications of nonviolent approaches to resistance and reform, and most of all, the deeply democratic convictions of transnational initiatives that have begun to construct the alternative paradigm of a global civil society.

We can expect many ebbs and flows, many relapses and pitfalls, endless discussion about the failure and character of democracy, and yet the cumulative drift of the normative project has been and remains dedicated to the deepening and the expansion of democracy in relation to all fields of human endeavor. It is virtually impossible to imagine humane governance as a global phenomenon without presupposing the increasing influence and acceptance of participatory politics, whether or not called "democracy," resting on the dignity and worth of the individual, but also of the group. Democracy, in these senses, provides the indispensable organizing principle, with the aim that it can be eventually presupposed, possibly to such an extent that the label can and will be dropped.

These ten dimensions of the normative project, some of recent origin, but all with many antecedents throughout the world, suggest the contours of humane governance. Their emergence remains . . . generally subordinate to globalization from above, acutely uneven, provisional, precarious, at the margins, but yet undeniable. Whether the dynamics of emergence will create a toppling of "the Berlin wall" of militarist, market-driven, materialist globalism is far from assured. At the same time, such a shift in fundamental prospects for governance is a sufficiently plausible outcome as to make the struggle to achieve it the only responsible basis for positive citizenship at this stage of history. Whether ours is an axial moment of normative restructuring of collective and individual life cannot yet be determined, but such possibilities inherent in the present situation provide us with the best and most realistic basis of hope about how to work toward human betterment, as understood and applied in many separate ways around the world.

Betty Reardon

SEXISM AND THE WAR SYSTEM

Making peace, in the deepest sense, requires us to acknowledge that the personal is political, and vice versa. Among the most personal human traits is gender, which has numerous implications—just beginning to be recognized—for social behavior, including but not limited to violence and oppression. In the following selection, longtime peace educator, feminist, and activist Betty Reardon examines some of the connections between sexism and the war system as well as some alternatives, including the importance of personal transformation.

The problems and issues to be explored in this examination of sexism and the war system are viewed through four major conceptual lenses: the

war system, sexism, feminism, and world order. Each concept comprises a set of subconcepts and the underlying assumptions that determine the connotations carried by the conceptual terms. I offer the following definitions not as an assertion of the essential meaning of the concepts but rather to clarify the terms as they are used in this work. They are offered as well to expose my own underlying assumptions and to support the thesis that the two phenomena, sexism and the war system, arise from the same set of authoritarian constructs. . . .

THE WAR SYSTEM: ENFORCEMENT OF PATRIARCHY

My use of the term "war system" refers to our competitive social order, which is based on authoritarian principles, assumes unequal value among and between human beings, and is held in place by coercive force. The institutions through which this force is currently controlled and applied are dominated by a small minority, elites who run the global economy and conduct the affairs of state. These elites are men from industrial countries, primarily Western, and for the most part educated to think in Western, analytic terms. Although their relationship is competitive within the elite structures, there is a common objective that holds the elites together: the maintenance of their own control and dominance. This purpose accounts for the degree of accommodation and cooperation that can be found among all elites. Their primary competition is therefore with the nonelites, the majority of the world's people. Control is maintained by force in the form of threat, intimidation, and, when necessary, violent coercion. The control system requires that only intimidation and threat of force be used whenever possible, in part to save the cost of violent coercion but mainly to keep the majority at a sufficient level of well-being to maintain their productive capacity.

This latter, fundamental purpose of maintaining productive capacity necessitates a level of subelites within the general hierarchical structure. These subelites, for example, heads of client states, military officers, or favorite wives, carry out the day-to-day management of the productive functions of the majority of the population. Their lot is sufficiently better than the majority, from whose ranks they are usually drawn, to convince them that service to

the elites and maintenance of the system is in their own best interest. They help keep the basic conflict between the elites and the majority submerged in cultural norms, traditional myths, and political ideologies. Their effectiveness depends on their remaining as removed as possible from the actual application of force, which is executed by more replaceable individuals. With the exception of those states so militarized that state violence need not be obscured, a general characteristic of the system is that the higher the level of command, the farther away it is from the actual application of violent force or the conduct of warfare. . . .

Militarism—the belief system that upholds the legitimacy of military control of the state—is based on the assumption that military values and policies are conducive to a secure and orderly society. It has served to legitimate both warfare and civil use of coercive force (i.e., national guards and militia) in the interest of "national security." It is not surprising, given the relationship between patriarchy and the war system, that the more militarist a society tends to be the more sexist are its institutions and values. Feminists have noted this relationship in such cases as Nazi Germany and, more recently, Chile.

Militarization—the process of emphasizing military values, policies, and preparedness, often transferring civil functions to military authority—assumes that when a society is in crisis or threatened, the crisis or threat can best be weathered by strengthening the military. Two significant indicators of militarization are public expenditures, particularly the percentage of total expenditures allocated to military purposes, and the discussion or application of military measures as solutions to problems and conflicts that are basically political or economic. It should be noted that women take virtually no part in the decision making regarding such policies and that increasing military spending at the cost of social expenditures impacts most negatively on women. It contributes significantly to the feminization of poverty. Sivard indicates that the majority of the world's poor will soon be women.

The militarization of post–World War II Euro-American society has paralleled the women's movement. Given the chronological relationship of the two phenomena and some of the working assumptions shared by feminists and the peace movement, this relationship is likely to be more than coincidental. It was to be expected that Phyllis Schlafly, heroine of the New Right, would take on the nuclear freeze movement in the wake of the defeat of the Equal Rights Amendment. Much of contemporary feminism that is anathema to the New Right springs from conceptual roots totally antithetical to the concepts of war, warfare, militarism, and militarization, which derive from negative masculine values. Militarism manifests the excesses of those characteristics generally referred to as *machismo,* a term that originally connoted the strength, bravery, and responsibility necessary to fulfill male social functions. Militarist concepts and values are upheld by patriarchy, the structures and practices of which have been embodied in the state, forming the basic paradigm for the nation-state system. Thus there is in all aspects of that system an inevitable sexist bias that is especially acute in matters related to security, the term all political units apply to self-preservation. Security is the impulse that produces the *military*— "structures of organized violence controlled by the state." . . .

The military, then, is the distilled embodiment of patriarchy; the militarization of society is the unchecked manifestation of patriarchy as the *overt* and *explicit* mode of governance. . . .

WORLD ORDER VALUES: INDICATORS OF MILITARISM AND SEXISM

World order studies inquire into the possibilities for abolishing war and developing a peaceful and human global order. This inquiry offers the greatest potential for the integration of feminism and feminist perspectives into both peace research and the political struggle for peace. The concept of world order studies . . . provides a normative approach to global problems. It projects and evaluates alternatives to the present system that could achieve world order values and open possibilities for the evolution of a more peaceful and just social order. Those who adopt a world order perspective view such evolution as progress toward the universal enjoyment of values that they see as fundamental criteria for the assessment of peace and justice and that they assert

should be the basic norms upheld by the structures of a transformed global system. As I will explicate in a later section, these values are somewhat wanting from a feminist perspective in minimal standards for humane norms and global transformation. They do, however, provide us with some basic guidelines for assessing the degree of those antitheses of peace and justice, *violence* (that is, the unnecessary and avoidable harm to life and well-being) and *oppression* (the humanly devised barriers to the exercise of choice and self-determination), which characterize and bind together sexism and the war system. A brief review of world order values is offered here to illustrate this point and to support the case that substantive progress toward either peace or justice cannot be achieved without the elimination of sexism.

Each of the five world order values—economic equity, social justice, ecological balance, political participation, and peace—can be used to demonstrate that the present global order, the war system, is maintained by violence and oppression, and that women are more victimized by the system than are men. The current severe frustration of these values also suggests the possibility that both increased militarization and the male-chauvinist backlash are symptoms of an authoritarian system responding to a threat to its continuation.

The degree to which economic equity is frustrated by the war machine has been clearly documented each year by *World Military and Social Expenditures,* edited annually by Ruth Sivard. . . . It provides data that demonstrate that global poverty is greatly exacerbated as a result of military spending. It also documents an alarming increase in militarization, which is revealed by the number of governments that have fallen under military control, thereby verifying the assertion that public expenditures are an indicator of militarism.

Structural design certainly figures into my notion of transformation, but its role in the total change process is secondary to that of significant changes in human relations. The fundamental values of equity and mutuality, which I advocate as the norms to guide the changes, would of necessity also influence social and political structures. The structural changes, however, should emerge from the changing relations rather than coming prior to them. In other words, structures should facilitate human relations and give institutional form to the fundamental values rather than dictate and control relations and values as they have in male-dominated society. Thus a blueprint is not part of these reflections on the question of transformation. The emphasis here is more on the need for personal and relational change. If we cannot change ourselves, I doubt we can change the world.

In this context transition strategies are means by which personal and relational changes are translated into social movement and political action. The personal and the political are thoroughly intertwined in the present reality and therefore cannot be divided neatly into two distinct separate arenas for change in any transition plan that purports to be headed toward genuine transformation. This intertwining of the personal and the political makes education, viewed as the process by which we learn new ways of thinking and behaving, a very significant component of the transition-transformation processes. Education is that process through which we glimpse what might be and what we ourselves can become. It is also the process through which we articulate what might be and through which we strive to become what we choose to be. Through it we learn to choose and to pursue choices. Education is transformative when it produces visions to be pursued (that is, the goal of the *transformation*) and when it develops the capacities to achieve the goal (that is, *transition* skills, the strategies for struggle). . . .

It has long been my belief that authentic transformation of the global order is as much a matter of emotional maturity as of structural change. The crux of the argument set forth in this book, that neither sexism nor the war system can be overcome independently from the other, lies in the assumption that structural, even revolutionary, changes in the public order without significant inner psychic changes in human beings will be ineffective, old wine in new bottles. . . .

This indeed is the lesson we learn from a long history of revolutions. Authentic transformations have occurred only when people themselves have changed their world-views, their values, and their behaviors as a basis for change in the social and political structures. Such changes usually involve the

society coming to perceive itself as a manifestation of a new set of human, sometimes cosmic, relationships. This assumption about the interrelationship of personal and political change, which has been a major influence on my approach to peace education, began as an intuition but has evolved into a fundamental hypothesis, one that is shared by other feminists.

This hypothesis is what lies at the base of feminist insistence that the personal circumstances of women have political roots and political significance. It is central to what some have perceived as an inordinate feminist emphasis on specific details of personal relationships between men and women and preoccupation with domestic social and economic policies that affect the everyday quality of life for women. Child care, abortion rights, and payment for housework, although conceptualized and expressed in terms of improving women's lot, are at base as structural as the concerns with such issues as peacekeeping forces and adjudication procedures that world order models have emphasized.

Such feminist proposals integrated into our concepts of transformation and transition could introduce into world order studies notions of the human and quotidian, the everyday lived experience of ordinary people, to which most people can relate more readily. It is at least one approach to overcoming the commonly held perception that world order models and peace research proposals lack relevance to the real world. It is, in fact, this lack of human detail that gives the pejorative connotation to the criticism that such academic visions of a peaceful and just world system are utopian. Feminist utopias provide flesh and bone, human and quotidian dimensions that enable us to catch a glimpse of what human life might be like in a preferred future. As the phrase "think global, act local" has characterized futurist efforts to involve people where "they're at" (that is, geographically and socially), feminists might include the human element in the phrase "think futuristically, act daily," giving the movement a different kind of time dimension, making it more relevant to the present and the personal.

Feminists also see the task of future building as preserving and nurturing the positive elements and small-scale changes we all perceive and participate in. A positive future most likely will be made up of these elements of the preferred present that reflect the requisite values, behaviors, and worldview changes that will constitute the larger transformation. Because of their more intimate physical connection to the life cycle, women understand that the future is not an abstract condition in a remote time. It is the process of becoming. Women know in their bones that the achievement of a preferred future requires us to act in the present on the basis of the norms and values we enshrine in our visions of transformation. . . .

As individual human development is cyclical, and often regresses at stages rather than progresses, so too a feminist view of transition is not a step-by-step linear progression but rather an organic, flowing and eddying notion of change. It is, I believe, this very notion of organic change with its expectation and understanding of recurrent regression that keeps women from despairing of their failures and infuses their continued struggle for a better life and for peace. I am, in fact, convinced that linear, step-by-step concepts of transition not only are bound to lead to severe disappointments, but are more likely to result in the despair that engulfs so many as the militarist negative trends increase in volume and speed. . . .

MASCULINE MODE, FEMININE MODE: SEPARATION AND CONNECTION

Gilligan points out how a masculine bias in the study of the different development emphases between men and women—men striving for separation and independence and women for connection and interdependence—has given us an unbalanced and inadequate notion of maturity. And, I would add, it has led to an overemphasis on individualism and the power to control, which so characterize the present dangerous stage of the war system, the arms race. These observations help us to see how the masculine bias actually has limited the conceptual repertoire and styles of problem resolution we bring to the arenas of politics and conflict. Individuation and separation have so determined our concepts of national interests that we are blinded to the many realities of interdependence that are the major determinants of

our present world situation. That we are willing to risk our very survival to defend the national interest is not so surprising in a masculine-biased system when we understand that "the morality of rights differs from the morality of responsibility in its emphasis on separation rather than connection, in its consideration of the individual rather than the relationship as primary." . . .

This significant difference in the types of morality that are developed by men and women provides us with an important insight into the causes of our present crises. It also suggests that transformation, the realization of global change, and transition, the process of achieving it, may well depend on the integration of masculine and feminine perspectives and modes in the processes of designing new structures and the political and educational programs to achieve them.

Finally, it seems to me, Gilligan's work lends further support to the hypothesis of reciprocal causation and provides grounds for the assertion that the structures of violence that constitute the war system are as much imbedded in the human psyche as in social structure. They are undoubtedly influenced by the attributes we use to guide the development of masculine identity and by masculine modes of public decision making. These factors are revealed only when the whole truth about the human experience is no longer filtered through an exclusive masculine bias, for "in the different voice of women lies the truth of an ethic of care, the tie between relationships and responsibility and the origins of aggression in the failure of connection." . . .

The masculine mode approaches transformation and transition of the global order in the same analytic abstract fashion as it approaches other intellectual issues. The two concepts are perceived as a discrete set of end circumstances and a specific sequence of strategies to achieve them. The transformation, the end circumstances, generally are described in terms of *specific* structures and processes. These very often take the form of models that frequently appear to feminist and third world eyes to be a rearrangement of traditional forms of power rather than a full and authentic transformation of the present reality.

Masculine models of transformation, frequently referred to as "system change," tend to be abstracted from everyday human conditions, to display a central concern with power arrangements, and to be preoccupied with the concept of sovereignty, an essentially patriarchal notion. Some focus much attention on determining which component of the revised structures will be endowed with the power and the right legitimately to use force, whether that force be armed or "nonviolent." Such models can be depicted by charts, diagrams, computer games, and institutional descriptions, but almost never do they have any explicit element of human relations or affective, emotional content, and few have displayed any cultural dimension.

The strategies set forth in the masculine mode for the transition process tend to be primarily political and economic. They are at their best in proposals for staged disarmament and plans for industrial conversion. They are conceived as steps to be taken in the public arena in a particular, incremental style (though of varying degrees of rapidity) and impacting primarily on public life. The value changes included in transition scenarios tend to be norms for social and public policies such as protection for human rights and procedures for conflict resolution. They are corporate rather than personal and conceived so as to have a direct impact on the public domain. The consequent effects of value changes on the private and personal spheres are given little if any more attention in world order transition strategies than in present public policy formation. This blindness to "secondary" consequences gives feminists, who do assess policy impact on women, cause for concern that the proposals are indeed more rearrangement than transformation. Indeed, it is this masculine preoccupation with the public and structural that has aborted the transformative potential of most twentieth-century revolutions. It kept them as just that: a revolution, a turning of the major power wheels that failed to produce changes in the fundamental global order. Such changes remove a particular group from political power but do not make connections to changes in the interpersonal realm nor to the nonmaterial sources of personal empowerment that feminism emphasizes. (It must be noted that some women researchers and futurists, myself included, have produced these same kinds of masculine scenarios.) The transition scenarios in

the masculine mode have always been far weaker, less convincing, and less relevant either to the goal or the present reality than are their visions of transformed structures. In general there is a significant disjuncture between the transformative visions and the plans for the process to achieve them. Masculine models of transformation exhibit little or no consideration of the personal and individual changes that will be required. It is my opinion that this weakness in world order modeling results from the lack of the human, explicit, behavioral elements that are characteristic of the feminine mode. . . .

Most feminist visions or models of the future world order are found not in academic essays, computerized games, graphs, or charts but in novels, poetry, works of art, and specific behavioral changes that women are currently making in themselves and seeking to help others to make. Women are significantly active in initiating political movements, particularly movements related to peace and justice, but they have yet to be as concerned with political strategy design and the devising of structural changes for the institutionalization of the kind of human interrelationships they seek. Yet their current efforts and their visions of healing and wholeness are in some ways far more transformative than the precise structural designs and abstract political processes that male researchers have offered to date.

TRANSCENDING POLARIZATION: RECONCILIATION AS A WORLD ORDER VALUE

To move toward a broader comprehension of the meaning of healing and wholeness in our fragmented world and to comprehend the full dimensions of the transformational task, we need to take note of the many damaging divisions and separations that are in large part a consequence of the masculine bias in science, politics, and social structures in general. We need to focus on the major separations and dichotomies in thought and social functions and the consequent inequity, conflict, and violence that this bias has produced. Among the deepest of these divisions that the feminine flow toward healing and wholeness call us to transcend are those between science and philosophy, fact and value, the individual and the community, the family and the state, the public and the private spheres, citizens and nurturers, and male and female social roles. For example, citizenship in a feminist future order would carry responsibility to nurture and enhance life as well as participate in politics and public affairs. . . .

What I am advocating here is a new world order value, reconciliation, and perhaps even forgiveness, not only of those who trespass against us, but primarily of ourselves. By understanding that no human being is totally incapable of the most reprehensible of human acts, or of the most selfless and noble, we open up the possibilities for change of cosmic dimensions. Essentially this realization is what lies at the base of the philosophy of nonviolence. If we are to move through a disarmed world to a truly nonviolent one, to authentic peace and justice, we must come to terms with and accept the other in ourselves, be it our masculine or our feminine attributes or any of those traits and characteristics we have projected on enemies and criminals, or heroes and saints.

If we advocate the equal value and dignity of all persons, we need also accept their shortcomings as well as their gifts and talents, and understand that all (even ourselves) are capable of changing. The question is whether we will be motivated to do so. My own belief is that this motivation is primarily a task for education, particularly for peace education. Indeed, we have seen little evidence of motivation to change either in the bastions of male chauvinism or in the entrenched militaristic social system. But without the possibility of such change there is little hope of escaping from the war system trap. Education is an enterprise based on hope and the possibility of change.

At its best, education, like the struggle for peace, is motivated by love. The facts that men and women continue to love each other, and that some even struggle to understand each other despite the overwhelming dimensions of the system that separates and alienates us from each other, are a tremendous source of hope. So, too, is the growing bonding among women transcending a socialization that separated and alienated them from each other, setting them into competition to win the favor of men. As men have bonded in the hunt and on the

battlefields and playing fields, women now bond in the feminist movement and in the peace movement, offering each other some of the love and support they have been socialized to lavish on husbands and children. They are supporting and nurturing each other through personal change and political challenge. Such sources of hope make it possible to believe we can change. It is this belief that feminists find empowering and from which we take a new definition of *power*: the capacity to change, to change ourselves and our environment.

Indeed, the empowerment of the powerless is the fundamental change required to transcend sexism and the war system. It would be the very antithesis of the present coercive use of power. It is one of the major motivations behind the feminist demand that women have control over their own bodies, the prime requisite of empowerment, and it clearly makes these women's issues world order issues. It means as well that world order must at last fully embrace that elusive fifth value, *participation*, as it moves toward the stronger, more transformative value of universal human empowerment. Only through this kind of process can we be liberated from the continued global dominance of the industrial male elites. Women's movements, anticolonial movements, and all forms of human rights movements are evidence that such a process is under way. All such movements begin with the refusal of the oppressed to continue to accept their inferior status as inevitable or deserved. Value of self, a primary value of feminism, is essential to the process of liberation and to the development of mature responsibility. . . . The most significant aspect of the process is recognizing the costs. Empowerment, self-respect, and authentic responsibility are not easily come by, not by individuals or societies. Nor do we have the specific strategies of empowerment at hand. However, given the commitment and the visions, feminist strategies are born out of specific contexts and conditions.

These examples hold forth the possibility of relating to others, and to the other, as full persons, not as enemies or objects. The focus was on both political objective, or social model, and on human relations. They seemed to combine the masculine abstract intellectual approach with the feminine concrete, practical approach. This, it seems to me, is what we need in transition strategies—a convergence of masculine and feminine styles of change.

There is a significant similarity between feminist peace strategists and male practitioners of nonviolence in their refusal to accede to the seemingly unchangeable, and their challenge to the authority of raw, coercive power. They have taken responsibility to ask the fundamental questions about the necessity of human suffering. Questioning, taking responsibility, empowerment, and value of self are attributes of maturity and transformation. They are evidence, too, of the convergence of positive masculine and feminine values, modes of thought, and styles of action. These developments are cited as signs of the hoped-for convergence of feminism and the peace movement, and to indicate that the possibilities for truly transformatory movements can be greatly enhanced by encouraging and widening this convergence. The possibility of a cultural transformation of unprecedented proportions is, indeed, emerging. The chances of making that possibility become a probability, of achieving a truly human future, will be enhanced by deeper study of the connections between sexism and the war system. The potential for transformation that I see in the knowledge such study would yield gives me hope at a time when ordinary politics and traditional scholarship offer none.

CONCLUSION: REPRODUCING THE FUTURE

Because one major purpose of this monograph has been to reflect on the life-enhancing possibilities of feminism and women's movements, the language of human reproduction provides an appropriate frame for the conclusion. The conception of a transformed society will be found in the actualizing of the central ideas that will give birth to that society. As male and female genetic material converge in the conception of an individual human life, so must masculine and feminine perceptions, modes, and participation merge into a conception of a truly human society. This conception can be politically symbolized by taking on as one goal the two major transformative tasks of our generation: achieving equality for women and complete disarmament. Achieving the first task would give social value to positive feminine human traits, and the accomplishment of the second would require denial of social value to the most negative masculine traits.

The gestation of the transformed society would be in the processes we devise to develop the basic conception into a living social order, capable of maturing into an entity no longer dependent on specific structures or controlled by the circumstances that led to its conception. Such processes are likely to be simultaneous and complementary behavioral and structural changes guided by the masculine values of justice and equality and the feminine values of care and equity. Transition strategies equal to this task can be designed only by men and women together working in a style of true mutuality.

The "cry of life" of the transformation might be the public articulation and institutionalization of the fundamental values derived from the parents. The birth would be symbolized, as have been the births of societies for centuries, by the inauguration of new governing structures. Such an inauguration might be the formal recognition of the institutional framework of a global peace system, derived as the result of the equal political participation of men and women in the maintenance and development of a disarmed and demilitarized world.

The maturity of such a peace system would be indicated by continuous reflection on and challenge to its rules and structures and by its capacity to change in response to new conditions leading to new stages of human maturation. Maturity is, in the last analysis, the capacity to transform, and to bring forth new life. Transformation is the continuous process by which human beings exercise choice, change reality, and find meaning. Transformation is life. Feminism chooses life.

Dalai Lama

A HUMAN APPROACH TO WORLD PEACE

Certain individuals, by virtue of their moral authority, are especially well positioned to prick the global human conscience. Among these, the Dalai Lama is especially prominent, with an impact not limited to his Buddhist followers. Thus, he has long stood for firm but nonviolent resistance to Chinese encroachment into Tibet, but beyond this, for the prospect that all human beings might liberate themselves from pain and suffering—not simply via an afterlife or longed-for future nirvana but through genuine love and compassion in this life.

When we rise in the morning and listen to the radio or read the newspaper, we are confronted with the same sad news: violence, crime, wars, and disasters. I cannot recall a single day without a report of something terrible happening somewhere. Even in these modern times it is clear that one's precious life is not safe. No former generation has had to experience so much bad news as we face today; this constant awareness of fear and tension should make any sensitive and compassionate person question seriously the progress of our modern world.

It is ironic that the more serious problems emanate from the more industrially advanced societies. Science and technology have worked wonders in many fields, but the basic human problems remain. There is unprecedented literacy, yet this universal education does not seem to have fostered goodness but only mental restlessness and discontent instead. There is no doubt about the increase in our material progress and technology, but somehow this is not sufficient as we have not yet succeeded in bringing about peace and happiness or in overcoming suffering.

We can only conclude that there must be something seriously wrong with our progress and development, and if we do not check it in time there could be disastrous consequences for the future of humanity. I am not at all against science and technology—they

have contributed immensely to the overall experience of humankind; to our material comfort and well-being and to our greater understanding of the world we live in. But if we give too much emphasis to science and technology, we are in danger of losing touch with those aspects of human knowledge and understanding that aspire toward honesty and altruism.

Science and technology, though capable of creating immeasurable material comfort, cannot replace the age-old spiritual and humanitarian values that have largely shaped world civilization, in all its national forms, as we know it today. No one can deny the unprecedented material benefit of science and technology, but our basic human problems remain; we are still faced with the same, if not more, suffering, fear, and tension. Thus it is only logical to try to strike a balance between material developments on the one hand and the development of spiritual, human values on the other. In order to bring about this great adjustment, we need to revive our humanitarian values. . . .

SOLVING HUMAN PROBLEMS THROUGH TRANSFORMING HUMAN ATTITUDES

Of the many problems we face today, some are natural calamities and must be accepted and faced

Office of H.H. the Dalai Lama.

with equanimity. Others, however, are of our own making, created by misunderstanding, and can be corrected. One such type arises from the conflict of ideologies, political or religious, when people fight each other for petty ends, losing sight of the basic humanity that binds us all together as a single human family. We must remember that the different religions, ideologies, and political systems of the world are meant for human beings to achieve happiness. We must not lose sight of this fundamental goal and at no time should we place means above ends; the supremacy of humanity over matter and ideology must always be maintained.

By far the greatest single danger facing humankind—in fact, all living beings on our planet—is the threat of nuclear destruction. I need not elaborate on this danger, but I would like to appeal to all the leaders of the nuclear powers who literally hold the future of the world in their hands, to the scientists and technicians who continue to create these awesome weapons of destruction, and to all the people at large who are in a position to influence their leaders: I appeal to them to exercise their sanity and begin to work at dismantling and destroying all nuclear weapons. We know that in the event of a nuclear war there will be no victors, because there will be no survivors! Is it not frightening just to contemplate such inhuman and heartless destruction? And, is it not logical that we should remove the cause of our own destruction when we know the cause and have both the time and the means to do so? Often we cannot overcome our problems because we either do not know the cause or, if we understand it, do not have the means to remove it. This is not the case with the nuclear threat.

Whether they belong to more evolved species like humans or to simpler ones such as animals, all beings primarily seek peace, comfort, and security. Life is as dear to the mute animal as it is to any human being; even the simplest insect strives for protection from dangers that threaten its life. Just as each one of us wants to live and does not wish to die, so it is with all other creatures in the universe, though their power to effect this is a different matter.

Broadly speaking there are two types of happiness and suffering, mental and physical, and of the two, I believe that mental suffering and happiness

are the more acute. Hence, I stress the training of the mind to endure suffering and attain a more lasting state of happiness. However, I also have a more general and concrete idea of happiness: a combination of inner peace, economic development, and, above all, world peace. To achieve such goals, I feel it is necessary to develop a sense of universal responsibility, a deep concern for all irrespective of creed, color, sex, or nationality.

The premise behind this idea of universal responsibility is the simple fact that, in general terms, all others' desires are the same as mine. Every being wants happiness and does not want suffering. If we, as intelligent human beings, do not accept this fact, there will be more and more suffering on this planet. If we adopt a self-centred approach to life and constantly try to use others for our own self-interest, we may gain temporary benefits, but in the long run we will not succeed in achieving even personal happiness, and world peace will be completely out of the question.

In their quest for happiness, humans have used different methods, which all too often have been cruel and repellent. Behaving in ways utterly unbecoming to their status as humans, they inflict suffering upon fellow humans and other living beings for their own selfish gains. In the end, such shortsighted actions bring suffering to oneself as well as to others. To be born a human being is a rare event in itself, and it is wise to use this opportunity as effectively and skillfully as possible. We must have the proper perspective, that of the universal life process, so that the happiness or glory of one person or group is not sought at the expense of others.

All this calls for a new approach to global problems. The world is becoming smaller and smaller—and more and more interdependent—as a result of rapid technological advances and international trade as well as increasing transnational relations. We now depend very much on each other. In ancient times problems were mostly family-size, and they were naturally tackled at the family level, but the situation has changed. Today we are so interdependent, so closely interconnected with each other, that without a sense of universal responsibility, a feeling of universal brotherhood and sisterhood, and an understanding and belief that we really are part of one big human family, we cannot hope to overcome the dangers to our very existence—let alone bring about peace and happiness.

One nation's problems can no longer be satisfactorily solved by itself alone; too much depends on the interest, attitude, and cooperation of other nations. A universal humanitarian approach to world problems seems the only sound basis for world peace. What does this mean? We begin from the recognition mentioned previously that all beings cherish happiness and do not want suffering. It then becomes both morally wrong and pragmatically unwise to pursue only one's own happiness oblivious to the feelings and aspirations of all others who surround us as members of the same human family. The wiser course is to think of others also when pursuing our own happiness. This will lead to what I call "wise self-interest," which hopefully will transform itself into "compromised self-interest," or better still, "mutual interest."

Although the increasing interdependence among nations might be expected to generate more sympathetic cooperation, it is difficult to achieve a spirit of genuine cooperation as long as people remain indifferent to the feelings and happiness of others. When people are motivated mostly by greed and jealousy, it is not possible for them to live in harmony. A spiritual approach may not solve all the political problems that have been caused by the existing self-centered approach, but in the long run it will overcome the very basis of the problems that we face today.

On the other hand, if humankind continues to approach its problems considering only temporary expediency, future generations will have to face tremendous difficulties. The global population is increasing, and our resources are being rapidly depleted. Look at the trees, for example. No one knows exactly what adverse effects massive deforestation will have on the climate, the soil, and global ecology as a whole. We are facing problems because people are concentrating only on their short-term, selfish interests, not thinking of the entire human family. They are not thinking of the earth and the long-term effects on universal life as a whole. If we of the present generation do not think about these now, future generations may not be able to cope with them.

COMPASSION AS THE PILLAR OF WORLD PEACE

According to Buddhist psychology, most of our troubles are due to our passionate desire for and attachment to things that we misapprehend as enduring entities. The pursuit of the objects of our desire and attachment involves the use of aggression and competitiveness as supposedly efficacious instruments. These mental processes easily translate into actions, breeding belligerence as an obvious effect. Such processes have been going on in the human mind since time immemorial, but their execution has become more effective under modern conditions. What can we do to control and regulate these "poisons"—delusion, greed, and aggression? For it is these poisons that are behind almost every trouble in the world.

As one brought up in the Mahayana Buddhist tradition, I feel that love and compassion are the moral fabric of world peace. Let me first define what I mean by compassion. When you have pity or compassion for a very poor person, you are showing sympathy because he or she is poor; your compassion is based on altruistic considerations. On the other hand, love toward your wife, your husband, your children, or a close friend is usually based on attachment. When your attachment changes, your kindness also changes; it may disappear. This is not true love. Real love is not based on attachment, but on altruism. In this case your compassion will remain as a humane response to suffering as long as beings continue to suffer.

This type of compassion is what we must strive to cultivate in ourselves, and we must develop it from a limited amount to the limitless. Undiscriminating, spontaneous, and unlimited compassion for all sentient beings is obviously not the usual love that one has for friends or family, which is alloyed with ignorance, desire, and attachment. The kind of love we should advocate is this wider love that you can have even for someone who has done harm to you: your enemy.

The rationale for compassion is that every one of us wants to avoid suffering and gain happiness. This, in turn, is based on the valid feeling of "I," which determines the universal desire for happiness.

Indeed, all beings are born with similar desires and should have an equal right to fulfill them. If I compare myself with others, who are countless, I feel that others are more important because I am just one person whereas others are many. Further, the Tibetan Buddhist tradition teaches us to view all sentient beings as our dear mothers and to show our gratitude by loving them all. For, according to Buddhist theory, we are born and reborn countless numbers of times, and it is conceivable that each being has been our parent at one time or another. In this way all beings in the universe share a family relationship.

Whether one believes in religion or not, there is no one who does not appreciate love and compassion. Right from the moment of our birth, we are under the care and kindness of our parents; later in life, when facing the sufferings of disease and old age, we are again dependent on the kindness of others. If at the beginning and end of our lives we depend upon others' kindness, why then in the middle should we not act kindly toward others? The development of a kind heart (a feeling of closeness for all human beings) does not involve the religiosity we normally associate with conventional religious practice. It is not only for people who believe in religion, but is for everyone regardless of race, religion, or political affiliation. It is for anyone who considers himself or herself, above all, a member of the human family and who sees things from this larger and longer perspective. This is a powerful feeling that we should develop and apply; instead, we often neglect it, particularly in our prime years, when we experience a false sense of security.

When we take into account a longer perspective, the fact that all wish to gain happiness and avoid suffering, and keep in mind our relative unimportance in relation to countless others, we can conclude that it is worthwhile to share our possessions with others. When you train in this sort of outlook, a true sense of compassion—a true sense of love and respect for others—becomes possible. Individual happiness ceases to be a conscious self-seeking effort; it becomes an automatic and far superior by-product of the whole process of loving and serving others.

Another result of spiritual development, most useful in day-to-day life, is that it gives a calmness

and presence of mind. Our lives are in constant flux, bringing many difficulties. When faced with a calm and clear mind, problems can be successfully resolved. When, instead, we lose control over our minds through hatred, selfishness, jealousy, and anger, we lose our sense of judgement. Our minds are blinded, and at those wild moments anything can happen, including war. Thus, the practice of compassion and wisdom is useful to all, especially to those responsible for running national affairs, in whose hands lie the power and opportunity to create the structure of world peace. . . .

INDIVIDUAL POWER TO SHAPE INSTITUTIONS

Anger plays no small role in current conflicts such as those in the Middle East, Southeast Asia, the North–South problem, and so forth. These conflicts arise from a failure to understand one another's humanness. The answer is not the development and use of greater military force, nor an arms race. Nor is it purely political or purely technological. Basically it is spiritual, in the sense that what is required is a sensitive understanding of our common human situation. Hatred and fighting cannot bring happiness to anyone, even to the winners of battles. Violence always produces misery and thus is essentially counter-productive. It is, therefore, time for world leaders to learn to transcend the differences of race, culture, and ideology and to regard one another through eyes that see the common human situation. To do so would benefit individuals, communities, nations, and the world at large . . . .

As all nations are economically dependent upon one another more than ever before, human understanding must go beyond national boundaries and embrace the international community at large. Indeed, unless we can create an atmosphere of genuine cooperation, gained not by threatened or actual use of force but by heartfelt understanding, world problems will only increase. If people in poorer countries are denied the happiness they desire and deserve, they will naturally be dissatisfied and pose problems for the rich. If unwanted social, political, and cultural forms continue to be imposed upon unwilling people, the attainment of world peace is doubtful. However, if we satisfy people at a heart-to-heart level, peace will surely come.

Within each nation, the individual ought to be given the right to happiness, and among nations, there must be equal concern for the welfare of even the smallest nations. I am not suggesting that one system is better than another and all should adopt it. On the contrary, a variety of political systems and ideologies is desirable and accords with the variety of dispositions within the human community. This variety enhances the ceaseless human quest for happiness. Thus each community should be free to evolve its own political and socioeconomic system, based on the principle of self-determination.

The achievement of justice, harmony, and peace depends on many factors. We should think about them in terms of human benefit in the long run rather than the short term. I realize the enormity of the task before us, but I see no other alternative than the one I am proposing—which is based on our common humanity. Nations have no choice but to be concerned about the welfare of others, not so much because of their belief in humanity, but because it is in the mutual and long-term interest of all concerned. An appreciation of this new reality is indicated by the emergence of regional or continental economic organizations such as the European Economic Community, the Association of South East Asian Nations, and so forth. I hope more such transnational organizations will be formed, particularly in regions where economic development and regional stability seem in short supply.

Under present conditions, there is definitely a growing need for human understanding and a sense of universal responsibility. In order to achieve such ideas, we must generate a good and kind heart, for without this, we can achieve neither universal happiness nor lasting world peace. We cannot create peace on paper. While advocating universal responsibility and universal brotherhood and sisterhood, the facts are that humanity is organized in separate entities in the form of national societies. Thus, in a realistic sense, I feel it is these societies that must act as the building blocks for world peace. Attempts have been made in the past to create societies more just and equal. Institutions have been established with noble charters to combat antisocial forces. Unfortunately,

such ideas have been cheated by selfishness. More than ever before, we witness today how ethics and noble principles are obscured by the shadow of self-interest, particularly in the political sphere. . . .

Such human qualities as morality, compassion, decency, wisdom, and so forth have been the foundations of all civilizations. These qualities must be cultivated and sustained through systematic moral education in a conducive social environment so that a more humane world may emerge. The qualities required to create such a world must be inculcated right from the beginning, from childhood. We cannot wait for the next generation to make this change; the present generation must attempt a renewal of basic human values. If there is any hope, it is in the future generations, but not unless we institute major change on a worldwide scale in our present educational system. We need a revolution in our commitment to and practice of universal humanitarian values.

It is not enough to make noisy calls to halt moral degeneration; we must do something about it. Since present-day governments do not shoulder such "religious" responsibilities, humanitarian and religious leaders must strengthen the existing civic, social, cultural, educational, and religious organizations to revive human and spiritual values. Where necessary, we must create new organizations to achieve these goals. Only in so doing can we hope to create a more stable basis for world peace. . . .

Finally, a few words about material progress. I have heard a great deal of complaint against material progress from Westerners, and yet, paradoxically, it has been the very pride of the Western world. I see nothing wrong with material progress per se, provided people are always given precedence. It is my firm belief that in order to solve human problems in all their dimensions, we must combine and harmonize economic development with spiritual growth.

However, we must know its limitations. Although materialistic knowledge in the form of science and technology has contributed enormously to human welfare, it is not capable of creating lasting happiness. In America, for example, where technological development is perhaps more advanced than in any other country, there is still a great deal of mental suffering. This is because materialistic knowledge can only provide a type of happiness that is dependent upon physical conditions. It cannot provide happiness that springs from inner development independent of external factors.

For renewal of human values and attainment of lasting happiness, we need to look to the common humanitarian heritage of all nations the world over. May this essay serve as an urgent reminder lest we forget the human values that unite us all as a single family on this planet. . . .

Desmond Tutu

NO FUTURE WITHOUT FORGIVENESS

Although there is no shortage of bad news in the world (readers are encouraged to suggest, .e.g., their "top ten"), there is good news as well. Thus, peace workers are fond of pointing out that many characteristics of human society that were long considered "natural" and therefore "inevitable" have given way and become so discredited as to appear peculiar social fossils: dueling, basing legal decisions upon "trial by personal combat," chattel slavery, the "divine right of kings." Modern times have also witnessed dramatic changes in circumstances that had appeared permanent features of the political landscape . . . until they disappeared, in some cases virtually overnight. Consider the end of the Cold War; the dissolution of the U.S.S.R. and with it, the end of Soviet hegemony over Eastern Europe; the end of long-standing dictatorships in Haiti, the Philippines, Indonesia, Korea, and elsewhere; as well as the (mostly) nonviolent demise of apartheid in South Africa, and the "Arab Spring" of 2010–2011.

Following the remarkable success in South Africa, newly installed President Nelson Mandela empowered a nationwide Truth and Reconciliation Commission, headed by Bishop Desmond Tutu, whose goal—largely successful—was to help that traumatized country face the future without being dragged down by the pain, resentment, and angers of the past. The process, based on the African concept of *ubuntu*—social cohesion and shared goals and responsibility—was extraordinary, involving public testimony about abuses, intimidation, and murder, in the hope of achieving national reconciliation. This example offers the possibility that one way to approach peace is to acknowledge the evils of the past, accept responsibility, and then move on. As Bishop Tutu shows, it is a terribly difficult but immensely rewarding process and one that might well be appropriate for every country.

In relations between individuals, if you ask another person for forgiveness you may be spurned; the one you have injured may refuse to forgive you. The risk is even greater if you are the injured party, wanting to offer forgiveness. The culprit may be arrogant, obdurate, or blind; not ready or willing to apologize or to ask for forgiveness. He or she thus cannot appropriate the forgiveness that is offered. Such rejection can jeopardize the whole enterprise. Our leaders were ready in South Africa to say they were willing to walk the path of confession, forgiveness, and reconciliation with all the hazards that lay along the way. And it seems their gamble might be paying off, since our land has not been overwhelmed by the catastrophe that had seemed so inevitable.

It is crucial, when a relationship has been damaged or when a potential relationship has been made impossible, that the perpetrator should acknowledge the truth and be ready and willing to apologize. It helps the process of forgiveness and reconciliation immensely. It is never easy. We all know just how difficult it is for most of us to admit that we have been wrong. It is perhaps the most difficult thing in the world—in almost every language the most difficult words are, "I am sorry." Thus it is not at all surprising that those accused of horrendous deeds and the communities they come from, for whom they believed they were committing these atrocities, almost always try to find ways out of even admitting that they were indeed capable of such deeds. They adopt the denial mode, asserting that such-and-such has not happened. When the evidence is incontrovertible, they take refuge in feigned ignorance. The Germans claimed they had not known what the Nazis were up to. White South Africans have also tried to find refuge in claims of ignorance. The former apartheid cabinet member Leon Wessels was closer to the mark when he said that they had not wanted to know, for there were those who tried to alert them. For those with eyes to see, there were accounts of people dying mysteriously in detention. For those with ears to hear, there was much that was disquieting and even chilling. But, like the three monkeys, they chose neither to hear, nor see, nor speak of evil. When some did own up, they passed the blame to others, "We were carrying out orders," refusing to acknowledge that as morally responsible individuals each person has to take responsibility for carrying out unconscionable orders.

We do not usually rush to expose our vulnerability and our sinfulness. But if the process of forgiveness and healing is to succeed, ultimately acknowledgment by the culprit is indispensable— not completely so but nearly so. Acknowledgment of the truth and of having wronged someone is important in getting to the root of the breach. If a husband and wife have quarreled without the wrongdoer acknowledging his or her fault by confessing, so exposing the cause of the rift; if a husband in this situation comes home with a bunch of flowers and the couple pretend all is in order, then they will be in for a rude shock. They have not dealt with their immediate past adequately. They have glossed over their differences, for they have failed to stare truth in the face for fear of a possible bruising confrontation. They will have done what the prophet calls healing the hurt lightly by crying, "'Peace, peace,' where there is no peace."[3] They will have only papered over the cracks and not worked out why they fell out in the first place. All that will happen is that, despite the beautiful flowers, the hurt will fester. One day there will be an awful eruption and they will realize that they had tried to obtain reconciliation on the cheap. True reconciliation is not cheap. It cost God the death of his only begotten Son.

Forgiving and being reconciled are not about pretending that things are other than they are. It is not patting one another on the back and turning a blind eye to the wrong. True reconciliation exposes the awfulness, the abuse, the pain, the degradation, the truth. It could even sometimes make things worse. It is a risky undertaking but in the end it is worthwhile, because in the end dealing with the real situation helps to bring real healing. Spurious reconciliation can bring only spurious healing.

If the wrongdoer has come to the point of realizing his wrong, then one hopes there will be remorse, or at least some contrition or sorrow. This should lead him to confess the wrong he has done and ask for forgiveness. It obviously requires a fair measure

---

[3] Jeremiah 6:14 and 8:11.

of humility, especially when the victim is someone in a group that one's community had despised, as was often the case in South Africa when the perpetrators were government agents.

The victim, we hope, would be moved to respond to an apology by forgiving the culprit. As I have already tried to show, we were constantly amazed in the commission at the extraordinary magnanimity that so many of the victims exhibited. Of course there were those who said they would not forgive. That demonstrated for me the important point that forgiveness could not be taken for granted; it was neither cheap nor easy. As it happens, these were the exceptions. Far more frequently what we encountered was deeply moving and humbling.

In forgiving, people are not being asked to forget. On the contrary, it is important to remember, so that we should not let such atrocities happen again. Forgiveness does not mean condoning what has been done. It means taking what happened seriously and not minimizing it; drawing out the sting in the memory that threatens to poison our entire existence. It involves trying to understand the perpetrators and so have empathy, to try to stand in their shoes and appreciate the sort of pressures and influences that might have conditioned them.

Forgiveness is not being sentimental. The study of forgiveness has become a growth industry. Whereas previously it was something often dismissed pejoratively as spiritual and religious, now because of developments such as the Truth and Reconciliation Commission in South Africa it is gaining attention as an academic discipline studied by psychologists, philosophers, physicians, and theologians. In the United States there is an International Forgiveness Institute attached to the University of Wisconsin, and the John Templeton Foundation, with others, has started a multimillion-dollar Campaign for Forgiveness Research. Forgiving has even been found to be good for your health.

Forgiving means abandoning your right to pay back the perpetrator in his own coin, but it is a loss that liberates the victim. In the commission we heard people speak of a sense of relief after forgiving. A recent issue of the journal *Spirituality and Health* had on its front cover a picture of three U.S. ex-servicemen standing in front of the Vietnam Memorial in

Washington, DC. One asks, "Have you forgiven those who held you prisoner of war?" "I will never forgive them," replies the other. His mate says, "Then it seems they still have you in prison, don't they?"[4]

Does the victim depend on the culprit's contrition and confession as the precondition for being able to forgive? There is no question that, of course, such a confession is a very great help to the one who wants to forgive, but it is not absolutely indispensable. Jesus did not wait until those who were nailing him to the cross had asked for forgiveness. He was ready, as they drove in the nails, to pray to his Father to forgive them, and he even provided an excuse for what they were doing. If the victim could forgive only when the culprit confessed, then the victim would be locked into the culprit's whim, locked into victimhood, whatever her own attitude or intention. That would be palpably unjust.

I have used the following analogy to try to explain the need for a perpetrator to confess. Imagine you are sitting in a dank, stuffy, dark room. This is because the curtains are drawn and the windows have been shut. Outside the light is shining and a fresh breeze is blowing. If you want the light to stream into that room and the fresh air to flow in, you will have to open the window and draw the curtains apart; then that light which has always been available will come in, and air will enter the room to freshen it up. So it is with forgiveness.

The victim may be ready to forgive and make the gift of her forgiveness available, but it is up to the wrongdoer to appropriate the gift—to open the window and draw the curtains aside. He does this by acknowledging the wrong he has done, so letting the light and fresh air of forgiveness enter his being.

In the act of forgiveness we are declaring our faith in the future of a relationship and in the capacity of the wrongdoer to make a new beginning on a course that will be different from the one that caused us the wrong. We are saying here is a chance to make a new beginning. It is an act of faith that the wrongdoer can change. According to Jesus,[5] we should be

---

[4] Vol. 2, No. 1 (New York, Trinity Church: Spirituality & Health Publishing).
[5] Matthew 18:22.

ready to do this not just once, not just seven times, but seventy times seven, without limit—provided, it seems Jesus says, your brother or sister who has wronged you is ready to come and confess the wrong they have committed yet again.

That is difficult, but because we are not infallible, because we will hurt especially the ones we love by some wrong, we will always need a process of forgiveness and reconciliation to deal with those unfortunate yet all too human breaches in relationships. They are an inescapable characteristic of the human condition.

Once the wrongdoer has confessed and the victim has forgiven, it does not mean that is the end of the process. Most frequently, the wrong has affected the victim in tangible, material ways. Apartheid provided the whites with enormous benefits and privileges, leaving its victims deprived and exploited. If someone steals my pen and then asks me to forgive him, unless he returns my pen the sincerity of his contrition and confession will be considered to be nil. Confession, forgiveness, and reparation, wherever feasible, form part of a continuum.

In South Africa the whole process of reconciliation has been placed in very considerable jeopardy by the enormous disparities between the rich, mainly the whites, and the poor, mainly the blacks. The huge gap between the haves and the have-nots, which was largely created and maintained by racism and apartheid, poses the greatest threat to reconciliarion reconciliation and stability in our country. The rich provided the class from which the perpetrators and the beneficiaries of apartheid came, and the poor produced the bulk of the victims. That is why I have exhorted whites to support transformation taking place in the lot of blacks.

For unless houses replace the hovels and shacks in which most blacks live, unless blacks gain access to clean water, electricity, affordable health care, decent education, good jobs, and a safe environment—things which the vast majority of whites have taken for granted for so long—we can just as well kiss reconciliation good-bye.

Reconciliation is liable to be a long-drawn-out process with ups and downs, not something accomplished overnight and certainly not by a commission, however effective. The Truth and Reconciliation Commission has only been able to make a contribution. Reconciliation is going to have to be the concern of every South African. It has to be a national project to which all earnestly strive to make their particular contribution—by learning the language and culture of others; by being willing to make amends; by refusing to deal in stereotypes by making racial or other jokes that ridicule a particular group; by contributing to a culture of respect for human rights, and seeking to enhance tolerance—with zero tolerance for intolerance; by working for a more inclusive society where most, if not all, can feel they belong—that they are insiders and not aliens and strangers on the outside, relegated to the edges of society.

To work for reconciliation is to want to realize God's dream for humanity—when we will know that we are indeed members of one family, bound together in a delicate network of interdependence. . . .

If we are going to move on and build a new kind of world community, there must be a way in which we can deal with a sordid past. The most effective way would be for the perpetrators or their descendants to acknowledge the awfulness of what happened, and the descendants of the victims to respond by granting forgiveness, providing something can be done, even symbolically, to compensate for the anguish experienced, whose consequences are still being lived through today. It may be, for instance, that race relations in the United States will not improve significantly until Native Americans and African Americans get the opportunity to tell their stories and reveal the pain that sits in the pit of their stomachs as a baneful legacy of dispossession and slavery. We saw in the Truth and Reconciliation Commission how the act of telling one's story has a cathartic, healing effect.

If the present generation could not legitimately speak on behalf of those who are no more, then we could not offer forgiveness for the sins of South Africa's racist past, which predates the advent of apartheid in 1948. The process of healing our land would be subverted, because there would always be the risk that some awful atrocity of the past would come to light that would undermine what had been accomplished thus far; or that people would say, "It is all right so far as it goes in dealing with the contemporary situation, but it is all utterly ineffectual because it has failed to deal with the burden of the past."

True forgiveness deals with the past, all of the past, to make the future possible. We cannot go on nursing grudges even vicariously for those who cannot speak for themselves any longer. We have to accept that what we do we do for generations past, present, and yet to come. That is what makes a community a community or a people a people—for better or for worse.

I have wished desperately that those involved in seeking solutions for what have seemed intractable problems in places such as Northern Ireland and the Middle East would not despise the value of seemingly small symbolic acts that have a potency and significance beyond what is apparent. I have been distressed to learn that some of those most intimately connected to the peace process in Northern Ireland have not been seen shaking hands in public, that some have gone to odd lengths not to be photographed together with those on the other side, their current adversaries. It was wonderful that, at the funeral of King Hussein of Jordan, President Ezer Weizman of Israel had the courage to shake hands with the leader of a radical Palestinian group. It was a gesture that helped to humanize his adversary, where before much had conspired to demonize him. A small handshake can make the unthinkable, the improbable—peace, friendship, harmony, and tolerance—not quite so remote.

I also hope that those who are at this moment enemies around the world might consider using more temperate language when describing those with whom they disagree. Today's "terrorist" could very well be tomorrow's president. That has happened in South Africa. Most of those who were vilified as terrorists are today our cabinet ministers and others sitting in the government benches of our National Assembly. If those we disagree with today are possibly going to be our colleagues tomorrow, we might begin by trying to describe them in language that won't be an embarrassment when that time of change does come.

It is crucial too that we keep remembering that negotiations, peace talks, forgiveness, and reconciliation happen most frequently not between friends, not between those who like one another. They happen precisely because people are at loggerheads and detest one another as only enemies can. But enemies are potential allies, friends, colleagues, and collaborators. This is not just utopian idealism. The first democratically elected government of South Africa was a government of National Unity made up of members of political parties that were engaged in a life-and-death struggle. The man who headed it had been incarcerated for twenty-seven years as a dangerous terrorist. If it could happen there, surely it can happen in other places. Perhaps God chose such an unlikely place deliberately to show the world that it can be done anywhere.

If the protagonists in the world's conflicts began to make symbolic gestures for peace, changed the way they described their enemies, and began talking to them, their actions might change too. For instance, what is it doing for future relations in the Middle East to go on constructing Jewish settlements in what is accepted to be Palestinian territory, when this causes so much bitterness and resentment among the Palestinians, who feel belittled and abused? What legacy does it leave for the children of those who are destined to be neighbors? I have asked similar questions when Arab nations have seemed so completely unrealistic in thinking they could destroy Israel. What a wonderful gift to the world, especially as we enter a new millennium, if true peace would come in the land of those who say *salama*, or *shalom*, in the land of the Prince of Peace.

Peace is possible, especially if today's adversaries were to imagine themselves becoming friends and begin acting in ways that would promote such a friendship developing in reality. It would be wonderful if, as they negotiated, they tried to find ways of accommodating each other's needs. A readiness to make concessions is a sign of strength, not weakness. And it can be worthwhile sometimes to lose a battle in order in the end to win the war. Those who are engaged in negotiations for peace and prosperity are striving after such a splendid, such a priceless goal that it should be easier to find ways for all to be winners than to fight; for negotiators to make it a point that no one loses face, that no one emerges empty-handed, with nothing to place before his or her constituency. How one wishes that negotiators would avoid having bottom lines and too many preconditions. In negotiations we are, as in the process of forgiveness, seeking to give all the chance to begin again. The rigid will have a tough time. The flexible, those who are ready to make principled compromises, end up being the victors.

I have said ours was a flawed commission. Despite that, I do want to assert as eloquently and as passionately as I can that it was, in an imperfect world, the best possible instrument so far devised to deal with the kind of situation that confronted us after democracy was established in our motherland. With all its imperfections, what we have tried to do in South Africa has attracted the attention of the world. This tired, disillusioned, cynical world, hurting so frequently and so grievously, has marveled at a process that holds out considerable hope in the midst of much that negates hope. People in the different places that I have visited and where I have spoken about the truth and reconciliation process see in this flawed attempt a beacon of hope, a possible paradigm for dealing with situations where violence, conflict, turmoil, and sectional strife have seemed endemic, conflicts that mostly take place not between warring nations but within the same nation. At the end of their conflicts, the warring groups in Northern Ireland, the Balkans, the Middle East, Sri Lanka, Burma, Afghanistan, Angola, the Sudan, the two Congos, and elsewhere are going

to have to sit down together to determine just how they will be able to live together amicably, how they might have a shared future devoid of strife, given the bloody past that they have recently lived through. They see more than just a glimmer of hope in what we have attempted in South Africa.

God does have a sense of humor. Who in their right minds could ever have imagined South Africa to be an example of anything but the most ghastly awfulness, of how *not* to order a nation's race relations and its governance? We South Africans were the unlikeliest lot, and that is precisely why God has chosen us. We cannot really claim much credit ourselves for what we have achieved. We were destined for perdition and were plucked out of total annihilation. We were a hopeless case if ever there was one. God intends that others might look at us and take courage. God wants to point to us as a possible beacon of hope, a possible paradigm, and to say, "Look at South Africa. They had a nightmare called apartheid. It has ended. Northern Ireland (or wherever), your nightmare will end too. They had a problem regarded as intractable. They are resolving it. No problem anywhere can ever again be considered to be intractable. There is hope for you too." . . .

Rebecca Solnit

VISION: REVOLUTION IS AS "UNPREDICTABLE AND AS BEAUTIFUL AS SPRING"

Among the most exciting (and surprising) recent events has been the worldwide emergence of numerous prodemocracy movements, nearly all of them spontaneous and locally organized, mostly nonviolent, and directed against long-standing dictatorships. Although there are good reasons to question the advisability of exporting democracy to other countries, it is impossible not to admire the courage and determination of indigenous movements, many of which have succeeded in overthrowing brutal tyrants. These movements have been especially pronounced among Arab countries, whose populations had long been considered either indifferent to their governments or for some reason incapable of rebelling successfully. The so-called Arab Spring of 2010–2011 proved otherwise.

Winston Churchill once observed that democracy is the worst possible system of government . . . except for all the others! Although this might be a Western, culture-bound viewpoint, the passion and courage with which prodemocracy activists have struggled to achieve representative government suggests that democracy may well be preferred by most people, given the opportunity. In any event, peace scholars have long observed that although democratic governments are no less war-prone than are autocracies, it is extremely rare for democracies to go to war against other democracies (the last clear case being the War of 1812, between the United States and Great Britain). The next selection, written in the heady enthusiasm of the Arab Spring, celebrates the promise of nonviolent, prodemocracy movements—especially in the Arab world, but with abundant potential for everybody.

Revolution is as unpredictable as an earthquake and as beautiful as spring. Its coming is always a surprise, but its nature should not be. Revolution is a phase, a mood, like spring, and just as spring has its buds and showers, so revolution has its ebullience, its bravery, its hope, and its solidarity. Some of these things pass. The women of Cairo do not move as freely in public as they did during those few precious weeks when the old rules were suspended and everything was different. But the old Egypt is gone and Egyptians' sense of themselves—and our sense of them—is forever changed.

No revolution vanishes without effect. The Prague Spring of 1968 was brutally crushed, but 21 years later when a second wave of revolution liberated Czechoslovakia, Alexander Dubcek, who had been the reformist Secretary of the Czechoslovakian Communist Party, returned to give heart to the people from a balcony overlooking Wenceslas Square: "The government is telling us that the street is not the place for things to be solved, but I say the street was and is the place. The voice of the street must be heard."

The voice of the street has been a bugle cry this year. You heard it. Everyone did, but the rulers who thought their power was the only power that mattered, heard it last and with dismay. Many of them are nervous now, releasing political prisoners, lowering the price of food, and otherwise trying to tamp down uprisings.

There were three kinds of surprise about this year's unfinished revolutions in Tunisia, Egypt, and Libya, and the rumblings elsewhere that have frightened the mighty from Saudi Arabia to China, Algeria to Bahrain. The West was surprised that the Arab world, which we have regularly been told is medieval, hierarchical, and undemocratic, was full of young men and women using their cell phones, their Internet access, and their bodies in streets and squares to foment change and temporarily live a miracle of direct democracy and people power. And then there is the surprise that the seemingly unshakeable regimes of the strongmen were shaken into pieces.

And finally, there is always the surprise of: Why now? Why did the crowd decide to storm the Bastille on July 14, 1789, and not any other day? The bread famine going on in France that year and the rising cost of food had something to do with it, as hunger and poverty does with many of the Middle Eastern uprisings today, but part of the explanation remains mysterious. Why this day and not a month earlier or a decade later?

Or never instead of now?

Oscar Wilde once remarked, "To expect the unexpected shows a thoroughly modern intellect." This profound uncertainty has been the grounds for my own hope.

Hindsight is 20/20, they say, and you can tell stories where it all makes sense. A young Tunisian college graduate, Mohammed Bouazizi, who could find no better work than selling produce from a cart on the street, was so upset by his treatment at the hands of a policewoman that he set himself afire on December 17, 2010. His death two weeks later became the match that lit the country afire—but why that death? Or why the death of Khaled Said, an Egyptian youth who exposed police corruption and was beaten to death for it? He got a Facebook page that said "We are all Khaled Said," and his death, too, was a factor in the uprisings to come.

But when exactly do the abuses that have been tolerated for so long become intolerable? When does the fear evaporate and the rage generate action that produces joy? After all, Tunisia and Egypt were not short on intolerable situations and tragedies before Bouazizi's self-immolation and Said's murder.

Thich Quang Duc burned himself to death at an intersection in Saigon on June 11, 1963, to protest the treatment of Buddhists by the U.S.-backed government of South Vietnam. His stoic composure while in flames was widely seen and may have helped produce a military coup against the regime six months later—a change, but not necessarily a liberation. In between that year and this one, many people have fasted, prayed, protested, gone to prison, and died to call attention to cruel regimes, with little or no measurable consequence.

GUNS AND BUTTERFLIES

The boiling point of water is straightforward, but the boiling point of societies is mysterious. Bouazizi's death became a catalyst, and at his funeral the 5,000 mourners chanted, "Farewell, Mohammed, we will avenge you. We weep for you today, we will make those who caused your death weep."

But his was not the first Tunisian gesture of denunciation. An even younger man, the rap artist who calls himself El General, uploaded a song about the horror of poverty and injustice in the country and, as the *Guardian* put it, "within hours, the song had lit up the bleak and fearful horizon like an incendiary bomb." Or a new dawn. The artist was arrested and interrogated for three very long days, and then released thanks to widespread protest. And surely before him we could find another milestone. And another young man being subjected

to inhuman conditions. And behind the uprising in Egypt are a panoply of union and human rights organizers as well as charismatic individuals.

This has been a great year for the power of the powerless and for the courage and determination of the young. . . . Causes are Russian dolls. You can keep opening each one up and find another one behind it. WikiLeaks and Facebook and Twitter and the new media helped in 2011, but new media had been around for years. Asmaa Mahfouz was a young Egyptian woman who had served time in prison for using the Internet to organize a protest on April 6, 2008, to support striking workers. With astonishing courage, she posted a video of herself on Facebook on January 18, 2011, in which she looked into the camera and said, with a voice of intense conviction:

> Four Egyptians have set themselves on fire to protest humiliation and hunger and poverty and degradation they had to live with for 30 years. Four Egyptians have set themselves on fire thinking maybe we can have a revolution like Tunisia, maybe we can have freedom, justice, honor, and human dignity. Today, one of these four has died, and I saw people commenting and saying, "May God forgive him. He committed a sin and killed himself for nothing." People, have some shame.

She described an earlier demonstration at which few had shown up: "I posted that I, a girl, am going down to Tahrir Square, and I will stand alone. And I'll hold up a banner. Perhaps people will show some honor. No one came except three guys—three guys and three armored cars of riot police. And tens of hired thugs and officers came to terrorize us."

Mahfouz called for the gathering in Tahrir Square on January 25th that became the Egyptian revolution. The second time around she didn't stand alone. Eighty-five thousand Egyptians pledged to attend, and soon enough, millions stood with her.

The revolution was called by a young woman with nothing more than a Facebook account and passionate conviction. They were enough. Often, revolution has had such modest starts. On October 5, 1789, a girl took a drum to the central markets of Paris. The storming of the Bastille a few months before had started, but hardly completed, a revolution. That drummer girl helped gather a mostly

female crowd of thousands who marched to Versailles and seized the royal family. It was the end of
the Bourbon monarchy.

Women often find great roles in revolution,
simply because the rules fall apart and everyone has
agency, anyone can act. As they did in Egypt, where
liberty leading the masses was an earnest young
woman in a black veil. That the flapping of a butterfly's wings in Brazil can shape the weather in Texas is
a summation of chaos theory that is now an oft-re-
peated cliché. But there are billions of butterflies on
earth, all flapping their wings. Why does one gesture
matter more than another? Why this Facebook post,
this girl with a drum?

Even to try to answer this you'd have to say
that the butterfly is born aloft by a particular breeze
that was shaped by the flap of the wing of, say, a
sparrow, and so behind causes are causes, behind
small agents are other small agents, inspirations,
and role models, as well as outrages to react against.
The point is not that causation is unpredictable and
erratic. The point is that butterflies and sparrows and
young women in veils and an unknown 20-year-old
rapping in Arabic and you yourself, if you wanted
it, sometimes have tremendous power, enough to
bring down a dictator, enough to change the world.

OTHER SELVES, OTHER LIVES

2011 has already been a remarkable year in which
a particular kind of humanity appeared again and
again in very different places, and we will see a great
deal more of it in Japan before that catastrophe is
over. Perhaps its first appearance was at the shooting
of Congresswoman Gabrielle Giffords in Tucson on
January 8th, where the lone gunman was countered
by several citizens who took remarkable action,
none more so than Giffords's new intern, 20-year-
old Daniel Martinez, who later said, "It was probably not the best idea to run toward the gunshots.
But people needed help."

Martinez reached the congresswoman's side
and probably saved her life by administering first
aid, while 61-year-old Patricia Maisch grabbed
the magazine so the shooter couldn't reload, and
74-year-old Bill Badger helped wrestle him to the
ground, though he'd been grazed by a bullet. One

elderly man died because he shielded his wife rather
than protect himself. Everything suddenly changed
and those people rose to the occasion heroically
not in the hours, days, or weeks a revolution gives,
but within seconds. More sustained acts of bravery
and solidarity would make the revolutions to come.
People would risk their lives and die for their beliefs
and for each other. And in killing them, regimes
would lose their last shreds of legitimacy.

Violence always seems to me the worst form of
tyranny. It deprives people of their rights, including
the right to live. The rest of the year so far has been
dominated by battles against the tyrannies that have
sometimes cost livess and sometimes just ground
down those lives into poverty and indignity, from
Bahrain to Madison, Wisconsin.

Yes, to Madison. I have often wondered if the
United States could catch fire the way other countries sometimes do. The public space and spirit of
Argentina or Egypt often seem missing here, for
what changes in revolution is largely spirit, emotion,
belief—intangible things, as delicate as butterfly
wings, but our world is made of such things. They
matter. The governors govern by the consent of the
governed. When they lose that consent, they resort
to violence, which can stop some people directly, but
aims to stop most of us through the power of fear.

And then sometimes a young man becomes
fearless enough to post a song attacking the dictator
who has ruled all his young life. Or people sign a
declaration like Charter 77, the 1977 Czech document that was a milestone on the way to the revolutions of 1989, as well as a denunciation of the
harassment of an underground rock band called the
Plastic People of the Universe. Or a group of them
found a labor union on the waterfront in Gdansk,
Poland, in 1980, and the first cracks appear in the
Soviet Empire.

Those who are not afraid are ungovernable, at
least by fear, that favorite tool of the bygone era of
George W. Bush. Jonathan Schell, with his usual
beautiful insight, saw this when he wrote of the
uprising in Tahrir Square:

> The murder of the 300 people, it may be, was the
> event that sealed Mubarak's doom. When people
> are afraid, murders make them take flight. But

when they have thrown off fear, murders have the opposite effect and make them bold. Instead of fear, they feel solidarity. Then they "stay"—and advance. And there is no solidarity like solidarity with the dead. That is the stuff of which revolution is made.

When a revolution is made, people suddenly find themselves in a changed state—of mind and of nation. The ordinary rules are suspended, and people become engaged with each other in new ways, and develop a new sense of power and possibility. People behave with generosity and altruism; they find they can govern themselves; and, in many ways, the government simply ceases to exist. A few days into the Egyptian revolution, Ben Wedeman, CNN's senior correspondent in Cairo, was asked why things had calmed down in the Egyptian capital. He responded: "[T]hings have calmed down because there is no government here," pointing out that security forces had simply disappeared from the streets.

This state often arises in disasters as well, when the government is overwhelmed, shut down, or irrelevant for people intent on survival and then on putting society back together. If it rarely lasts, in the process it does change individuals and societies, leaving a legacy. To my mind, the best government is one that most resembles this moment when civil society reigns in a spirit of hope, inclusiveness, and improvisational genius.

In Egypt, there were moments of violence when people pushed back against the government's goons, and for a week it seemed like the news was filled with little but pictures of bloody heads. Still, no armies marched, no superior weaponry decided the fate of the country, nobody was pushed from power by armed might. People gathered in public and discovered themselves as the public, as civil society. They found that the repression and exploitation they had long tolerated was intolerable and that they could do something about it, even if that something was only gathering, standing together, insisting on their rights as the public, as the true nation that the government can never be.

It is remarkable how, in other countries, people will one day simply stop believing in the regime that had, until then, ruled them, as African-Americans

did in the South here 50 years ago. Stopping believing means no longer regarding those who rule you as legitimate, and so no longer fearing them. Or respecting them. And then, miraculously, they begin to crumble. In the Philippines in 1986, millions of people gathered in response to a call from Catholic-run Radio Veritas, the only station the dictatorship didn't control or shut down. Then the army defected and dictator Fernando Marcos was ousted from power after 21 years.

In Argentina in 2001, in the wake of a brutal economic collapse, such a sudden shift in consciousness toppled the neoliberal regime of Fernando de la Rúa and ushered in a revolutionary era of economic desperation, but also of brilliant, generous innovation. A shift in consciousness brought an outpouring of citizens into the streets of Buenos Aires, suddenly no longer afraid after the long nightmare of a military regime and its aftermath. In Iceland in early 2009, in the wake of a global economic meltdown of special fierceness on that small island nation, a once-docile population almost literally drummed out of power the ruling party that had managed the country into bankruptcy.

CAN'T HAPPEN HERE?

In the United States, the communion between the governed and the governors and the public spaces in which to be reborn as a civil society resurgent often seem missing. This is a big country whose national capital is not much of a center and whose majority seems to live in places that are themselves decentered.

At its best, revolution is an urban phenomenon. Suburbia is counterrevolutionary by design. For revolution, you need to converge, to live in public, to become the public, and that's a geographical as well as a political phenomenon. The history of revolution is the history of great public spaces: the Place de la Concorde during the French Revolution; the Ramblas in Barcelona during the Spanish Civil War; Beijing's Tiananmen Square in 1989 (a splendid rebellion that was crushed); the great surge that turned the divide of the Berlin Wall into a gathering place in that same year; the insurrectionary occupation of the Zocalo of Mexico City after corrupt presidential elections and of the space in Buenos Aires that gave the Dirty War's most open opposition its name: Las Madres de la Plaza de Mayo, the Mothers of the Plaza of May.

It's all very well to organize on Facebook and update on Twitter, but these are only preludes. You also need to rise up, to pour out into the streets. You need to be together in body, for only then are you truly the public with the full power that a public can possess. And then it needs to matter. The United States is good at trivializing and ignoring insurrections at home. The authorities were shaken by the uprising in Seattle that shut down the World Trade Organization meeting on November 30, 1999, but the actual nonviolent resistance there was quickly fictionalized into a tale of a violent rabble. Novelist and then-*New Yorker* correspondent Mavis Gallant wrote in 1968: "The difference between rebellion at Columbia [University] and rebellion at the Sorbonne is that life in Manhattan went on as before, while in Paris every section of society was set on fire, in the space of a few days. The collective hallucination was that life can change, quite suddenly and for the better. It still strikes me as a noble desire. . . . "

Revolution is also the action of people pushed to the brink. Rather than fall over, they push back. . . . Much of the insurrection and the rage in the Middle East isn't just about tyranny; it's about economic injustice, about young people who can't find

work, can't afford to get married or leave their parents' homes, can't start their lives. This is increasingly the story for young Americans as well, and here it's clearly a response to the misallocation of resources, not absolute scarcity. It could just be tragic, or it could get interesting when the young realize they are being shafted, and that life could be different. Even that it could change, quite suddenly, and for the better.

There was a splendid surliness in the wake of the economic collapse of 2008: rage at the executives who had managed the economy into the ground and went home with outsized bonuses, rage at the system, rage at the sheer gratuitousness of the suffering of those who were being foreclosed upon and laid off. In this country, economic inequality has reached a level not seen since before the stock market crash of 1929.

Hard times are in store for most people on Earth, and those may be times of boldness. Or not. The butterflies are out there, but when their flight stirs the winds of insurrection no one knows beforehand. So remember to expect the unexpected, but not just to wait for it. Sometimes you have to become the unexpected, as the young heroes and heroines of 2011 have. I am sure they themselves are as surprised as anyone. Since she very nearly had the first word, let Asmaa Mahfouz have the last word: "As long as you say there is no hope, then there will be no hope, but if you go down and take a stance, then there will be hope."

Victoria Bonney Goodwin

ANTIWAR ACTIVISTS, WHERE ARE YOU?

Democracy is based on citizen participation, in return for which, governance is supposed to reflect the popular will. And yet, a paradoxical consequence of democracy is that it often leads citizens to *avoid* personal involvement, assuming that others—especially the "experts"—will do what is right and necessary. Moreover, despite the fact that young people are widely assumed to be most involved in political activism in general and antiwar activism in particular, the reality is that voting participation is typically lowest among people ages eighteen to twenty-five, and that ever since the Vietnam War (in large part, perhaps, because of the absence of a military draft), young people have been notably *under*represented in antiwar activism. The following selection, written by a college student, appeared as an op-ed article in the *Boston Globe* newspaper. It is a question—and a plea—that readers of this book might well take to heart.

My fellow young Americans, the evidence is mounting that this war we are fighting in Iraq is not a "just" war. No, this is a dirty fight, and we're in it for the long haul. But I guess that's the problem— "we" are not in it at all.

"We" are here in our land of iPods and cell phones, luxuriating in our apathetic comas while our soldiers are over there.

I know what you're thinking. You have that magnetic yellow ribbon on your SUV, and, boy, if that is not uber-effective I do not know what is. But let me ask you, if you'd just put your podcast on pause and cell phone on silence for a moment, is this all enough?

Two wars ago, during the Vietnam disaster, there was Generation Activist. The youth of America rallied against "the man." How did they do it? They didn't have e-boards or e-mail, for that matter.

Yet somehow, this archaic mob of longhairs and peaceniks managed to mobilize. They marched on the National Mall. They protested everywhere, even in bed (refer to your hippie handbook, under John Lennon and Yoko Ono's "bed-in"). Their methods were not always nonviolent, but they were creative and incorrigible.

Why is Generation Apathetic unable to have the same resounding roar?

For starters we have a woman from Generation Activist doing our dirty work. Former flower child Cindy Sheehan[6] is out on the front lines with a pack of her patchouli-wearing alliances. What is the youth of America doing in the meantime?

We are watching it on our car television sets thinking about the jerk in front of us who is not driving fast enough.

It's not our fault that we all have Attention Deficit Disorder. We are conditioned like Pavlov's dogs to jump at the sound of "You've got mail!" But we are in dereliction of our duty as a thorn in the side of authority. Our parents shouldn't have to bail us out of everything. So while we appreciate the help of Cindy and her comrades, this is our fight.

It's not only apathy that is killing the spirit of our generation, it's the execution of our dissidence. For some reason the youth of America think that violence is the most effective method of rebellion (albeit something we learned from our PlayStations).

That brings us to another nifty way that the young inactivists of America are making life easier for our elected warmongers—E-Marches.

Yes, E-Marches are the newest way to protest your government. All it takes is a double click, and you will be part of a simulated march on Washington.

Oh, dear, sweet, well-intentioned youth, don't you see? Just as easily as you signed up to electronically protest your senators, they can delete you from their in-box. The Internet is a resource for sports scores, CliffsNotes, and porn—not a venue for modern dissent.

We are a generation with potential coming out of our ears. We could move mountains if only we'd turn off our televisions. They only tell us we are powerless and to just give up.

---

[6] Editor's note: Ms. Sheehan's son was killed in the Iraq War, after which she became an influential antiwar activist. Prior to this, she had simply been an "ordinary citizen."

So this is what you have to do. Tomorrow when you stop into Starbucks for your venti latte and the person behind the counter gives you your change, look at it. Look closely. There, written on your bills is our American mantra in a defunct language.

It says, *E Pluribus Unum*, which means, "out of many, one." Let this be your daily reminder. Generation Apathetic, we are in this boat together.

It's up to us to chart a course. We cannot live our lives on cruise control.

STUDY QUESTIONS

1. What are some important lessons to be learned from peace movements of the past, and how might they inform peace movements of the future?
2. What do you see as one or more likely scenarios for the world in the near future? The distant future?
3. What would you *like* to see as one or more likely scenarios for the world in the near future? The distant future?
4. Many people claim that "peace begins with me." Discuss some pros and cons of this attitude.
5. Suggest a classification of peace movements other than those presented in this chapter.
6. Describe differences between the anti–Iraq War peace movement and its earlier anti–Vietnam War counterpart. Try to explain these differences and discuss what lessons, if any, might be learned as a result.
7. Insofar as the twenty-first century has been lacking in peace, to what extent is it appropriate to blame the United States? Where else might blame fairly be placed?
8. If peace studies did not exist, perhaps it would be necessary to invent it. Try your hand at inventing peace studies as though it did not exist; consider education, practical action, connections to other traditions, etc.
9. Look deeply into one or more of the poems included in this chapter, and/or suggest some others; to what extent does their imagery add to your intellectual grasp of the issue? What are some "futuristic" novels that might also fit into this chapter?
10. Have you been treating the material in this book as anything other than just one more text to be studied, learned from, tested and graded on, and then filed away somewhere? If so, why? If not, why not?

SUGGESTIONS FOR FURTHER READING

Boyte, Harry C. 2008. *The Citizen Solution: How You Can Make a Difference*. St. Paul: Minnesota Historical Society Press.

Brock, Peter. 1991. *Studies in Peace History*. Syracuse, NY: Syracuse University Press.

Carter, April. 1992. *Peace Movements: International Protest and World Politics since 1945*. New York: Longman.

Cortright, David. 2008. *Peace: A History of Movements and Ideas*. New York: Cambridge University Press.

Downton, James V. 1997. *The Persistent Activist: How Peace Commitment Develops and Survives*. Boulder, CO: Westview Press.

Fry, Douglas P. 2007. *Beyond War: The Human Potential for Peace*. New York: Oxford University Press.

Guigni, Marco. 2004. *Social Protest and Policy Change: Ecology, Antinuclear, and Peace Movements in Comparative Perspective*. Lanham, MD: Rowman & Littlefield.

Reardon, Betty. 1993. *Women and Peace: Feminist Visions of Global Security*. Albany: State University of New York Press.

Rochon, Thomas R., and David S. Meyer, eds. 1997. *Coalitions & Political Movements: The Lessons of the Nuclear Freeze*. Boulder, CO: L. Rienner.

Zisk, Betty H. 1992. *The Politics of Transformation: Local Activism in the Peace and Environmental Movements*. Westport, CT: Praeger.

Index

(Note to the reader: A few basic words and phrases, such as "war," "peace," and to a lesser extent, "United States," are not listed in this index because they appear—or are implied—on nearly every page.)